Focus on Computer Graphics

Tutorials and Perspectives in Computer Graphics

Edited by W. T. Hewitt and W. Hansmann

Springer
Berlin
Heidelberg
New York
Barcelona
Budapest
Hong Kong
London
Milan
Paris
Tokyo

Fabio Paternó (Ed.)

Interactive Systems: Design, Specification, and Verification

1st Eurographics Workshop
Bocca di Magra, Italy, June 1994

With 176 Figures

 Springer

Focus on Computer Graphics

Edited by W. T. Hewitt and W. Hansmann
for EUROGRAPHICS –
The European Association for Computer Graphics
P. O. Box 16, CH-1288 Aire-la-Ville, Switzerland

Volume Editor

Fabio Paternó
Istituto Consiglio Nazionale delle Ricerche
36 Via S. Maria, I-56126 Pisa, Italy

CR Subject Classification (1991): I.3, D.2, F.3

ISBN-13: 978-3-642-87117-7   e-ISBN-13: 978-3-642-87115-3
DOI:10.1007/978-3-642-87115-3

Library of Congress Cataloging-in-Publication Data
Interactive systems: Design, specification, and verification/ Fabio Paternó. – Berlin; Heidelberg;
New York; Barcelona; Budapest; Hong Kong; London; Mailand; Paris; Tokyo: Springer, 1995
(... Eurographics workshop; 1) (Focus on computer graphics)

NE: Paternó, Fabio [Hrsg.]; European Association for Computer Graphics: ... Eurographics
workshop

Cover: Konzept & Design, Ilvesheim, Germany
Typesetting: Camera ready copy by authors/editor
SPIN 10131049   45/3142 – 5 4 3 2 1 0 – Printed on acid-free paper

Preface

Background

Monastero S. Croce in Bocca di Magra, near La Spezia and Tuscany was the venue for the Eurographics workshop on Design, Specification, and Verification of Interactive Systems, held June 8–10, 1994. Monastero S. Croce is a monastery run by monks and nuns of the Carmelite Order. The tranquility of the retreat house with its uninterrupted views of the sea and mountains beyond, coupled with the hospitality which is characteristic of the monastic order, produced an ideal environment in which to hold the workshop.

The purpose of the workshop was to review the state of the art in design, specification and verification of interactive systems, to compare different existing approaches in the field, in order to identify principal requirements, the most suitable notations, and to indicate the results that can be obtained from their use. In the call for participation, the following topics were identified to be of interest for the workshop discussion:

- Foundations and reference models for interactive systems
- Verification of user interfaces, application of theorem-provers
- Methodologies for abstract design, comparative studies of methods/description techniques
- Specification of human-computer interaction, multi-modal user interfaces and virtual realities
- Design of graphics systems and window systems
- Formal description of users' related properties
- Model-based user interface software tools

The workshop was attended by 33 participants drawn from 11 European and American countries. Most came from universities or public research institutes and some from industry. Twenty papers were selected for the final program from 32 submissions. Ten of them were presented, the other ten were considered in the discussion sessions of the workshop as the aim was to promote discussion rather than paper presentations. All twenty papers are included in this volume.

Structure

The workshop was run over a two and a half day period, with papers presented on the first one and a half days, followed by discussion in working groups and a closing plenary session in which reports of the working groups were received and future progression of the work was discussed. Summaries of the working group sessions are included in this book.

Each of the first two days opened with invited presentations. On the first day Jim Foley spoke about UIDE (User Interface Design Environment) an environment which starts from data models and pre/post conditions to automatically generate a user interface. These conditions allow the management of the large number of states in which a system can be. The environment supports a range of functionality (automatic generation of interaction objects, dynamic control of their enabling and disabling, generation of help, support of correctness-preserving transformation). This tool was considered an interesting reference point for all the new tools which are being developed in this area.

On the second day, Phil Barnard spoke about interactions with advanced graphical interfaces and the development of latent human knowledge. His approach draws upon a parallel model of the human information processing mechanism. A number of specific issues were considered in the blending of multimodal information and sensory information. Another very important issue was how formal methods might also be used for representing the properties of user cognition. The talk was illustrated with some excellent animations of the model.

The paper presentations were organized around three topics, and are summarized below.

Modelling in Design of Interactive Systems

In this section the use of abstractions and models for supporting the work of software designers in the development process of Interactive Systems was considered. Different starting points for obtaining useful information for this purpose were analyzed: visual programming, task analysis, conceptual design and so on. Modelling approaches using abstractions for basic interaction objects such as PAC or Interactors were used in several contexts. Another important theme was how to bridge the gap from the conceptual design of Interactive Systems to the determination of software implementation. The necessity of a structured approach to modelling was recognized. For this purpose two main approaches were identified: a task-centred approach where the system functionality is organized in such a way as to reflect user tasks and object-oriented modelling. In abstract modelling and design an important issue is to connect components both at the conceptual and the architectural levels. Thus attention was focused on possible relationships and composition operators. Another important issue discussed was how to integrate task analysis and functional requirements. The model-based approach was emphasized and illustrated by different approaches, for example an approach based on entity-relationship-attribute model (ERA) and on an activity chaining graph (ACG) resulting from the task analysis and an approach based on data-flow diagrams and attributed grammars to model the behaviour of the user interface.

Tasks and Specification

This session was more oriented to introducing the user point of view in the modelling and design of user interfaces. Thus notations for specifying user tasks and for deriving further information from them were considered. In particular approaches for investigating properties about the relationships between the information presented by the system and that required by the user in order to perform some tasks were discussed. Even the problem of using abstractions as a means to hide details of tasks at various levels was considered, trying to identify which are the possible general abstraction levels which should be used. The importance of usability in the early phases of design rather than a post-hoc usability assessment was noted. This means comparing different design options in the various phases of the development process of an Interactive System. A particular design situation is defined by choosing an appropriate value for each design option among a set of possible values. Determining such a value heavily depends on the task description. Several usability requirements were considered (error tolerance, memory requirements, selection feedback,...). Furthermore the problem of comparing and combining different modalities was discussed. It was recognized that whereas the enabling technologies for multimodal representation are growing rapidly, there is a lack of theoretical understanding of the principles which should be observed in mapping information from some task domain into presentations at the user interface in a way which optimizes the usability of the interface. Even if such a mapping is tried, there is no method for guaranteeing the usability of the product in every design situation, though particular cases have already been investigated.

Formal Specification

In this part of the workshop different notations and approaches to formal specification of Interactive Systems were compared. By formal notation is meant a notation whose semantics have been mathematically defined. Both software engineering notations and specific notations for HCI were considered. A wide range of approaches were considered and discussed; starting with logic for the analysis of distributed actions, which is especially useful for groupware applications. The use of Petri nets included in an object-oriented framework is useful for verifying properties such as absence of deadlock, predictability, reinitiability and availability of a command. Algebraic model of interaction which are at a level of abstraction and genericity to the various functional models but which try to capture more explicitly essential characteristics of direct manipulation such as IO synchronization and dependence. Specific applications such as interactive knowledge based systems were considered as case study in which models and approaches previously developed were evaluated.

Working Groups

In the second part of the workshop participants were divided into three working groups.

One group was on Users (end-users of systems). It had to consider issues such as how to include user perception in the specification of Interactive Systems and the effect on the design. Other problems to consider were general usability issues and the role of user tasks.

The group on the Role of Formalisms considered problems such as neutral descriptions/ freedom from notational bias; domain modelling; trade-off between cost of learning and pay-off for each notation (textual, visual); role of formal methods, notations in design, temporal modelling and reasoning. Here specific classes of applications were identified where it is particularly recommended to use formal methods. For example safety critical applications because in these cases the cost of a failure is very important with respect to the cost of the development.

Finally the group on Role of Development Environments focused on who are the users for these kind of environments, what kind of tools are necessary, which are the development models able to integrate software engineering and human-computer interaction concepts, place of formalism in these models, criteria for acceptability and use of task modelling. Here several types of designers were identified and for each of them current support by automatic tools was compared with improved support which should be included in future generation tools.

Pisa, June 1995   F. Paternó

Program Committee

S. Bagnara

D. Duce

G. Faconti

E. Fiume

M. Gangnet

P. ten Hagen

M. Harrison

R. Hartson

D. Olsen

F. Paternó (chair)

P. Sukaviriya

A. Sutcliffe

M. Tauber

Table of Contents

Part I

Invited Presentations and Discussions

Part I

General Presentation and Discussion

1 History, Results, and Bibliography of the User Interface Design Environment (UIDE), an Early Model-based System for User Interface Design and Implementation

James D. Foley

Piyawadee "Noi" Sukaviriya

ABSTRACT

UIDE, the User Interface Design Environment, was conceived in 1987 as a next-generation user interface design and implementation tool to embed application semantics into the earlier generation of User Interface Management Systems (UIMSs), which focused more on the look and feel of an interface. UIDE models an application's data objects, actions, and attributes, and the pre- and post- conditions associated with the actions. The model is then used for a variety of design-time and run-time services, such as to: automatically create windows, menus, and control panels; critique the design for consistency and completeness; control execution of the application; enable and disable menu items and other controls and make windows visible and invisible; generate context-sensitive animated help, in which a mouse moves on the screen to show the user how to accomplish a task; generate text help explaining why commands are disabled and what must be done to enable them; and support a set of transformations on the model which change certain user interface characteristics in a correctness-preserving way.

The model-based approach represented by UIDE is considered promising for four reasons. First, the model is specified in a non-procedural fashion at a higher level of abstraction than the code which the model replaces, thus replacing verbose procedural code with terser declarative knowledge. Second, many of the services provided automatically as a consequence of having the UIDE model, such as help, would typically have to be added after the application has been constructed. Changes to the application would have to be reflected back into those services. Third, when the model changes, all of the above uses of the model can be changed automatically. Finally, some of the design-time services provided by the model would not otherwise be available at all.

1.1 Introduction

UIDE was first developed in 1987, and has subsequently evolved through at least three generations, each of which represents an evolution of modeling concepts and an advance in our understanding of model-based user interface development tools.

UIDE contains meta-knowledge about an application and its relation to the application interface that is presented to the user. UIDE's *application model* represents actions which can be invoked by users, their operational constraints, and data objects on which the actions operate. An example is deleting a circle in a CAD program. UIDE's *interface model* represents interface components, actions which users apply to these interface components, and operational constraints on these actions. An example is selecting the delete action from a menu. The mappings from the application model to the interface model are also represented. UIDE as a whole is a collection of modeling entities and a set of tools which use the entities to specify interfaces, control dialog sequencing at runtime, and generate context-sensitive help. The heart of our UIDE research is to develop high-level semantic representations which can capture application and interface operations and objects. The representations then are used by various tools which enable UIDE to provide support for the user interface design process from its conception on through to application execution.

In this paper collection, we present the development of UIDE from 2 points of view: chronologic, and thematic. The two organizations help fit each paper both into a temporal context and a subject context. The chronology traces the development of UIDE from 1987 to 1994, through implementations in LISP, ART, and C++. We have continually added modeling constructs to UIDE so that it can perform more and more design-time and run-time functions. The thematic organization discusses and organizes the papers based on the major purpose of the UIDE model as discussed in the particular paper: application modeling, interface modeling, automatic help generation, adaptive user interfaces, transformations of user interfaces, automatic generation of user interfaces, automatic evaluation of user interfaces, and specifying the model by demonstrational techniques. Please note that many papers are cited in both the Chronology and Themes sections. Readers can use these cross references to find, for example, where a paper from a theme fits in the context of time, or vice versa.

1.2   The UIDE Chronology

Software tools for simplifying or expediting the development of user interfaces have been studied for many years: see [FOLEY90, Chapter 10] for a brief review. The term *User Interface Management System*, or *UIMS*, was often associated with such tools. Typically, compiler parsing techniques were used to define sequences of allowable user actions, employing formalisms such as regular expressions, state machines, BNF and augmented transition networks. Working at this low level of abstraction proved to be both tedious and inappropriate for the new generation of direct manipulation, WYSIWYG interfaces.

Two seminal dissertations were published in the mid-1980's. Mark Green's 1985 dissertation [GREE85] postulated an interesting but unimplemented user interface specification language including pre and post conditions for each user action. Scott Hudson's HIGGINS UIMS [HUDS86] used a data model as the basis for controlling a user interface.

At the same time, Jim Foley was despairing that the previous generation of UIMSs would have any impact, and was inspired by Green's and Hudson's move to a higher level of abstraction in representing user interfaces. Foley developed a vision of using a single representation combining and extending elements of Green's and Hudson's work, with the resulting model being usable for a much richer set of purposes than had previously been conceptualized by UIMS researchers. Hence, the objective of UIDE is to create an environment where knowledge about an application is captured early in the design process and then used throughout the design and implementation cycle.

The initial framework for UIDE is presented in [Foley et al.,1987, *A Knowledge Base for User Interface Management Systems*] presented at the SIGGRAPH Workshop on Software Tools for User Interface Management. The paper describes the concept of specifying an interactive graphics application program in terms of objects, actions on objects, and pre- and post-conditions on actions. A notation, IDL (Interface Definition Language, similar to the more recently-developed IDL used by the Object Management Group to describe objects) is introduced, as are a series of correctness-preserving transformations on the IDL description of an application. The transformations include adding modal and/or default attribute values, inserting a currently-selected object or currently-selected set of objects concept into the application, and specializing or generalizing commands. A second paper, [Foley et al., 1987,

Transformations on a Formal Specification of User-Computer Interfaces], elaborates on the transformations and their precise definition.

The first version of UIDE was implemented in LISP on a VAX, by Srdjan Kovacevic, Christina Gibbs, and Won-Chul Kim. Emphasis was on the representation (an internal form of IDL) and the transformations, with a text-oriented interface to the application. The transformations mentioned above were developed in this version.

The second generation UIDE was implemented in ART, the Automatic Reasoning Tool, by Kevin Murray, Srdjan Kovacevic, Christina Gibbs, and Won Kim. ART is a frame- and rule-based expert system shell implemented in LISP. This version re-implemented the transformations, making extensive use of ART's pattern matching to find frames which needed to be changed by a particular transformation. The version included simple rules for automatically generating a crude graphical user interface from the specification, involving menu selection, direct manipulation, text type-in, and slider manipulation. This meant that once the application was specified, the designer could transform the application and then "test drive" it without having to explicitly design the interface. Also included was a simple help capability, based on the actions' pre-conditions, to explain why a command was disabled and what to do to enable it. Post-conditions were used to give a simple account of some of the semantics of an action. The interface description could be printed in IDL for subsequent analysis.

The internal representations and some of the capabilities of this ART-based version of UIDE are described in [Foley et al., 1988, *A Knowledge Base for User Interface Management Systems*]; more in-depth discussions are found in [Foley et al., 1991, *UIDE – An Intelligent User Interface Design Environment*], the published version of an earlier paper presented at the March 1988 SIGCHI – AAAI ash Lockheed workshop organized by Joe Sullivan and Sherman Tyler, *Architectures for Intelligent Interfaces: Elements and Prototypes*.

Using this second generation of UIDE, Sukaviriya and Moran applied key-stoke analyses to different versions of the same application, with the versions being created by applying the transformations. This provided a very fast way to explore a space of design alternatives. The task sequence needed to perform the analysis was given by example on the automatically-generated user interface. The task sequence was then transformed along with the interface, to maintain consistency between the two for the keystroke analysis. This work is mentioned in [Foley et al., 1988, *A Knowledge Base for User Interface Management Systems*; Foley et al., 1991, *An Intelligent User Interface Design Environment*].

With the ART-based version, Kovacevic, for his Ph.D. dissertation, refined the model considerably, developing a finer granularity of specification and transformations which could exploit the granularity. His work is reported in [Kovacevic, 1992, *A Compositional Model of Human-Computer Interaction* ; Kovacevic, 1993, *TACTICS for User Interface Design: Coupling the Compositional and Transformational Approach*]. In addition, Kovacevic showed that the UIDE representation could be used to generate an ATN-based natural language parser for a textual interface to UIDE-modeled applications [Kovacevic, 1991, *A Compositional Model of Human-Computer Dialogues*]. With the ART-based version, Kim for his Ph.D. dissertation developed a sophisticated automatic layout tool, DON, which used semantics in the application model to help designers choose between dialog boxes and menus, and to help them layout dialog boxes according to semantic groupings and graphic layout rules [Kim et al., 1990, *DON: User Interface Presentation Design Assistant*t; Kim, 1993, *Knowledge-based Framework for an Automated User Interface Design Environment* ; Kim et al., 1993, *Providing High-level Control and Expert Assistance in the User Interface Presentation Design*].

The third generation of UIDE was implemented in Smalltalk-80 by Noi Sukaviriya to explore automatic, run-time generation of context-sensitive animated help [Sukaviriya et al., 1990,

Coupling a UI Framework with Automatic Generation of Context-sensitive Animated Help; Sukaviriya, 1991, *Automatic Generation of Context-sensitive Animated Help*]. The objective was to support, as part of UIDE, a general, application-independent means to create context-sensitive animated help based on the UIDE model. The system, called CARTOONIST, used many of the second-generation UIDE modeling entities. The significant additions included extending the UIDE model to distinguish two levels of representation the application and the interface levels; generalizing the use of pre- and post-conditions for planning via back-chaining (to create a plan for presenting the help); and explicitly representing the application and interface context so that the help plan could indeed be context-sensitive. The pre- and post-condition representation was changed to use a first-order predicate language.

At this stage, it became clear that some of the research concepts of UIDE were indeed viable, as demonstrated by private-sector support for UIDE. But, it was also clear that the technology-transfer path from the proprietary ART system and LISP to the world of real software was at best difficult. License fees, operating system upgrades, access to new and/or better interface toolkits, audio and voice technology were all, at best, difficult. Hence, with support from Sun Microsystems and Siemens Corporation, we moved UIDE to C++, thereby creating the third (and current) generation of UIDE.

While building the third generation, we also conducted a series of trials of various concepts as separate C++ implementations, portions of which were ultimately included in UIDE. These include:

- Using pre- and post-conditions attached to widgets to sequence dialog control [Gieskens, 1991, *Controlling User Interface Objects Through Pre- and Postconditions*; Gieskens et al., 1992, *Controlling User Interface Objects Through Pre- and Postconditions*]
- Automatic layout of dialog boxes using an application data model [de Baar, 1991, *Towards Integrating Application Design and User Interface Design*; de Baar et al., 1992, *Coupling Application Design and User Interface Design*]
- Automatic generation of textual, context-sensitive help from predicates attached to objects [de Graff, 1992, *Context-sensitive Help as an Integral Part of a User Interface Design Environment* ; de Graff et al., 1993, *Automatic Generation of Context-sensitive Textual Help*].

In the process of re-building the UIDE environment, numerous design revisions and additions were incorporated to compensate for the luxury of the loosely-typed, interpretive ART and Smalltalk environments in the strictly-typed, compile-link-run C++ environment. Run-time support such as automatic dialog sequencing works reasonably well [Sukaviriya et al., 1993, *A Second Generation User Interface Design Environment: The Model And The Runtime Architecture*; Sukaviriya et al., 1993, *A Model-based User Interface Architecture: Enhancing a Runtime Environment with Declarative Knowledge*], and automatic generation of "why" help, audio and animated help, have been thoroughly integrated and refined [Spaans, 1993, *Integration of Automatically Generated Context-sensitive Animated and Textual Help into UIDE*; Sukaviriya et al., 1993, *Automatic Generation of Multimedia Help in UIDE: the User Interface Design Environment*].

Yet a fourth UIDE generation is now being developed. The new generation, called MASTERMIND, integrates HUMANOID and UIDE. HUMANOID is another powerful model-based user interface environment developed by Pedro Szekely, Bob Neches, and Ping Luo at the Information Sciences Institute of the University of Southern California. The integration captures the best characteristics of each system [Neches et. al, *Knowledgeable Development Environments Using Shared Design Models*]. Developing the new generation and further enhancing its capabilites is a three-year effort funded by ARPA, the Advanced Research Project Agency. MASTERMIND will be built on top of a C++ version of Garnet, Brad Myers' user interface toolkit. References to MASTERMIND can be found in many of the UIDE papers, and vice-versa.

1.3   UIDE Themes

In this section, UIDE papers are organized around various themes: the modeling itself, and the various uses to which the model is put: application modeling, interface modeling, integrated, more sohpisticated application and interface modeling, automatic help generation, adaptive user interfaces, transformation of user interfaces, automatic generation of user interfaces, automatic evalutaion of user interfaces, and specifying the model via demonstrational techniques.

1.3.1   First-Generation UIDE: Application Modeling

The first generation UIDE represented only the application model, with its two sub-models: the data model describing objects in an application or task domain, and the control model describing the actions that may be performed on objects in the data model. [Foley et al., 1988, *A Knowledge Base for User Interface Management Systems*; Foley et al., 1989, *The User Interface Design Environment - A Computer Aided Software Engineering Tool for the User-Computer Interface*; Foley et al., 1991, *UIDE – An Intelligent User Interface Design Environment*]. Predicate-based preconditions and postconditions of actions are used to represent the semantics of actions, and to control the run-time execution of an application [Gieskens et al., 1992, *Controlling User Interface Objects Through Pre- and Postconditions*].

1.3.2   Second-Generation UIDE: Application and Interface Modeling

The second generation UIDE models both application and interface semantics, hence the control model and the data model are present for both the application and the interface domains [Sukaviriya et al., 1993, *A Second Generation User Interface Design Environment: The Model And The Runtime Architecture*; Sukaviriya et al., 1993, *A Model-based User Interface Architecture: Enhancing a Runtime Environment with Declarative Knowledge*; Sukaviriya et al., 1993, *A Comprehensive Look at the Usage, the Model, and the Architecture of UIDE: the User Interface Design Environment*; Sukaviriya et al., 1993, *A Model-based and Direct-Compositional-based Interface Design Environment: Integration of GaTech's UIDE and Siemens' SX/Tools*]. The implementation language is C++ rather than the earlier LISP and ART. A formal specification has been established to link the application tasks to the interface tasks, allowing multiple ways to perform an application task, possibly with different input devices. Dialog sequencing is controlled automatically from the semantic information specified by designers as pre- and post-conditions, both in the application and interface model. Also, being incorporated into the system is the ability to trace user interactions using the UIDE application and interface model. These traces will be used for adapting the appearance, behavior, and help of the interface.

1.3.3   Third-Generation UIDE: UIDE + HUMANOID = MASTERMIND

MASTERMIND, which stands for **M**odels **A**llowing **S**hared **T**ools and **E**xplicit **R**epresentations to **M**ake **I**nterfaces **N**atural to **D**evelop, is the merger of UIDE and MASTERMIND discussed earlier. The new model combines the strengths of both models [Neches et al., 1993, *Knowledgeable Development Environments Using Shared Design Models*]. MASTERMIND implemention began in late 1994.

1.3.4   Automatic Help Generation: CARTOONIST, AUTOHELP

The concept of context-sensitive animated help was developed in a small prototype as part of Sukaviriya's dissertation proposal [Sukaviriya, 1988, *Dynamic Construction of Animated Help from Application Context*]. The first version of a model-based automatic generation of procedural help was implemented in a system called Cartoonist as Sukaviriya's dissertation at The George Washington University [Sukaviriya et al., 1990, *Coupling a UI Framework with Automatic Generation of Context-sensitive Animated Help*]. Cartoonist built on the original UIDE representation of actions, parameters, pre- and post-conditions, and objects. Cartoonist refined UIDE's knowledge base to support the planning process for context-sensitive construction of help messages at run-time, and introduced a hierarchical high-level representation separating the application and the interface domains. The separate models allow interface and help generation mechanisms to remain application-independent. Cartoonist uses animation of a mouse icon moving on the screen, with button clicks when appropriate, and a keyboard icon showing character strings being typed in to demonstrate to end-users how to perform actions within the user's current context.

A separate prototype of help on why an object in an interface is disabled was developed using the pre- and post-conditions associated with objects [de Graff et al., 1993, *Automatic Generation of Context-sensitive Textual Help*]. The concept was later revised, redesigned, and integrated in the C++ version of UIDE, retrieving application semantic information directly from action pre-conditions. Animated help has been re-implemented in the C++ UIDE platform using the same principles as Cartoonist. In addition to the animation, descriptions of procedures are extracted from the knowledge base and played as an audio narration of the animation. The combined and growing help system in UIDE is currently called AutoHelp [Sukaviriya et al., 1993, *Automatic Generation of Multimedia Help in UIDE: the User Interface Design Environment*].

To facilitate the provision of animated help, Bharat created a general-purpose animation server [Bharat et al., 1993, *Animating User Interfaces Using Animation Servers*], which can be used with UIDE or any other UNIX/X-based application.

1.3.5   Adaptive User Interfaces

The UIDE model can be used as the start of a user's model of an application. By tracking user action sequences, insights into what the user understands and does not understand can be garnered. Two papers describe how we expect to provide adaptive user interface behavior [Sukaviriya et al., 1993a, *Supporting Adaptive Interfaces in a Knowledge-Based User Interface Environment*, Sukaviriya, 1993, *From User Interface Design to Supporting Intelligent and Adaptive Interfaces: an Overhaul of UI Software Architecture*; Sukaviriya et al., 1993b, *A*

Built-in Provision for Collecting Individual Task Usage Information in UIDE: the User Interface Design Environment].

1.3.6 Transformations of User Interfaces

One important early use of the model is in the context of correctness-preserving transformations which allow different points in user interface design space to be quickly visited [Foley et al., 1987, *Algorithms to Transform the Formal Specification of a User-Computer Interface*; Foley, 1987, *Transformations on a Formal Specification of User-Computer Interfaces*]. A menu of transformations (establish currently-selected object paradigm, specialize commands, create modal attribute) is presented to the user interface designer, who can then invoke a transformation and within seconds begin executing an interface with the newly-created characteristics. The transformations quickly do what otherwise could take several hours of coding.

Kovacevic, for his Ph.D. dissertation, refined the model considerably, developing a finer granularity of specification and transformations which could exploit the granularity. Kovacevic's UI model identifies and classifies components of a UI and structuring principles for composing them into a functional UI. His model establishes explicit relationships between UI components and application components (captured in the UIDE model), which enables automatic generation of user interfaces. Furthermore, the look-and-feel of a UI is explained in terms of how UI components are configured and can be controlled by applying transformations. This integrated knowledge representation of the application and its interface enables additional design assistance, such as a design critic detecting potential ambiguities. His work is reported in [Kovacevic, 1992, *A Compositional Model of Human-Computer Dialogues*]. In addition, Kovacevic showed that the UIDE representation could be used to generate an ATN-based natural language parser for a textual interfaces to UIDE-modeled applications [Kovacevic, 1993, *TACTICS - A Model-based Framework for Multimodal Interaction*].

1.3.6.1 Automatic Generation of User Interfaces: DON and AUTO-DEVGUIDE

Given a UI model, it is possible to create interface elements for the model. DON [Kim et al., 1990, *DON: User Interface Presentation Design Assistant*; Kim et al., 1993, *Providing High-level Control and Expert Assistance in the User Interface Presentation Design*] does global layout of dialogue boxes, applying graphics design considerations such as balance, weight, and symmetry. Using a generate and test strategy, many alternative designs are created and evaluated. The best designs are presented to the UI designer for selection and possible modification with an interactive design tool.

Auto-DevGuide [de Baar et al., 1992, *Coupling Application Design and User Interface Design*] is a rule-driven extension to Sun Microsystem's DevGuide user interface design tool. The system accepts a data model and uses the rules to select appropriate dialogue box widgets, such as sliders, scrolling lists, and buttons. The rules are adapted from OpenLook, and hence automatically enforce the OpenLook style guide. This approach ensures a higher degree of UI design consistency than would otherwise be possible. The same approach can be used with other style guides, such as MOTIF. Gray increased the sophistication of the system by using sequential and hierarchical dependencies among interface objects to order them in the dialogue box [Gray et al., 1993, *Grouping and Ordering User Interface Components*].

1.3.6.2   Automatic Evaluation of User Interfaces: Keystroke and GOMS analysis

A UI model can be used as input to human performance models. This is a powerful predictive tool which can speed up the rapid prototyping and testing process by converging more quickly on a final "best" design.

The UIDE model has been used in this way for keystroke model analysis and for GOMS analysis. In the keystroke analysis work, which can predict speed of use for expert users performing routine tasks, we allowed the designer to create a task scenario by example, using an interface generated automatically by UIDE. Then, after the designer modifies aspects of the UI design (interaction techniques and devices, applying transformation), the modified model could be analyzed for speed of use to predict which design variation would be fastest for the user. This provided a very fast way to explore a space of design alternatives. The task sequence needed to perform the analysis was transformed with the interface to maintain consistency between the two for the keystroke analysis. An overview of the keystroke analysis work is reported in [Foley et al., 1989, *The User Interface Design Environment - A Computer Aided Software Engineering Tool for the User-Computer Interface*; Foley et al., 1991, *UIDE – An Intelligent User Interface Design Environment*].

More recently, we have collaborated with Dave Kieras at the University of Michigan to apply his NGOMSL tool for GOMS analysis to UI Models from UIDE [Byrne et al., 1993, *Automating Interface Evaluation*]. GOMS estimates the learning time for an interface, as well as execution times for tasks, including more complex tasks than can be analyzed with the keystroke model.

Mike Bryne implemented USAGE (the UIDE System for semi-Automated GOMS Evaluation), which translates the UIDE model into an NGOMSL model. That all the information needed by NGOMSL is present in UIDE is significant in that it indicates a certain kind of completeness of the model. A separate task scenario is entered into NGOMSL, and the analysis is performed. In one example, execution times for different interface designs ranged from 37 to 47 seconds: a 25% difference predicted by the model without actual testing of any of the three interfaces studied. Of course, the estimates could be wrong, but validation studies typically show good correlation between measured results and the predictions. In some cases the rank ordering and ratios of predictions are correct, with their absolute values being incorrect.

1.3.6.3   Specifying the Model via Demonstrational Techniques

Specifying a model is tedious. We are developing notational, by-example and by-interview techniques for facilitating the process [FRAN93a, FRAN93b, SADUN93]. The key idea of Frank's work is to demonstrate the user interface, inferring from the demonstration the underlying model. The model is made available to the designer for further refinement - in contrast to typical demonstrational systems, in which "what you demonstrate is what you get." In the case of Sadun's work, a graphical notation representing a different set of modeling abstracts is shown to the user after a demonstration. The graphical notation can be edited, and is animated during user interface execution to show the flows of control. This is intended to facilitate debugging and modification.

1.4   Acknowledgements

The development of UIDE is a continuing endeavor. We extend our sincere thanks to all who have participated over the years: Hernan Astudillo, Krishna Bharat, Terry Bleser, Bob Braudes, Michael Byrne, Dennis deBaar, Steven Chang, Martin Frank, Christina Gibbs, Daniel Gieskens, J. J. "Hans" de Graaff, Mark Gray, Todd Griffith, Erwin Hansen, Ray Johnson, Won-Chul Kim, Srdjan Kovacevic, Thomas Kuhme, Erica Liebman, Lucy Moran, Kevin Murray, Jeyakumar Muthukumarasamy, Alberto Rama, Spencer Rugaber, Hikmet Senay, John Sibert, Anton Spaans, and Uday Sreekanth.
Initial support for this work came from the Interactive Systems program of the National Science Foundation, under grants DMC-8420529, and IRIS-8813179. Subsequent support has been provided by Digital Equipment Corporation, Schlumberger Foundation, Siemens Corporation, Software Productivity Consortium, Sun Microsystems, and US West.

1.5   References

This first set of references is to previous work on user interface management systems.

[FOLE90]   Foley, J., A. van Dam, S. Feiner, and J. Hughes, *Computer Graphics: Principles and Practice,* Addison-Wesley, Reading, MA, 1990.
[GREE85]   Green, Mark, *The Design of Graphical User Interfaces*, Technical Report CSRI-170, University of Toronto, Toronto, Canada, 1985.
[HUDS86]   Hudson, S. and R. King, A Generator of Direct Manipulation Office Systems, *ACM Transactions on Office Information Systems*, 4(2), April 1986, pp. 132–163.

The following is a complete list of all UIDE papers. This collection contains a subset of these papers. Those not included tend to overlap the papers we have selected to include here. Many of these papers are available electronically from ftp http. Also, a hard copy collection of many of the papers is available for $ 25.00 (prepaid by check in US currency), from the authors.

[BHAR93]   Bharat, K; and P. Sukaviriya. Animating User Interfaces Using Animation Servers. In *Proceedings of ACM SIGGRAPH 1993 Symposium on User Interface Software and Technology*, 1993.
[BYRN93]   Byrne, M., S. Wood, P. Sukaviriya, J. Foley, and D. Kieras, Automating Interface Evaluation, *Proceedings CHI'94 - SIGCHI 1994 Computer Human Interaction Conference*, ACM, New York, NY, 1994, pp. 232– 237.
[DEBA91]   deBaar, D. *Towards Integrating Application Design and User Interface Design.* Master's Thesis. Delft University of Technology. Delft, the Netherlands. 1991.
[DEBA92]   deBaar, D; J. Foley; and Kevin Mullet. Coupling Application Design and User Interface Design. *Proceedings CHI'92 - SIGCHI 1992 Computer Human Interaction Conference.* ACM, New York, NY, 1992, pp. 259–266.
[DEGR92]   de Graff, J.J. *Context-sensitive Help as an Integral Part of a User Interface Design Environment.* Master's Thesis. Delft University of Technology. Delft, The Netherlands. 1992.

[DEGR93]   de Graff, J.J.; P. Sukaviriya; and C. van der Mast. Automatic Generation of Context-sensitive Textual Help. *Technical Report GIT-GVU-93-11*. Atlanta, Georgia: Graphics, Visualization, and Usability Center, Georgia Institute of Technology, 1993.

[FOLE87a]   Foley, J. Transformations on a Formal Specification of User-Computer Interfaces. In ACM SIGGRAPH Workshop on Software Tools for User Interface Management, in *Computer Graphics*, 21(2), April 1987, pp. 109–113.

[FOLE87b]   Foley, J.; W. Kim; and C. Gibbs. Algorithms to Transform the Formal Specification of a User-Computer Interface. In *Proceedings INTERACT '87, 2nd IFIP Conference on Human-Computer Interaction.* Elsivier Science Publishers, Amsterdam, pp.1001–1006.

[FOLE87c]   Foley, J. Models and Tools for Designers of User Computer Interfaces. In *Theoretical Foundations of Computer Graphics and CAD*, R. Earnshaw, Ed., Springer-Verlag, Berlin, 1987.

[FOLE88]   Foley, J., C. Gibbs, W. Kim, and S. Kovacevic. A Knowledge Base for User Interface Management Systems. *Proceedings CHI '88 - 1988 SIGCHI Computer-Human Interaction Conference.* ACM, New York, 1988, pp. 67–72.

[FOLE89]   Foley, J.; W. Kim; S. Kovacevic; and K. Murray. The User Interface Design Environment - A Computer Aided Software Engineering Tool for the User-Computer Interface. *IEEE Software*, Special Issue on User Interface Software, 6(1), January 1989, pp. 25–32.

[FOLE91]   Foley, J.; W. Kim; S. Kovacevic; and K. Murray. UIDE – An Intelligent User Interface Design Environment. In J. Sullivan and S. Tyler, Eds.,*Architectures for Intelligent Interfaces: Elements and Prototypes*, Addison-Wesley, 1991, pp. 339–384.

[FRAN93a]   Frank, M. and J. Foley. Model-Based User Interface Design by Example and by Answering Questions. *Proceedings INTERCHI 1993*, ACM, New York, 1993, pp. 161–162.

[FRAN93b]   Frank, M. and J. Foley, Model-Based User Interface Design by Example and by Interview, Proceedings of UIST'93, Nov. 1993, pp. 129–137.

[FRAN94]   Frank, M. and Foley, J. A Pure Reasoning Engine for Programming By Demonstration. In *Proceedings of UIST'94, ACM Symposium on User Interface Software and Technology*, (November 2–4, Marina del Rey, California) ACM, New York, 1994.

[par GIES91] Gieskens, D. *Controlling User Interface Objects Through Pre- and Postconditions* . Master Thesis. Delft University of Technology. Delft, The Netherlands. 1991.

[GIES92]   Gieskens, D. and J. Foley. Controlling User Interface Objects Through Pre- and Postconditions. In *Proceedings CHI'92 - SIGCHI 1992 Computer Human Interaction Conference*, ACM, New York, NY, 1992, pp. 189–194.

[GRAY93]   Gray, M.; J. Foley; and K. Mullet. Grouping and Ordering User Interface Components. GVU Center working paper, 1993.

[KIM90]   Kim, W. and J. Foley. DON: User Interface Presentation Design Assistant. In *Proceedings SIGGRAPH 1990 Symposium on User Interface Software and Technology (UIST '90)*, pp. 10–20.

[KIM93a]   Kim, W. *Knowledge-based Framework for an Automated User Interface Design Environment*t. Ph.D. Dissertation, George Washington University, Washington, DC, 1993.

[KIM93b]   Kim, W. and J. Foley. Providing High-level Control and Expert Assistance in the User Interface Presentation Design. In *Proceedings INTERCHI 1993*, ACM, New York, pp. 430-437.

[KOVA92a]   Kovacevic, S. A Compositional Model of Human-Computer Dialogues. In Blattner M. and Dannenberg R. (Eds.), *Multimedia Interface Design*, ACM Press, New York, 1992.

[KOVA92b]   Kovacevic, S. *A Compositional Model of Human-Computer Interaction*. Ph.D. Dissertation, George Washington University, Washington, DC, 1992.

[KOVA93]   Kovacevic, S. TACTICS for User Interface Design: Coupling the Compositional and Transformational Approach. *Technical Report GIT-GVU-93-43*. Atlanta, Georgia: Graphics, Visualization, and Usability Center, Georgia Institute of Technology, 1993.

[NECH93]   Neches, R.; J. Foley; P. Szekely; P. Sukaviriya; P. Luo; S. Kovacevic; and S. Hudson. Knowledgeable Development Environments Using Shared Design Models. In *Proceedings of the Intelligent Interfaces Workshop*, Orlando, Florida, January 4-7, 1993, pp. 63-70.

[SADU93]   Sadun, E. and J. Foley. *DJASA: Interactive Notation for Dynamic Interfaces*. Poster paper, CHI '94.

[SENA93]   Senay, H.; P. Sukaviriya; and L. Moran. Planning for Automatic Help Generation. In Proceedings *of IFIP Working Conference on Engineering for Human Computer Interactions*, Napa Valley, California, August, 1989.

[SPAA93]   Spaans, A. *Integration of Automatically Generated Context-sensitive Animated and Textual Help into UIDE*. Master's Thesis. Delft University of Technology. Delft, the Netherlands. 1993.

[SUKA88]   Sukaviriya, P. Dynamic Construction of Animated Help from Application Context. In *Proceedings UIST '88 Conference*, 1988, ACM, New York, NY, pp. 190–203.

[SUKA89]   Sukaviriya, P. Context-Sensitive Animated Help, video presented at CHI'89. Austin, Texas, May 1989. (SIGGRAPH video tape 57).

[SUKA90]   Sukaviriya, P. and J. Foley. Coupling a UI Framework with Automatic Generation of Context-sensitive Animated Help. In *Proceedings SIGGRAPH 1990 Symposium on User Interface Software and Technology (UIST '90)*, pp. 152–166.

[SUKA91]   Sukaviriya, P. *Automatic Generation of Context-sensitive Animated Help*. Ph.D. Dissertation, George Washington University, Washington, DC, 1991.

[SUKA93a]   Sukaviriya, P. and J. D. Foley. Supporting Adaptive Interfaces in a Knowledge-Based User Interface Environments. In *Proceedings of the Intelligent Interfaces Workshop*, Orlando, Florida, January 4-7, 1993, pp. 107–114.

[SUKA93b]   Sukaviriya, P.; J. Foley; and T. Griffith. A Second Generation User Interface Design Environment: The Model And The Runtime Architecture. In *Proceedings INTERCHI 1993*, ACM, New York, pp. 375–382.

[SUKA93c]   Sukaviriya, P. From User Interface Design to Supporting Intelligent and Adaptive Interfaces: an Overhaul of UI Software Architecture. Submited and accepted for the *Knowledge-based Systems Journal*, In press.

[SUKA93d]   Sukaviriya, P. and J. D. Foley. A Built-in Provision for Collecting Individual Task Usage Information in UIDE: the User Interface Design Environment. In M. Schneider-Hufschmidt, T. Kühme, and U. Malinowski (eds), *Adaptive User Interfaces: Principles and Practice*, Amstradam : North Holland, 1993.

[SUKA93e]   Sukaviriya, P.; M. Frank; J. Muthukumarasamy; and A. Spaans. A Model-based User Interface Architecture: Enhancing a Runtime Environment with Declarative Knowledge. *Technical Report GIT-GVU-93-12*. Atlanta, Georgia: Graphics, Visualization, and Usability Center, Georgia Institute of Technology, 1993.

[SUKA93f]   Sukaviriya, P.; A. Spaans; J.J. de Graaff; and J. Muthukumarasamy. Automatic Generation of Multimedia Help in UIDE: the User Interface Design Environment. *Technical Report GIT-GVU-93-36*. Atlanta, Georgia: Graphics, Visualization, and Usability Center, Georgia Institute of Technology, 1993.

[SUKA93g]   Sukaviriya, P.; T. Kühme; J. Muthukumarasamy; M. Brenner; and H. Astudillo. A Model-based and Direct-Compositional-based Interface Design Environment: Integration of GaTech's UIDE and Siemens' SX/Tools.

2 Interactions with Advanced Graphical Interfaces and the Deployment of Latent Human Knowledge

Phil Barnard
Jon May

ABSTRACT

Advanced graphical interfaces are increasingly dynamic, multimodal and involve multi-threaded dialogues. This paper provides a theoretical perspective that can support an analysis of the issues involved in their use: the Interacting Cognitive Subsystems (ICS) framework. This framework is used to examine alternative ways in which information from different data streams can be blended within perception, thought and the control of action. The potential applicability of the core constructs to interface design is considered. The paper concludes by outlining a specific strategy for bringing this form of understanding into closer harmony with the formal methods community in computer science.

2.1   Introduction

2.1.1   The design problem

As human interfaces to information technology become increasingly advanced, the representational and communicative capabilities they embody have broadened considerably. We can no longer consider interfacing to be a simple matter of issuing commands – by lexical or graphical means – and ensuring that a user understands the consequent change in display state. Advanced graphical interfaces are increasingly dynamic, multimodal and involve multi-threaded dialogues. These interfaces may incorporate video communications technologies, computer controlled films or dynamic animations, intelligent agents, voice input and so on. The end users of such technologies must actively interpret what their full range of senses tell them, remember what a range of computer and human agents are doing, and carefully craft rather complex response patterns – often 'social' in nature. As designers, software engineers must now develop complex communicative environments. In doing so they must pose and answer a full range of questions about the complete interactive system, incorporating devices and users, operating in one or another domains of application – such as air traffic control, computer-aided design, computer supported co-operative work, or computer games.

In thinking about the issues raised, it is natural first to consider the domain tasks and explicit knowledge that a user must already have or needs to acquire in order to use an interface effectively. What is the relevant domain and task knowledge? How is the deployment of such knowledge constrained by limitations on human memory or upon human abilities to do more than one thing at a time? Providing answers to such questions has been the traditional contribution of human factors and cognitive engineering approaches to the design, development and evaluation of computer interfaces.

In the context of advanced systems it is also necessary to consider how the human mental mechanism integrates information over modalities (voice and vision) or over sources and locations (as when a pointing gesture is used to resolve reference to an item). Tone of voice, facial expression or accompanying gestures may radically alter the appropriate interpretation of a message and other factors such as the attribution of agency. The perceived emotional or social status (yes – even of computers!) can radically change the properties of interactions.

Much of the relevant human knowledge that governs these considerations is 'latent' and its analysis lies outside the capabilities of most current approaches to cognitive engineering.

2.1.2   Latent knowledge and its relevance to the design of advanced graphical interfaces

While our overt knowledge of the procedures and properties of interfaces helps to determine what we can achieve with them and what we can explain to, or teach others, latent knowledge plays a powerful role in user performance. It acts throughout the human mental mechanism systematically to constrain perception, thought and the control of action. For example, when things happen in the world, they are typically perceived as unified 'events'. We see a flock of birds fly across our field of view; we hear someone shout our name; or we may feel drops of rain on our face. We can interpret these events as unitary even though the information that we receive about them is clearly not unitary: constituent information can be separated in space and in time, or it can originate in different sensory 'modalities'. In a tennis game, we may see a ball approaching and, at the point of contact, both hear and feel its impact on the racquet. We are able to bring constituents together by learning to recognise the invariant structural patterns that typify events 'in the world' [28].

There is a substantial literature on the unification of information within individual modalities like vision [18] or audition [11, 17]. Although rather less is known about it, there is more than ample evidence that multimodal integration supports a whole range of human understanding. When we watch an accomplished ventriloquist, there is a spatial separation between the source of the voice and the position of the dummy. The audience will nevertheless understand the action as a single fused event sequence focused on the dummy. For decades billions of people have been happy to watch events on television while the sound accompanying them has come from a small speaker to one side of the screen. A thunderclap follows a flash of lightning by an unpredictable number of seconds, but we can understand them as a consequence of the same event, and can even make productive use of information about the temporal disparity. Although we can be aware that multimodal integration is taking place, the latent knowledge that determines its real time operation is often not readily accessible. Some explanations rely upon very general abstractions like the Gestalt principles of common fate and proximity. So, for example, Radeau [41] argues that "the rules underlying auditory-visual pairing could state that if elements from two different sensory modalities have the same temporal patterning, are asynchronous and come from locations which are not too far apart in space, then they can probably be assigned to the same event".

The consequences of systematic departures from normality may be all too accessible. The misalignment of voice and lip movements that occurs when the soundtrack of a film goes out of synchrony is highly disruptive, because we 'see' one speech stream and 'hear' another. Other instances may be equally inaccessible to conscious awareness. When the speech information we hear is at variance with the lip movements of the speaker, a listener may 'hear' what was seen, or may blend the two sources to perceive a word that was neither seen nor heard (e.g. [30]). If we place a finger on one hand in a glass of hot water and a finger on the other hand in a glass of cold water until temperature adaptation occurs, then place both fingers into a third glass of warm water, the resulting sensations conflict. The *same* water feels cold to one finger and hot to the other (see [37]).

Although some of these examples may appear somewhat esoteric, interest in the fusion of information within and between human sensory modalities is not simply of academic interest. Multisensory fusion is vital in advanced robotics and, of course, in virtual reality and telepresence systems. Current computer system design is preoccupied with developing multimedia and multimodal forms of interaction. Video, dynamic animation, speech modes, head 'mice', data gloves, force feedback and other forms of haptic information exchange are increasingly being bolted on to traditional text and gesture based interactions. Designers keen on illustrating how such technology might play a part in a tourist information system might, for example, show how two, very small video windows of different parts of the town can be simultaneously running on the screen, accompanied, of course, by a single informative voice over. At the same time, the user may actually be accessing a database of train times. All of these 'new' classes of system involve the management of multiple 'streams' of information, either within the same or in different modalities. At the heart of the vast majority of the systems are advanced graphical interfaces. Observation of existing 'demonstrator' applications suggests that computerised 'events' may not always be accompanied by an appropriate fusion of related information or by an appropriate separation of unrelated streams. If such systems are to be effective, they must be kept within the limits of normal human capabilities for handling multiple sources of information.

2.1.3   Structure of the paper

This paper will be broadly concerned with the capabilities, and limitations of the deployment of latent human knowledge in interface usage. The paper will not provide direct advice to designers on specific issues. Rather, the intention here is to provide a broader view of how the human information processor may function to deploy its latent knowledge in perception, thought and the control of action. Our wider objective is to develop an explicit account of the uni-modal and cross-modal blending of information. In the specific context of HCI, this endeavour contributes directly to the development of techniques for the approximate modelling of cognitive activity based upon Interacting Cognitive Subsystems – ICS (e.g. [5, 34]).

The remainder of this paper is divided into three main sections. The next section is theoretical and reviews those features of the ICS framework that are relevant to the blending of information sources to form unified streams of data. The following section (2.3) focuses on the four types of representational blending that occur within the ICS architecture. In each case potential applicability to interface design is discussed. A summary of the main points to emerge from our preliminary application of the ICS framework to these issues is presented in section 2.4, which also outlines an agenda for bringing this form of understanding into closer harmony with the design and formal methods communities in computer science.

2.2   Interacting Cognitive Subsystems

Interacting Cognitive Subsystems (ICS) is a part of a theoretical movement within cognitive psychology (e.g., [47]) that represents the human information processing mechanism as a highly parallel organisation with a modular structure. The ICS architecture contains a set of functionally distinct subsystems, each with equivalent capabilities, yet each specialised to deal with a different class of representation. These subsystems exchange representations of information directly, with no role for a 'central processor' or 'limited capacity working memory'. The assumption is that we are dealing with a *system* of distributed cognitive resources, in which behaviour arises out of the co-ordinated operation of the constituent parts. In order to be able to discuss specific issues concerned with the different forms of representational blending, it is essential to have a general overview of the architecture and its operation.

2.2.1   The systemic organisation

As a fundamentally systemic approach to mental processing, ICS is comprehensive: it encompasses all aspects of perception, cognition, and emotion, as well as the control of action and internal bodily reactions. Acting together, nine component subsystems deal with incoming sensory information, structural regularities in that information, the meanings that can be abstracted from it, and the creation of instructions for the body to respond and act both externally, 'in the real world', and internally, in terms of physiological effects. Figure 2.1 outlines the overall architecture whilst Table 1 lists the nature of the mental representations that each subsystem processes. The subsystems can be classed as *peripheral* if they exchange information with the world via the senses or the body (the Sensory subsystems AC, VIS, and BS; and the Effector subsystems ART and LIM), or *central* if they only exchange information with other subsystems (the Structural subsystems MPL and OBJ; and the Meaning subsystems PROP and IMPLIC).

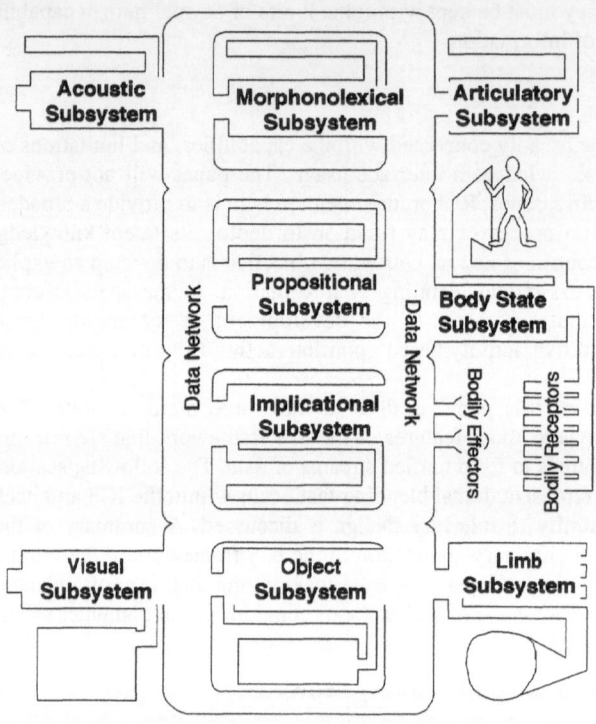

Figure 2.1:   The systemic organisation of ICS

2.2.2   The internal structure of each subsystem

Although each of these subsystems deals with a different class of information, they have the same basic internal structure (Figure 2.2). The representations they receive arrive at an *input array,* where they are *copied* into an *image record,* while simultaneously being operated on by a number of *transformation processes.* The input array brings together all the information currently represented in the form appropriate for its subsystem, and so its content is dynamically changing from moment to moment. The Copy process continually transfers this information, without changing it, to the Image Record, which acts as a memory 'local' to the subsystem. Any representation that has ever been received at the input array of the subsystem is registered in the record, and in the long-term any communalities and regularities of the varied representations can be abstracted from this stock of past experience. In the shorter-term, it presents an 'extended representation' of the transient information on the input array, making available derivatives such as a rate of change of a representation or repeated occurrences of the same patterning within the constituent structure of those representations.

PERIPHERAL SUBSYSTEMS
a) Sensory

(1)	Acoustic (AC):	Sound frequency (pitch), timbre, intensity etc. Subjectively, what we 'hear in the world'.
(2)	Visual (VIS):	Light wavelength (hue), brightness over visual space etc. Subjectively, what we 'see in the world' as patterns of shapes and colours.
(3)	Body State (BS):	Type of stimulation (e.g., cutaneous pressure, temperature, olfactory, muscle tension), its location, intensity etc. Subjectively, bodily sensations of pressure, pain, positions of parts of the body, as well as tastes and smells etc.

b) Effector

(4)	Articulatory (ART):	Force, target positions and timing of articulatory musculatures (e.g., place of articulation). Subjectively, our experience of subvocal speech output.
(5)	Limb (LIM):	Force, target positions and timing of skeletal musculatures. Subjectively, 'mental' physical movement.

CENTRAL SUBSYSTEMS
c) Structural

(6)	Morphonolexical (MPL):	An abstract structural description of entities and relationships in sound space. Dominated by speech forms, where it conveys a surface structure description of the identity of words, their status, order and the form of boundaries between them. Subjectively, what we 'hear in the head', our mental 'voice'.
(7)	Object (OBJ):	An abstract structural description of entities and relationships in visual space, conveying the attributes and identity of structurally integrated visual objects, their relative positions and dynamic characteristics. Subjectively, our 'visual imagery.'

d) Meaning

(8)	Propositional (PROP):	A description of entities and relationships in semantic space conveying the attributes and identities of underlying referents and the nature of relationships among them. Subjectively, specific semantic relationships ('knowing that').
(9)	Implicational (IMPLIC):	An abstract description of human existential space, abstracted over both sensory and propositional input, and conveying ideational and affective content: *schematic models* of experience. Subjectively, 'senses' of knowing (e.g., 'familiarity' or 'causal relatedness' of ideas), or of affect (e.g., apprehension, desire).

Table 1.   The subsystems within ICS and the type of information with which they deal (based on [6]).

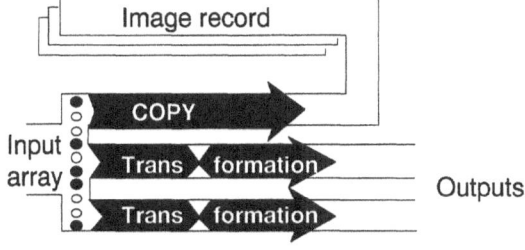

Figure 2.2:   The internal structure of each subsystem

While the Input Array, the Copy process and the Image Record are crucial in defining the internal function of each subsystem, the Transformation processes are the key to the function of the overall, systemic organisation. In normal operation, these transform the information represented on the input array into a different representation, for use by another subsystem. The VIS subsystem, for example, contains a VIS→OBJ transformation process that uses the information contained within the sensory, Visual representation to derive the more abstract, Object representation. The transformation processes within a subsystem are independent, and so can act simultaneously, on the same part of the input array, or on a different part. A consequence of this is that each subsystem can produce multiple, different output representations at the same time, each from a different transformation process. A single transformation process can only produce one output at a time, though, since it can only process a single coherent stream of data. This constraint is an important one, and the definition of a 'coherent' stream will be discussed later.

2.2.3   Configurations of processing

Since the subsystems are specialised to receive information represented in a particular way, none of these subsystems can do much on its own. In practice, cognition is the consequence of several subsystems functioning in a chain, or configuration, each taking its input representation and producing an output representation for use by a subsequent subsystem. The parallel nature of the architecture means that information 'flows' through this configuration, rather than pulsing in steps. The flows that are possible are defined by the outputs that each subsystem can produce, a crucial constraint of the architecture. The particular transformation processes 'allowed' within ICS have been systematically derived. Only those processes that are both logically plausible (given the nature of the information held within each representation) and empirically justified (given the experimental and phenomenological evidence about human cognition) are contained in the architecture. The internal structures, transformation processes and systemic organisation of ICS are brought together in Figure 2.3.

The subsystems dealing with vision (VIS) and hearing (AC) produce one output reflecting the structural regularities of their native representations (for OBJ and MPL respectively), and another output reflecting its global patterning (for IMPLIC). The latter outputs provide information of both 'cognitive' and 'affective' significance. The structural subsystems (OBJ and MPL) produce effector representations (for LIM and ART, respectively), and derive the referential, or semantic, level of meaning (for PROP) from their native representations. Note that these two subsystems do not produce Implicational representations. To enable skilled reading and naming of objects, the OBJ subsystem is able to recognise the shape of words and letters and to produce their corresponding MPL representation. However, it is assumed that there is no corresponding inverse transformation (from a word to its shape, MPL→OBJ). The third sensory subsystem is the Body State subsystem (BS). This subsystem can produce Implicational representations that reflect bodily and skeletal states. It can also produce effector representations (ART and LIM) to provide proprioceptive feedback during motor action. Unlike the processing of visual and acoustic information, there is *no* subsystem corresponding to the structural level (OBJ & MPL) for body state information.

Of the two Meaning subsystems, IMPLIC uses its schematic representations to derive a more detailed referential meaning appropriate to the current situation and state (for PROP) and to produce affective responses in the body via the SOM (somatic) and VISC (visceral) representations. These are not directly received by any of the other subsystems, but the consequences of the action of these processes are, of course, indirectly sensed by BS. The referential level of meaning, PROP, is unique in neither receiving representations from sensory subsystems, nor producing effector representations. Instead, it receives representations from each of the other central subsystems, and produces output for each of them. This gives it a central role in many of information flows underpinning thought. The remaining two subsystems, ART and LIM, directly control the articulatory and skeletal musculatures, and do not produce representations for other subsystems. However, as with somatic and visceral states, the bodily consequences of their outputs may be sensed by BS and fed back both locally and to the Implicational subsystem.

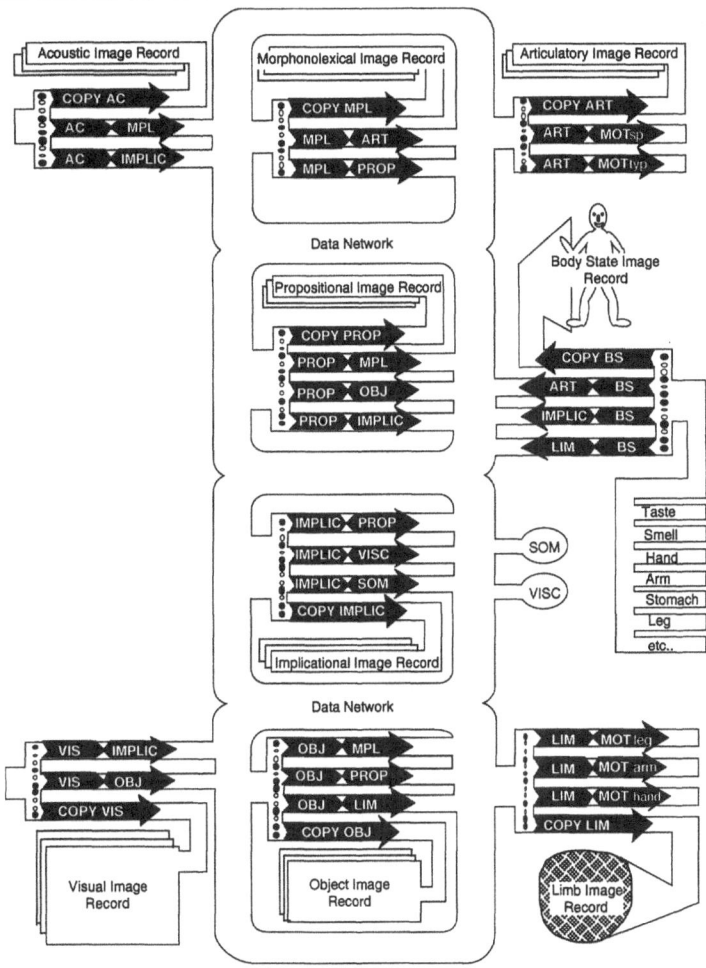

Figure 2.3: An overall view of the ICS architecture, showing the transformation processes.

2.2.4   Integrating information over sources and over time

The transformation processes shown in Figure 2.3 can be organised into a significant range of simple and complex configurations. The more complex configurations can include cyclical exchanges of representations between pairs and even triplets of central subsystems (e.g., PROP→IMPLIC & IMPLIC→PROP, and OBJ→MPL, MPL→PROP & PROP→OBJ). The configurations that are possible are systematically constrained by the availability of resources, since any given process can only be doing one thing at a time [3]. It should be also be clear from the figure that all central and effector subsystems receive inputs from at least two others.

The sensory subsystems can also receive their inputs from multiple sensory 'transducers', in that we have two eyes and ears, and many sources of proprioceptive information. Consequently, any one process can receive input about the same event from different sources, each source may provide different information about that event. These are available to be blended together, or fused, to form a richer representation than any single source can provide. The potential for multiple inputs to subsystems provides the first way in which the integration of information can be dealt with in the ICS architecture, and so allows us to reason about the types of multimodal information that can be cognitively useful.

Integration of information also occurs as a consequence of the internal structure of subsystems. In Figure 2.2, the operation of transformation processes was illustrated through the direct transformation of information on the input array into an output code. In addition, the transformation processes can also make use of information held in the image record and produce an output representation on the basis of these stored representations. This has several implications. Most obviously, it enables a form of episodic long-term memory, and supports the abstraction of regularities in the history of input to a subsystem. In the very short term, it also allows the transformation process to operate upon an 'extended representation' rather than upon the moment to moment contents of the input array. Since the Copy process is continually transferring information from the input array to the image record, this enables the Copy process and a transformation process to operate serially, with the image record acting as a short-term 'buffer' between the input array and the transformation process. The buffered mode of operation is mainly useful where the representation on the input array is changing too quickly for the transformation process to use, or where it is the nature of the change that is relevant to the transformation rather than the information itself. In this sense, buffered processing supports the integration, or blending of information, over time within a single source as well as over sources at one time.

One effect of the buffered mode of operation is to allow the transformation process to produce output at its natural processing rate, and to cope with variation in the timing of input data flow. A further constraint arising from the architecture of ICS is that, within a subsystem, only one transformation process can access the image record at a time, whether for revival of long-term records or for operation in buffered mode. It is also assumed that buffering helps co-ordinate the rate of flow throughout a configuration.

The differences between the direct and buffered modes of operation have subjective consequences. The Copy process gives rise to a general sense of conscious awareness of arriving information, but the operation of transformation processes is assumed not to be available to our conscious experience. Since there are normally Copy processes active in each of the subsystems, we can be diffusely aware of information at several different levels of representation, and we can even be aware of uncorrelated streams of information, depending upon the particular configural flows of information that are active at the time. In contrast, the buffered mode of operation corresponds to *focal awareness* of the extended representation: if any process within a configuration is operating in buffered mode, then the extended representation that it is operating upon will be the subjective focus of attention. Since only one process within a configuration can be buffered at a time, it follows that our focal awareness, will be restricted. We can nevertheless remain diffusely aware of the activity of the Copy processes throughout the system.

In summary, the architectural principles underlying ICS allow integration of information in two ways: in direct processing by the blending of information from different sources, and in buffered processing by transformation processes using an extended representation from the image record, hence supporting the integration of information over time. The consequences of the integration depend, of course, upon the nature of the information being integrated, and this corresponds to the subsystem at which integration is occurring. The differentiation between forms of integration consequently mirrors the differentiation between the types of subsystem, being divisible at a gross level between peripheral and central integration.

2.3   Peripheral integration

The peripheral subsystems (see Table 1) are those that exchange information with the physical world (both internal and external to the body). The Sensory subsystems (AC, VIS and BS) do not receive representations from other subsystems, and the Effector subsystems (LIM and ART) do not produce representations for other subsystems to use directly. These two groups of subsystems are consequently assumed to have different roles in the integration of information. In brief, Sensory integration cannot be cross-modal, since each Sensory subsystem only receives information from its own set of transducers, while Effector integration is limited to the blending of intended actions with proprioceptive feedback.

2.3.1   Sensory Integration

As described above, the Sensory subsystems do not receive representations from other subsystems, but only from their sensory transducers. In consequence, these subsystems cannot integrate information from different modalities, although they can integrate multiple streams of information produced from within the capabilities of their respective transducers.

When an orchestra is playing, for example, the Acoustic subsystem can produce output that is a composite of the sound of all of the instruments, or it can 'focus in' on one particular sound, perhaps the strings or the percussion. Within these streams of information, it is not usually easy for a novice listener to focus in to attend to a particular violin, although it is usually possible to distinguish different percussive instruments. At a different level, a similar effect occurs in our processing of speech information. Different formants within a stream from a single source blend to form a percept that corresponds to a vowel sound. The knowledge deployed in these forms of integration is characteristically not available to conscious introspection, but is implicit or latent within the processing mechanism itself.

Figure 2.4:   Visual integration (left) and differentiation (right)

Similarly, the Visual subsystem is able to operate upon representations of a flock of birds flying through the sky, and to attend to one particular bird. There are also situations where the Visual subsystem is unable to differentiate between different constituent elements of a visual scene. The left of Figure 2.4 shows an example of this: two overlapping rectangular areas forms, each composed of arrow-heads of different orientations. The Visual subsystem is easily able to resolve each constituent element of the areas where they do not overlap, but in the overlapping region, where their constituent elements intersect, a new 'xx' form is created which cannot be resolved visually into its two component parts (although it can be resolved 'conceptually', which will be discussed later). What the visual system 'sees' here is the integrated, or blended, form. The rectangular areas on right of Figure 2.4, where the arrowheads have different form, remain differentiated. Were the regions to be placed on separate overhead projector foils and one passed over the other, more dynamic forms of integration can be experienced with, for example, the precise perceptual 'blend' achieved from the pair on the left changing over time to resemble zig-zags and squares. The kinds of blends that can be achieved within the sensory subsystems are constrained by the information provided by the receptors in terms of range and constituent form. So, for example, individuals can only hear or see things within well defined wavelength limits and internal resolution.

2.3.2   Effector Integration

Like the sensory subsystems, the effector subsystems (ART and LIM) communicate with the external world, in that they produce representations that cause the articulatory and skeletal musculatures to carry out actions. Unlike the sensory subsystems, their input arrays receive representations from other subsystems. Each receives one stream of representations from the appropriate structural subsystem (MPL→ART and OBJ→LIM) and another from the Body State subsystem (BS→ART and BS→LIM). The output of the structural subsystems defines the intended speech or action, while the output of the Body State subsystem represents proprioceptive feedback about the current state of the musculatures. Clearly, if the LIM subsystem is receiving representations from OBJ about a hand movement, it needs to have the information about the current position of the hand to be able to construct the appropriate motor representation. Similarly, the ART subsystem needs to know where the tongue is in the mouth and what the lips are doing before it can construct a representation for the production of the sounds specified by MPL.

Unlike the integration of representations by the sensory subsystems, where the same event, or consequences of the same event, were being brought to the sensory input arrays by different transducers, effector integration brings together two representations of different origin, and of potentially different content and structure. One will be internally derived, representing intended action, and one will be externally derived, representing the actual position and motion of the bodily parts. This is not a problem most of the time, for in normal co-ordinated performance the proprioceptive feedback reflects the actions that have just been carried out. As long as the structural subsystems are producing a coherent output data stream, and actions are being carried out roughly as intended, the proprioceptive feedback will be compatible with it, and so will be integrable.

In normal motor action or in speech, we are rarely aware of the many little compensatory adjustments that we continually make to our posture and movements, or of the many different ways in which we make a speech sound, depending upon the sound that has preceded it and the sound that is to follow it. Corrections to motor output can occur extremely rapidly, driven by the proprioceptive feedback from BS, without disturbing the 'planning' stream arriving from the structural subsystem. For example, if the lower lip is perturbed during speech, adjustments occur not only in that lip, but also in the upper lip, within 36-72 ms of the perturbation [1]. The adjustment occurs on the very first trial, showing that it is not learnt during the experiment, and its nature is determined by the speech that is being produced, showing that it is a functional response related to the planned speech, not a reflex. Monster, Herman & Altland examined the effects of adding a force to the ankle joint, finding that a load torque of 1.4 kg-m in either direction produced a 4° error in perceived position, with the sole of the foot feeling more flexed than it actually was [36]. Under ischaemic anaesthesia of the arm (cutting off blood flow to remove sensation), people report its perceived position to be closer to the body than it actually is, with the degree of error increasing as duration of ischaemia increases [25]. Muscular exertion can also produce distorting after-effects, as in the Kohnstamm effect. To experience this, stand in a doorway, with your arms at your sides. Keeping your arms straight, push against the door frame with the backs of your hands for 10 to 20 seconds. When you step out of the doorway, your arms will 'feel' light, and will seem to rise almost effortlessly. Once again much of the 'key knowledge' deployed by the human information processing mechanism is latent.

As with sensory integration, the precise forms of effector integration will be constrained by the nature of the human skeleton and musculatures – there are only two arms and two legs with well defined degrees of freedom in the movements that can be achieved. Many of the points concerning the integration of information in the control of action may appear obvious as, indeed, may many of those points covered in the previous subsection on sensory integration. Nonetheless, achieving an understanding of the operation of these processes is of key importance to design. The dot matrix printer illustrates how technology can be developed to support the blending of constituents of characters into increasingly well defined and fully integrated form. In contrast, variability 'in peoples' sensory abilities frequently goes unrecognised in design. The capabilities of the visual and auditory coding space decline with age and other factors. The genetics of colour vision radically alter how colours are resolved by a particular individual. Many systems and information displays, like graphs, are produced in which it is very difficult for a significant proportion of users to distinguish colours that mark vital contrasts. Similarly, the environment in which perception and action occur may move beyond normal limits, as when a pilot is flying on instruments in altered gravitational conditions. In all these and other instances, it is important to understand the properties of the underlying mechanism.

As each new advance occurs, new challenges are posed with renewed opportunities for problematic design. In one relatively recent example, in order to get a large map onto a small screen, compression algorithms were proposed to enable a large area to be shown concurrently with a high resolution representation of a focussed part of that area. A user controllable fish-eye lens solved this "representational" part of the problem. However, the dynamic distortion of the objects and scales represented introduced substantial difficulties with the basic perceptual processing of the visual information [33]. In one sense, virtual reality and telepresence systems share an important property with the early dot matrix printer: a requirement to increase resolution in the relevant human coding spaces. A designer may have a choice between updating the constituent graphic elements of a basic visual unit individually as they are computed, or to wait and update the constituents of the whole unit simultaneously. The choice may radically affect how features are blended in both space and time.

2.4   The structure of representations

To explain why certain representations can be integrated but not differentiated, and others can be differentiated but not integrated, we need to consider their structure. The subsystems in ICS all share the same functional architecture. While the contents of their representations differ, all can be treated as following a common set of structural rules. ICS treats a representation as consisting of a number of basic units, which may have constituent elements (a substructure) and be grouped together in some way (a superstructure). One of the basic units will be the 'psychological subject' of the representation, and the others will form its predicate structure. The psychological subject is the 'theme' of the representation: the element of the scene to which attention is directed.

This applies for representations received by each of the subsystems. In the Visual example shown in Figure 2.4, the psychological subject of the representation may be one of the arrowheads, one of the double-cross forms, one of the larger rectangular areas, or the overlapping area (and there are other possibilities). If an arrowhead or a double-cross is the psychological subject, then the changing hues and brightness levels within it and around its edges will be its substructure; the rows, diagonals and columns it belongs to will form its superstructure; and the other 'pools' of brightness and darkness within these superstructural groups will form the basic units within its predicate structure. If one of the larger regions is the psychological subject, then its textural constituents will form its substructure; the other regions with differing constituent elements will form the predicate structure; and together the figure as a whole will form their superstructure.

Since the Visual subsystem deals with low-level information about brightness, hue, and so on, its representation cannot 'split up' the intersecting black lines of the double-crosses to 'see' the original arrowheads: to do this, we need the information that would be obtained by transforming the Visual representation into an Object representation, where lines or differing orientation can be represented. If the arrowheads were of different hues, however, the Visual representation of a double-cross would include substructural detail sufficient to allow only the parts in one hue to form the psychological subject: in the right of Figure 2.4, the arrowheads can be 'seen' within the double-crosses. The structure of the Object representations that can be produced from the figure are shown in Figure 2.5.

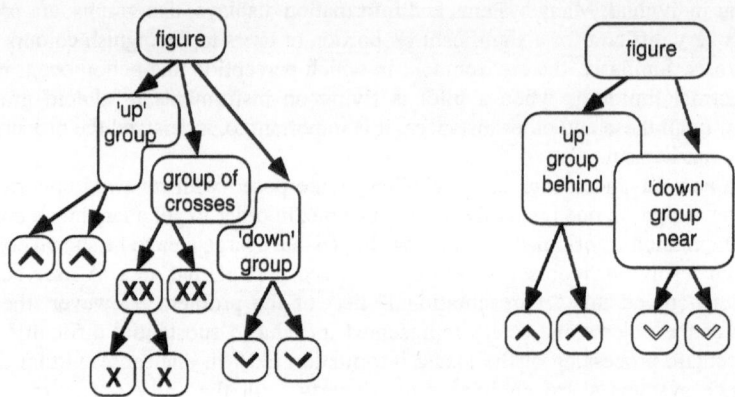

Figure 2.5: The structures of object representations resulting from Figure 2.4

In the Acoustic orchestral example, a psychological subject may be formed from the overall sound of the music, in which case the constituent 'voices' within the music would be the substructure. If one of these voices were taken as the psychological subject, the other voices would form the predicate structure, and the music as a whole the superstructure. The nature of the constituent elements of the voice would then determine whether or not a further 'thematic transition' could be made to bring one of them to the fore as a new psychological subject. In the case of the strings, their acoustic forms would probably not present enough discriminating detail to allow this transition to take place, and like the different arrowheads in Figure 2.4, they would 'overlap' to form an integrated whole. The acoustic forms of different percussive instruments might be more discriminable, and if so would be differentiated as basic units.

These two sensory examples have shown how differences in the external data can affect the theme or subject of the representation. The representations of the central subsystems can also be influenced by internally generated streams of information, and so thematic transitions can be 'willed', allowing attention to be directed. Even in the left of Figure 2.4, the double-cross forms can be 'taken apart' at a structural level to focus on the 'up' and 'down' parts separately. This 'central integration' is discussed further in section 2.5.

2.4.1   Coherent data streams

The notion of structure is the key to the definition of a coherent data stream. A crucial point in the arguments about integration of information is the constraint that a single transformation process can only operate upon a single coherent data stream at any given time. If two data streams cannot be integrated into a common representation, a transformation process will not be able to produce an output representation that is based upon both of them, and only one will pass onwards for subsequent processing. So in the classic case of the cocktail party phenomenon [14], there may be many people speaking in the same room concurrently. However, at any given point in time, only one of these can be recoded through to the MPL subsystem and from there to subsequent processing of its meaning.

At the level of the sensory representations, the nature of the representations is largely a property of the neuroanatomy of the sensory transducers. Events in the 'real world' that cannot be discriminated by our senses necessarily form integrated basic units, and hence a single data stream, while discriminable events form differentiated basic units, and separable data streams. In Visual representations, brightness, hue and spatial organisation are the delimiting dimensions; in Acoustic representations, the frequency, timbre, intensity, and onset; in Body State representations, the type of stimulation, its location (and hence the density of receptors at its site), intensity, onset, and so on (see Table 1). At the central representations, the structure depends more upon the nature of the information flow, a factor to which the discussion will return later.

This should not be taken to mean that the separation or integration of data streams within the sensory subsystems is largely a matter of the underlying 'neural wiring'. Integration will occur because there are topographic and dynamic patterns that recur in the external world or the internal world of the body [28]. Within the ICS framework, a transformation process 'learns' to map inputs onto outputs. So for example, the Acoustic to Morphonolexical transformation (AC→MPL) extracts regularities in the underlying sound stream which, in this case, come to form key contrasts in the structural description of the 'sounds' used by the linguistic community in which the individual lives. These regularities are captured by distinguishing substructure, basic units and superstructures at each level of representation. For example, frequency patterns in sound over time represent the formant structures of speech sounds. While aspects of the substructures of these sounds will reflect properties of the human vocal tract, the way in which they are put together to form basic units of speech sounds and their superstructure depends upon experience.

As it moves through successive transformations, the nature of the information changes. When transforming a representation of sound (AC) to a structural description of sounds (MPL) the elemental acoustic information is discarded – the basic units of the input representation become the substructure of the output representation, and the superstructure of the sound stream indicates the basic units. Conversely, a transformation to an effector representation (e.g. MPL→ART) involves the reverse process, of taking an abstract structural description of the sound and computing more detailed articulatory representation necessary for the subsequent motor control of speech. This all depends upon experience with the appropriate sounds, and very young pre-speech children babble in the full range of human vocalisations, attempting to imitate the speech they hear. Eventually they hear themselves producing the appropriate set of sounds, and the inappropriate sounds cease to be part of their articulatory repertoire. Still later, we cease even to be able to differentiate between speech forms that are not used in our native languages.

The integration and differentiation of sensory representations according to these structural invariants necessarily constrains the structure of the output representations. In this respect, the products of processes constrain the higher level invariances that can be abstracted in exactly the same way as sensory transducers. Although these interdependencies are potentially rich, the architecture of ICS and its associated view of information representations enable us to frame theoretically motivated distinctions about the coherency of data streams. They also enable us to understand in more precise terms the part that might be played by the classic Gestalt principles of 'common fate' and 'proximity' that were mentioned earlier in section 2.1.2. Within the ICS framework, the principle of common fate can be defined more precisely as a property of sets of basic units within a representation (not necessarily a sensory representation). When basic units behave with highly similar characteristics over time, or are part of some invariant within the representational space, they can be interpreted as single superstructural element. Even though proximity as a concept is most obvious when applied to spatial location, it can equally well be applied to auditory representations, as well as to central representations. To be useful, the dimensions on which units are 'proximal' must be thought of as those of the 'space' within which they are represented.

In summary, at any level of representation constituents represented on the input data array can be blended into a single data stream by a transformation process if they can be interpreted as a basic unit, given the learning history of the subsystem. The blending of units into a coherent data stream occurs when a transformation process imposes a superordinate structure upon the basic units. The imposition of this structure will again depend upon the learning history of the process and the ways in which basic units have come together in those structures in the past.

2.4.2   Integration of coherent data streams

Given the structural organisation of representations, we can now start to account for phenomena, of the sort introduced earlier, which involve the integration of information to form a single data stream. The birds flying in a flock across the sky can be interpreted in sensory representations (VIS→OBJ) as a unified superstructure of basic units with shared dynamic properties, as can points of light moving in a co-ordinated way [18]. Similarly, the formants in speech sounds can be represented as basic units, made up of energy distributions in sound space, with a superstructural organisation representing phonemes. Some blends occur because the information is not distinguished on the data array (e.g. low level localisation; psycho-acoustic fusion; critical flicker frequency), while other blends occur because information on the data array systematically co-occurs, giving rise to phenomena associated specifically with speech [17].

At the other extreme, the ICS architecture is capable of understanding thunder and lightning as constituents of the same event at a deeper, propositional level, in terms of their onset asynchrony. Features such as the intensity and unexpectedness of the event may have affective constituents that blend at an affective, Implicational level (see Table 1). The blending of information within the central subsystems is capable of occurring over a very much longer duration and is also likely to be 'interactive', incorporating the effects of the individual's own actions. Again, such 'interactivity' is not purely a property of the processing of information by central subsystems. Systematic effects of integration and differentiation occur at shorter durations. In between examples of psychoacoustic forms of integration and thunder and lightning, forms of integration that depend upon morphonolexical and articulatory representations would be expected.

Delaying auditory feedback of our own voices can have extremely disruptive effects on normal articulation of speech [29], maximally so at delays of around 200msec. At very small delays, or those exceeding around 300msec, the effects can be negligible. If the delay is small, buffered representations can be used to overcome the disparity, and to treat the acoustic feedback and the intended speech as part of the same data stream. At the longer delays, the acoustic feedback is so different to the intended speech that the two streams are clearly differentiated, and do not interfere. Between these limits, conditions are presumably created where the superstructure of the acoustic representation is similar enough to that of the intended speech to allow integration, yet the content of the basic units (intensity, for example) is far enough from the intended speech to suggest that there has been some problem in articulation (that the onset of the sounds was incorrect, for example). Interestingly, non-speech sounds can have equivalent effects when the overall rhythm of the feedback is driven by the speech output [27] – perhaps illustrating here how 'common fate' in the superstructure of acoustic representations can itself contribute to blending.

There can be additional problems in identifying data streams when there are multiple sources of feedback. Within the architecture of ICS, feedback about voice also occurs internally via the products of the BS→IMPLIC and BS→ART processes. The model therefore suggests that blending of articulatory constituents can be influenced by affective and oral routes, in addition to auditory feedback. This helps us to understand why stutterers are often strongly influenced by anxiety [16] as well as oral sensory feedback. With instruction and practice, people can learn to cope with delayed auditory feedback, relying on the proprioceptive information from the mouth and tongue instead of auditory information to co-ordinate their speech [2].

2.5   Central Integration

As with the peripheral subsystems, integration of information by the central subsystems corresponds to the nature of the representations dealt with by the subsystems in question. The structural subsystems, MPL and OBJ, integrate information reflecting the structure of sound and visual space respectively, while the Meaning subsystems, PROP and IMPLIC, integrate referential and schematic information. Unlike the peripheral subsystems, the central subsystems can exchange information with each other, and can form cyclical configurations. The representations that they receive are highly likely to have been influenced in part by their own outputs. The potential for integration is correspondingly much greater, and so we shall describe each of the four central forms of integration in turn.

The OBJ subsystem receives input from visual processing (VIS→OBJ) and propositional processing (PROP→OBJ). It also acts as an interchange between information flow interpreting the visual environment (OBJ→PROP) and that involved in structuring output for the subsequent control of skeletal movement by the LIM subsystem (OBJ→LIM). No direct integration of multimodal sources occurs at this subsystem, since there are no sensory BS→OBJ or AC→OBJ processes, and no central MPL→OBJ process. Any effects of multimodal origin of information at this subsystem must therefore be indirect, with the configuration of information flow passing through the PROP subsystem.

In many ways, the MPL subsystem is an analogue of the OBJ subsystem, but in the domain of sound. It acts as an interchange point between the comprehension (MPL→PROP) and production of language (MPL→ART). In another important respect it differs quite markedly. The MPL subsystem takes crossmodal input (from OBJ→MPL) but produces no reciprocal output back to the OBJ subsystem. Unlike OBJ, it is possible for MPL to integrate multimodal information, although apart from Acoustic representations it is limited to receiving representations about word forms and the recognition of well-known objects or scenes.

Alone among the four central subsystems, the PROP subsystem neither receives information directly from sensory subsystems nor produces output for effector systems. Just as the OBJ and MPL subsystems act as a mediating point between sensory 'input flows' and effector 'output flows', the PROP subsystem mediates the flow of information between the structural subsystems and the higher level schematic representations of the implicational subsystem. It is able to do this in both directions, both receiving representations from the structural subsystems to produce IMPLIC representations, and receiving IMPLIC representations to produce structural representations. This gives it a pivotal role in most 'cerebral' configurations, and in all that include a cyclical loop. Although as far as multimodal integration is concerned, PROP is only able to blend the structurally organised output of MPL and OBJ rather than the lower-level output of AC and VIS, its ability to bring them together with representations derived from the schematic content of IMPLIC means that it is the key to giving implicit, latent knowledge a more explicit form.

In marked contrast, the Implicational subsystem is deeply multimodal. It receives input from sound (AC→IMPLIC), vision (VIS→IMPLIC), and proprioception (BS→IMPLIC), as well as the products of referential, semantic meaning (PROP→IMPLIC). The information received directly from the sensory subsystems is quite distinct from that which comes through the sequential analysis of sentences (via MPL and PROP) or the spatial analysis of visual scenes (via OBJ and PROP). While these indirect representations convey considered, or inferred, affective content, the direct inputs from sensory subsystems concern broad 'gut reactions' to the general tone of voice, facial expression, arm gestures, and bodily arousal. In fact, as discussed below, the directness of these sensory inputs to IMPLIC means that the IMPLIC→PROP process may provide an output that can be integrated with the structural subsystems' output to PROP, before PROP is able to produce an IMPLIC representation that would give a more 'rational' schematic view of the representations' referential content.

2.5.1   Object Integration

As described in the previous section, inputs of direct multimodal origin do not arrive at the object subsystem. In order to understand many effects of intermodal conflict, such as the ventriloquism effect and its analogues [41], it is necessary to look elsewhere within the architecture. The object subsystem is able to produce different output representations, and since it is a central subsystem, it can operate in cyclical configurations with the propositional subsystem and this does have some consequences for integration.

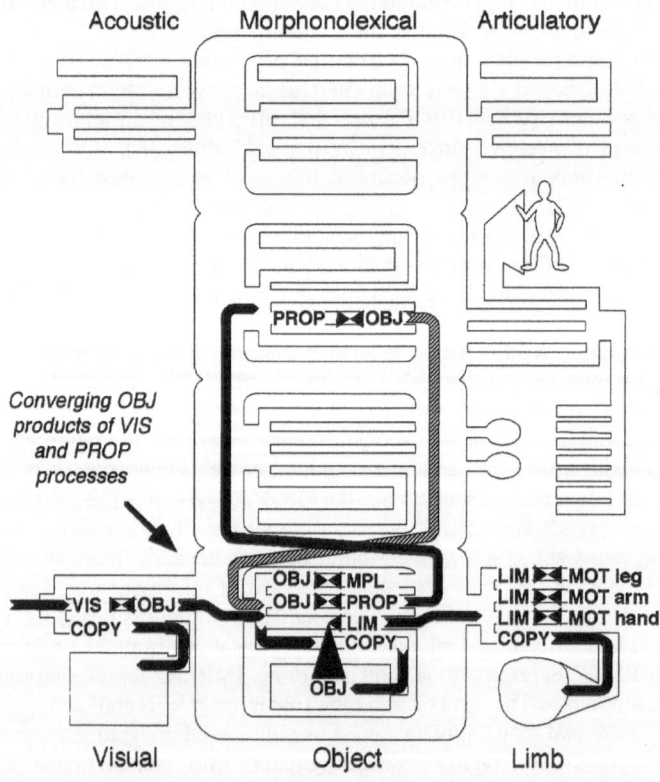

Figure 2.6:   Converging object products of visual and propositional processing activity

Figure 2.6 shows a configural flow for motor action under the direct control of a visual source of information. This would be the sort of configuration controlling the hitting of a tennis ball on a particular trajectory in the real 3-d world or even in 2-d world of a computer game. The Visual representation of the ball, moving through space is transformed by the VIS→OBJ process, forming the primary input to the OBJ input array. The ball is almost certainly moving too fast for the OBJ→LIM transformation to use this representation directly, and in any case the actual position of the ball is not as relevant as its velocity and acceleration, which are derivatives of these moment to moment representations. To have access to this information, and enable the individual's motor actions to begin in time for their racket to intercept with the tennis ball, the OBJ→LIM process must act in buffered mode, processing the extended representation in the image record.

At the same time as the OBJ→LIM process is producing its representations of intended action, the OBJ→PROP process is able to produce a referential interpretation of the structural representation. Since the OBJ→LIM process is accessing the image record, the OBJ→PROP process can only operate upon the information on the input array. This may mean that it is unable to keep up with the speed at which the representations arrive, and that the referential output of the process is not as smooth as it would be if it were buffered, having a more 'snapshot' nature. It also means that the referential representations it produces are not based upon the derivative information available from the extended representation, and so are different in content as well as nature to the products of the OBJ→LIM process. As the solid arrow in Figure 2.6 indicates, once they have been produced, they enter the input array of the PROP subsystem, where they can be operated on by the PROP→OBJ process. These centrally generated OBJ representations will now be based upon a referential interpretation of the visual scene, rather than the raw visual information. Since the OBJ→PROP process can operate on any part of the representations arriving at the OBJ input array, the products of this reciprocal PROP→OBJ process may now include information derived from the position of the opponent's arm as they hit the ball, or of their position on the court, instead of being based on the velocity of the ball. Whatever the content of the PROP representations, the PROP→OBJ process will use the individual's referential, rule-like experience of tennis playing to feed back new OBJ representations via the downward, hatched arrow in Figure 2.6.

Like the output of the VIS→OBJ process, the products of the PROP→OBJ process also arrive at the input array, and so provide an opportunity for information integration to take place. Just as with sensory and effector integration, central integration can only occur if the data streams are compatible: if they provide conflicting or irreconcilable information, the transformation processes will simply not be able to produce any useful output. In this example, the referentially mediated OBJ representations (of, say, the opponent's actions) are highly likely to be closely correlated with can be integrated with the representations derived from the raw visual information (of the consequences of their actions), and so they should form a single coherent data stream with few conflicts. The extended representation in the image record contains these integrable representations, not solely the products of the VIS→OBJ process. In consequence, the OBJ→LIM process of a skilled tennis player is able to operate on the basis of more than basic, visuomotor reactions. It can blend in the referential knowledge derived from their experience of playing tennis – for example, to recognise from their opponents' posture, action and position that a ball is likely to have spin, and so to predict its trajectory more accurately.

This is not the whole story, of course, for vision is not the only sense active during a game of tennis. As noted earlier, the impact of the tennis ball is also heard and felt. Bodily effects and the sound of the impact individually influence Implicational understanding (via BS→IMPLIC and AC→IMPLIC), and bodily effects also provide feedback to movement control (BS→LIM), but these sources cannot form an integrated data stream at the *object* level of representation, since there are neither direct paths from AC or BS to OBJ, nor from IMPLIC to OBJ. For these sources of information to be used by OBJ→LIM, they will have to pass through PROP, as we shall describe in the section on Propositional Integration.

In summary, the OBJ subsystem can integrate over bottom up, visual information (from VIS→OBJ) and top-down, referential information (from PROP→OBJ). This provides a way that propositional mappings and image records can come to influence the processes of visual interpretation. Standard texts (e.g. [24]) often make use of simple but powerful demonstrations. Presenting scenes containing a Jersey cow or a Dalmatian dog as a pattern of dots or blobs against a similar background can make the 'object' percept hard to establish. In Figure 2.7, for example, the Visual information is inadequate for an Object representation to be formed easily. However, once the 'object' is known, it is subsequently impossible not to see the pattern involving that 'object'. In this case, where the picture shows two ducks swimming on the River Cam, stored referential knowledge about the appearance of ducks can be automatically mapped to the OBJ input array (PROP→OBJ) to constrain the interpretation of input.

Figure 2.7:   Propositional knowledge about this scene can make it easier to form an object representation.

Similarly, in Figure 2.4, the double-cross forms in the left-hand overlapping region cannot be resolved at a visual level into their component arrowheads, but once we 'know' what they consist of, the PROP→OBJ input allows the integrated OBJ representation to 'attend' to either the upward pointing part of the form, or the downward pointing part (note, though, that it is harder still to attend to both at once). The same route allows the overlapping arrowheads in the right-hand region to be 'seen' as double-cross forms, albeit multicoloured. This is what was meant earlier by the word 'conceptually'. This form of propositional, top-down control over perception is a pervasive part of our everyday cognitive activity, normally helping us to impose order on what may be an incomplete or ambiguous sensory data stream. The many visual illusions and ambiguous figures (e.g., the Necker Cube) that fill textbooks on perception testify to its role.

The tennis example was useful in emphasising how the dynamic nature of cognition is central to the integration of information, since it results from the concurrent activity of independent processes transforming a flow of representations. The particular streams of representations being integrated in that example make it a little harder to discuss the role of structure, since there are many different tennis playing situations, and the role of PROP→OBJ depends on the skill and experience of the individual tennis player. The structure of the representations being provided to OBJ by VIS and PROP is still crucial, though, as the following, more static, example indicates.

In the left hand part of Figure 2.8, it is easy to see one of the elements 'popping-out' from its companions, yet in the right hand part, it is quite hard on first sight to find the unique element. The two arrays have been carefully controlled to balance their visual characteristics, and the substructural features of each element, but the superstructures are clearly different. Taking the left-hand side first, VIS→OBJ is able represent each element as a three dimensional cube, with the majority of them having the same orientation. The array as a whole can consequently be seen as having the orientation of its constituent elements: the superstructure of the OBJ representation takes on the common attributes of its basic units. One of the elements does not have the same attributes however, and so VIS→OBJ cannot represent it as part of this superstructural group, even though it is spatially 'within' it. In consequence, it 'pops-out'. The bias of the VIS→OBJ process is to represent disparities within the visual scene as the theme of the representations it constructs for OBJ, since these are in practice likely to be the 'figure' against the 'background'. In this example the odd element out will typically become the psychological subject of the OBJ representation, and the rest of the array, with its common superstructural description, its predicate structure.

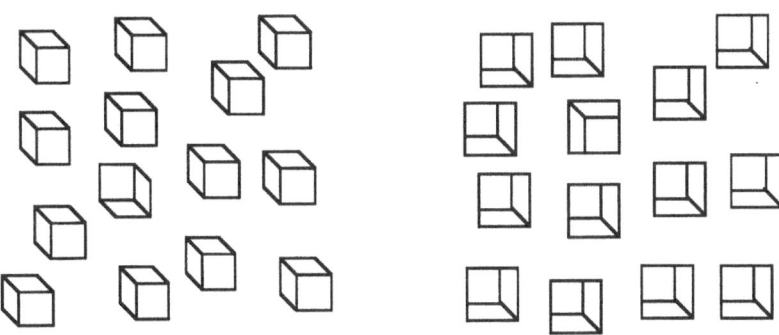

Figure 2.8: Examples of visual 'pop-out' that vary according to the visual and propositional information about the superstructure of the object representation

In the right hand part of Figure 2.8 the visual information is different. The basic units of the visual representation now no longer have the characteristics that allow VIS→OBJ readily to produce three-dimensional representations, and so it is able to produce a common, two-dimensional superstructure for the OBJ representation that adequately fits all of its basic units. None of them 'pop-out'; the incongruous element has to be found by searching the array. Here we can show the role of PROP→OBJ upon the formation of the structure of the integrated OBJ representation. As soon as you 'know' referentially that the elements in the right hand array are 'square holes in a flat surface', the OBJ→PROP & PROP→OBJ loop is able to add three dimensional information to the OBJ input array: the superstructure of the representation now becomes a three dimensional form with the basic units 'descending' into it. Now one of them can immediately be 'seen' to descend in an incompatible way, and it 'pops-out' of the array. In this case 'pop-out' can be seen to be a property of the OBJ representation, depending upon the integration of PROP→OBJ and VIS→OBJ representations.

The exact way in which a scene is structured obviously exerts a major influence on the way in which the constituent elements appear when displayed upon a computer screen. They also constrain the way in which people search for a specific target. In a very simple example, a typical task for a text based display is to present a listing of filenames in a directory. In many systems an attempt is made to make use of the full screen display by writing names alphabetically across lines with a tab separating each item on the line. With a large list, many lines are presented, and the overall appearance created is of several *columns* of items. Under these circumstances users tend to direct their search down the columns rather than use the normal reading strategy of moving across the lines. Since the column strategy is at variance with the alphabetic listing across the page, this makes it hard to locate specific targets accurately and rapidly. This is not simply a problem for graphically challenged display technologies. Similar effects have been discussed in the context of button organisations within hypertext systems, and have been identified in conjunction with subject-predicate analyses [34, 35]. Indeed, as graphical interfaces become more advanced the number of ways in which these problems arise will undoubtedly increase.

A transformation process in OBJ that has not been mentioned in this discussion is OBJ→MPL, which produces representations of the names of objects, and the sound of words or word parts in reading. The absence of a direct route from MPL→OBJ means that the structural representations of sounds do not play a role in the integration of object representations. The converse is not true. When people read words, for example, the transformation from an OBJ to an MPL representation is not subject to the same temporal dynamics as spoken speech, which produces an MPL representation from the raw AC representations. This has very strong implications for multimodal integration, particularly in the context of advanced graphical systems.

2.5.2   Morphonolexical Integration

Figure 2.9 shows how information flows come together at the Morphonolexical system. Like the other structural subsystem, OBJ, the MPL subsystem receives information flow from sensory (AC→MPL) and referential sources (PROP→MPL). Unlike OBJ, MPL also receives input from a crossmodal source, OBJ→MPL. This asymmetry has its origins in language processing and supports the skill of reading.

Just as OBJ plays a crucial mediating role in visuomotor action, co-ordinating the intended motor actions with the visual scene, MPL is central to the production of speech, co-ordinating intended speech with the acoustic scene: the general noise level, the individual's immediately recent speech acts, and the speech acts of others. There is a direct analogy between the buffered OBJ→LIM process in the tennis example of Figure 2.6, and a buffered MPL→ART process in the production of speech. There is also an analogy between the OBJ→PROP & PROP→OBJ cycle integrating with the VIS→OBJ flow to influence object perception, and the MPL→PROP & PROP→MPL cycle integrating with the AC→MPL flow to influence our perception of the acoustic world. There are very strong effects of context on the recognition of spoken words, particularly when the speech is degraded on a noisy channel. Just as what we see depends upon what we expect to be seeing (cf. Figure 2.7), what we 'hear' depends upon what we referentially 'expect' to be hearing.

This key role of the MPL subsystem in controlling speech results in its transformation processes operating at a rate compatible with the flow of transient, acoustically derived representations. The structural nature of these representations is dominated by temporal relationships. In contrast, in reading, the objects are written words, which are less transient entities, in two dimensional space. The products of OBJ→MPL processing generated in the course of reading cannot be handled directly by MPL processes, since they are on the wrong time base: the sequential patterning of the MPL basic units is not equivalent to that of normal speech processing. The mechanism copes with this by using buffered processing, either of MPL→ART, if the words are to be read aloud directly, or of MPL→PROP if referential comprehension is intended.

This model of reading supports the theoretical analysis of classic modality differences in short term memory [3], where the last item of aurally presented lists of words is usually recalled with greater accuracy in serial recall tasks than the last item in visually presented lists. An auditory list allows a direct flow of Acoustic, through MPL to Articulatory representations, resulting in consistent, temporally ordered representations in the proximal part of the Articulatory image record that can be revived to support short-term memory retrieval tasks. The buffering of the MPL transformation provides a basis for explaining the effects obtained on the last item of a visually presented list of written words.

However, there are circumstances under which a full 'auditory' recency effect occurs with visual material [13, 48]. These circumstances involve lip-read material. Barnard [3] argues that these effects are obtained because lip-read information, although visual in origin and hence processed by VIS→OBJ and OBJ→MPL, is on the same time-base as speech, and so can be transformed directly by the relevant processes in the MPL subsystem. Crossmodal effects occur when a redundant item (a suffix) is presented to be lip-read at the end of an aurally presented list [48], but only if the inter-item timing allows them to be dynamically interpretable as constituents of the same data stream, and so integrable by MPL transformations.

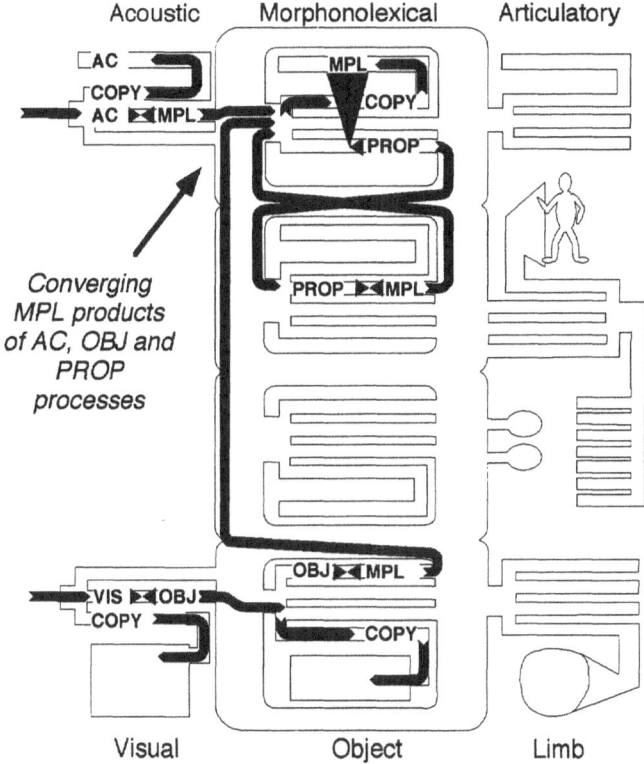

Figure 2.9: The converging MPL products of acoustic, propositional and object-based processing. Here the configuration is for the comprehension of speech, where the individual is listening to the form of the information in the speech stream (buffered at MPL).

This general analysis of information flow receives considerable support from another classic phenomenon, this time explicitly dealing with multimodal integration: The McGurk effect [30, 31]. In the basic McGurk effect video recording techniques are used to alter the relationship between lip movement and heard speech. Acoustic information for one utterance is presented with the visual information for another. Initially, subjects were instructed to watch the speaker and repeat what had been said. The subjects in this study [31] experienced neither intermodal conflict nor domination of information in one modality by information in another. The two sources 'fused' to yield a unified percept. So, for example, when the sound of /ba-ba/ was dubbed onto lip movements for the utterance /ga-ga/, 80% of pre-school children and 98% of adults reported hearing /da-da/. Dubbing /ga-ga/ onto /ba-ba/ also produced illusions, with subjects reporting that they heard /gab-ga/ or /bag-ba/. Similarly, presenting the sound of /pa-pa/ with the lip movements for /ka-ka/ elicited /ta-ta/ as the dominant response; here the reverse dub resulted in such responses as /pak-pa/ and /kap-ka/.

Visual dominance theories or an acoustic averaging hypothesis for similar dichotic fusions [17] cannot explain this effect. Information flow within the ICS architecture provides an explanation: crossmodal integration occurs through the convergence of multimodal sources at the MPL input array. Since the arriving representations can fit a common structural description, and are on the same time base, integration into a coherent data stream is possible. The integrated structure that results will be dependent upon the content of the representations that are to be integrated, and the dynamic status of the processing activity that is to operate on the integrated structure. The McGurk effect has now been widely investigated and the precise character of the effect does appear to vary, being dependent on detailed linguistic influences in some circumstances [30], and on the actual language involved. There are reports for example that the effect is hard to obtain with Japanese [45] due to its syllabic structure; but that it does occur in English when voices of one gender are dubbed onto lip movements of the opposite gender [23].

As advanced graphical interfaces develop, multimodal characteristics assume massive importance. Superficially, the synchronisation of voice in video film, in videophone conversation, in the use of animated characters who 'speak', and even in ventriloquism, are all cases within the ICS framework where multimodal integration could be occurring at the MPL level. However, the bulk of the evidence suggests that multimodal integration at the MPL level must be subject to very tight temporal constraints, and also depends upon detail being abstracted from lip-read information about the linguistic forms being articulated.

While voice asynchrony in high definition films may well cause considerable discomfort, the visual information in very small video images presented on computer screens (e.g. see Figure 2.12) may be quite inadequate to convey the kind of articulatory contrasts that lead to real time blending on the input array of the MPL subsystem. Animated faces, videoconferencing images [46], or the mouth movements of a ventriloquist's dummy would not be detailed enough to let OBJ→MPL produce the detailed MPL representations that are necessary for blending of individual speech sounds to occur. Nevertheless, the overall superstructure and rhythm of the visual stream might be sufficiently well correlated with the Acoustically derived MPL representations for blending of larger units of speech to occur, allowing the speech stream as a whole to be propositionally attributed to a particular visual source, without causing crossmodal conflict at the level of the individual sounds.

An exact synchronisation of video and audio outputs dealing with speech may not be necessary, unless both sources are of sufficiently high fidelity that any offset would cause differentiation of data streams at the MPL level. Their superstructure and the temporal dynamics of the data streams may be sufficient to ensure an attribution of voice and moving image to a single source. However, rapidly improving technology means that larger images of 'speaking faces' are being incorporated into new systems. For these graphic displays, detailed lip movements may be readily discernible, forming a basis for direct blending, conflict or temporal offset on the input array of the MPL subsystems. Along with increased size may come greater requirements for achieving close synchrony between sound and vision.

Even in situations where the visual and acoustic data cannot be reconciled at a superstructural level, it may be possible cognitively to attribute a speech stream to a visual object. In the same way that the VIS representations could not integrate the differently coloured arrowheads, and a higher-level OBJ representation was required, the MPL representation will not be sufficient, and the higher-level PROP representation will be involved.

2.5.3   Propositional Integration

As noted earlier the propositional subsystem takes no direct input from sensory sources, but the role it plays in the indirect integration of information derived from multimodal sources should not be underestimated. This level of representation deals with abstract referents, their properties and semantic inter-relationships. We have already described the role of the PROP subsystem in cycles with OBJ and MPL, providing a referential stream of information to be integrated with and inform our structural interpretation of sensory data. It also plays a directly integrative role in its own right.

The PROP subsystem receives input from OBJ, MPL and IMPLIC sources. Each of these deals with information originating in sensory subsystems. The relevant data flows are highlighted in Figure 2.10. If there are no conflicts between the data flows from OBJ→PROP and MPL→PROP, and if they are compatible with the schematic models active at the implicational level, then multimodal events can be understood indirectly in terms of their integrated PROP representations.

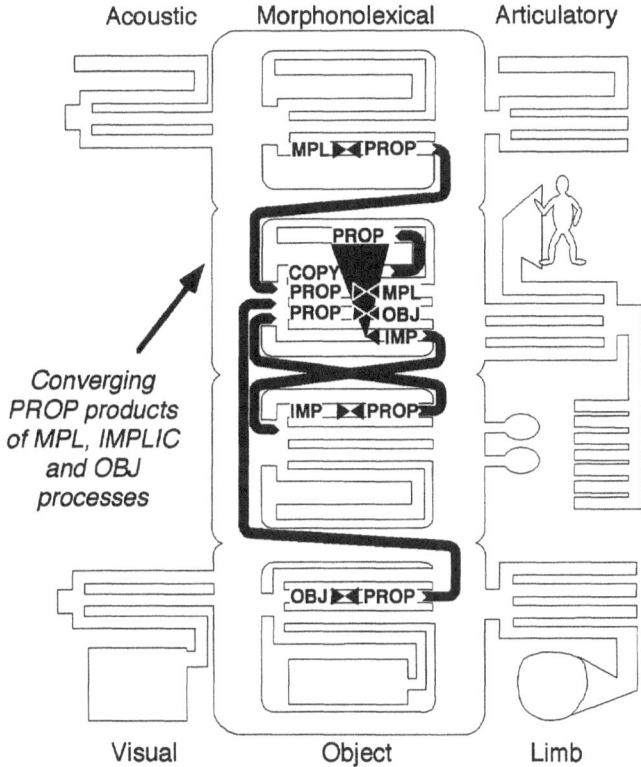

Figure 2.10:   Converging propositional products of MPL, OBJ and IMPLIC processes.

Our 'perception' of thunder and lightning being related to the same environmental event really comes down to a propositional understanding in which the structurally interpreted sensory information is semantically integrable as consequences of a single environmental referent. Likewise, a language stream can be attributed to an animated non-human referential agent so long as they combined agent/speech representation is within the bounds of schematic models of what is reasonable. It is perfectly acceptable behaviour to see and understand a cartoon tree as capable of speaking to you, but it would take very special circumstances for it to be acceptable for you to be seen talking to a real tree in a real park.

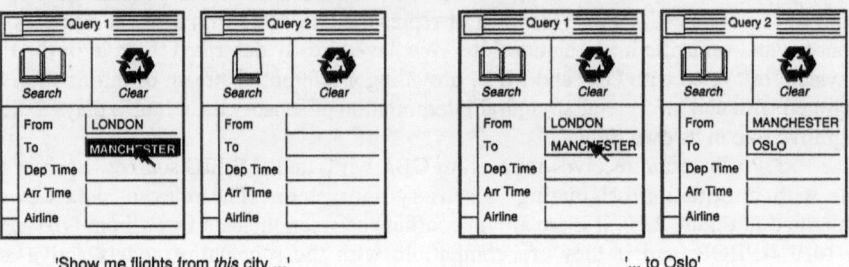

'Show me flights from *this* city ...'   '... to Oslo'

Figure 2.11: A flight information system that allows deictic reference (Nigay, 1994)

In normal discourse, we understand what is said in relation to some frame of reference – and more often than not, the frame of reference involves the external world. Reference to things in the world is an integral part of communication – deixis. We refer to things 'out there' by pointing or by sharing very particular forms of semantic common ground. In terms of the ICS architecture, deictic reference is resolved through the integration and blending of propositional information from different sources (OBJ→PROP; MPL→PROP). Some prototype computer interfaces explicitly support deictic expression. For example, the flight information system illustrated in Figure 2.11 might allow a user to ask for 'flights from this city to Oslo' verbally, co-ordinated with mouse motions that point at the name of the origin city elsewhere on the screen [38, 39].

This kind of application is interesting to analyse for a number of reasons. Pointing with a particular interface device while simultaneously talking is a novel skill combination for most people, even though we can point with our own hands and talk, and would require some experience and learning to acquire. More important are the technological constraints imposed by current speech recognition systems. These systems typically take a significant amount of time to recognise a word and provide feedback about its identity. Even when trained they are also subject to significant error rates. The delay may well be crucial for appropriate deictic fusion at the propositional level. With significant delays, users are likely to become impatient and, where possible, achieve the same ends by other means.

For such systems to be effective the recognition technologies may have to attain a level of performance commensurate with the 'normal' requirements for propositional integration. With advanced graphical interfaces, and particularly those developed in the context of computer supported work, pointing may have far less deictic precision than that normally attained with a mouse. Figure 2.12 combines a graphical workspace in which a user is pointing with arm and finger to an item in the display. In such circumstances, the referent of a verbal statement "this one" can be quite ambiguous and understanding depends on the extent to which a range of cues intersect to minimise the propositional ambiguity [7].

In the broader experimental literature on multimodal events, a great deal of effort has been devoted to understanding what happens with inter-modal conflicts in attributes of sound sources and light sources, such as their spatial or temporal separation [41]. Very often, the tasks require people to exercise considerable judgement. So, for example Rock & Victor [43] asked people to grasp a square whilst simultaneously viewing it through a lens that contracted its image to half size. Subjects were then asked to match what they had experienced to one of several alternatives. Their judgements were more biased by what they had seen than by what they had felt. Indeed, in many cases 'visual dominance' is often assumed in the resolution of multimodal conflicts. This is by no means universally the case. In other circumstances, Walker

& Scott [50] showed that people judge a light as of shorter duration than an tone of identical duration. The form of analysis evolving here would suggest that many of the cases of inter-modal conflict are best understood not in terms of the information processing of sensory or structural representations – but rather as a consequence of cyclical central processing in which propositional attributions may be derived from various integrations of information originating in OBJ, MPL and IMPLIC processing activity.

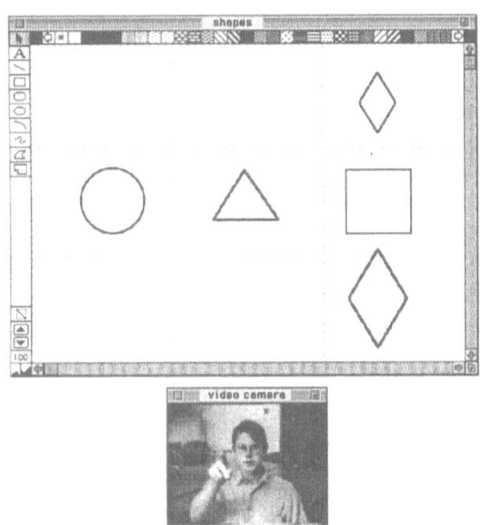

Figure 2.12: A mock-up of a 'shared drawing' package that encourages its users to make deictic references.

The cycles that PROP can make with OBJ and MPL have already been discussed, but it should now be clear that PROP is able to bring these two cycles of activity together. In fact the two cycles can in principle act independently, with their representations remaining differentiated at the PROP input array, and only one (or even neither) of PROP→OBJ or PROP→MPL being buffered. This means that it is quite possible for someone to play tennis, with an OBJ⇔PROP cycle helping them hit the ball, while engaging in a conversation with their opponent and using an MPL⇔PROP cycle to co-ordinate the referential meaning of their speech. What will not be possible, since only one of the processes within PROP can access the image record at a time, is for image record access to occur in both cycles simultaneously. In practice, when the PROP⇔OBJ cycle needs to access experientially derived referential information about tennis, the player will have to momentarily disengage their PROP→MPL process from buffered mode, and so pause the production of intended speech. Similarly, a need to access referential information to drive the speech stream will prevent PROP→OBJ from using the image record. The MPL→ART process will continue to drive the articulatory mechanisms, and OBJ→LIM the motor mechanisms, and so this interchange of buffering will only cause delays in either the speech or play if critical referential activity is required in both streams at the same time. Then the tennis player will have to pause their speech, or risk missing their shot.

In addition to the cycles with the structural subsystems, PROP can both receive representations from IMPLIC and produce IMPLIC representations in return, allowing it to form a third cyclical configuration, PROP⇔IMPLIC. Indeed, propositional representations can rarely, if ever, be sensibly considered in isolation from the processing of the schematic representations of IMPLIC. The cycle between these two levels of meaning is so pervasive within human cognition that it is known as the 'central engine' of cognition. This cycle is also important in bringing latent schematic knowledge into referential form, which is required for it to be verbally expressed (since it is assumed that there is no direct IMPLIC→MPL process).

2.5.4   Implicational Integration

A sweeping, rather dismissive gesture of the hand is over in a moment and almost certainly contributes to a propositional understanding of a speech stream, not by detailed parsing of its spatio-temporal attributes, but by direct apprehension of some quality of the movement (VIS→IMPLIC followed by IMPLIC→PROP). In the same way, facial expressions indicate the mood of the speaker, or provide clues as to how a listener is reacting to what you are saying. Similar representations may be abstracted from tone of voice (AC→IMPLIC) or even from feelings in the body, such as running vigorously on the spot whilst being persuaded to try harder (BS→IMPLIC). All of these sorts of information can be integrated into a unified data stream at this most abstract level of representation within the ICS architecture (Figure 2.13).

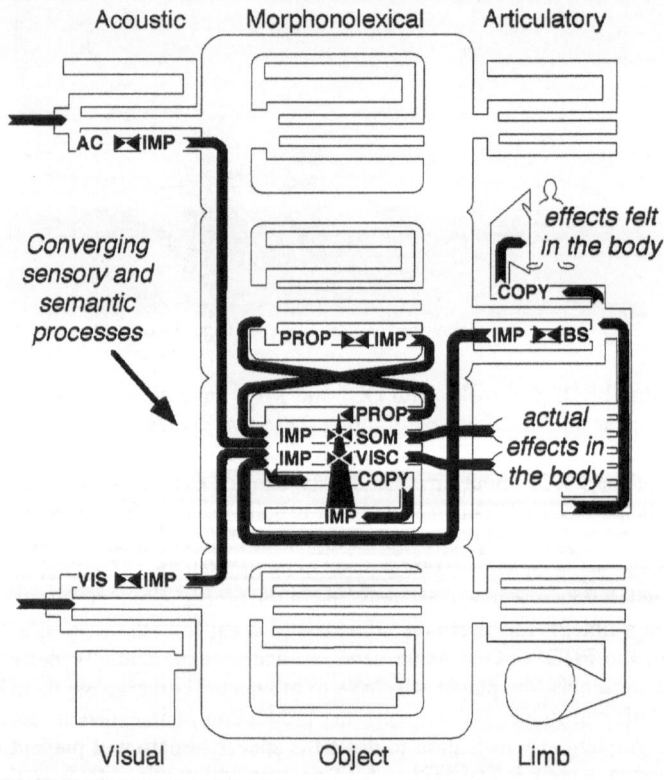

Figure 2.13 Sensory and semantic inputs converging at the Implicational level.

It is at the implicational level that cognition and affect inter-relate most clearly. So, for example, affective judgements about the sound quality of walkman tape recorders tend to be more positive when the subjects are doing arousing physical exercise than when they are at rest [15]. Following the integration of this sensory input to IMPLIC, consequences can then flow back to the PROP subsystem. It is important to note that the other output from IMPLIC only maps to the somatic (SOM) and visceral (VISC) representations to produce responses in the body. Its influence on OBJ and MPL representations, and so their integration with affective information, can only occur indirectly, through the mediation of PROP. Similarly, structural interpretations of the sensory data cannot directly influence its affective representation, but must be channelled through PROP, hence the importance of the PROP⇔IMPLIC central engine.

The basic units of the implicational level of representation are holistic concepts and properties, which come together to form schematic models of a rather generic kind (see Table 1). It also the level of representation at which cognitive and affective concerns come together [49]. Like any other type of representation within ICS, incoming representations can be integrated by transformation processes to form a coherent stream of data. This depends on the way an individual's learning experience has led to the formation of basic units at this level and their combination into higher level superstructures. The form and content of the schematic models constrain our judgement, decision making and overt behaviour.

The effects of implicational integration are general. Information about relative visual positioning and sound localisation contribute to the overall generic specification of the physical environment within which we are operating. Properties of facial expression, tone of voice and bodily context will contribute to setting the interpretative context for incoming utterances. The influences of pattern based factors like facial expression and tone of voice can be illustrated by reference to a simple example of how sensory information can contribute directly, via the VIS→IMPLIC and AC→IMPLIC processes, to the kind of holistic meaning represented at the implicational subsystem. Figure 2.14 shows two shapes. When asked 'which one is Uloomo and which one is Takete?', the majority of people point to the form composed of round elements as Uloomo, and the form composed of angular lines as Takete [19]. The visual characteristics of the shapes and the acoustic and articulatory characteristics of the sounds seem to match in this particular way, and not the other way around: 'Uloomo' connotes a generic quality of roundness, and 'Takete' conveys a similar generic quality of sharpness. The very difficulty people have in justifying their assessments is characteristic of the involvement of IMPLIC representations, set apart as they are from verbalisation without the mediation of PROP.

Figure 2.14: Two 'connotative' shapes (after Davis, 1961)

Implicational information derived from visual sources may also inter-relate and blend with Body-State and Propositional considerations. There is, for example, a massive literature on mood, memory and judgmental effects . To take but one case, asking people 'how do you feel' when the weather is sunny generally produces more positive responses than when it is raining [44]. The pleasantness of an individual's physical environment is assumed to provide a continual affective input via VIS→IMPLIC and BS→IMPLIC to the 'central engine' of propositional and implicational processing. The basic judgemental effect can be radically altered through the creation of specific propositional representations. If *before* asking them how they feel, their attention is directed to their environment by being asked 'what's the weather like?', the effects of weather on their subsequent judgement of how they feel can be removed [44]. Answering the question about the weather requires PROP→IMPLIC and IMPLIC→PROP processes to assess the status of the weather, and what it means qualitatively. When they answer the later question, any weather related affective representations at IMPLIC will be schematically linked with the earlier question, and will be less likely to produce latent or implicit effects on the a judgement of their own 'overall state' [49].

At first glance, the relevance to design issues in human-computer interaction of somewhat esoteric aspects of the connotative meaning of visual form, facial expression and the weather may appear somewhat remote. However, with both simple technologies [4] and advanced interfaces, this is far from the case. For example, Figure 2.15 shows a schematic view of an hypothetical military radar-screen. Here it is easy to recognise which shapes are intended to represent formations of friendly aircraft or ships and to recognise those intended to represent the enemy. In this context, connotation via the sensory-schematic-referential chain can be extremely useful in communicating abstract information quickly, a factor recognised by the earlier investigators of such displays [40].

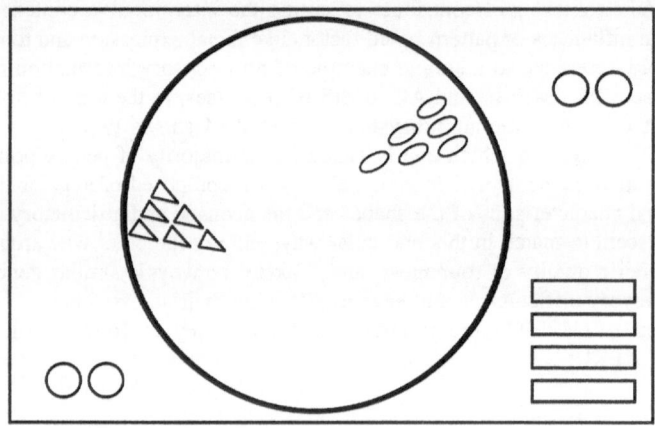

Figure 2.15: A schematic view of a military radar screen, showing friend and enemy formations using connotative forms

Processing in the Implicational subsystem also plays a vital role in the overall co-ordination of communicative behaviour, and so is of considerable significance for the development of computerised systems that are intended to support collaborative work. Since the sensory subsystems send their output directly to IMPLIC, it can arrive before the structural and referential subsystems have interpreted its explicit content. The affective tone of a message may be interpreted and fed back to PROP in advance of the structural subsystems' contribution. Gesture, gaze and intonation, for example, have long been regarded as playing a key role with respect to the management of dialogue. They are also associated with the expression of meaning and with more generic social signalling. Both content and timing are important. Beattie [9], for example discusses the differential distribution of speech focused movements and gestures. Lexically related gestures tend to occur an average of 800msec in advance of the word to which they are related [12]. Although such advance gestures could be related to planning, it is equally plausible that they provide the listener with a context for interpreting the speech.

The use of facial cues to add information about a speaker's affective meaning to the content of their speech is functionally useful when dealing with a person whose facial appearance does correlate with the meaning of their speech. When this correlation is missing, or inappropriate, as is possible in computer generated facial expressions, it can cause problems. Walker et al [51], for example, compared two versions of a synthesised on-screen face accompanying auditory questions (Figure 2.16) with a plain text version of the same questions. Users who were asked questions by the talking faces spent longer writing, wrote more comments, and made fewer mistakes than those responding to textual questions. In addition, users who saw a 'stern' face (the right-hand face in Figure 2.16) spent longer, wrote more, and made fewer mistakes than those who saw the 'neutral' face (left hand side), but they liked the experience and the face less. Here the affective content of the face changed the way that subjects interpreted the situation as a whole, with the vaguely negative tone of the stern face giving a neutral question and answer session the characteristics of an inquisition.

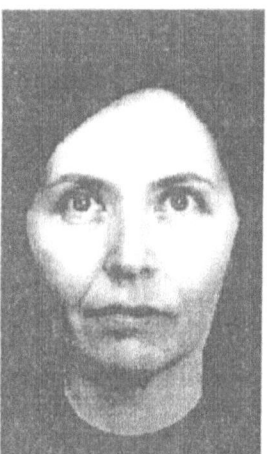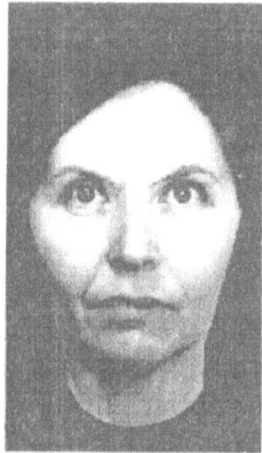

Figure 2.16: a neutral (left) and stern (right) synthesised face, used to accompany auditory questions to computer users (from [15]; reproduced with the permission of the Association for Computing Machinery).

These direct sensory-affective routes are not the only way that affective content can be generated. The PROP→IMPLIC route is just as important, particularly given the possibility for direct feedback via the central engine cycle which can iteratively reinforce its contribution. Referential representations at PROP, derived from structural interpretations of the environment (from OBJ→PROP and MPL→PROP), can provide the sources for the PROP→IMPLIC transformation. In this case, implicit or latent knowledge about the world can be elicited, and unless their attention is drawn to the source of the information, as in the case of the weather question discussed earlier, people remain unaware of its origin, and even its effects upon their subsequent behaviour. For example, when people of different status talk to each other, there is some evidence that the higher status person will tend to use a different proportion of nouns to verbs in their speech than will the lower status person. Change their respective status and they will adjust their speech style. Neither of them will be aware of any change [22]. Similarly, adults when talking to children will automatically adjust their speech style to use shorter, high frequency words. There are many examples of this form [42]. In the context of a meeting, a manager will tend to take up a dominant physical location relative to other participants. Speech cues, location and even dress sense may all contribute to the blending of information to form a particular schematic model.

Within the ICS framework, implicational representations express generic meanings. Their broader function is to capture high level communalities about the world and the self, rather than the specific details. Under circumstances that hinge upon to the integration of multimodal information at the implicational level, the key issue is not whether a specific implicational 'cue' is available, but whether the integrated representation remains adequate to deliver appropriate implicational basic units, and the schematic models to which they contribute. As the applications of advanced graphical systems extend to encompass all domains of human endeavour, it will be increasingly important to supplement our understanding of the mental processing of perceptual form and propositional meaning with an understanding of the role of the wider, holistic meaning that is captured in implicational concepts and their often personal significance. It has long been known that successful computer games are highly engaging [32]. Excitement, curiosity, fantasy and enjoyment are constructs that resonate more closely with implicational rather than propositional meaning.

2.6   Conclusion

2.6.1   Summary

This paper has been concerned with a range of cognitive issues that may arise in the design of advanced graphical interfaces. The concept of advanced graphical interfaces has been taken in its widest sense, encompassing links between graphical presentations and the full range of input and output modalities that can be associated with their use. At the outset, the intention was to convey an understanding of the issues raised rather than to provide detailed design advice. To support that understanding a conceptual framework was presented. This framework is a unified theory of human information processing incorporating two fundamental aspects. The first aspect was a theory of information *flow*. The elements of this theory were basic mental processes organised into subsystems, each concerned with a specific domain of mental life, from sensation through central processing to the effector control of action. Individual subsystems were in turn organised within a wider, superordinate architecture.

The second aspect of the framework involved a theory of information and its *representation*. As with the internal organisation of processes within subsystems, it is assumed that the information represented within all mental codes is organised according to a common set of principles. Representations in each code are formed out of basic units. These basic units are themselves built from constituent elements whose properties reflect the nature of the underlying coding space – be it in a sensory, central or effector domain. The basic units are themselves constituents of a superordinate structuring of the information. This superordinate structuring is governed in part by thematic considerations. Each representation is assumed to be about something (the psychological subject) that is linked to other constituents (the predicate).

The theory of information flow is also closely linked to the theory of representation. First, the flow of information depends upon processes which transform information from one code to another. As such the coding systems are related. With a change from sensory to structural codes information about the sensory constituents is discarded and the sensory superstructure signals the basic units of the structural code. Exactly the same thing happens in the transformation of structural to propositional and in the transformation from propositional to implicational codes. In moving from implicational through propositional and structural codes to effector output, the respective transformation processes accomplish the inverse. The properties of the flow also link quite directly with the thematic structure of representations. The patterns of flow within the architecture are a crucial determinant of the inputs received by a process. This constrains the properties of the central and effector mental codes, since flow patterns determine how information from different sources comes together and blends.

It is upon this last point that the current paper has been focussed. Within the ICS framework, it is assumed that conscious experience is associated with the operation of the copy processes. The actual action of the underlying transformation processes is 'unconscious'. Of course, since information produced by one process will be copied into the image record of a subsequent subsystem, the products of that process will be available to conscious experience, but mediated by a copy process in a different subsystem. Since the elements of an input code are discarded when producing an output code, the *products experienced* at the subsequent level cannot directly represent how those elements came together. The constraints governing combination, fusion or blending of constituent elements are inherent, and consequently the knowledge deployed is 'latent' within the process. It will not directly be reflected in the products of that processing activity. If related streams fail to fuse, the separate products will, of course, be available to conscious experience at the next level of representation.

The arguments presented here have covered a very broad range. The particular illustrations were selected to demonstrate the relevance of the material to the resolution of issues in the design of advanced graphical interfaces. Hopefully, they went further and illustrated the potential utility in design of the kind of deeper understanding offered by cognitive theory. However, for such utility to be realised, means must be available to make the theory useful in the context of systems design, software engineering processes and human factors evaluations.

2.6.2   Relating cognitive theory to evaluation, design processes, and software engineering.

The general idea of utilising cognitive theory in design has long been an objective of research in HCI. Theories have often proved to be of limited scope and difficult to apply in a manner that guides design processes effectively [33]. The concluding section of a long paper is no place to pursue the relevant arguments in detail. It is nonetheless appropriate to provide some pointers. As a part of a long term inter-disciplinary collaboration, three strategies have been pursued for connecting the form of theory presented here to practical processes of design.

The first strategy is to develop heuristics for analysing practical design scenarios based upon the theoretical techniques. It is then necessary to convey those heuristics and the products of the application into design processes. So, for example, heuristics can be described in a technical manual for decomposing the structure of information on displays and principles described that support inferences about user performance with those structures. The products of analyses based upon these sorts of heuristics can them be incorporated into representations that support design. Design Rationales can, for example, be specified in the form of a notation based upon Questions Options and Criteria. Work done as a part of the AMODEUS project has illustrated how the heuristic analysis of design scenarios based upon ICS techniques can come to form criteria in a design space [10].

This first kind of strategy clearly relies upon the training and availability of people who are skilled in the relevant techniques and it is unlikely that this would be a real option for many design teams. An alternative strategy is to build software tools to support design which effectively embody those theoretical skills. This second strategy has also been pursued for some years [8, 34]. Production system techniques are used to automate the process of collecting information about a design space. The same techniques are used to represent theoretical heuristics. As with the skilled expert, these production rules can then build explicit models of the kinds of cognitive activity that will occur during the different mental phases in the performance of an interactive task. This can then be used to provide a predictive evaluation of user performance and theoretically motivated advice about design solutions.

A third strategy is to seek more direct means for interlinking the techniques of cognitive science with those of computer science. In one tactic, methods have been sought to represent interactions using formal methods [26]. In this approach, particular interactional requirements are precisely formulated. Their consequences can then be explored, on the one hand, by reference to an appropriate models of the interactive behaviour of the computer system, and on the other hand to a model of user cognition. Another more direct tactic has also been explored. ICS is constrained by principles of information flow and information representation, with sufficiently adequate precision to be modelled using formal methods of software engineering. Interactor theory in computer science [21] can be used as a basis for this formal specification. In fact, using the MATIS system of Figure 2.11 as an example, Duke et al. [20] have shown how cognitive and system theory can be directly combined. Using a deontic extension of modal action logic, key constraints on the information flow imposed by the ICS model of user cognition were represented axiomatically. Key aspects of the behaviour of the MATIS computer system were formally represented in equivalent axiomatic terms. With both user and system models represented in the same language, they could be directly combined into a third, syndetic model. This third model represents the axioms governing the conjoint behaviour of the user and the system.

Naturally, much remains to be done to convert these strategies into everyday design methods. However, the opportunities to relate cognitive theory to the kinds of software engineering techniques described throughout this volume are certainly there to be grasped.

Acknowledgement

The research reported in this paper was carried out within the AMODEUS project, ESPRIT BRA 7040, funded by the European Union. We are grateful both for their financial support and for the opportunity to work in a strongly interdisciplinary context. Information about the project, and access to many project documents, is available electronically:

http://www.mrc-apu.cam.ac.uk/amodeus/
ftp://ftp.mrc-apu.cam.ac.uk/pub/amodeus/

References

[1] Abbs, J.H. & Gracco, V.L. (1984). Control of complex motor gestures: Orofacial muscle responses to load perturbations of lip during speech. *Journal of Neurophysiology, 51,* 705-723.

[2] Attanasio, J. S. (1987) Relationships between oral sensory feedback skills and adaptation to delayed auditory feedback. *Journal of Communication Disorders*, 20, 391-402.

[3] Barnard, P.J. (1985) Interacting Cognitive Subsystems: A psycholinguistic approach to short term memory. In A. Ellis (Ed.) *Progress in the Psychology of Language*, (Vol. 2), Chapter 6, London: Lawrence Erlbaum Associates, 197-258.

[4] Barnard, P. and Marcel, A.J. (1984) Representation and understanding in the use of symbols and pictograms. In R. Easterby and H. Zwaga (Eds.), *Information Design: The Design and Evaluation of Signs and Printed Material*, 37-75. John Wiley: Chichester.

[5] Barnard, P. & May, J. (1993) Cognitive Modelling for User Requirements. In Byerley, P., Barnard, P. & May, J. (Eds.) *Computers, Communication and Usability: Design Issues, Research and Methods for Integrated Services*. Chapter 2.1, pp 101-146, Amsterdam: North Holland, Studies in Telecommunications.

[6] Barnard, P.J. and Teasdale, J.D. (1991) Interacting cognitive subsystems: A systemic approach to cognitive-affective interaction and change. *Cognition and Emotion, 5,* 1-39.

[7] Barnard, P., May, J. & Salber, D. (1994) Deixis and points of view in Media Spaces: an Empirical Gesture. AMODEUS project document UM/WP19;submitted for publication.

[8] Barnard, P., Wilson, M. and MacLean, A. (1988) Approximate modelling of cognitive activity with an Expert system: A theory based strategy for developing an interactive design tool. *The Computer Journal, 31,* 445-456.

[9] Beattie, G. (1983) *Talk*. Milton Keynes: Open University Press.

[10] Bellotti, V., Buckingham-Shum, S., MacLean, A., & Hammond, N. (1994) Multidisciplinary Modelling In HCI Design … In Theory and In Practice, *Amodeus Project Document ID/WP 34;* submitted for Publication

[11] Bregman A. S. & Rudnicky, A.I. (1975) Auditory Segregation: Stream or Streams? *Journal of Experimental Psychology: Human Perception and Performance*, 1, 263-267.

[12] Butterworth, B & Beattie, G. (1978) Gesture and silence as indicators of planning in speech. In: Campbell, R. N. & Smith. P.T., *Recent Advances in the Psychology of Language: Formal and Experimental Approaches*. New York, Plenum.

[13] Campbell, R. & Dodd, B. (1980) Hearing by Eye. *Quarterly Journal of Experimental Psychology*, 32, 85-99.

[14] Cherry, E. C. (1953) Some experiments on the recognition of speech, with one and two ears. *Journal of the Acoustical Society of America*, 25, 975-979.

[15] Clark, M., Millberg, S.,& Ross, J. (1983) Arousal cues arousal-related material in memory: Implications for understanding effects of mood on memory. *Journal of Verbal Learning and verbal Behaviour*, 22 633-649.

[16] Craig, A. (1990) An investigation into the relationship between anxiety and stuttering. *Journal of speech and hearing disorders, 55,* pp. 290-294.

[17] Cutting, J. E. (1976) Auditory and Linguistic Processes in Speech Perception: Inferences from Six Fusions in Dichotic Listening. *Psychological Review*, 83, 114-140.

[18] Cutting, J. E. (1981) Six Tenets for Event Perception. *Cognition*, 10, 71-78.

[19] Davis, R. (1961) The fitness of names to drawings. *British Journal of Psychology*, 52, 259-268.

[20] Duke D.J. , Barnard P.J. Duce D.A. and May, J. (1994) Syndetic Models For Human-Computer Interaction. *Amodeus Project Document* ID/WP35; submitted for publication.

[21] Duke, D. J. & Harrison, M. D. (1993). Abstract Interaction Objects. *Computer Graphics Forum*, 12 (3).

[22] Fielding, G. & Fraser, C. (1978) The Language of Interpersonal relationships. In Markova, I (ed) The social context of language, Chichester: Wiley.

[23] Green, K., Kuhl, P. Meltzoff, A & Stevens, B. (1991) Integrating speech information across talkers, gender, and sensory modality. *Perception and Psychophysics, 50,* 524-536.

[24] Gregory, R. (1971) *The Intelligent Eye.* London: Weidenfeld & Nicolson.

[25] Gross, Y. & Melzack, R. (1978) Body Images: dissociation of real and perceived limbs by pressure cuff ischemia. *Experimental Neurology, 61,* 680-688.

[26] Harrison, M.D. and Barnard, P.J. (1993) On defining requirements for interactions. In A. Finkelstein (Ed.), *Proceedings of IEEE International Workshop on Requirements Engineering* New York: IEEE, 50-54, 1993.

[27] Howell, P. & Powell, D. J. (1987) Delayed auditory feedback with delayed sounds varying in duration. *Perception and Psychophysics*, 42, 166-172.

[28] Köhler, W. (1947) *Gestalt Psychology.* New York: Liveright.

[29] Lee, B. (1950) Effects of delayed speech feedback. *Journal of the Acoustical Society of America, 22,* pp 824-826.

[30] MacDonald, J. & McGurk, H. (1978). Visual influences on speech perception processes. *Perception and Psychophysics*, 24, 253-257.

[31] McGurk, H. & MacDonald, J. (1976) Hearing lips and seeing voices. *Nature*, 264, 746-748.

[32] Malone, T (1982) Heuristics for designing enjoyable user interfaces: Lessons from computer games. In *Human Factors in Computing Systems.* ACM: Washington, 63-68.

[33] May, J. & Barnard, P. (1995) The case for supportive evaluation in design. *Interacting With Computers, 7* (in press).

[34] May, J., Barnard, P.J., and Blandford, A. (1993) Using Structural Descriptions of Interfaces to Automate the Modelling of User Cognition. User *Modelling and Adaptive User Interfaces, 3(1)*

[35] May, J., Barnard, P.J., Boecker, M. and Green, A.J. (1990) Characterising structural and dynamic aspects of the interpretation of visual interface objects. In *ESPRIT '90 Conference Proceedings* (pp.819-834). Brussels (November 1990), Dordrecht: Kluwer Academic Publishers.

[36] Monster, A.W., Herman, R. & Altman, N.R. (1973). Effects of the peripheral and central 'sensory' component in the calibration of position. In J.E. Desmedt (Ed.) *New developments in electromyography and clinical neurophysiology* (vol. 3). Basel: Karger.

[37] Munn, N. (1961). *Psychology: The fundamentals of Human Adjustment*, London: George Harrap.

[38] Nigay, L. (1994). *Conception et Modélisation Logicielles des Systèmes Interactifs.* Ph.D. Thèse de l'Université Joseph Fourier, Grenoble. 350 pages.

[39] Nigay, L., Coutaz, J. & Salber, D. (1993) MATIS: a Multimodal Airline Travel Information System. *AMODEUS Project Document* SM/WP10.

[40] Provins, K, Stockbridge H, Forrest, D. & Anderson, D. (1957) The representation of aircraft by pictorial signs. *Occupational Psychology*, 31, 21-32.

[41] Radeau, M. (1992). Cognitive Impenetrability in Auditory Visual Interaction. In: *Analytic Approaches to Human Cognition.* Alegria, J., Holender, D., Junça de Morais, J. and Radeau, M. (eds.). Amsterdam: Elsevier Science Publishers, BV. 41-55.

[42] Robinson, W. P. (1972) *Language and Social Behaviour* Harmondsworth: Penguin Books.

[43] Rock, I & Victor, J. (1964) Vision and Touch: an experimentally created conflict between the two senses. Science, 143, 594.

[44] Schwarz, N. & Clore, G.L. (1983) Mood, misattribution, and judgements of well-being: Informative and directive functions of affective states. *Journal of Personality and Social Psychology*, 45, 512-523.

[45] Seikiyama, K. & Tokura, Y. (1991). McGurk effect in non-English listeners: Few visual effects for Japanese subjects hearing Japanese syllables of high auditory intelligibility. *Journal of the Acoustical Society of America,* 90, 1797-1805.

[46] Sellen, A. (1992) Speech patterns in video-mediated conversations. In Proceedings of CHI '92 ACM: New York, 49-59.

[47] Shallice, T. (1988) *From Neuropsychology to mental structure.* CUP: Cambridge.

[48] Spoehr, K. & Corin, W. (1978) The stimulus suffix effect as a memory coding phenomenon. *Memory and Cognition,* 6, 583-589.

[49] Teasdale, J. & Barnard, P.J. (1993) Affect, Cognition and Change: Re-modelling depressive thought. Hove: Lawrence Erlbaum Associates.

[50] Walker, J & Scott, K. (1981) Auditory-visual conflicts in the duration of lights tones, and gaps. Journal of Experimental Psychology, Human Perception and Performance, 7, 1327-1339.

[51] Walker, J.H., Sproull, L. & Subramani, R. (1994) Using a Human Face in an Interface' In Proceedings of CHI'94, pp. 85-91. ACM: New York.

3 Users

D.A. Duce

3.1 Participants

P.J. Barnard
N.O. Bernsen
M. Cooper
D.A. Duce (Rapporteur)
D.J. Duke
G.F. Faconti
R. Hartson (Chairman)
P. Markopoulos
C.R. Roast

3.2 Discussion

3.2.1 Introductory Remarks

Interactive systems involve more than just computer software; they increasingly make assumptions that concern users' cognitive abilities, as in visualization systems or virtual reality. In this context the term 'user' means the end user of a system. Discussion of the topic started from the following set of headings:

- perception;

- effect on design;

- relationship to specification;

- usability issues;

- tasks.

In his invited presentation, Dr Barnard used some rather sophisticated AV equipment which enabled him to control a Macintosh interface projected onto a screen, using a laser pointer. The chairman initiated discussion by reflecting on the difficulty of double-clicking on a file icon using such a pointing device, because of the high probability of moving the pointer between clicks. He also reflected on the difficulty that the speaker had had in locating a particular file. In order to open a file, the icon had to be visible; the problem is to find the icon! This involves cognitive user actions - pattern matching and recognition. This preamble opened into a discussion on the adequacy of a presentation (visual or otherwise). Does the presentation build on the user's implicit or explicit knowledge? Does it support the user's knowledge about the metaphors used in the system? Such knowledge is often implicitly captured during design. There is a need for notations not only in order to record such knowledge, but also to provide an evaluative ability, for example the ability to detect ambiguity. Other factors that may affect use of the system were noted. These covered physical, cognitive, environmental and communicative issues.

3.2.2   Analysis in Design

Whilst an analytical framework helps in evaluating a design, the point was made that when analysis identifies a problem *it is highly desirable that the framework then suggests a solution.* Without this, the designer again has to revert to an empirical approach. Thus, a criterion by which to judge an analytical techniques is 'does it give substantive input to redesign?'

It was noted that check lists can be very helpful in design in some circumstances, without requiring a large amount of theoretical machinery. There are classes of errors that arise just because some generic issues have not been considered by the designers. A checklist of issues can be helpful for eliminating such kinds of errors from a design. There are other domain specific errors which a checklist would not help the designer to detect.

If a particular way in which to represent a design is chosen, does that then lock the designer into a particular region of the design space? Very good designers (the top 5%, say) will design very good solutions. The issue facing this community is how to support the other 95%, the average designers. Can representation techniques be found that will lead the designer to a good design? A requirement to make something stand out in a visual interface is of little use without an understanding of what it is that causes a feature to stand out; this is a form of reification for designers. Guidelines alone are often ambiguous and difficult to interpret. It is the underlying cognitive principles which are important; for example, if an icon is not standing out, then why is that?

3.2.3   Design and Craft

The proximity of the monastery to Cararra, a source of high quality marble for centuries, prompted the observation that designers are skilled craftsmen, just like marble scupltors!

There is a need to scope what is given to designers, there is no way to capture everything that a designer might encounter. An example was given concerning the design of the processor box of a certain make of computer. There is a recessed channel just below the top of the box, which just happens to be about the same width as a floppy disc. Would theory ever have predicted that users would try to insert floppy discs into this channel in the belief that it contained the entry to the disc drive?!

The craftsman analogy was pursued further. No design aids are ever likely to raise an average designer to the level of the Michelangelo of User Interface Design, but what one can hope to do is to enhance the capabilities of the average designer. Even 'Sistine Chapels' need solid craftsmen to support the master.

The analogy holds well for interface development too, Most software is large enough that no one person can do the whole interface. 'Masters' are needed to solve the most difficult problems, decide the metaphors, etc. and skilled workers and apprentices are needed to fill in the details (and there are lots of impediments to usability lurking in the details!).

It was pointed out that craftsmen make prototypes first; for example the sculptor will make sketches and models before embarking on the 'real thing'. One cannot predict all the problems from scratch; prototypes help to tease out problems. However, prototyping is not just about reification. It is necessary to provide the right abstractions for the prototype. Should a sculptor make a prototype using plasticine, LEGO or mashed potatoes? Some of those materials have the right properties, i.e. embody appropriate abstractions, others do not. Craftsmen must understand the properties of their material. Likewise, through abstraction, the designer should be able to reflect back to the salient points. The question 'Are the right abstractions in the prototype?' was seen as a key question. Some examples were discussed.

How does one know what the salient aspects are? Such knowledge was seen to come from a variety of sources, for example experience, theoretical understanding. The properties of the human visual system, for example, and the distance from which overhead foils are to be viewed, allow one to work out whether foils containing characters of a particular size will be legible by viewers in a particular age range).

The role of design rationale within design representation was discussed. Design rationale was seen as a way to make design decisions and reasoning explicit. Making decisions and reasoning explicit was seen as a way to encourage designers to explore more of the design space and hence to increase the likelihood of finding a better solution. There was seen to be a need to explore in principled ways rather than a scatter-gun approach. 'What is the principled way forward, what am I really trying to do and how could it be done in a systematic way' were felt to be key questions for a designer to address.

In relation to usability issues, many representations have been developed over the last 20 years which are tightly scoped to particular design problems. There is a need to develop notations which will address the next generation of problems. Keystroke models, for example, are not appropriate for interfaces based on graphics, parallelism and gesture. Notations have lagged behind problems and there is a tendency to invent a new notation for each new design problem.

It is also easy to focus on a narrow set of issues. For example, consistency. Consistency in interfaces is a good thing, but consistency alone is not enough, there are plenty of examples of interfaces that are consistent, but still unusable.

Some would argue that design is purely an empirical problem. Designers such as Michelangelo worked empirically. There are some hard problems here. When applying analytical techniques, it is easy to run into a brick wall and stop at that point, rather than stepping back and trying to identify and characterize the problem. There is a danger in analysis of concentrating on the problems that we can solve well; what is necessary is to characterize the problems we cannot solve and move towards new techniques with wider applicability. There should be some common understanding of the limitations of existing techniques which constitute requirements that future models and techniques should strive to address. The paper by Dearden and Harrison addresses the limitations of some techniques in the context of modelling interactive case memories.

What are we focusing models on? One cannot talk about usability, say, in an abstract sense alone. There need to be notions of what constitutes usability. One of the key current research questions was felt to be 'what are the ideas and concepts on which to base the next generation of interactive systems?' It is clear that such systems will be 'richly interactive'. Models such as the keystrokes model are the wrong way to think about gestural systems, say, where there is a much higher level feedback loop than in keystrokes. There was seen to be a certain irony in criticisms that formal methods are not appropriate at low levels of the system, when concern is shifting to much higher level concepts.

3.2.4 Temporal Aspects

Temporal aspects of systems are becoming much more important, for example in multimedia and virtual reality systems. Even with temporal notations, it is difficult to relate events to actions. Temporal logic supports qualitative reasoning about time, but does not have a concrete metric of time. Temporal logic was felt to be good for describing high level requirements, but does not help in describing what happens when things go wrong. The notion of the 'grain' of a formalism introduced in Alan Dix's talk, which captures the idea that a formalism may do some things well and other things not at all, was seen to be important. As in any undertaking, it is important to know what factors will be important and to choose the right tools for the job.

3.2.5   Formalism and Models

It was noted that over the years 'quantitative data drives out qualitative' and this is usually at the cost of crucial salient features. It was felt to be extremely important to have notations which convey *understanding*. It is very easy to miss out key ideas in generating a lot of formalism. Formalism does not guarantee consistency or completeness. Formal methods grew up to describe the functional parts of a system and there is no *a priori* reason to suppose that such methods will also work for the user interface, though work on applying formal methods to complete systems described in the papers by Duke, Harrison, Barnard and Blandford was noted.

It is useful to look at a microcosm of HCI research, the ESPRIT Amodeus project, which brings together both system and user modellers. In the early days of the Amodeus, the accusation was made that user modelling techniques did not of themselves produce insight and design suggestions, but rather these came from the craft skill of those applying the techniques, not from the theory. This can be equally applied to formal methods, the method does not tell you what to represent, that comes from the skill of the analyst. This is unfortunate, but true - and true about many other kinds of methods, formal and otherwise.

It was noted that some effort has been invested over the last 20 years in describing vending machines. To make this work, the user involvement is abstracted away. The real problem is to embed the functional parts which belong to the user.

Equally, one must not expect that all the key points will come out in one go. One of the positive outcomes of the Amodeus project, seen by the members of the project team in the discussion group, has been the ability to pick up pieces and ideas from the different models represented in the project. There are some interesting conditions necessary for this to happen; it is all too easy for the inventors of techniques to become adversarial in their defence of their invention. Iteration was seen as an important factor in the development of techniques.

Formal methods give a particular kind of insight, for example thinking about pre-conditions for operations explicitly acts as a forcing function for thinking about the failure modes of the system. A key question is 'what value do you get from a particular approach?'

3.2.6   The Road to Good Designs

What will help a designer to get onto the path of a good design? It may be, for example, that by examining the claims about psychological behaviour that are built into the design, a good direction may emerge. Even if there is time to investigate only a small number of claims in-depth, the designer may still learn a lot about the design and the design space.

It was observed that people who are good at doing theory in design will come up with good claims, but in the hands of a novice, the same exercise will be nugatory. Another key question is 'how transferable are techniques from their creators?'

'Designing to constraints' was felt to be an important theme. The narrower the scope of a design project, the happier designers feel about it. People want smaller design spaces because they can be managed more effectively. Note that there is a tension in design between focussing effort on a small space, and prompting designers to consider new solutions. The issues here are not just about transferring knowledge, but include management of the complexity of the design space so that designers can cope with it.

3.2.7 Concluding Thought

Finally the group came up with an important observation:

> Formal methods are the interface to a formal model. Do the notations do this successfully? Do they convey the insight that is behind the formal model?

4   Role of Formalisms

M.D. Harrison

4.1   Participants

Remi Bastide
Andy Dearden (Chair)
Alan Dix
Bob Fields
Michael Harrison (Rapporteur)
Philippe Palanque
Juan Carlos Torres

4.2   Discussion

Many of the papers presented at the workshop were concerned with the use of formal notations in specifying interactive systems. This working group was tasked with the problem of considering the role of this work and establishing an agenda for further work. More specific topics that were suggested for the group were:

- neutral descriptions;

- domain modelling;

- trade-off between ease of learning and what the technique will deliver;

- role in design;

- temporal modelling and reasoning.

All the discussion groups were asked to present conclusions in terms of a statement of the key issues and problems, and an analysis of the strengths and weaknesses of the various approaches. The discussion began by organising the topics to be discussed. Temporal ordering and reasoning were of particular interest to the group and hence it was discussed first. There then followed a more general discussion of trade-off and role.

4.3   Temporal modelling and reasoning

4.3.1   Why is time important?

The group felt that three issues make timing an important area for consideration.

1. Timing affords an opportunity to make an effective link with psychological models. There are well established cognitive models that deal with timing at a keystroke level. These models provide an opportunity to develop compatible system models that incorporate time.

2. Safety critical systems demand an analysis of whether tasks or actions can be carried out within specific time limits. This issue is particularly important when considering dynamic control systems. Properties of such systems include "liveness properties" such as whether it is possible for an operator to carry out a series of actions before a deadline. Another "safety property" is the *pace* of the interaction.

3. Multi-modal interaction provides capacity for supporting multiple streams of input at the same time. Here time may be considered in the context of so called "temporal windows" for blending these multiple streams. For example, it is necessary to identify the time interval in which the spoken utterance "put that ..." relates to a gesture that points to the object which is to be "put".

4.3.2   What sort of time modelling?

It was agreed that a number of aspects should be emphasised in any modelling approach. The list is not complete but rather represents the course which the discussion took.

sequencing: take a cashpoint machine where it may be necessary to guarantee that the cash is withrawn only after the card is withdrawn in order to prevent widespread loss of cash cards. A requirement would be that the ordering of events be constrained.

parallelism: take a guillotine machine where it is necessary (for safety reasons) to guarantee that both the user's hands must be kept from the blade at "cut time". This may be ensured by requiring the user to push two buttons at the same time using both hands.

intrusion errors: It may be appropriate to legislate that sequences of actions are not shared between similar tasks. The problem here would be to avoid another form of error where a user intends to achieve one objective but, because a subsequence of the actions is familiar as a means of achieving another objective, achieves the other objective instead. These sorts of errors are called "intrusion errors".

hard real time: When dealing with what an operator is capable of achieving we may be concerned with time evaluation and quantitative models of time. For example, it may be necessary to quantify "immediate" response for a variety of actions and ensure that the implemented system supports it.

assessing expertise: It may be necessary to calculate the speed at which input is being created to assess expertise of the user.

real world feedback: Perhaps the system should be designed to produce realistic feedback commensurate with what happens in interaction with real-world systems. There is a concern with the specification of time restriction: where we want to be able to ensure that users meet deadlines.

In retrospect it is clear that the first two items relate to ordering requirements rather than timing.

It was noted that it is difficult to formulate requirements and specifications that are constrained by time criteria. It is difficult to use time quantitatively so that a detailed specification of the system may be produced that satisfies the time criteria. Requirements change as the specification gets closer to the implementation. What seems to be "synchronisation" at one level becomes another kind of property at a more detailed level. Furthermore there is a possibly difficult relationship between refinement and other properties of interactive systems. For example *initiative* may reside with the system because the system keeps the user waiting. It would be worth exploring other places where there is interaction between timing and other properties.

4.3.3   What are the timing issues?

The group chose a set of questions about systems that are likely to be asked and have timing implications. These were:

- *How fast is the system running?* This question relates to response time and the speed at which actions must be completed.

- *How do I deal with time critical input?* This relates to the speed at which actions must be completed. It also relates to how various parallel modalities are related in time - the temporal window issue mentioned earlier.

- *How much time does the user have?* This question is related to the user orientated problem of assessing the capability of the user under time and workload demands.

- *Does my system evolve spontaneously over time?* This question is concerned generally with the dynamic properties of systems though it is of particular interest in adaptive systems where the adaptation occurs at the system's initiative.

The group noted that at the time of the meeting there was very little published literature within Human Computer Interaction on notions of *time*. However, existing time based formalisms may lend themselves to further study. For example, several Petri-net extensions allow modelling and reasoning about time in a quantitative manner. Stochastic Petri nets, for example, have been extensively studied and used for performance evaluation and analysis of real-time and telecommunication systems.

4.4   Trade-offs and pay-offs

The group discussed particular positive and negative features of the formalisms that were being used by members of the working group in their research. A future agenda should include a more complete and consistent discussion of these trade-off issues.

4.4.1   Petri Nets

The *Petri net* community, represented by Bastide and Palanque, noted that a steep "learning curve" is associated with Petri Nets, but that they are useful for analysing interactive systems. The framework is particularly useful for checking reachability properties such as path checking. They are not useful for bringing out relationships between the state and the display of an interactive system. Petri nets tend to be difficult to read. Hierarchical structure is often unclear and it is not clear from the description where the interactive system starts and ends. It was noted that careful structuring of the specification could bring out the meaning more clearly.

4.4.2   Interactors

The *interactors* community was represented by Dearden, Fields and Harrison. They commented that there is also a "learning curve" problem here. A notion of state is explicit in the form of description and therefore history and other contextual properties are more easily expressed. Because this specification technique makes a clear distinction between state and display, *visibility* properties and recoverability properties are more easily expressed.

4.4.3   Algebraic Specification

Torres briefly described his work on the application of *algebraic specification* to interactive systems. Here a synchronization mechanism is included within the specification. The method has not, as yet, been used for real applications, however theoretical properties have been investigated. The modular nature of algebraic specification imposes a hierarchical working method. This may be an advantage (it enforces structure), but it is also a restriction (it may be difficult to use for exploratory specification). The notation also incorporates display information, and so is would be possible to analyse *visibility*. On the other hand, algebraic specification is a high level specification method – it assumes no underlying model. This could be an advantage, as it does not impose any restriction on design, but it is also a drawback because it is more difficult to express the specification, and to derive a design from it.

4.4.4   General Implementation Issues

From the point of view of implementation, the refinement of Petri net descriptions would produce a system in which there is an embedded model (like the User Interface Development Environment discussed by Foley) whereas Interactors support refinement to other more concrete system specifications. The approach of algebraic specification is similar to that of interactors and has been developed particularly within the Larch framework.

Interactors are undeveloped and do not have effective tool support. In the specific context of flexible manufacturing systems Petri Nets are supported by Grafcet. The utility of these techniques for large scale problems has not been demonstrated.

4.5   Where have formal notations been used?

Formal notations in general have been used effectively in safety critical applications where the cost of failure is potentially greater than the cost of development. Praxis systems have said that formally specifying parts of an air traffic control system has led to a tenth of the errors compared with informal techniques, with a tenth of the maintenance cost. Their project cost as much to develop as would have been the case using conventional methods. Recent work has been carried out in the context of the Esprit Amodeus 2 project to develop techniques that would enable more efficient specification of the interactive components of the Praxis air traffic control system.

4.5.1   Safety critical systems

There was discussion of the need for specifications that can draw out the relationship between simulation and reality. Current methods do not adequately deal with real life issues that affect the way people recognise the reality of systems. One property that was mentioned under this category was "proximity" in input.

It was also noted that there is a relationship between formal methods and human reliability assessment. Mention was made of a project sponsored by British Aerospace at York that is concerned with understanding this connection more effectively. It was noted that specifying systems, so that problems of transferring tasks between agents can be made explicit, was not currently possible. For example, such a specification would help the designer decide when to make a pilot cross check as a standard procedure when the Head up Display falls below acceptable levels of reliability. Apart from the work in UAN (described by Hartson and Mayo) there is little contact between system modelling and task analysis in general.

5 Role of Development Environments

Piyawadee "Noi" Sukaviriya

5.1 Participants

David	Bell
Hans	de Bruin
Thomas	Elwert
Mark	van Harmelen
Virpi	Hassinen
Ales	Limpouch
Fabio	Paterno
Siegfried	Schreiber
Noi	Sukaviriya
Roger	Took
Jean	Vanderdonckt

5.2. Initial Discussions

Our group was asked to discuss about these aspects of design environments:
   Who are the users?
   What kind of tools should we provide?
   Development models (SE & HCI)
   Places for formalisms
   Criteria for acceptability
   Task modeling

Our group defined "a development environment" as an environment where interactive applications are defined, evaluated, and implemented. A point worth noting here is that our group defined "a development environment" as a place where both application and application interface are developed, implying that the two processes should be done in an integrated manner and with consideration of each other. We defined "users" of our environments as application designers and the word "end-users" as those who use the applications after they are developed by designers. We defined an interactive application as consisting of roughly two parts – the application interface and the application program which implements the functionality. The interface of an application consists of both the static and dynamic aspects of the interface.

The mission of our group, simply put, is to draw a scope for development environments. The scope is for us to realize where our research accomplishments stand relative to the demands of the entire design process, how can existing research and technology be integrated in design environments, and what are sensible future directions. In order to achieve these goals, we first brainstormed on the outstanding problems in the design process, the issues each of us considers important, and the techniques, instruments, tools, and/or assistance that are necessary for the design process. Soon enough, we generated a rather long list, perhaps made longer by different perspectives each of us brought to the table. This is perhaps an indication that research in development environments is still far from being of adequate service to the real world. It also indicates the fact that computational resources are not being used at their full capacity to better support the interface design process.

Here we highlight some of the items in the list we generated: incrementally evaluating interfaces with clear results leading to guidelines to improve the quality of interfaces, knowledge needed to support the design of complex systems such as computer-aided design, geographical information systems, computer-supported collaborative work, etc., managing the design of a complex system, mapping from task analysis results to design scenarios, portability issues that users of development environments must consider when designing user interfaces, documentation of user interface design, and support for involving end users in the design process. This list is also know as our "wish list," as we generated it from thinking about the kind of support we wished to have while we did our design work. We hope that all of these issues will be addressed in the future.

At this point in our discussion, we attempted to be more systematic in our approach. We turned the discussion around by listing out categories of designers – users of developments environments. For each designer category, we described the activities this person does, listed the kind of tools needed to support these activities, listed the research areas which currently support this person's activities, and finally identified the research needed to better support this person's tasks.

We agreed on 3 groups of designers: 1) human factors people consisting of task analysts and human factors/usability engineers; 2) software engineers consisting of requirement analysts, formal specifiers, system modellers, and software developers; and 3) user interface designers consisting of presentation designers (graphics artists) and dialog designers. We also mentioned end-users as being an important part of the design process. However, since our group focused on design support tools and we did not envision end-users as being users of the development environments, we dropped the end-user category.

One observation though, we ended up having four types of users under the software engineering category. That is twice more than those in the human factors and the user interface design categories. This may well be from the fact that the group members, and as a matter of fact the workshop attendees in general, were mainly software engineers. Some argued that human factors and user interface design categories are more closely related to each other and that the two of them combined strikes a better balance between what is called "Software Engineering Design" and "User Interface Design."

A major chunk of discussion time was spent on collecting ideas about tools and technology currently available for these different classes of designers, related on-going research topics, and the needs of the future. The following discussion notes are organized based on designer categories.

5.3.   Designers and Their Tools

5.3.1   Human Factors

5.3.1.1   Task Analysts

These are designers who perform initial interactions with users. Currently, task analysts use techniques such as functional analysis, user requirement analysis, and ethnographic studies to help them understand the structure and constraints of user tasks. We need to provide tools which support task modeling and which capture the results of task and user requirement analyses early in the design process. The support in this area which is obviously insufficient is on tools and representations to capture task analysis results. The current lack in this area is on guidelines of how to map task analysis results to design models, especially interaction models.

5.3.1.2 Human Factors/Usability Engineers

These designers interact with both users and task analysts in order to understand initial task requirements and the user cultures, and to make sure these constraints are incorporated in the final design of the interface. Human factors/usability engineers apply human factors guidelines, interface style guides, and organizational style guides to interfaces. We noted that problem-solving tasks still lack human factor guidelines to help design interactions for them. Future contribution to designing this type of tasks may be drawn from cognitive science research.

Techniques and findings from psychology research such as keystroke analysis, cognitive complexity theory, cognitive walk-through, effectiveness of learning from multimedia presentation, error predictions, etc., may be employed by human factors/usability engineers to improve interfaces. However, these techniques are often not incorporated in design environments so as to be easily accessible. Also, some of these techniques are still at their infancy and are still far from being applicable to real world problems. For example, more research is needed to understand enough to evaluate user interactions with multimedia and multi-modal interfaces. And while research may not yet provide overall solutions when we need them, support for using metaphors in design may serve as an alternative technique to make interfaces easy to learn and to use.

Human factor/usability engineers are also involved with prototyping interfaces. Currently, two classes of tools are available for prototyping interfaces – widget-bound and free-form tools. The former class consists of tools such as Motif dialog builders. These tools are very functional, supporting the design of both the presentation and behavior of interfaces. These tools however, do not support interface paradigms beyond those limited by their toolkits. The latter class consists of tools such as Macromedia Director[1], which are less functional as interface prototyping tools, but do not impose boundary on the design space and creativity. The tools in this class also allow interface behavior to be prototyped, but it may require more work to duplicate behavior since the tool does not provide as much automatic support as those depending on the known behavior of a limited set of widgets. A combination of these two classes of tools will result in a much better prototyping environment allowing interface designs to be more aesthetic and direct.

Post-design evaluations from user task and performance recording is also rather important for human factor/usability engineers. Currently this can be done by instrumenting program code to generate desired user performance data. This cannot be easily accomplished when dealing with proprietary software. Some research prototypes can produce task-based event recordings but these systems are not yet publicly available. When they are, human factors engineers need to be able to control the history and statistical recordings without having to program, and at the levels that suits their analyses.

---

[1] Macromedia Director is a commercial multimedia authoring tool with an emphasis on animation techniques and organizational support for creating animated scenes.

5.3.2   Software Engineering

5.3.2.1 Requirement Analysts

Working with task analysts and user requirement analysts produce a set of goals, conditions, and constraints which need to be satisfied in the application. Currently, requirement analysts use analytical techniques such as functional, data, and object-oriented analyses to aid in their work. These techniques need to be incorporated into tools which help integrate analysis results into the design representation.

5.3.2.2 Formal Specifiers

Formal notations such as predicate logic, algebraic specifications [2, 4] state-based approach [8, 14] process-based notations [6, 9] and hybrid notations [7] are mathematically-based notations which formal specifiers use to analyze a system and its interfaces. These formal notations are often hard to specify correctly in the first run; automatic syntax and semantic checking would remarkably increase formal specifiers' productivity. Support in this direction has begun to appear but certainly more work would be welcome. Also, automatic support for managing changes over time and automatic design transformations are needed.

Though the specifications of a reasonably sized application are structured in nature, it is rather long and large due to the textual nature of formal notations. This makes it difficult for formal specifiers to search for components. A syntactically-oriented search support would make design revisions more fruitful. Also, support for multiple views, such as syntactic organization, communication structures, structures of object relationships characterized by an is_a or a has_a relation, etc., of the same structure would allow designers to single out various aspects of a design and selectively work on one aspect at a time. Views of specifications when dynamically coupled with runtime execution are harder to provide, but would be most feasible in the case of process specifications. This could also be enhanced with possibilities to visualize and test out alternative action sequences at any point during runtime. These dynamic views could be provided through design simulation. A good example of dynamic simulation is the LOTOS simulator. In this system, possible actions are visualized and the tool allows designers to select one of the possible actions to see what actions are possible as the consequence.

5.3.2.3 System Modellers

System modellers are those designers whose job is to map requirements and abstract specifications into specifications of system components. They identify system components, compositional rules for these components, and specify dynamic characteristics of systems. Formal notations are often used to specify and evaluate their designs. System modellers sometimes are concerned with system efficiency through components and architecture as well.

When dealing with the design of interactive applications, system modellers also deal with the specifications of user interface systems. They specify and evaluate interactions among interface components, and between interface and application components. Tools using formal notations, with abstractions designed towards interactive systems, would allow formal notation support to be applied more to the interface domain.

We noted here that the task of specifying and evaluating dialogs are also shared by task analysts and dialog designers. We think the areas where development environments will particularly contribute in the future are information infrastructure and software which allow design results to be shared by different types of. Another contribution will be in methodology, and in the support to structure and manage modeling work. Currently, two approaches are being discussed – object-oriented and task-driven. A useful support would be to allow results from the two approaches to be combined and/or overlapped, allowing designers to see two different orientations of the same design. This could well be the beginning of supporting software engineering and HCI design in the same environment. That is, system modellers may need to see an application in an object-oriented view , while human factors engineers may want to see the design from the end-users point of view. The later may be procedural and hence differ from the system view in some applications. These two approaches nevertheless do not include solutions for managing a large design. Support for managing a large and complex design is definitely needed in design environments.

5.3.2.4 Software Developers

Software developers provide correct and efficient implementations of system components as identified by system modellers. They are also responsible for implementing user interface components and behavior as defined by presentation and dialog designers. Implementation of the user interface is only required if it is beyond the capabilities of the underlying toolkits and/or support in interface runtime environments. Current tools used by software developers are programming languages, debugging environments, software development environments, library of routines, existing user interface toolkits or widgets, interface development environments such as Visual Basic, and operating system support. A step further would be to provide software developers with tools which assist in transformations from high-level specifications (e.g. algebraic specifications) to implementations in a target programming language. Another class of useful tools are interface environments which can operate from high-level specification of interactions. Such tools can free programmers from the low-level programming tasks and help map dialog designer's specifications directly to executable interface behavior.

5.3.3   User Interface Design

5.3.3.1 Presentation Designers

Presentation designers work with dialog designers and human factors/usability engineers to come up with aesthetic surface features of interfaces. Presentation designers as defined in this discussion group do not design the dynamic behavior and the interaction part of an interface. Currently available tools are bit-map editors, drawing programs, scanners, and pencil and paper for mocking up interfaces. The more directly usable the end products from presentation designers are, the better the tools. Presentation designers have the knowledge and skills to compose pretty pictures; they however need support to incorporate inputs from other design activities such as functional requirements, user culture and workload, limitations of underlying toolkits, etc. Critics incorporated into basic drawing tools would help to keep the design bound within functional constraints and implementation limitations. Guidelines developed from psychology and human factors studies are also useful in this design process. Lastly, presentation designers need support to maintain the tie between domain components and the current design.

5.3.3.2 Dialog Designers

As mentioned previously, there are 2 classes of tools available for prototyping interfaces. Dialog designers share these prototyping tools with human factors/usability engineers. However, their responsibilities are different. Dialog designers use these tools to prototype and test new dialogs. Tools such as Motif dialog builders do not allow new interactions to be prototyped. Manual tools for rapid prototyping interfaces such as Macromedia Director allow design sketching and interaction prototyping, but the resulting interfaces are not readily executable as truly functional interfaces.

Researchers have been developing computer-aided tools for modeling dialogs, such as model-based tools and notation-based tools. Model-based tools such as TRIDENT [1], BOSS [12], HUMANOID [16], UIDE [3, 15], Druid [13], MIKE [11], MICKEY [10], and ITS [18], often emphasize rapid prototyping from frame-oriented models filled in by designers. They allow dialogs to be prototyped and results to be readily available for execution. Notation-based tools such as UAN [5], Petri-nets, and State-transition diagrams, place more emphasis on formal notations. They allow dialogs to be prototyped but the implementation is not driven directly from the notations. In general, extending these tools to design new interaction techniques is often too hard, and sometimes are even impossible.

Though support in dialog design is often weak in accommodating the creation of new interaction techniques, it is often extensible through hard work and often devious programming. Knowledge of which interaction techniques should be used for which kinds of tasks is absent in current research. Knowledge of how to map tasks to interaction media, styles, and techniques, support for evaluating completeness, consistency, and the quality of an interface as a whole, and support for workload analysis are very much needed in order to come up with easier-to-use interfaces.

5.4.   Inter-Relationship Among Design Activities

Towards the end of our discussion, we drew a figure of the design activities and how they are inter-related. This was after a short discussion about how responsibilities of these designers tend to overlap significantly. Figure 5.1 illustrates the result. Please note that the interactions among different design activities are much more inter-twined than that portrayed in the Venn diagram in Figure 5.1. For lack of a better illustration, we decided to keep it. An alternative diagram is proposed by van Harmelen [17]. Harmelen's diagram shows flows of information from one type of designers to others and serves as a good model for showing when some of the interactions among different designers are likely to occur in the design process. It also gives an idea of where design iterations are needed, which is not shown in the diagram below. However, Harmelen's diagram does not help visualize the true nature of interactions among activities, and hence does not serve the purpose of our discussion in the same fashion as the diagram in Figure 5.1.

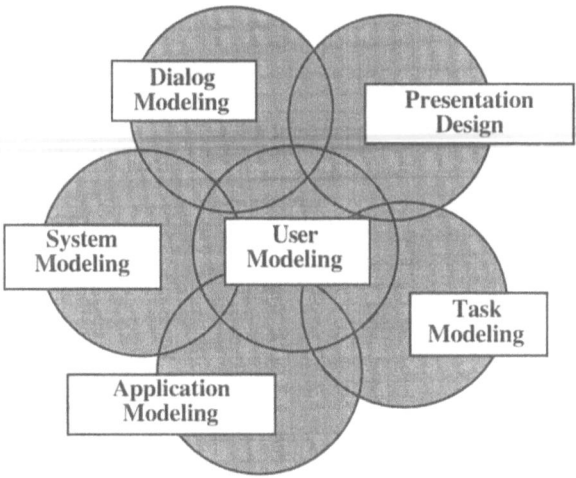

FIGURE 5.1. Diagram of Interactive Application Design Activities.

When our group plotted the activity diagram, we did it based on activities, not classes of designers. By changing our focus to the kind of modeling which designers would do, user modeling and application modeling showed up naturally as major design activities. We had mentioned neither of these two activities in the responsibility list we came up with earlier for different designers. Task modeling was mentioned quite often, but was not explicitly referred to as application modeling. This is an indication of the difference in the views of software-engineering-oriented and HCI-oriented researchers. We both think that we model the underlying application but the labels of these two activities actually show the different mind sets these two types of researchers have. In fact, there is a big overlap between software-engineering application modeling and HCI task modeling. It is the task of this workshop to continue refining the similarities and differences, and to draw out the concrete components which make "domain modeling" by these two groups of researchers similar and distinguishable. In addition to similarities and differences, we also want to identify when the two groups use the same concepts with different labels, and when the same labels are used for different concepts. Also, when we use the same concepts, do we require drastically different tools and evaluation criteria for our work?

5.5.   Miscellaneous

In addition to all the discussions mentioned up to this point, we also mentioned classes of applications as a factor which may shape development environments into different emphases, that is, we foresee that there will be different kinds of customized development environments – each specialized for a certain class of applications. Characteristics of various classes of applications will definitely place more or less demand on various aspects of application interfaces, levels of control over interaction design, design activities, and a suite of tools which are appropriate for the characteristics. One generic development environment is not likely to satisfy all application interface designs. If it were so, this environment would either be too complicated to use, or too limited to be useful.

During the workshop, we hoped that at the end we would see different emphases on various tools and activities for different classes of applications. Application classes such as highly interactive applications, multiple-interface applications, highly interactive graphics such as CAD and GIS, and multiple-user applications such as those in CSCW, were considered. Unfortunately, time did not permit us to go back and analyze relationships between application classes and tools. Also, the granularity of concepts from various design activities in terms of tools and techniques were not refined and were not concrete enough to help us identify demands on tools and activities for different application classes.

5.6.   Conclusions

It is clear from our discussion that no single person can cover the whole spectrum of the interface design process for large and sophisticated applications. A design team needs multiple designers with various expertise and it is important to emphasize interaction among various design activities. Such design teams are currently used, but the development environments they use are still very heterogeneous requiring duplicate efforts, does not prevent information loss, and hinders information sharing. Many design activities do not even have support tools.

In an ideal environment for a large application design where there is at least one person holding each design expertise (as we identified), an integrated environment will function as a facilitator allowing design results to be shared and enhanced by these designers. Duplicate efforts can be avoided. With a suite of tools available, designers must be allowed to work with tools which fit their needs and only work on parts of the design which are of concern to them. Design environments so far have not achieved this goal. Considerable amount of effort is still required to make the ideal design scenario happen.

Some of the design activities are rather domain-independent and can be done once and reused for various applications. Dialog designers, for example, may be able to capture a variety of reusable interactions in a library. With the right architectural support and well-designed information infrastructure, some of the expertise may be provided through reusable primitives and/or automated tools. This will take away some of the burden in the design process and will allow a smaller, less complete design team to place more emphasis on the domain-dependent aspects of the design.

Regarding, places for formalisms in design environments, we identified them as being techniques applicable in various design activities such as dialog modeling, system modeling, and task modeling. Figure 5.2 illustrates the relationship between formalisms and the bigger scope of the overall design activity. The benefits of using explicit formal notations are precision and unambiguous specification of interfaces. Mathematically correct descriptions of an interface can explain the behavior of the interface thoroughly and serve as good evaluation techniques. The explicit notation also provides possibilities for reasoning on the notation. The contribution of formalisms is clear, but they alone only help part of the whole design process.

It would be helpful if the work of generating formal notations can be partially automated. It will be even more useful if formal notations can be used bi-directionally – that is, notations can be translated into an executable interface, and a mock-up interface by graphics artists or human factor engineers can be parsed and notations generated. This will make the design process more flexible, as the design process often does not start out with knowing exactly what a design is going to be like. Describing a design in formal notations at an early stage of a design may not be possible.

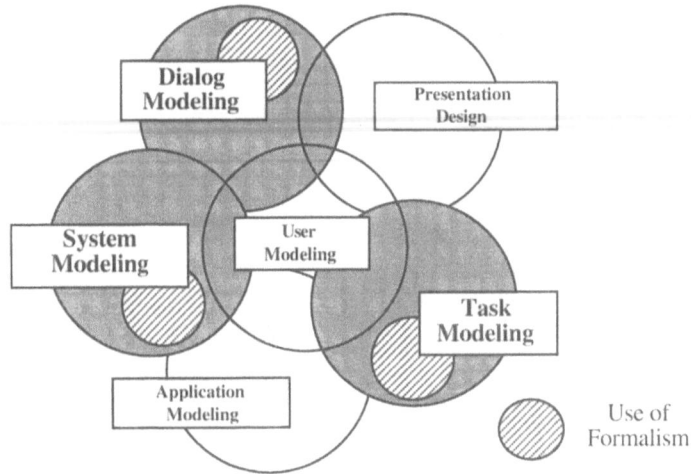

FIGURE 5.2. Contribution of Formalisms in Design Activities.

As for places for the model-based design research, we drew Figure 5.3 to depict the areas which have been explored by the model-based design approach. HCI-oriented models partially cover human factors guidelines, user task representations, automatic support for presentation designs, and end-user characteristics. HCI-oriented models, however, tend to cross over more heterogeneous design activities and serve as a beginning point for design activity integration. HCI-oriented models have not been able to support each design activity as extensively as they should have. System-oriented models cover a narrower scope but provide a more thorough support in dialog design, system architecture, and application functionality modeling. In overall, much more research and labor work in design integration is still needed to advance the state-of-the-art of development environments to their next generation.

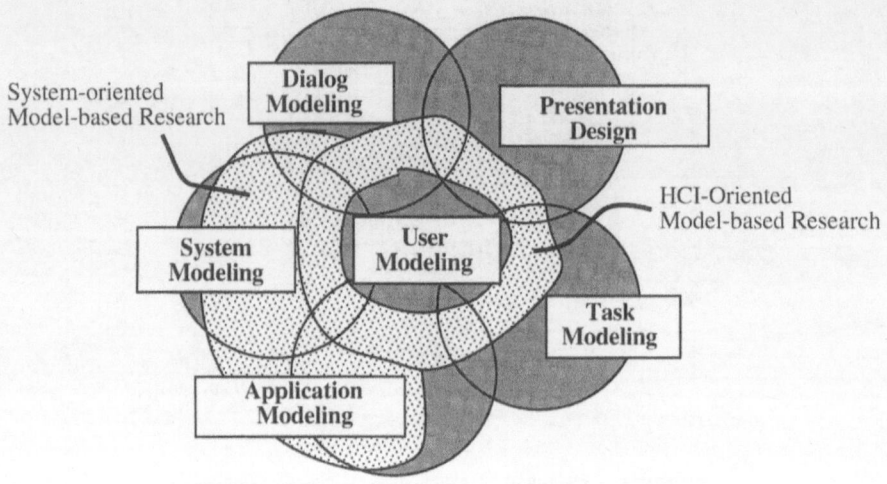

FIGURE 5.3. Areas Covered by Model-based Design Environments.

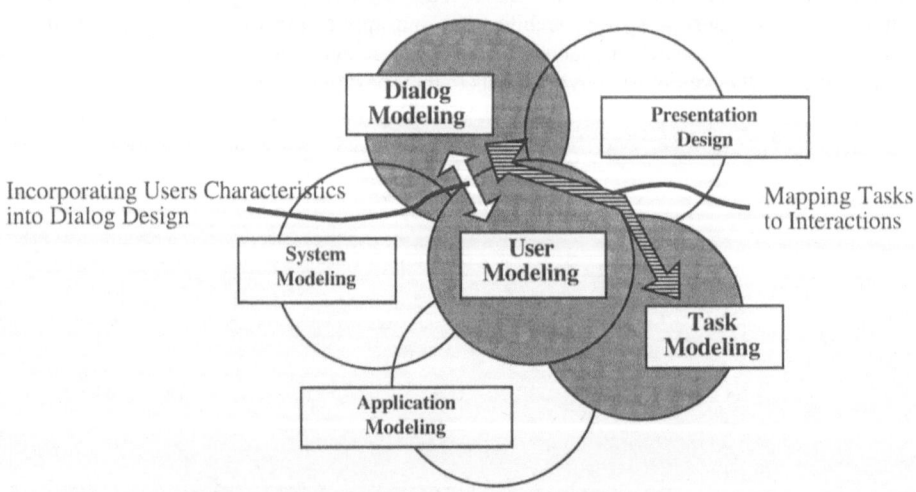

FIGURE 5.4. Depiction of Under-explored Cross Design Activities.

Finally, an issue which kept coming back through out the discussion was the lack of knowledge as well as tools and techniques to map from task models to dialog models. Without unlocking this part of the design process, our knowledge of the design process will remain incomplete. The shaded arrow in Figure 5.4 depicts this missing link in the design process. Supporting integrated design activities in a seamless environment is not likely to finish without filling in this gap first.

Another issue which came up towards the end of our discussion was the currently weak incorporation of user modeling into design activities. The other arrow in Figure 5.4 depicts this missing link.

The missing links in Figure 5.4 are the two issues which our group considered most important and which require immediate attention from researchers to build up knowledge in these areas.

5.7. Our Last Words

Building interface development environments is not a matter of developing nifty tools. The task of providing a comprehensive and well-integrated design environment is a big and challenging goal. Advances in this research area do not come from building more tools, but from understanding how existing research areas interact, from designing new environments which allow designs to be shared and designers to get a leverage from each other's work, and from identifying new research areas which arise as we attempt to integrate different principles in a comprehensive environment. Though our group discussion went into great detail about tools and techniques to support each class of designers, the exercise we went through reinforces the importance of integrating the overlapping design activities and interactions among designers. We (explicitly or not) came to a consensus that development environments are means to make the design process more complete and less time consuming. Our discussion gave us a better understanding of how design activities interact, which interactions we can understand and support well, and which we do not. Understanding the interdisciplinary nature of these new integrated environments is the key to success in development environment research. Researchers in this area are embarking on a rather under-explored territory of how design activities interact, and how tools can be used to facilitate the interactions. Our task is not at all easy, as we are not sure whether anyone, or even all of us combined, really understands the overall design process well – the design process which starts from task modeling, to system modeling, and ends at user interface modeling. Or is that the sequence really?

5.8.   References

[1]   Bodart, F.; Hennebert, A.; Provot. I.; Leheureux, J.; Vanderdonckt., J. A Model-Based Approach to Presentation: A Continuum from Task Analysis to Prototype. In: this book.

[2]   Ehrig, H. and Mahr, B. Fundamentals of Algebraic Specifications. Vol. 1. Equations and Initial Semantics. Spring Verlag, 1985.

[3]   Foley, J.D.; C. Gibbs; W.C. Kim; and S. Kovacevic. A Knowledge-based User Interface Management System. In *Proceedings of Human Factors in Computing Systems, CHI'88*. May 1988, 67-72.

[4]   Futatsugi, K; Goguen, J.A.; Jouannaud, J.-P., and Mesequer, J. Principle of OBJ2. Proceedings of the 1985 Symposium on Principles and Languages.

[5]   Hartson, R.; Mayo, K. A Framework for Precise, Reusable Task Abstractions. In: this book.

[6]   Hoare, C.A.R. Communicating Sequential Processes. London : Prentice Hall International. 1985.

[7]   Information Processing Systems - Open Systems Interconnection - LOTOS - A Formal Description Technique Based on Temporal Ordering of Observational Behavior - ISO/IS 807. ISO Central Secretariat. 1988.

[8]   Jones, C.B. Systematic Software Development Using VDM. London : Prentice Hall International. 2nd Ed. 1990.

[9]   Milner, A.J. Communications and Concurrency. New York: Prentice Hall. 1989.

[10]   Olsen, D. A Programming Language Basis for User Interface Management. In *Proceedings of Human Factors in Computing Systems, CHI'89*. May 1989, 171-176.

[11]   Olsen, D. MIKE: The Menu Interaction Kontrol Environment. *ACM Transactions on Graphics* 5,4 (1986): 318-344.

[12]   Schreiber, S. The BOSS-System: Coupling Visual Programming with Model Based Interface Design. In: this book.

[13]   Singh, G. and Green, M. A High-Level User Interface Management System. In *Proceedings of Human Factors in Computing Systems, CHI'89*. May 1989, 133-138.

[14]   Spivey, J.M. Understanding Z: A Specification Language and its Semantics. London : Cambridge University Press. 1989.

[15] Sukaviriya, P; J.D. Foley; and T. Griffith. A Second Generation User Interface Design Environment: The Model and the Runtime Architecture. In *Proceedings of Human Factors in Computing Systems, INTERCHI'93.* 375-382.

[16] Szekeley, P.; P. Luo; and R. Neches. Facilitating the Exploration of Interface Design Alternatives: the HUMANOID Model of Interface Design. In *Proceedings of Human Factors in Computing Systems, CHI'92.* May 1992, 507-515.

[17] van Harmelen, M. Object-oriented Modelling and Specification for User Interface Design. In: this book.

[18] Weicha, C.; Bennet, W.; Boies, S.; Gould, J.; Greene, S. ITS: A Tool for Rapidly Developig Interactive Applications. *ACM Transactions on Information systems* 8,3 (1990):204-236

Part II

Modelling in Architectural Design of Interactive Systems

6 A Model-Based Approach to Presentation: A Continuum from Task Analysis to Prototype

François Bodart
Anne-Marie Hennebert
Jean-Marie Leheureux
Jean Vanderdonckt

ABSTRACT

This paper presents a complete model-based approach to the building of presentation for a business oriented highly interactive application. This approach is considered complete in the sense that it supports a continuum from task analysis to a first prototype without disruption. The main steps involved in the proposed methodology include a task analysis performed as a hierarchical decomposition of the interactive task into sub-tasks, a specification of the functional requirements and its integration with task analysis results, a writing of an activity chaining graph which graphically depicts the information and function flow within the task, the selection of an interaction style, the definition of presentation units, the selection of abstract interaction objects, their transformation into concrete objects to be placed before generating a first prototype. The described methodology not only consists of the definition of these steps, but also shows how computer-aided tools can automatically generate the presentation of such an interface.

6.1 Introduction

TRIDENT (Tools foR an Interactive Development EnvironmeNT) is a methodology and a support environment for developing highly interactive business oriented applications [3,4,23]. This methodology consists of a set of :

- *processes* that define a complete and continuous approach for developing such applications;

- related *products* that result from these processes;

- basic *models* on which the processes are grounded;

- interactive *tools* that support the processes and that help the designer to build the user interface in an automated or computer-aided way.

These four facets have proved to be necessary since merely having tools to produce the user interface (e.g. by automatic generation, by demonstration) is not believed to be enough. A methodology in which these facets are gracefully integrated is needed [10,11]. To obtain this goal, the TRIDENT methodology should meet at least five requirements :

1. to extend classical application development methodology [2] and environment to the development of user interface;

2. to provide autonomy (separation) between the application domain functions and the user interface [9];

3. to provide a separation between the conversation and presentation components of the dialogue in the user interface [3];

4. to use explicitly a set of ergonomical rules to drive and to generate the definition of the presentation [3];

5. to directly derive conversation and presentation from task analysis [3,21].

The user interface, or dialogue, is consequently divided into presentation and conversation. The *presentation* forms the static visual layout of the dialogue, made up of interaction objects. The *conversation* is responsible for the dynamic behaviour of these interaction objects that can be manipulated by the final user (e.g. input responses). This paper is devoted to a model-based approach to presentation in TRIDENT.

This approach consists of a complete methodology which runs continuously from a task analysis of the future application to a visible and working prototype of the presentation. It relies mostly on an extended entity-relationship attribute model and a task model, which can be graphically depicted by an activity chaining graph. Different processes (some manual, some computer-aided, some automated) are performed to produce the presentation model of the dialogue.

This presentation model, from which the final user interface will be generated, is graphically represented as a hierarchy of presentation units containing interaction objects. Both data and interface models can be specified with a specification language called DSL (Dynamic Specification Language). To illustrate this model-based approach, a relatively simple example is detailed trough the different processes.

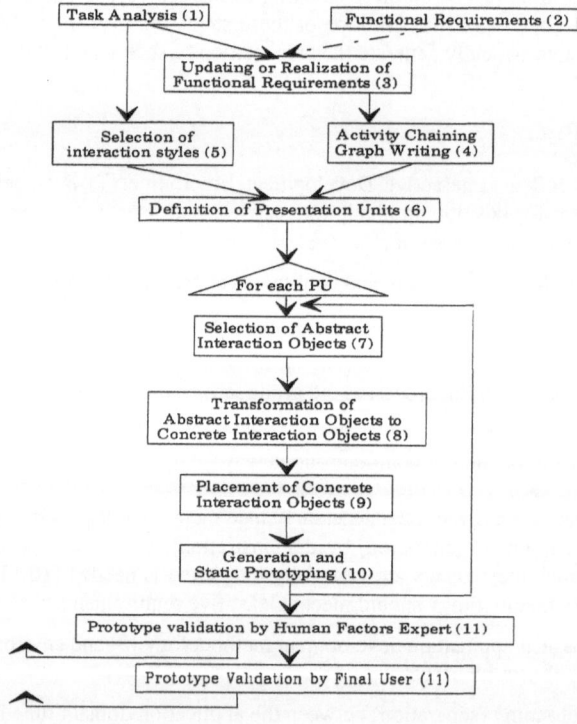

FIGURE 6.1. Overview of the model-based approach to the presentation in TRIDENT.

6.2   Overview of TRIDENT Methodology

The methodology includes two model-based approaches for the dialogue : one for the conversation and one for the presentation. Model-based approach is examplified in [19,20]. The model-based approach to the **conversation** is introduced in [3]. It basically starts from a task model (which is shared with the presentation) in order to build a hierarchical object-oriented architecture of dialogue objects [4]. A similar approach can be found in [7]. Each dialogue object is responsible for one piece of the global conversation. The behaviour script of each dialogue object is formally specified by a rule-language expressed in the first order predicate logic (see [16]) that can be partially depicted graphically by state-transition diagrams [18]. These diagrams allow an asynchronous representation of the task model in the conversation [12]. The model-based approach to the **presentation** will be discussed in this paper (Figure 6.1). Each process, denoted by a rectangle in Figure 6.1, is described in the following numbered sections : the products of each process, the underlying model if any, and the existing tool if any. This description is sometimes summarized for the benefit of a broader demonstration of how these processes are connected.

6.3   Task Analysis

The task analysis should build the foundations of every complete methodology as recommended in [21,22]. In TRIDENT, the task analysis starts from field studies and interviews with potential or existing users in order to understand their tasks. Let us consider a company selling clothes by phone. Let us examine for example the task "Phone order" extracted from the Product Management domain. The text of this task, resulting from interviews, is reported here with the left border [13].

When a customer makes a phone order to the company, three steps are performed :
Identification of the customer
When a customer calls, the operator asks the customer whether s/he is already a registered customer of the company.

If the customer is a **new** one, s/he provides firstname, lastname and complete address.
If the customer is an **old** one and still **knows his/her identification number,** s/he tells the operator what this number is. The operator then searchs this id. through the company's database. Registration of identification numbers over the phone is often fraught with human error. Therefore, searching such numbers can be unsuccessfull. Three cases may occur :

1. the provided id. exists in the database and is the right one. The operator reads the customer's complete address to be further acknowledged by the customer : if the customer moved, s/he is now able to provide the new address;
2. the provided id. exists in the database and is a wrong one. In order not to get on the customer's nerves and not to worry him/her, the operator then asks the first- and lastname, trying to locate the customer with this more precise information. The operator may either succeed (in this case, the customer's address is read and could be modified if necessary) or fail (in this case, the operator adds a new record to the database);
3. the provided id. does not exist in the database : similarly, the operator assumes the caller to be a new customer and thus creates a new entry.

If the customer is an **old** one and **does not know his/her identification number**, the operator asks the first- and lastname trying to locate the customer. By analogy, the search may either succeed or fail.

In all cases, the identification number of the customer is available as soon as the customer is identified.

The definition of the order

For each product requested, the customer provides the product number and the quantity to the operator. For each product, the operator dictates the label of the article until each product number and label match.

The record of the order

Once the customer has been identified and the order has been defined, no matter what the order, the operator asks the customer the mode of payment (which can be cash, by credit card or by bank transfer) and the delivery date. The operator finally records the order.

The task analysis then proceeds with a precise definition of :

1. a hierarchical decomposition of the interactive application into interactive tasks. These tasks are recursively decomposed into sub-tasks according to decomposition criteria which preserve consistency, completeness, and human cognitive work load. The last level of decomposition of this hierarchy highlights the actions needed to perform the task (e.g. automatic, manual or interactive actions). Once finished, the task analysis allows the specification of related goals (e.g. identification), actions (e.g. database search), and objects (e.g; customer) for each task and sub-task. Figure 6.2 shows a possible decomposition of the task described above.

> Application Product Management Application
> Interactive task : Phone order
> Sub-task 1 : Identification of a customer
> Action 1 : modify the address of a customer
> Action 2 : search a customer by identification number
> Action 3 : search a customer by firstname and lastname.
> Sub-task 2 : Definition of the order
> Sub-task 3 : Record of the order

FIGURE 6.2. Hierarchical decomposition of an interactive task

2. the relations existing between the user and the interactive system, for each sub-task;

3. the following attributes for each interactive task :

   - pre-requisite (minimal/moderate/maximal) : whether the user needs special pre-requisite to accomplish the task;

   - productivity (low/medium/high) : whether the task is accomplished a couple, some or many times;

   - objective environment (existent/non existent) : whether physical task objects (e.g. source document) exist;

- environment reproducibility (practicable/unpracticable) : whether the objective environment could be metaphorized;
- task structure (low/medium/high) : whether the task is poorly, somewhat or highly structured in the sub-tasks;
- task importance (low/medium/high) : whether this particular task is critical for the whole interactive application;
- task complexity (low/medium/high) : whether the task requires little, some or a great deal of human skill (e.g. motor, cerebral, cognitive, verbal).

In the example, the interactive task "Phone order" might be characterized by pre-requisite=moderate, productivity=high, objective environment=non existent, environment reproducibility=unpracticable, task structure=high, task importance=medium, task complexity=low.

4. the user stereotypes. A stereotype abstracts a particular category of users in the population. The main reason for introducing different stereotypes is that the same task can be accomplished in very different ways by very different users according to their habits and skills. A similar assumption is done in ADEPT [13] and in the model of User Characteristics described in [6], p. 47. For each stereotype considered, the following attributes are given :

- task experience (elementary/medium/complex) : whether the user already possesses previous experience for the task;
- system experience (elementary/medium/complex) : whether the user already uses other similar systems;
- motivation (low/medium/high) : whether the subjective satisfaction factor of the user is low, medium, or high;
- experience of a complex interaction media (elementary/medium/complex) : whether the user already masters some interaction media whose behaviour is not necessarily familiar (e.g. keyboard, function keys, rotators).

In the example, a possible stereotype of the company operator might be characterized by task experience=medium, system experience=elementary, motivation=medium, experience of interaction media=complex.

5. the description of the workplace in terms of the following attributes :

- process type (mono-processing/multi-processing) : whether the interactive task could be interrupted;
- process capacity (low / medium / high) : whether concurrent tasks are allowed.

6.4   Functional Requirements

Classical development methodologies traditionally include the definition of functional requirements. If the task analysis and the user stereotypes, especially, specify the operational requirements, this process is responsible for writing the functional requirements. TRIDENT provides different models for different purposes [2]. An entity-relationship-attribute (ERA) model, extended and built on database theory and software engineering practive, describes the object structure and relations to be manipulated by the user. Each ERA model can be input either graphically (Figure 6.3) with a direct-manipulation editor or with a suited specification language (Dynamic Specification Language) (Figure 6.4). ERA model is appropriate for the information modeling part of the functional requirements. For the function modeling part, the hierarchical decomposition of the interactive task is considered : a function is required for each action. A function refers to an internal function belonging to the Semantic Core Component of the application.

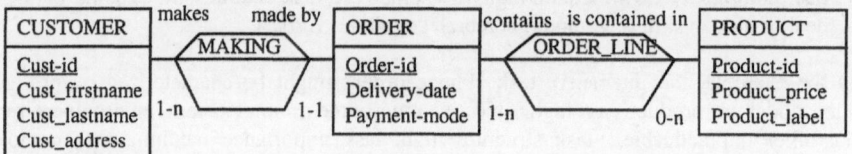

FIGURE 6.3. An Entity-Relationship-Attribute model for the interactive task "Phone order"

```
DEFINE ENTITY Customer;
  CONSISTS OF Cust_id, Cust_firstname, Cust_lastname, Cust_address;
  IDENTIFIED BY Cust_id;
DEFINE ENTITY Order;
  CONSISTS OF Order_id, Delivery_date, Payment_mode;
  IDENTIFIED BY Order_id;
DEFINE ENTITY Product;
  CONSISTS OF Product_id, Product_price, Product_label;
DEFINE GROUP Cust_address;
  CONSISTS OF Street, Number, Zip_code, City;
DEFINE RELATION Making;
  RELATES Customer AS Makes WITH CONNECTIVITY 1-N;
  RELATES Order AS Made_by WITH CONNECTIVITY 1-1;
DEFINE RELATION Order_line;
  CONSISTS OF Quantity;
  RELATES Order AS Contains WITH CONNECTIVITY 1-N;
  RELATES Product AS Is_contained_in WITH CONNECTIVITY 0-N;
DEFINE ELEMENT Quantity;
  DOMAIN OF VALUE ARE N(2);
DEFINE ELEMENT Cust_id;
  DOMAIN OF VALUE ARE N(6);
DEFINE ELEMENT Cust_firstname;
  DOMAIN OF VALUE ARE A(30);
DEFINE ELEMENT Cust_lastname;
  DOMAIN OF VALUE ARE A(20);
DEFINE ELEMENT Street;
  DOMAIN OF VALUE ARE X(30);
DEFINE ELEMENT Number;
  DOMAIN OF VALUE ARE N(4);
DEFINE ELEMENT Zip_code;
  DOMAIN OF VALUE ARE 1000 THRU 9999;
DEFINE ELEMENT City;
  DOMAIN OF VALUE ARE A(32);
DEFINE ELEMENT Order_id;
  DOMAIN OF VALUE ARE N(6);
DEFINE ELEMENT Delivery_date;
  DOMAIN OF VALUE ARE X(8);
  FORMAT IS "##-##-##";
DEFINE ELEMENT Payment_mode;
  DOMAIN OF VALUE ARE "Cash","Credit card","Bank transfert" WITH CARDINALITY 3;
DEFINE ELEMENT Product_id;
  DOMAIN OF VALUE ARE N(6);
DEFINE ELEMENT Product_price;
  DOMAIN OF VALUE ARE N(5);
DEFINE ELEMENT Product_label;
  DOMAIN OF VALUE ARE X(30);
```

FIGURE 6.4. The specification of the ERA model for the interactive task "Phone order"

6.5   Updating or Realization of Functional Requirements

Since the functional requirements are inherited from classical methodologies and from software engineering, they should be smoothly integrated within the methodology. In the past, designing an interactive application started from these requirements in order to derive the operational requirements (as in task analysis).

Today, there is a shift of focus : the task analysis should be the starting point for deriving the functional requirements and not vice versa. If both task analysis and functional requirements have been done separately, they are merged during this process. If the functional requirements have already been done, they should be updated according to the task analysis in order to avoid incompleteness and inconsistencies. If the functional requirements have not yet been done before, they could be derived here from the task analysis.

6.6   Activity Chaining Graph Writing

Task analysis and functional requirements help to draw an *activity chaining graph* (ACG), which is a graph describing the information flow between the application domain functions which are necessary to perform the task goal highlighted in the task analysis. The ACG provides several benefits, the most important of which is to define clearly a functional invariant for the interactive task, independently of user stereotypes. Should the task be performed, this functional and business logic should be followed, no matter the user.

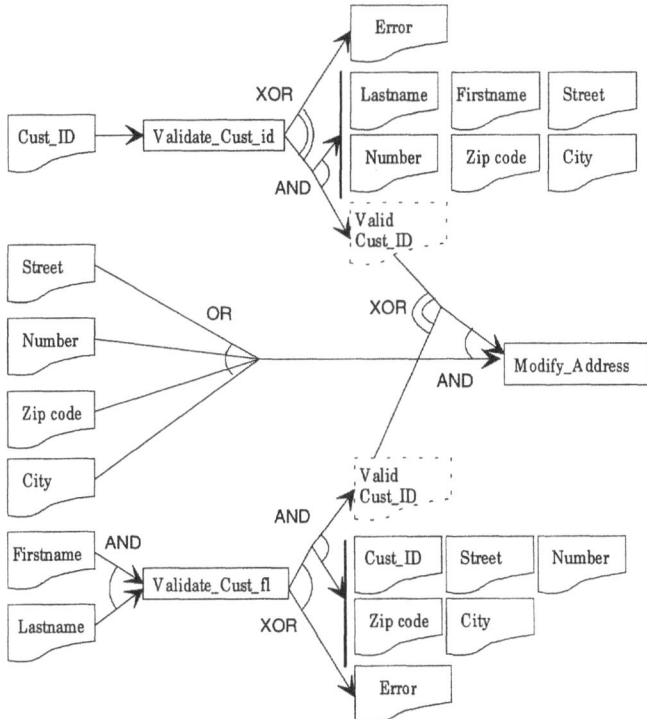

FIGURE 6.5. The ACG of the sub-task "Identification of a Customer"

The ACG establishes a basic contract between the person who is responsible for the Semantic Core Component and the one who is responsible for the Dialogue Component [4]. This process is the focal point for the connection between user-oriented concepts (e.g. task, sub-task, action, object) and application-oriented concepts (e.g. information and function). The ACG of the sub-task "Identification of a customer" is given in Figure 6.5. In this figure, each rectangle denotes a terminal function identified in the task analysis and each piece of paper represents a piece of information coming either from the ERA model or the application. Information located at the left, respectively at the right, of each function is called *input information*, respectively *output information*. Information drawn in plain line denotes *external information* (i.e. visible and manipulable by the user), whereas information drawn in dotted line denotes *internal information* (i.e. not visible by the user and produced by the application). Internal information typically covers system messages, organisation messages and decision points.

Three types of links allow us to combine input and output informations : AND links allow a conjunction of information, OR links allow a disjunction of information, and XOR links allow a disjunction with mutual exclusion. Figure 6.5 is interpreted as follows : to validate a customer with the identificaton number, the system needs the information "Cust_id". As a result, the function "Validate_Cust_id" returns either a failed search (in this case, an error message is generated) or a successfull search (in this case, the following set of informations is produced : the internal information "Valid Cust_id" to trigger the function "Modify_address" and the external informations firstname, lastname, street, number, zip code, city). ACGs can be graphically edited with the graphical direct-manipulation editor.

6.7   Selection of Interaction Style

Another process that could be achieved in parallel with other processes is the selection of interaction style(s) which is (are) appropriate for conducting the task with the different user stereotypes. Common interaction styles include : natural language, command language, query language, questions/answers, function keys, menu selection, form filling, multi-windowing, direct manipulation, iconic interaction,...
A single interaction style could be selected for performing each interactive task, but a composite interaction style, made up of a combination of several others, might also be appropriate. This is often the case when different user stereotypes with varying attributes are in competition. This process consists of two sub-processes :

1. the setting of the following dialogue attributes [8,10,11,22] that are relevant to the current interactive task. This setting can be decided manually by the user interface expert or interactively with a software tool that automatically suggests these attributes from task attributes, user stereotypes and workplaces attributes as indicated in the task analysis :

   - *dialogue control* which can be internal, external or mixed;
   - *dialogue mode* which can be sequential or asynchronous;
   - *function triggering mode* which can be :
     automatic if the user interface has the initiative,
     manual if the user has the initiative :
       implicit if automatically deduced from the user actions (e.g. field exit),
       explicit if resulting from a dedicated user action (e.g. control manipulation) :
         displayed if the action provides a visible feedback (e.g. an "Ok" pushbutton),
         undisplayed if the action does not have any visual cue (e.g. F10 function key);
   - *metaphor* which can be conversation based or graphic based.

In the example "Identification of a customer", dialogue control could be mixed, the dialogue mode could be asynchronous, function triggering mode could be manual explicit displayed, and metaphor could be conversation based.

2. the derivation of interaction style from dialogue attributes.

ADEPT [14] is a good example of such a tool for defining these attributes interactively and then deriving the interaction style with production rules. In TRIDENT methodology, the most appropriate interaction styles are expressed in tables that match the different values of the dialogue attributes for each interaction style. If the combination of the current values of dialogue attributes is found in the tables, the corresponding interaction style is selected.

Otherwise, interaction styles that minimize the standard deviation according to the dialogue attributes are selected. Though command language, function keys, menu selection, form filling, and multi-windowing are only interaction styles currently available to generate the presentation in TRIDENT, this step could be achieved more broadly in every target environment. In our example, multi-windowing and form filling could be selected together.

6.8   Definition of Presentation Units

Once the appropriate interaction style(s) has (have) been selected and the ACG has been completed, we are ready to start the definition of the presentation (Figure 6.1). The presentation is recursively structured into *Presentation Units* (PU). By definition, a PU consists of an input/display world decomposed into windows (not all necessarily present at the same time) in order to perform a sub-task of the interactive task by satisfying the human requirements of the user. Consequently, one PU is defined for each sub-task in each interactive task. Sub-tasks that have been discovered in the task analysis possess a special status. They form a part of the task that is significant from the point of view of the user only. Special criteria have to be used to outline these sub-tasks in the task decomposition.

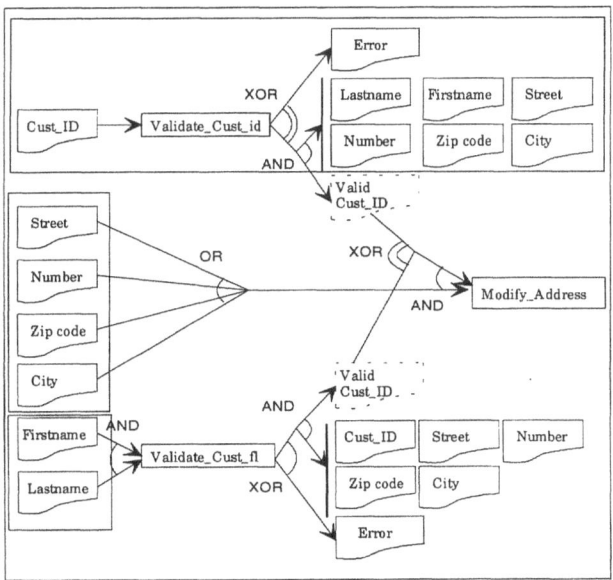

FIGURE 6.6. Some Presentation Units on the ACG of the sub-task "Identification of a Customer"

In the example, there could be three PUs :

1. PU1: Identification of a customer;

2. PU2 : Definition of the order;

3. PU3 : Record of the order.

Each PU is composed of one or multiple logical windows and has a basic window from which the user intiates the conversation. One advantage of the ACG is that we are able to draw the scope of presentation units on it. Figure 6.6 shows multiple alternatives for PUs. Drawing a slope around the functions and related information provides the ability to clearly visualize which information would be input and/or displayed in the PU and which function would be triggered. One may imagine as many PU as necessary since drawing a PU on the ACG is theoretically free. Six important categories of PU can be chosen :

- maximal PU : when all functions and informations are gathered in one PU only;

- minimal PU : when each piece of information with or without function is presented in a separate PU;

- input/output PU : when all input information and all output information for each function are split into two PUs ;

- functional PU : when all input and output informations are grouped in one PU for each function;

- grouped PU : when atomic PU (minimal, input/output, functional) are grouped;

- free PU : when the definition of the PU does not obey to any of the above categories.

Drawing any PU on the ACG is an easy job (Figure 6.6). What would be more interesting is as automatically as possible to suggest to the designer the PU which may be chosen according to the interaction styles and the ACG configuration. TRIDENT provides three types of assistance in order to draw PUs which will result in a user-friendly presentation and which are very much concerned with human factors :

1. PU criteria to identify a suitable starting PU that does not generate cumbersome or overcrowded presentations;

2. PU selection according to interaction styles : some PU categories are more appropriate to specific interaction styles and some PU categories are absolutely impossible to realize within specific interaction styles. The following PU are recommended :

   - questions/answers : minimal PUs

   - command language : input/output PUs

   - form filling : functional, maximal or free

   - menu selection : functional, maximal or free;

3. PU grouping strategy that works on ACG in finding dynamic paths that are consistent from a cognitive and semantic point of view : different algorithms dealing with graph theory concepts are now under investigation and validation.

PUs are to be defined for each sub-task of each interactive task. The content of PU can be viewed at two conceptual levels :

1. at the *physical level*, a PU is made of *Concrete Interaction Objects* (CIO) which are the graphical objects for input and display data the user can see, feel and manipulate ([6], p. 41). CIO is synonymous to a control, a physical interactor, a widget or a presentation object [19]. CIOs belong to the Physical Toolkit [4] which is the equivalent of the Run-time system ([6], p. 55)

2. at the *logical level*, a PU is made of *Abstract Interaction Objects* (AIO) which abstract both presentation and behaviour of CIOs as recommended in [6], p. 55. AIOs belong to the Virtual Toolkit [4] which is the equivalent of the Abstract Model ([6], p. 55). ADEPT [14] also employs these abstraction levels.

PU is the corner-stone of the complete presentation model to be refined in the following processes. More precisely, once the information and function content of the PU has been defined, the logical PU will be completely defined in terms of AIOs leading to the definition of physical PUs in terms of CIOs.

6.9   Selection of Abstract Interaction Objects

AIOs are illustrated extensively in [4,23]. AIO are divided into six sets according to their very first nature (Table 6.1).

AIO sets	AIO elements (some)
action	menu, menu item, menu bar, pulldown menu, cascade menu
scrolling	scroll arrow, scroll cursor, scroll bar, frame
static	label, separator, group box, prompt, icon
control	edit box, scale, dial, check box, switch, radio box, spin button, push button, list box, drop-down list box, combination box, table
dialogue	window, dialogue box, expandable dialogue box, radio dialogue box, panel
feedback	message, progression indicator, contextual cursor

Table 6.1. Table of Abstract Interaction Objects

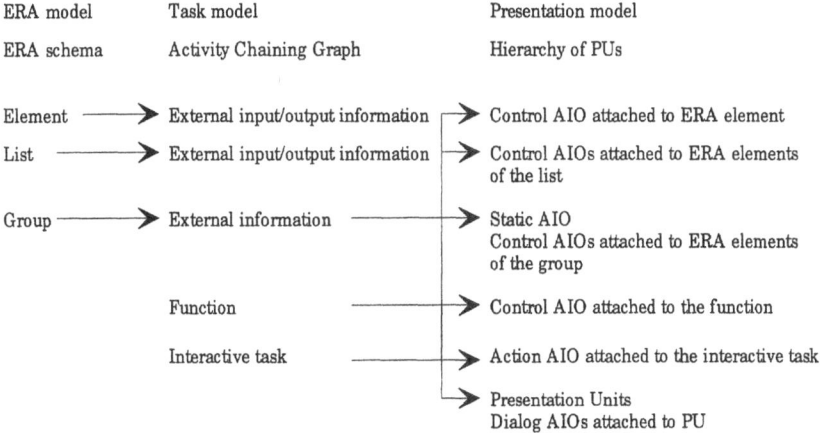

FIGURE 6.7. Selection of AIO from ERA and task models

The goal of AIO Selection is to choose appropriate AIOs according to the extended ERA model specified in the Functional Requirements, and the task model defined in the task analysis. Figure 6.7 shows how different concepts from the extended ERA model are mapped onto concepts belonging to the ACG. Once this mapping has been established, AIO are selected to obtain the complete presentation model in terms of AIO.

The selection of AIO is based on decision tables of selection rules that select an appropriate AIO from the specifications contained in the ERA model [23]. Several decision tables are provided for :

- selecting AIO for element input/display;
- selecting AIO when the workplace should be considered;
- selecting AIO for specific element input/display;
- selecting AIO for list input/display;
- selecting AIO for group input/display;
- selecting AIO for triggering functions.

The decision table for selecting AIO for element input/display supports nine data types : hour, date, boolean, graphic (e.g. icon, image), integer, real, alphanumeric, sound, and video. In our example, the selected AIO are the following :

elements	Cust_id, Cust_lastname, Cust_firstname, Street,Number, Zip_code, City	Edit box
group	Cust_Address	Group box
functions	Validate_Cust_id and Validate_Cust_fl	Pushbutton "Search"
	Modify_Address	Pushbutton "Modify"
		Presentation Unit
Identification_Customer		Window with Default Pushbuttons

TRIDENT contains an expert system reponsible for the selection of AIO. The selection can be full automatic or computer-aided with forward, backward and bidirectional chainings. Decision tables are graphically represented by decision trees. Similar and complete selection approaches are found in UIDE [1,14].

6.10 Transformation of Abstract Interaction Objects into Concrete Interaction Objects

Since the selection has been made in terms of AIO, AIO should be converted to CIOs for the particular physical target environment (e.g. OSF/Motif, Microsoft Windows, Open Look). Transformation of AIOs into CIOs for a particular environment is achieved using a matching table. The presentation is consequently designed from the view of interaction needs and requirements, not from the available set of CIOs.

Degradation can be expected when a rich AIO is matched onto a poor CIO, not because the previous AIO is not appropriate enough for this purpose, but because the corresponding CIO may not exist in the target environment. For example, if the expert system selects a sound control system for a sound element, this particular control may be not present in all environments. An other example concerns the table AIO. This interaction object is normally not present in the OSF/Motif environment, but such an object can be set up in a class.

Portable environments (e.g. SUIT, Open Interface, Galaxy, XVT) should be considered to offer a balance of CIOs available across a wide variety of platforms. We are considering the SUIT (Simple User Interface Toolkit) environment in which customized CIOs have been implemented so that they can be reused in other platforms. Such CIOs include a drop-down list, a combination box, a scrolling list box, a scrolling combination box, special dialog boxes.

6.11 Placement of Concrete Interaction Objects

This process deals with the question : how to place and to lay out CIOs in presentation units according to visual design principles and guidelines. The answer is detailed extensively in [5]. DON [15] is a pionneer of this question. Most of the time, CIOs are laid out manually within the graphical editor of the physical environment. On the other hand, a software tool can generate a first layout to be further refined by the visual designer. This approach is followed in DON and in TRIDENT. Three dimensions of an effective layout of CIO exist in the expert system :

1. the localization of CIO : where should they be placed?

2. the dimensioning : with which dimensions should they be formatted and displayed?

3. the arrangement : in which order should they be laid out?

Fifteen mathematical geographic relations are progressively added in the specifications of the AIO in order to define an abstract layout that will result in a visually appealing layout :

- horizontal/vertical sequencing;
- left, right, top, bottom justifications;
- horizontal, vertical centrations;
- horizontal, vertical uniformizations;
- diagonal, horizontal, vertical, proportional, total equilibria.

Two placement strategies have been investigated so far : a static strategy and a dynamic strategy. The **static placement** strategy is a strategy which automatically designates placement either in a two-column or a grid-based structure. This strategy assists the sequencing of information, promotes visual continuity and balances input/output into two columns according to a predefined format. This logical format consistently designates the placement for the following CIOs in the PUs : title, screen identifier, screen body, including labels, prompts, CIOs (messages, command box, push buttons). Several shortcomings of this strategy lead us to introduce a dynamic strategy [5]. The **dynamic** placement strategy consists of computer-aided placement which is based on a right/bottom strategy and on heuristics. Step-by-step placement can be presented to the visual designer in order to avoid undesirable layouts. Main criteria of this strategy are :

- to allow a see-and-place computer-aided generation,
- to reduce unused blank spaces,
- to deal with complex dialogue boxes,
- to optimize reading time,
- to reduce ocular movement on the screen,
- to guide the user visually through CIOs by visual continuity;

6.12   Generation and Static Prototyping

The generation of the user interface in TRIDENT is to a degree computer-aided. Once the presentation has been generated, the designer is able to test a static prototype : all CIOs can be tried individually, though without any global interaction and without attached function. The PU related to the sub-task "Identification of a customer" is reproduced in Figure 6.8. In this static prototype, the user can type information in the edit boxes and press the push buttons, but no function will be triggered.

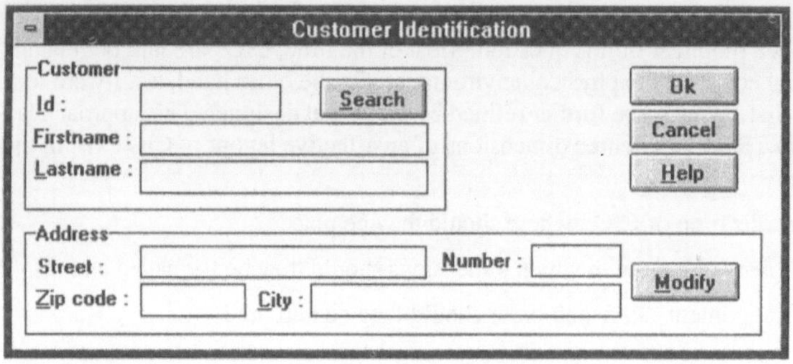

FIGURE 6.8. Result of the generation of PU "Identification of a customer"

Once again, the result of the generation completes the last stage in the specification of the presentation. The specification of the PU reproduced in Figure 6.8 is the following :

```
DEFINE PRESENTATION-UNIT Customer_Identification;
   CONSISTS OF Customer_Identification_Window; (* Only one window in this PU *)
   DIALOGUE MODE IS ASYNCHRONOUS;
   TRIGGERING MODE IS EXPLICIT MANUAL DISPLAYED;
   CONTROL IS MIXED;
   METAPHOR IS CONVERSATION;

DEFINE INTERACTION-OBJECT Customer_Identification_Window;
   IS INSTANCE OF Window;
   IS COMPOSED OF Customer_GroupBox, Address_GroupBox, Ok_PushButton,
                  Cancel_PushButton, Help_PushButton;

DEFINE INTERACTION-OBJECT Customer_GroupBox;
   IS INSTANCE OF GroupBox;
   IS COMPOSED OF Id_Label, Id_EditBox, Firstname_Label, Firstname_EditBox,
                  Lastname_Label, Lastname_EditBox, Search_PushButton;
   IS COMPONENT OF Customer_Identification_Window;

DEFINE INTERACTION-OBJECT ID_Label;
   WORDING IS "Id.";
   MNEMONIC IS "I";
   PROMPT IS ":";
   IS INSTANCE OF Label;
   IS COMPONENT OF Customer_GroupBox;

DEFINE INTERACTION-OBJECT Id_EditBox;
   MAX-LENGTH IS 6; (* See specification of the domain of element Cust_id *)
   LINEARITY SIMPLE;
   IS INSTANCE OF EditBox;
   IS COMPONENT OF Customer_GroupBox;
   IS ATTACHED TO Cust_id; (* Attachment to the ERA element Cust_id *)
...
DEFINE INTERACTION-OBJECT Address_GroupBox;
   IS INSTANCE OF GroupBox;
```

```
IS COMPOSED OF Street_Label, Street_EditBox, Number_Label, Number_EditBox,
               Zip_code_Label, Zip_code_EditBox, City_Label, City_EditBox,
               Modify_PushButton;
IS COMPONENT OF Customer_Identification_Window;
IS ATTACHED TO Cust_Address; (* Attachment to the ERA group Cust_Address *)
...
DEFINE INTERACTION-OBJECT Modify_PushButton;
  WORDING IS "Modify";
  MNEMONIC IS "M";
  STATUS INACTIVE; (* Push button should be desactived according to the ACG *)
  STYLE NORMAL;
  IS INSTANCE OF PushButton;
  IS COMPONENT OF Address_GroupBox;
  IS ATTACHED TO Modify_Address; (* Function attached to an action identified in
                                    the task analysis *)
...
```

The complete generated presentation produced presentation units whose screen captures are illustrated in Figure 6.9.

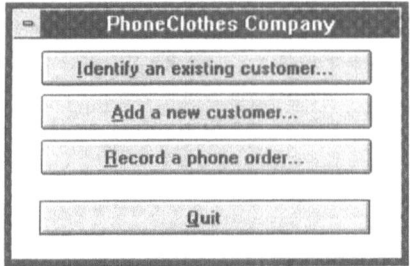

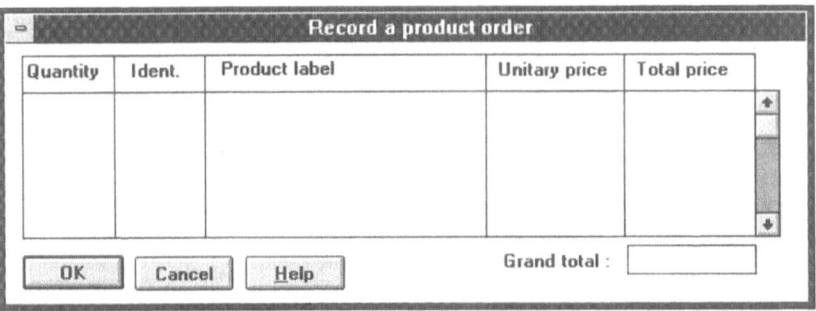

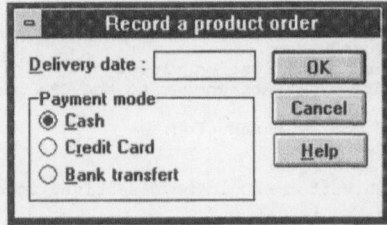

FIGURE 6.9. Result of the generation of all PUs for the task "Phone order"

As explained in section 6.7, multiple interaction styles can be selected. If command language and functions keys are added, the PU "Identification of a Customer" can have the presentation of Figure 6.10.

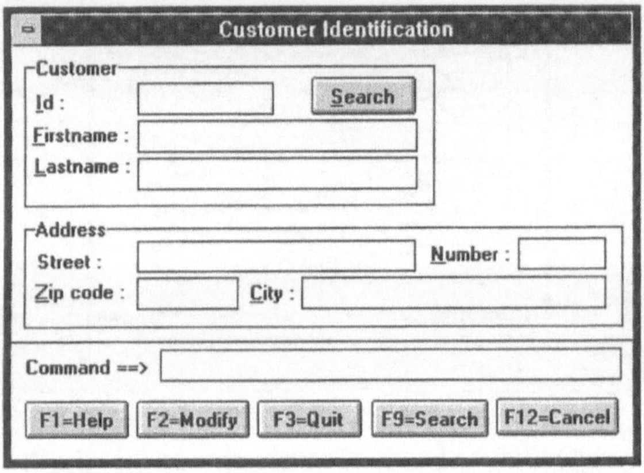

FIGURE 6.10. Result of the generation of PU "Identification of a Customer" with multiple interaction styles.

6.12   Prototype Validation by Human Factors Expert and Final User

The working prototype leads to a validation by :

- the human factors expert who can conduct a usability study to check user compatibility, styleguide compliance,...

- the final user who can provide remarks about compatibility between the interactive task and real-world task.

The observations of these experimentations can imply a return to virtually any previous process, leading to redesign, respecification and regenration.

6.13   Conclusion

The complete model-based approach which has been described here represents a first real attempt to start from the task analysis to reach a real prototype. The main contribution of this methodology is the modelling, with the ERA model, and the use of the ACG to connect user interface tasks with application informations and functions. Other strong points include :

- the definition of a task model to be graphically represented by an activity chaining graph,
- the derivation of dialogue attributes for each interactive task from task analysis;
- the selection of presentation units from the activity chaining graph,
- the use of the Abstract Interaction Object concept,
- the computer-aided selection and placement of interaction objects,
- the ability to edit the result of the generation.

Though this approach is believed feasible, it is now under ongoing experimentation with several case-studies outside the business-domain : medicine, insurance, decision-support systems. Not all processes of the TRIDENT methodology are computer-aided. Thus, we concentrate our extending implementation to the entire system and to validate the results with the user's point of view and the human factors expert's point of view.

6.14   Acknowledgements

The authors would like to thank the anonymous reviewers of Eurographics Workshop for their helpful comments. This work was partially supported by the FIRST research program of "Direction Générale des Technologies et de la Recherche du Ministère de la Région Wallonne", Ref. RASE/SCHL319/Conv. 1487 and by the "Informatique du Futur" project of "Service de la Politique et de la Programmation Scientifique" under contract N°IT/IF/1. Any opinions, findings, conclusions or recommendations expressed in this paper are those of the authors, and do not necessarily reflect the view of the Belgian Government.

6.15   References

[1] D.J. de Baar, J.D. Foley, K.E. Mullet, *Coupling Application Design and User Interface Design*, in Proceedings of CHI'92, Monterey, 3-7 May 1992, pp. 259-266.
[2] F. Bodart, Y. Pigneur, *Conception Assistée des Systèmes d'Information*, 2nd ed., Masson, Paris, 1989.
[3] F. Bodart, A.-M. Hennebert, J.-M. Leheureux, I. Provot, B. Sacré, J. Vanderdonckt, *Architecture Elements for Highly-Interactive Business-Oriented Applications*, in Proceedings of EWHCI'93, Moscow, 3-7 August 1993, pp. 151-173.
[4] F. Bodart, A.-M. Hennebert, J.-M. Leheureux, I. Provot, B. Sacré, J. Vanderdonckt, *Architecture Elements for Highly-Interactive Business-Oriented Applications*, in L. Bass, J. Gornostaev and C. Unger (Eds.), Lecture Notes in Computer Science, Vol. 753, Springer-Verlag, Berlin, 1993, pp. 83-104.
[5] F. Bodart, A.-M. Hennebert, J.-M. Leheureux, J. Vanderdonckt, *Towards a Dynamic Strategy for Computer-Aided Visual Placement*, in Proceedings of AVI'94, Rome, 1-4 June 1994, ACM Press, to be published.
[6] D.A. Duce, M.R. Gones, F.R.A. Hopgood, J.R. Lee (Eds.), *User Interface Management and Design*, Proceedings of the Workshop on User Interface Management Systems and Environments, Lisbon, 4-6 June 1990.
[7] P.J.W. ten Hagen, J. Derksen, *Parallel Input and Feedback in Dialogueue Cells*, in User Interface Management Systems, Proceedings of the Workshop on User Interface Management Systems, G.E. Pfaff (Ed.), Seeheim, 1-3 November 1983, Springer-Verlag, Berlin, 1983, pp. 109-124.
[8] H.R. Hartson, *Advances in Human-Computer Interaction*, Vol. 1, 2, 3, Ablex Publishing Corp., Norwood, 1985.

[9] H.R. Hartson, D.H. Johnson, R.W. Ehrich, *A Human-computer Dialogueue Management System*, in Proceedings of INTERACT '84, B. Shakel (Ed.), Elsevier Science Publishers B.V., Amsterdam, 1985, p. 379-383.

[10] H.R. Hartson, D. Hix, *Toward empirically derived methodologies and tools for human-computer interface development*, International Journal of Man-Machine Studies, Vol. 31, 1989, pp. 477-494.

[11] H.R. Hartson, *User Interface Management Control and Communication*, IEEE Software, January 1989, pp. 62-70.

[12] H.R. Hartson, A.C. Siochi, *Task-Oriented Representation of Asynchronous User Interface*, in Proceedings of CHI'89 Austin, 30 April - 4 May 1989, pp. 183-188.

[13] A.-M. Hennebert, *Comment commander chez Téléphonachat?*, internal report, Institut d'Informatique, 2 March 1993.

[14] P. Johnson, S. Wilson, P. Markopoulos, J. Pycock, *ADEPT- Advanced Design Environment for Prototyping with Task Models*, in Proceedings of INTERCHI'93, Amsterdam, 24-29 April 1993, p. 56.

[15] W. Kim, J. Foley, *DON: User Interface Presentation Design Assistant*, in Proceedings of UIST'90, Snowbird, 3-5 October 1990, pp. 10-20.

[16] D.R. Olsen, *A Programming Language Basis for User Interface Management*, in Proceedings of CHI'89, Austin, 30 April - 4 May 1989, pp. 171-176.

[17] D.R. Olsen, *Propositional Production Systems for Dialogue Description*, in Proceedings of CHI'90, Seattle, 1-5 April 1990, pp. 57-63.

[18] I. Provot, *Spécification du comportement des objets de contrôle*, internal report, Institut d'Informatique, 17 Dec. 1993.

[19] P. Sukaviriya, J.D. Foley, T. Griffith, *A Second Generation User Interface Design Environment: The Model and The Runtime Architecture*, in Proceedings of INTERCHI'93, Amsterdam, 24-29 April 1993, pp. 375-382.

[20] P. Sukaviriya, J.D. Foley, *Supporting Adaptive Interfaces in a Knowledge-Based User Interface Environment*, in Proceedings of IWIUI'93, Orlando, 4-7 January 1993.

[21] A.G. Sutcliffe, *Task Analysis, Systems Analysis and Design: Symbiosis or Synthesis?*, Interacting with Computers, Vol. 1, No. 1, 1989, pp. 6-12.

[22] A.G. Sutcliffe, *Human-Computer Interface Design*, MacMillan, 1988.

[23] J. Vanderdonckt, F. Bodart, *Encapsulating Knowledge for Intelligent Automatic Interaction Objects Selection*, in Proceedings of INTERCHI'93, Amsterdam, 24-29 April 1993, pp. 424-429.

7 Modeling and Analyzing Human-Computer Dialogues with Protocols

Hans de Bruin, Peter Bouwman and Jan van den Bos

ABSTRACT
A new object-oriented model for modeling and analyzing human-computer dialogues is presented. In this model, dialogues are distributed over a number of objects all running in parallel, and each object maintains the state of a sub-dialogue. The dialogue model is based on only a few concepts: autonomous concurrent objects, communicating with each other via message passing, and the behavior of an object is recursively defined in terms of protocols. Protocols, a concept derived from the concurrent object-oriented language Procol, describe the interaction patterns with an object using an augmented regular expression notation. This dialogue model is targeted to concurrent multi-threaded event-driven dialogues. In addition, dialogues can be quite naturally visualized and interactively specified using graphical direct manipulation techniques.

7.1 Introduction

Human-computer dialogues denote the structure of the conversations between the human and the computer. Three abstraction levels can be identified in human-computer dialogues: the lexical, syntactical, and semantical level. In the design of interactive systems, the term dialogue usually refers to the syntactical aspects of a system. The dialogue part of an interactive system is the intermediary between the semantical part of a system, the application, and the lexical part of a system, the presentation.

Several programming techniques have been developed for designing and implementing dialogues. In particular, object-oriented techniques have been quite successfully applied to the implementation of highly interactive end-user driven graphical direct manipulation (DM) user interfaces. In object-oriented systems, the human-computer dialogues are distributed over a number of objects, each one maintaining the local state of a sub-dialogue. However, the use of programming techniques for specifying dialogues has a number of problems. Firstly, it is difficult to reveal the structure of a dialogue from a piece of code. Secondly, it is almost impossible to analyze dialogues in order to prove certain properties because the lexical and semantical aspects are interwoven in the code with the syntactical (dialogue) aspects of an interactive system. For these reasons, specialized dialogue notations have been developed for modeling and/or analyzing dialogues at a much higher abstraction level. Dialogue notations come in many forms, and can be roughly separated in two categories:

- Diagrammatic, e.g., State Transition Networks (STN);

- Textual, e.g., grammars, event response systems, and process algebras.

Diagrammatic dialogue notations are typically used for modeling and design purposes, they can reveal the structure of a dialogue at a glance. In contrast to textual dialogue notations, diagrammatic notations often have an informal character, and consequently are less suitable for analysis purposes.

The increasingly popular DM Graphical User Interfaces (GUI) have brought a great deal of user-friendliness to the end-user. However, developing such interactive systems is not an easy task, because the interaction style has shifted from internal, computer controlled dialogues to external, end-user controlled dialogues in which the end-user can be engaged in multiple sub-dialogues simultaneously. Not all dialogue notations can cope with this complexity adequately. The demands on dialogue notations become even stronger with the advent of new technologies. Interface technology is rapidly evolving, introducing new types of user interfaces with a multitude of interaction devices as in multi-media applications, and with multiple users as in Computer Supported Cooperative Work (CSCW) systems.

In this paper we present a new dialogue model, well-suited for modeling and analyzing dialogues in a concurrent, event-driven, and object-oriented context. This dialogue model lends itself naturally to graphical specifications using DM techniques. The model is based on the concepts found in the concurrent object-oriented language Procol [14], and is extended with concepts for modeling event-driven interactive systems. In Procol, all objects run in parallel and they can be distributed over an arbitrary number of processors. The central concept in Procol is the protocol, describing the legal interaction patterns with an object using an augmented regular expression notation. A protocol is an active entity. Each object is equipped with an individual protocol that manages the access to the object.

The dialogue model is used in DIGIS [13, 5], a graphical UI design environment which can be characterized as follows:

- Targeted to UI designers with little or no programming experience;

- It is a complete environment, it addresses all aspects of UI design;

- The UI is designed with DM techniques;

- No restrictions on the type of UI.

DIGIS enforces a strict separation between the application (the semantics) and the UI (the presentation and the dialogue). The application is modeled in an object-oriented way. DIGIS allows a UI designer to quickly construct various kinds of UIs for a particular application, ranging from simple menu-driven form-oriented UIs to highly interactive graphical DM UIs where the end-users have the illusion that they are directly manipulating application objects.

The DIGIS requirements on a dialogue model can be summarized as follows:

- Suitable for specifying concurrent, end-user driven, multi-threaded dialogues;

- Suitable for interactively specifying the dialogue with DM techniques, e.g., drag-and-drop techniques;

- Suitable for automatically analyzing dialogues;

- Understandable by UI designers with a cognitive ergonomics background.

Although a wealth of dialogue notations exists, no existing notation can fulfill all DIGIS requirements in a satisfactory way. For this reason we have developed a more powerful dialogue notation. A comparison between this notation and some well-known dialogue formalisms can be found in section 7.5.

The outline of this paper is as follows. First we discuss the underlying computational model of the dialogue notation. Then we show how dialogues can be interactively constructed with graphical DM techniques. Next we discuss how dialogues can be analyzed in order to prove properties of human-computer dialogues. Finally we compare our work with other dialogue notations.

7.2 Computational Model

In this section we present the computational model of the dialogue notation. The model is based on only a few concepts: autonomous concurrent objects, communicating with each other via message passing, and the behavior of an object is recursively defined in terms of protocols. A formal model provides the basis for automatically analyzing dialogues. It is also an executable model, i.e., it can be regarded as a very basic object-oriented programming language. Indeed, if this notation is used for textual specifications, it would be rather restricted and lacks the expressive power found in ordinary object-oriented languages. However, the model was not developed with textual specifications in mind. Besides, the full power of a programming language is hardly required in dialogue specifications. As we shall see in section 7.3, the simplicity of the model adds much to the possibility to interactively specify dialogues with drag-and-drop DM techniques without actually constraining the dialogue designer.

The dialogue notation is used in DIGIS for modeling and analyzing the behavior of agents in a concurrent environment. The software architecture, i.e., the implementation or run-time model, of interactive systems constructed with DIGIS [4] is based on the PAC model [3]. A PAC consists of three components: *Presentation*, defining the input-output behavior, *Abstraction*, implementing the functional core (application), and *Control*, responsible for dialogue control and maintaining the consistency between the Presentation and Abstraction. The PAC model is a multi-agent model. A complete interactive system is recursively decomposed into a hierarchy of PACs (see Figure 7.1). Each PAC provides an abstraction at a certain level. The PACs at

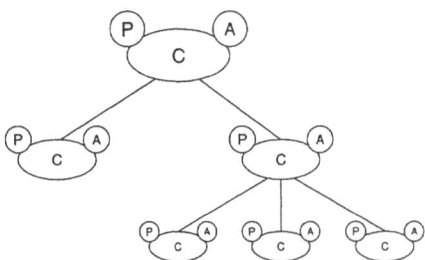

FIGURE 7.1. The PAC model.

the bottom level of the hierarchy implement elementary interactions with the end-user, while a PAC at the top level implements the application domain specific functionality of an interactive system.

Modeling interactive systems as a collection of agents is advantageous for several reasons. An agent defines the unit for modularity. This means that an agent can be replaced by another one without affecting the rest of the interactive system. Furthermore, since each agent is a stand-alone processing unit, agents may run concurrently, possibly on a number of processors. Therefore, the PAC model is well-suited for implementing multi-threaded dialogues, handling multiple interaction devices simultaneously, and supporting multiple users in CSCW systems.

The PAC model is silent about the programming techniques or languages to be used for implementing PACs. However, since each PAC encapsulates a clear concept of state and behavior, PACs are naturally designed and implemented with object-oriented techniques. The dialogue notation described in this paper can be used to formally describe the behavior of PAC agents in an object-oriented way.

The computational model of the dialogue notation is explained with the help of an abstract syntax. It is called abstract for two reasons. Firstly, the syntax is invisible in interactive specifications. Secondly, as said before, the model can be regarded as a basic concurrent object-oriented programming language. However, we do not wish to invent yet another object-oriented programming language. Instead, the model is defined in such a way that it can be superposed on any suitable host language, for instance, (concurrent) C(++) or Smalltalk. The syntax should be adapted to adhere to the style conventions of the actual host language.

7.2.1   Basic Concepts

In this section we explore the basic concepts of the model which are derived from the object-oriented programming language Procol. The computational model of Procol is based on many concurrent objects acting as servers. The access to an object is protected with a protocol describing the legal interactions patterns with the object.

Protocols

A protocol manages the access to an object, and is specified as an augmented regular expression over object method terms. A protocol expression is constructed with 5 operators: interleave ($\|$), guard (:), repetition ($*$), sequence (;), and selection ($+$) (in decreasing precedence). Parentheses may be used to overrule the precedence of an operator, or to enhance the readability. The semantics of protocol expressions are summarized in Table 7.1, where E and F are arbitrary sub-expressions over object method terms.

Protocol expression	Operator	Meaning
E $\|$ F	interleave	E and F may occur interleaved
E + F	selection	E or F is selected
E ; F	sequence	E is followed by F
E $*$	repetition	Zero or more times E
φ : E	guard	E only if φ is true

TABLE 7.1. Semantics of protocol expressions.

In addition, a bounded repetition operator is supported as a notational shorthand:

$$E[m, n] \ where \ 0 \leq m \leq n \ with \ m, n \ integers \ or \ n = *$$

At most one method in an object may be active at any one time: the one-at-a-time principle. After a method has been processed, the guards in the protocol are evaluated, and the new set of acceptable interactions with the object is determined.

For example, a file server object can be specified as follows:

```
FileServer =
    declare
        string        name;
    protocol
        input
            ( open(name) ; read⇒(string text) * ; close )*
    methods
        open =
            // open the file
        end open

        read =
            // read from the file
        end read

        close =
            // close the file
        end close
end FileServer
```

The protocol of the file server states that it is impossible to read from, and to close an unopened file. After the file is opened, an arbitrary number of strings can be read from the file, or the file may be closed. A new file may be opened only after the file is closed.

A few syntactical and semantical remarks are in order here. Two kinds of methods are defined in the protocol of the file server: a method without a reply, e.g., open(name), and a method with a reply, namely, read⇒(string text). Parentheses may be omitted if an input argument list is empty, as is the case in the read and close methods. When an incoming message has been accepted by the protocol of an object, the message arguments are copied to the appropriate instance variables.

There are three important benefits of protocol protection. Firstly, protocols bring security: interactions with an object are guaranteed to occur following the well-defined interactions patterns described in a protocol. Secondly, related to the first argument, objects are easier to design. For instance, in the implementation of the read method we do not have to check whether a file is opened or not. Thirdly, a protocol documents an object, describing when and how to use the services provided by an object.

The advantages of specifying protocols with regular expressions are that they are compact, and they are easy to visualize. Regular expressions are less powerful than grammars. For instance, it is impossible to count parentheses with a regular expression. Another disadvantage is that regular expressions are not really suitable for describing interleaved behavior. To overcome these deficiencies, a protocol can be specified with the augmented regular expression operators guard (:) and interleave (∥). Consider, for example, a simplified protocol of an Automated Teller Machine (ATM):

```
( card ; pincode[1,3] ; valid_pincode : amount )*
∥
cancel *
∥
help *
```

The guard valid_pincode assures that it is only possible to withdraw an amount of cash if the customer has entered a valid pin-code. By using the interleave operator, it is easy to specify that a customer is allowed to cancel a transaction or to ask for help after each step in the standard ATM procedure.

Message Passing

In contrast to Procol, objects communicate with each other by sending asynchronous messages. The choice between synchronous and asynchronous message passing is a difficult one. Synchronous message passing implies synchronization between the sender and the receiver. Therefore, concurrent object-oriented systems based on synchronous message passing are often easier to design and to analyze than systems based on asynchronous message passing. On the other hand, the degree of parallelism in a system with asynchronous message passing may be higher than in the synchronous case because a sender does not have to wait for a receiver willing to accept a message. We have chosen to use asynchronous message passing because our dialogue model has a communication primitive (see section 7.2.2) which is most naturally based on asynchronous communication principles. Furthermore, if needed, synchronous message passing can be easily expressed in terms of asynchronous message passing.

In principle, nothing can be said about the arrival time of an asynchronous message at the receiver. However, this complicates modeling even the simplest communications between two objects in a natural way. Consider, for example, an object A repeatedly sending characters to object B. Due to the nature of asynchronous communication, the characters may arrive at B in a different order than sent by A. For this reason, we use a *restricted* form of asynchronous message passing that preserves the partial ordering of communications sent from A to B. Asynchronous message passing implies message buffering, and conceptually, each object is equipped with a message buffer in which unprocessed incoming messages are stored (see Figure 7.2.a). An

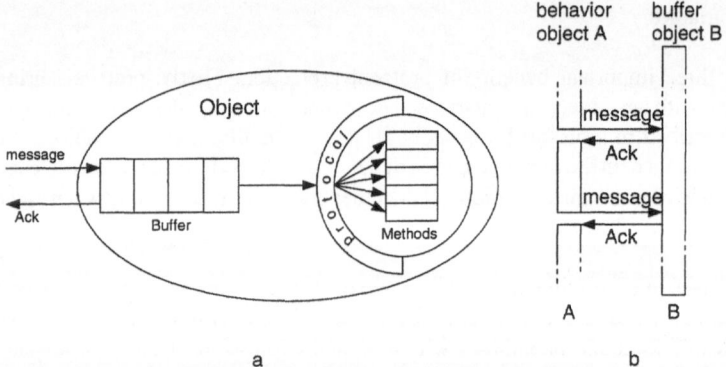

FIGURE 7.2. Asynchronous message passing.

object A sending a message to object B is blocked until an acknowledgement has been received from B, indicating that the message has been stored in the message buffer of B. Only after the receipt of the acknowledgement, object A can proceed, for instance, by sending another message to B. In this way, the messages sent from object A to object B are received in the same order at B (see Figure 7.2.b). This does not necessarily mean that messages are *processed* by a corresponding method in the receiver in the same order. The protocol determines the set of acceptable messages. Access to the object is granted on a first-come-first-served basis of acceptable messages. In conclusion, message passing in this model has a synchronous and an asynchronous flavor: synchronous message *buffering* but asynchronous message *processing*.

Two basic communication primitives are supported: the send and the request. An asynchronous message is sent to an object by issuing, for example:

```
var.open("MyFile")
```

The message open is sent to an object referred to by the variable var. A request is split in two asynchronous sends operating in lockstep. An object issues a request in the following way:

```
var.read⇒(result)
```

The result of the request is stored in one or more variables, in this case the variable result. The receiving object replies by means of a special asynchronous return message specified by the ! (bang) primitive:

```
!(text)
```

The requester is blocked and cannot be engaged in other communications during a request until a reply has been received. Thus, from the requester's point of view, a request is a synchronous communication primitive. After the receiver has sent an asynchronous reply, it continues to execute the post actions of a method, if any. A reply does not alter the protocol state of the requester.

7.2.2 Modeling Event-Driven Interactive Systems

In the previous section we have discussed the basic communication principles between objects. In this section we introduce two important concepts for modeling event-driven systems: output protocols, and sub-protocols.

Modeling the External Behavior of an Object

The programming language Procol encourages a client-server model of computation. A system based on this client-server model consists of a collection of cooperating objects, taking roles as clients and servers. The initiating role lies by the client, the server humbly waits until requested by a client to perform one of its duties. A server is free to delegate a request from a client to another server, and behaves as a client to this server. In this client-server model, the external behavior of a server is fully specified by the declarations and the input protocol. By just looking at the declarations and the input protocol, we know how to use the services provided by an object. For instance, the external behavior of a file server is documented as follows:

```
FileServer =
    declare
        string      name;
    protocol
        input
            ( open(name) ; read⇒(string text) * ; close )*
end FileServer
```

Event-driven servers are hard to describe in such a client-server model. Consider, for example, a user interface object like a button. Clearly, a button can be regarded as a server for clients which need to be notified when the end-user has activated the button by means of a mouse click. We observe that the initiating role has moved from the client to the server, that is, the button. An input protocol now only partly describes the external behavior of an object. What is missing is a description of the notification messages, the output behavior of an object. The output behavior of an object is captured in an output protocol, defined as an augmented regular expression over notification messages, or notifications for short. For example, the output protocol of a button can be described as follows:

```
( arm ; ( disarm ; arm )* ; activate [0,1] ; disarm )*
```

This output protocol states that a button must first be armed before it can be activated, and eventually an armed button is disarmed. An object can send notifications by means of an asynchronous !! (bang-bang) notification message. The notification is multi-cast to all objects which expressed their interest in this message. For instance, a button sends the `activate` notification as follows:

    !!activate

All incoming messages are handled by the input protocol of an object. Therefore, the input protocol is the natural place for declaratively expressing the interest in particular notifications from servers:

    server.notification↦method

We refer to this as input-output protocol linkage, a notification from a server is mapped on a method of a client. Input-output protocol links are established at run-time, that is, a link is established as soon as the variable `server` refers to a server object. If the variable `server` gets a new value, i.e., refers to another server, the old link is removed and a new one is established. An example of input-output protocol linkage is shown below:

```
YesNoBox =
    declare
        PopUpWindow      window;
        Label            label;
        Button           yesbutton,nobutton;
        string           str;
    protocol
        input
            prompt(str) ;
            ( yesbutton.activate↦doit + nobutton.activate↦dont )
        output
            yes + no
    methods
        prompt =
            do
                // Create the yesbutton, the nobutton, and a label showing the prompt.
                // Create a pop-up window.

                window.popUp
            end prompt

        doit =
            do
                window.popDown ;
                !!yes
            end doit

        dont =
            do
                window.popDown ;
                !!no
            end dont
    end YesNoBox
```

This Yes-No dialogue box is initialized by sending the message `prompt`, resulting in the creation of a yes and a no button, and a label showing the prompt. When the yes and no button come into existence, the declaratively defined input-output protocol links are established. The Yes-No dialogue box provides a yes-no notification abstraction as defined in the output protocol.

The external behavior of a server is completely defined by the declarations, and the input-output protocol. It is interesting to see how objects described by their input-output behavior can be used to build abstractions on abstractions. For instance, a simple button object maps low-level mouse events to an arm-activate-disarm abstraction. The Yes-No dialogue box in its turn increases the abstraction level by mapping button activations to a yes-no abstraction.

The external behavior in the form of input-output protocols can be used to formally describe the surface or lexical level of an interactive system. This is an attractive feature for incorporating existing UI building blocks in a system. The output protocol and input-output protocol linkage formalize and generalize the callback mechanism found in, for instance, X-toolkit widgets.

In a typical interactive system, the initiating role can lie by a client as well as by a server. We therefore prefer not to speak of clients and servers, instead we would like to view an object as an agent, capable of reacting to notifications and requesting other agents to carry out some activity.

Modeling the Internal Behavior of an Object

In an event-driven system, an agent is activated as a result of the receipt of a notification from some agent, which reacted to a notification itself, and so on, until we end at an elementary agent: the end-user or an external hardware device. A method is usually specified in terms of services provided by other agents. In an event-driven system, agents provide these services by sending notifications. The notifications sent by agents occur in an unpredictable order and must be synchronized in the method in some way. As we have seen, an input protocol is well-suited for synchronization purposes. Thus, a method can be defined in terms of a sub-protocol over sub-methods. Applying the argument recursively, the sub-methods can be defined by means of a sub-sub-protocol, and so on, until a nested method can be defined solely in primitive actions. Only a few primitive actions are defined:

- communication primitives: asynchronous send, synchronous request, asynchronous reply (!), and asynchronous notification (!!) as discussed in the previous sections.

- instantiating primitive: new var

  A new dialogue object is created and var now refers to this object. An object can be initialized by sending the appropriate messages as defined in the input protocol of the object. The destruction of objects is not supported since it is possible to incorporate terminating methods in the input protocol of an object in such a way that the object cannot respond to communications anymore. Readers concerned with space efficiency may assume that the space of a unreferenced object is reclaimed by a garbage collector.

- assignment primitive: (expr) $\Rightarrow$ (var)

- host language escape primitive: {/* host language statements */ }

  The escape primitive is provided to use features of the host language. It is of no importance to the model, meaning that it can be ignored in an analysis.

The (sub-)protocols synchronize the notifications received from other agents. In a way, the protocols implement flow control, they control the allowed message flow between a collection of cooperating agents. Thus, event-driven human-computer dialogues can be modeled as a collection of autonomous agents, communicating with each other via message passing, and the behavior of a method is recursively defined in terms of protocols until a nested method can be defined as simple sequences of primitive actions (see Figure 7.3). A nested method is called a *protocol method* unless it is defined solely in terms of primitive actions, in which case it is called

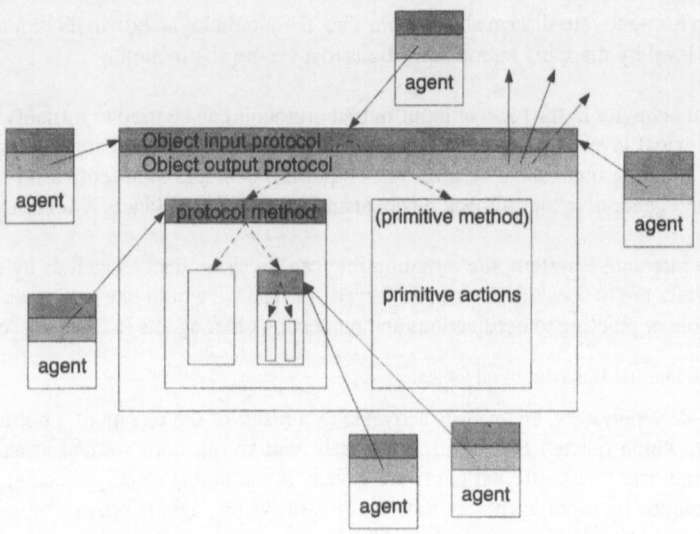

FIGURE 7.3. Recursively defining the behavior of an object with (sub-)protocols.

a *primitive method.*

Unfortunately, the idea that all control can be specified with protocols is too simplistic. Consider, for example, an agent receiving an integer, say, x. Dependent on whether $x \geq 0$ or $x < 0$, two different primitive action sequences must be performed. Clearly, there is a need for programming language control structures, like if-then-else and while-do, to define the behavior of a primitive method. However, we wish to formulate a model rather than defining a programming language. Instead of incorporating programming language control constructs in the model, the behavior of a primitive method is described by a regular expression over primitive actions. Regular expression operators are strongly related to programming language constructs, e.g., the selection $(+)$ operator corresponds to the if-then-else control structure, repetition $(*)$ corresponds to while-do, and sequences of actions can be represented by the sequence operator $(;)$. Returning to the example, the behavior of a method, activated by receiving a message with x as message argument, can be described as:

```
MyObject =
    declare
        int    x;
    protocol
        input
            m(x)
    methods
        m =
            do
                (
                    // regular sub-expression for the branch (x ≥ 0)
                    // for instance, a sequence of primitive actions,
                    // using the regular expression operator (;)
                )
                +
                (
                    // regular sub-expression for the branch (x < 0)
                )
        end m
    end MyObject
```

A regular expression formally describes the *possible* behaviors of a primitive method. If this method was to be executed, the system would have the choice to either execute the sequence of primitive actions for the branch ($x \geq 0$) or to execute the branch ($x < 0$). In order to turn the formal specification into an executable specification, we can add guards, in such a way that all choices are eliminated. For instance, method m can be defined with guards as:

```
m =
    do
        x ≥ 0 : (
            // regular sub-expression for the branch (x ≥ 0)
        )
        +
        x < 0 : (
            // regular sub-expression for the branch (x < 0)
        )
    end m
```

The advantage of using this scheme for specifying primitive methods is that everything in the model is expressed by means of regular expressions. Agreed, the use of programming control structures, like if-then-else, is more compact (one condition versus two complementary conditions). Nonetheless, we have chosen to use regular expressions because guards are only used for turning a formal specification of a primitive method into an executable specification. As we shall see in section 7.4, they can be safely ignored in an automatic analysis for proving dialogue properties. For analysis purposes, a regular expression notation that clearly states the possible behaviors is more appropriate than a programming language like notation.

We have made a distinction between protocol methods and primitive methods. In many practical cases, a sub-protocol can be activated only after some initializing statements have been executed, such as the creation and initialization of supporting agents. Protocol methods and primitive methods can be unified as shown below:

```
m =
    declare_opt
    do_opt
    protocol_opt
    methods_opt
    final_opt
    end m
```

The optional *do* section is executed first, then the sub-protocol is activated and incoming messages are handled by the sub-methods defined in the methods section. A sub-protocol is defined in the same way as an input protocol. After the protocol has terminated, the optional *final* section is executed. The *do* and *final* sections are defined in terms of a regular expression over primitive actions, as described above. The *protocol* and *method* sections are optional. If they are not defined, the method is a primitive method. In this way, protocol and primitive methods can be uniformly specified. A protocol or a regular expression terminates when it is in a state with no continuations.

7.2.3   Example

In the previous section we have discussed the concepts for modeling event-driven systems. A small, but realistic, example is given here for demonstrating how to use these concepts for modeling and realizing such interactive systems. The human-computer dialogues are distributed over a number of agents, each one implementing a well-defined sub-dialogue as specified in the protocols of these agents. Consider an application with a graphical user interface as depicted in Figure 7.4.a. The user interface consists of a main window with a menu-bar. When the end-user clicks on the file menu item, a pull-down menu is revealed, showing the well-known file handling

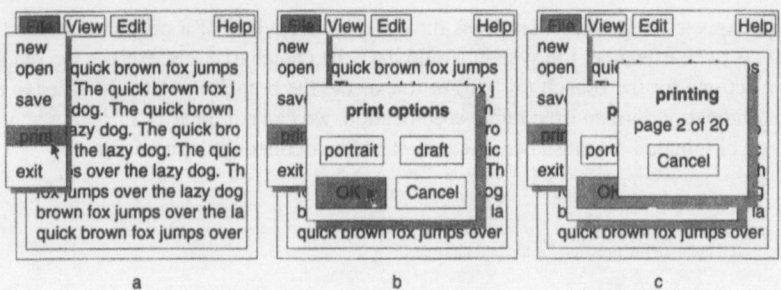

FIGURE 7.4. Scenario for printing a file from a menu.

options such as open, save, and print. In this example we take a closer look at printing a file. A print option dialogue box is popped-up when the end-user activates the print menu item (see Figure 7.4.b). The end-user can set the desired print options and press the ok button indicating that the file may be printed. The file is sent to the printer and a print monitor box is popped-up showing the progress (see Figure 7.4.c). The end-user may decide at any time to cancel the print job by pressing the cancel button.

A schematic overview of the objects involved is given in Figure 7.5. The central role is played

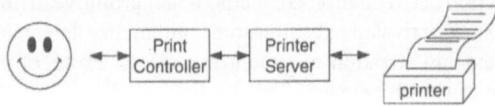

FIGURE 7.5. Overview of the objects involved for printing a file.

by the PrintController object, the human-computer dialogues are handled by this object. The PrinterServer object deals with the details of printing files and exceptions such as running out of paper. The external behavior of the printer server is specified as follows:

```
PrinterServer =
    declare
        string          filename;
        boolean         portrait,draft;
    protocol
        input
            ( print(filename,portrait,draft) ; cancel [0,1] ) *
        output
            ( printing(int currentpage,int lastpage) * ; ready ) *
    end PrinterServer
```

The printer server starts printing when the message print has been received. It counts the number of pages in the file, and repeatedly sends a printing notification when a new page is printed. The ready notification is sent when there are no more pages left. A print job can be cancelled at any time by sending the cancel message.

The interactions with the end-user are handled by the print option and print monitor dialogue boxes. The external behavior of these dialogue boxes are specified as shown below:

```
PrintOptionBox =
    protocol
        input
            popUp ; popDown
        output
            (
                orientation(boolean portrait) +
                quality(boolean draft)
            ) * ;
            ( ok + cancel )
end PrintOptionBox

PrintMonitorBox =
    declare
        int     currentpage,lastpage;
    protocol
        input
            popUp ; update(currentpage,lastpage) * ; popDown
        output
            cancel [0,1]
end PrintMonitorBox
```

The PrintController object is the intermediary between the end-user and the PrinterServer object, and must react to notifications from both sides:

```
PrintController =
    declare
        string                  filename;
        PrinterServer           server;
    protocol
        input
            print(filename,server) *
    methods
        print =
            declare
                PrintOptionBox      optionbox;
                boolean             portrait,draft;
            do
                new optionbox ; optionbox.popUp
            protocol
                (
                    optionbox.orientation↦orientation(portrait) +
                    optionbox.quality↦quality(draft)
                ) * ;
                ( optionbox.ok↦ok + optionbox.cancel↦cancel )
            methods
                orientation =
                    // boolean portrait is implicitly set
                end orientation

                quality =
                    // boolean draft is implicitly set
                end quality

                ok =
                    declare
                        PrintMonitorBox     monitorbox;
                        int                 currentpage,lastpage;
                    do
                        new monitorbox ; monitorbox.popUp ;
                        server.print(filename,portrait,draft)
                    protocol
                        server.printing↦printing(currentpage,lastpage) * ;
                        server.ready↦ready
                        ‖
                        monitorbox.cancel↦cancel
                    methods
                        printing =
                            do
                                monitorbox.update(currentpage,lastpage)
                            end printing
```

```
              ready =
                 // do nothing
              end ready

              cancel =
                 do
                      server.cancel
                 end cancel
              final
                 monitorbox.popDown
           end ok

           cancel =
              // do nothing
           end cancel
        final
           optionbox.popDown
      end print
   end PrintController
```

It is interesting to see that the print controller is completely event-driven, and that the dialogues are exclusively controlled by the (sub-)protocols. In this example we assume that the print controller and an appropriate printer server have already been created. The print dialogues start by sending the print message to the PrintController object as a result of activating the print menu item in the file menu.

7.3   Interactively Specifying Dialogues with DM Techniques

In the previous sections we have presented the computational model of the dialogue notation, we are now in the position to explain how a dialogue designer can interactively specify a dialogue with DM techniques. We first present the basic concepts followed by an example specification session and a discussion on interactive specification techniques.

7.3.1   Basic Concepts

The basic idea is to construct interaction diagrams describing the behavior of an object and the interactions with other objects. An example interaction diagram is depicted in Figure 7.6, showing the behavior of a Yes-No dialogue box, the interactions with supporting objects such as buttons and a window, and the interactions with an agent that uses the abstractions provided by the Yes-No dialogue box. The behavior of an object is represented as visualizations of regular expressions denoting the control flow . The visualizations of the regular expression operators are shown in Figure 7.7. Regular expressions are expressed in terms of primitive building blocks, or primitives for short, as depicted in Figure 7.8. A message is received in a so called *inlet* primitive representing a method invocation. Objects are instantiated by "sending " a message to a special kind of inlet: the *creation inlet*. Actually, this is a notational convenience for object instantiation, since it is impossible to send messages to objects which do not exist yet. The sequences of primitives between inlets describe the behavior of a method. A method is typically defined in terms of the send, the request, and the notification primitives. The latter is called an *outlet* primitive, and it can be linked to an arbitrary number of inlets in other objects.

The input and output protocols, and the behavior of the methods are all contained in a single diagram. Such a diagram can be translated to a textual and/or graphical representation where these three facets are separated. In many cases, a dialogue designer is interested in the external behavior rather than the internal behavior of an object. For example, the external behavior of a button object in the form of input and output protocols is visualized in Figure 7.9.a. To reduce

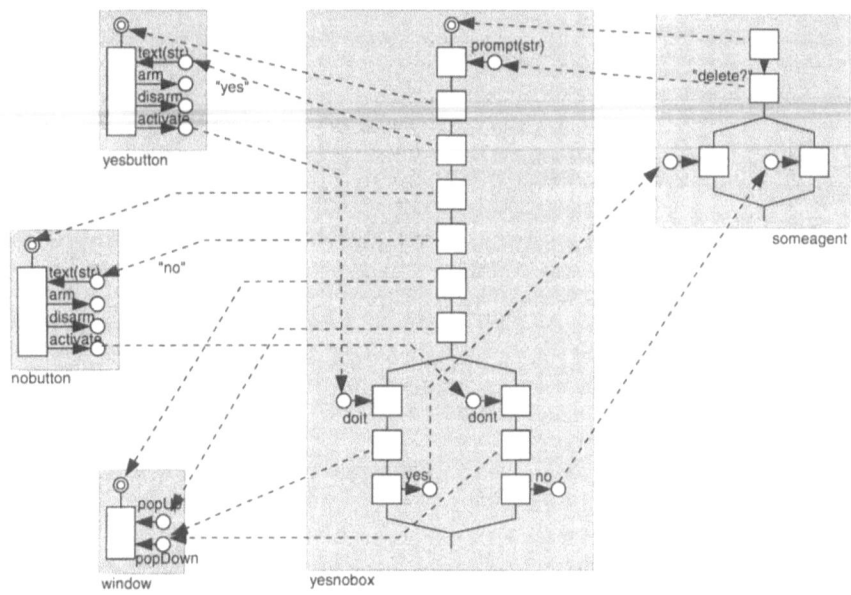

FIGURE 7.6. Example interaction diagram.

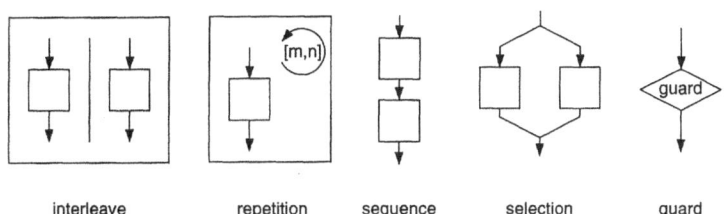

interleave   repetition   sequence   selection   guard

FIGURE 7.7. Graphical representations of regular expression operators.

the required screen space for visualizing interaction diagrams, objects may be collapsed in a single block only giving an enumeration of the inlets and/or the outlets (see Figure 7.9.b).

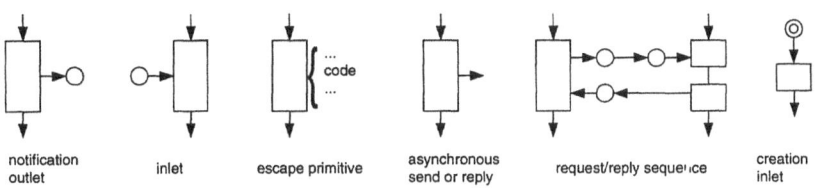

notification
outlet   inlet   escape primitive   asynchronous
send or reply   request/reply sequence   creation
inlet

FIGURE 7.8. Graphical representations of primitives.

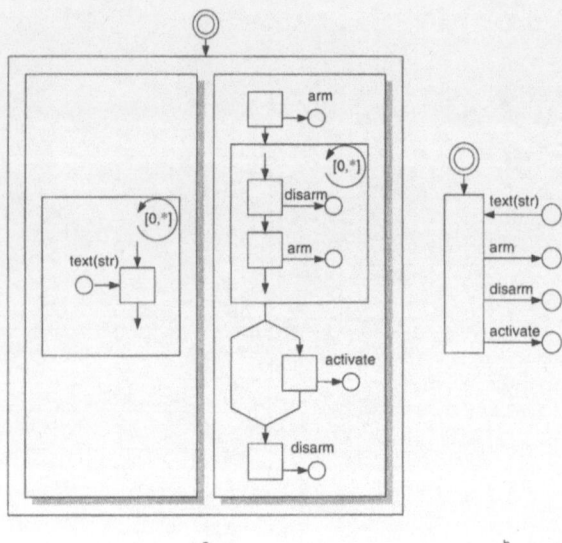

FIGURE 7.9. External behavior of a button object.

7.3.2   Specifying the Print Controller

To get an idea of the construction process of interaction diagrams, we give an artist's impression of the interactive specification of the print controller dialogue (see section 7.2.3). Interaction diagrams are constructed by dragging primitives (inlets, outlets, etc.) to a construction area, and by applying the appropriate regular expression operators to them, such as sequence, selection, and repetition. In this example we take a closer look at the construction of the print method of the print controller. For constructing the print method, the designer first drags a number of inlet primitives to the construction area (see Figure 7.10.a). A multi-way selection branch is constructed by selecting an arbitrary number of inlets and choosing the right operation from the operation menu (see Figure 7.10.b and 7.10.c). Letting the designer choose an operation from a menu has the advantage that no inconsistent interaction diagram can be constructed. In a similar way, the multi-way selection branch is incorporated in a loop (see Figure 7.10.d). The loop can then be appended to another block for constructing a sequence. The order of the sequence is deduced from the order in which the blocks were selected: the block first selected will appear first in the resulting diagram. When the behavior of the print method has been defined, the designer can proceed by establishing the input-output protocol linkages with the print option box by clicking on an appropriate outlet and dragging a rubber-banded arrow to an appropriate inlet (see Figure 7.11). Care has been taken to reduce typing effort to a minimum when constructing an interaction diagram. New outlets introduced into a diagram under construction get a unique label, but can be overruled by the designer. After linking an outlet to an inlet, the name of the inlet automatically takes the name of the outlet, but again, it can be overruled by the designer. Message arguments of an inlet can be linked to arguments of an outlet, a send, or a request primitive using the same drag-and-drop techniques as in linking outlets to inlets.

A dialogue designer can zoom in on an inlet in order to construct a nested protocol method. For instance, by first selecting the ok inlet, and then activating the zoom operation from the menu, a new construction area is popped-up. The dialogue designer proceeds by specifying the behavior

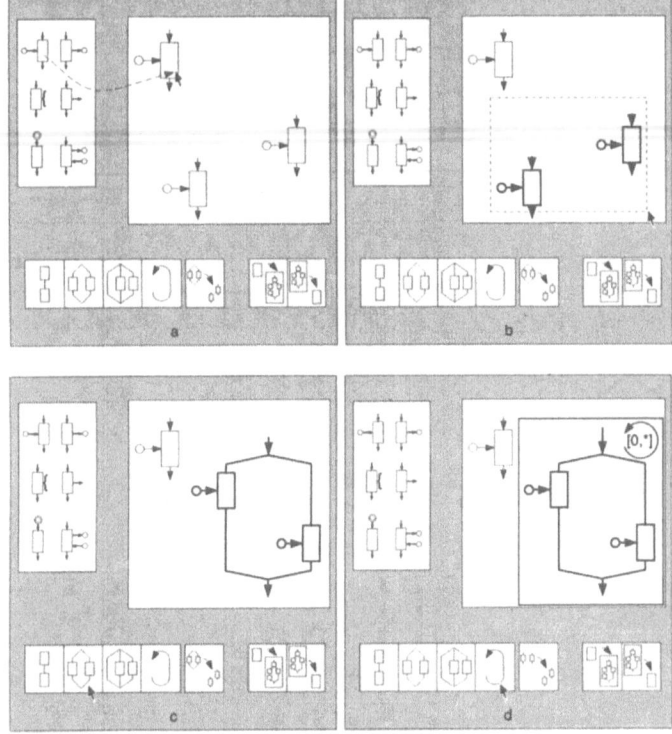

FIGURE 7.10. Interactively constructing an interaction diagram.

of the ok method in this construction area.

7.3.3   Discussion on Interactive Specifications

Interactive programming techniques can, according to Myers [11], be divided in three categories:
programming by examples (PBE), programming with examples (PWE), and visual programming (VP). In PBE, a system infers the program from input-output specifications or sample
traces of execution. In contrast, PWE systems do not infer, examples for all possible sequences
must be given. In VP systems, a program is specified in two or more dimensions using graphical
techniques. Textual languages are not considered two dimensional, because they are compiled
or interpreted in a one dimensional fashion.

The interactive specification techniques for constructing interaction diagrams should be classified as visual programming. However, the term programming suggests a rather low abstraction
level. We prefer to view interactive dialogue specifications as visual specification or visual modeling techniques.

The advantages of VP are well understood, but at the same time VP is often criticized. The most
prominent disadvantages being:

Difficulty with large programs or data: The visual representations of corresponding textual
language constructs often consume a tremendous amount of screen space. This disadvantage does not apply to the specification of interaction diagrams. Only a few objects are

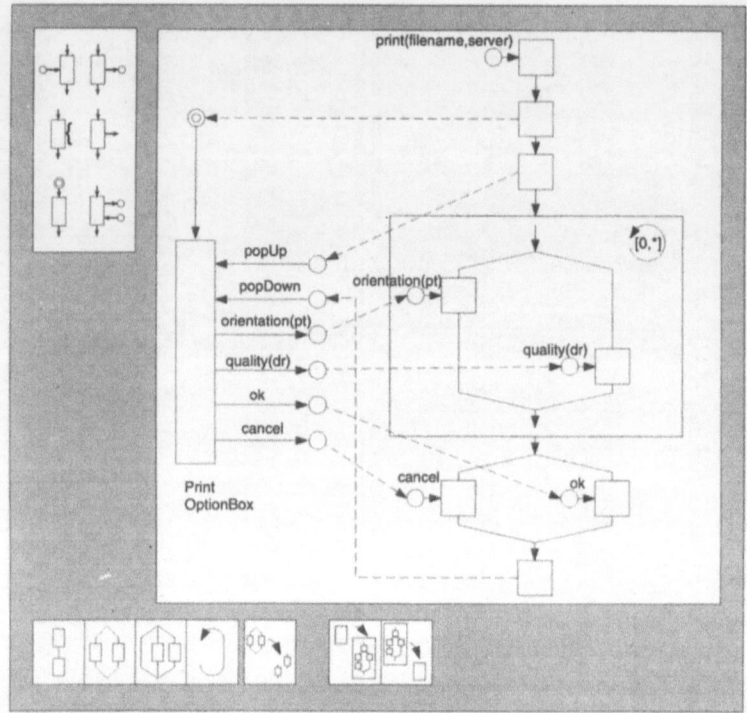

FIGURE 7.11. Linking outlets to inlets.

involved in typical interactions. Furthermore, abstraction mechanisms, such as collapsing and zooming in on sub-protocols, are provided to reduce the required screen space.

Lack of functionality: Many VP system work only in a limited domain. This is true in our case. However, the interactive specification techniques were developed for the limited domain of dialogue control specification in the first place. All conceivable dialogues can be specified with interaction diagrams.

Unstructured programs: Many VP systems promote unstructured programming practices, e.g., goto statements and global variables. This disadvantage does not apply to our model. State and behavior are encapsulated in objects, and protocols are used for message flow control purposes.

7.4 Analyzing Dialogues

In dialogue analysis we are concerned with issues like reachability, reversibility, consistency, and completeness. A formal basis is required for (automatically) proving properties of human-computer dialogues. For instance, in a command-driven interactive system, we can verify that every command is terminated with a press on the return key. However, there is little hope that dialogue analysis tools can give exact quality rankings of human-computer dialogues. For example, it is possible that a tool detects inconsistencies in dialogues, but the dialogue designer might have designed these dialogues on purpose because they increase the flexibility and they may not be perceived as inconsistencies by the end-user. Therefore, analysis tools should be used to pinpoint weak spots in a dialogue design to be interpreted by the dialogue designer.

The ability to automatically analyze the dialogue is important in DIGIS to provide for context-sensitive help. In DIGIS, the application is modeled in an object-oriented way, that is, the application appears to the UI as a collection of objects, although the application need not necessarily be implemented in an object-oriented way. The only way to achieve a goal in the application is to execute a task. The most elementary tasks are the basic tasks, defined in terms of operations on application objects. The execution of a basic task results in the achievement of an elementary goal. Higher level tasks are crafted on top of lower level tasks, and ultimately basic tasks. Given a sequence of low level or basic tasks, it is possible to infer the set of higher level tasks and the associated higher level goals the end-user is currently trying to achieve. This set can be presented in some way to the end-user in order to give context-sensitive help. However, just presenting this set to the end-user is not sufficient. Besides telling the end-user *which* higher level goals he is trying to achieve, the end-user must be informed of *how* to achieve these goals. This requires an analysis of the human-computer dialogues. In particular, the interaction sequences resulting in the activation of lower level tasks, required to complete a higher level task, must be deduced.

In our dialogue model, the dialogue is distributed over a number of concurrent objects. The structure of the dialogue is formally described in the (sub-)protocols and in the primitive methods of these dialogue objects. Dialogue objects are the intermediaries between application and presentation objects. For analysis purposes, we assume that the objects at the application and presentation level are described by their external behavior in the form of input-output protocols. This makes it possible to differentiate between dialogue objects, described by their internal and external behavior, and application and presentation objects which are purely defined by their external behavior.

Analyzing dialogues in a distributed concurrent environment is much harder than in a deterministic environment. However, the dialogue model has several features that help to manage the complexity. First of all, the protocols synchronize the messages received from other objects. Secondly, the dialogue model is strongly typed, that is, we know the behavior of the objects we are communicating with. Thirdly, communication links are explicitly established in input-output protocol linkages.

The problem of finding all interaction sequences that can lead to the activation of tasks for giving context-sensitive help can be reformulated as follows. Given a method in some dialogue object, find all interaction sequences with objects at the presentation level that result in the invocation of this method. Finding all interaction sequences means that every possible alternative must be statically investigated. The guards in protocols and primitive methods are ignored in a statical analysis, i.e., they are assumed to evaluate to true. Consider, for example, the following input protocol:

a ; (guard$_1$:b + guard$_2$:c) ; d

The sequences that lead to the activation of method d can be written as:

a;b;d + a;c;d

That is, a regular expression is rewritten in the form:

sub-expr$_1$ + ... + sub-expr$_n$

using the rewrite rules:

$$p ; (q + r) = p;q + p;r$$
$$(q + r) ; s = q;s + r;s$$
$$(p + q)* = (p*q*)*$$

Regular expressions in this form denote the possible traces that lead to the activation of a method. The next step is to recursively rewrite a trace in terms of interaction sequences with other objects, until all traces are expressed in terms of interactions with presentation objects. Finding the traces is certainly not a straightforward process, but the lack of space does not permit us to elaborate on this.

7.5   Related Work

Dialogue notations come in many forms, and each one has its strengths and its weaknesses. Some dialogue notations are diagrammatically oriented, such as State Transition Networks (STN), others are more textually oriented, such as grammars, production systems, and process algebras. Diagrammatic notations are often used for modeling and design purposes. Dialogue specifications based on a formal (textual) model are eligible for analysis purposes. Properties of dialogue notations to be assessed include items as descriptive power, the possibility to analyze dialogues, concurrency, modularization, sequencing, and interleaving.

Many dialogue notations have their origins in internally controlled command-driven systems. The application is in control, and the end-user must stick to the interaction patterns provided by the application. In particular, grammars, such as BNF, and STNs have been used to describe the human-computer dialogue in such applications. With the advent of graphical DM user interfaces, the control has shifted from the application to the end-user. In these systems, the end-user has many degrees of freedom and can be engaged in multiple sub-dialogues simultaneously. Because grammars and STNs are not really suitable for describing such interleaved dialogues, the ability to adequately specify the human-computer dialogues with these notations is greatly reduced. Consequently, grammars and STNs have been augmented to deal with the stronger demands on dialogues. Grammars, for instance, have been extended with permutation constructs to allow interleaving [12]. Augmented Transition Networks (ATN) and Recursive Transition Networks (RTN) have been developed to increase the descriptive power of STNs. However, they still suffer from state explosion when describing interleaved behavior. This problem is addressed in Generative Transition Networks (GTN) [2]. GTNs stresses on the regularity in dialogues, the arcs required for implementing interleaved dialogues are generated from a higher level description. Another successful approach for taming the state explosions are statecharts [7]. Statecharts are composed of hierarchies of STNs which may run in parallel.

Interactive systems can be divided in three components: the presentation, the dialogue, and the application component [6]. This monolithic approach to developing interactive systems has been recently abandoned in favor of multi-agent architectures. Multi-agent architectures offer better support in modularization and multi-threaded dialogues involving multiple interaction devices and multiple users. In multi-agent architectures, an interactive system is structured as a collection of cooperating agents, usually organized as an hierarchy. Each agent maintains the local interaction state. Typical examples of multi-agent architectures are PAC [3] and MVC [10]. The dialogue model described in this paper can be used for modeling and analyzing interactive systems based on a multi-agent architecture. The external and internal behavior of an agent or object is formally described with protocols using an augmented regular expression notation. A similar approach has been taken by Jacob [9], where each object has an associated STN for describing dialogues at the object level. Ordinary regular expressions have the same descriptive power as STNs. However, regular expressions are more compact and offer higher level abstractions such as repetition and selection which must be explicitly specified with states and arcs in STNs. Note that both STNs and regular expressions can be augmented to enhance the descriptive power and to support interleaving.

A production system is another dialogue formalism that is frequently used in object-oriented contexts [8]. A production system consists of a collection of production rules of the form: if *condition* then *action*. A rule is said to fire when a condition is satisfied, the associated actions of a rule are then executed. Production systems are good at describing interleaved behavior, but they perform poorly at sequencing.

A dialogue notation that deals equally well with sequencing and interleaving is the process algebra eventCSP [1]. A subset of CSP (Communicating Sequential Processes) is used in eventCSP to describe concurrent and sequential dialogues. The formal basis of CSP and the readability of eventCSP dialogue descriptions provide a strong basis for modeling and analyzing dialogues. However, the lack of modularization constructs for encapsulating local state, such as objects, makes eventCSP less suitable for modeling large distributed interactive systems.

7.6   Discussion

We have discussed a new human-computer dialogue model. It is both a formal and an executable model, and therefore can be used for modeling, analyzing, and implementing human-computer dialogues in an event-driven, distributed environment. We have developed a general purpose concurrent object-oriented language based on the ideas described in this paper. This language, called Talktalk, is superposed on Smalltalk, and is used as the implementation language for the graphical UI design environment DIGIS which is a highly interactive system itself. The implementation of DIGIS gave us the opportunity to validate the effectiveness of the dialogue model concepts.

Does the dialogue notation satisfy all DIGIS requirements? Yes, it fulfills the hard and easy to verify requirements like the suitability for modeling and analyzing dialogues in distributed environments, the ability to construct dialogues with graphical DM techniques, etc. But there is still work to do in proving that the dialogue notation is usable by UI designers who do not necessarily have substantial programming experience. All we can say at this moment is that the few concepts in the model are easy to grasp. After all, agents are very much like persons, they react to events and request other persons to carry out some activity. On the other hand, the behavior of an agent must be unambiguously specified in detail, which is certainly not a straightforward task.

If we ignore concurrency for a moment, most dialogue notations have the same descriptive power. It is the ease of specification, the expressive power, that counts. We believe that object-orientedness in combination with graphical DM techniques provides the required expressiveness for modeling and analyzing end-user driven human-computer dialogues.

7.7   References

[1]   Heather Alexander. Structuring dialogues using csp. In Michael Harrison and Harold Thimbleby, editors, *Formal Methods in Human-Computer Interaction*, number 2 in Cambridge Series on Human-Computer Interaction, chapter 9, pages 273–295. Cambridge

University Press, Cambridge, England, 1990.

[2] Gilbert Cockton. Designing abstractions for communication control. In Michael Harrison and Harold Thimbleby, editors, *Formal Methods in Human-Computer Interaction*, number 2 in Cambridge Series on Human-Computer Interaction, chapter 8, pages 233–271. Cambridge University Press, Cambridge, England, 1990.

[3] Joëlle Coutaz. PAC; an implementation model for dialog design. In *Proceedings Interact*, pages 431–436, Amsterdam, the Netherlands, 1987. North Holland.

[4] Hans de Bruin and Peter Bouwman. The software architecture of DIGIS. In Gavriel Salvendy and Michael J. Smith, editors, *Advances in Human Factors/Ergonomics*, volume 19B, pages 244–249, Amsterdam, the Netherlands, August 8–13, 1993. Proceedings of the Fifth International Conference on Human-Computer Interaction (HCI '93), Orlando, Florida, Elsevier.

[5] Hans de Bruin, Peter Bouwman, and Jan van den Bos. DIGIS; a graphical user interface design environment for non-programmers. In Roger Hubbold and Robert Juan, editors, *Computer Graphics Forum, Conference Issue*, volume 12–3, pages 13–24, Oxford, England, June 6–10, 1993. Proceedings Eurographics '93, Barcelona, Spain, NCC Blackwell.

[6] Mark Green. Report on dialogue specification tools. In G. Pfaff and P. J. W. ten Hagen, editors, *User Interface Management Systems*, pages 9–20. Springer-Verlag, Berlin, Germany, 1985.

[7] David Harel. Statecharts; a visual formalism for complex systems. *Science of Computer Programming*, 8:231–274, 1987.

[8] Ralph D. Hill. Event response systems; a technique for specifying multi-threaded dialogues. In *Proceedings SIGCHI+GI'87: Human Factors in Computing Systems*, pages 241–248. ACM, April 5–9 1987.

[9] Robert J. K. Jacob. A specification language for direct manipulation user interfaces. *ACM-TOG (Transactions on Graphics)*, 5(4):283–317, October 1986.

[10] Glenn E. Krasner and Stephen T. Pope. A cookbook for using the model-view-controller user interface paradigm in Smalltalk-80. *Journal of Object-Oriented Programming*, 1(3):26–49, August 1988.

[11] Brad A. Myers. *Creating User Interfaces by Demonstration*, volume 22 of *Perspectives in Computing*. Academic Press, Boston, Massachusetts, 1988.

[12] Jan van den Bos. Abstract interaction tools; a language for user interface management systems. *ACM-TOPLAS (Transactions on Programming Languages and Systems)*, 10(2):215–247, April 1988.

[13] Jan van den Bos and Chris Laffra. Project DIGIS; building interactive applications by direct manipulation. *Computer Graphics Forum*, 9(3):181–193, September 1990.

[14] Jan van den Bos and Chris Laffra. Procol; a concurrent object language with protocols, delegation and persistence. *Acta Informatica*, 28:511–538, September 1991.

8   Bridging the Gap from Conceptual Design to Software Design

W. David Hurley

ABSTRACT

Designers need a bridge across the gap from conceptual design of the interactive system they want to build to software design of the system that will be built. A suitable framework for such a bridge would be a representation scheme that unifies design information from disparate conceptual spaces and supports automated determination of software design. This paper presents a representation scheme that explicitly represents conceptual designs of user interface, functional core, and the internal dialogue between them. In particular, it makes precise distinctions among a wide variety of possible concept structures. These distinctions have direct implications for software design. A detailed example demonstrates an automated capability to deduce aspects of software design, including correspondence and control requirements, software construction, and communication mechanisms.

8.1. Introduction

Designers need a bridge across the gap from conceptual design of the interactive system they want to build to software design of the system that will be built. The bridge should support sharing design information among designers in different roles [1]. It should also help designers rapidly determine the impact on software design of changes to the conceptual designs of the user interface and functional core, from minor refinements to complete reconceptualizations, and the determination must be automated [2].

A suitable framework for such a bridge would be a representation scheme that unifies design information from disparate conceptual spaces. To build this framework, two key issues must be addressed: (1) identifying the design information to be represented, and (2) defining a scheme for representing the information.

So far, little progress has been made in identifying the relevant design information. Several researchers have pointed out that in order to make better decisions, designers need clear and precise information about the abstract (independent of software design) structure of the internal dialogue between the interactive human-computer dialogue subsystem, or user interface, and the non-interactive computational subsystem, or functional core [3, 4, 5]. Coutaz and Balbo [6] have identified three structural characteristics that impact software design: (1) the nature of the information exchanged between the user interface and functional core — either elementary or structured; (2) correspondence — the direction of information flow between objects in the user interface and functional core required for maintaining related values, such as a temperature reading in the functional core and the position of a graphical pointer in a visual gauge; and (3) connectivity — the cardinality of the relationships between functional core objects and their presentation objects. Their results suggest three areas for further work: (1) distinguishing the ways information could be structured, (2) extending correspondence to include the kinds of information involved, and (3) refining connectivity to remove ambiguous interpretations.

Considerable progress has been made in defining schemes for representing design information. Software engineering provides abstract models, such as entity-relationship models and object models [7]. User interface software technology provides techniques based on software engineering models or specialized models [3, 8]. An area of active research is agent models as a unifying paradigm from user interface design to software implementation, e.g., [9, 10]. One knowledge-based scheme represents the conceptual designs of a functional core and a user interface, and provides tools for producing conceptual design specifications and applying rules to analyze them [11]. This work provided a platform for developing the results introduced in this paper.

A common deficiency of previous work is an inadequate treatment of "structure" — in both conceptual design and software design. For software design, coarse treatments of construction, e.g. [12, 13], distinguish two kinds of composition based on whether the states of parts objects are encapsulated within the composite object (hierarchical composition) or are accessible by another object (structural composition). More refined treatments, e.g. [14], distinguish four kinds of hierarchical composition: exclusive or shared, based on whether an object is part of only one composite object; and dependent or independent, based on whether the existence of the component object depends on the existence of the composite object.

For conceptual design, more abstract relationships are needed to describe concept structures. Some recent work uses entity-relationship models. Chudziak et al. [15] use a fixed set of relationships to distinguish variations of structure, but they distinguish relationships by their names, which leads to ambiguity. Dijkstra [16] formalizes structuring rules, but overly restricts the nature of structured elements; for example, all structured elements must contain components, which precludes modeling an object whose entire contents can be removed.

The results introduced here extend previous results three major ways. First, the identified design information augments and elaborates upon the characteristics presented by Coutaz and Balbo. Second, the treatment of relationships accommodates a wider variety of structures for both conceptual design and software design. Third, new rules codify knowledge for analyzing conceptual designs to deduce aspects of software design.

8.2. An Illustrative Example

This section introduces an example that will illustrate the results presented in this paper. The example involves the PAC method for conceptual design of an interactive system [17]. This method was selected because it is gaining wide acceptance and it can be described briefly, as follows: The abstract model in PAC structures an interactive system into three parts: Presentation, which corresponds to the user interface; Abstraction, which corresponds to the functional core; and Control, which corresponds to the internal dialogue. The PAC model supports decomposition into object-triads similar to the model-view-controller triads in Smalltalk but at the conceptual level. A presentation object (p-object) handles input and output as perceived by the user, an abstraction object (a-object) handles some media-invariant aspect of the system functionality, and a control object (c-object) maintains the mapping and consistency between the p- and a- objects.

An example borrowed from [17] and illustrated in Figure 1 applies PAC to a pie-chart presentation. P1 provides for output, a circular shape and a color for each piece of the pie, and for input, mouse actions that the user performs to change the size of the pieces. A1 is comprised of an integer value within the range of two integer limits. C1 maintains consistency between A1 and P1. For instance, if the user modifies the size of a piece, C1 initiates the update of the integer value. If some other object, say in the functional core, modifies the value in the A1, the control object takes care of adjusting the size of the pieces.

One of the advantages of the PAC model is its support for designing compound objects from elementary ones. Figure 2 illustrates a super pie chart, which presents an integer value not only as the size of a slice of pie but also as an integer string, in P2. P12 is made up of P1 and P2. C12 keeps C1 and C2 consistent: when C12 receives information from one, it notifies the other. A12 contains information that is contained in A1 and A2.

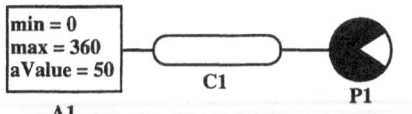

FIGURE 8.1. Pie chart [adapted from Coutaz 87]

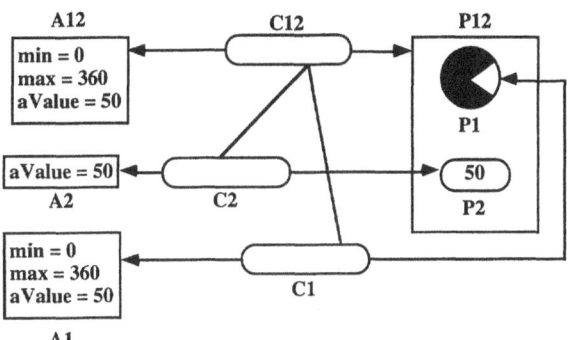

FIGURE 8.2. Super pie chart [adapted from Coutaz 87]

The conceptual design shown in Figure 2 suggests that the software construction mechanisms for P12, C12, and A12 would be different, but the differences are unclear. The purpose of this example is not to show that formalized representations are more precise than informal diagrams or that the process of formalizing promotes greater clarity of thought — we all know that. Rather, the purpose is to show how the results presented in this paper bring these advantages to the domain of interactive systems.

Consider the following interpretation of Figure 2: C1 and C2 access P1 and P2, respectively; therefore, P1 and P2 would not be encapsulated within P12, which rules out hierarchical composition. P12 does not access P1 and P2, which rules out structural composition also. So, what would be the construction mechanism for P12? Also, only C12 accesses C1 and C2; could they be encapsulated within C12? Finally, A12 has no explicit relationships with A1 or A2. Would A12 share or duplicate the information in A1 and A2?

Other interpretations of Figure 2 lead to similar questions, which must be answered consistently to support software design. We need a more precise specification of the conceptual design, one that leads to clear and precise implications about software construction, e.g., using the results to be presented in this paper. Section 3 gives an overview of the representation scheme. Section 4 discusses what conceptual design information is specified. Section 5 describes the design knowledge for analyzing specified information. Section 6 applies these results to the super pie chart. Section 7 states conclusions.

8.3. Representation Scheme

The representation scheme extends the entity-relationship model with pre-defined abstractions for modeling the elements of an interactive system and the relationships among them, provides structuring rules that prescribe how the abstractions can be combined in a model, and includes a knowledge representation language for expressing design information in terms of the abstractions. Detailed discussion of the original scheme is found in [11]. Section 4 will present the extended treatment of relationships. The paragraphs below briefly summarize the other aspects.

The two fundamental structural abstractions are concept — a thing or situation in a domain of discourse, and relationship — a directed connection or association involving concepts. Kinds of concepts include the following system-theoretic abstractions: An element is a concept capable of behaviors that may change its traits or qualities. A system is an element that has a boundary, components (a set of elements), and a structure over the components. An open system is a system in which exchanges of material, information, or energy take place across the boundary between the open system and its environment.

Structural abstractions (concepts and relationships) are represented as types in a term subsumption representation (TSR). A type is a structured-object representation similar to a frame, but unlike frame systems, the TSR can determine automatically whether one type (or term) subsumes (is more general than) another. The TSR provides several kinds of properties (like slots) and facets; supports single, strict inheritance of structural characteristics; and automatically maintains a correct type structure through subsumption, inheritance, and consistency checks. An important aspect of the TSR is that it uses names of types only for the convenience of humans; it distinguishes types by the semantics of their properties.

8.4. Conceptual Design Information

Conceptual design specifications for interactive systems are produced by generating subtypes of existing concept types (type Concept and its descendents) to represent systems and components, and using pre-defined relationship types to describe their structure. For example, an interactive system might be modeled as a descendent of type OpenSystem with three components: a user interface, an internal dialogue, and a functional core; each component would be a descendent of type OpenSystem. A relationship type would be selected that precisely expresses the intended semantics of "components." The following discussion examines three categories of information: construction, correspondence, and connectivity.

14.4.1. Distinguishing Kinds of Structure

Relationship types describe those associations or connections among concepts that have implications for software design. Table 1 summarizes selected relationship types and their properties. It gives a semantic interpretation for each property, values each property can be assigned, and what aspects of a situation the values distinguish. For example, every relationship type has properties sourceTypes and targetTypes to specify the participating source and target types, respectively; whether the participants are types or instances of types; and the range of cardinality for each participant.

Presentation relationships (type Presentation and its descendents) account for the notion that features of a user interface reflect features of a functional core. Interaction relationships inherently imply run-time interaction between related elements. ExistencePragmatics relationships account for a pragmatic intention to have elements created or destroyed together.

Of particular interest in this work, meronymic inclusion relationships extend meronymic relations defined in cognitive science to explain ordinary English-speaking use of the phrases "part of" and "has part" [18]. Table 2 shows distinguishing values of properties for selected whole-part relationships. Whole-part relationships with a targetTypes cardinality of 1:1 describe a situation in which the whole has exactly one part (of the participating type). Whole-part relationships with a targetTypes cardinality of 1:many describe a whole that has at least one part. These total relationships are interpreted to mean that removing the last part destroys the whole.

TABLE 8.1. Selected relationship types and properties

Type	Property	Interpretation	Possible Values	Situations Distinguished
Relationships	sourceTypes	identifies participating source types	a set of concept types	types or instances; the range of cardinality
	targetTypes	identifies participating target types	a set of concept types	types or instances, and the range of cardinality
Presentation Relationships	medium	presentation involves a physical medium	text, graphics, animation, image, video, sound	physical medium
	surrogacy	source is surrogate of (stands for) the target	---	---
Interaction Relationships	interaction	flow of information, material, or energy from source to target	prompting	source requests something from the target
			communication	source transfers information to the target
			conveyance	source transfers material to the target
			transmission	source transfers energy to the target
			access	source has access to the target or to information about it
	reachability	a kind of access: ability of the source to change traits of the target	direct, indirect	whether changes are direct results or side effects
	effect	a kind of access: ability of the source to create or destroy the target	creation, destruction	the effect
	observability	a kind of access: availability to the source of information about traits of the target	direct, indirect	whether observations are results of retrieval operations or automatic receipts of information
Existence-Pragmatics Relationships	existence-Effect	source and target are created and destroyed together	---	cardinality determines propagation of effect
Inclusion Relationships	inclusion	generic notion of inclusion	spatial, meronymic	kind of inclusion
	functional	organization of parts supports functional role of the whole	yes, no	whether condition holds
	separable	parts removable without changing the identity of the source	yes, no	whether condition holds

TABLE 8.2. Selected whole-part relationships

Functional	Separable	sourceTypes Cardinality	targetTypes Cardinality	Relationship Name
no	yes	0 : 1	0 : many	Collection-Members
no	yes	0 : 1	1 : 1	InherentCollection-Member
yes	no	0 : 1	1 : many	InherentIntegralElement-Components
yes	no	1 : 1	1 : many	InherentIntegralElement-InherentComponents
yes	no	0 : 1	1 : 1	InherentIntegralElement-Feature
yes	yes	0 : 1	0 : many	IntegralElement-Components
yes	yes	1 : 1	0 : many	IntegralElement-InherentComponents

Whole-part relationships with a sourceTypes cardinality of 1:1 or 1:many are onto relationships. They require each part to belong to a whole. In contrast, a sourceTypes cardinality of 0:1 or 0:many indicates that a part can exist without a whole.

The Boolean-valued property separable distinguishes whether parts can be removed without changing the identity of the source (here, the whole). Although not obvious from Table 2, the value of this property is independent of cardinality. The Boolean-valued property functional distinguishes whether the organization of the parts supports the functional role of the whole. In Table 2 the two collection relationships are nonfunctional.

14.4.2. Deducing Correspondence Requirements

The conceptual design information needed to deduce software design requirements for maintaining related information includes the relationship properties medium, surrogacy, separable, sourceTypes and targetTypes (see Table 1), and temporal information in element types. Some temporal information pertains only to elements themselves: whether the existence of an element is permanent (cannot be destroyed at run time) or temporary (can be destroyed at run time), whether an element is persistent (existence preserved between activations of a system), and whether each attribute (a property whose value may differ among instances of a type; also called an instance property) is dynamic (value changeable at run time) or static (value unchangeable at run time).

Element types also contain three items of information that characterize temporal aspects of their participation in a relationship. First, a property describing a relationship from A to B is static, in the direction from A to B, if B is to be the same element while the relationship is in effect; otherwise it is dynamic. Second, the property lists any attributes involved in the relationship. For instance, if file icons represent files and their names, then there is a presentation relationship from FileIcon to File that involves the file attribute name. The property lists the attribute name. Third, the property describes the involvement of an attribute in a relationship: it is static if the attribute value is inherently static, dynamic if the attribute value is inherently dynamic and is changeable while the relationship is in effect, and nondynamic if the attribute is inherently dynamic but is unchangeable while the relationship is in effect.

14.4.3. Deducing Connectivity

A conceptual design specification can be analyzed mechanistically to determine the connectivity between user interface and functional core objects. For example, suppose that element types File, MenuItem, and FileIcon, along with relationship type Visualization, which has sourceTypes to targetTypes cardinalities of 0:1 to 1:1, are used to specify that a file can be represented by a file icon and by a selectable item in a menu. In the specification, the relationship Visualization would be used to describe the connection from FileIcon to File and from MenuItem to File. The computed connectivity from functional core to user interface would be 1-to-n.

However, a conceptual design specification makes explicit distinctions that connectivity alone cannot make. In the above example, it is clear that the connectivity of 1-to-n results from multiple presentations (menu item and file icon) of a single functional-core object (a file) and not from a decomposition of a single functional-core object into multiple presentation objects. This distinction has implications for software design (see [6]).

8.5. Automated Analysis

Design knowledge is codified as rules for analyzing a conceptual design specification to deduce aspects of software design. For clarity, a few example rules are given below in prose.

A correspondence requirement is a requirement to maintain related information. The following rule deduces a requirement for the internal dialogue to maintain mappings from user interface objects to functional core objects:

IF an element in the user interface has a relationship to an element in the functional core
    AND the relationship is static to an element whose existence is permanent
    AND the relationship involves a (physical) medium
    AND the existence of the element in the user interface is temporary
THEN the internal dialogue must store and update a dynamic set of static mappings

In this rule, the individual mappings between elements are static, but the sets of mappings are dynamic because individual mappings could be added or deleted at run time.

Control is a systems science notion based on reachability and observability (Table 1). Control requirements are requirements to compensate for a lack of control in certain situations. The following rule describes one such situation:

IF the internal dialogue must store and update the value of an attribute of an element in the functional core
    AND either the functional core or the environment has reachability to that attribute
THEN the internal dialogue requires indirect observability of that attribute.

Indirect observability is automatic receipt of information (either notification the value changed or receipt of the new value).

Visibility is reference by one element to an external resource of another [12]. It is deduced from the presence of an access relationship (property interaction has value access) between elements. Because relationships are directed, the analysis can deduce both one-way and two-way visibility (it is not necessarily symmetric). Visibility is used to distinguish two kinds of whole-part inclusion. The first kind, which corresponds to hierarchical composition, is encapsulated whole-part inclusion:

IF an element A has a relationship to an element B
    AND the relationship involves inclusion
    AND the relationship is functional
    AND any element that has visibility to element B is element A or a component of A
THEN element B can be an encapsulated component of element A.

The second kind is unencapsulated whole-part inclusion:

IF an element A has a relationship to an element B
    AND the relationship involves inclusion
    AND the relationship is functional
    AND some element, other than A or a component of A, has visibility to element B
THEN element B must be an unencapsulated component of A.

Of course a software designer could encapsulate B by converting accesses to B to accesses to A.

Independent and dependent composition are deduced from temporal properties of elements and properties of relationships that imply existence dependency — the cardinalities of the sourceTypes and targetTypes properties, the value of the property separable (if any), and the presence or absence of the properties existenceEffect and surrogacy. Shared and exclusive composition are deduced by a system-wide examination of whole-part relationships. For brevity, example rules are omitted.

8.6. Returning to the Illustrative Example

This section develops a conceptual design specification for the PAC example. For brevity, the design is expressed in sequentially-numbered prose statements, with one figure that shows a tool presentation. First, some pragmatic assumptions about PAC triplets:

P a visual representation of A.   [1]

P and C are created and destroyed together (exist only in pairs).   [2]
C exists only for (i.e., to support the presentation of) its associated A.   [3]
The statements refer to types but are interpreted as statements about instances of types; for example, statement 1 is read as "Instances of type P are visual representations of instances of..."

Also for brevity, statements about certain details are omitted, such as the generation of subtypes and the formation of triplets P1-C1-A1, P2-C2-A2, and P12-A12-C12, which are structurally similar to the P-A-C triplet (statements 1-3); and the values of the existence properties (permanent for types A1 and A2; temporary for all other types).

A1 has three attributes: max and min, which are static, and aValue, which is dynamic.   [4]
A2 has one attribute: aValue, which is dynamic.   [5]
A12 is nonfunctional (see Table 1) composite of exactly one A1 and exactly one A2.   [6]
The existence of A12 is contingent on the existence of C12.   [7]
P1 has one attribute: angularExtent, which is dynamic.   [8]
P1 presents a visualization of the aValue attribute of A1.   [9]
P2 has one attribute: displayValue, which is dynamic.   [10]
P2 presents a natural visual representation of the aValue attribute of A2.   [11]
P12 is a functional composite of exactly one P1 and exactly one P2.   [12]
PAC_Example-FunctionalCore can modify the aValue attributes of any A1 or any A2.   [13]
PAC_Example-FunctionalCore is a functional composite of zero or more A12.   [14]
PAC_Example-UserInterface is a functional composite of zero or more P12.   [15]
C1 gets automatic receipt of information about the dynamic attributes in P1 and A1.   [16]
C1 can modify the values of the dynamic attributes in P1 and A1.   [17]
C2 gets automatic receipt of information about the dynamic attributes in P2 and A2.   [18]
C2 can modify the values of the dynamic attributes in P2 and A2.   [19]
C12 is a functional composite of exactly one C1 and exactly one C2.   [20]
C12 constrains the aValue attributes in A1 and in A2.   [21]
PAC_Example-InternalDialogue is a functional composite of zero or more C12-objects   [22]

The tools are used to generate the types for the p-, c-, and a- objects, and using only predefined relationships, to express the information in statements 1 through 22. Figure 3 shows a graphical view of P12, which looks much like an entity-relationship diagram. The reader can find relationships that account for most of the statements in this example.

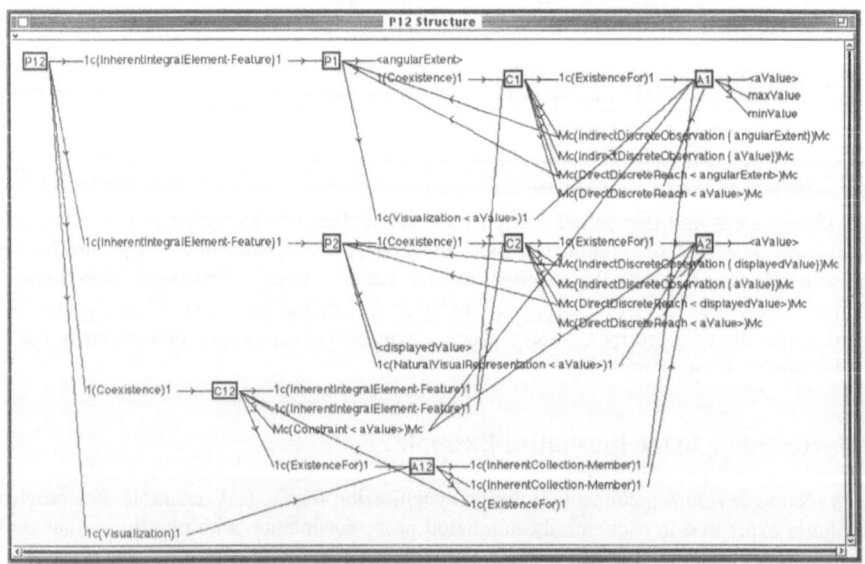

FIGURE 8.3. Graphical view of P12 structure

When invoked to analyze this conceptual design specification, the Analyzer tool generates a multi-part report; Table 3 shows excerpts. Part 1 states information about the proposed user

TABLE 8.3. Results of automated analysis

Analysis of PAC_Example

1 User Interface Design:
 The user interface has the following interaction styles:
   'direct manipulation'
 The user interface has surrogates representing the following functional core information:
   P1 -> A1: aValue.
   P12 -> A12.
   P2 -> A2: aValue.

2. Internal Dialogue — Correspondence Requirements:
 The internal dialogue must store & update the following dynamic sets of static mappings from temporary user interface components to permanent functional core components:
   P1 -> A1
   P2 -> A2
 The internal dialogue must store & update the following dynamic sets of static mappings (source-to-target existence dependency):
   P12 -> A12
 The internal dialogue must maintain (temporarily or permanently store and update) the following attributes:
   P1 -> A1: aValue.
   P2 -> A2: aValue.

3. Control Requirements:
 The internal dialogue must maintain (store & update) but can never control the following functional core attributes:
   A1: aValue.
   A2: aValue.

4. Detailed Design:
 The following modifications to the functional core can be implemented with simple messages:
   C1 -> A1: aValue.
   C2 -> A2: aValue.
 The following automatic receipts of information from the functional core can be implemented with discrete active mechanisms:
   C1 -> A1: aValue.
   C2 -> A2: aValue.
 For the user interface, the following lists composite types and their encapsulated components:
   PAC_Example-UserInterface -> P12.
 For the internal dialogue, the following lists composite types and their encapsulated components:
   C12 -> C2.
   C12 -> C1.
   PAC_Example-InternalDialogue -> C12.
 For the functional core, the following lists composite types and their encapsulated components:
   PAC_Example-FunctionalCore -> A12.
 For the user interface, the following lists composite types and their un encapsulated components:
   P12 -> P2.
   P12 -> P1.
 For the functional core, the following lists composite types and their unencapsulated components:
   A12 -> A2.
   A12 -> A1.

interface. Part 2 states correspondence requirements for the internal dialogue; it must maintain two kinds of dynamic sets of static mappings, and it must store and update two attributes (statements 9 and 11). Part 3 states deduced control requirements; the internal dialogue must maintain two functional core attributes it cannot control (it lacks exclusive reach access — statement 13).

Part 4 of Table 3 states deduced aspects of detailed design. The software construction mechanism for P12 should be unencapsulated whole-part inclusion. This deduction is expected because P12 cannot encapsulate its components (statements 17 and 19). C12 can encapsulate C1 and C2. This deduction is valid at the level of software design. Although implementing indirect observability (statements 16 and 18) requires awareness of C1 and C2 (to send them information), the awareness could be at the system level rather than at the programmer level if the run-time connections between objects are established implicitly rather than programmed (e.g., with Smalltalk's dependency mechanism).

The conceptual design explicitly specifies that A12 is a collection (nonfunctional composite) of two components: one A1 and one A2. Thus the attribute aValue appears twice in A12. This approach reflects the PAC intention of facilitating the construction of compound objects. Because C12 ensures their consistency (statement 21), no coding changes to A1 or A2 are required. Table 3, Part 4 concludes that the software construction mechanism for A12 should be unencapsulated whole-part inclusion, which is expected (statements 17 and 19).

8.7. Conclusions

The representation scheme provides a suitable framework for a bridge from conceptual design to software design. It unifies design information in disparate conceptual spaces and supports an automated capability for deducing aspects of software design. The design information expressible in this scheme makes precise distinctions among a wide variety of possible concept structures, elaborates the notion of correspondence, and makes distinctions that connectivity cannot make. The analysis capability directly supports design independence: it allows user interface and functional core designers to focus on their conceptual designs, ignoring the impact of their decisions on software design, which is handled automatically.

We are optimistic that the results of this work can evolve into the basis for a full-blown development environment for interactive systems. Work is progressing in three directions. First, we are formalizing a design space of choices for software design; for example, it will include design architectures such as model-view-controller. Second, we are accounting for dynamics, which involves adding abstractions (for behavior, control, and communication) and codifying knowledge about the propagation of operations over relationships. Third, we are extending the tools with front ends that support designer role-oriented specification techniques, such as UAN [19].

8.8. References

[1] G. Cockton. Critical issues: conceptual design. In J. Larson and C. Unger, editors, Engineering for Human-Computer Interaction: Proceedings of the IFIP TC2\WG2.7 Working Conference on Engineering for Human-Computer Interaction, IFIP Transactions A-18, pages 405-410. Elsevier Science Publishers, 1992.

[2] J. Nielsen. Iterative user-interface design. IEEE Computer, 26(11):32-41, 1993.

[3] L. Bass and J. Coutaz. Developing Software for the User Interface. The SEI Series in Software Engineering. Addison-Wesley, 1991.

[4] H. R. Hartson and D. Hix. Human-computer interface development: concepts and systems for its management. ACM Computing Surveys, 21(1):5-92, 1989.

[5] W. M. Newman and E. A. Edmonds. The Separable User Interface: a Conversation. In E.A. Edmonds, editor, The Separable User Interface, Computer and People Series, part 7, pages 347-355. Academic Press, 1992.

[6] J. Coutaz and S. Balbo. Applications: adimension space for user interface management

systems. In S.P. Robertson, G.M. Olson, and J.S. Olson, editors, CHI'91 Conference, Reaching Through Technology. ACM Press, 1991.

[7]   A. M. Davis. Software Requirements: Analysis and Specification. Prentice-Hall, 1990.

[8]   M. Harrison and H. Thimbleby, editors. Formal Methods in Human-Computer Interaction. Cambridge Series on Human-Computer Interaction. Cambridge University Press, 1990.

[9]   L. Bass, G. Cockton, and C. Unger. IFIP Working Group 2.7 user interface engineering: areference model for interactive system construction. In J. Larson and C. Unger, editors, Engineering for Human-Computer Interaction: Proceedings of the IFIP TC2\WG2.7 Working Conference on Engineering for Human-Computer Interaction, IFIP Transactions A-18, pages 1-11. Elsevier Science Publishers, 1992..

[10] R. K. Ege and C. Stary. Designing maintainable reusable interfaces. IEEE Software, 9(6):24-32, 1992.

[11] W. D. Hurley. Toward an infrastructure for managing interactive software design. Journal of Computer and Software Engineering, 2(1):3-27, 1994.

[12] G. Booch. Object Oriented Design: With Applications. The Benjamin/Cummings Series in Ada and Software Engineering. Benjamin/Cummings, 1991.

[13] T. Minoura, S. Choi, and A. Srivastava. The SAOS approach to software lifecycle support. In S.K. Chang, editor, Fifth International Conference on Software Engineering and Knowledge Engineering. Knowledge Systems Institute, 1993.

[14] M. Magnan and C. Oussalah. Object evolution. In S.K. Chang, editor, Fifth International Conference on Software Engineering and Knowledge Engineering. Knowledge Systems Institute, 1993.

[15] J. Chudziak, H. Rybinski, and J. Vorbach. Towards a unifying logic formalism for semantic data models. In R. Elmasri and V. Kouramajian, editors, Twelfth International Conference on Entity-Relationship Approach. ER Institute, 1993.

[16] J. M. M. Dijkstra. On complex objects and versioning in complex environments. In R. Elmasri and V. Kouramajian, editors, Twelfth International Conference on Entity-Relationship Approach. ER Institute, 1993.

[17] J. Coutaz. PAC, an object oriented model for dialog design. In H.-J. Bullinger, B. Shackel, editors, Human-Computer Interaction — INTERACT '87. Elsevier Science Publishers, 1987.

[18] M. E. Winston, R. Chaffin, and D. Herrmann. A taxonomy of part-whole relations. Cognitive Science, 11: 417-444, 1987.

[19] H. R. Hartson, A. C. Siochi, and D. Hix. The UAN: A user-oriented representation for direct manipulation interface designs. ACM Transactions on Information Systems, 8(3):181-203, 1990.

9 A Human-Computer Collaboration Paradigm For Bridging Design Conceptualization And Implementation

Ping Luo

ABSTRACT

In this paper, we describe a human-computer collaborative environment called MIDAS that defines a new division of labor between human designers and computers. The environment leverages the strengths of both collaborative parties, while compensating for their weaknesses and smoothing the transition from higher level design abstraction to lower level design activities and implementation. The environment has the following tangible features: (a) it lets designers explicitly express their conceptual design intentions and helps them map the high-level intentions into interface implementations; (b) it lets human designers control design decisions and handles a pyramid of details for them during design; and (c) it provides flexible work and control flow for opportunistic design.

9.1 Introduction

As of today, neither humans nor computers alone can effectively handle the complexity of interface development. Like most designs that involve great amount of creativity, user interface design is an *ill-structured* problem, that is, interface design requirements are incomplete and ambiguous, with poorly defined goals. In addition, they lack of well-specified criteria for evaluating solutions, and have no definite mechanism for applying evaluation criteria [31].

Interface design is also a search process in a design space containing a huge number of alternatives. This space is defined by design decisions on, for example, the operations an application supports; the objects of interest to the application; the presentation of these objects, operations, and the parameters of the operations; choices of gestures that invoke the operations and that supply the parameters of the operations; and so on. As a high-level concern is iteratively decomposed into many lower level ones, more design issues need to be addressed and more and more design alternatives are available. Consequently, the size of design exposure increases rapidly, and the size of the design space explodes combinatorially.

Because of the ill-structured nature and complex design space involved in interface design, and because of the lack of an effective technology to tackle these problems, designers are too often exposed to a large number of irrelevant and cumbersome tasks that distract them from their design focus. In practice, the most often used interface design method is trial and error. With it, designers are constantly buried by details, and they are forced to continually validate proposed solutions, restructure design problems, and reschedule tasks to be performed. This inevitably consumes a great deal of human mental resources and thus reduces the reachable solution space and the quality of designs sought.

Current interface design tools have not been able to help designers deal effectively with ill-structured interface design problems globally, i.e., high-level design conceptualization, intermediate design refinement, low-level implementation, and transitions across different levels of design abstraction. Today's high-level design tools cannot effectively tackle ill-structured interface design because they restrain designers to high-level conceptual design activities only. These tools separate design conceptualization from implementation, implicitly imposing a top-down design approach. Also, they are *isolated* from interface construction tools and provide little transition from design conceptualization to refinement and implementation. Research has shown that the top-down design approach is inadequate for ill-structured design problem domains and that the lack of transition discourages opportunistic design [11, 12, 14, 33].

Tools that facilitate low-level design and implementation and that support paradigms of intertwined design and implementation [6, 33] do not provide an adequate balance between providing high-level design automation and giving designers extensive control over interface design. Interface builders (e.g., [24, 25]) and automatic interface generation systems (e.g., [2, 10, 13, 26, 30]) represent tools of this kind. Interface builders offer designers extensive control over certain tasks (such as defining the properties of a push button: shading, color, label, font, size, and so on) with an iterative development paradigm. However, they require designers to handle too many details (e.g., dim the presentation of an operation when the operation is not executable) even if they are routine, distracting, or sometimes irrelevant to the current design focus. Furthermore, these tools do not support high-level interface design activities; designers cannot use them address conceptual design concerns (e.g., the semantics of an operation that affects presentation, behavior, and sequencing of interface objects).

In contrast, automatic generation systems insulate designers from the details by automating *all* decision making during interface development; designers have little control over the design. However, because interface design is ill-defined, capturing sufficient knowledge to automate all the decision-making processes is impossible and, consequently, the automatic systems are not yet practical to generate high-quality interfaces for a wide range of applications.

This paper reports our effort to bridge the gap between design conceptualization and implementation by enabling designers to explicitly express their conceptual design intentions and assisting them to map their high-level design goals into implementations of functioning user interfaces. The framework developed by this research leverages the strengths and complements the weaknesses of both computer and human designers. It off-loads regular and tedious tasks to computers, meanwhile giving human designers extensive and flexible control over design decisions.

The system described in this paper, MIDAS, provides a human-computer collaborative interface development environment that defines a division of labor to let humans and computers work from their strengths in design. In this collaborative environment, the human focuses on design exploration, decision making, and design evaluation. These tasks involve experience, heuristics, and personal subjective practice where humans are superior to any automated tools. The computer focuses on providing high-level design automation (such as maintaining a task agenda, detecting interactions among design decisions, and decomposing high-level design into design refinements) and on performing low-level routine tasks. These tasks are well defined, often tedious and distracting to human designers, but can be handled better by a computer (than by unexperienced and unknowledgeable designers).

The rest of the paper is organized as follows. In the next section, we review in detail the related work that both motivates and enables our research. We then describe the framework of MIDAS and its architecture in supporting human-computer collaboration. With an example, we demonstrate some of the strengths enabled by the system that implements our framework. We briefly discuss the current status of the system, our conclusions, and our future work at the end.

9.2   Related Work

Other than the tools identified in the previous section, there are three interface development strategies: human collaboration mechanisms, model-based interactive systems, and human-computer collaborative environments. This section reviews some of the related work that inspires our research and provides us with the enabling technology to approach the problems identified in this review.

9.2.1 Human Collaboration Mechanism

Research in computer-supported cooperative work (CSCW) studies the technology of supporting human-human collaboration in computer-mediated environments. When applied to engineering domains, CSCW provides a desirable technology for design collaborations among human designers for sharing design space, both locally and remotely, and recording the decision making process in order to capture design issues, solutions, and rationale.

CSCW systems (in engineering design domains) mainly focus on one of the two phases of a (software) development cycle, early conceptual design or implementation. The conceptual design environments (e.g., gIBIS [5] and QOC [1]) provide effective mechanisms for recording and retrieving design issues, solutions, and rationales generated during design negotiation. The recorded information could be used to guide and constrain the ongoing design activities throughout the lifecycle of software development.

Current CSCW systems that support implementation (e.g., TelePICTIVE [19]) provide mechanisms for sharing the same workspace and manipulating the same design artifacts synchronously from remote sites. In contrast to CSCW high-level design systems, these tools are geared toward concrete implementation issues.

Systems such as XNetwork [28] try to bridge the above two extremes by associating issues with design artifacts. They let designers focus on specific artifacts, design issues, and negotiations. However, because of the chosen domain, after reaching design decisions, designers have to implement the designs *off-line*.

MIDAS differs from these systems in the following ways:

- *It supports interface design from conceptualization to implementation.* With it, designers can initiate design tasks by explicitly expressing conceptual design issues and, with the help of MIDAS, smoothly map the conceptualization into interface implementations.

- *It provides a flexible work flow.* MIDAS offers top-down, bottom-up, and middle-out approaches for interface design and enables designers to shift freely between these paradigms during design. It also allows designers to work anywhere between totally inside or outside of the environment. With these features, opportunistic design activity becomes more natural to perform.

- *It offers high-level automation.* Acting as an active assistant, MIDAS manages interface design activities in order to off-load routine, distracting tasks from designers in many ways: by decomposing high-level tasks into simpler ones; by keeping track of the status of design activities; by offering designers different means to realize a design; and by preparing tools for interface implementation. With these features, opportunistic design becomes easier to manage.

9.2.2 Model-based Approach

Model-driven approaches (e.g., UIDE [10], APT [18], Mike [26], SAGE [29], UofA* [30], and HUMANOID [35, 36]) use declarative interface models to facilitate interface design with sophisticated services throughout the interface development lifecycle. These models explicitly describe characteristics of interfaces; therefore, by analyzing and annotating the models, the model-driven approaches can provide advanced services that would be impossible in a conventional programming paradigm, where interface specification is implied by procedure code. Examples of the services provided by this type of approach are design exploration aids during conceptualization, refinement, and implementation; design guidance; critics; and end-user help.

Interface modeling focuses on issues of user-interface application semantics, interface presentation, interactive behavior, and dialogue sequencing. Semantics describes objects of interest, operations for manipulating the objects, and the parameters required by the operations. Presentation addresses how to display application objects and operations under various conditions. Behavior defines the type of interactions the interface will support (including, for example, regions on the display that the interactions are active, interactive events that trigger and terminate the interactors, and the actions that the interactors perform). Sequencing can be explicitly modeled or can be derived from the semantic models at run-time.

Model-based systems can be further divided into two categories: automatic interface generation systems (e.g., APT [18], Mike [26], SAGE [29], and UofA* [30]) and design exploration aids (e.g., UIDE [10] and HUMANOID [35, 36]). Systems that generate interfaces automatically completely insulated designers from detailed design activities. They hide interface design complexity by automating *all* design decisions (that otherwise would have to be made by human designers); however, they give designers little control over design decisions.

Unfortunately, the ill-structured nature of interface design creates several hard-to-overcome barriers to effective automation of interface design. It is hard to specify definite and complete interface design goals, difficult to define specific criteria to control the automation of interface generation, and impossible to tell an automated system about personal preference and application-specific considerations that affect the weighting of alternatives. Consequently, it is impractical to construct rules for automatic generation systems that can effectively and automatically carry out decision making and design evaluation. In fact, the interfaces generated by these systems either are limited to certain presentations (such as the pane- and menu-style interfaces generated by Mike and UofA*) or limited to certain types of application (such as tables and charts, produced by APT and SAGE, which do not provide interactive input) because the main display areas of application interfaces are too difficult to be generated automatically.

MIDAS distinguishes itself from the above systems in several aspects: (a) it aims to strikes an adequate balance between offering high-level automation and providing designers with extensive control over design decisions; (b) it provides a shorter interface development cycle by making explicit the control of the interface model over the generated interface; and (c) it is a generic interface development environment.

Design exploration aids, the second type of model-based systems, bring design activities to a higher level than graphical interface specification tools do. They facilitate interface design at different levels of design abstraction and in a much broader range, from supporting design exploration, to providing designers with tighter control over design decisions, and to providing help to end-users of the interface software products.

UIDE [10] and HUMANOID [35, 36] are instances of such systems. Both of them offer much richer interface models to address design issues across the full life cycle of interface software development. UIDE's model describes application objects of interest, operations to manipulate the objects, inputs required by the operations, and pre- and post-conditions of the operations. By utilizing the declarative interface models, UIDE can transform an existing interface model to alternative interface designs without changing the functionality of the applications [8, 10]. By reasoning on the model, UIDE can critique a given design's consistency and completeness [3]. The run-time status of UIDE's models is used to detect end-users' difficulty during their interaction with the interface generated from UIDE's model. When a problem is found, UIDE will derive a sequence of help (based on pre-conditions and post-conditions of the related operations) and animate help information, as if the end-users are interacting with the interfaces to perform the operations [32].

In contrast, the HUMANOID model emphasize more on (a) operations that applications provide (referred to as *application semantics*), (b) presentation methods that are sensitive to the application semantics and run-time application data structures, (c) interactive behavior that an interface provides for manipulating objects of interest, and (d) sequencing and side-effects of the operations and the interactions.

HUMANOID's interface model has two layers, the generic and the application-specific extension layer. The generic layer provides a rich library of sophisticated models that cover general interface design concerns. The application-specific extension is provided by designers to address application-specific interface design (using the vocabulary defined in the generic layer). With the powerful object inheritance mechanism of the interface model, designers can focus on application-specific modeling and specify as much or as little information as they wish. The aspects left unspecified by designers will be filled in by the generic model through inheritance.

Associated with the interface model is a run-time system that always executes the current interface model, thereby generating the functioning interface defined by the model — even when the model is incomplete and sketchy, early in a design. This lets designers obtain a functional view of the interface model very early, when a design is still conceptual and easy to change. Also, with the run-time system, developers do not need to write code to update the display. They specify declaratively the dependencies between presentation methods and application data structures. HUMANOID uses this information to dynamically reconstruct interface displays whenever the application data structures change during run time.

In contrast to other model-based interface design systems, HUMANOID has an interactive modeling environment that offers sophisticated graphical modeling tools to reduce the cost of obtaining the benefits of modeling. Like interface builders, these tools support iterative design and hide the syntax of the modeling language. However, HUMANOID tools also facilitate the understanding of the interface model and are capable of generating functioning interface prototypes from partial interface specifications.

Because interface design is a human-in-the-loop process, a handy, interactive design tool alone does not necessarily assure that a wider range of designers will produce good interfaces. As Carrol notes in [4], the fundamental problem has always been that without explicit goal-and-process management, a design process is indistinguishable from trial-and-error thrashing.

To use any of the aforementioned design tools that provides extensive control over the design process, designers must be highly skillful and knowledgeable. They must know how to break down high-level design goals into activities that are supported by the tools, how to resolve interactions among these activities, and how to weed out irrelevant factors and focus on important issues. Although the HUMANOID interactive modeling environment combines the strengths of interface builders and model-driven programming, it is not immune to this problem when used for interface design. Our experience tells us that decomposing design intentions into system-supported design activities is a difficult task (if it can be done at all by inexperienced designers). The expressivity and flexibility of a powerful model such as the one UIDE and HUMANOID provide will not be utilized effectively unless designers are experienced on both design and modeling issues.

9.2.3 Human-Computer Cooperative Environment

Cooperative design environments (e.g., Framer [15] and DETENTE [37]) offer design guidance and design management with the paradigm of *human-computer* collaboration. They utilize the knowledge of design process to guide design activities. Since design is managed by the systems, human designers need not possess the knowledge or work to maintain an agenda of necessary tasks during design.

The core idea of these systems is to overcome the problems of both autonomous expert systems and human problem solving. Autonomous expert systems require sufficiently complete domain knowledge, but capturing knowledge to such a great extent in an ill-structured problem domain (such as interface design) is itself a complex problem with no solution. Thus, using autonomous agents to handle interface design problems is impractical. On the other hand, human problem solving is limited by cognitive capability. Humans tend to use the first solution they find, and they are unaware and unable to keep all relevant factors in mind when making decisions. The collaborative systems cope with both problems by providing external knowledge to human designers and leading them to detailed implementations.

MIDAS is superior to these systems in that it is equipped with a much more sophisticated engineering model of interface design that is general to a wide range of interface styles and design activities, not limited to specific application frameworks or interface presentations and behaviors. This model provides designers with a vocabulary for expressing conceptual design issues, maps conceptual design activities into specific sequences of implementation tasks, and guides the system to analyze and monitor the properties of the interface design artifacts. This enables the system to support arbitrary levels of design decomposition/composition, to offer designers a flexible control flow, and to let designers initiate design tasks. Thereby, the system realizes a much more collaborative human-computer collaboration paradigm, with the human in control and the computer in assisting when needed.

As shown above, each of the reviewed approaches has its unique contributions and provides the enabling technology to overcome the weaknesses of the others. The following sections present our work on combining these strengths and compensating for the weaknesses.

9.3   Managing Interface Design via Agendas/Scenarios

Our framework, MIDAS, uses several in-house tools to manage interface design [16]. Novel features enabled by MIDAS are: (a) it lets designers explicitly express their design intentions, helps them iteratively map these intentions into the space of design refinements, and leads designs into the refinements and implementations of functioning interfaces; (b) it manages the design task by keeping track of design activities, maintaining an up-to-date design agenda, and preparing design choices for current design issues; and (c) it enables designers to shift freely among various design paradigms, provides them with extensive control over design decisions, yet still insulates them from those irrelevant, distracting details.

MIDAS utilizes the HUMANOID declarative interface model and its interactive modeling techniques. It extends the scale of HUMANOID's interface model to the engineering model of interface design, intention, and process (design model for short). To provide active and context-sensitive design assistance, MIDAS monitors both kinds of models (the interface model and the design model) and maintains an agenda of design goals to be achieved, together with the methods to achieve them. (The generic task/activity management is provided by Agendas/Scenarios developed by the IN-USE group at ISI [23].)

9.3.1 Architecture

MIDAS has four integrated substrates: (1) an explicit interface model that separates interface design concerns into self-contained dimensions and that lets designers describe their design at many levels of design abstraction and on most (if not all) aspects of interface designs; (2) an interactive, iterative modeling system that lets designers build an interface model incrementally and that helps designers to understand modeling issues through different views of the model; (3) a library of design goals that describes design intentions, encapsulates design tasks and processes, and maps high-level design goals into specific modeling tasks; and (4) a management system that maintains an up-to-date design agenda by monitoring the status of interface models, design tasks, and design processes. Each of these components is described and defined in more detail in the following sections.

9.3.1.1 Interface Model

The interface model facilitates interface design by factoring design into semi-independent dimensions in order to minimize interactions among different design concerns [35]. It lets designers concentrate on the design issues of their choices and provides designers with a rich vocabulary for describing interface design at many levels of design abstraction. With the modeling language, designers can work only on the design issues they care about and only at the levels of design abstraction they feel comfortable with.

A run-time system of the model always executes the current interface model. It produces functioning user interfaces from the model and keeps the interfaces up-to-date as a design progresses. Thus, at any time during modeling, designers always have functioning interface examples for testing and evaluating the impact of the decisions they make. This feature eases design and enables us to build an iterative modeling environment supporting design-evaluation-redesign iteration.

9.3.1.2 Interactive Modeling Environment

The interactive modeling environment reduces the cost of modeling in many ways by hiding the syntax of its underlying modeling language and by facilitating the understanding of interface models:

- It realizes the idea of "modeling without programming" [34]. With the integrated interactive tools [17, 36], designers can conduct all aspects of interface modeling without programming. Thus it makes modeling accessible to designers who do not know how to code interface models.

- It supports the concept of "multiple visual design notations" [12, 36] that makes correct models easier to produce. These multiple visual notations include detailed views of all aspects of an interface model, structural views of part-whole relations of a complex interface model, and functional views of a model, i.e., the actual interfaces generated from the model, through which designers can test and evaluate the model that controls the interface at run time.

- It provides a kind of "what-if" capability that makes modeling easier to understand. This notion includes (1) the ability to identify relationships among components of an interface model and components of an interface generated from the model, (2) the facility to let designers modify and test a piece of a model before installing changes into the current design, and (3) support for searching in parallel for design solutions along different paths.

9.3.1.3 Engineering Model of Design

The engineering model of design declaratively describes conceptual activities extracted from a wide range of activities of daily interface development. This model describes conceptual design intentions, captures processes and tasks, and offers operational units to realize the described intentions. In addition, this engineering model is understood and shared by both the computer and the human designers and serves as a common ground for establishing human-computer collaboration. With this model, designers explicitly express their conceptual design intentions and concerns; the computer helps designers map the declared intentions into specific engineering steps that implement functioning interfaces and automates the management of interface design. In addition, this engineering model is highly reusable for a wide range of interface designs and is supplied by the system, rather than being provided by the interface designers who use this system.

In MIDAS, goals and their decompositions are explicitly modeled and organized into a hierarchy. At the top of the hierarchy are intention-oriented goals capturing high-level design intent. These goals are decomposed iteratively into implementation oriented goals. A goal has at least one method, a description of (a) how to further decompose the goal (to implement a complex design), (b) how to automate a simple, routine task to satisfy the goal (to implement a simple design), or (c) how to set up the underlying interface modeling tools for designers to make implementation directives that realize the goal. Because the goal decompositions lead high-level, conceptual design intentions to specific implementational activities (supported by the HUMANOID interactive modeling environment described above), MIDAS uses this design model to automate design management (described in the next section).

Such an engineering model is constructed via task identification and task modeling. Task identification is conducted by a series of design walk-through of existing interface software. Based on the identified tasks, a set of design goals that present interface design intentions is extracted. (These goals and tasks are then categorized into *generic* design issues and *specific* implementation issues. Generic issues are common to a wide range of interface designs, regardless of the underlying interface representation and interface implementation tools. In contrast, specific issues depend on the internal interface representation and on the interface construction tools.) In task modeling, these identified tasks and goals are modeled declaratively with a scripting language provided by Agendas/Scenarios, and the models are then compiled into a library that, during interface design, is shared by both human designers and the computer and is used to guide Agendas/Scenarios to automate task management.

The goal model has the following important characteristics:

- It provides a vocabulary that is close to the human mental model of design and that can be used to explicitly describe design intentions. This model also helps designers explore design space while assisting them to map their design conceptualization into refinement and implementation.
- It supports both goal decomposition and composition. The decomposition factors a complex design issue into many simpler ones that are easier to solve. The composition enables designers to work on simpler problems first and then assemble their solutions to the simpler problems into solutions for the complex ones. Decomposition and composition support top-

down and bottom-up approaches respectively; their combination supports middle-out design.

- It provides implementable methods for achieving goals, by decomposing complex goals into subgoals that are easier to achieve, by automating simple tasks to satisfy the goals, and by preparing the underlying engineering environment in which designers make implementation directives.

- Methods created within the goal model connect conceptual design activities with actual interface implementation tasks. The methods capture knowledge about the engineering tools that are used to carry out conceptual tasks. MIDAS can use this knowledge to prepare the underlying engineering environment for designers to make implementation directives that drive corresponding tools to manipulate relevant design artifacts. This benefits design by reducing the designers' need for specific skills and knowledge. MIDAS hides the internal structure of the interface modeling language from human designers, so that they can work at a higher level without having to map their conceptual tasks into actual artifacts and the tools to manipulate the artifacts. The computer handles those routine tasks that require detailed skills to use the right tools in the right contexts following specific sequences. Again, this focuses designers more on design issues, much less on tools.

- Goals monitor design artifacts. The satisfying conditions of goals are predicates whose values are determined by the properties of the interface model. In other words, the conditions depend on the properties of the model and the status of goals should be reactive to changes made to the properties of the model. We realize this in MIDAS by using constraint-based formulas [21] to implement the satisfying conditions. These formulas establish value constraints that guide a constraint system to propagate changes to the interface model, which in turn triggers the agenda management system (described below) to validate the status of design activities. Because these formulas analyze the properties of interface design artifacts rather than watching particular events that cause the changes to the properties, the satisfaction of goals does not rely on specific ways of obtaining the desired properties. This feature allows designers to modify the design artifacts freely by using either the methods provided by the goals, the tools equipped by the underlying environment, or whatever tools and means designers find convenient to use. Furthermore, this also ensures that the enactment MIDAS introduces aims at facilitating design, not restricting designers to a small set of means it recognizes.

In addition to the above characteristics, this engineering model is highly reusable, which greatly reduces our effort on modeling. Equally important, it enables different design paradigms by allowing the construction of sophisticated design goals out of less sophisticated goals (bottom-up approach) and by decomposing them into simpler ones (top-down). The reusability also encourages design exploration by proposing intermediate-level design goals on an existing design (middle-out). And of course, with the same set of highly reusable goals, one can combine different paradigms flexibly.

9.3.1.4 Agenda Management

The agenda manager is provided by a generic, domain-independent activity management system called Agendas/Scenarios [23]. As described above, the engineering model explicitly describes goal decomposition, methods, and applicability and satisfying conditions of goals and methods. By utilizing the engineering model, the agenda manager automates the following tasks, to off-loading to the computer distracting and irrelevant tasks that designers would otherwise have to handle:

- monitoring the interface models under design, keeping track of the design processes encapsulated in the design model, and validating activity status as the design progresses;

- enforcing activity synchronization when the nature of design requires it;

- posting applicable goals and presenting applicable methods for achieving the goals as design progresses; and

- upon request, executing the methods to decompose corresponding goals or set up a proper context for using appropriate underlying interface construction tools to implement the goals.

9.4   Example

The example in this section provides more details about MIDAS' collaboration with human designers. Although the example is seemingly simple and commonly used, it is not supported on-line by any other tools that we are aware of. It clearly illustrates MIDAS' ability to let designers explicitly express their intentions and assist them to realize these intentions by letting them focus on high-level design issues, by helping them map their design intentions into implementations, and by automatically managing various of design activities.

Figure 1 shows an object browser (built with the HUMANOID interface model) for presenting attribute-value pairs of a frame-like object. The application has one command, *Quit*, for exiting the application.

Consider a situation in which a second command, *Browse*, is added to the application model (for displaying in a new browser window an object that is the value of some slot). *Browse* requires one parameter, referred to as an input in HUMANOID, *Object to Browse*, to pass along the object for browsing. (Since the HUMANOID interface model separates interface design concerns into several semi-independent dimensions, designers can add the command *Browse* to the *Object Browser* application model without worrying about other aspects of the design at this time.)

The scenario of this example is to enhance the current interface design by providing a mechanism for end-users to access the *Browse* command through the interface of *Object Browser*. (Although constructing the object browser and adding a command to an application are interesting scenarios, for shortening our discussion, this example starts from here, after the browser has been constructed and the *Browse* command added to the application.)

Notice that "providing a mechanism for end-users to access the *Browse* command" is an abstract, conceptual requirement and is incompletely defined. Also notice that adding this functionality needs requires a middle-out approach rather than top-down or bottom-up. Furthermore, the approach by which an application interface (the object browser in this case) is constructed is irrelevant to whether MIDAS can help in enhancing (or refining) a design of

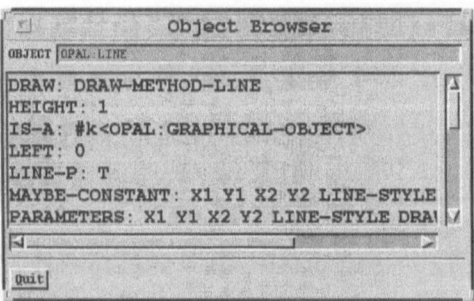

Figure 1. A sample object browser.

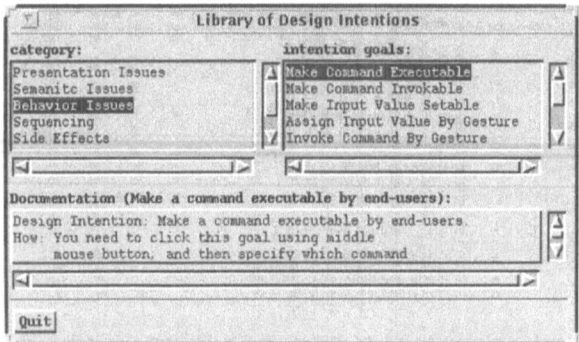

Figure 2. The window of the design intention library.

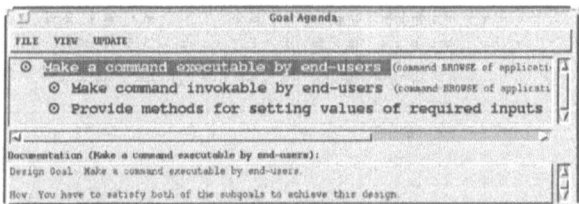

Figure 3. Initial agenda after Make a command executable by end-users is posted.

the application interface.

Unlike conventional tools that force designers to jump into implementation details, MIDAS allows designers to explicitly express their intentions in a vocabulary closer to their conceptual mental model. In this example, the designers would choose Make Command Executable from the library of intentions (Figure 2) and post it (by mousing on it and specifying the context information, the *Browse* command in this case) to a Goal Agenda (Figure 3).

In response to the posted goal, MIDAS helps designers manage design activities by triggering the Agendas/Scenarios run-time system to carry out the following tasks (most of which otherwise have to be carried out regularly and manually by designers). First the system uses the engineering model of the design to prepare a to-do list (in terms of subgoals) for the posted goal and presents the list on the agenda window. It then checks against the interface model to validate the status of the elements in the to-do list. Again, this validation process is guided by the model of design, or more specifically by the predicate conditions specified in the goals. The validation partitions the goals (in the to-do list) into satisfied and unsatisfied goals, and then further classifies the unsatisfied goals into routine and non-routine. Routine goals capture regular design activities that can be automated by the system without human designers' guidance and directives. These goals have methods that the system performs to satisfy them. Unlike the routine tasks, non-routine goals capture design activities that either need further decision making or involve personal preference and subjective practice, for which an automated system cannot provide a sufficiently satisfiable solution (such as the hot-spot for selection). Thus, non-routine activities remain unsatisfied.

Figure 3 shows the initial goal agenda after the goal Make a command executable by end-users is posted for the command *Browse*. Each item displayed in the agenda window presents a goal. To the left of each item is an icon showing the status of the goal. The icon of a circle with a dot at the center represents an unsatisfied goal; the icon of a circle with an

```
Make Command Executable              Invoke Command By Gesture
    subgoals                             subgoals
        Make Command Invocable               when Specify/Create Gesture Interactor
        Make All Inputs Value Setable            subgoals
                                                     Define Strokes For Gesture
Make Command Invocable                       Specify Hot Spot
    options                                  Specify Events
        Invoke Command By Button             ...
        ...
    Invoke Command By Gesture
```

Figure 4. Pseudo definition for the goal in Figure 3.

(a) 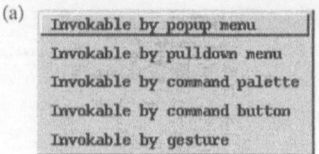 (b)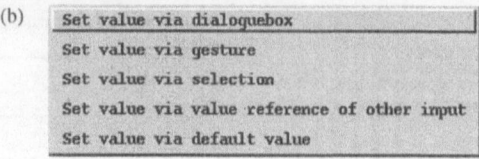

Figure 5. Methods in popup menus. (a) Means to realize the goal `Make command invokable by end-users`. (b) Means to realize `Provide methods for setting values of required inputs`.

arrowhead means a satisfied goal. When the status of a goal changes as the design progresses, its icon also changes to reflect the current status of the goal (as we will see later).

Notice that two more goals, `Make command invokable by end-users` and `Provide methods for setting values of required inputs`, are posted under the goal the designers just posted. They are subgoals decomposed from the top-level goal (refer to Figure 4). The ability of the agenda manager to automate the process of goal decomposition facilitates design in that it reduces the human designer's mental burdens. With this feature, designers do not have to know (or spend time to find out) how to break down a high-level design goal into smaller pieces; they can focus more on decision making and evaluating trade-offs among the possible design choices.

In addition to serving as an output medium for presenting the status of current activities, the agenda interface also gives designers a means to achieve the goals. When the status icon of a goal is moused on, a menu pops up presenting all the system-defined methods (see Figure 5). Designers can choose any of the methods to realize the goal.

Again, this shows how the system compensates for human cognitive weaknesses, such as short-term memory and inability to retrieve unknown information in situations where the human does not even know all possible design choices. With this mechanism, designers need not memorize design choices at each design branching point; the system presents the available choices to them.

It is important to note that, unlike other (usually well-defined) engineering domains, in interface design most of the different means for realizing a design intent can and should co-exist, i.e., they are not exclusive to one another.[1] Our engineering model captures this characteristic and allows designers to choose many methods to realize a goal. For example, in the current context, designers can use gestures and popup menus to invoke the *Browse* command. This lets designers implement multiple design solutions or explore design solutions along many directions in parallel. In these situations, the agenda manager keeps track of all

---

1. Systems designed for domains in which procedures for carrying out tasks are well defined rarely require this feature because their end-users will probably never try to realize an already achieved goal with different approaches.

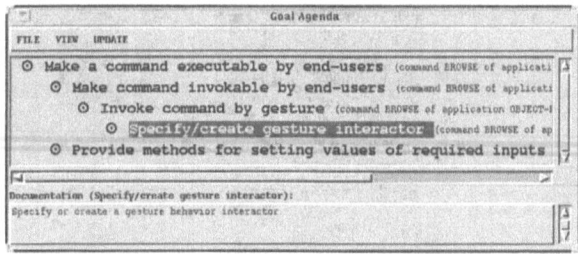

Figure 6. Agenda after `Invokable by gesture` is selected.

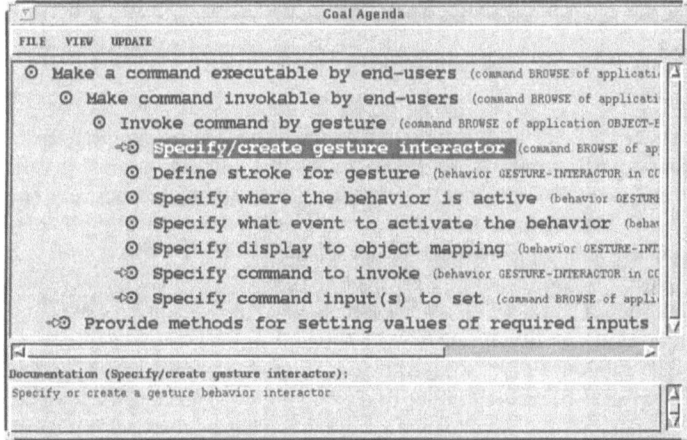

Figure 7. Agenda after an interactor is created.

design threads.

In our example, when the designers select the method *Invoke by gesture* (in Figure 5a), the system posts a new subgoal `Invoke command by gesture`. Again, the newly posted goal is automatically decomposed (according to the goal model in Figure 4) as in Figure 6.

There are two means for achieving the subgoal `Specify/create gesture interactor`: *use an existing interactor* or *create a new interactor*. When the designers choose the first means, the system will present them with all the existing interactors; when they choose the second, the system prompts them for the information needed to create a new interactor. Figure 7 shows the agenda after the designers chose the second means, supplied needed information, and directed the system to carry out the task.

The agenda in Figure 7 illustrates how MIDAS automatically sequences design activities. In this case, as soon as the goal `Specify/create gesture interactor` is satisfied, the system posts more subgoals under `Invoke command by gesture`. These subgoals, capturing the tasks of parameterizing a gesture interactor, were blocked by `Specify/ create gesture interactor` before the subgoal was satisfied, i.e., before the interactor was available.

Notice that in Figure 7 three other goals are satisfied (each of them has an icon of an arrow in a target). Two of them are subgoals of `Invoke command by gesture`, and the other one

(a)   (b)

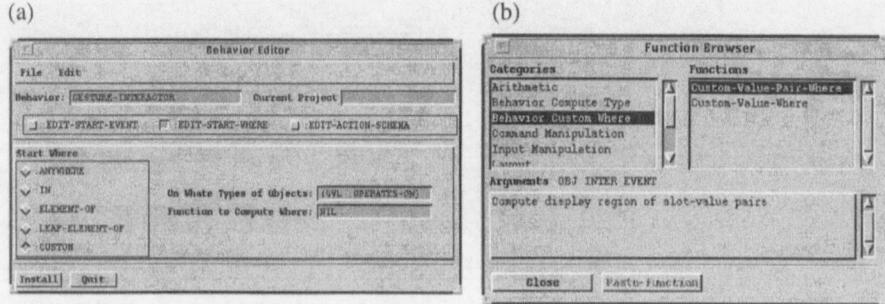

Figure 8. (a) is a HUMANOID tool for editing interactive behaviors; (b) is a function browser for specifying proper functions that compute the region of the hot-spots.

is Provide methods for setting values of required inputs, a subgoal of the top-level goal.

This illustrates MIDAS' ability to help designers manage design activities, by monitoring interface models, keeping track of design threads, and automatically validating the task agenda. These goals are automatically satisfied for following reasons: (1) The system knows what command is to be invoked by the gesture, and it automatically fills in the information, thus meeting the satisfying condition of the subgoal Specify command to invoke. (2) Similarly, since the command has only one input, the system knows by default that the value of this input should be set by the same gesture (of course, designers can change this default if they do not like it), and thus satisfies the subgoal Specify command input(s) to set. (3) The subgoal Provide methods for setting values of required inputs is satisfied because the value of the only input *Object to Browse* of command *Browse* is set by the gesture that invokes the command. That is, the occurrence of (3) is a direct consequence of (2), even though the designers did not explicitly address the design issue of (3).

When the designers choose the method of subgoal *Specify where the behavior is active*, the system invokes the HUMANOID interactive modeling environment for defining the region for the behavior (as shown in Figure 8). As demonstrated here, methods of goals are the bridges that connect conceptual activities with actual implementation tasks. When such a method is invoked, MIDAS sets up an appropriate environment and invokes the right tools. Thus, by issuing implementation directives, designers can realize design goals by carrying out conceptual design activities. With this service, designers do not have to know what tools of the underlying systems they should use and how to set up the environment to the corresponding context. Again, they stay at the conceptual level and focus on decision making, even when they need to carry out specific implementation tasks.

It is important to point out that the methods provided by MIDAS aim to facilitate designers rather than constrain them to specific means of conducting interface development. Designers do not have to use these system-provided means to achieve their design goals. They can use whatever tools they feel comfortable with (e.g., Emacs), and they can use any method to achieve the goals. They can achieve some goals using the provided methods, others with their own. Within a goal, it is even possible to combine the provided methods with the designers' own. However, when the tasks are carried out, as long as the interface model (or design artifact) has the desired properties, MIDAS will update the task agenda accordingly.

This feature is enabled by the sensitivity of the satisfying conditions of goals to the interface models. That is, when a piece of interface model changes, the corresponding conditions of

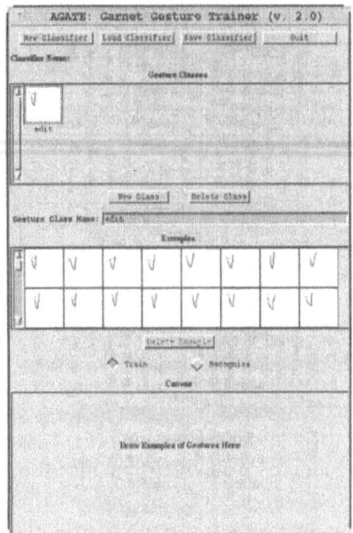

Figure 9.AGATE, the Garnet gesture trainer.

goals that depends on the properties of the piece of model will be validated. Thus, no matter how the models are altered, as soon as the manipulated model is installed into the run-time environment, the agenda manager will validate the existing task agendas (as described previously for goal Provide methods for setting values of required input). This feature is necessary to free designers from the system-furnished methods and let them work outside of the methods offered by MIDAS. Furthermore, this feature ensures that the system only enforces what has to be done, not how it has to be done — which, we strongly believe, is an important requirement for human-computer collaboration.

MIDAS also gives designers the freedom to work on issues in any order, and even on several issues in parallel, that is, they do not have to finish a task before they can start a new one. This freedom encourages designers to explore the space of interface design opportunistically, in accordance with the flow of thought in humans' mind in the process of creative design [11].

We need to point out that even though most of the methods provided by MIDAS connect conceptual design activities with the HUMANOID interface development environment, the mechanism is generic and can interface to any tool. Figure 9 is the window of AGATE, the Garnet gesture trainer, invoked by method *Train gesture* of goal Define stroke for gesture.

Figures 2 through 8 illustrate the way MIDAS leads interface designers toward specific design activities supported by the underlying software construction system. Following these paths, high-level design intentions are mapped into sequences of specific activities. Throughout the design process, the computer collaborates with human designers: designers concentrate mostly on decision making and the system focuses mostly on task agenda management.

After the designers have performed all the necessary tasks to satisfy the remaining subgoals, *Invoke command with gesture* is satisfied, as are its parent goal and the topmost goal. When all the goals are met, the object browser will have the desired functionality (shown in Figure 10).

To further refine the current design, designers can post other design intentions by referring to the current application interface (e.g., "make this object selectable" or "invoke that command

(a)   (b)

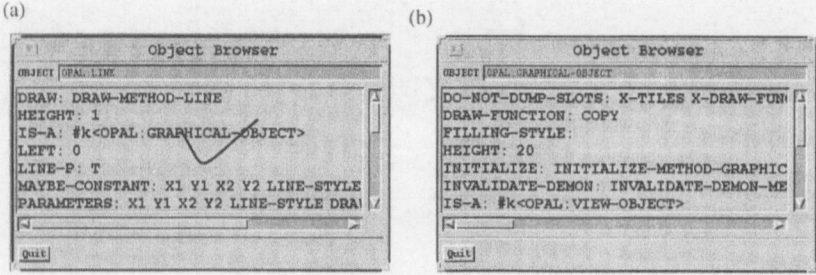

Figure 10. The sample object browser with gesture interactor to invoke the *Browse* command for browsing a gestured object in another browser window. When gesturing a check mark on a frame object, Graphical-Object as shown by (a), another browser window pops up showing the details of the object (b). Gesturing on View-Object in (b) will bring up a third browser window showing the object.

by pull-down menu"). Furthermore, designers can feed an interface model into MIDAS and let the system derive a straight top-down decomposition of interface design tasks (based on the structure of the interface model) as if the interface model had been constructed top-down by following the derived agenda. With the decomposed goal hierarchy, designers can manipulate the interface model by using the methods associated with the goals. That is, they can continue the interface development left from a previous session even if the model has produced by others.

9.5   Conclusion

The human-computer collaborative paradigm presented here contributes to interface software design with the following unique features:

* *It provides a library of design intentions close to a human's mental model of design.* Designers can initiate interface software design by pulling from this library the elements that represent their design intentions. As our example shows, designers can explicitly describe their conceptual intention of making a command executable by the end-users.

* *It helps designers map their top-level design goals into interface software.* The system automates design management by proposing goal decompositions, presenting choices of design decisions, preparing executable design resolutions, and keeping track of the status of design threads (as shown in Figures 2-8).

* *It compensates for the cognitive weakness of human designers and leverages their strength in design.* MIDAS offers extended services through high-level design automation. However, it does so only to the degree of off-loading cumbersome and distracting tasks to let designers focus on decision making and evaluation of the trade-offs between different design choices. At any time during design, designers have extensive control over design decisions on all the aspects of design.

* *It opens a new avenue to deal with ill-structured design.* HUMANOID supports opportunistic design by providing multi-disciplinary design approaches and multi-level design abstraction. By managing multiple, complex design issues, MIDAS makes opportunistic activities easy to perform.

9.6   Current Status and Future Work

MIDAS currently has about thirty top-level goals that capture conceptual design intentions. Although the size is small, the coverage is substantial and the design support is quite flexible. Most of these high-level goals can be (and are actually) used as subgoals of other goals to support even high-level design intentions. (For example, *Invoke Command by Gesture* is itself a top-level goal and a subgoal of *Make Command Invokable*, which in turn is a subgoal of *Make Command Executable*).

Flexibility: We have tested many ways to conduct the object browser sample application. These different approaches include straight top-down, mixed top-down and bottom-up, composing by reusing existing constructs, enhancing an existing interface (middle out), and combinations of all the above.

Design Exploration: We have used MIDAS in obtaining many (more than ten) different interfaces of the sample object browser application. These interfaces have different presentations, behaviors, and interaction sequencing.

Coverage: We have built several other applications with the system by re-engineering and re-implementing existing applications. We believe that MIDAS can be used to develop a wide-range application that requires sensitive presentation and interactive behaviors. (The application interfaces in Figures 1 and 2 are created with MIDAS.)

One weakness of the system is in supporting specific tasks such as layout. This weakness is not internal to the framework developed, but inherited from the underlying interactive modeling tools. Our plan for approaching this problem is to employ "demonstrational" and "by example" technology.

This research can be pursued in many directions, including: (a) improving the agenda interface to support more complex interactions for filtering displayed agenda items, manipulating the status of design activities, and restructuring activities; (b) integrating into MIDAS a critiquing system for identifying potential design problems; (c) using feedback both from an informal usability study and from the test-bed of more complex design tasks to improve the overall system; (d) studying the support of interface design beyond WIMP (windows, icons, menus, and pointers) style; and (e) controlling goal decomposition by employing design guidelines and cognitive user models.

9.7   Acknowledgements

I want to thank Robert Neches and Pedro Szekely for their support on this research; David Benjamin for enhancing the original Agendas/Scenarios system; and James Landay and Brad Myers at CMU for providing the programming interface to AGATE. I also want to thank Sheila Coyazo for helping me with the writing of this paper. The research reported in this paper was supported by ARPA through Contract Numbers NCC 2-719 and N00174-91-0015. The contents represent the opinions of the author, and do not reflect the official positions of ARPA or any other government agency.

9.8   References

1   V. Bellotti. Integrating theoreticians' and practitioners' perspectives with design rationale. In *Proceedings INTERCHI'93*. pp. 101-106. April 1993.

2   W. Bennett, S. Boies, J. Gould, S. Greene and C. Wiecha. Transformations on a dialog tree: Rule-based mapping of content to style. In *Proceedings UIST'89*, pp. 67-75, November 1989.

3   R. Braudes. A Framework for Conceptual Consistency Verification. *D.Sc. Dissertation*. Dept. of EE&CS, The George Washington University, Washington, DC 20052, 1990

4   J.M. Carroll. Creating a design science of human-computer interaction. *Interacting with Computers*. 1993. v5. N1. pp. 3-12.

5   J. Conklin and M.L. Begeman. gIBIS: A hypertext tool for exploratory policy discussion. *ACM Transactions on Office Information Systems*. 1988, v6, n4. pp.303-331.

6   S. Draper and D.A. Norman. Software engineering for user interfaces. *IEEE Transactions on Software Engineering*. pages 252-258. March 1985.

7   G. Fischer, A.C. Lemke, and T. Mastaglio. Critics: An emerging approach to knowledge-based human-computer interaction. *Int. J. Man-Machine Studies* (1991) 35. pp.695-721.

8   J. Foley, C. Gibbs, W.C. Kim, and S. Kovacevic. Formal Specification and Transformation of User-Computer Interfaces. *Report GWU-IIST-87-10*. July 1987.

9   J. Foley, et. al. *Computer Graphics: Principles and Practice*. Addison-Wesley Publishing Company. 1990

10 J. Foley, W.C. Kim, S. Kovacevic, and K. Murray. UIDE - An intelligent user interface design environment. *Intelligent User Interface*, J.W. Sullivan & S.W Tyler, Ed., Addison Wesley, Pages 339-384, 1991.

11 R. Guindon. Knowledge Exploited by experts during software system design. *Int. J. Man-Machine Studies*. pp. 279-304. 1990

12 R. Guindon. Requirements and design of DesignVision, an object-oriented graphical interface to an intelligent software design assistant. In *Proceedings ACM SIGCHI'92*. pp. 499-506. May 1992.

13 P. J. Hayes, P. Szekely and R. Lerner. Design alternatives for user interface management systems based on experience with COUSIN. In *Proceedings ACM SIGCHI'85*. pp. 169-175. April 1989.

14 B. Hayes-Roth and F. Hayes-Roth. A cognitive model of planning. *Cognitive Science*. 1979, 3. pp. 275-310.

15 A. C. Lemke and G. Fischer. A cooperative problem solving system for user interface design. *Proceedings of AAAI-90*. pp.479-484.

16 P. Luo, P. Szekely, and R. Neches. Management of interface design in humanoid. In *Proceedings INTERCHI'93*. April 1993.

17 P. Luo, P. Szekely, and R. Neches. Iteratively Design User-Interface Application Semantics. *ISI working paper*.

18 J. Mackinlay. Automating the design of graphical presentations of relational Information. *ACM Transactions on Graphics*. pp.110-141. April 1986.

19 D. Miller, J. Smith, and M. Muller. TelePICTIVE: Computer-supported collaborative GUI design for designers with diverse expertise. *Proceedings UIST'92*. pp. 151-160. November 1992.

20 A. Morse and G. Reynolds. Overcoming current growth limits in UI development. *CACM* 36, 4 (April 1993), pp 73-81.

21 B. A. Myers, et. al. Garnet: Comprehensive support for graphical, highly-interactive user interfaces. *IEEE Computer* 23(11), pp. 71-85, November, 1990.

22 R. Neches, J. Foley, P. Szekely, P. Sukaviriya, P. Luo, S. Kovacevic, and S. Hudson. Knowledgeable development environments using shared design models. *The 1993 International Workshop on Intelligent User Interfaces (IWIUI'93)*. January 4-7, 1993.

23 R. Neches, D. Benjamin, J. Granacki, B. Harp, and P. Szekely. Agendas/Scenarios: A Reusable, Customizable Approach to User-System Collaboration in Complex Activities. *ISI working paper*.

24 Neuron Data, Inc. 1991. *Open Interface Toolkit*. 156 University Ave. Palo Alto, CA 94301.

25 NeXT, Inc. 1990. *Interface Builder*, Palo Alto, CA.

26 D. Olsen. MIKE: The menu interaction kontrol environment. *ACM Transactions on Graphics*, vol 17, no 3, pp. 43-50, 1986.

27 D. Olsen, Jr. *User Interface management Systems: Models and Algorithms*. Morgan kaufmann Publishers. 1992.

28 B. Reeves and F. Shipman. Supporting communication between designers with artifact-centered evolving information spaces. *Proceedings CSCW'92*. pp. 394-401. October 1992.

29 S. Roth and J. Mattis. Data characterization for intelligent graphics presentation. *In Proceedings ACM SIGCHI'90*. pp. 193-200. April 1990

30 G. Singh and M. Green. A high-level user interface management system. In *Proceedings ACM SIGCHI'89*. pp. 133-138. April 1989.

31 H.A. Simon. The structure of ill-structured problems. *Artificial Intelligence*. 1973, 4. pp. 181-201.

32 P. Sukaviriya and J. Foley. Coupling a UI framework with automatic generation of context-sensitive animated help. In *Proceedings of UIST'90*. October 1990, pp. 142-146.

33 W. Swartout and R. Balzer. On the inevitable intertwining of specification and implementation. *CACM* 25, 7 (July 1982), pp. 438-440.

34 P. Szekely. Template-based mapping of application data to interactive displays. In *Proceedings UIST'90*. October 1990, pp. 1-9.

35 P. Szekely, P. Luo, and R. Neches. Facilitating the exploration of interface design alternatives: The HUMANOID model of interface design. In *Proceedings ACM SIGCHI'92*. May 1992, pp. 507-515

36 P. Szekely, P. Luo, and R. Neches. Beyond interface builders: Model-based interface tools. In *Proceedings INTERCHI'93*. April 1993.

37 D.A. Wroblewski, T.P. McCandless, and W.C. Hill. DETENTE: Practical support for practical action. *Proceedings of ACM SIGCHI'92 Conference on Human Factors in Computing Systems*. pp. 195-202. April 1991.

10   A Tool-Supported Approach to the Refinement of Interactive Systems

F. Paternó
A. Leonardi
S. Pangoli

ABSTRACT
In this paper we present an approach to support developers in the refinement of specifications of Interactive Systems. We begin with a formal specification of user tasks. We then obtain an architectural description of the corresponding Interactive System in terms of the composition of interaction objects, and finally we generate the prototype of the user interface. We describe the first results in the development of a tool for supporting designers through these phases by using graphical representations and automatic translations among different types of descriptions.

10.1   Introduction

There is an increasing need for automatic tools that can support designers and developers of Interactive Systems to manage the complexity of software development, such as software for interacting with users. Such tools could be used by software designers of Interactive Systems who want to take into account the user's point of view when producing these types of artefacts.

It is widely recognised that systems are easier to use if their functionalities are designed to reflect the logical organisation of user tasks.

We believe that another important point is the use of formal notations, as they force designers to clarify their specifications right from the first steps in the refinement process of a system. However, our experience in the application of formal methods has shown that to obtain more reliable results these methods should be tool-supported as a pencil-and-paper approach alone is limited, especially with large size specifications.

In the software engineering field there are several automatic tools that help to design, specify and verify concurrent systems by formal notations such as the Concurrency Workbench [7] and LITE [10]. Our goal is to develop a similar tool but specifically oriented towards Interactive Systems, so that we can evaluate their typical properties and design these systems with their typical architectural models.

In this paper we present a tool, the Interactive System Workbench, which we are building to support the refinement of Interactive Systems. Its main features are:

- To assist designers of user interfaces, beginning with abstract specifications expressed in terms of user tasks, and throughout all the stages until the related software has been prototyped.

- To specify user tasks and their relationships with the support of a formal notation. We use LOTOS [2] for this purpose, which is a notation for concurrent systems developed to specify the temporal relations among the interactions of the system considered. Other notations for task specification have similar constructs (UAN [12] and MAD [17] for example).

- The toolkit used for prototyping user interfaces is based on a clear architectural model and its interaction objects (interactors) are semantics-oriented rather than appearance-oriented, thus facilitating the refinement from task descriptions to software interaction objects.

The resulting environment accounts for the fact that user interfaces are characterised by appearance and behaviour. The behaviour can cause problems that are very difficult to manage, as it is the result of the internal architecture of the system which is obtained by composing hundreds of interaction objects. The first phases are therefore dedicated to a clear specification and refinement of the relationships in terms of temporal ordering of events, and, communication and synchronization among the components. The appearance is left to a graphical editor, which is similar to those that are widely available in the last stage of prototyping.

10.2   Related Works

Adept [18] is a tool with similar objectives to ours which begins with a task analysis performed by TKS to obtain user interfaces. However, unlike our environment it does not have a semantics-based, task-oriented toolkit of interactors for prototyping. UIDE [11] is a model-based environment where in the application model the designer describes the functionality of an application as a set of actions that are associated with pre- and post-conditions, parameters and parameter constraints. In UIDE the interaction objects are dependent on widgets of current toolkits which communicate by call-backs with a dialogue manager. Recent developments in UIDE [4] allow designers to have automatic support for a GOMS-based analysis in order to predict learning and execution times.

In [9] a semi-formal account of the work that the user wishes to accomplish is specified by means of a task-context model. This is then refined into an abstract dialogue model to describe the behaviour of the user and the system. The dialogue model is specified using a notation based on a production system and is supported by a software tool.

Mackinlay [13] has developed a tool for generating 2D representations of relational information depending on the user's purposes. BOZ [6] is one of its evolutions which begins with task specification in order to obtain more suitable graphical representations.

Our environment is based on visual representations. Visual representations of the LOTOS formal notation have already been proposed [3], but as they are based on one-to-one mapping between operators and graphical symbols the resulting diagrams may be too complicated. Since we only use a subset of the operators of the notation we have used simpler graphic symbols.

10.3   The Refinement Approach

A task is a crucial element which allows us to link the user to the system. The basic concept is that if the logical organisation of software systems reflects the structure of user tasks, then the systems will be easier to use and more comprehensible.

Complex tasks are usually subdivided into simpler tasks. The result of task decomposition can be used to obtain two types of descriptions of interactive systems:

The *interactional description*, where possible user actions, system feedback, and their temporal ordering are identified.

The *architectural description*, where the basic components of the system and their relationships in order to support the given tasks are indicated.

UAN is a notation which was specifically developed to obtain interactional descriptions; while LOTOS is a more general purpose notation, which can be used to obtain both types

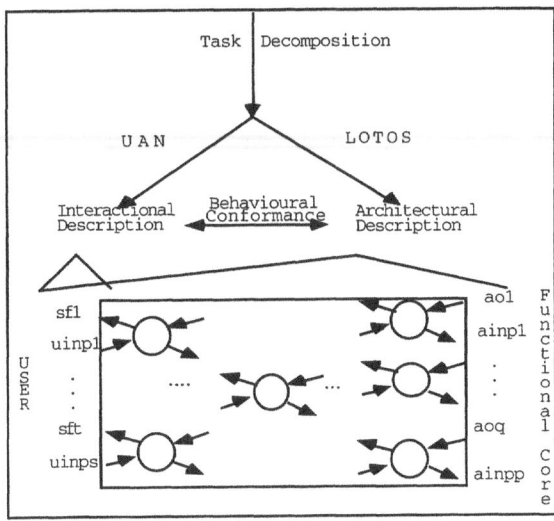

FIGURE 10.1. Approaches to the Design of Interactive Systems

of descriptions. In our case LOTOS is used to derive architectural descriptions following a specific basic model for interaction objects.

Clearly, if we take both an interactional and an architectural description of the same system they should be consistent, in the sense that a behavioural conformance should be verified. This means that if we take the architectural description and we hide the actions related to the synchronization among interaction objects, and among interaction objects and the functional core, we should obtain the interactional description. An approach to apply correctness preserving transformations in order to obtain an architectural description equivalent to a starting interactional description is described in [1].

We propose combining these two approaches: UAN as an approach to evaluate, especially from a usability point of view, existing software and as documentation for users who want to know how to perform specific tasks; and LOTOS and related tools as a notation for the design, specification and verification of the software related to the development of Interactive Systems.

Using formal notations as documentation for users may seem a problem because at first sight they do not appear to be very straightforward or comprehensible. However, if users want precise answers to specific questions, such as the actions to execute for a specific task, they are the most reliable tool.

Figure 1 shows how we follow task decomposition using LOTOS, which gives an architectural description (LOTOS could also be used to obtain an interactional description but here we are interested in designing the underlying system). It is possible to apply LITE tools [10] to the LOTOS abstract description to simulate and verify properties.

Firstly, our tool provides graphical and automatic support for task specification. The basic tasks are then refined into specifications of interaction objects. Finally, these are refined into software interaction objects. The work area of the initial layout of the tool (Figure 2) is divided into two parts: one for task specification, the other for graphical architectural specification. These can be considered as two different views of the Interactive System to develop (one for the user's view of the functionality, the other for developer's

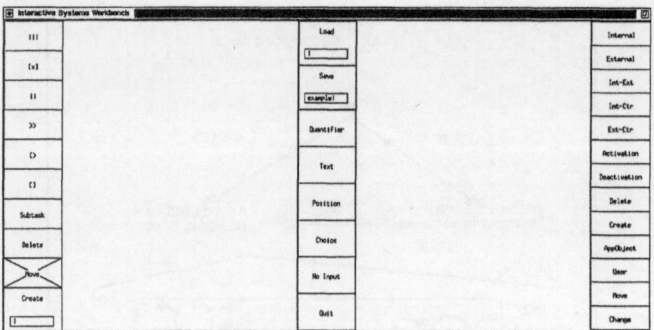

FIGURE 10.2. The Initial Layout of the Tool

view of the corresponding system). In the middle, there is a tree of menus which allows the designer to navigate in the set of implemented interaction objects available.

10.4   Task Description

During the task description phase the designer can indicate a task in terms of its subtasks and define the temporal relationships among tasks. The LOTOS operators which we use for this are: *interleaving* (T1 ||| T2, T1 and T2 actions can be performed in any possible order), *full synchronization* (T1 || T2, for any action T1 and T2 have to synchronise), *sequential composition* (T1 >> T2, T2 is performed when T1 has been completed), *disabling* (T1 [> T2, T1 is disabled at the beginning of T2), *synchronization* (T1 |[x1, ..., xn]| T2, T1 and T2 need to synchronise at the x1, .., xn communication gates), *choice*, (T1 [] T2, it is possible to choose between the T1 and T2 behaviours).

LOTOS was developed in the software engineering field, but it is suitable for describing any system characterised by reactions to external events. Proof that its operators are useful for describing human-computer interactions is that different notations developed for task specifications have similar operators: UAN has operators for sequential, repeating disjunction, order independence, one-way interleavability, mutual interleavability, and concurrent tasks; MAD has operators for sequential, parallel, alternative and iterative tasks.

The basic idea in our work environment is that designers start to sketch the logical organisation of the system after a rough task analysis. They should then use a formal notation to specify the results of this analysis. This forces designers to clarify the requirements of their system. They thus have to identify more abstract tasks and specify their temporal relationships precisely.

Our tool provides a graphical environment where instances of symbols associated with tasks can be created by indicating how a high level task can be refined into more basic tasks. To create a user (sub)task, the designer simply types its name in the *create* box; the top level task is the application itself, which is in turn decomposed into a hierarchy of subtasks.

When the desired level of abstraction is reached, the temporal relationships between tasks can be expressed simply by graphically linking two subtasks and indicating the appropriate LOTOS operator. The resulting description is a tree-like structure which can be interpreted as the first steps in the refinement process of the corresponding Interactive

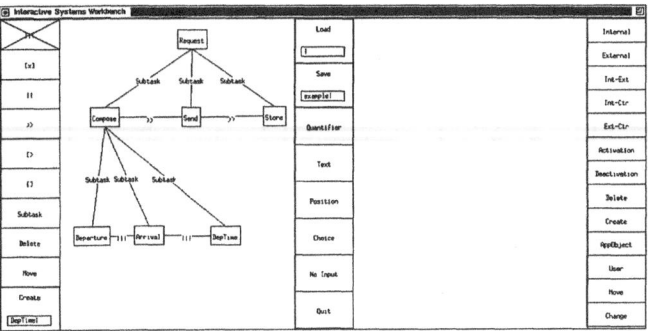

FIGURE 10.3. An Example of Task Decomposition

System.

Figure 3 shows a brief example of task refinement. The global task is to provide a request for a flights data base. The first step refines this into composing a request, sending the request, and showing the result. These tasks should be performed in sequence. The composing request is then further refined and the towns of departure and arrival, along with the date are specified. The actions related to these tasks can be carried out in any order.

The designer can perform a set of operations on the graphical representations of tasks (rectangles with the task name inside): creating new instances, deleting, defining their component actions, modifying a position on the screen, saving a representation on a file, and loading from a file.

10.5   Architectural Description

The first phase of task specification is useful for indicating the main temporal constraints among the components of the Interactive System that is being developed.

Interactive Systems are composed of a User Interface System and a Functional Core. The User Interface System consists of a set of interactors. The Functional Core has a set of application objects which can be modelled according to other application-driven models. In addition, there are *conceptual objects* which create the interface between the two components. They map data from one side in calls to the functionality of the objects on the other side.

One of the main goals of our environment is to provide support for obtaining the description of a system as a composition of interactors. We follow a specific architectural model which was originally formally specified and analysed [14], and then implemented into a toolkit which itself has been implemented using an object-oriented programming language [16] that reflects the formal specification.

In our view an interactor is an object that can receive data from both the user and the application side and generate results of its processing on the opposite side. It has triggers to explicitly indicate when to produce a result; these triggers are, however, optional. If they are missing it means that whenever an interactor receives some data from one side then the interactors generate the result on the opposite side. A more detailed discussion on our view of interactors can be found in [15].

The interactors in our toolkit are classified according to their semantics rather than

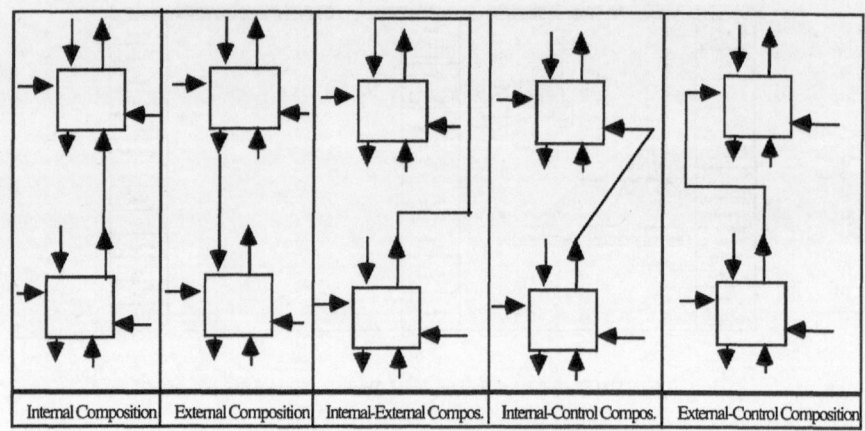

| Internal Composition | External Composition | Internal-External Compos. | Internal-Control Compos. | External-Control Composition |

FIGURE 10.4. The Set of Possible Composition Operators

their appearance, as is the case with most current toolkits. By *semantics-oriented* we mean that they are classified in relation to the information they provide the application with. This concept is very close to the definition of the task that they support, since a task can be considered as a user-desired modification of the state of the application. Since the semantics of an interactor identifies the basic task that it can carry out we provide a useful support to facilitate the task-to-interactors mapping. Basic tasks that are the result of task decomposition can be associated with classes of available interactors that perform the functionality required. In fact, with our tool it is possible to navigate within the tree of the interactors available. Our software interactors are characterised firstly by the basic task they can support, then by the type of appearance they provide, and finally by the type of feedback they can generate. It is thus easy to identify which interaction object can support the given task. If none of the available interactors is suitable then it is straightforward to identify where to extend the toolkit.

The resulting Interactive System cannot be obtained simply by one-to-one mapping from tasks to interactors. Thus the designer is given the opportunity to edit the architectural description further in order to give a more detailed description of the organisation of its components by adding new interactors and modifying their compositions. For this purpose a set of composition operators have been mathematically defined [15] according to which part of the interactors they compose: the result of the input part is given to the input part of another interactor (*internal-composition*), the result of the output part is given to the output part of another interactor (*external-composition*), the result of the input part is given to the output part of another interactor (*internal-external composition*), the result of the input part of one interactor is the input trigger event of another interactor, (*internal-control composition*), the result of the input part of one interactor is the output trigger event of another interactor (*external-control composition*), the result of the input part of one interactor makes one or more interactors reactive (*activation composition*), and the result of the input part of one interactor deactivates the behaviour of one or more interactors (*deactivation composition*).

The specification of the compositions among interactors is stored in the tool by a matrix representation where rows and columns are associated with sending and receiving interactors, and the element in the matrix is associated with the type of composition and

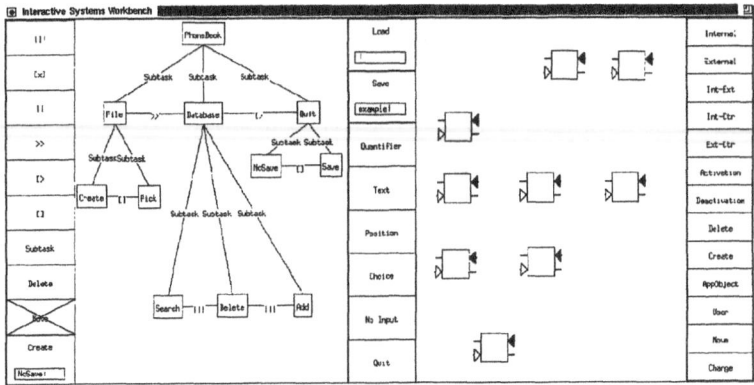

FIGURE 10.5. Task Description of the Example

the data types that are exchanged.

When designers pass to the part of the Interactive Systems Workbench dedicated to the architectural specification, they can load a file with the result of the task specification. This is interpreted, and the result is visualised in the architectural area for further editing. The interpretation currently consists in associating an interactor with each basic task and understanding that if two tasks need to synchronise this implies that the corresponding interactors need to be composed. The tool provides a specific graphical symbol to indicate that two interactors need to be composed. When the symbol has been selected, the designer can indicate one of the five possible types of composition which can be selected from the menu on the right hand side; the corresponding connections are then visualised.

10.6 An Example

To show how our system currently works we will consider a brief example. We have a data base that manages a list of phone numbers. Each record has a phone number, a name, an address, an age, and a generic information field.

The generic task of managing the phone number data base can be described by the following LOTOS expression:

specification database [create, pick, searc, ad, delet, qui] : *exit*
behaviour
Loadfile[create, pick] >> (DataBase[searc, ad, delet] [> Quit[qui])
where
process Loadfile[create, pick] : *exit* := create; exit [] pick; exit *endproc*
process DataBase[searc, ad, delet] : *noexit* := searc; Search [searc] ||| ad; Add [ad] |||
delet; Delete [delet] *endproc*
process Search [searc] : *noexit* := searc; Search [searc] *endproc*
process Add [ad] : *noexit* := ad; Add [ad] *endproc*
process Delete [delet] : *noexit* := delet; Delete [delet] *endproc*
process Quit[qui] : *exit* := qui; exit *endproc*
endspec

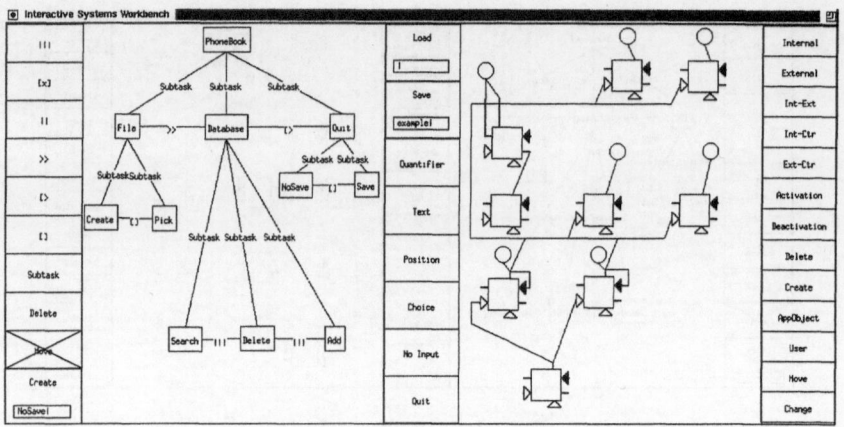

FIGURE 10.6. Architectural Description of the Example

The LOTOS expression indicates that the user can load a file by creating a new one or by selecting an existing one. Once this task is terminated, the user can interact with the data base by interleaving the tasks that involve searching for information, adding new information or deleting previously stored information. These tasks can be continuously performed until the quit task is performed. When the designer has finished specifying the task, he/she can ask the system to automatically start the development of a corresponding architectural description. The first result is to obtain a description with one interactor for each basic task (leaves in the task tree), as shown in Figure 5. This rule is applied except when a choice operator between two tasks is found. In this specific case the two tasks are refined into three interactors. As no synchronization was indicated in the task specification then no connection is indicated in the automatically generated architectural specification.

This rough description, which identifies a tentative set of interactors, can then be reworked by the designer. We thus obtain the definitions of the connections and we can also identify the devices and the application functionality used to carry out the interactions desired. The new architectural description obtained is shown in Figure 6. In the interactor graphical representations white or black heads of arrows also appear. These are associated with enabling (white head arrow) and disabling (black head arrow) signals. There is also a small trinagle in the lower-right hand side of the graphical representation of the interactors, which indicates that they directly interact with users.

From the architectural description we have enough information to generate the resulting user interface (Figure 7). It allows the user to select a file and visualise its contents in a window. A scrollbar can be used if all the contents cannot be visualised in the window. There are two Edit interactors, one to insert a value to search for in the data base, the other to store a new record. These two interactors communicate directly with the application object, while the results from the functional core are passed directly to the FileEdit interactor. In this example the functional core supports operations for loading a file, for loading all records where one field contains a given value, and for saving a record.

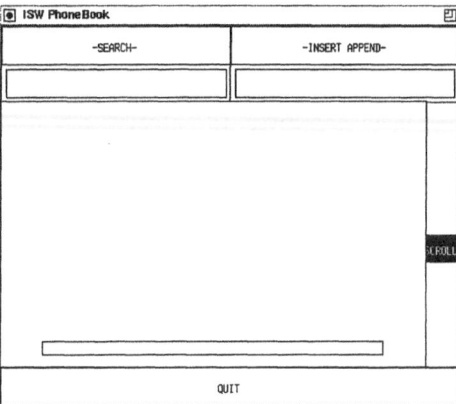

FIGURE 10.7. The Initial Layout of the Example

It is possible to create a new file or insert a new element at the bottom of a specific file. To do this the user needs to specify the name of the file to use and then the fields to store.

The data in a file can be completely visualised by inserting the given name into the central dialogue box. The top-left dialogue box allows the user to search for all the records in the data base that contain a given value (for example all the phone users who live in a given town). Figure 8 shows an interaction which visualises the result of loading a file and adding a new record.

10.7   Conclusions

We have presented a proposal for the refinement of Interactive Systems based on formal notations, an architectural model for interaction objects, along with a related implementation of a task-oriented toolkit and a visual environment. Our approach is supported

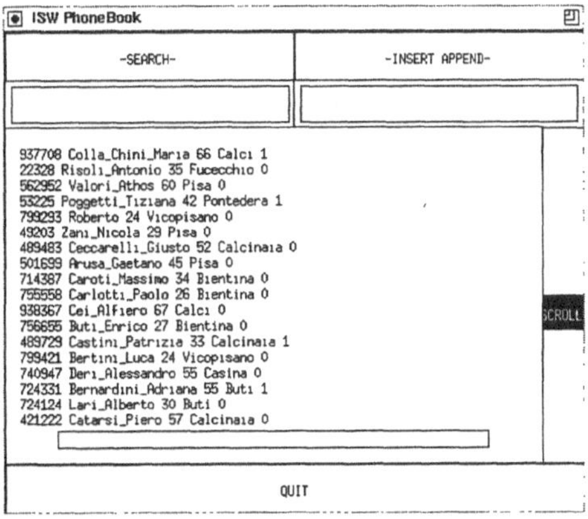

FIGURE 10.8. An Example of an Interaction

by an automatic tool which makes use of graphical representations of tasks and interaction objects. The resulting environment is a tool in its early stages which can be used by designers to manage the complexity of software interactive systems by a systematic approach supported by a direct manipulation environment.

Future work has three main objectives: to automatically demonstrate properties at different stages in the refinement process, to generate user interfaces which incorporate usability concepts, and to support user interfaces with automatic task-oriented help.

10.8   References

[1] C.Bernardeschi, A.Fantechi, F.Paterno'.   Application of Correctness Preserving Transformations for Deriving Architectural Descriptions of Interactive Systems from User Interface Specifications, Proceedings of the Seventh International Conference of Software Engineering and Knowledge Engineering, June 1995, Rockville, Maryland, USA.

[2] T.Bolognesi, E.Brinskma. Introduction to the ISO Specification Language LOTOS, Computer Networks & ISDN Systems, 14, 1987, pp.25-59.

[3] T.Bolognesi, D.Latella, Techniques for the Formal Specification of the G-LOTOS Syntax, Proceedings of the IEEE Workshop on Visual Languages, 1989, pp.43-49.

[4] M.Byrne, S.Wood, P.Sukaviriya, J.Foley, D.Kieras, Automating Interface Evaluation, Proceedings ACM CHI94, pp.232-237.

[5] N.Carlsen, L.Bass, G.Cokton, P. ten Hagen, On Defining the Application Interface to the UIMS: A Conceptual Framework for Interactive Software Systems in User Interface Management and Design, D.Duce and others (ed.), 1991.

[6] S.M.Casner, A Task-Analytic Approach to the Automated Design of Graphics Presentations ACM Transactions on Graphics, Vol.10, N.2, April 1991, pp.111-151.

[7] R.Cleaveland, J.Parrow, B.Steffen. The Concurrency Workbench in Automatic Verification Methods for Finite State Systems, LNCS 407, Springer Verlag, 1990, pp.24-37.

[8] J.Coutaz, F.Paterno', G.Faconti, L.Nigay A Comparison of Approaches for Specifying Multimodal Interactive Systems Proceedings Workshop ERCIM on Multimodal Human-Computer Interaction, Nancy, November 1993.

[9] A.Monk, M.Curry, Discount dialogue modelling with Action Simulator In Cockton, G., Draper, S.W. and Weir, G.R.S. (Eds.), Computers and People 9: HCI'94 Proceedings, Cambridge: Cambridge University Press, pp. 327-338.

[10] P.van Eijk, The Lotosphere Integrated Environment Proceedings 4th International Conference on Formal Description Techniques (FORTE'91), Sidney, November 1991, North Holland, pp.473-476. 1991.

[11] J.D.Foley, W.C.Kim, S.Kovacevic, K.Murray, UIDE-An Intelligent User Interface Design Environment. In Architectures for Intelligent Interfaces: Elements and Prototypes. Eds. J.Sullivan and S.Tyler, Reading, MA: Addison Wesley, 1991.

[12] R.Hartson, P.Gray, Temporal Aspects of Tasks in the User Action Notation, Human Computer Interaction, Vol.7, pp.1-45.

[13] J.Mackinlay, Automating the Design of Graphical Presentations of Relational Information, ACM Transaction on Computer Graphics, Vol.5, N.2, April 1986, pp.110-141.

[14] F.Paterno', G.Faconti, On the Use of LOTOS to Describe Graphical Interaction, People and Computer VII, pp.155-173, Proceedings HCI Conference 1992, York, Cambridge University Press

[15] F.Paterno', A Theory of User-Interaction Objects, Journal of Visual Languages and Computing, Vol.5, N.3, pp.227-249, 1994.

[16] F.Paterno', A.Leonardi, A Semantics-Based Approach the Design and Implementation of Interaction Objects, Computer Graphics Forum, Vol.13, N.3, pp.195-204, 1994.

[17] S.Sebillotte, D.Scapin, From Users task Knowledge to High Level Interface Specification Proceedings WWDU92, Berlin.

[18] S.Wilson, P.Johnson, P.Kelly, C.Cunningham, P.Markopoulos, Beyond hacking: a Model Based Approach to User Interface Design, in J.Alty, D.Diaper, S.Guest (eds.), People and Computer VIII, Proceedings of HCI'93, Cambridge University Press, 1993, pp.217-231.

11 The BOSS System: Coupling Visual Programming with Model Based Interface Design

Siegfried Schreiber

ABSTRACT
Due to the limitations of WYSIWYG User Interface Builders and User Interface Management Systems model based user interface construction tools gain rising research interest. The paper describes the BOSS system, a model based tool which employs an encompassing specification model (HIT, Hierarchic Interaction graph Templates) for setting up all parts of the model of an interactive application (application interface, user interaction task space, presentation design rules) in a declarative, designer oriented manner. BOSS offers an integrated development environment in which specifications are elaborated in a graphical, visual–programming–like fashion. Through a refinement component a specification can be transformed according to high–level design goals. From a refined specification BOSS generates automatically user interfaces using modified techniques from compiler construction.

11.1 Introduction

Currently, there are two categories of tools supporting the development of user interfaces:

The first category, to which belong most of the available User Interface Builders and User Interface Management Systems, follows a so called bottom–up approach. The task of building a user interface starts with the assembly of the static layout of the desired interface using a WYSIWYG editor. This approach has several drawbacks:

- Only static portions of user interfaces like menus or dialogue boxes can be built easily. In most cases, however, user interfaces have to support applications, where complex structured objects are dynamically created, destroyed or manipulated. Keeping the user interface layout consistent with the application and dialogue state is often poorly supported.

- WYSIWYG interface tools do not encapsulate common software-ergonomic rules, style–guide compliance [21] of user interfaces has to be checked "by hand".

- the design of an alternative user interface (e.g. for a different class of users) is often as time consuming as the original design, because a lot of layout details have to be reconsidered.

The second category of user interface tools tries to overcome these drawbacks. Model based user interface tools or user interface generators [19, 27, 8, 30, 12, 28, 5, 2] follow the notion of generating automatically an executable user interface out of a declarative description (model) of the properties of an interactive application (application interface, user interaction task space, presentation design rules).

Model based tools claim the following benefits:

- adopting the principle of separating logical from layout structure, also known from related research domains like document architecture [7, 26], user interface designers are freed from the burden of making presentation design commitments (e.g. designing menus or dialogue boxes) at early stages of the design process, thus being able to design user interfaces centered around the concepts of users and tasks.

- rapid prototyping of working interfaces (not just display mock-ups) is well supported by model based tools, even if the specification is not worked out in all details [30].

However, as reported in [9], current model based tools are rarely used by interface designers, as they "often use cryptic languages for the model specification" [9]. Moreover, interface designers often have to learn different specification techniques for setting up different parts of the model. The BOSS System (BOSS is the acronym of "Bedienoberflächenspezifikationssystem", the German translation of "user interface specification system") tries to overcome these drawbacks by the following means:

- Unlike other model based systems, BOSS uses an encompassing specification model (HIT, Hierarchic Interaction graph Templates) to cover all parts (see above) of the model of an interactive application. HIT is well–suited for supporting different roles of persons in user interface design: Application analysts describe the structure of the task space, which an interactive application offers to its users. Human factors experts express presentation design rules capturing software ergonomic guidelines in a constructive manner.

- HIT combines properties of two well–known software construction methods: dataflow diagrams and dynamic attribute grammars. HIT is an adaequate compromise between a designer oriented and an implementation oriented specification model: designers can express their notions in a declarative, natural manner. Application analysts, e.g., describe the user interaction task space in a way closely related to phsychologically motivated modelling approaches in HCI (e.g. [22]). From a given specification, efficient implementations are generated automatically.

- Based on the same specification the specification refinement component of BOSS generates automatically different kinds of user interfaces according to high level design goals (e.g. support a particular class of users). The refinement component supports transformations, which change the behaviour and presentation of an user interface in a global way.

- BOSS is not tailored to any specific application domain (e.g. business oriented systems [12, 2]), but can also handle interfaces with e.g. animated, interactive graphics and application specific objects.

- BOSS offers an Integrated Development Environment (IDE), in which specifications are elaborated graphically in a visual–programming–like fashion. The IDE of BOSS supports very tight specification / generation / evaluation cycles and therefore increases the usability of the system.

- BOSS supports the systematic development of user interfaces from early activities (e.g. task analysis) to presentation design and implementation. As BOSS allows the derivation of "standard" user interfaces out of task–level descriptions, user interfaces can be tested and evaluated at early stages in the development process.

Figure 11.1 shows a human factors expert setting up presentation design rules in the IDE of BOSS (for an explanation of figure 11.1 see section "presentation design").

The paper is organized as follows: first we give an overview about model based interface design with the BOSS system. Then we outline the specification of an example to illustrate the use of the HIT specification model at the various states in the interface design process. Finally, we discuss the specification refinement component of BOSS.

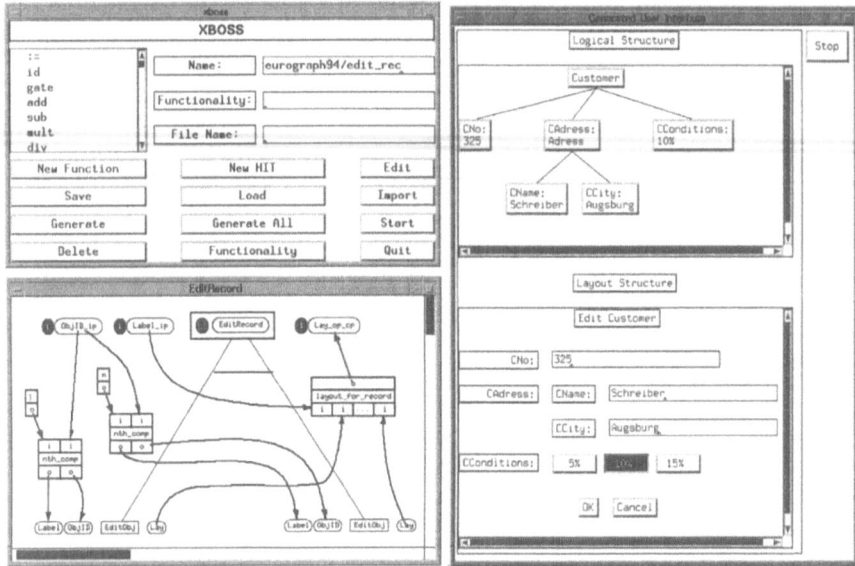

FIGURE 11.1. Specification session of a human factors expert with the BOSS–IDE

11.2   Model Based User Interface Design with BOSS: An Overview

Figure 11.2 shows the overall architecture of the BOSS system, which is made up of a design–time part and a run–time part. The design–time part describes the user interface development process using BOSS. The runtime–part shows how a end–user interacts with a generated user interface.

11.2.1   The Structure of the Model of an Interactive Application

In model based interface tools like BOSS the model of an interactive application captures all knowledge which is needed to support the user interface development process at various stages of the UI lifecycle (e.g. analysis, design, usage). The model structures the space of properties of interactive systems into design dimensions corresponding to different roles of persons in user interface design [15, 3] (see figure 11.2):

- Description of the Application Interface (AI), i.e. specifying application data structures and functions relevant for the user interface (role of application analyst).
- Description of the space of interaction tasks users can perform within the application interface. This User Interaction Task Space (UITS) is a structured, high–level description of "what a user can do with a system", which does not consider presentation aspects (role of application analyst).
- Presentation Design (PD, role of human factors expert), i.e. description of the mapping of the task–level state of the interactive application (logical structure) to an appropriate (according to software ergonomic rules) presentation (layout structure).

It is important to note that setting up the model is not a sequential process starting with AI and being finished with PD. When designing an interactive application from scratch, we might want to start with identifying potential classes of end users and the tasks they want to accomplish (user centered interface design process [13]). Breaking down

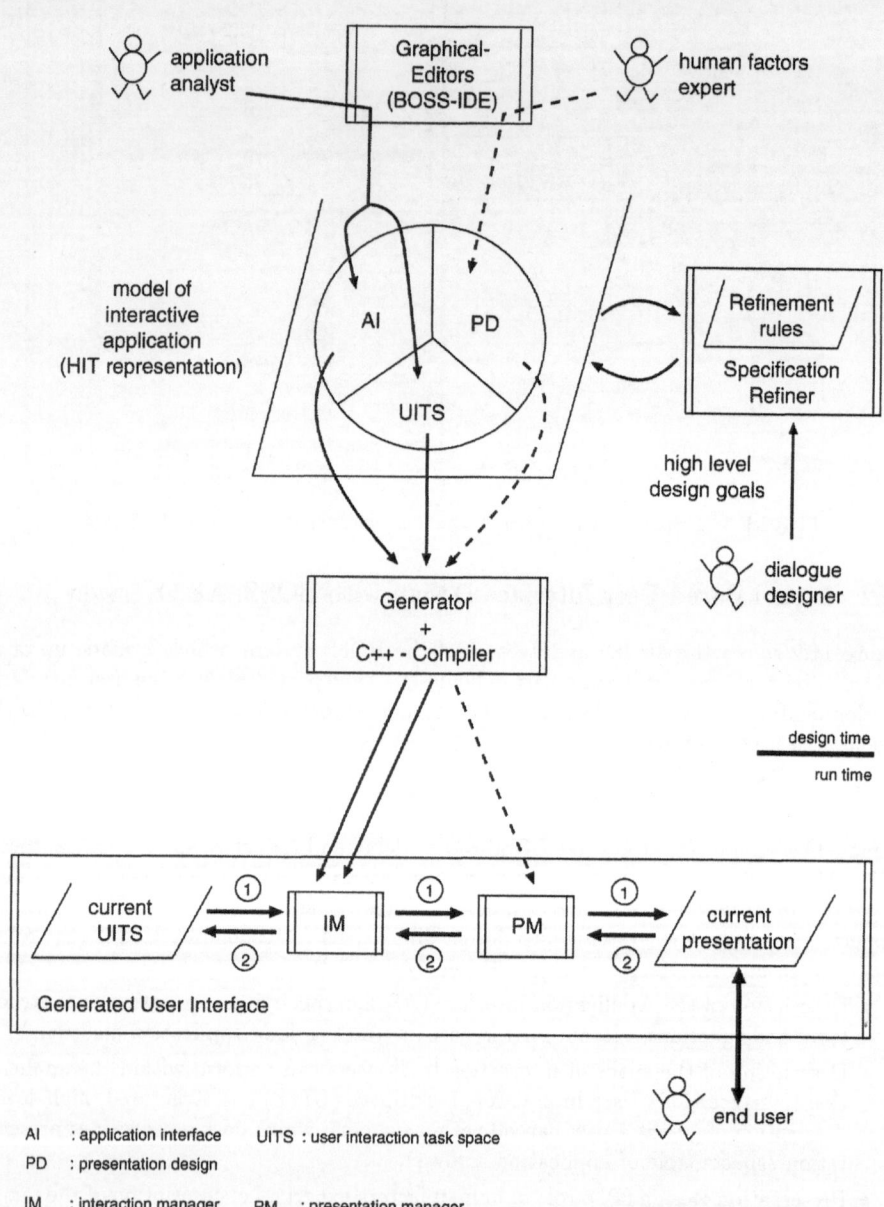

FIGURE 11.2. Architecture of BOSS (communication with application omitted

complex tasks into simpler ones results in functions which can be carried out without user interaction and become therefore part of AI.

Also the parts of the model are to some extent application independent. Typically, the model part PD contains rules how to present "generic" interaction tasks like entering data instances or triggering application functions. As such interaction tasks appear in almost every user interface, PD can be regarded as the specification of a reusable user interface style guide, of which many (but not all) parts can be used within different applications. It is a main goal of the BOSS system to increase the level of reusability also for the design dimensions AI and UITS by providing means for specifying reusable "building blocks" for the composition of AI and UITS.

Although AI, UITS and PD belong to different UI design dimensions similar kinds of information have to be described:

- At each level structural information is modeled. In AI, complex application data structures are built from "simpler" ones. The UITS dimension captures how (i.e. by which temporal relation) simpler tasks are composed to complex tasks. Recursion is used to model arbitrary deep nested structures.

- Structural descriptions have to be enriched by semantic information to model e.g. data structures which have to fulfill semantic constraints (semantic data models). When modelling the UITS, not only the syntactical task structures (i.e. task–subtask relations) have to be described. It is also necessary to model context sensitive (e.g. under which conditions a task may be executed) and data flow dependencies between tasks (on which input data does a task operate, what output data is delivered by the task, by which interactions a user transforms input into output data).

Every part of the model has to be represented explicitly by a certain specification model. The BOSS system employs only one encompassing specification model (HIT, Hierarchic Interaction graph Templates) for the representation of all parts of the model of an interactive application.

11.2.2   The HIT Specification Model: An Overview

The HIT specification model combines properties of object–oriented and rule–based specification techniques. A HIT–specification consists of a set of basic data type and function definitions and a set of templates called HITs (Hierarchic Interaction Graph Template). Within a specification, HITs are used mainly for two purposes:

- HITs may serve as prototypes for creating objects (HIT–instances) maintaining their own state, reacting in response to external messages and being connected with other objects in an object structure (object–oriented view). In the context of user interface design, these object–oriented properties are employed e.g. for describing objects representing instances of those user interaction tasks, which are part of the user interaction task space UITS.

- HITs may be used for specifying rules describing the transformation of input data into output data (rule–based view). The rule–based properties of the HIT specification model are important in the context of presentation design, where rules capturing software–ergonomic guidelines e.g. for the presentation of application data have to be defined.

The HIT specification model shares properties with extended data flow diagrams used for the specification of information systems [23, 16, 29] and techniques known from compiler construction like dynamic and higher order attribute grammars [10, 6, 1]. In their "original" application domain these specification techniques are known for combining intuitivity with efficiency.

A definition of a HIT consists of a structural (syntactical) and a semantic part.

The structural definition describes how a HIT h is constructed from "simpler" HITs $h_1, ..., h_n$ using operators like construction of records ("parallel" composition, $h = rec(h_1, ..., h_n)$) alternatives ($h = alt(h_1, ..., h_n)$) or sequences ($h = seq(h_1, ..., h_n)$). As in attribute grammars, this structural description is enriched by semantic information. Associated with a HIT, there are various kinds of data flow constraints between the following entities:

- slots (in the context of attribute grammars named attributes) representing the state of an HIT instance. A slot stores either a data instance (e.g. a instance of a HIT) or a reference to another slot. Certain slots of a HIT are distinguished: Through its input-, input/output- and output- parameter slots a HIT instance shares parts of its state with related HIT instances in an object hierarchy. Input slots may be modified by an external entity (e.g. a human user), the values of output slots are relevant to the environment.

- message ports for receiving events from external entities and for the distribution of messages across a structure of HIT-instances (building communication structures). A HIT containing input slots, message ports or component-HITs with input slots or message ports is said to be interactive. Interactive HITs, input slots and message ports are called interactions. Interactions in a HIT instance can be enabled (allowing users to interact) or disabled. Together with the output slots, the interactions define the observable state of an HIT instance.

- rules defining either a directed equation in a "spreadsheet-like" manner (i.e. one-way constraints which should hold at every time) or a transaction caused by an external entity (e.g. an application function called by an user). A rule invokes either an external function or an instance of a HIT. A rule may have a precondition which is normally the precondition of the called function.

To encourage reusage of HITs in different contexts a HIT may parametrized (like template classes in C++). Each component of a HIT may be annotated with arbitrary information, which may be used by tools reasoning about specifications. E.g. for a transaction rule in an HIT being part of UITS the estimated frequency of use is an important information for presentation design.

The lifetime of a particular HIT-instance i is determined by the structural context of i (i.e. whether i is part of e.g. a sequential or alternative HIT instance) and by an applicability condition depending on the values of the input parameter slots and a termination condition depending on the so called termination slots, which are usually a subset of the output parameter slots. With these mechanisms a set of HITs describes an object space changing dynamically to satisfy the semantic context conditions given by applicability and termination conditions. E.g. when a HIT $h = alt(h_1, ..., h_n)$ consisting of the alternatives $h_1, ..., h_n$ is instantiated, only one of those alternatives with satisfied applicability condition is instantiated too. This results in a dynamically growing and shrinking tree of HIT-instances (and therefore in a dynamically growing and shrinking data flow graph). A tree of HIT-instances is called consistent when (among other criteria), at each node, the applicability condition is satisfied and the termination condition is not satisfied.

The HIT specification model incorporates a few extensions by which the behaviour of an user interface can be specified in a "fine grained" way, like

- the behaviour of rules wrt. to violated preconditions can be tailored
- rules may demand their input parameters in a particular order. This causes interactions like input slots to be enabled only if they supply (directly or indirectly) a parameter position of a demand rule, which is currently required
- interactions may be temporarily blocked by other interactions to realize modal forms of dialogue.

Moreover, "generic" UI features like UNDO/REDO are supported (for more details see [25]). Normally these "advanced" features are not employed by user interface designers directly, but are used for the automatic refinement of given specifications (see figure 11.2).

11.2.3 Specification Refinement and Generation of Efficient Programms

As shown in figure 11.2 BOSS offers a refinement component which performs transformations on the model according to high level design goals entered by a dialogue expert. The refinement layer will be discussed in detail later.

From the refined UI specification a generator builds the components Interaction Manager (IM) and Presentation Manager (PM) of the running user interface. During this generation process, the completeness and consistency of the model is checked. If, e.g., there is an application function in AI which does not appear in the UITS, the UITS is not complete wrt. the application interface. Consistency of the model is violated, if e.g. a sequential task in the UITS is represented by the sequential HIT $h = seq(h_1, h_2)$ and there are data flow dependencies from h_2 to h_1.

From each specified HIT a corresponding C++ – class with appropriate constructors, destructors, members and member functions is generated using modified techniques from compiler construction like incremental attribute evaluation [31] or pre–generation of evaluation strategies. At run time, unlike in other model based interface tools, no time and memory expensive techniques like unification and resolution are employed.

The interaction manager IM is composed of those C++ object classes, which are generated out of the HITs constituting the design dimensions AI and UITS. Therefore, the IM component manages task–level user interaction at run time. The presentation manager PM is built from the C++ classes generated from the HITs in PD and is capturing software ergonomic rules in a constructive, executable manner.

11.2.4 Runtime Architecture of Generated User Interfaces

As shown in figure 11.2, a generated user interface contains, besides the components IM and PM, at least the two "data bases" Current UITS and Current Presentation, which provide two different views on the state of the user interface of an interactive application:

- Current UITS denotes the state wrt. the user interaction task space UITS. Current UITS is capturing knowledge about the tasks the user has completed, is currently working on and has to complete to achieve a certain goal.
- Current Presentation is a representation of the Current UITS in terms of Abstract Interaction Objects (AIO) [5] like abstract buttons or menus.

Current UITS and Current Presentation are coupled by the components IM and PM through the information flows labeled with "1" and "2" in figure 11.2:

- information flow "1" denotes the construction of a presentation by the presentation manager PM. Every time, when Current UITS (logical structure) changes a corresponding Current Presentation (layout structure) is created and presentation objects are bound to all the observable objects of the logical structure. As outlined below the Current UITS is represented as a consistent tree of HIT instances, which can be treated as a "normal" data instance within the HIT specification model. Therefore, the process of constructing the Current Presentation according to software ergonomic guidelines can be specified within HIT.

- information flow "2" shows how a user changes the Current UITS. Through the Current Presentation the user instantiates a HIT (normally the HIT encapsulating the top–level task decomposition of the interactive system) by indicating its current input parameter values. Starting with this toplevel HIT instance, the interaction manager IM constructs a consistent tree of HIT instances, which becomes the Current UITS. The user interacts with this Current UITS by triggering transaction rules, by changing (through interaction objects in the presentation) the values of input slots or by sending messages to message ports of a HIT instance. If the Current UITS becomes inconsistent through these interactions the IM constructs a new and consistent Current UITS. If, e.g., in an instance $i = seq(i_1)$ of the sequential HIT $h = seq(h_1, h_2)$ the instance i_1 of h_1 has terminated, an instance i_2 of h_2 is created as child of i. In this context, the interaction manager IM can be regarded as a task–oriented parser, which analyzes a stream of basic user interactions in terms of those higher level task units given in the UITS description.

11.3   Model Based User Interface Design with BOSS: An Example

To illustrate the use of the BOSS system at the various levels of interface design, we outline the specification of an example: a simple Order Management System (OMS), which handles customers, products and orders.

11.3.1   Modeling the Application Interface (AI)

The AI consists of a structural and a functional part. Figure 11.3 shows the semantic data model (structural part) of the OMS in a grammar–like notation.

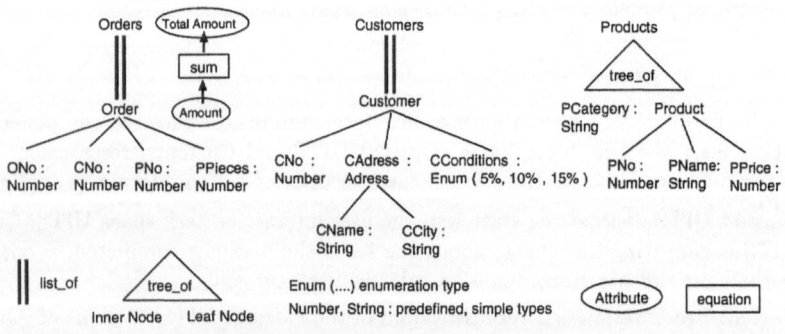

FIGURE 11.3. Semantic data model of the OMS

Based on predefined, simple data types (here: *Number, Enum(...), String*), complex data structures are built using operators for constructing records, alternatives, lists, trees. Data structures may be assigned additional semantic information via attributes and attribute evaluation rules (usually directed equations). In our example the attribute *TotalAmount* of *Orders* holds the *sum* of the values of all orders in the order–list *Orders*. Every time, when an instance of *Orders* is modified (e.g. by the insertion of a new order) *TotalAmount* is kept up to date.

The functional part of the application interface consists of the functions which the OMS exports to the user (see figure 11.4). A function is described by indicating its formal

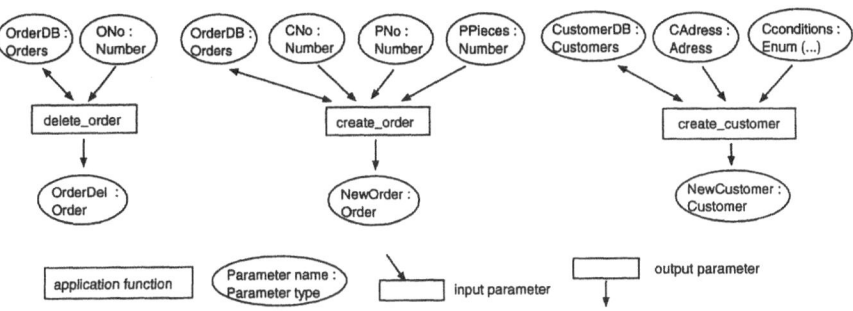

FIGURE 11.4. Application Functions of the OMS

input, input/output and output parameters and a precondition on the values of its input parameters. In our example *create_order* creates a new order and *delete_order* is used for removing existing orders. New customers are created with *create_customer*. *create_order* and *delete_order* modify their input/output parameter *OrderDB*, which is denoted by the double–headed arrow. Preconditions describe constraints on the input parameter values of a function. For the function *delete_order*, e.g., we demand that the parameter *ONo* (the number of the order to be deleted) denotes an existing order in the parameter *OrderDB*.

It is important to note, that BOSS uses no pre– and postcondition mechanism for describing the sequencing of functions in a task. This kind of information is expressed in an explicit manner when modeling the UITS.

11.3.2   Representing the UITS

Within the HIT specification model application analysts describe the User Interaction Task Space (UITS) in a two step process closely related to phsychologically motivated modelling approaches in HCI (e.g. [22]):

- First, the structure of the UITS is described. Complex user interaction tasks (e.g. interaction with the entire OMS) are decomposed into simpler tasks until the level of application functions is reached. Within HIT such a task hierarchy is modeled in a grammar–like, structured manner as a set of HITs. Each task corresponds to a HIT. The task structure is represented by the structure of the HIT, i.e. the composition (e.g. sequential or parallel) of "simpler" HITs it consists of.

- In the second step the structural description of the UITS is enriched by semantic information to relate the entities given from AI with user interaction. Within HIT, user interaction in a task is described by defining data flows between user inputs (input slots, interactive HITs), functions (rules) and data stores (slots). A task can be regarded as accomplished if the termination condition of the HIT is satisfied.

From the point of view of the interaction manager IM the UITS description models all possible sessions (sequences of basic interactions) between an user and an interactive application. Due to the explicite, declarative HIT representation of the UITS BOSS can determine how a particular task is accomplished by analyzing the task structure and by following the data flows backward from termination slots to input slots and interactive HITs. This knowledge can be exploited in various ways, e.g. for the generation of a context sensitive help system.

Figure 11.5 shows the HIT representation of the OMS toplevel task decomposition, which an application analyst would draw comfortably with the integrated development environment of BOSS. If not stated otherwise the applicability and termination conditions of a specified HIT are *true* and *false* per default.

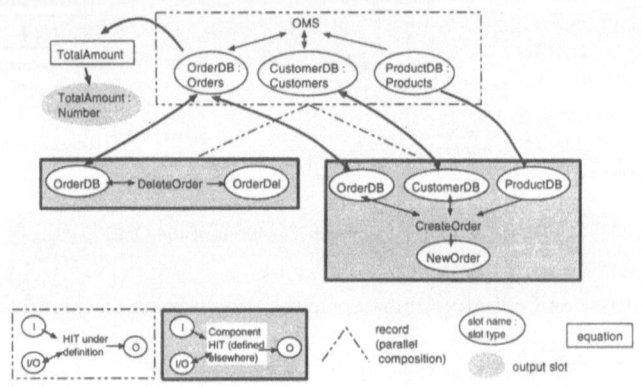

FIGURE 11.5. Toplevel Task Decomposition of the OMS represented as a HIT

The environment of the OMS is given by the "data bases" *OrderDB*, *CustomerDB* and *ProductDB*, which are input *(ProductDB)* and input/output *(OrderDB, CustomerDB)* parameters of the HIT *OMS*. The OMS supports the independent subtasks *CreateOrder* and *DeleteOrder* working on the same data bases as the *OMS* (indicated by the data flows in figure 11.5). As the user should be permanently informed about the amount of all orders in *OrderDB*, we introduce an output slot *TotalAmount*, whose value is computed by an equation rule (see 11.2.2) accessing the value of the attribute *TotalAmount(OrderDB)* of *OrderDB*. Every time when the attribute *TotalAmount(OrderDB)* changes (e.g. when a new order is created), the value of the slot *TotalAmount* is recomputed automatically via incremental attribute evaluation. This change is propagated automatically by the presentation manager PM to the interaction object displaying the value of *TotalAmount*.

The component HITs *CreateOrder* and *DeleteOrder* of the HIT *OMS* represent mutually independent subtasks in the order management system. When the HIT *OMS* is instantiated and becomes part of Current UITS, instances of *CreateOrder* and *DeleteOrder* are created too, as *OMS* is structured in a record–like manner.

In the task *CreateOrder* (see figure 11.6) new orders are added to the system by invoking the application function *create_order* represented by a transaction rule. While an equation–rule (see above) is evaluated automatically to satisfy constraints which should

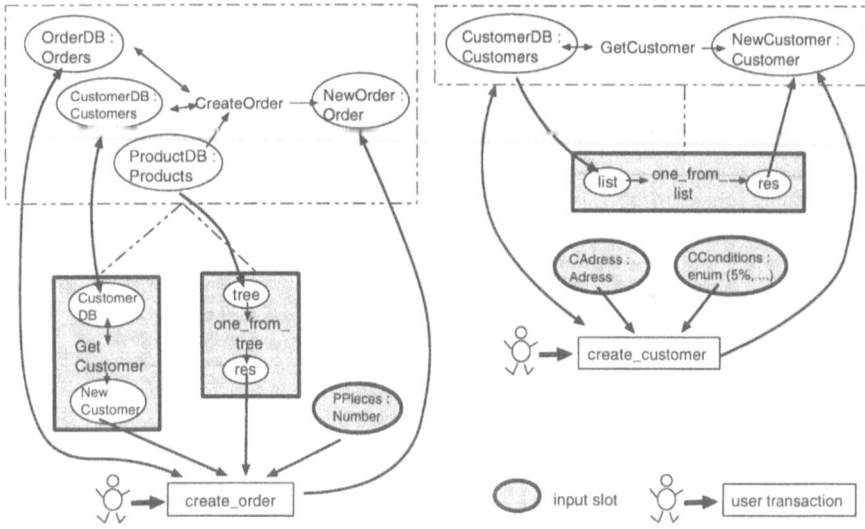

FIGURE 11.6. HIT representation of the tasks CreateOrder and GetCustomer

hold at every time, a transaction has to be triggered explicitly by an user. For the input parameter *PNo* of *create_order* users should be allowed to enter only products from the product data base *ProductDB*. This is accomplished by introducing an *one_from_tree*–HIT ensuring that users can enter only values from a given tree (here: *ProductDB*, which is organized hierarchically as a tree of products, see figure 11.6). The input parameter *CNo* can be entered through a *one_from_list* selection from the customer data base *CustomerDB*. If a "new" customer has not been found in *CustomerDB* users should be able to create a new customer account becoming automatically the required parameter for *create_order*. This behaviour is encapsulated in the HIT *GetCustomer* shown also in figure 11.6, where the output parameter slot *NewCustomer* is connected to an *one_from_list* HIT and to the result of the *create_customer* transaction.

Representing the user interaction task space UITS within the HIT specification model is a designer–friendly and problem–oriented way to describe the task–level dynamics of an interactive application. Of course, in practice, the UITS has a much richer structure than in our OMS. This complexity is handled by application analysts by composing the UITS in a graphical, visual–programming–like manner out of reusable, simple structured building blocks like e.g. *GetCustomer*. HITs like *one_from_list* and *one_from_tree* denote interaction tasks, which appear in almost every UITS e.g. to ensure preconditions of application functions. Therefore they are part of a standard task library, which supports an application analyst in setting up the UITS. The specification of the presentation of such standard interaction tasks belongs to the dimension of presentation design.

11.3.3 Presentation Design with HITs

In model based interface tools presentation design does not mean the direct composition of a particular user interface display, but consists of setting up executable rules for constructing presentations. Within the area of model based tools, there are two approaches for presentation design (PD):

- generation of the static interface layout out of knowledge available at designtime (e.g. [14, 2, 5, 12])
- specification of the presentation of the current system state (e.g. [30])

As shown in 11.2, BOSS follows the second approach as it allows specifying context sensitive presentations [18] depending on data available only at run–time (e.g. data instances which are interactively constructed by the user, adaptive presentations). In the BOSS system presentation design means specifying the presentation manager PM (see figure 11.2), which maps the Current UITS (task–level state, logical structure) to the Current Presentation (layout structure) built from so called Abstract Interaction Objects (AIO) [5]. As Current Presentation has to allow users to interact with Current UITS (e.g. by changing the values of input slot instances), this involves the specification

- of application specific interaction objects, if necessary. As HIT combines concepts like modeling object structures and evaluation of one–way constraints (i.e. directed equations), which are often used in graphical toolkits, application specific objects with e.g. interactive graphics can be described within the HIT specification model.
- of the selection of appropriate interaction objects by which e.g. a user triggers transactions, modifies the values of input slots or by which the values of output slots are displayed.
- of the composition of those selected interaction objects into a presentation which visually reinforces the logical structure. E.g. for an input slot storing a "complex" data instance, the interaction objects building up the presentation generated to allow users to edit that instance should be arranged according to the logical data structure.

Current UITS is represented in the BOSS system as a consistent tree of HIT instances, which is treated as normal data instance within HIT. Therefore, the presentation manager PM may be specified within the HIT specification model. With BOSS, human factors experts identify common user interaction tasks like browsing through large object structures (e.g. *one_from_list*, *one_from_tree*) or editing data instances. Software–ergonomic guidelines determining the presentation of these tasks are represented in a constructive, formal and unambigous manner as a set of HITs in the BOSS system. This can be regarded as the formal representation of an reusable UI style guide.

To show how the HIT specification model is used in the context of presentation design, let us regard an example: The presentation manager PM may be specified through a HIT *PresentTaskInstance*, which requests as input parameter the HIT instance to be presented (e.g. the root of Current UITS) and produces a presentation built from predefined AIO like buttons or menus or from application specific interaction objects. In each HIT instance, which is part of the Current UITS, an enabled input slot stands for the elementary interaction task "edit a possibly complex structured object". The HIT *EditObj* (see figure 11.7), which is part of the definition of *PresentTaskInstance*, defines generic presentations for editing arbitrary objects. *EditObj* consists of a couple of alternative HITs arranged in a decision–tree–like structure according to the structure of the object to be edited. The HIT *EditObj* requests as input parameters the object instance to be edited *(ObjID)* and a optional label *Label* and produces a presentation *Lay*, by which a user can edit *ObjID*.

The composition activity in presentation design involves deriving possibly complex layout constraints from logical structures. Figure 11.1 shows a human factors expert working with the BOSS–IDE at the specification of the HIT *EditRecord*, which handles the presentation of editing an object constructed in a record–like manner (expressed in the applicability–condition *record_type(ObjID)*, see figure 11.7). For each component of *ObjID*

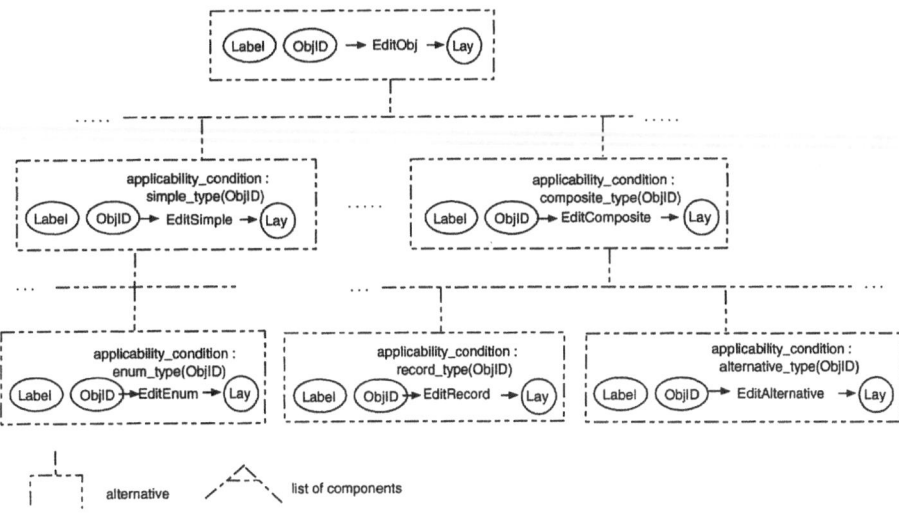

FIGURE 11.7. HIT representation of EditObj in a decision–tree–like structure

a presentation is constructed recursively by *EditObj*. The component presentations are composed by the equation–rule *layout_for_records*, which performs in our example just a horizontal alignment between the label (i.e. the name of the record component) and the vertical alignment of the component presentations. The function *nth_comp* yields the n-th component of a record and its name. The window on the right side of figure 11.1 shows a user interface automatically generated by BOSS containing two different presentations of *EditObj*. In the upper part, a human factors expert edits an instance of the data structure *Customer* (see figure 11.3) in its logical structure, the lower part shows the presentation produced by *EditRecord*. The radio buttons for editing the component *CConditions*, e.g., are generated by the HIT *EditEnum* (see figure 11.7), as *CConditions* is an instance of an enumeration type.

Please note that the example does not consider information like spatial constraints (e.g. screen size) or user preferences, which have much influence on presentation design [5]. As there are often many possibilities for determining presentations, the HIT specification model allows to find the "best" solution employing techniques from dynamic programming. A noninteractive, alternative HIT is assigned a cost function to choose the branch yielding the lowest costs among all applicable branches.

11.4   Specification Refinement Through High–Level Transformations

The parts AI and UITS of the model of an interactive application describe the so called logical structure of the user interface, which is a high level description of "what a user can do with the system". There are quite a lot of degrees of freedom for determining concrete dialogue and presentation characteristics of an interface supporting user interaction in a given UITS.

As stated above the HIT specification model provides means for user interface designers in the role of dialogue experts to tailor the behaviour of user interfaces in a fine grained way (specification refinement). It is, however, a quite tedious task to do this specification refinement "by hand", as high level design goals like "build an interface for a certain class of users" have to be expressed in a consistent manner by the means provided by the underlying specification model (e.g. determining in which order the parameters of an application function should be entered).

To overcome this drawback, BOSS offers a specification refinement component (see figure 11.2) for the automatic refinement of "underspecified" models. To be able to do so, a model based user interface construction tool like BOSS has to

- organize possible user interface properties in a designspace with (almost) independent design dimensions. A vector in this designspace denotes the properties of a particular interface.
- maintain knowledge of mapping high level design goals to a vector in the designspace.
- maintain knowlegde about the transformations in the underlying specification model to achieve a desired property in a certain design dimension.

Figure 11.8 shows a part of the designspace currently implemented in the BOSS specification refinement component:

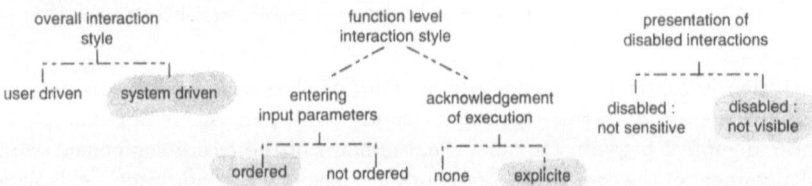

FIGURE 11.8. Designspace for determining user interface properties at different abstraktion levels

The dimensions in this designspace denote the following properties:

- *overall interaction style* defines the characteristics of an user interface in a rather global manner. A system–driven [15] interaction style guides a novice user in walking through the UITS. In an user–driven [15] interaction style expert users are almost free in exploring the UITS on their own. E.g. mutual independent tasks can be carried out in an interleaving fashion.
- *function level interaction style* defines the user interface characteristics at a fine grained level, adressing the following questions: Should input parameters be entered in a particular order? Should the user acknowledge explicitly the execution of the function? Moreover, transformations like CSO (Currently Selected Object) or CSC (Currently Selected Command) offered by UIDE [8] belong to the dimension function level interaction style.
- *presentation of disabled interactions* deals with presentation level characteristics like: Which presentation style is appropriate for interactions disabled in the current system state? Should they be not visible at all or visible, but not sensitive for user interactions?

Let us have a look on some of the underlying transformations performed by the specification refinement component to approximate the overall interaction style system driven. Typically the transformations performed include transformations on the structure of the UITS. Figure 11.9 shows an example of such a structural transformation rule. The trans-

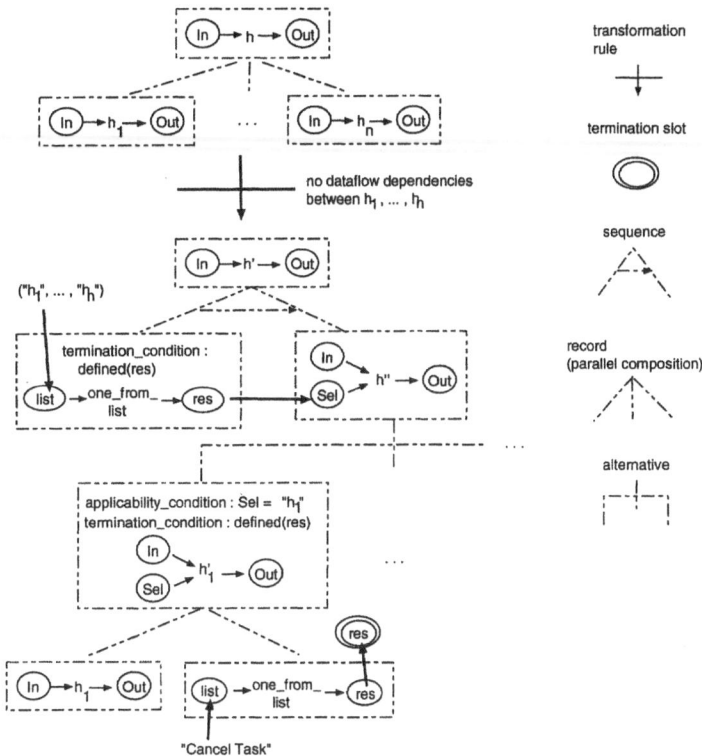

transformation rule

termination slot

no dataflow dependencies between $h_1, \ldots, h_n$

sequence

record (parallel composition)

alternative

FIGURE 11.9. Sample transformation rule to approximate system driven behaviour

formation rule in 11.9 may only be applied to a record HIT $h = rec(h_1, \ldots, h_n)$ where there are no dataflow dependencies between the components $h_1, \ldots, h_n$. From the point of view of the UITS model part h represents an interaction task with mutually independent subtasks. The rule transforms h into the sequential HIT h'. Through the first component of h' (a *one_from_list* selection) users have to select first, which task they want to accomplish. The alternative HIT h'' ensures that, after the selection, an instance of the selected task becomes part of the Current UITS. If the HIT h_i ($1 \leq i \leq n$) has no termination condition, h_i is augmented by a HIT h'_i which allows users to terminate the task.

At a "fine grained" level the property system driven in the dimension overall interaction style is mapped to demand graph evaluation strategies known from incremental attribute evaluation [31] or data flow machines. In the following we will outline how system driven interaction behaviour is approximated through demand evaluation: Figure 11.10 shows the two demand transaction rules t_1 and t_2. A interaction (input slot, message port, interactive HIT) connected to a demand rule is enabled only if it is connected with a currently required parameter position. If the result of the t_2 transaction is required, the input slot i_1 is to be enabled first, as i_1 is required for executing t_1 and t_1 supplies the first parameter position of t_2. The flow of enabling is depicted in figure 11.10. From the user's point of view this flow of enabling means, that the interactive application demands all information from the user, which is needed to accomplish a certain task (i.e. system driven behaviour).

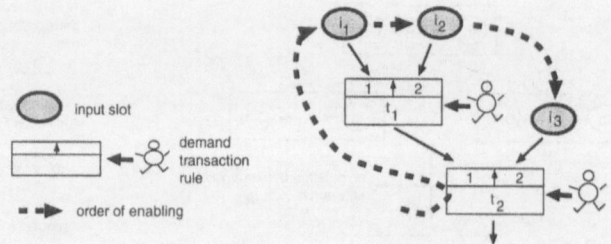

FIGURE 11.10. Approximating system driven behaviour through demand rules

Overall the vector in the designspace shown in figure 11.8 approximates the high level design goal "build an interface for an user with little semantic knowledge" [4] (i.e. a user with low experience with the application domain). The refinements shown in figures 11.9 and 11.10 represent the HCI principle, that unexperienced users should be guided by the system when accomplishing a task. In the OMS specification from figures 11.5 and 11.6 users can accomplish the subtasks *CreateOrder* and *DeleteOrder* in an interleaved fashion, being allowed to enter all required information in arbitrary order. For less experienced users it would be more appropriate, if the system informs the user about the available tasks, let the user choose one of these tasks, and .demands step by step all information required to accomplish the task. Figure 11.11 shows snapshots of an interactive session with the OMS, after it has been refined according to the system–driven style shown in figure 11.8. The presentations shown below are automatically derived by the presentation manager PM from the Current UITS (i.e. the task–level state of the user interface) at two consecutive states.

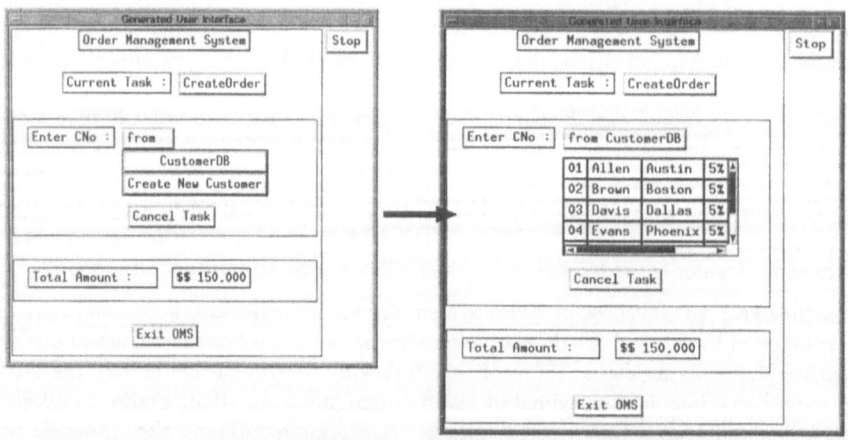

FIGURE 11.11. Two snapshots of a system driven session in the OMS

As the OMS provides two independent tasks *CreateOrder* and *DeleteOrder* (see figure 11.5) the structural refinement rule can be applied. Users have to state first in a system driven session, which task they want to accomplish. Selecting *CreateOrder* from an generated menu (layout representation for the *one_from_list* selection introduced by the structural refinement rule) causes the task *CreateOrder* to be enabled. In our function level dialog style the parameter *CNo* of *create_order* is requested (see figure 11.6). This enables the task *GetCustomer* which provides two alternatives for indicating the customer (see figure 11.6). In our example we want to take the customer from the *CustomerDB* (see figure 11.11), which causes the corresponding *one_from_list* HIT to be enabled. As in our presentation style only enabled interactions become visible in the user interface layout, a possible presentation of the task *one_from_list* appears now (see figure 11.11). The button labeled "Cancel Task" is the presentation of the *one_from_list* selection introduced in the refinement rule to let users terminate a task. After the users pushes *Cancel Task* the OMS is in its beginning state (users can select again the task they want to accomplish).

11.5 Related Work

In HIGGENS [11] the semantic data model is used to derive views as abstract representations of user interface displays. MIKE [19], Mickey [20] and UofA* [27] generate user interfaces out of a description of application actions and parameters. Compared to these systems, which had much influence on the development of BOSS, BOSS allows to exert more control over the different aspects of an interactive application's model, therefore increasing the bandwith of user interfaces, which can be generated.

ITS [32] enriches the traditional three layer UIMS architecture by a style layer describing the mapping of dialogue content to style. In contrast to BOSS, ITS offers no integrated development evironment and no graphical specification techniques. ITS employs different notations for describing dialogue content and presentation design rules.

UIDE [8, 28, 9] and HUMANOID [30, 17], recently joint in the MASTERMIND–project [18], offer an encompassing design model for the specification of an interactive application's properties, upon which various tools offer support at design–time (e.g. generating menus and dialogue–boxes) [14] and run–time (e.g. animated help). BOSS differs from MASTERMIND in the use of an encompassing specification model to represent all parts of the user interface design model, in the support of semantic data models, in the application of adapted generation methods from compiler construction to produce efficient C++–Code, in the rather explicit representation of user interaction task space and in the use of techniques from dynamic programming (mainly for presentation design). Although BOSS can determine via dataflow analysis how even quite complex tasks have to be accomplished, the current implementation of BOSS (ca 80000 lines of C++ code) does not offer yet the capabilities of UIDE in the domain of animated help.

ADEPT [13] provides a task and user oriented design model for user interface specification and generation. Again, BOSS differs from ADEPT in the use of an encompassing specification model also suited for presentation design. Compared to ADEPT the aspect of data flow is emphasized in BOSS. The level of the UITS description of BOSS is, regarding the degree of abstraction, between the task and the AIM (Abstract Interface Model) level of ADEPT.

11.6 Acknowledgements

This work has been supported by Siemens Corporate Research and Development, Department of System Ergonomics and Interaction (ZFE ST SN 51). I would like to thank Werner Schreiber, Bernhard Bauer and Frank Lonczewski for their useful comments and suggestions on draft versions of this paper.

11.7   References

[1] H. Alblas and B. Melichar, editors. *Attribute Grammars, Applications and Systems.* Springer LNCS 545, 1991.

[2] H. Balzert. Der JANUS–Dialogexperte: Vom Fachkonzept zur Dialogstruktur. *Softwaretechnik 93*, 13(3), 11 1993.

[3] L. Bass, C. Cockton, and C. Unger. IFIP Working group 2.7 User Interface Engeneering: A Reference Model for Interactive System Construction. In J. Larson and C. Unger, editors, *Engeneering for Human-Computer Interaction*. North Holland, 1992.

[4] L. Bass and J. Coutaz. *Developing Software for the User Interface* . Addison–Wesley, 1991.

[5] F. Bodard, A.M. Hennebert, J.M. Leheureux, I. Sacre, and J. Vanderdonckt. Architecture Elements for Highly–Interactive Business–Oriented Applications . In L. Bass, J. Gornostaev, and C. Unger, editors, *Human–Computer Interaction: EWHCI 93 Proceedings* . Springer LNCS 753 , 8 1993.

[6] P. Deransart, M. Jourdan, and B. Lorho. *Attribute Grammars: Definitions, Systems and Bibliography* . Springer, 1988.

[7] J. Eickel. Logical and layout structures of documents. *Computer Physics Communication*, 61:201–208, 1990.

[8] J. Foley, W. C. Kim, S. Kovacevic, and K. Murray. UIDE – An Intelligent User Interface Design Enironment . In *Intelligent User Interfaces*. Addison-Wesley, 1991.

[9] M. Frank and J. Foley. Model–Based Interface Design By Example and By Interview . In *Proceedings of the UIST 93, ACM Symposium on User Interface Software and Technology* . ACM , 11 1993.

[10] H. Ganzinger. *Optimierende Erzeugung von Übersetzerteilen aus implementierungsorientierten Sprachbeschreibungen*. PhD thesis, Technische Universität München, 1978.

[11] S. Hudson and R. King. A generator of direct manipulation office systems. *ACM Transactions on Information Systems*, 4(2):132–163, 1986.

[12] C. Janssen, A. Weisbecker, and J. Ziegler. Generating User Interfaces from Data Models and Dialogue Net Specifications . In *ACM Interchi 93 Proceedings* . ACM, 1993.

[13] P. Johnsen, S. Wilson, C. Kelly, and P. Markopoulos. Beyond hacking: a model based approach to user interface design . In *BCS HCI 93 Conference*. Cambridge University Press , 1993.

[14] W.C. Kim and J.D. Foley. Providing High-level Control and Expert Assistance in the User Interface Presentation Design . In *ACM INTERCHI'93 Proceedings* . ACM, 1993.

[15] J.A. Larson. *Interactive Software: Tools for building interactive user interfaces.* Prentice Hall, 1992.

[16] S. Lauesen and M.B. Harning. Dialogue Design Through Modified Datafow and Data Modelling . In *VHCI 93 Proceedings* . Springer LNCS 733, 1993.

[17] P. Luo, P. Szekely, and R. Neches. Beyond Interface Builders: Model–Based Interface Tools . In *ACM Interchi 93 Proceedings* . ACM, 1993.

[18] R. Neches, J. Foley, P. Szekely, P. Sukaviriya, P. Luo, S. Kovacevic, and S. Hudson. Knowledgeable Devolopment Environments Using Shared Design Models . In *Intelligent User Interfaces 93* . ACM, 1993.

[19] D. R. Olsen. MIKE: The Menu Interaction Kontrol Environment. *ACM Transactions on Graphics*, 5(4):318 – 344, 1986.

[20] D. R. Olsen. A programming language basis for user interface managment. In *ACM CHI 89 Proceedings*. ACM, 1989.

[21] *OSF/Motif Style Guide Release 1.1* . Open Software Foundation, 1991.

[22] S.J. Payne and T.R.G. Greene. Task–Action Grammars: A Model of the Mental Representation of Task Languages . *Human–Computer Interaction* , 2, 1986.

[23] S. Peretz. ADISSA: Architectural Design of Information Systems based on structured analysis. *Information systems*, 13(2):193–210, 1988.

[24] S. Schreiber. Specification and Generation of User Interfaces with the BOSS-System . In A. Cypher and J. Gornostaev, editors, *Proceedings East-West International Conference on Human-Computer Interaction EWHCI'94* . ICSTI Moscow, 8 1994. Also in: Human Computer Interaction, Selected Papers EWHCI'94 Conference, Springer LNCS 876 .

[25] S. Schreiber. The BOSS–System: A Tutorial Introduction . Technical report, Technische Universität München, to appear 1994.

[26] W. Schreiber. Prosaische Logik für Dichter und Denker – Textverarbeitung maßgeschneidert . *Forschung für Bayern*, (6), 1993.

[27] G. Singh. A high-level user interface management system. In *ACM CHI 89 Proceedings*. ACM, 1989.

[28] P. Sukaviriya, J. D. Foley, and T. Griffith. A second generation user interface design environment: The model and the runtime architecture. In *ACM INTERCHI 93 Proceedings* . ACM, 1993.

[29] A.G. Sutcliffe and M. McDermott. Integrating methods of human–computer interface design with structured sytems development . *Int. Journal of Man–Machine Studies* , 34, 1991.

[30] P. Szekely, P. Luo, and R. Neches. Faciliating the Exploration of Design Alternatives: The HUMANOID Model of User Interface Design . In *ACM CHI 92 Proceedings*. ACM, 1992.

[31] T. Weiske. SICK: Inkrementelle Auswertung von Attributgrammatiken . In G. Snelting, editor, *Sprachspezifische Programmierumgebungen: Workshop der Fachgruppe Implementierung von Programmiersprachen, T.H. Darmstadt 6.4 – 8.4.88* , 4 1988.

[32] C. Wiecha. ITS: A Tool for Rapidly Developing Interactive Applications . *ACM Transactions on Information Systems*, 8(3), 1990.

12 A Model-Based User Interface Architecture: Enhancing a Runtime Environment with Declarative Knowledge

Piyawadee "Noi" Sukaviriya
Jayakumar Muthukumarasamy
Martin Frank
James D. Foley

ABSTRACT

A model-based user interface environment refers to an interface design and execution environment which utilizes declarative semantic knowledge about application interfaces. We capture in the *application model* tasks which will be performed by users, their operational constraints, and objects on which these tasks operate. We capture in the *interface model* interface components, application-independent interface tasks, and operational constraints on these tasks. Mapping from the application to the interface model serves as a means to construct an interface to an application. Modeling components in the interface model are coupled with executable components, thereby forming working interfaces. They also support intelligent behavior such as partially automatic control sequencing, automatic generation of textual and animated help, and recordings of statistical and chronological command usage history. The modeling components in UIDE are task-oriented. Specifying an interface through these components not only eliminates the low-level programming from the interface creation process, but also makes the design process centered around user tasks.

12.1. Introduction

A model-based user interface architecture is a design and/or a runtime architecture which utilizes computer processable representation of an application interface. This means that information such as user tasks, application functionality, application objects, presentation objects, object behaviors, etc., can be represented. One of the benefits of having such a representation is that interface environments can reason about different aspects of the application which are related to user interfaces. For example, user interface control can be automated by inferring the semantic dependency from the application model in the runtime environment. Intelligent support such as automatic generation of help and recordings of user's action history can be provided utilizing the model. For these benefits to be supported across different applications, the architecture needs a schematic representation in which various applications can be specified. Our current model has such a representation which captures user operations and data objects within an application, how this level of information maps to interface operations and objects, and how information flows from one level to the other.

The research prototype reported in this paper is an extension to UIDE, the User Interface Design Environment [7, 8]. UIDE is designed to aid interface designers to create, modify, and generate interfaces to applications through high-level specifications. The purpose of the environment is to support the interface design process through its life cycle – from its inception to its execution. This support is made possible using a model which describes various details of an application interface including partial application semantics. Some of the research work done with UIDE are automatic layout of menus and dialog boxes [15, 5] and an automatic transformation among different interface paradigms [16]. The first generation UIDE was reported in [7, 8]; its emphasis has been on the design support, and not so much on the runtime environment. Also, its declarative knowledge emphasized how to capture application semantics but lacked a representation of the interfaces which it supported. We have expanded our research to strengthen the quality of runtime support which can be automatically provided from the model. We also added a representation of interface objects and their behavior so it can be reasoned about. For the past several years, we have changed the implementation platforms from an expert system shell called Automatic Reasoning Tool [13] to Smalltalk-80 and to C++; the latter choice is made to take advantage of better speed performance, easy integration with interface toolkits of our choice, as well as opportunities to easily adopt emerging input/output technology. The C++ environment currently has a greater emphasis on the runtime environment. We continue to call it UIDE, though the name has become rather misleading as the "D" in "Design" is no longer the sole focus of our research.

Four years ago, we started the C++ development by building a few small and separated C++ prototypes which take advantage of application knowledge to provide automated behavior. Details of these prototypes can be found in [5] on design assistance which automatically lay out menus and dialogue boxes, in [9] on using pre- and post-conditions to control interface objects at runtime, and in [6] on automatic generation of textual help. Our research focus has centered around UIDE's representation and the design of a comprehensive user interface architecture which functions with the representation. That is, once designers specify an application interface through the UIDE representation, the runtime architecture would understand the specification and can control the interface accordingly. The UIDE architecture has been revised to work in the C++ and the X environment. We expect the representation and the architecture to evolve over time, as more benefits are likely to be discovered from having processable application semantic knowledge available at runtime.

Since detailed UIDE's representation model was reported in [25], we will only give an overview of the model components in this paper. We will later focus on the runtime architecture, discussing how an interface is created and controlled. We will then briefly explain the currently supported runtime benefits which leverage off from having the model available at run-time such as automatic generation of context-sensitive help and recordings of user's statistical and chronological command usage history.

12.2. The Declarative Model

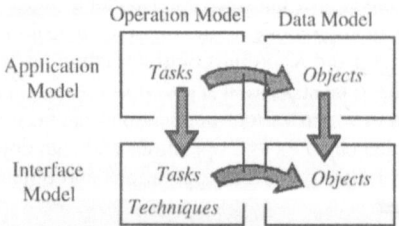

FIGURE 12.1. A basic scheme of UIDE's application model, interface model, and their interconnections.

We use a two-level view as a basis for representing an application interface. Both levels of representation consist of the **operational** model and the **data** model. The operational model contains declarative information about tasks which users can perform. The data model contains objects on which tasks operate. The distinction between the operational and the data models is similar to that of the original UIDE representation model. The top-level representation as shown in Figure 12.1 is referred to as the **application** model, which includes information about user tasks and objects specific to a particular application. This level of representation is usually interface independent and remains the same though interface descriptions have been changed to accommodate different interface paradigms.

The bottom-level representation is referred to as the **interface** model, which includes information about chosen interface tasks and objects which form an interface to the application. It also includes interaction techniques which specify low-level tasks to be performed with various input devices on interface objects. There are commonly used interface tasks, interface objects, and interaction techniques which share the same properties and behavior when used in various application interfaces. Contents of interface objects or sequencing of interface tasks (which influences sequencing of interface objects, i.e., when a dialog box should pop up) on the contrary can be customized and stored in the interface model of an application.

A single task representation is used in the operational model at all levels. A task is defined with a label and its parameters stating inputs which are needed for the task and outputs which the task produces. Each task can also be defined with pre-conditions stating which conditions must be true before the task can be invoked. A task can also be defined with post-conditions, which state the consequences of the task. Each object in the data model has a set of attributes. A class-subclass hierarchy and a part-whole hierarchy are supported in the data model.

It is the interconnection between tasks in the application model and the interface model which glues pieces of an interface together in a way that is meaningful to an application. The connections between tasks and objects are established through task-parameter relationships. The mapping from objects in the application model to objects in the interface model states how objects are presented in an interface. (In many cases this link is just a pointer from an application object to an interface object. For example, a logic gate in a circuit design application points to a bitmap object which symbolically represents the object and where it is placed on a design. In cases where multiple views of an object can be presented, a list of pointers can be stored with an application object.) Some interface objects such as buttons or menus indirectly connect to application actions through interface actions associated with them. The mapping from the application to the interface forms a task hierarchy which the end-users must follow.

The mapping from the application's operational model to the interface's operational model is one-to-many. That is an application task is often mapped to a set of interface tasks. These interface tasks can be thought of as procedural steps to achieve the application task. The order in which these interface tasks must be performed (by end-users) is dictated by sequencing specifications. For example, if an object can be selected after a menu item is selected, the two interface tasks are strung together through a sequential operator. The sequence specifies how the interface should flow, in addition to the pre-defined pre-conditions (such as an object can be selected if it is not hindered by other windows) and post-conditions (such as a button is highlighted once it is selected).

Figure 12.2 illustrates a view of the topology of connection from an application task to interface tasks. Every interface task is connected to at least one interaction technique. The interaction techniques at the bottom have their implementation duos; when users perform these techniques on specified interface objects at runtime, information flows from interaction techniques to the application task model.

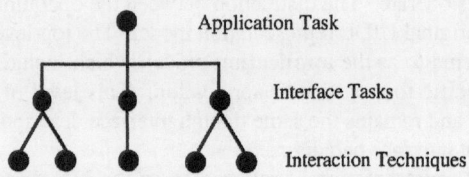

FIGURE 12.2. A mapping from an application task to interface tasks.
Perpendicular links denote a sequencing relation. Angular links denote alternatives

The concept of representing tasks with parameters is not all new. Cousin [11], MIKE [20], MICKEY [21], UofA* UIMS [22], and HUMANOID [27] use descriptions of commands and parameters to automatically generate interfaces. Their approaches center around the same essential concepts of task and parameter descriptions. However, all of these systems except HUMANOID discard the semantic information once interfaces are generated. Once the semantic information is lost, it cannot be reasoned about at run-time.

Also, the systems mentioned except UIDE have one-to-one mapping from their command descriptions to corresponding interface tasks and do not have detailed descriptions of interface tasks beyond commands and parameters.

HUMANOID and UIDE use pre-conditions for action descriptions to determine when an action is enabled and can be performed by the user. Both HUMANOID and UIDE also have explicit descriptions of application objects. We have partially consolidated the representations and runtime capabilities of HUMANOID and UIDE in a new system called MASTERMIND; its early proposal was documented in [19].

12.3. Examples of UIDE Representation

Figure 12.3 is a snapshot of a phone application interface, one of the interfaces developed with UIDE. By the appearance of this interface, one would think that it does not differ from one which is created using one of the available graphical interface builders plus some additional programming. In fact, this interface is internally very different because it has an underlying model. The interface components are those which have appearance on the screen while other components in the model are functional and most often are not prominent in an interface.

In this phone interface, the user must turn on the Speaker before using the phone. To make a call, the user clicks on the button labeled Call, enters a phone number, and then selects OK.

The data model of this interface consists of objects which can be seen mostly in the interface. The task model consists of actions which can be performed on these objects. Objects in Figure 12.3 such as buttons, text fields, scroll bar, etc., are represented as objects in the model. The buttons *Call, Hang Up, Speaker On, Speaker Off*, etc., are objects of class **Button**. Each button has the same attributes *Label, Width, Height, X, Y*, and *Owner* with their values set accordingly. Objects at this level are called *interface objects*, and they include objects such as those provided by standard X-based toolkits such as Motif, and those which are application specific, such as file icons in a file management application, or various types of gates in a circuit layout application. Objects in standard toolkits have pre-defined behavior with built-in user input handling mechanisms. Application-specific objects do not have behavior and it must be specified by designers. Internally dealing with these two types of objects at runtime is rather different. Not much implementation is required for built-in toolkit widgets. Application-specific objects however require UIDE's runtime architecture to handle input events for them and distribute them correctly according to the designer's specification. However, from the designer's point of view, we attempt to hide this difference and let designers model these objects in a homogeneous fashion. The difference only lies in that behavior cannot be added to pre-defined widget objects.

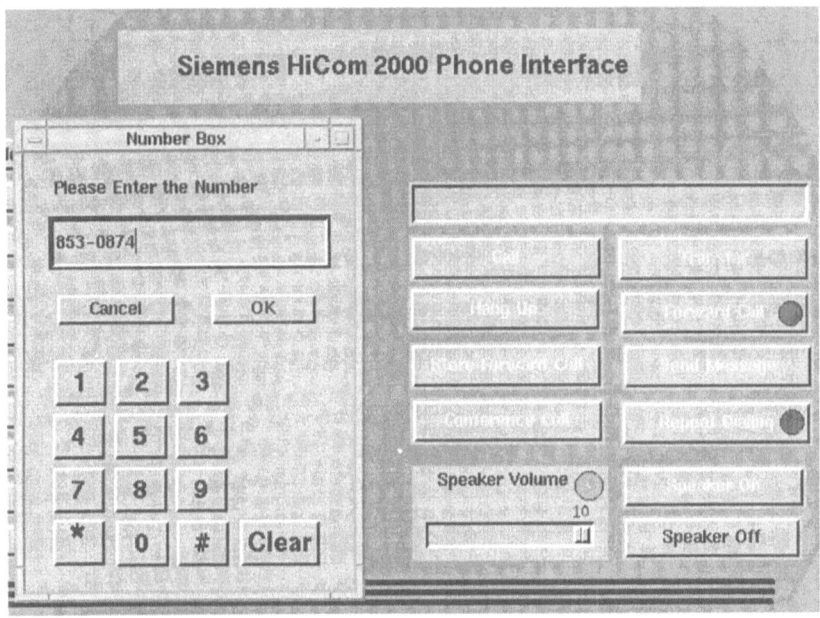

FIGURE 12.3. A Screen from a Phone Interface Created with the UIDE Model and SX/Tools as the Graphical Interface Front-End.

12.4. Creating a Model of an Application and its Interface

Currently the application and the interface model are created by parsing in textual inputs. An application model parser reads in descriptions of application tasks and generates a structure consisting of tasks, parameters, and pre- and post-conditions. Descriptions of interface tasks and interaction techniques are pre-defined and stored in the *Interface Library* using the same task structure as in the application model. An interface model parser reads in information which links application tasks to interface tasks and interaction techniques. This parser pulls related information from the *Interface Library* and decorates the declarative model for the run-time environment. Figure 12.4 shows a flow diagram of how the application and interface models are created from textual inputs.

It is our design decision to keep the interface model and the application model in 2 separate files. Doing so allows an application to remain the same while it is coupled with multiple interface files. This is useful when multiple interfaces are needed for different platforms, different users, or different interface paradigms.

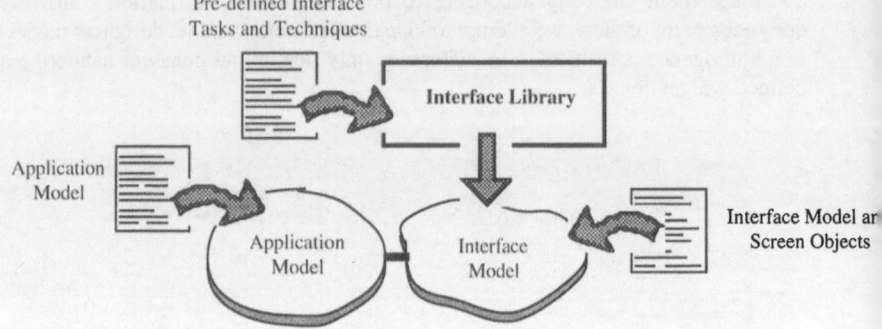

FIGURE 12.4. A Diagram Showing Input Files which are the Sources for Creating the Runtime Model.

In UIDE, a designer creates an interface for an application by first describing objects and tasks in the application. Figure 12.5 shows examples of some application tasks defined for the phone interface in Figure 12.3. The task representation in UIDE right now can handle hierarchical application task specification, but the run-time architecture currently only deals with one level of application tasks.

```
Task:  Call-with-a-Number
{
        Goal:  "To place a phone call at the number indicated"
        Parameter  (input phoneNumber, string)
        Preconditions: "status(Speaker, ON) & not status(Phone, IN-USE)"
        Postconditions: "status(Phone, IN-USE)"
}

Task: Hang-up
{
        Goal:  "To hang up the current connection."
        Preconditions:      "status (Phone, IN-USE)"
        Postconditions:     "not status (Phone, IN-USE)"
}
```

FIGURE 12.5. Textual Input for some Application Tasks.

In Figure 12.6, we show how connections to the interface are specified in the interface model file. From the top of the figure, *Call-with-a-Number* has 2 subtasks – *SelectCommand* and *EnterString*. In this scenario, the *SelectComand* interface task can be performed by one of these techniques - *MouseSelectButton* or *VoiceCommand*. For the *MouseSelectButton* technique, the button is set to "Call-button" and for the *VoiceCommand* technique, the voice string is set to "Call." For the other subtask *EnterString*, a text string is to be entered in a dialog box "Number-Box" in a text field "Phone-number-field." The post-conditions of these actions are: when the *String-Text-Field* technique is performed, the *text* entered will be transferred to the *value* parameter of the *EnterString* interface task. The *value* parameter is then transferred to the *phone-number* parameter of the *Call-with-a-Number* task.

```
Task: Call-with-a-Number
{
  Subtasks:      SelectCommand  EnterString
}

Task:  Call-with-a-Number.SelectCommand
{
  Subtasks:      MouseSelectButton I VoiceCommand
}

Task-Technique:  Call-with-a-Number.SelectCommand.MouseSelectButton
{
  Initialization:  button = "Call-button"
}

Task-Technique:  Call-with-a-Number.SelectCommand.MouseSelectButton
{
  Initialization:  VoiceCommand = "Call"
}
...
....
Task-Technique:   Call-with-a-Number.EnterString.String-Text-Field
{
  Initialization:  textField = "Phone-number-field",
                   dialogBox = "Number-Box"
  Postconditions: "assign(EnterString.value, String-Text-Field.text)"
}

Task-Subtask:   Call-with-a-Number.EnterString
{
  Postconditions: "assign(Call-with-a-Number.phone-number, EnterString.value)"
} .
```

FIGURE 12.6. An Example of Textual Descriptions of the Interface Model.

```
Prototype:  Name-Number-Pair            Object Call-button : Button {
{                                          Label:     "Call";
  <string>     FirstName;                  X:         250;
  <string>     LastName;                   Y:         100;
  <string>     PhoneNumber;                Width:     70;
}                                          Height:    50;
                                           Owner:     "Main-Window";
// This is an example of how an instance   }
// would be created.

Jane : Name-Number-Pair
{
          FirstName     Jane;
          LastName      Smith;
          PhoneNumber   777-8888;
  <string> Her-Birthday    "November 16";
}
```

FIGURE 12.7. Example of Specifications of an Object Prototype and Object Instances

Figure 12.7 shows an example of object prototype definition and object instances in the interface model of the phone application. (Objects in the application model are defined in the same syntax.) Interface objects for graphical user interfaces normally refer to objects of which prototypes are pre-defined, such as buttons, menus, menu items, etc. When an object of a pre-defined prototype is specified, a declarative instance of the object is created and its contents initialized. New prototypes of objects can be defined as well as shown in Figure 12.7. Notice here that we do not create new classes of objects in C++ as a result. These objects are merely stored as a set of attribute-value pairs which can be reasoned about. If objects in an interface are rather sophisticated, the actual object class must be implemented to make the interface work as desired. We will omit details of this aspect in this paper. Finally, since we use the prototype-instance paradigm, new attributes can be easily added to an existing prototype of object when an instance is defined. An example of this is shown in the object which stores Jane's number in Figure 12.7.

Specifying all necessary details of application-interface connections requires quite a bit of understanding of which tasks are appropriate for which interface objects, which interface tasks are appropriate for different kinds of application tasks, which parameters each task has, and how parameter values should flow among tasks. The current design process through textual specifications is rather tedious and still requires quite a bit of knowledge of the representation; this may not be misleading to the designers. For example, a click-button technique must be associated with a button to create a click-able button, which is already implemented in Motif. This seems like an unnecessary step. Some of these mappings to existing toolkits could be automated in the future. Also, graphical, model-based user interface tools which automatically create textual specifications while interfaces are created visually would free designers from these syntax obligations. It would also allow them to switch between the bottom-up and the top-down approaches.

12.5. The Architecture

UIDE is object-oriented; tasks, techniques, parameters, objects, pre-conditions, and post-conditions are represented and stored as objects. These objects are linked together to maintain semantic relationships among related components. We maintain two facets of an object – the declarative facet and the functional facet. So far, we have explained the declarative part of our modeling components, which is used for reasoning at runtime. Some of these objects, such as interface objects and interaction techniques, are coupled with their implementation partners and work as functional objects in the runtime environment as well. The functional side of these components and how they fit together in an architecture are the key parts which make up a running interface. These are also the parts which are likely to require a re-implementation when there is a platform or toolkit change.

The architecture of the UIDE's runtime environment is shown in Figure 12.7. Siemens's S/X tools[1] with its server-client user interface architecture [17] is used as the graphical front-end to UIDE. The UIDE Runtime Controller maintains the model and interprets the models for sequencing control. The Runtime Controller communicates to SX/Tools through the Protocol Handler, which is implemented on top of the Xlib protocol [29]. The UIDE model and the Runtime Controller are implemented independently of toolkits used in the interface. The

---

[1]SX/Tools is written in C++ and is part of a commercial product VisualDialog marketed by Siemens Nixdorf, Munich, Germany.

interface runs as a separate process and communicates with UIDE through the protocol handler. Messages from the UIDE Runtime Controller to the graphical interface front-end are those which normally control the sequencing of an interface such as displaying objects, undisplaying windows, or disabling buttons and menu items, etc. Messages from the front-end interface would be those which inform the Runtime Controller what the user has done, i.e., an object was just clicked upon, an object has been dragged, etc.

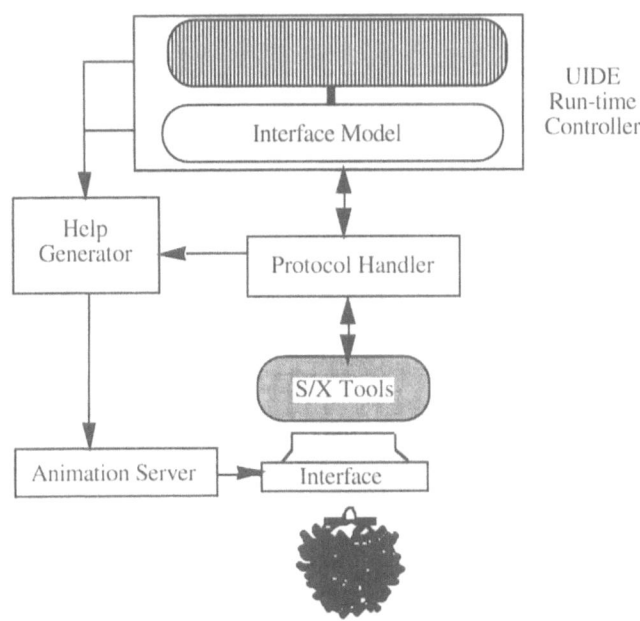

FIGURE 12.7. UIDE Architecture Using Siemens SX/Tools as the Graphical Front-End.

UIDE maintains the runtime context in 2 parts as shown in Figure 12.8 – one concerns the application program itself, and the other concerns the context of the interface to the application. Within the application context, a list of application tasks, their related semantic components, and the declarative part of application objects are maintained. The interface context has a similar structure which maintains a list of interface objects, interface tasks, and interaction techniques in the interface to the application. In each context, a blackboard is implemented to maintain information concerning the status of the environment, such as what are the currently selected objects, what is the task being performed etc. A blackboard is a list of text strings, each of which represents a predicate.

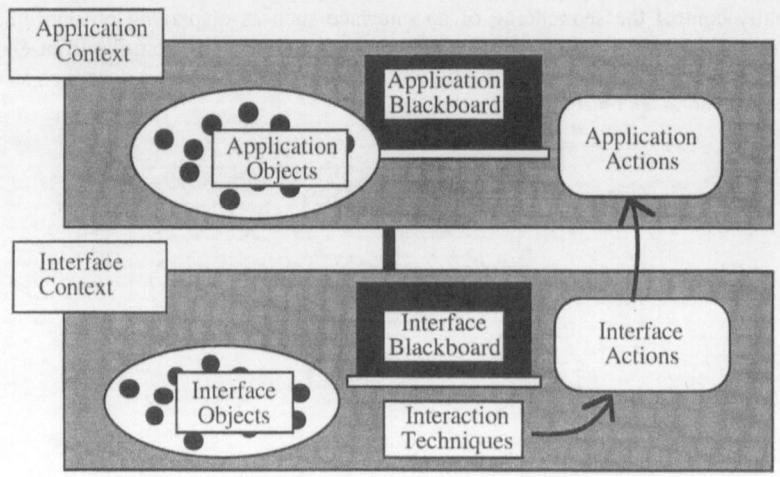

FIGURE 12.8. A Close-up Look at the Run-time UIDE Model.

12.5.1. Processing Input Information

UIDE keeps track of which application tasks are enabled or disabled at all times. An application task is enabled if its pre-conditions are satisfied within the current context. Preconditions, described in predicate calculus, are evaluated against the contents of the blackboard and the declarative object representation. The declarative object representation behaves as an extension to the blackboard; it keeps track of facts about objects which exist at runtime. When an application task is enabled, interface tasks connected to it are enabled. If interface tasks are defined such that they be performed sequentially, the first in the sequence will be enabled. Connected interaction techniques are enabled accordingly.

Upon the user completing an interaction technique, such as clicking, on an object, the graphical interface front-end sends a message to UIDE Runtime Controller that the "click" technique was completed upon the object. The Runtime Controller searches in the model for the corresponding technique among the enabled tasks. Once found, the connected interface task is informed. For example, if the object the user just clicked on happens to be a button, the *SelectCommand* interface task is likely to be notified. Parameter information may also be passed along in case some information from the technique is to be used in the application context. For example, if the technique happens to be a *click-position* technique, the (x,y) coordinates will be passed on to the interface task. This information flow must be specified in the model file as post-conditions of interface tasks, as mentioned in the previous section.

The interface action which gets notified will have its post-conditions evaluated, the results of which may change the condition in the interface blackboard. UIDE checks from the application context for the task which must be performed next. Let's say the first task in a sequence has already been performed, it will enable the next task in the sequence. Once all interface tasks have been performed, the application routine associated with the application task is invoked. This is done by UIDE sending a message to the application, which runs as a separate process.

The communication between UIDE and the application is synchronous. Once the application sends a message back, UIDE executes the post-conditions of the task and this often results in changes to the application blackboard. Currently, the application cannot pass back data yet. This turns out to be quite a limitation in the current architecture.

12.5.2. Application Routines

Application routines can be associated with application tasks defined in the UIDE model. Figure 12.9 shows how an application routine is specified. As you can see, the designers must specify the routine's name and the application's name to which UIDE should send the message to invoke the routine. The designer must also specify routine parameters and their types. This is for UIDE to create an appropriate message with data when an application routine is about to be invoked. Currently, each application routine is required to unpack the message string passed to it and know how to convert it into the actual parameter values.

```
Task: Call-with-a-Number
{
    Goal: "To place a phone call at the number indicated"
    Parameter (input phoneNumber, string)
    Preconditions: "status(Speaker, ON) & not status(Phone, IN-USE)"
    Postconditions: "status(Phone, IN-USE)"
    Application-Routine:  Phone:Call_by_Number {
        Parameters:    (int phoneNumber string);
    }
}
```

FIGURE 12.9. An Example of Application Routine Specification

12.5.3 Automatic Dialog Sequencing

Let's assume from the scenario above that some parameters of the application task are still not specified. Upon realizing that more interface tasks need to be performed for an application task, the application context passes control to the interface context. The next interface task whose pre-conditions are met becomes enabled. The interface objects which are connected to associated interaction techniques are enabled. For example, if the next input parameter must be entered through a text field in a dialog box, UIDE will pop up the dialog box and enable the text field. What needs to be done to an object when it is enabled is part of the interaction technique definition. Right now it is not intuitive to change or add to this information. We have not worked on the designer's interface yet in this respect.

Any interface object can be effected by changes to the current context. UIDE has to constantly check which objects are enabled and which are not. Evaluating pre-conditions of all interface tasks is definitely inefficient. Currently, UIDE only re-evaluates pre-conditions of those interface actions connected to the enabled application tasks. In case a task is being performed, only those objects associated with interface tasks in the sequence are checked. A more appropriate evaluation strategy in the future would be to narrow the evaluation scope down to screens. That is, only application tasks associated with the current screen are evaluated.

Notice that the automatic sequencing control depends on the pre- and post-conditions which are associated with tasks. Pre- and post-conditions provide a mechanism for designers to specify semantic dependency among tasks. For example, a task may be enabled only when certain values are specified. For example, in a train reservation system, SELECTED(city1, ORIGIN) and SELECTED(city2, DESTINATION) means cities must be selected as origin and destination for a task (associated with this condition) to be enabled. Pre-conditions can also depend on values previously entered. For example, if EXIST(x, TEMPERATURE) & STATUS(x, greater-than(100)) is specified, the task associated with this condition is enabled only when the temperature value is above 100.

One of our earlier C++ prototypes [9] uses a predicate mechanism to maintain dependencies between objects in an interface. The prototype is also based on predicates but these predicates are associated directly with objects. This approach has its advantage that the code which enables/disables objects no longer needs to be written. The same is true in the current UIDE. The current model, however, removes the semantic dependency specification from objects on the screen. The semantic dependency is defined with application tasks and remains the same regardless of which interfaces are specified for the application. This makes it even better since the semantic dependency is maintained in the application model where it belongs, and no longer needs to be re-specified when there is a change in interface object sets or interface paradigms.

12.6. Benefits of Having a Declarative Model

12.6.1. Automatic Generation of Context-sensitive Help

Another C++ prototype which generates textual help for 2 questions, **why** an interface object is disabled and **how** to enable a disabled object, is reported in [6]. The help system uses pre-conditions which are associated with widgets as a basis for explaining the reasons why a widget is disabled at runtime. It uses a text template associated with each predicate as a basis for generating text. The answer to how a widget can be enabled is generated using a simple planner to derive a series of actions which, when chained together, satisfies the unsatisfied pre-conditions.

Context-sensitive animated presentation of how to perform an action was implemented utilizing the Smalltalk-80 version of the knowledge model [23, 24]. The help system, Cartoonist, synthesized the current context and the procedural descriptions of the knowledge model to come up with animation scenarios which explained how to perform actions. A planner was also used to derive scenarios involving additional actions which satisfied conditions which were not true in the current context.

We are currently working on integrating animated help with textual help generation. We are working on three major improvements over our previous prototypes. First, the textual WHY help generation is being revised to work with the full knowledge model. Pre- and post-conditions are now inferred from interface and application actions associated with a disabled object. Second, the textual help on HOW to enable an object is now derived from actions in both the application model and the interface model. Animated help is integrated with this help for showing interaction techniques on interface objects, while textual explanations are derived from associated interface and application actions. And lastly, help on HOW to perform an action is derived in a fashion similar to Cartoonist, with a better planner and a more efficient predicate representation. All these kinds of help generation are automatically generated and will be made available in the same environment.

12.6.2. Recording of User Task Usage Information

Another piece of work currently being developed is using the knowledge model as a framework to record user task usage patterns within UIDE. As described in Section 12.5 on the way input information is processed in the current architecture, it is easily seen that each time an interaction technique is completed, each time an interface action is completed, and each time an application action is completed, UIDE is discretely aware of these occasions. We take advantage of the fact to record user completion of actions at different levels of abstractions. Following are different kinds of information available through the task recording mechanism.

Statistical History of Interactions

Upon the successful completion of each application action, the counter for this action is incremented. All interface actions and interaction techniques which are used for this particular invocation are considered completed and their corresponding counters are incremented.

Two kinds of statistics could be recorded with regards to interface actions and interaction techniques. One is their usage in relation to the actions to which they are bound. This recording allows the system to have information such as "has this technique been used for this action by this user?" or "which interface action is used more often to invoke this command?" The other statistic is global across actions in an application. At any point in time, this statistic would provide information such as the number of times an interaction technique has been used in this application, or whether most commands are invoked through accelerator keys, etc. Since interface actions and interaction techniques can be used in various applications, this information could be useful in understanding how well users will handle a new application with interface elements they are already familiar with.

Chronological History of Interactions

Chronological history can be recorded rather straightforwardly in UIDE. Each action, once performed, can be recorded with associated parameter values chosen. Timestamps can be recorded. Interface actions and interaction techniques can also be recorded. The chronological recording would feed in research prototypes for intent recognition work such as Edwards [1], EAGER [4], SINIX [14] and LEXITUS [12].

Chronological recording of help requests can be recorded separately. It is merely a list of actions for which help is requested and timestamps when the requests occur.

12.7. Future Directions

Visual interfaces have their strength in caching some of the information which would otherwise have to be memorized on the screen. Direct manipulation user interface builders such as DevGuide [26] and Prototyper [3] make designing an interface one step easier. Some direct manipulation tools such as DialogEditor [2] and Peridot [18] are intelligent and they make the interface design process less tedious and less repetitive. These tools facilitate a bottom-up approach of interface design while UIDE emphasizes a top-down approach. These tools are not model-based tools and provide no assistance beyond laying out interface objects on the screen. VisualWorks [28] is close to what we would like to see; it partially creates the underlying model when an interface object is created. This makes creating an interface in the MVC paradigm [10] possible without having to understand it first.

Creating the model in UIDE using textual input is still very cumbersome, and the connection from the model to the actual interface are not easily seen. A necessary future direction is to develop visual tools which would make specifying the application model, creating an interface and its model, and connecting the two models together, much easier to visualize. We have started working in this direction.

Re-designing and switching platforms for UIDE turns out to be fruitful to us. Separating the application model from its interface, and coupling the interface model with its implementation partner, for instance, are two good design decisions. As preferences for toolkits and platforms tend to shift over time, we need to be able to maintain our prototype without having to throw away code every time these preferences change. We redesigned UIDE into modules, making each piece replaceable with comparable technology. Some of these pieces are the graphical interface front-end, the protocol handler, the animation server, and the voice recognition utility. This redesign allows us to experiment with toolkits with slightly different behavior, or different interface paradigms for the same application. With the current architecture, it is clear that porting UIDE to a different platform would be fairly straightforward with pieces requiring re-implementation easily identified. It is foreseeable that this architecture could also support multiple interfaces simultaneously for the same application. Figure 12.10 illustrates how the UIDE architecture may look like in the future.

12.8. Conclusions

A model-based user interface architecture embeds semantic information about an application and its interface in the runtime architecture. Taking advantage of this declarative knowledge, the system can provide intelligent user interface support. UIDE is an example of a model-based user interface architecture. In this paper, we described the UIDE application and interface models, and how interface can be constructed through the specification used in these models. We also described how declarative information in the model enables intelligent support such as automatic generation of context-sensitive help and recording of user command usage pattern. These two benefits open doors for future research such as adaptive interfaces, adaptive help, and perhaps others as well.

In addition to these benefits, the modeling components in UIDE can be used as a set of primitives to program an interface. These primitives take away the burden of programming an interface; they allow designers to think in terms of, but not necessarily restricted to, abstract functions in the application domain as well as in the interface domain. A visual interface tool without a model often makes designers think too much about physical details and layout of an interface; designers can easily get distracted from the actual tasks an interface is designed for. A model-based user interface design seems to bring out a more user-oriented design process, while the benefits which it introduces at runtime are more than convincing that a model should be part of the user interface architecture in the future.

12.9. Acknowledgments

This work has been supported by the Siemens Corporate R&D System Ergonomics and Interaction group of Siemens Central Research Laboratory, Munich, Germany, the Human Interface Technology Group of Sun Microsystems through their Collaborative Research Program, and Digital Corporation. The work builds on earlier UIDE research supported by the National Science Foundation grants IRI-88-131-79 and DMC-84-205-29, and by the Software Productivity Consortium. We thank our colleagues, both present and in the past, of the Graphics, Visualization, and Usability Center for their contributions to various aspects of the UIDE project: Spencer Rugaber, Hernan Astudillo, J.J. "Hans" de Graaff, Anton Spaans, Mark Gray, Srdjan Kovacevic, Ray Johnson, Todd Griffith, and our visiting researcher from Siemens, Thomas Kühme.

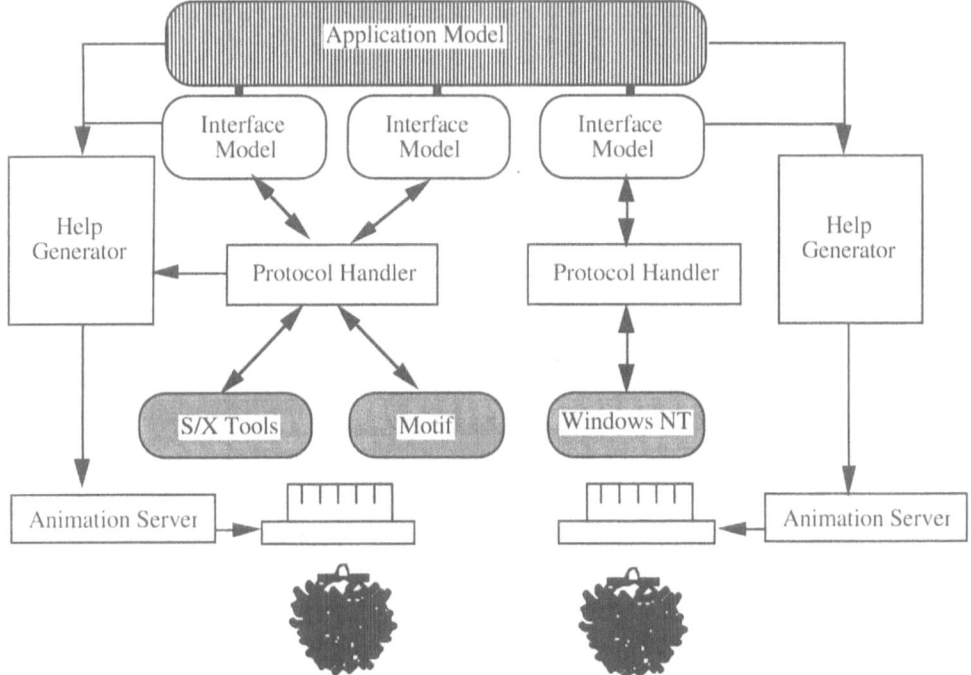

FIGURE 12.10. Future UIDE Architecture where Various Toolkits Could be Used as UIDE Front-Ends.

12.10. References

[1] Bos, E. Some Virtues and Limitations of Action Inferring Interfaces. In *Proceedings of the ACM SIGGRAPH Symposium on User Interface Software and Technology*. November 1992, 79-88.

[2]   Cardelli, L. Building User Interfaces by Direct Manipulation. In *Proceedings of the ACM SIGGRAPH Symposium on User Interface Software and Technology*. Banff, Alberta, Canada. October, 1988, 152-166.

[3]   Cossey, G. *Prototyper*. SmetherBarnes, Portland, Oregon, 1989.

[4]   Cypher, A. Eager: Programming Repetitive Tasks by Example. In *Proceedings of Human Factors in Computing Systems, CHI'91*. 1991, 33-39.

[5]   de Baar, D.; J.D. Foley; and K.E. Mullet. Coupling Application Design and User Interface Design. In *Proceedings of Human Factors in Computing Systems, CHI'92*. May 1992, 259-266.

[6]   de Graaff, J.J.; P. Sukaviriya, and A.P.G. van der Mast. Automatic Generation of Context-sensitive Textual Help. Submitted to UIST'93.

[7]   Foley, J.D.; C. Gibbs; W.C. Kim; and S. Kovacevic. A Knowledge-based User Interface Management System. In *Proceedings of Human Factors in Computing Systems, CHI'88*. May 1988, 67-72.

[8]   Foley, J.D.; W.C. Kim; S. Kovacevic; and K. Murray. UIDE–An Intelligent User Interface Design Environment. In *Architectures for Intelligent Interfaces: Elements and Prototypes*. Eds. J. Sullivan and S. Tyler, Reading, MA: Addison-Wesley, 1991.

[9]   Gieskens, D. and J.D. Foley. Controlling User Interface Objects Through Pre- and Post-conditions. In *Proceedings of Human Factors in Computing Systems, CHI'92*. May 1992, 189-194.

[10] Goldberg, A. Information Models, Views, and Controllers. *Dr. Dobb's Journal of Software Tools*, 15(7) : 54-61, July 1990.

[11] Hayes, P.J.; P. A. Szekeley; and R.A. Lerner. Design Alternatives for User Interface Management Systems Based on Experience with COUSIN. In *Proceedings of Human Factors in Computing Systems, CHI'85*. April 1985, 169-175.

[12] Hoppe, H. U. Intelligent User Support Based on Task Models. *Adaptive User Interfaces: Principles and Practice*. Amsterdam : North Holland Elsevier, 1993.

[13] Inference Corporation. *ART Reference Manual*. Inference Corporation, Los Angeles, CA, 1987.

[14] Kemke, C. Representation of Domain Knowledge in an Intelligent Help System. In *Proceedings INTERACT'87, 2nd IFIP Conference on Human-Computer Interaction*. 1987 215-220.

[15] Kim, W.C., and J.D. Foley. Providing High-level Control and Expert Assistance in the User Interface Presentation Design. In *Proceedings of Human Factors in Computing Systems, INTERCHI'93*. 430-437.

[16] Kovacevic, S. A Compositional Model of Human-Computer Dialogues. In *Multimedia Interface Design*. Eds. M.M. Blattner and R.B. Dannenberg, New York, New York: ACM Press, 1992.

[17] Kühme, T. and M. Schneider-Hufschmidt. SX/Tools - An Open Design Environment for Adaptable Multimedia User Interfaces. In *Proceedings of EuroGraphics'92, Computer Graphics Forum*. Vol. 11, No. 3. 1992.

[18] Myers, B. Creating Interaction Techniques by Demonstrations. *IEEE Transactions on Computer Graphics and Applications* 7 (September 1987): 51-60.

[19] Neches, R.; J.D. Foley; P. Szekeley; P. Sukaviriya; P. Luo; S. Kovacevic; and S. Hudson. Knowledgeable Development Environments Using Shared Design Models. *Proceedings of Intelligent Interfaces Workshop*, Orlando, Florida, January 4-7, 1993.

[20] Olsen, D. MIKE: The Menu Interaction Kontrol Environment. *ACM Transactions on Graphics* 5,4 (1986): 318-344.

[21] Olsen, D. A Programming Language Basis for User Interface Management. In *Proceedings of Human Factors in Computing Systems, CHI'89*. May 1989, 171-176.

[22] Singh, G. and Green, M. A High-Level User Interface Management System. In *Proceedings of Human Factors in Computing Systems, CHI'89*. May 1989, 133-138.

[23] Sukaviriya, P., and J.D. Foley. Coupling a UI Framework with Automatic Generation of Context-Sensitive Animated Help. In *Proceedings of the ACM SIGGRAPH Symposium on User Interface Software and Technology*. October 1990,. 152-166.

[24] Sukaviriya, P. *Automatic Generation of Context-sensitive Animated Help*. A Ds.C. Dissertation, George Washington University, 1991.

[25] Sukaviriya, P.; J.D. Foley, and T. Griffith. A Second Generation User Interface Design Environment: The Model and the Runtime Architecture. *Proceedings of Human Factors in Computing Systems, INTERCHI'93*. April 1993.

[26] SunSoft. *OpenWindows™ Developer's Guide 3.0 User's Guide*. Sun Microsystems, Inc. Part No:800-6585-10, Revision A, November 1991.

[27] Szekeley, P.; P. Luo; and R. Neches. Facilitating the Exploration of Interface Design Alternatives: the HUMANOID Model of Interface Design. In *Proceedings of Human Factors in Computing Systems, CHI'92*. May 1992, 507-515.

[28] VisualWorks. ParcPlace Systems. Mountain View, California

[29] Xlib Reference Manual. Ed. Adrian Nye. California : O'Reilly & Associates, Inc., 1992.

13   Object-Oriented Modelling and Specification for User Interface Design

Mark van Harmelen

ABSTRACT
Specification using object-oriented modelling is a useful technique for user interface design when it is placed in an appropriate methodological context. While designing a user interface, a designer can use object-oriented models to record, refer to and communicate user interface design information, namely, abstractions describing application domains, computer systems and their interactive components. This paper describes (a) the rationale for modelling; (b) a user interface design methodology, Idiom, which integrates modelling activities with other more traditional user interface design activities; (c) a notation for object-oriented modelling which includes the ability to append formal or informal descriptive properties to a model; (d) a brief example illustrating the kinds of models that are constructed during user interface design; and, (e) a discussion of experience with modelling in Idiom.

13.1 Introduction

Object-oriented modelling techniques can significantly enhance the user interface design process by recording abstractions of application domains, systems and their interactive components during the design process, making these available for reference and communication. However, in order to be useful for this purpose, modelling can not be used in isolation from the general processes of user interface design; modelling must be applied together with appropriate user interface design techniques. Thus, while this paper primarily describes the use of object-oriented modelling techniques for user interface design, it also places this modelling in a methodological perspective; showing how object-oriented models of key components in the user interface design process are being integrated into Idiom, a user interface design methodology.

This section provides a rationale for modelling and defines terms. Idiom is introduced in the next section. Thereafter, an object-oriented modelling notation is presented and used in a discussion of the structure of interactive systems. Modelling is illustrated by developing a model of a simple interactive CAD system. Interaction sequences are then introduced as a means of specifying detailed design, linking detailed user interface design to object-oriented models of interactive systems. Finally, there is a brief discussion of experience with modelling interactive systems.

13.1.1   Why model?

There are good reasons to encourage and adopt the use of object-oriented modelling during the design process. Object-oriented modelling provides abstractions to capture and record salient characteristics of application domains and computer systems. In the author's and colleagues' view, once the object-oriented approach is acquired it seems both natural and easy to use. During the design process models can be used to record design decisions, serve as a reference to the current state of the design, and provide a means of communicating the design to others. The models can provide answers to designers' questions about the scope, behaviour and interactive capabilities of the system as it is currently envisaged. For these purposes, models record the state of the design at any point in the design process being constructed by a series of incremental changes to reflect the current state of design knowledge.

Descriptive properties can be added to an object-oriented model to provide extra information about the model, thereby enhancing its usefulness. Properties may be either (i) informal natural language descriptions which provide easily accessible documentation about the system being modelled, or (ii) formal mathematical descriptions which increase the precision of the modelling notation. The variable degree of formality provided by different kinds of properties is particularly good for the user interface community which has little familiarity with formal descriptions. In modelling within Idiom designers can initially augment their models with properties expressed in natural language. Within the same framework there is a growth path to more precise description techniques using a formal notation. This variability and notational growth path is important for user interface design, a field which is viewed from perspectives as divergent as 'art', 'engineering' and 'mathematics'.

13.1.2   Systems, object-oriented modelling and specifications

A *system* is some part of the world that is of interest to a designer for a particular period. Important systems for user interface designers are *application domains* and *computer systems*. A designer can create a *model* to record the behaviour of an existing system, or to specify the behaviour of a system which is still to be built. Models are created using a *notation*. The particular notation used depends on the designer's view of the world and systems in the world.

In the object-oriented view, systems are composed of *objects* which may have relations between them. A *part-of relation* indicates that one object is part of another object. A *general relation* indicates some other more general relationship between objects. Objects which have the same characteristics have a common *type* which defines the objects' characteristics and behaviour. An *inheritance relation* between two types indicates that the *subtype* in the relation inherits the characteristics of the *supertype*. Each object has *attributes* which are inaccessible from outside the object, and *methods* which provide services, including changing attribute values. Any method can utilize the services of another method that is in the same object or in an object connected by a part-of or a general relation. Methods provide services by manipulating attributes, relations, creating new objects, destroying old objects, and invoking other methods. Methods may have arguments and may return values.

In moving from the general object-oriented approach to object-oriented specification, there is a shift in emphasis. Speaking formally, we should be concerned with *operations* upon types, rather than methods. Any specification of the behaviour of operations can be expressed in terms of the effects on a *state*. The state consists of *state variables*, which we will continue, for convenience, to call attributes. We are not concerned with details of implementation; specifications define system behaviour but do not say how the behaviour is implemented. The advantage of specifications is that they avoid the extra overhead of implementation detail, and are characterized by "precision and conciseness" [7, p xiv].

13.2   Idiom

Idiom, a user interface design methodology, is presented in overview form to show how modelling can be integrated into a user interface design methodology.

13.2.1   Background

Description of software systems using object-oriented techniques is, for example, described in [2], [10], [12], and [14]. Formal properties for object-oriented models are discussed in [13]. User interface design methodologies include those discussed in [4], [9] and, as a 'development lifecycle', in [11]. [9] introduces the idea of using objects in a user model, and [4] recommends using them in a conceptual model. However, none of the above develop this idea to include a notation for modelling, nor do they explore specification of interactive systems using object-oriented modelling. Some of the techniques that have been integrated into Idiom are well-known, e.g., task analysis [3], [8]. [11] is partly about how techniques can be integrated into a framework for software and user interface design.

Idiom builds on and integrates the above sources, providing a user interface design methodology that meets requirements for:

- A holistic user interface design methodology utilizing both object-oriented modelling and, optionally, object-oriented implementation techniques;

- A user interface methodology which accommodates the mutual informing that occurs during user interface design;

- A methodology allowing the design and specification of systems which use graphical interaction;

- A methodology which uses graphical notations for its modelling component and for specifications of user interactions;

- A methodological framework that can use different degrees of formalism in its models.

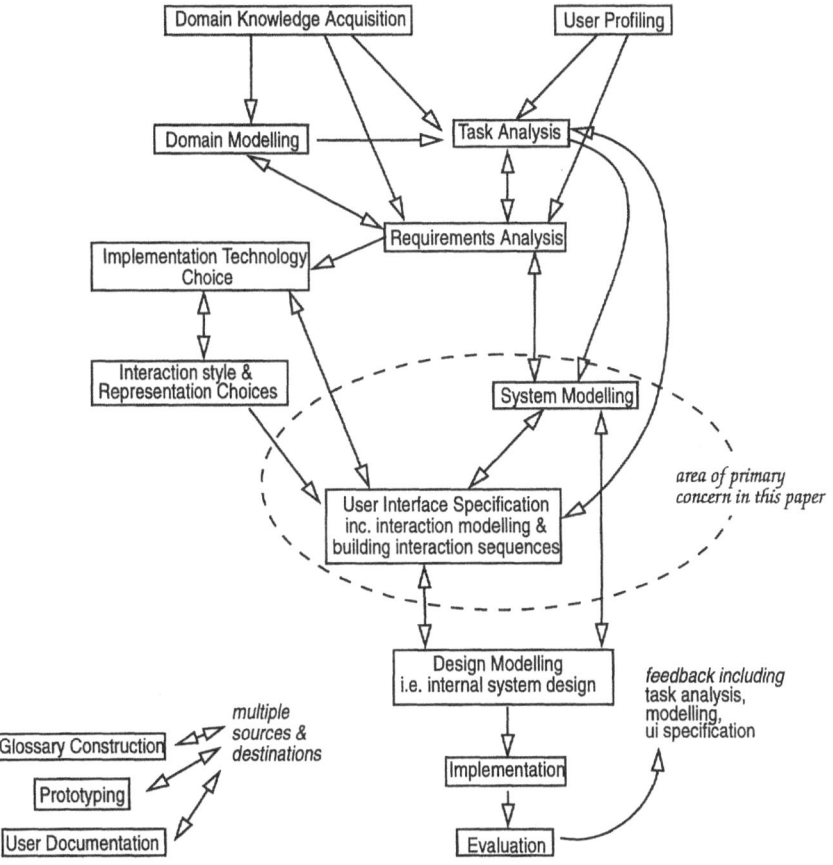

FIGURE 13.1. Top level activities and major information flows in Idiom

13.2.2   Information flow in Idiom

Figure 13.1 shows a top level view of Idiom and the major information flows in the methodology. Idiom is composed of *design techniques*; a *design activity* is the application of a design technique. In general, each block in figure 13.1 represents a design activity, but the user interface specification block contains several techniques which are mentioned below.

Information flow is important in Idiom. One activity may make information available to another activity; frequently activities are mutually informing [6]. Figure 13.2 illustrates *mutually informing activities* A and B — performing A generates design information pertinent to B, and *vice versa*. In Idiom different design activities are concurrently interleaved according to the designer's experience, the current state of the developing design, informing activities, and a few guidelines. In such a freely ordered methodology, it is necessary to impose a completion order on design activities in order to allow design activities to be scheduled in a commercial environment.

13.2.3   Models in Idiom

Four kinds of object-oriented models are used in Idiom: The *domain model* specifies the application domain that is of interest to the designer. This model is the basis for the *system model* of the computer system that is being designed; the types in the system model are a subset of those in the domain model. The system model only contains specifications of objects that the user will be expected to understand, use and manipulate. The type definitions in the system model must contain operations that correspond to user actions. System modelling has been called conceptual design [4], system analysis, or object-oriented analysis [10]. Since the system model does not specify how the user will interact with the system, it must be augmented with an *interaction model*, which provides some of the information about the way in which a user can interact with the application. The interaction model forms part of a larger user interface specification. If Idiom is also used as an implementation methodology, there must be a *design model* from which the generation of code is a trivial matter. The design model is a *reification*, i.e. transformation, of the system and interaction models. Design modelling is also known as object-oriented design, as in [10].

The completion order for modelling in Idiom is first the domain model, then the system and interaction models, then, if need be, the design model.

13.2.4   Overview of user interface specification in Idiom

The overall process of user interface specification includes:

- Construction of domain and system models; this is conceptual design in many user interface design methodologies;

- Construction of the interaction model, for aspects of interaction: Transaction and view structures, composability etc., as discussed in subsequent sections.

- Specification of other components of the interactive system: Menus, dialogue boxes etc.

- Connection of the model to other components in Idiom: The interaction sequences and the task analyses.

FIGURE 13.2.   Information flows between mutually informing design processes

The last three activities above correspond to the user interface specification activity in figure 13.1. This consists of a set of interrelated design activities, which include construction of an interaction model, as well as scenario generation and detailed design using interaction sequences, interaction technique design (including menu and feedback), cursor design, screen/window layout, error message/dialogue design, and help system design.

Other activities in figure 13.1 are closely allied to user interface specification: Choice of I/O devices and interaction style, system modelling, and task analysis. Consideration of these is beyond the scope of this paper.

13.2.5 Components of specifications

There is a second way of looking at specification in Idiom, looking not at the process of specification, but at the results that can be expected from the methodology.

There are a set of design artifacts that can be expected from Idiom. These are related to each other in significant ways that allow mutual informing and enable various consistency checks on a completed design. These artifacts are shown in figure 13.3.

On the left hand side of the figure are the domain and system models, as well as the interaction model, which augments the system model by specifying view structures and transactions in the interactive application. In combination, the system model and interaction model are, after reification, implemented as an interactive system with a user interface that is described by the interaction sequences shown at the bottom of the figure. The main concern in this paper is the use of the domain, system and interaction models to design and specify interactive systems and their user interfaces.

On the right hand side are coarse- and fine-grained task analyses. The coarse-grained task analysis captures the tasks that users perform in the domain, and coarse-grained tasks correspond to operations on types in the domain and system models. However, fine-grained tasks

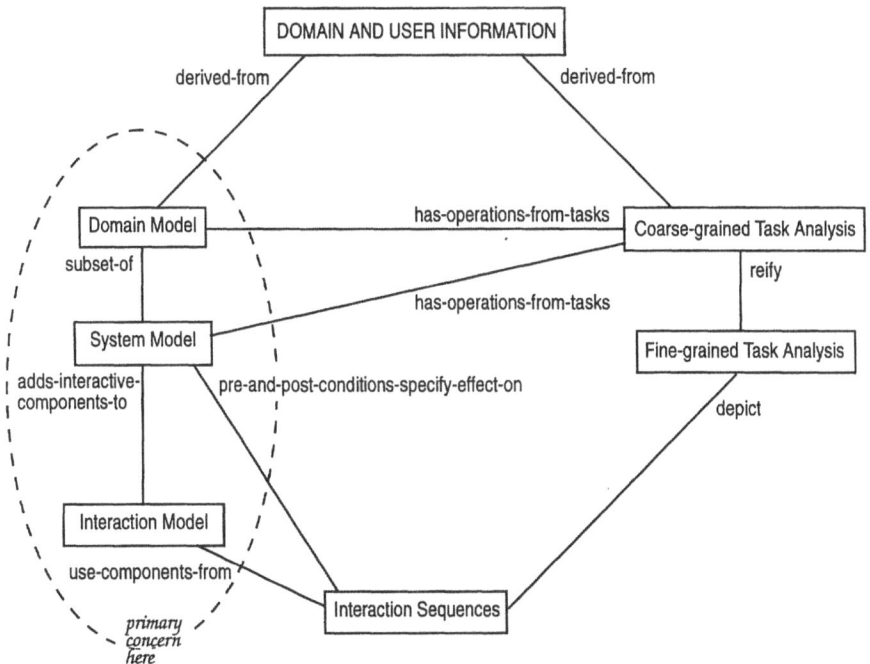

FIGURE 13.3. Some of Idiom's design artifacts

are at a level of granularity that pertains to both the presentation of the user interface and interaction with it. Fine grained tasks appear in the interaction sequences, but operations corresponding to these tasks do not appear in any model; we are not interested in the implementation of these tasks, rather in their effect on the system model. Thus, fine-grained tasks, with their associated feedback, are captured in a graphical form in the interaction sequences, and the pre- and post-conditions on interaction sequences specify the effects of the interaction sequences, and thus tasks, on both the system and interaction models.

The interaction model shows how the views that are depicted in the interaction sequences are composed of information derived from the system model, what their update frequency is, and some of the interaction techniques that may be attached to particular views.

13.3 Types and Models

13.3.1 Types

Types are collections of objects which have the same externally observable behaviour. All the objects of the same type respond to the same (sequences of) messages in the same way.

In Idiom, a type is specified using four different constituents:

- A *name* for the type;

- A set of *attributes* that model the state of an object;

- A set of *operations* that can be invoked on any object of the type;

- A set of *properties* that describe characteristics of and constraints on the object's state and, possibly, on associated objects. Properties may also specify pre- and post-conditions for operations.

  The properties may be written with different degrees of formality: Most interface designers will want to use natural language statements to express properties, but it is possible to use predicate calculus for this purpose.

During design activities, it is possible and often desirable to specify only those constituents that are relevant to the specification task in hand.

Graphically, a type is depicted thus:

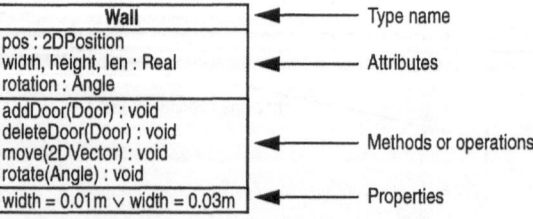

FIGURE 13.4. A type depicted graphically

A type merely specifies behaviour and does not define the internal implementation of the objects of that type. Thus it is sufficient, at one level, to be concerned only with the operations on and properties of a type. However, during modelling, properties are often expressed in terms of attributes which represent an abstract object state. Later, a type may be implemented by one or more classes which contain internal implementation details — variables capturing the state of an object and code implementing behaviour. Although most object-oriented analysis and design methods use objects specified by classes, there are significant advantages to modelling using objects specified by type. Firstly, one is concerned with **rela-**

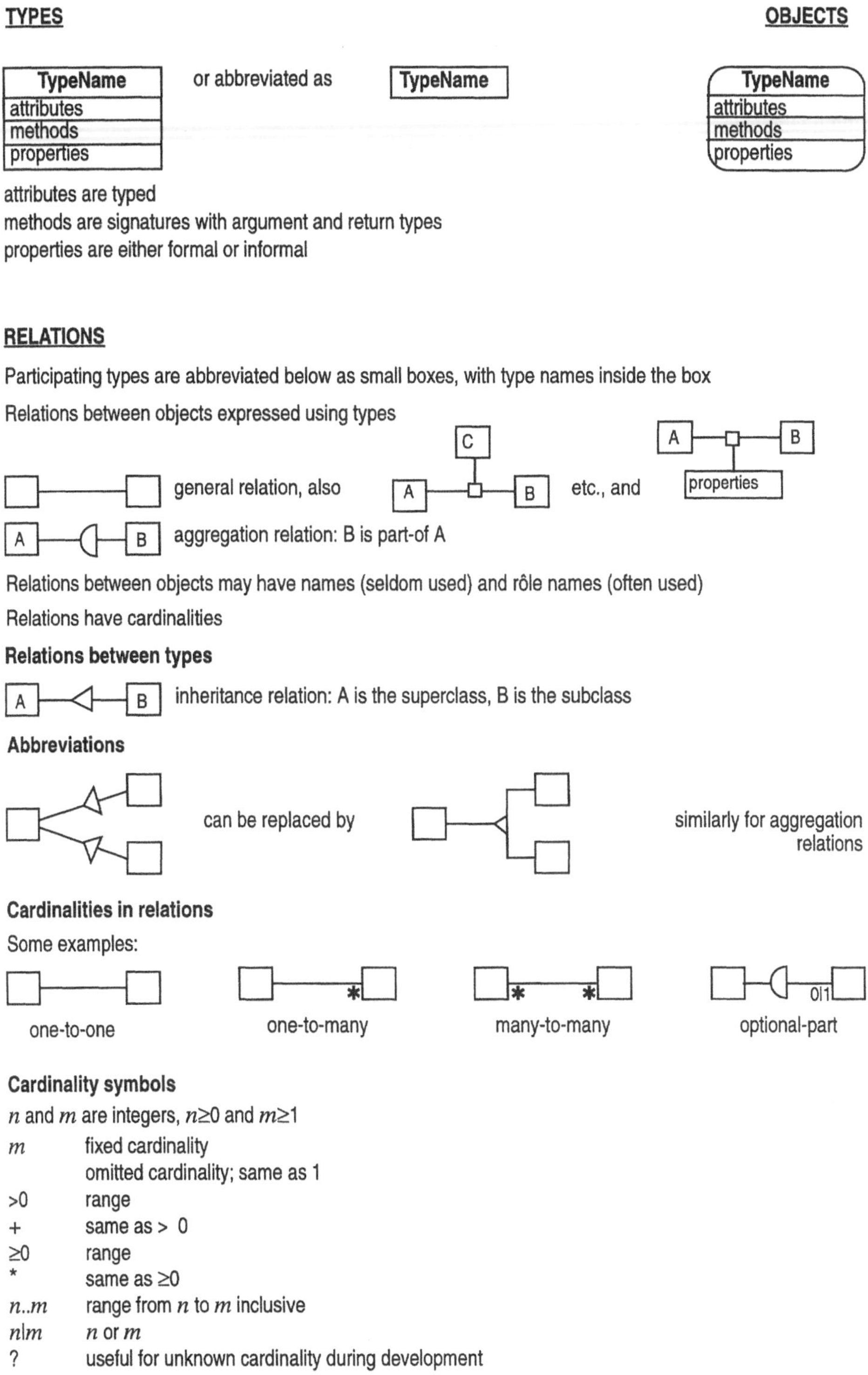

TYPES

OBJECTS

TypeName
attributes
methods
properties

or abbreviated as | TypeName |

TypeName
attributes
methods
properties

attributes are typed
methods are signatures with argument and return types
properties are either formal or informal

RELATIONS

Participating types are abbreviated below as small boxes, with type names inside the box

Relations between objects expressed using types

general relation, also   etc., and

aggregation relation: B is part-of A

Relations between objects may have names (seldom used) and rôle names (often used)

Relations have cardinalities

Relations between types

inheritance relation: A is the superclass, B is the subclass

Abbreviations

can be replaced by   similarly for aggregation relations

Cardinalities in relations

Some examples:

one-to-one   one-to-many   many-to-many   optional-part

Cardinality symbols

n and m are integers, $n \geq 0$ and $m \geq 1$

m	fixed cardinality
	omitted cardinality; same as 1
>0	range
$+$	same as > 0
≥ 0	range
$*$	same as ≥ 0
$n..m$	range from n to m inclusive
$n\vert m$	n or m
?	useful for unknown cardinality during development

FIGURE 13.5. Components of type diagrams (inset for objects in object diagrams)

tively simple specifications of behaviour, rather than more complex implementation concerns. Secondly, as explained below, use of types allows use of polymorphism, a valuable design technique. Classes should only be introduced at a later stage if there is a need to design and code an implementation that uses an object-oriented or object-based programming language.

13.3.2   Models

A *model* specifies the behaviour of some system of interest at a particular level of detail, during some period. An *object-oriented model* specifies behaviour using types which specify [i] the behaviour of individual objects in the system being modelled, and [ii] relations between these objects. An object-oriented model is capable of representing a system over time. Like the system, the model may change dynamically with respect to the numbers and types of objects in the model, and the associations between those objects. These dynamically changing networks of associated objects are specified in a template-like form by a *type diagram* (often called a class diagram in the object-oriented analysis and design literature). Different elements appearing in type diagrams appear in figure 13.5. To give a feeling for the use of a type diagram, both figures 13.6 and 13.7 show a type diagram and an *object diagram*; a snapshot of a model at a particular point in time. The object diagram shows one network of related objects corresponding to the specification in the type diagram.

There are two kinds of relations between objects. Firstly, the *aggregation relation* specifies that one object is composed of other objects. We can use this relation to specify that, for example, a filing cabinet is composed of a case, drawers, and a locking mechanism. Secondly, other relations can show that objects are related to each other in a way that does not imply aggregation or composition. While these relations might be called non-aggregation relations, they are more often called *general relations*. One might use such relations to model ownership or use of objects.

Object-oriented models may, as well as having relations between objects, have relations between types. The only kind of relation allowed between types is the *inheritance relation*. An inheritance relation associates two types, a *supertype* and a *subtype*. The supertype specifies methods, attributes, properties and relations that are inherited by the subtype. Inheritance is a useful technique that allows us to re-use existing type specifications when creating

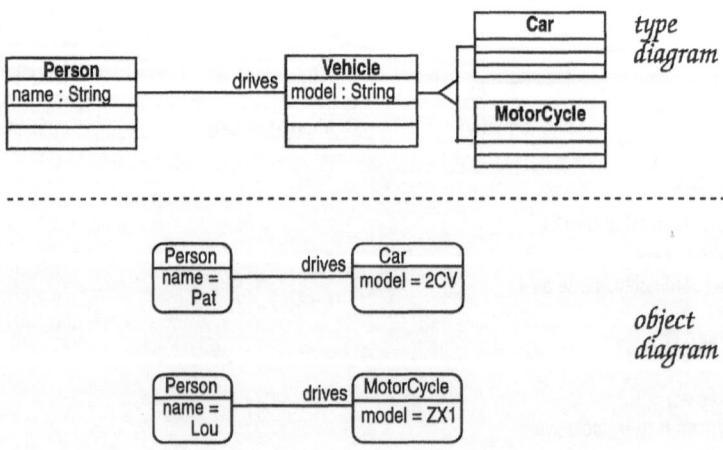

FIGURE 13.6. Polymorphism in action (instances of Person drive instances of different subtypes), also showing inheritance of a relation

new types, and to take advantage of polymorphism (see below).

In general the relationship between types and subtypes is as follows: *s* is a subtype of type *t* if and only if for all objects of type *s*, those objects are also of type *t*. We can refer to *t* as the supertype of *s*.

America and van der Linden [1, p 164] give a fuller definition of a subtype (some symbol substitution is made for readability in the quote):

"The type *s* is a subtype of *t* if

1. The object properties of *t* are among those of *s*.
2. For each method m_t of *t* there is a corresponding method m_s of *s*, such that

- m_t and m_s have the same name

- m_t and m_s have the same number of arguments

- The ith parameter type of m_t is a subtype of the ith parameter type of m_s (the contravarient parameter type rule)

- Either both m_t and m_s have a result type or neither has one

- If there is a result type then the result type of m_s is a subtype of the result type of m_t (the covarient result type rule)."

Polymorphism is the consequence of the type–subtype relationship. Since all objects of a subtype also conform to the supertype, one can use an object of the subtype whenever one might expect to use an object of the supertype. Thus, in modelling we can use a common supertype to show how objects of different types are handled. This is illustrated in figure 13.6. Polymorphism has implications for later re-design; it is possible to specify systems which allow future design extensibility because of polymorphism. Thus, in the example of figure 13.6, one might later add Truck as the third subtype of Vehicle. As mentioned above, lack of polymorphism is one reason why Idiom does not advocate modelling using classes: Although subclasses inherit from superclasses, enabling re-use of the superclass' definitions and behaviour, it is possible to define a subclass using non-conformant inheritance, where the instances of the subclass do not behave in the same way as instances of the superclass. This means that we lose the general ability to exploit polymorphism.

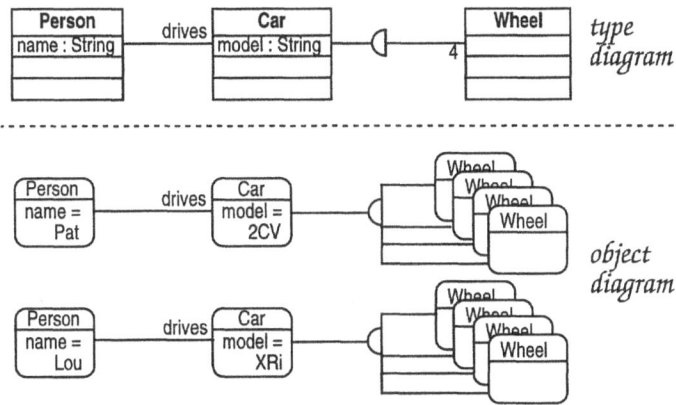

FIGURE 13.7. Type diagram and some corresponding object diagrams illustrating cardinality

13.3.3 More about Relations

General and part-of relations may have one or more *rôle names*, which indicate the relationship of objects to each other. In discussing rôle names, we limit ourselves to the consideration of binary general relations, where two types are associated. At our level of analysis, all relations are implicitly bi-directional, and two rôle names allow convenient bi-directional reading of relations. However, it is possible to be less formal and use one rôle name, if it implies the other rôle name, and if the missing rôle name is not to be used in a property. Thus, in figure 13.7 the rôle name **drives** is used for a general relation, indicating that, for objects belonging to types of **Person** and **Vehicle**, a person drives a vehicle. Note the rôle name position. The missing rôle name at the other end of the relation can be inferred to be something like **drivenBy**.

Cardinality symbols may appear at each end of general and part-of relations, and a missing symbol indicates a cardinality of one; see figure 13.5. The **drives** relation in figure 13.6 is one-to-one, specifying that a driver drives exactly one vehicle, and *vice versa*. The wheels relation in figure 13.7 is one-to-four: Every car has among its constituent parts exactly four wheels

Relations in which a type participates are inherited by the type's subtypes. This can be seen by comparing the type and object diagrams in figure 13.6, and seeing the source and destination of the relation with rôle **drives**.

13.3.4 More about properties

The properties may record method behaviour, invariants on objects, and invariants on relations. Properties may contain object identifiers, type names, attribute names, rôle names, and logical operators. Formal properties may use model-oriented [1] or algebraic specification techniques, although the later use of attributes in object-oriented implementations strongly leans Idiom towards the use of model-oriented properties. Formal and informal properties can be intermixed.

Most designers and design clients will neither understand nor use formal properties, but will find natural language properties valuable. The Idiom method is to start with natural language properties, and, **if** properties are formalized, to maintain a natural language version of each formal property. The natural language version enhances accessibility for non-mathematical designers and clients, while the formal version provides increased accuracy for technically sophisticated designers.

To compare informal and formal properties, [14] defines formal properties for a system model for a factory scheduler. In this model, one informal invariant on task objects is:

> The manufacturing time for a batch of devices is the set-up time for the device being manufactured plus the inter-device production time multiplied by the number of devices in the batch

A formal version of this property is:

> end-start = yield.what.latency + yield.what.interval*yield.q

The latter is much briefer, but at the cost of readability, even if the relevant type diagram is available. Various properties, including both formal and informal properties, appear as part of the example developed later in this paper.

---

1.   A second meaning to the word model: 'Model-oriented' specifications use a model to represent a state, together with invariants on the model and conditions on operations. Thus, a model-oriented specification can specify behaviour of a type.

13.4 The Structure of Interactive Systems

While designing interactive systems, we choose a subset of the domain objects to be represented and manipulated by an interactive application. Having done this, we need to envisage the representation of the domain objects on a display surface for viewing and/or manipulation by the users of the system. Consequently, the developing design of an interactive system requires extra types to allow for presentation and interaction. A structure of types and relations that is only used for presentation is called a *view structure*, and one that is also used for modification is called a *transaction*. These are discussed below.

13.4.1 The core of an interactive system

In an object-oriented model of an interactive system, a core of types represents the system's concerns with domain objects whatever they may be — e.g. elements of buildings will be represented in the core of an architectural CAD system. Objects having these types form a *core* in an interactive system. 'Core' is an alternative, somewhat colloquial name for the system model. In the example that follows, both terms are used.

At a high level of detail, the user interface has the function of providing the user with the means of viewing and manipulating core objects (see figure 13.8).

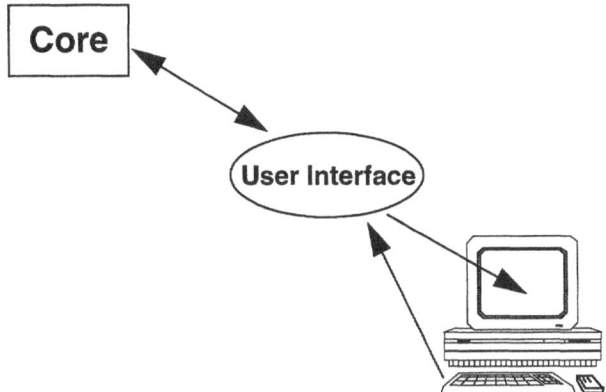

FIGURE 13.8. Interactive system structure

Methods of or operations on the core objects (i) represent changes that can be made to the domain objects being represented in the interactive system, and (ii) provide the means for the user interface to obtain information about the state of those objects.

The core objects should always represent a state that is valid and permissible in the domain of interest. Thus, for example, there are no unsupported ceilings in a building. Since the core should be consistent, every operation which alters core objects must change the core from one valid state to another valid state in just one operation.

13.4.2 Transactions and view structures

Unfortunately, human users are limited in the things that they can do at one time. Thus to re-arrange a building, a user of an architectural CAD system is unlikely to be able to specify the re-arrangement in one step. He or she may have to make a sequence of modifications which temporarily leave the building in a structurally inconsistent state, perhaps moving walls while leaving a roof unsupported. A *transaction* allows an object to be changed from one valid state to another, possibly in steps which allow a user to manipulate an inconsistent object at the user interface [13].

There are two kinds of transactions, classified according to how they work:

- A *core transaction* first gathers all the information needed to perform a change to the core, then it invokes an update operation on the core.

- A *copy transaction* first makes a copy of (part of) the core, creating an object of a similar type in which intermediate 'inconsistent' states are allowed and supported. Secondly, stepwise changes are interactively made to the copy. Thirdly, to change the core, a consistency check is run to see if the transaction is consistent with regard to core constraints, and, if so, an update operation is invoked on the core. Figure 13.9 illustrates the operation of a copy transaction.

Transactions may contain a range of objects which have nothing to do with the domain of interest *per se*. Thus, a typical transaction might contain objects representing whatever the transaction is being used to edit, as well as objects required for interaction, for example, cursor position, selection markers, and cut-copy-paste buffers.

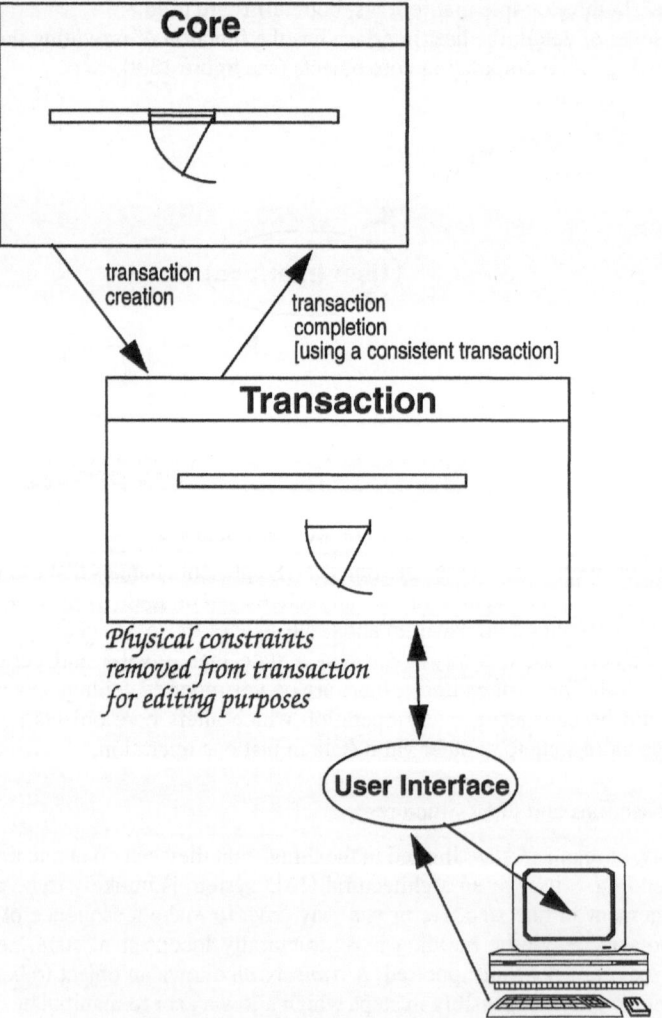

FIGURE 13.9. Transaction-based interactive system structure

Good user interfaces incorporate undo facilities. Undo is generally transaction-based. Each transaction may either be *completed* (i.e. *committed*) or *cancelled*. The completion of a transaction:

- Stores undo information to enable the complete transaction to be undone later as a result of a user command. Often there is only one level of undo; if so, previous undo information is discarded before storing the new undo information;

- Throws away undo information for operations and embedded transactions done within the completed transaction.

The cancellation of a transaction:

- Throws away undo information for operations and embedded transactions done within the cancelled transaction;

- Leaves other undo information unchanged.

Software engineering principles dictate that in order to preserve flexibility, maintainability, and re-usability of the core, the transaction must encapsulate all transaction-related operations. It is worth stressing that responsibility for the details of initiation and completion of the operations should reside in the transaction. The core only provides general purpose access and update facilities.

View structures are similar to transactions, but they only display information and do not allow modifications to be made.

13.4.3   Views

Transactions and view structures are built from views. A *view* is a projection of some information from one or more objects. For example, if we are rendering a wire frame model of some three dimensional information, we might utilize a projection that transforms 3D information into 2D information (see figure 13.10).

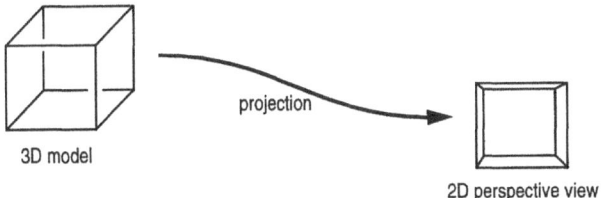

FIGURE 13.10. Model, projection, and view

In discussing views, we need to introduce some terminology: One common use of *model*[1] defines it as one or more objects which have a projection applied to them to create a view. A *view* therefore consists of one or more objects which contain information that has been projected from a model. A *projection* may select and/or transform model information for use by a view. In a well structured object-oriented system, the projection operation is part of the responsibility of the view, which queries the model for the relevant data and transforms that data to create the view's state. In this way the model is re-usable with different view struc-

---

1.   A third meaning of the word model, as explained in the text. The term model and the model-view dyad are derived from the Smalltalk MVC (Model-View-Controller) triad. However, MVC is implementation-oriented, here models and views are purely used in specifications.

tures and transactions, since it is not concerned with the needs of particular views.

It is possible and often desirable to create a hierarchy of views: We might be interested in

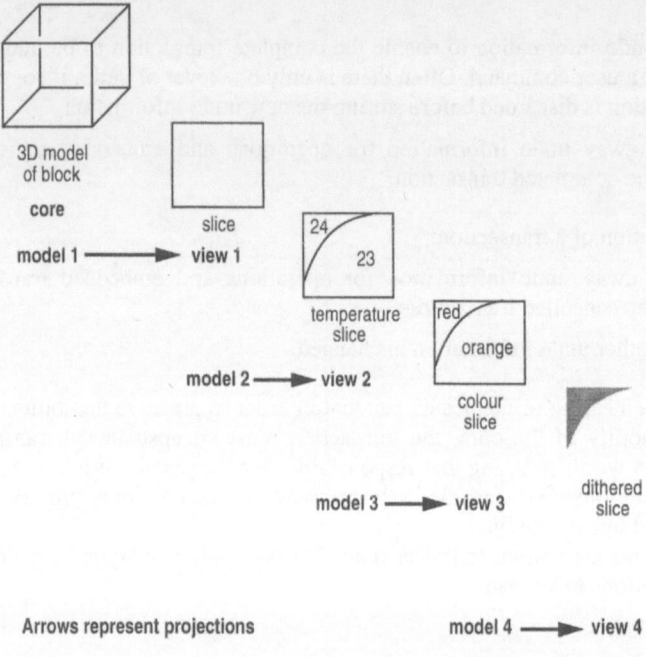

Arrows represent projections   model 4 ━━━▶ view 4

FIGURE 13.11. Recursive model and view hierarchy

displayed heat maps of a slice through some block of material. In this example, depicted in figure 13.10, we might specify a system in which we (1) start with the block, (2) create a slice through the block, (3) map temperatures onto the slice according to external heat sources and sinks, (4) map colours onto the temperature map of the slice to represent the temperatures, and (5) finally perform dithering to be able to represent the colours on a limited colour-resolution colour output device. Here the original block represents the core and is the model for the slice view. The slice view is the model for the temperature view and so on.

A view has the following responsibilities:

- When it is created, to extract data from the model using operations on the model, and if necessary, to transform this data;   [i]

- To similarly keep itself consistent with the model whenever the model changes. The model informs all its views each time it changes.   [ii]

If a view, *view1*, participates in a transaction, and *view1* is also a model for another view, *view2*, then *view1* may also be required to:

- Map changes invoked by *view2* into changes on *view1*'s model.

Interactive programs need to display data, and thus the ultimate view in any chain of one or more views must be displayable. For example, the dithered view in figure 13.10 is displayable. Any such *displayable view* has responsibilities:

- [i] and [ii] above;

- to render a visual representation of itself on a display surface or via a display subsystem (such as a window manager).

If a displayable view is participating in a transaction, it may have responsibilities to:

- Map user input events back to its model

13.5 An Example

In this section, we examine the application of object-oriented modelling techniques by developing an example of a very simple interactive application; an architectural CAD system.

The system allows a user to manipulate designs consisting of walls which may optionally contain doors. Walls may abut, but may not overlap. Placing a door in a wall requires that there is sufficient space in the wall on either side of the door to support a lintel over the door. (A lintel is a beam that is placed over a gap in a wall to support the wall over the gap.) The lintel space required on either side of the wall is 0.3m. Doors are required to open at least 90° without impediment from either a wall or a door that might be partially or fully open.

13.5.1   Domain model

The domain model is simple, as befits a simple example. Figure 13.12 shows that an architectural design is composed of one or more walls, and walls may contain doors. The types which respectively represent these are **ArchDesign**, **Wall** and **Door**. Informal properties in **ArchDesign** and **Wall** express the constraints on the domain. An architectural design containing nothing (i.e having no walls) is considered to be a design wherein either no design work has been done as yet, or an explicit choice has been made to build nothing. Consequently it is important to allow for a zero cardinality for the **walls** rôle.

13.5.2   System model

We can adopt this domain model unchanged as the system model for the example.

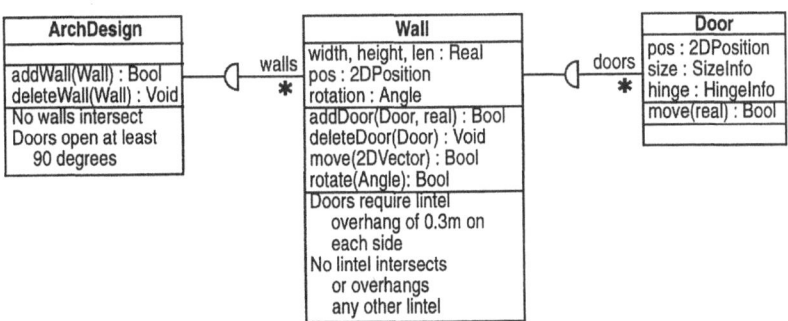

FIGURE 13.12. Domain and system models

13.5.3   Interaction model

Domain and system models only specify objects and abstract tasks, making explicit what is frequently called "conceptual design". However, user interface designers also need to specify the detailed design of an interface, relating the detailed design to the conceptual design. Specification of an interaction model helps in this process.

An interaction model may contain both transactions and view structures. The interaction model addresses:

- Numbers of, composition of, and update strategies for transactions and view structures;
- Relation of these to each other and to the core;
- Which transactions and views appear in windows.

This is not all the information that is required to specify a user interface, but it establishes the basis of the interactive application, and provides a framework for the remaining components of the detailed user interface design.

The interaction model for the architectural CAD system is developed in subsequent subsections. As we will see, besides being useful for specification of interfaces, interaction modelling can result in the generation of useful informing information for concrete, detailed user interface design.

Formulating the interaction model

One general issue when using an editing system to edit constrained application data (architectural data, molecular modelling data, software engineering data, and so on) is this: Should a user be continually constrained to generate legal designs, or should it be possible to temporarily violate design constraints as part of the overall design process?

Applying this question to our very limited architectural CAD domain, should the design be constrained by an editor so that doors are always correctly inserted in walls? Here 'correct insertion' means that a door is co-planar with the wall, that the base of the door is at the base of the wall, that there is sufficient wall space on both sides of the door to support the lintel, and that the door can open fully without encountering a fixed obstacle. To implement this requires a snap-dragging style of editing; as a cursor is moved across the design space, any door being 'dragged' snaps to the nearest legal position. Similar interactive considerations apply to wall manipulation, as well as to door and wall creation.

The alternative editing style is that a user may move a door regardless of design constraints on positions for doors. Thus it is possible for a user to position a door in space or overlapping some other architectural element (a door or wall) during a composite editing operation, leaving it there until he or she is ready to insert it in a legal position in a wall. Similarly, walls may be temporarily positioned over other walls and/or doors.

Depending on circumstances, a user interface designer might choose one of three different editing styles; snap-dragging editing, free-movement editing, or editing with the ability to change between these editing styles. An abstract model of the CAD system can capture the choice of one of these interaction styles without showing details of implementation, and without the designer needing to specify the interaction style using scenarios or natural language description.

For example, the interaction model in figure 13.12 only allows for a door to be inserted in a space in a wall; there is no allowance for freely positioned doors. This is specified by the properties on InteractDesign and InteractWall. However, in figure 13.14, the properties in Interact-Design have been relaxed, and doors need not only be inserted in walls. Thus doors and walls may be positioned wherever a user desires; figure 13.14 shows a model suitable for a free-

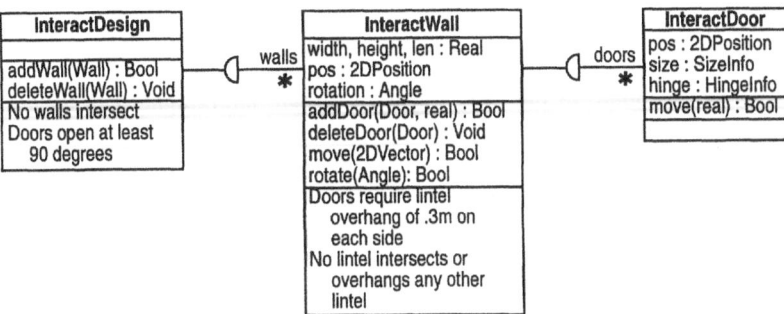

FIGURE 13.13. Snap-dragging interaction model

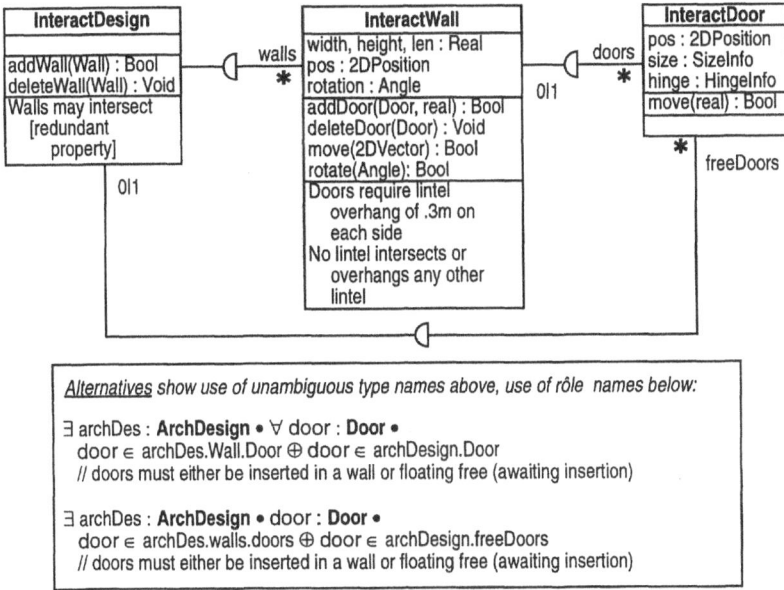

FIGURE 13.14. Free-dragging interaction model

movement editor. The model still allows for doors to be inserted in walls; allowing a wall to be moved together with any inserted doors, but raising the issue of how doors are inserted and removed from walls. This issue will be resolved below. A formal property is used to specify that a door is either positioned in a wall or is freely positioned, but may not simultaneously be both. The free-movement model is used as the basis for the interaction model in the example being developed here.

Aside: Flexibility in specifications

For a user interface designer, there is considerable flexibility in expressing the ideas central to the developing design. For example, the designer can take advantage of:

- *Abstraction*: The doors in walls each need to have their hinges on a particular side and need to open in a certain way. This is important because of the requirement that doors must be able to open ninety degrees. Rather than worry about low-level details of representing hinge and opening direction information, this information can simply be abstractly represented as an attribute, hinge, of type HingeInfo. Later, if need be, the designer can reify the abstraction by adding a detailed representation for the hinge information.

- *Underspecification*: In the early stages of design, the designer can leave methods unspecified, assuming, for the moment, that various useful methods exist. For example, a wall will need, at some stage, to compute its physical shape. The designer can assume that there are appropriate methods to help in this computation: When a wall needs to know about its physical shape, it can find out the size of a gap for a door by invoking one of the door's methods.

- *Variable levels of formality*: Formal and informal properties may be intermixed. See 12.3.4 for an example of a formal property and a corresponding informal property.

- *Flexibility in Specification*: Properties may be expressed in different ways. Figure 13.15 shows how the formal property in the free editing model has been moved and transformed to become a property appearing in type InteractDesign:

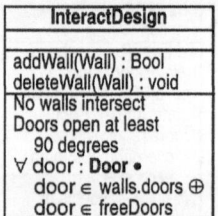

FIGURE 13.15. Moved property for free interaction model

We could even remove the need for the property if we used a type diagram utilizing inheritance:

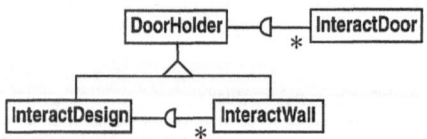

FIGURE 13.16. An equivalent way of specifying free-movement

However this particular type structure may appear counter-intuitive to user interface designers and to clients, since there is no real world object that corresponds to a DoorHolder.

Aside: Specification informs detailed user interface design

The process of design is one of generating information, and some of the information generated during interaction model design is useful outside that activity, informing detailed design activities.

For example, considering the free-movement interaction model, it is possible to move walls around together with their contained doors, to overlap walls with other walls, to move free doors on top of walls or other free windows. This information is directly extracted from the model. There are consequences for detailed user interface design: Moving walls together with contained doors seems a nice labour-saving touch, but leaves detailed user interface design questions of how to insert a door in a wall (where constraints apply), how to remove a door from a wall, and how to reposition a door in its containing wall

It is important to consider concurrently the interaction model and low-level design details to ensure that the interaction model supports the desired low-level interaction. As an illustration, while formulating the CAD example, the sequence of design events was as follows: The model of figure 13.14 was formulated, and then it was observed that the model still allowed doors in walls, rather than being a totally free model without any doors in walls. It was observed that moving walls with inserted doors was a nice side-effect which could ease interaction in some circumstances. But what about the problems of inserting a door in a wall or removing a door from a wall? Should there be modes or commands to do this? After a moment's consideration it seemed that this was a bad idea leading to too many commands being available at the interface, possibly slowing down user interaction, or resulting in a user becoming lost in 'command space'. Dragging was then used as a solution to avoid extra commands for inserting, moving and removing doors.

The dragging solution is as follows: Drag a door close to a wall and it snaps into the wall at the closest legal position, or one of two legal positions if there are two equidistant legal positions. Drag an inserted door along its wall and it snaps to the nearest legal position in the wall. Drag it away from the wall and it is pulled out of the wall. All of these dragging operations require a tolerance; if the cursor is closer to a wall than the tolerance, then the user is assumed to be inserting a dragged door into a wall or changing its position in the wall. If a user is dragging a door and moves the cursor outside the wall's tolerance zone, then the door jumps out of the wall to the cursor position. The user might be further assisted if there was hysteresis in conjunction with the tolerance:

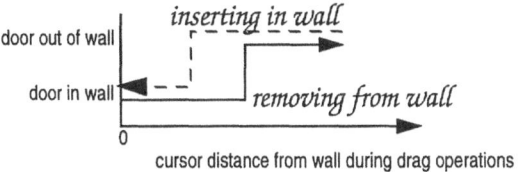

FIGURE 13.17. Drag Hysteresis

How, then, to move a door that is currently in a wall, rather than moving the wall itself? The easiest solution is to use selection before movement. Clicking a mouse button with the cursor over a door in a wall selects the door, clicking over a wall, in that part of the wall that does not contain a door, selects the wall. Movement of a door or wall is via the standard way of dragging a selected object.

If a user wants to position a door in a wall and there is no legal space inside the wall for the door, and the cursor is inside the tolerance zone, then what should happen? Some kind of feedback is appropriate, perhaps (i) the door should stay positioned next to the wall, or (ii) it should be shown over the wall and cursor, but at right angles to the wall, or (iii) free doors should be rendered in a different colour or style, or (iv) if the user releases a mouse button to erroneously terminate the drag operation (with the cursor over a wall with no space), a dialogue box appears to inform the user that the door has not been inserted in the wall. The choice of one or more of these alternatives can be delayed until a later stage in the design, or preferably, until user testing has been performed in conjunction with prototype systems.

13.5.4 Relating the system and interaction models

From a specification and software engineering perspective, there are distinct labour-saving advantages to being able to re-use specifications. Effective re-use relies, *inter alia*, on stability. A model which captures the essential characteristics of the application domain tends to be stable over time. Consequently, the approach recommended here is to start by modelling the domain, to use some or all of the domain as the system model or core of an interactive system, and then to proceed by adding an interaction model to the system model to create a model of an interactive system.[1] If the interactive details change during or after design, the core system model remains the same, and it can be re-used with a new interaction model during the design of the new interactive system.

If we are concerned with developing any kind of system that utilizes a transaction that loosens constraints on a core, then we need to design a structure that uses a copy transaction on the core for the loosened constraints. In editing systems this transaction is part or all of the interaction model. If the domain model has been used as a framework within which to capture properties of both domain objects and relations between domain objects, and these have been propagated through to the system model, then these properties can be used as the basis for consistency checks on the transaction before committing the changed transaction to the core. Of course, in order to keep the core independent of any transactions, consistency checking must be specified and implemented as part of the transaction's operation.

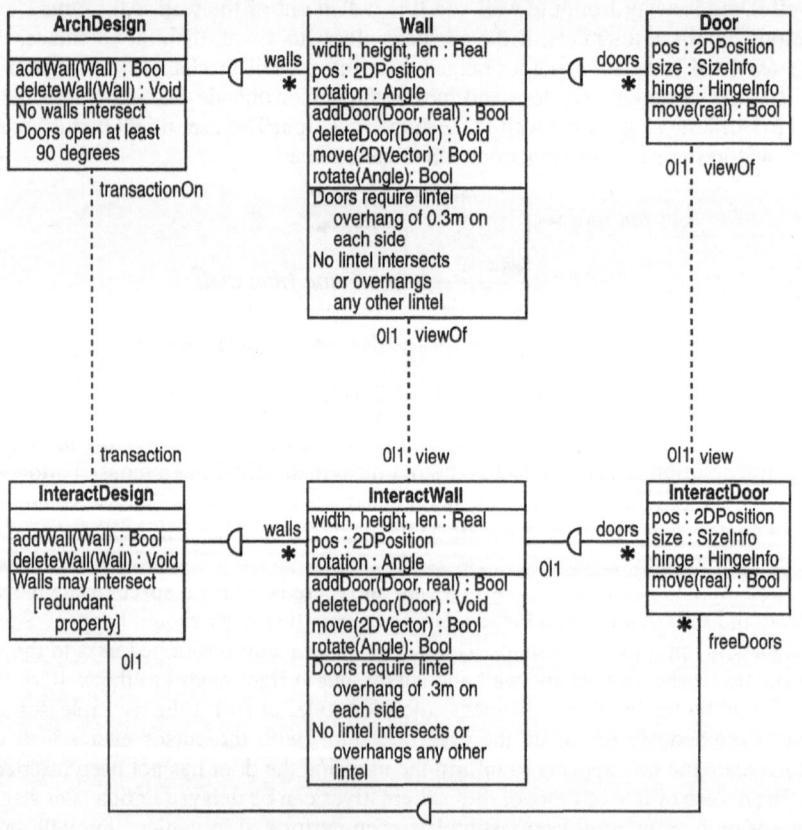

FIGURE 13.18. Relating domain model to interaction model

---

1.   The presence of a core or system model in a larger model of an interactive system is part of a specification provided by the larger model. Beyond specifying the behaviour of that system, the composition of the larger model says nothing about internal details of interactive system implementation. This allows for a variety of different implementation techniques to be used to implement interactive systems specified by object-oriented models.

Figure 13.18 relates the architectural domain system model to a transaction that is the free-movement interaction model shown in figure 13.14. The system model or core appears at the top of figure 13.18, with the transaction below it. New relations appear as dashed lines. To relate the core to the transaction we can simply use one or more relations labelled with the roles **transaction** and **transactionOn**. Figure 13.18 uses this relation between the core object of type **ArchDesign** and a transaction of type **InteractDesign**.

When considering a transaction, types in the transaction should be associated with types in the transaction's model (in this case the core), enabling easy recognition of the types in the model that are projected to form particular views. Thus, in figure 13.18, constituent parts of the model and the transaction have been associated using a relation with roles **view** and **viewOf**. Cardinalities have to be added to these relations, since deleting a wall from the transaction means that we have to allow for a **Wall** without an **InteractWall**, and adding a wall to the transaction means that we have to allow for an **InteractWall** without a **Wall**. Relevant changes are made to the model (in this case the core) after the transaction is committed. A consistent transaction adheres to the properties in the transaction's model, and only a consistent transaction may be committed, updating its model. After a consistent transaction is committed, all doors and walls in the transaction have corresponding doors and walls in the model, with **view** relations between them.

In some models, a full treatment might also show that a transaction has a proper subtype which is its model. This level of detail is considered unnecessary for user interface design purposes. However, for reference, it is:

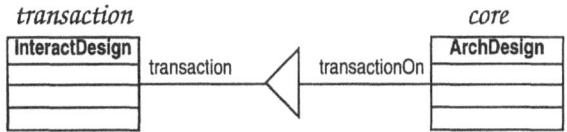

FIGURE 13.19. Type–subtype relationship for designs

Later implementation concerns

The approach of using a system model and a transaction on that model may initially seem to imply that, in an implementation, the transaction has to be explicitly created by a user to gain access to the data in the core, even if the access is only for perusal purposes. This need not be true. The implementation may or may not incorporate the system model as a distinct entity. If the implementation does incorporate the system model, automatic creation of a transaction can happen for consistent core data at application start-up, allowing perusal. If the implementation does not incorporate the system model, the transaction must be the implementation's core. In such a case, the system model still has validity in the specification as the source for any constraints that might be applied to the transaction during consistency checking.

13.5.5 Continuing to specify the interaction model

At this stage specification of the interaction model is not yet finished. The remaining issues include: Selection; view composition within displayable views; and cardinalities for displayable views. These and other issues are addressed below.

Selection

Any editor which uses the common "select object—apply command" style of interaction requires a means of specifying which objects are selected at any point in time. Again, for reasons of re-use, selection mechanisms should not be incorporated into the core or system model. Selection is part of the editing actions which are applied to a transaction on the core, and thus selection mechanisms properly belong to transactions

One general way of dealing with selectable objects of different types is to create a type that may be selected, called SelectableObject, and to make any existing type that is to be selectable within a transaction be a subtype of SelectableObject. Then add a type, Selection, that exploits polymorphism to keep track of the objects that have been selected.

This approach has been used in figure 13.20, where Selection is used as a placeholder to keep track of selected objects of types InteractWall and InteractDoor. New relations are shown using dotted lines.

The chosen selection mechanism captures and reveals more detail about interaction with

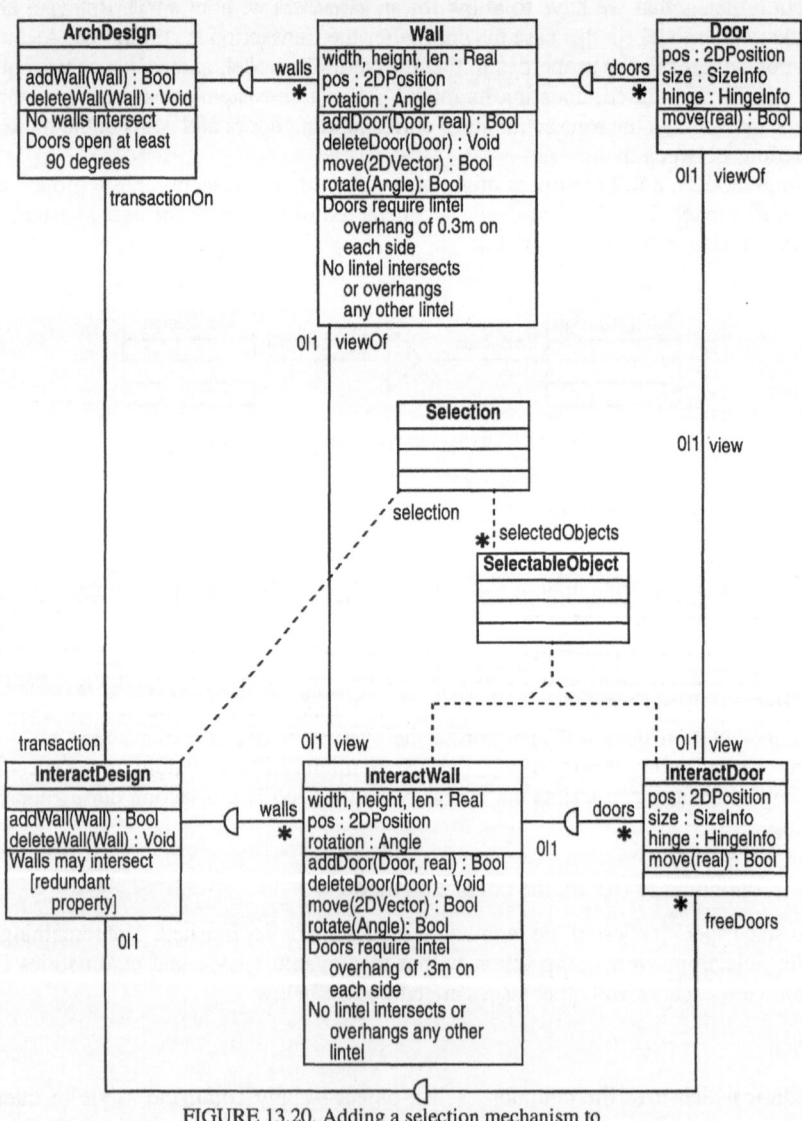

FIGURE 13.20. Adding a selection mechanism to
the interaction model

the application; in the example, zero or more selectable objects may form the selection, and these objects may have different types. However, selection actions and feedback are depicted in interaction sequences; see section 13.6.

Feedback

Feedback mechanisms which are responsible for objects which have a transitory existence, for example, dragged feedback shapes and rubber objects displayed within windows, can be modelled in a way that is very similar to the modelling of a selection mechanism. This is left as an exercise for the reader.

However, selection feedback itself is part of the responsibility of displayable objects, which are added to the interaction model below (see figure 13.20). Detail about selection feedback is irrelevant to the interaction model, and does not appear in the model.

On the other hand, how both kinds of feedback are displayed is of paramount importance, and consequently the interaction sequences (section 13.6) show both kinds of feedback as they are perceived by the user.

Visibility in interaction models

Projections of core objects will generally need to be seen by the user of a system, and we can easily specify how they appear in windows. In our example we need to display plans which contain representations of walls and doors. The simplest possible scheme is shown in figure 13.21, where the entire architectural design is shown in a window containing free-movement walls and doors.

The corresponding type diagram is shown in figure 13.22. There, a **Window**'s contents consist of a **DisplayablePlanView**, which in turn consists of displayable plan elements of type **DisplayableWall** and **DisplayableDoor**.

DisplayableWall and **DisplayableDoor** have methods for display (represented as display(): void), and methods to transform user input into actions on their models in the transaction (not represented). Should the visual representation or input handling change, then only **DisplayableWall** and **DisplayableDoor** need change, not **InteractWall** and **InteractDoor** in the transaction.

Attributes describing window size and position, and all consideration of the window bar have been omitted from **Window**, using a design strategy of omitting extraneous detail.

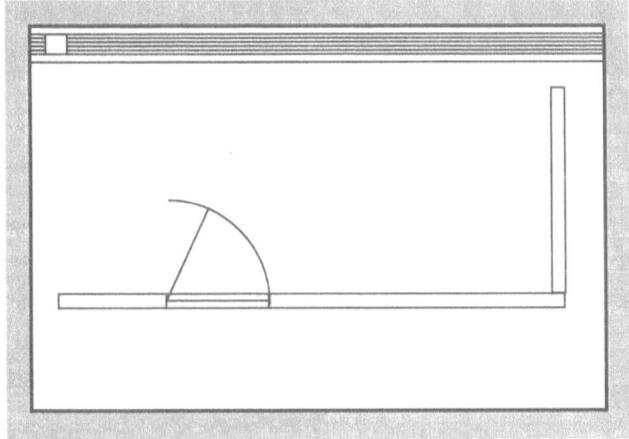

FIGURE 13.21. Simple window display,
showing all the objects in the design space

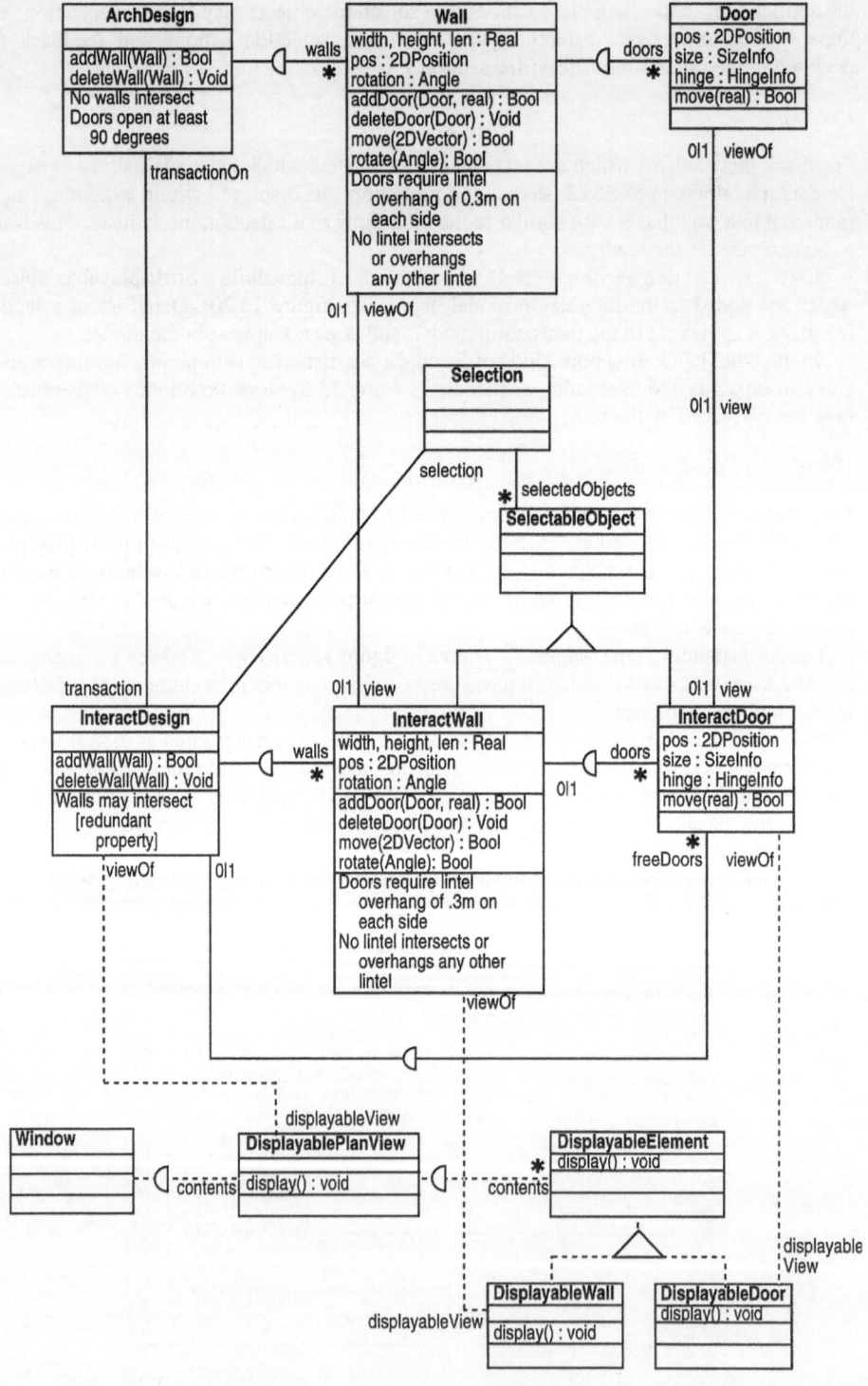

FIGURE 13.22. Adding displayable objects and a window

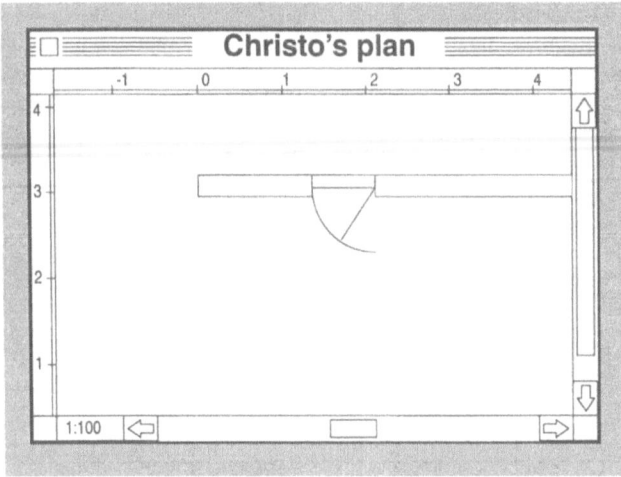

FIGURE 13.23. More complex window display,
capable of scrolling and changing scale

The window in figure 13.21 is basic; there are no facilities to control the scale or displayed area of the plan. We can develop the example to rectify this, considering finer-level details of a user's interaction with the system; here feedback as to the state of the view and means of controlling the state of the view is added to the interaction model.

Figure 13.23 shows a window incorporating interaction techniques for view control; there are two scroll bars, two rulers showing positional information, and a scale display which also doubles as the means by which a pull-up menu can be invoked to change the scale. A plan view appears in a sixth area of the window; part or all of a plan is displayed, depending on scale and scrolling. Various type-subtype relations are crucial in being able to compose composite views in this way — figure 13.24 shows how an object of type DisplayableView may be composed of zero or more objects of type DisplayableView or its subtypes.

This composability is exploited in figure 13.25, which depicts the components required for the window in figure 13.23. In figure 13.25, an object of type RulerScrollScaleView is displayed in a window. A RulerScrollScaleView is composed of two ScrollBars, two Rulers, a ScaleView, and a DisplayableView or any subtype thereof — in this case, DisplayableplanView. Some details of ScrollBar and Ruler are omitted; the type structure could be expanded to include these details, but they are not needed to explain the operation and rôle of objects belonging to these types

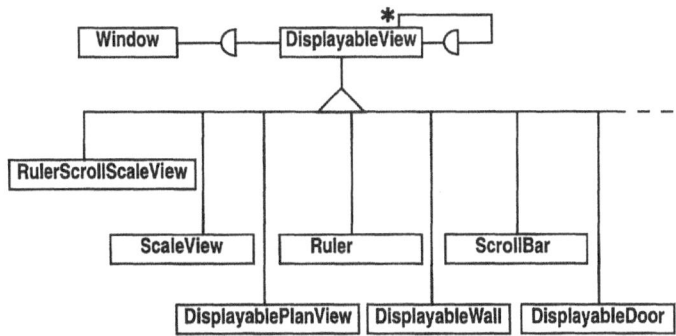

FIGURE 13.24. Type-subtype structure to compose displayable views

in the user interface specification.

One of the advantages of the object-oriented approach is that, once specified, components like the **RulerScrollScaleView** can be re-used by exploiting the polymorphism that allows any view to be used as the **contains** component of **RulerScrollScaleView**. Thus **RulerScrollScaleView** could be used to display a view of any information that can be usefully displayed with scroll bars, rulers, and a scale. Another advantage of the object-oriented approach is that it is not strictly

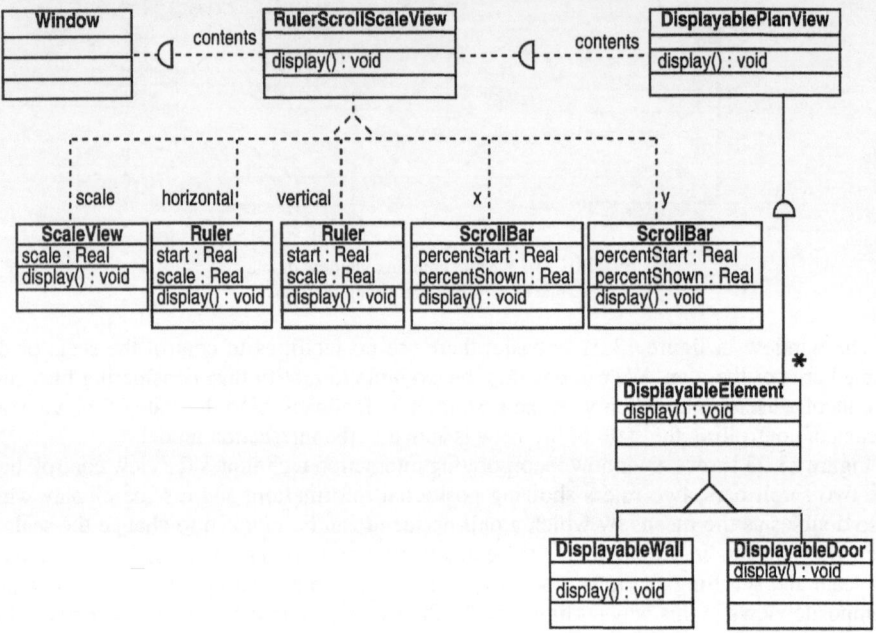

FIGURE 13.25. Increased display complexity for the window in figure 13.23

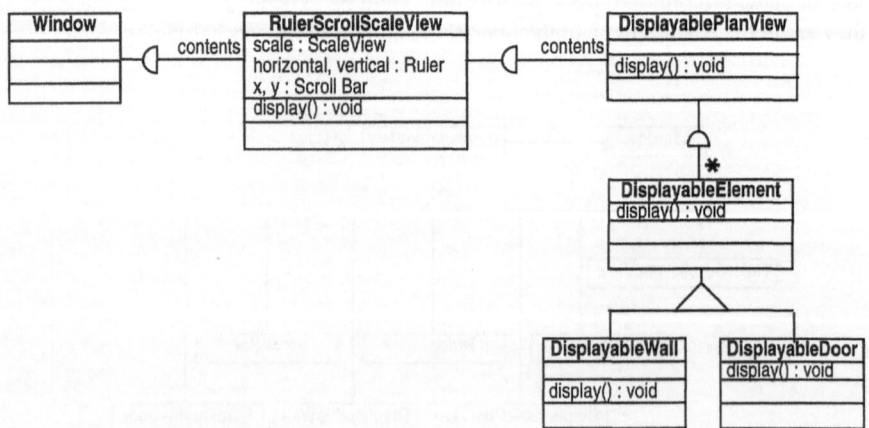

FIGURE 13.26. RulerScrollScaleView in use with hidden extraneous detail

necessary to show the associated types that help constitute **RulerScrollScaleView**; they can be mentioned as attributes of the type (as in figure 13.26), or even completely omitted once the type has been defined.

Multiple views and transactions in interaction models

The interaction model can record information about the number of different kinds of windowed displays that can appear in the system. This includes information as to the number of transactions and view structures in the system, what they display (as we have seen above) and their update frequency. Additionally, we can also specify if the user can work on one or a different number of architectural designs simultaneously.

Recall, from section 13.4.2, that a transaction and a view structure are similar in that they are each composed of information that is obtained from their model. Furthermore, the data maintained in each transaction or view structure is updated from the appropriate model as the model's data changes. However, a transaction can be used to change a model, whereas a view structure merely shows information from the model. As shown below (in figure 13.31), this difference can be shown in type diagrams using an experimental notation that utilises arrowed relations.

It is easy to invent an illustrative view structure for the CAD system, to provide a perspective rendition of a developing architectural design. For the moment, we will make this view structure display the core (i.e. system model), so that we do not have to be concerned with problems of representing perspective views of transactions containing inconsistent architectural design data that is being edited. A type diagram for this structure is outlined in figure 13.27. The most that the users can hope to see using this view structure is a consistent architectural design as captured by the object structure in the core, regardless of the current state of any edits being made via a transaction on the core.

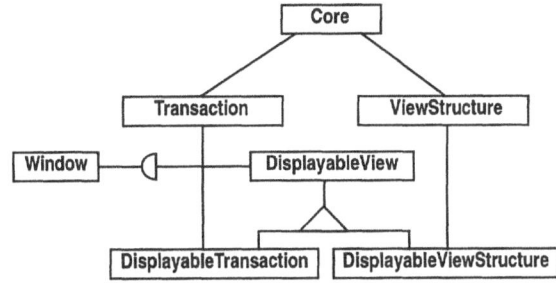

FIGURE 13.27. Core, transaction and view structure for irregular update.

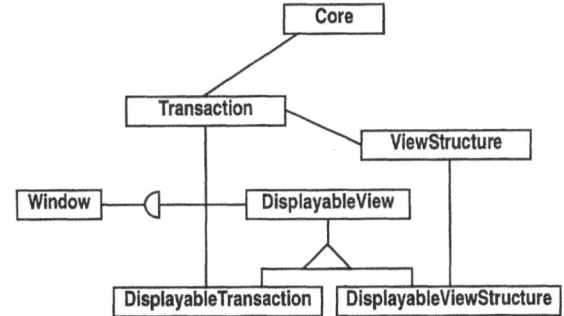

FIGURE 13.28. Core, transaction and view structure for continual update.

An alternative strategy is to make the view structure dependent on the transaction. This scheme is shown in the type diagram of figure 13.28. While this raises questions of how to display (if at all) inconsistent architectural data in a perspective drawing, the scheme does have the advantage of showing the most recently edited architectural data.

All of the relations in figures 13.27 and 13.28 have default cardinalities of one at each end of the relations, indicating that there is always a transaction for editing and a view structure for perspective display. From a user interface design point of view, this is limiting, and we can use cardinalities to show the allowable number of windows with different kinds of contents. Figure 13.29 uses cardinalities to show how two different windowing schemes are represented in type diagrams. The left-hand scheme shows an optional transaction that appears in one window only. The right-hand scheme shows an optional transaction that can be represented in one or more windows. This is the most useful scheme for the CAD example developed in this paper — multiple plan views of an edited transaction are useful to depict different parts of "the plan" at different scales, as shown in figure 13.30. Returning to figure 13.29, the unnamed type is DisplayableView. Its name has been omitted to emphasize the pertinent parts of the type diagrams, and an experienced designer could even go as far as omitting DisplayableView altogether, and showing the inherited aggregation relation between Window and DisplayableTransaction.

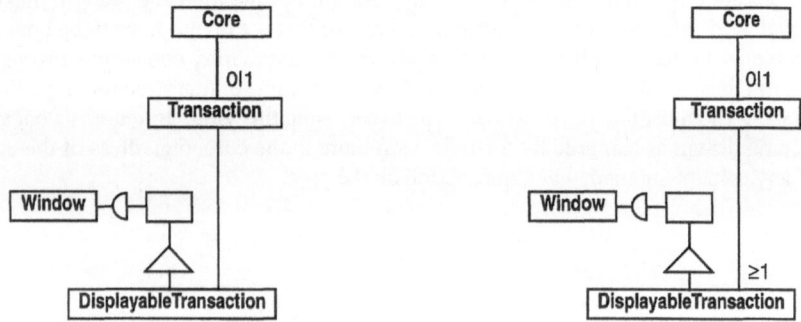

FIGURE 13.29. Single and multiple displayable transactions on an optional transaction

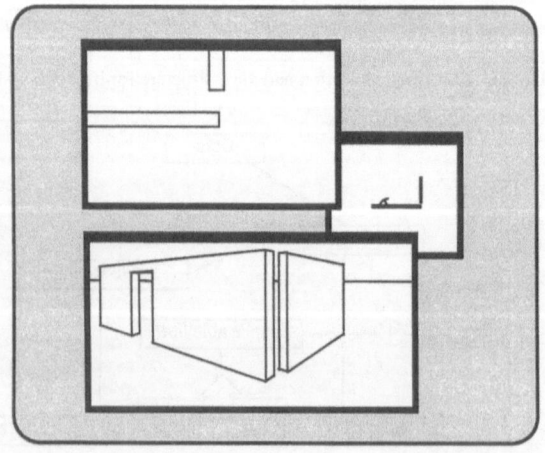

FIGURE 13.30. A sample display surface.

More than one architectural design

So far we have confined ourselves to systems which manipulate one architectural design, but if we require an interactive system that can deal with more than one plan we need to use a type which represents an anchor for the system and its multiple architectural designs. Figure 13.31 shows a model for such a system for zero or more architectural designs. As above, each design may have one or more plan editing windows, and zero or more perspective views. In any such scheme, we need to modify the treatment of selections from the approach suggested in figure 13.20 to one where Selection is related to the System, rather than to any individual InteractDesign. This will allow cut and paste across architectural designs

Augmenting the notation

Currently the notation for relations is being experimented with, using an augmented notation for transaction and view relations. If there is a projection of information, then a solid arrow is used in the projected direction. If the projection is a transaction, then a hollow-headed arrow is used to show the direction of propagation of change back from the transaction.

Figure 13.31 shows this experimental notation, which primarily seems to be of help in overall system models of the kind shown in figures 13.27-13.29 and 12.31, in circumstances where rôle names are not being used.

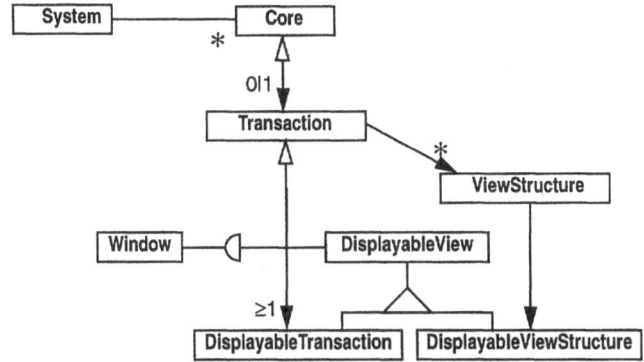

FIGURE 13.31. Multiple architectural designs,
experimental notation for views and transactions

13.6 Interaction sequences

Interaction sequences show the dynamics of prototypical user interaction with a system that is being modelled. They are composed of screen snapshots, or parts thereof, interspersed with user interactions. As such they are somewhat similar to a graphical form of the textual User Action Notation [5]. Interaction sequences may also have optional pre- and post-conditions. A *pre-condition* specifies some condition (or set of conditions) which must be true before the user interactions in the interaction sequence are performed, and a *post-condition* specifies what must be true after an interaction sequence is finished. Pre- and post-conditions can be expressed informally, in natural language, or using some formalism.

While interaction sequences are a useful means of specifying the dynamics of detailed user interface design, they have a greater significance in Idiom. Here pre- and post-conditions are added to interaction sequences to enable the effects of user actions to be linked to the system and interaction models. Since interaction sequences are also linked to the fine-grained task analysis, they provide a means of linking tasks to effects on the models.

Figure 13.32 shows a few example interaction sequences. The choosing pointing interaction sequence shows how a user interaction can affect the interaction model, putting the interface into a pointing and selection mode as a result of a menu selection. The selection sequence shows how a wall is added to the selection in the interaction model, and the selection feedback associated with walls. The movement sequence shows how a selected wall may be moved. Finally the wall creation example shows how a rubber rectangle represents the wall during creation. In all examples the pre- and post-conditions are expressed using a semi-formal notation describing the state of the model of the interactive system.

13.7 A note on task analysis

While task analysis is largely out of the scope of this paper, and, indeed, is the least developed of all the aspects of Idiom, it is worth noting that Idiom has used a very simple GOMS-like decompositional task analysis language, without the predictive elements of GOMS.

This language has been useful and pertinent to the Idiom method. In the context of object-oriented modelling and specification, one of the major benefits is informing the operations in the domain and system models. This informing occurred in the context of the example of this paper; there were no delete operations in the domain and system models until the relevant classes' operations were compared with a high-level task analysis.

NOTATION

mouse button	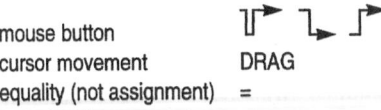
cursor movement	DRAG
equality (not assignment)	=
logical and	∧

In post conditions old values (values at the time of the pre-condition) are $\overline{\text{overlined}}$

CHOOSING POINTING

pre: cursor.location inside menu.pointingModeButton.area

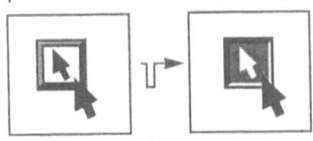

post: interactionMode = POINTING

SELECTING A WALL

pre: cursor.location inside wall.selectionArea ∧ interactionMode = POINTING

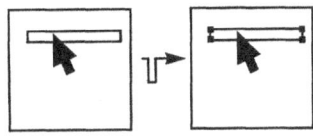

post: selected = wall

MOVING A WALL

pre: selected = wall ∧ cursor.location inside wall.selectionArea ∧
interactionMode = POINTING

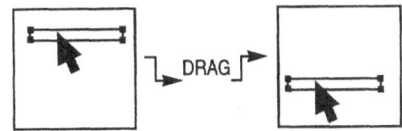

post: selected = wall ∧ wall.pos = $\overline{\text{wall.pos}}$ + dragVector

CREATING A WALL

pre: cursor.location inside planArea ∧ interactionMode = WALLCREATION

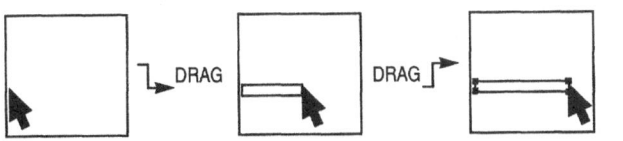

post: card { Wall } = card { $\overline{\text{Wall}}$ } + 1 ∧ wall selected ∧ interactionMode = SELECTION

FIGURE 13.32. Interaction sequence examples

13.8 Experience

Parts of Idiom, including its modelling techniques, have been used in the design of a handful of systems, including diverse research examples. Experience with the design of these systems has been positive. However, application of techniques from Idiom has been done 'on demand', rather than Idiom having been systematically applied to the problems. Nonetheless, it is felt that Idiom can be used systematically for the kind of development that one or two people might undertake over a period of six months to a year. For larger projects Idiom has not been given the kind of testing that it needs for claims of large-scale industrial strength to be substantiated; Idiom needs to be used in larger developments that require a team of people working for a year or more.

As a result of experience to date, the author feels that object-oriented modelling provides suitable abstractions for user interface design, and Idiom and its modelling techniques are of real use in designing user interfaces and interactive systems. In this respect, models provide useful user interface design information, both as that captured in the models, and as that informing other user interface design activities.

Interaction sequences have long been one of the author's favorite user interface description notations; they usefully summarize much detailed design information. With the addition of pre- and post-conditions, they may have the additional advantage of being able to link object-oriented models of interactive systems to the detailed design of these systems; supplying information about the applicability and results of user interactions while illustrating these interactions with prototypical interaction information.

There are, however, disadvantages to Idiom: Firstly, object-oriented modelling requires both an object-oriented perspective and modelling skills. These take time to acquire; as a rough guide, up to six months may be needed before good models are constructed. Secondly, the construction of design artifacts which rely on drawing (modelling, interaction sequences, window screen/layouts) is tedious using even the best of general purpose computer drawing facilities. This is due to the overhead in manipulating specialized diagrams using non-specialized drawing functions. For example., moving a type requires separate operations to move the endpoints of that type's relations, and altering a snapshot in an interaction sequence requires alteration of all subsequent snapshots in the sequence.

13.9 Acknowledgments

Alan Wills has provided me with advice about object-oriented modelling and formal specifications. In particular, I must give him credit for integrating cores, transactions and properties within object-oriented specifications. Matsushita Electronic Industrial Co. Ltd. and Fuji Xerox Information Systems Ltd. gave me time, space and resources to consider object-oriented systems between mid-1991 and mid-1992; some of the ideas presented here were formulated during that time. Finally, Rex Hartson kindly read this paper and provided me with many perceptive and thoughtful comments.

13.10 References

[1] America, P., & van der Linden, F., A Parallel Object-Oriented Language with Inheritance and Subtyping, *OOPSLA/ECOOP'90*, pp161-168.

[2] Booch, G., *Object-oriented Design with Applications*, Benjamin/Cummings Publishing, 1991.

[3] Card, S.K., Moran, T.P., Newell, A., *The Psychology of Human-Computer Interaction*, Lawrence Erlbaum, 1983.

[4] Foley, J.D., van Dam, A., Keiner, S.K., & Hughes, J.F., *Computer Graphics: Principles and Practice*, Addison-Wesley, 2nd Ed., 1990.

[5] Hartson, H.R., Siochi, A.C., & Hix, D. The UAN: A User-Oriented Representation for Direct Manipulation Interface Designs, *ACM TOIS*, 8(3), July 1990, 181-203.

[6] Henderson, A., A Development Perspective on Interface Design and Theory. In Caroll, J.M., *Designing interaction: psychology at the human-computer interface*, Cambridge University Press, 1991, 254-268.

[7] Jones, C.B., *Systematic Software Development Using VDM*, Prentice/Hall, 1986.

[8] Kieras, D., Towards a Practical GOMS Model Methodology for User Interface Design. In Helander (Ed.), The Handbook of Human Computer Interaction. North Holland, 1990, 137-157.

[9] Newman, W.M., & Sproull, R.F., Principles of Interactive Computer Graphics. McGraw-Hill, 1973

[10] Rumbaugh, J., Blaha, M., Premeriani, W., Eddy, F., & Lorensen, W., Object-oriented Modelling and Design. Prentice Hall International, 1991.

[11] Schniderman, B., Designing the User Interface: Strategies for Effective Human-Computer Interaction. Addison-Wesley, 2nd Ed., 1992

[12] Wilfs-Brock, R., Wilkerson, B., & Wiener, L., *Designing Object-Oriented Software*, Prentice-Hall, 1990.

[13] Wills, A., Structure of interactive environments, in Brereton, P., *Software engineering environments*, Ellis Horwood, 1988.

[14] Wills, A., *Object-oriented Software Engineering*, Object*ENGINEERING* Course Notes, 1991.

Part III

Users, Tasks and Specification

Part III

14 Why Are Analogue Graphics and Natural Language Both Needed in HCI?

Niels Ole Bernsen

ABSTRACT

The combined use of language and analogue graphics for the expression of information probably is as old as language itself. The paper addresses the question why we need both the expressions of natural language and analogue graphics for the representation of information. It is argued that analogue graphics and natural language have the complementary expressive virtues of specificity and focus, respectively. Their corresponding lack of focus and specificity, respectively, explain why (a) both have developed a number of mechanisms for coping with these deficiencies and (b) why their combination may often have superior expressive power. Since specificity follows from the analogue character of analogue graphics rather than from their graphic character, analogue sound and touch representations are analysed to explore whether results from the analysis of analogue graphics and their complementarity with natural language can be transferred to other analogue modalities of expression. The paper exemplifies the comparatively new field of Modality Theory.

14.1 Introduction

Natural language can be used to represent virtually anything and it may therefore seem enigmatic why analogue graphical expressions are sometimes preferred to natural language expressions for certain representational purposes. On the other hand, once the expressive power of analogue graphics has been realised, it may become less evident why natural language representations would ever be needed if it were not for the fact that speaking or writing is often more practical than drawing or creating animations and videos. The answer to these two questions seems to reside in two complementary features of natural language and analogue graphical expression. The features are that natural language expressions are focused but lack specificity while analogue graphical representations are specific but lack focus. This paper attempts to clarify the issues involved and to explore some of the consequences of the basic distinction between specificity and focus.

The work described forms part of the European ESPRIT Basic Research project GRACE which ultimately aims at providing a sound theoretical basis for usability engineering in the domain of multimodal representations. Whereas the enabling technologies for multimodal (including virtual reality) representation are growing rapidly, there is a lack of theoretical understanding of the principles which should be observed in mapping information from some task domain into presentations at the human-computer interface in a way which optimises the usability of the interface, given the specific purposes of the computer artifact being designed. Part of the research agenda of GRACE is to analyse in depth the differences in expressive power between different generic representational modalities such as (spoken or written) natural language and analogue graphics [3, 2].

The plan of the paper is as follows. Sect. 14.2 provides the concepts needed in the analysis to follow. Sect. 14.3 presents the distinction between specificity and generality. Sect. 14.4 presents the distinction between focused and unfocused representation. Both specificity (cum lack of focus) and focus (cum lack of specificity) are representational virtues, and their respective representational implications are described in Sects. 14.5 and

14.6. Since both representational virtues have their corresponding weaknesses, it is not surprising that the widespread use of natural language and analogue graphics has lead to the invention of mechanisms which to some extent serve to remedy those weaknesses (Sect. 14.7). On the other hand, given those weaknesses, one obvious way of trying to eliminate them is to combine the representational modalities of natural language and analogue graphics into multimodal representations (Sect. 14.8). The representational virtue of specificity in analogue graphics turns out to be due not to their graphical character but to their analogue character. Analogueness, however, is a property not only of graphics but of other representational modalities as well. The implications for sound and touch are explored in Sect. 14.9. Finally, Sect. 14.10 is a review of results.

14.2   Some Relevant Concepts

Some of the central concepts we shall need are explained in this section.

14.2.1   External and Internal Representations

The representations or representational modalities we shall be dealing with are primarily external representations, that is, they are embodied in some medium of expression such as graphics, acoustics or haptics, and are hence external to the human cognitive system and intersubjectively accessible. This is true of written or spoken words and sentences and of analogue graphics on computer screens or on paper. External representations are considered as representations by the human cognitive system and are primarily, as far as we are concerned, produced by data structures in computers and other items of information technology. It is important not to confuse external representations with the representations which are internal to the human cognitive system. Spoken or written natural language, when considered as external representations, are generally non-analogue. This does not preclude that the internal representations evoked by natural language are to some extent and in some sense analogue representations. External representations are interpreted as representations by an observer, and interpretation is an internal cognitive process. The properties of specificity and focus central to this paper derive from the fact that natural language and analogue graphics provide very different means of supporting the interpretation of external representations. For this reason, we cannot avoid the issue of internal representations entirely in what follows.

14.2.2   Analogue and Non-Analogue Representations

The distinction between analogue and non-analogue (external) representations designates the difference between representations, in whatever modality, which represent through sharing at least one dimension of information with what they represent and representations which represent through conventional pairing between representation and what is represented. Most analogue representations, such as photographs or diagrams, share many dimensions of information with what they represent, whereas others, such as graphs, share only one or a few dimensions of information with what they represent. As long as we focus only on external representations, the analogue/non-analogue distinction is clear in most cases. In practice, however, the distinction sometimes can be difficult to draw primarily because of the existence of levels of abstraction in analogue representation, whether the representation be a sound, a piece of graphics such as a diagram or a tactile/kinaesthetic one. A highly abstract diagrammatic representation, say, of a computer network showing servers, terminals, wiring, etc., may have so few recognisable topological similarities with what it represents that it may just as well, arguably, be considered a non-analogue representation of what it represents. The less recognisable similarity there is between what is represented and its representation, the more we may have to rely on additional knowledge of the representational conventions used in order to decode particular representations. In the limit, where we find, i.a., natural language, we have to rely exclusively on representational conventions.

Another problem in applying the analogue/non-analogue distinction is that it is sometimes unclear how real are the states of affairs which appear to be represented in analogue representations. The equator, for instance, is nearly always represented on maps, but what does this representation correspond to? An arbitrary triangular icon, on the other hand, perhaps resembles many triangular shapes to be found in nature or culture, so is it really arbitrary after all or is it rather a highly abstract analogue representation? These two examples may be distinguished using the criterion that the equator on the map does represent a fixed topological property of the globe whereas the triangular icon really is intended as being arbitrary - one might just as well have used a circle or something else again. What matters are exclusively the representational conventions imposed on it. In any case, the 'reality' represented in analogue representations is certainly more comprehensive than the tangible world of spatio-temporal objects, situations, processes and events. In another example, a conceptual graph does have a topology but in this case it appears justified to assume that the topology is not an analogue representation of conceptual relations because such relations do not themselves appear to be topological. Conceptual graphs, therefore, are non-analogue diagrams. However, it is not evident at this point that the topology criterion just described will be able to resolve all problems about the analogue versus non-analogue character of particular external representations. We may have to accept the existence of an undecidable 'grey' area between analogue graphical diagrams and non-analogue graphical diagrams which are often alternatively called 'abstract' or 'conceptual' diagrams. The sound and touch domains may pose similar decidability problems.

14.2.3   Arbitrary and Non-Arbitrary Representations

The distinction between non-arbitrary and arbitrary representational modalities marks the difference between external representations which, in order to perform their representational function, rely on an already existing system of meaning and representations which do not do so. The reason why this distinction tends to be overlooked is that, in most cases, it coincides with the distinction between analogue and non-analogue representation. For the purpose of this paper, however, it is important to note that the external representations of spoken and written language constitute exceptions to this rule. They are non-analogue and non-arbitrary.

The separation between the analogue/non-analogue distinction, on the one hand, and the arbitrary/non-arbitrary distinction, on the other, does seem quite important. It provides a broad and intuitive justification of why natural language can compete successfully with graphics for many representational purposes in human-computer interfaces and elsewhere. Despite being non-analogue considered as a form of external representation, natural language builds on an already existing system of meaning. If one does not understand the particular natural language in question, one does not have access to its corresponding system of meaning, but the system of meaning 'is' there nevertheless. And the separation between the analogue/non-analogue and arbitrary/non-arbitrary distinctions demonstrates that explanations of why, e.g., natural language modalities are in some cases inferior, and in others superior, to analogue graphical modalities cannot simply be provided by appealing to the analogue/non-analogue distinction.

14.2.4   Representational Modalities

We need not go deeply into the question of what is 'really' an external representational modality. The problem is not that the question is particularly difficult to answer but, rather, that the term 'modality' is being used in widely different ways in the literature. Explicating one's favoured sense of 'modality', therefore, is both an exercise in contrastive semantical decision-making and an effort in conceptual analysis. Elsewhere [4], a 'pure' (or unimodal) modality has been characterised as consisting of a specific medium and a profile constituted by its properties as selected from the following list of binary opposites: analogue/non-analogue, arbitrary/non-arbitrary, static/dynamic, linguistic/non-linguistic. A 'medium' is a physical substrate having a set of perceptual qualities accessible to humans such as a set of visual properties. 'Pure' modalities can be combined into multimodal representations. Given this conceptual apparatus, e.g., spoken language, written language and analogue static graphics come out as different pure representational modalities. It is possible that the current confusion surrounding the notion of 'modality' in the literature is due to the assumption that modalities are entities characterisable through one single property, if we could only identify that property. By contrast, the medium/profile notion of modalities assumes that modalities are complex-property entities.

14.2.5   The AG Domain

We know that natural language is capable of representing virtually everything, including 1-D, 2-D and 3-D spatial domains, the temporal domain and both concrete non-spatial and so-called abstract (non-spatial) domains. Analogue graphics can represent that to which they have an analogue relationship, i.e., the spatio-temporal domain, temporal events and processes being of course best represented in dynamic analogue graphics. The discussion below deals with natural language representations of the representational domain of analogue graphics which for the sake of brevity may be called the AG domain. It is important to note that the AG domain is significantly broader than the domain of access of human vision. Scientific visualisation, for instance, enables the visualisation of many spatio-temporal domains to which human vision has no access, such as intonation patterns in spoken language.

14.2.6   Limitations to Analogueness

Analogue graphics are not analogue, purely and simply. There are always limitations to the analogue mapping between analogue graphics and what they represent, even in the cases of photographs and videos. These limitations derive from aspects such as the degree of selective abstraction of the graphics, their degree of resolution and their spatial dimensionality. Yet other sources of lack of analogue mapping between analogue graphics and what they represent should be disregarded here since they deal with different phenomena. One example is one and the same object being viewed from one perspective and analogously represented from a different perspective. Another, one and the same object being viewed from one distance and analogously represented from a different distance.

14.3   Specificity Versus Generality

One of the two related, main differences between the respective representational powers of natural language and analogue graphics seems to be the specificity of analogue graphics vs. the generality of natural language expressions.

Natural language represents the AG domain through its individual expressions drawing upon an arsenal of more or less shared, general and stereotypical internal representations (or concepts) based for the most part on common visual experience. Being general and stereotypical, these representations always leave open and undetermined a certain inter- pretational scope (cf. [5]). A description in natural language normally leaves out a wealth of individual features of the entities in the AG domain which it describes. Recipients may or may not mentally or otherwise fill in by themselves the details omitted in the descrip- tion and thereby exploit or avoid to exploit the interpretational scope of the description. The term 'interpretational scope' should in this context be interpreted in a rather strong sense. Our general concepts may be structured in many ways as frames, scenarios, scripts, image schemata, etc., but, strictly speaking, even conceptual features such as defaults belong to the interpretational scope of concepts rather than to their core meaning.

The interpretational scope of a particular description in natural language can be incre- mentally narrowed and determined through the addition of further linguistic expressions. In the AG domain, however, this process tends to be lengthy and complex whenever the aim is to render all the properties of the entities being described. Arguably, the expression- addition process will in principle never succeed in providing a representation which is in- formationally equivalent to an analogue graphical representation of the same entities. One way of ensuring informational equivalence would be to require that the natural language description allows an exact and intersubjective, analogue graphical reconstruction of the AG domain described. One may attempt to devise exceptions to this principle of non- equivalence, but even if such exceptions do exist they will be unimportant by comparison to the domain where the principle holds. For instance, it might, perhaps, be possible to reconstruct the informationally equivalent analogue graphics corresponding to the follow- ing description: "A perfect circle with a diameter of 2 centimeters drawn in completely black ink and in a perfect 1 millimeter wide brush stroke". Even in this case more needs to be said on, e.g., the nature and structure of the surface on which the analogue graphics were drawn.

Analogue graphics, on the other hand, represent the AG domain through representing details of individual entities. Analogue graphics represent that over which the correspond- ing, abstract and general natural language expressions are abstractions and generalisa- tions. To be sure, the extent to which this is the case depends on the degree of abstraction of the analogue graphics used, on their degree of resolution and their spatial dimension- ality. However, to the extent to which analogue graphics represent individual detail, no interpretational scope is left open. In this sense, analogue graphics are specific as com- pared to the corresponding natural language expressions, and independently of the degree of abstration of the graphics and their degree of resolution. Remember that we are always comparing a piece of analogue graphics with its corresponding natural language descrip- tion or descriptions. This having been said, it is of course the case that, to the extent that analogue graphics embody some degree of abstraction and lack of resolution, they themselves leave open an interpretational scope. So the fact that both natural language and analogue graphics may leave open an interpretational scope should not be miscon- strued as stating that, given a certain level of abstraction of a piece of analogue graphics, its meaning may be identical or informationally equivalent to that of the corresponding natural language expression. This is virtually never the case. However abstract a piece of analogue graphics is, the meaning it expresses is always more specific than that of the corresponding linguistic expression. In a simple example, there are infinitely many specif- ically different graphic ways of representing an angle of 60 degrees. These all fall within the interpretational scope of the otherwise exact natural language expression 'an angle of 60 degrees'.

The example just provided helps clarity what is meant here by 'the linguistic expression corresponding to a piece of analogue graphics'. In using natural language we hardly ever attempt to go to the length of trying to provide descriptions which are informationally equivalent to some analogue graphical representation in the AG domain. Instead, we use expressions such as 'an angle of 60 degrees' and such expressions are sufficient for the communicative purpose at hand. However, such expressions leave open large interpretational scopes. Had we been using analogue graphical representations for the same communicative purpose instead, parts of the interpretational scope left open would have been closed.

Speaking now of internal representations, it would seem to follow directly that the internal representations to be posited by cognitive science as constituting the general meaning or sense of natural language expressions are not 'analogue' in the sense in which analogue graphics is analogue. These meanings or senses are generally like variables rather than constants. This is how they succeed in subsuming indefinite numbers of specifically different instances. And since the contents of our perceptual experience are never like variables but always consist of specific instances, the general meanings of natural language expressions cannot be analogue. A specific mental model created by some individual of a state of affairs in the AG domain which has been expressed through a general expression in natural language, on the other hand, might well be analogue in more or less the sense of analogue graphics. However, such a mental model would be one which exploited the interpretational scope of the natural language expression in question. To avoid any misunderstanding it may be pointed out here that, just like analogue graphics, mental models of entities in the AG domain may be quite abstract and low-resolution and do not have to incorporate more specificity than done by the most selectively abstract piece of analogue graphics.

The distinction between specificity and generality may be said to reflect a difference between 'direct' and 'indirect' external representation. Natural language represents the AG domain indirectly in the sense of representing via the general concepts of natural language. Analogue graphics, by contrast, represents the AG domain directly in the sense of not having to represent this domain via general concepts.

14.4   Unfocused Versus Focused Representation

The second main difference between the respective representational powers of natural language and analogue graphics seems to be the focused nature of the representations provided by natural language vs. the unfocused nature of analogue graphics.

Natural language expressions and descriptions are focused as compared with the corresponding analogue graphics. This contrast is closely related to that of the generality of natural language expressions vs. the specificity of analogue graphics. Natural language expressions focus on a particular aspect of what is being represented and leave open an interpretational scope. Analogue graphics close the representational scope and, for that very reason, do not focus. In the example of Sect. 14.3 above, the purely graphic representation of an angle of 60 degrees does not tell whether it is the 60 degrees which matter (and they would have to be measured first) to the representer, whether what matters is the fact that an angle is being represented or whether what is being represented is something third. When, on the other hand, natural language is being used to state the fact that an angle is 60 degrees, no irrelevant detail is involved and the statement is focused. It is important to note that 'focused' does not imply 'picking out a particular detail'. 'Focused' does imply picking out something which is then being expressed, but it need not be a detail of a larger whole and might just as well be the larger whole itself. Focusing, in other words, may operate at any level of detail.

Specificity implies that many different representational purposes may be satisfied by one and the same analogue graphic representation which, therefore, remains unfocused until further information has been provided. The viewer may happen to focus on particular aspects of the analogue representation but, barring contextual implications, is in no position to know if this is the focus intended by the representer. Focusedness implies that only one representational purpose is at least, and normally, being intended which, therefore, remains otherwise unspecific and leaves open an interpretational scope.

14.5 Implications of Specificity

Representational specificity is a powerful property of analogue graphics. This section explores some of its implications in terms of useful properties of analogue graphics. So far, no principle has been found which might help establish an exhaustive list of such implications. Implications are stated in a somewhat coarse-grained format leaving out more or less obvious qualifications which would need to be made in an exhaustive presentation. In this and the following section (Sect. 14.6), the reader should bear in mind that we are only speaking about implications of specificity and focusedness, respectively. That is, we are only dealing with the strengths of representation deriving from these properties in analogue graphics and natural language, respectively. In Sect. 14.7 we shall take a full view of analogue graphic and natural language expressions.

14.5.1 Representational Exhaustiveness

The potential of analogue graphics for achieving representational exhaustiveness, or one-to-one mapping with what is represented, follows from their specificity and is limited by their dimensionality as compared with the dimensionality of what is represented as well as by their degrees of abstraction and resolution. A 2-D map, for instance, cannot provide 3-D specifics; or a piece static graphics such as a process diagram [1], while somehow capable of representing movement, cannot provide its specifics. Process diagrams seem to represent movement and processes through the way they are being read (or interpreted) by people who use their domain knowledge to exploit the interpretational scope of the diagrams. Given their lack of specificity, the internal representations evoked by natural language expressions lack the potential for representational exhaustiveness.

14.5.2 Smooth Mapping

The specificity of analogue graphics allows them to smoothly map what is to be represented into the representation, their smooth mapping potential only being limited by their dimensionality and degrees of abstractness and resolution. Smooth mapping preserves whatever continuous transitions between properties are needed for the representational purpose at hand. The internal representations evoked by natural language expressions, being general and having an interpretational scope, lack the property of smooth mapping.

14.5.3 Direct Measurement

The specificity of analogue graphics allows direct measurements to be performed on the representation, which reflect the properties of what is represented. The potential for direct measurement is bounded by dimensionality and by the degrees of abstractness and resolution of the graphics. The internal representations evoked by natural language expressions, being general and having an interpretational scope, lack the property of direct measurement.

14.5.4   Approximate Inference

The specificity of analogue graphics allows approximate inferences to be performed on the representation, which reflect the properties and qualities of what is represented. The potential for approximate inference is bounded by dimensionality and by the degrees of abstractness and resolution of the graphics. Natural language expressions, being general and having an interpretational scope, lack the property of allowing approximate inference. However, natural language expressions do allow a form of approximate inference via the stereotypical concepts they evoke. Such inferences can be performed as well on the corresponding analogue graphics.

14.5.5   Direct Entity Identification

The specificity of analogue graphics provides the informational basis for subsequent direct identification of the particular entities represented. The generality and stereotypical character of the internal representations evoked by natural language expressions makes difficult the subsequent identification of the particular entities represented. This is why the police prefers photographs of robbers to linguistic descriptions. It is true that we manage pretty well in everyday life with natural language expressions for entity identification. The reason why we do so seems to be the widespread use of (linguistic) indexical reference, definite description and proper names (see below). The police would normally prefer to know the full name of a robber rather than his or her linguistic description.

14.5.6   Easy Update Connectivity

The introduction of a new entity into a piece of analogue graphics immediately allows an updating of its spatial (or spatio-temporal) relationships to all other entities represented. The introduction of a new piece of information into a series of natural language expressions describing something in the AG domain enforces the use of more or less complex inferences in order to update the internal representation of what is being described.

14.5.7   Substitution for Direct Experience

The specificity of analogue graphics means that they can be used as substitutions for direct perceptual experience, for instance in enhanced reality or virtual reality technologies. The internal representations evoked by natural language expressions, being general and having an interpretational scope, lack this property.

14.6   Implications of Generality and Focusedness

Just as representational specificity is a powerful property of analogue graphics, generality and focusedness are powerful representational properties of linguistic expressions. This section explores some of their implications in terms of useful properties of natural language. So far, no principle has been found for establishing an exhaustive list of such implications.

14.6.1   Abstraction

Abstraction allows natural language to 'directly' represent abstractions over experience in the AG domain. Such abstractions cannot be represented in analogue graphics. A simple example is that it is impossible to graphically represent colour in general. Because of their inherent specificity, analogue graphics have a limited potential for representing abstractions as compared to the corresponding natural language expressions. This is a profound advantage of linguistic expression which seems to reflect the fact that our repertoire of internal representations includes a large number of general and stereotypical concepts in the AG domain in addition to specific mental models. Such concepts can be conceived of as organised into abstraction hierarchies. The colour green, for instance, is already an abstraction which cannot be represented as such in analogue graphics. At a higher level of abstraction, the concept of colour subsumes all our abstract concepts of individual colours. At a still higher level, the concept of visual properties of entities (almost) subsumes the abstract concept of colour together with other concepts. Natural language allows us to freely focus on the appropriate level of abstraction.

Whereas colour in general cannot be represented in analogue graphics, the full colour spectrum can be represented in analogue graphics to an arbitrary degree of resolution. Generalising this observation, it would seem that any part of the AG domain can be represented in analogue graphics, to an arbitrary degree of exhaustiveness, namely as collections of specific instances. After all, the AG domain concepts of natural language are built from specific observed instances by the neural circuitry of the brain. However, communication in natural language would be impossible if we always had to include information on such specifics. Instead, natural language makes it possible to navigate freely at the abstraction levels above the specifics in the AG domain to realise particular communicative purposes at the constant price of operating within an interpretational scope.

14.6.2   Relevance Decidability

Given their non-focused character, it can be difficult to decide with respect to a piece of analogue graphics what is and what is not relevant to a specific representational or communicative purpose. It can therefore be difficult or impossible to identify the representational purpose behind a piece of analogue graphics in the first place. Given their focused character, the corresponding natural language expressions do not raise this problem. This is not to deny, of course, the existence of irrelevant discourse. But natural language is 'made for relevance', i.e., for making relevant descriptions at appropriate levels of abstraction. Relevance does not pose a problem for linguistic expression in the sense in which specificity poses a problem for natural language. There is reason to believe that far more cases of communication error arising through the use of natural language arise from lack of specificity than from lack of relevance (cf. [5]). "Be (sufficiently) specific!" is a much more important injunction to include in a practically oriented set of conversational postulates than is the injunction "Be relevant!".

14.6.3   Beyond the Analogue Media

Natural language expressions can represent many types of entity which lie outside not only of the AG domain but outside of the representational potential of external analogue media as a whole, including highly abstract concepts such as 'truth' or 'justice'. Given the notion of abstraction hierarchies of Sect. 14.6.1 above, even such concepts would seem to have some basis in specific occurrences. However, the properties of those specific occurrences that make them suitable for creating abstractions such as 'truth' or 'justice' cannot be captured in analogue media of representation.

14.6.4   Reasoning

Natural language expresses a number of important logical and epistemic operators which have no obvious equivalents in the domains of external analogue media, such as 'not', 'or' or 'if-then', and which can be essential to the realisation of specific purposes of information representation or communication. Again, the properties of specific occurrences or situations that make them suitable for creating such abstractions cannot be captured in analogue media of representation. To some extent, the importance of logical and epistemic operators for the representation of information has been taken into account in the graphic medium. A common solution is to add standardised abstract iconic representations to analogue graphics. For instance, a cigarette with a big X across it means that smoking is not allowed. Because of their standardised character, such abstract icons act as non-analogue and non-arbitrary external representations just like those of natural language (cf. Sect. 14.2 above).

14.7   Deficiency-Handling Mechanisms

The complementarity between natural language and analogue graphics representations has two main implications which will be discussed in this section and Sect. 14.8, respectively. The first is that each type of representation includes a number of mechanisms which are internal to that mechanism and whose function is to 'patch up' their respective deficiencies of expression. Thus, a number of focusing mechanisms have evolved in analogue graphics and natural language makes use of various specificity mechanisms for achieving increased specificity. These types of mechanism enable analogue graphics and natural language to overcome, to some extent, their respective, inherent expressive deficiencies and hence to realise a broader scope of information representation. And both types of mechanism can be seen to inherit their respective deficiency-handling capabilities from the complementary representational type. The second implication is that the multimodal combination of the two types of external representation offers many opportunities for benefiting from the strengths of each.

Viewing the mechanisms to be presented below as deficiency-handling devices is of course to adopt one perspective on those mechanisms among other, equally possible perspectives. Undoubtedly, some or most of these mechanisms have been present during the entire life-time of the representational types we are considering. The purpose of presenting those mechanisms as deficiency-handling devices is to emphasise the complementarity between specificity and focus. From another, equally valid and compatible, perspective, the isolated use, for a large variety of purposes, of each of the natural language or analogue graphics representational modalities can be seen as an effort to achieve as much specificity and focus as possible within the basic representational constraints on a particular modality. From this latter perspective, one is likely to emphasise the extent to which specificity and focus in particular instances of natural language or graphical representations are matters of degree.

14.7.1   Focusing Mechanisms in Analogue Graphics

Perhaps not surprisingly, given what has been said above, but worth pointing out anyway is the fact that the focusing mechanisms of analogue graphics all appear to trade analogueness for focus. Each focusing mechanism achieves its results by decreasing the analogue relationship between representation and what is represented. This happens at a price, of course, namely that focused analogue graphics, in various ways and to varying degrees, loose many of the virtues of specificity pointed out in Sect. 14.5 above. The primary advantage obtained by focusing, on the other hand, is an increase in relevance decidability which thus lets analogue graphics share one of the important advantages of natural language. A second advantage obtained through some types of focusing is that analogue graphics succeed in approaching the abstract representational qualities of natural language (cf. Sect. 14.6.1 above).

Selective Removal of Specificity

Selective removal of specificity is a useful mechanism for increasing the focus and hence the communicative relevance of analogue graphics. For instance, if one cannot clearly see from a piece of analogue graphics which kind of dog or tree is being represented, it may be contextually likely that what is represented is simply a dog or a tree. A step upwards in the abstraction hierarchy has thus been achieved. Removing background and other communicatively irrelevant entities from a piece of analogue graphics equally serves to enhance their focus. The filtering of information in order to make important features or structures appear more prominently represents a combination of selective removal of specificity and aspect enhancement (see below). What has been called here selective removal of specificity is often termed 'selective abstraction'. Note that this is not abstraction in the sense in which natural language expressions are abstract because specificity is being preserved in the process. However, selective removal of specificity shares with linguistic abstraction the effect of opening an interpretational scope which may be why the term 'abstraction' is often being used (ambiguously) in both cases.

Dimensionality Reduction

Dimensionality reduction is a form of selective removal of specificity. Many representational or communicative purposes can be achieved by using a lower spatio-temporal dimensionality than that characterising the entities being represented. For instance, many spatial layouts do not require representation in 3-D; many spatio-temporal processes and events can be expressed purely in the spatial domain and even 2-D representations are often sufficient for doing that.

Enhancing Aspects for Saliency

Analogue graphics have many different mechanisms for enhancing certain aspects of what is represented. Such mechanisms serve to increase the comparative saliency of certain aspects in the context of the graphics as a whole. In static graphics, relative enhancement of contours, differences in colouring, encircling, distortion of proportions, foregrounding, static simulation of dynamic zooming, and scaling and selective enlargement of entities all serve this purpose. These mechanisms can also be used in dynamic graphics which have an additional repertoire for aspect enhancement including dynamical change of colours, contours, shapes and sizes, zooming and scaling, blinking or oscillation, movement and so on. In addition, as indicated earlier, we have a small arsenal of standardised abstract (non-analogue, non-arbitrary) icons some of which can be used for saliency-enhancement. The most common example is the use of arrows for focusing purposes in analogue graphics. In books for bird-watchers, for instance, it is common to use arrows to point to discriminatory features among otherwise closely resembling species. Without these arrows, the analogue graphical bird representations provided would be less than half as useful for the support of species identification tasks, which offers a powerful illustration of the non-focused character of analogue graphics.

246 Niels Ole Bernsen

Dwelling and Repetition

Dwelling and repetition are two other focusing mechanisms which are primarily used in dynamic graphics but which may be used in static graphics as well.

14.7.2 Specificity Mechanisms in Natural Language

When using natural language for representational purposes one nearly always faces the problem of how to sufficiently reduce representational scope. Obvious examples include the description of complex spatial layouts or faces, but the problem is much more general and failure to solve it often causes communication error. It seems likely that, e.g., underspecified instructions lead to much wasted effort in the workplace. We have seen that the use of focusing mechanisms in analogue graphics happens at the price of reducing analogueness. The use of specificity mechanisms in natural language, on the other hand, does not necessarily happen at a price such as reduced focus or generality. And when a price has to be paid, its nature depends on the particular specificity mechanism used.

Lengthy Description

Increasing the comprehensiveness of a description (instruction, etc.) is a key method for reducing the interpretational scope of linguistic expressions. As remarked earlier, one virtually never achieves complete specificity this way. However, specificity sufficient for a given communicative purpose can often be achieved. The widespread use of summaries, repetition, statements of 'key points' and so on, testifies to the fact that the longer a description (instruction, etc.) becomes, the easier it becomes for recipients to loose its overall focus. The architecture of the standard news article in newspapers is that of a staged increase in (length and) specificity of description.

Interestingly, even though natural language is, by itself, a focused type of representation it also has mechanisms for focus enhancement. In the written natural language modality which exploits the graphical medium of expression, this is done through the use of graphical mechanisms such as underlining, italics, different font sizes, relative positioning of text bits, etc. In principle, all the analogue graphics saliency-enhancement mechanisms might be used as we do to some extent when annotating text written by others. It is common knowledge that these mechanisms are often misused, i.e., used unnecessarily, which serves to re-emphasise the inherent focusing power of natural language. In spoken language, focus can be marked through acoustic mechanisms such as change of rhytm or loudness of expression.

Indexical Reference

Indexical reference designates the strongest family of specificity mechanisms in natural language. In the broad sense of indexical reference with which we are concerned, indexical reference ties linguistic expressions to something specific which is or can be known from past, present or future experience. In tying linguistic expression to experience, indexical reference makes use of proper names, definite descriptions (e.g., "it's on the table in the living room") and indexicals. Extra-linguistic acts of indexical reference such as pointing serve the same purpose of tying language to experience in order to achieve specific internal representation of the topics of discourse. In the AG domain, the use of linguistic indexicals can be viewed as analogous to combining linguistic expressions and analogue graphics (e.g., "this is my sister Charlotte"). Descriptions of entities in the AG domain are of course strongly supported by indexical reference. However, when indexical reference to specific entities in the AG domain is used for illustration rather than identification (see Sect. 14.8 below), the specificity of the entities referred to may easily cause a decrease of generality and focus which then has to be remedied, for instance through the use of several different illustrations or by lengthening of the accompanying linguistic description.

Metrics

The inclusion of more or less exact metric properties of entities in linguistic descriptions is an important means of reducing interpretational scope. As suggested by the analysis of the example of an angle of 60 degrees in Sect. 14.4 above, use of metrical properties appears to be a necessary, but virtually never a sufficient condition for achieving fully specific natural language representations.

Use of Metaphor and Analogy

The difficulty of completely representing specific entities in the AG domain linguistically explains why the use of metaphor and analogy may dramatically increase the specificity of natural language descriptions. What a metaphor or an analogy contributes is to add, in a single word or phrase, an entire complex of features to the description which has already been provided. This can be much more efficient than one's having to painstakingly add literal expression upon literal expression to constrain interpretational scope. For instance, if a male person is correctly described as resembling a mole in face and posture it may be possible to pick out that person from a large crowd without the need of any further information.

14.8 The Integration of Natural Language and Analogue Graphics

The integration of natural language and analogue graphics for purposes of information representation in the AG domain offers the opportunity of combining the virtues of each generic form of representation. In such integrated multimodal representations, analogue graphics, whether static or dynamic, contributes specificity of representation and natural language contributes focus of representation, i.e., the virtues listed in Sects. 14.5 and 14.6 above are being combined. Adding to the power of combined representation, natural language can be used in expressing relevant information from outside the AG domain including abstract concepts and concepts facilitating reasoning in the AG domain. Moreover, many common types of multimodal linguistic/analogue graphics representation consist of combinations of linguistic expression and analogue graphics to which focusing mechanisms have been applied. In principle, of course, all the deficiency-handling mechanisms described in Sect. 14.7 above can be applied in multimodal representations. The result is a form of multimodal representation which can represent information in a way which is adequately focused and adequately specific at the same time. In the limit, such combinations can adequately substitute for direct experience in the AG domain and may hence serve as reality enhancements and substitutes for, e.g., training purposes. Let us review some well-known combination mechanisms.

14.8.1 Annotating

Naming of geographical locations on maps, entity parts in a diagram or persons in photographs, insertion of feature names or descriptions, defining the interpretation of graphical elements, or using written language 'bubbles' in cartoons are examples of linguistic annotation of analogue graphic representations. Other important forms of annotation of analogue graphics are the use of accompanying written or spoken natural language text. Annotation makes it possible to obtain the focus needed for a given representational purpose without loss of specificity.

14.8.2   Illustrating

Illustrating and annotating mirror one another. In annotation, it is the analogue graphics which are central to the representation and natural language serves to focus the graphical representation for a given communicative purpose. In illustrating something, it is the linguistic representation which is central to the representation and the analogue graphics are used for providing specific models of the subject-matter of linguistic representation. When this subject-matter is one of general concepts (in the AG domain) and/or reasoning with such concepts, illustration is all that analogue graphics can provide. Illustration supports the creation of appropriate mental models of the subject-matter at issue while linguistic expression more or less successfully prevents the loss of generality and focus. Books on mushrooms, for instance, can get people killed if this is not done properly.

Both annotation and illustration are widely used in what is commonly known as 'multimedia' representations of information.

14.8.3   Mutual Disambiguation and Redundancy

A third way of combining linguistic expression and analogue graphics is to make them disambiguate each other. A common example is the combination of word icons and analogue graphical icons in computer interfaces. Both are equally central to the multimodal representation they jointly constitute.

In this paper we have been mainly dealing with natural language and analogue graphics and their combinations as used for the 'output' representation of information on, e.g., computer screens. In all such scenarios, the user is a passive recipient of information and the representer's task is one of optimising focus and specificity for given communicative purposes. Researchers have begun to explore combinations of natural language and graphics as input modalities to computers (e.g., [8, 7]). This line of work does not seem likely to change the main points made in this paper.

14.8.4   Abstract or Conceptual Graphics

Strictly speaking, this topic lies outside of the scope of this paper. It may however be remarked that the combination of linguistic expressions and non-analogue, arbitrary graphical structures such as points, lines, boxes, etc. is a widely used method of combining general conceptual information expressed in written natural language with useful properties of non-linguistic graphical expression such as perspicuous ordering, segmentation, grouping and so on. Visual programming languages exploit this method.

14.9   Specificity as a Consequence of Analogueness: Implications for Sound and Touch

The specificity of analogue graphics seems to derive from its analogue character rather than from its graphic character. Analogueness is a property of other representational modalities than those of static or dynamic, diagrammatic or non-diagrammatic analogue graphics. This observation opens the perspective that other analogue representational modalities, such as analogue sound and touch, share many of the 'virtuous' properties of analogue graphics which derive from their specificity. This, indeed, seems to be the case. If we reconsider the seven properties of analogue graphics identified in Sect. 14.5 above, we find that six of these are characteristic of analogue sound and touch as well. They are:

- representational exhaustiveness;

- smooth mapping;

- direct measurement;

- approximate inference;

- direct entity identification;

- substitution for direct experience.

Only the property of easy update connectivity seems to be questionable with respect to touch and sound.

Furthermore, analogue sound and touch share the limitations of analogue graphics noted in Sect. 14.6 above with respect to:

- relevance decidability;

- abstraction;

- confinement to the analogue medium; and

- lacking capability for representing logical and epistemic operators.

The non-focused character of analogue sound and touch representations raises the question to what extent we find the same focusing mechanisms in the AS (analogue sound) and AT (analogue touch) domains as we found in the AG domain. The mechanisms were:

- selective removal of specificity;

- dimensionality reduction;

- enhancing aspects for saliency;

- dwelling and repetition.

Selective removal of specificity, enhancement for saliency and dwelling and repetition can be used in the AS and AT domains just as in the AG domain. Selectively specific sound diagrams, for instance, constitute a useful addition to the representational repertoire of current computers. Sound, being one-dimensional, cannot be subjected to dimensionality reduction. The dimensionality of touch is a complicated issue which will not be pursued here. As in the AG domain, use of these mechanisms in the AS and AT domains imply reduction in analogueness of representation.

Lacking in specificity, natural language needs the same specificity-enhancement mechanisms in the AS and AT domains as were needed in the AG domain:

- lengthy description;

- indexical reference;

- metrics;

- use of metaphor and analogy.

In other words, the basic distinction between specificity and focus appears to generalise rather smoothly into a characterisation of the basic differences between the use of spoken and written (and touch, for that matter) natural language, on the one hand, and the use of analogue representation in the AG, AS and AT domains, on the other.

Several implications seem to follow. The first is that analogue sound and touch representations may individually profit from being combined with natural language representations in the same ways as can analogue graphics, i.e. through the mechanisms of:

- annotating;

- illustrating;

- mutual disambiguation and redundancy.

Abstract or conceptual sound or touch 'diagrams' may not currently be widely used, but they are certainly possible in principle.

The second implication is that the integration of analogue graphics, sound and touch can be used to increase the scope of external representation towards the achievement of true virtual reality representation. However virtually real such representations become, linguistic representations will preserve their complementary virtues. These can be used, therefore, for annotating combined AG, AS and AT domain representations just as the latter can be used for illustrating abstract and general linguistic representation.

14.10   Concluding Discussion

The distinction between specificity and focus seems to be quite fundamental to the understanding of the representational capabilities and limitations of natural language, on the one hand, and analogue graphics, sound and touch representations on the other. Mapping out some of the implications of this distinction, as has been attempted above, seems to provide a principled basis for addressing the representational strengths and weaknesses of a multitude of interface and other representational modality combinations some of which are only now becoming technologically feasible. While the number of pure generic interface modalities are relatively limited and can be analysed in a principled manner, their actual or possible multimodal combinations are many and diverse [3, 2]. There seems to be no way of coping with this complexity other than through departing from the analysis of a small number of basic properties such as those of specificity and focus. In this way, we may be able to arrive at principled answers to many questions in the comparatively new field of modality theory, among which the celebrated puzzle: "When is a picture worth a thousand words?" (cf. [6]). The answer to this one has, in fact, been indicated above.

Acknowledgements

The work described in this paper was carried out under Esprit Basic Research project 6296 GRACE whose support is gratefully acknowledged. Discussions on Michael May's GRACE work on graphical features and types led the author to the hypothesis of the complementarity of specificity and focus and to the derivation of the features mentioned in Sects. 14.5 and 14.6, most of which had been identified by Michael. Kenneth Holmquist has provided valuable comments on an earlier draft.

14.11   References

[1] N.O. Bernsen. Matching Information and Interface Modalities. An Example Study. Technical Report Deliverable 2.1.1, Esprit Basic Research project GRACE, 1993.

[2] N.O. Bernsen. Modality Theory: Supporting multimodal interface design. In *Proceedings from the ERCIM Workshop on Multimodal Human-Computer Interaction*, Nancy, November 1993.

[3] N.O. Bernsen. A research agenda for modality theory. In R. Cox, M. Petre, P. Brna, and J. Lee, editors, *Proceedings of the Workshop on Graphical Representations, Reasoning and Communication*, pages 43–46, Edinburgh, August 1993. World Conference on Artificial Intelligence in Education.

[4] N.O. Bernsen. Foundations of multimodal representations. A taxonomy of representational modalities. *Interacting with Computers*, 6(4):347–371, 1994.

[5] N.O. Bernsen and B. Svane. Communication failure and mental models. In *Proceedings of the 13th Scandinavian Conference on Linguistics*, 1992.

[6] E. Hovy and Y. Arens. When is a picture worth a thousand words? Allocation of modalities in multimedia communication. In *Paper presented at the AAAI Symposium on Human-Computer Interfaces*, Stanford, 1990.

[7] E. Klein and L.A. Pineda. Semantics and graphical information. In D. Diaper, editor, *Human-Computer Interaction - INTERACT '90*, Amsterdam, 1990. Elsevier.

[8] J. Lee and H. Zeevat. Integrating natural language and graphics in dialogue. In D. Diaper, editor, *Human-Computer Interaction - INTERACT '90*, Amsterdam, 1990. Elsevier.

15 Modelling Interactive Systems and Providing Task Relevant Information

Bob Fields
Michael Harrison
Peter Wright

ABSTRACT

This paper presents an approach to the specification of interactive systems which supports reasoning about properties that emerge from the interaction between a system and a user. In particular, properties about the relationship between the information presented by the system and that required by the user in order to perform some task are studied. This gives rise to requirements being placed on the user's memory for effective use of the system which can be employed to compare different design choices. The techniques and notations are illustrated with a simple example from the domain of desktop office systems.

15.1 Introduction

This paper continues a discussion of *interactor*-based formal descriptions of interactive systems. The main concern is how to fold human aspects of the design of the system into the specification. The development of user interactors that capture procedures that will be required to achieve user objectives and also capture cognitive resources are considered. This description is used to assess and analyse likely difficulties in the specification of the system. In some senses, this work can be seen as a response to the agenda established in the paper by Runciman and Hammond [10].

Formal notations and modelling techniques allow designs to be documented with precision; formality allows reasoning – in this case about usability. As the concern is with models and specifications rather than completed systems, the process is intended as a contribution to the early phases of design, rather than a post-hoc usability assessment. This, however, raises the problem of how to interpret the ill-defined notion of "usability" in a formal context. [11] does this by proposing a means of assessing system designs (or alternatively, of iteratively improving a design) by a consideration of how tolerant a system is of user errors. This, however, isn't a complete characterisation of what usability is about, and in some application domains tolerance of a system to operator errors is not one of the significant concerns. In this paper a more complete means of capturing the behaviour of an interactive system and the user of such a system in a formal and precise way is described. A means of comparing different design options is outlined, using memory requirements as an assessment of the ease with which a user will be operate the system.

A system is modelled as a collection of communicating objects or *interactors*, each of which has an internal description based around private state, an external description based on the interaction sequences it can perform with its environment and a *rendering* which defines how the internal state is made perceivable to the environment (see [4]). Some system-level interactors can be taken as "given" descriptions of the environment in which the system and user will interact. Such objects are not really part of the system or the design, but impose requirements and constraints on the system and may be necessary for the formulation of certain usability properties. The same concepts can be used to describe aspects of the user's task as are used to define the system. Hence an interactor is also used to describe a component of user behaviour, such as a task to achieve some system goal.

The notation used is a combination of VDM [9] for an object's internal specification and CSP [7] for describing its external behaviour. This choice on notation was made for purely pragmatic reasons (being based on earlier work [1]), and a number of other options are equally valid; the important point is that both system and environmental entities are represented in terms of the events and renderings through which they interact with other entities, and in terms of some state-based notion of internal behaviour.

15.2   Spelling Checker Example

The example used here is the activity of checking the spelling of a document in a word processor. The aim is to show how system-level requirements emerge from an understanding of this task and assertions about the characteristics of users who may perform it. As the main emphasis is on performing analyses on design representations early in the lifecycle, rather than, say, performing usability evaluations of completed products, analysis and modelling can be carried out independently of any particular implementation.

The first step in this process is to decompose the domain into a number of independent objects or *interactors* (see, for example, [6]), each representing some aspect of the work to be performed. In this example, three objects are identified, as shown in Figure 15.1. The *WP* object represents functionality associated with word processing and document editing, the *Checker* object with looking up words in a dictionary suggesting alternatives for misspellings and the *User* object with deciding whether words not found in the dictionary or suggested alternatives are, in fact, correct. The names given to these objects suggest that an allocation of functionality between the system and user has been made. The intention at this stage in a development could, however, be to represent the main areas of function, without making decisions about the exact boundary between user and computer, in which case, more neutral names would be chosen.

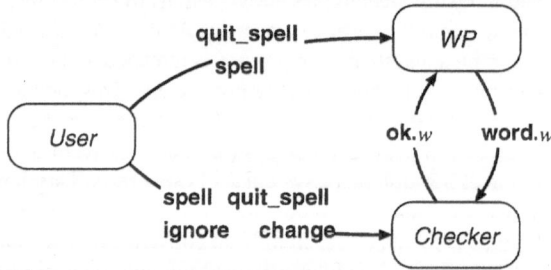

FIGURE 15.1. Structure of the spelling checker dialogue

The user initiates the spell checking task by issuing a spell event, and terminates it with a quit_spell event. The *WP* object represents the body of the word processing application (or at least, the aspects of its behaviour which are important for the description of the checking activity) and generates word events which cause a word in the document to be passed to the checker object for matching against a dictionary or presentation to the user. The *Checker* object responds to a word event by echoing an ok event back to *WP* which contains the original word or a correction for inclusion into the word processor's document. When the checker receives a word via a word event, it checks for its presence in a dictionary. If present, it is immediately echoed on the ok channel, otherwise it is presented, along with an alternative suggestion for the word, in the rendering of the checker object. The user may reply with one of two events: ignore if the word is to be left unchanged in the document (causing an ok event to emanate from the checker with the original word) or **change** if the original word is to be replaced by the alternative which the checker has suggested (leading to an **ok** with the new word). Note that it may seem more natural to regard the *WP* entity as taking a more passive rôle in the spell checking interaction. All communications would be initiated by the *Checker* object and words to be checked read by *Checker* from the rendering of *WP*. The presentation here, on the other hand, simplifies the replacement of mis-spelt words in the document.

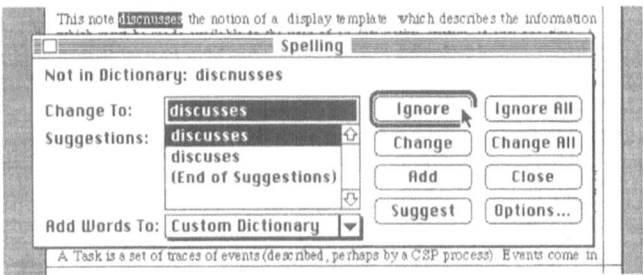

FIGURE 15.2. Microsoft Word Spelling Checker

Figure 15.2 is a screendump showing an example of a real implementation of this type of interface component: the spelling checker of Microsoft Word on the Macintosh. The window with the title **Spelling** corresponds to the *Checker* object and the window behind is the *WP* object. The **Ignore** and **Change** buttons correspond to events in the model of Figure 15.1 and the **Close** button activates the **quit_spell** event. The situation depicted in Figure 15.2 is just after an event of the form "word!*discnusses*" has been generated by the *WP* object, and this word, and the the suggested correction, "discusses" are presented to the user.

15.3   An Interactor Specification

Using the "Agent" Notation

In this section the entities mentioned above are defined using a combination of the VDM [9] model-based specification language and the CSP [7] process algebra which resembles the *Agent Language* of [1]. For each object, a CSP process is given which defines the possible *external* behaviours, in the form of traces of events, which may be observed about the object. In the second part of an agent description, a model of the system's *internal state* and a collection of *operations* which act on the state are given in the VDM notation. For each event in the CSP external specification there will be an operation of the same name in the VDM internal specification, defining the effect an external event has on the entity's internal state. Read events correspond to operations with parameters and write events to ones which return results. In fact, Abowd's agent notation goes further than this and [1] also has a *communications specification* which makes the link between the internal and external models in a more elaborate and general way.

15.3.1   The WP Interactor

The first object to be described is a simple model of the word processor system as a whole. If fact, only those aspects of its behaviour which are relevant from the point of view of the the spelling check functionality will be considered.

The *WP* object can engage in a number of user-level events: **spell** and **quit_spell** mark the beginning and end of spell checking activity, and insert, forward and set_mark are operations for editing the document. word and ok are events which allow communication between *WP* and the spell checker and are not available to the user.

---

interactor *WP*
events

spell , quit_spell , word.._ , ok.._ , insert.._ , forward , set_mark

external behaviour

$(\mu X \bullet \text{spell} \longrightarrow \mu Y \bullet (\text{word}!w \longrightarrow \text{ok}?w' \longrightarrow (Y \,\square\, \text{quit\_spell} \longrightarrow X))) \;\|$
$(\mu X \bullet \text{insert}?w \longrightarrow X \mid \text{forward} \longrightarrow X \mid \text{set\_mark} \longrightarrow X)$

The external behaviour of the word processor consists of two parallel processes, one of which engages in quit_spell events only after a corresponding spell, and word and ok events in that order, between a spell and a quit_spell.

The *WP* object maintains three state attributes: *doc* represents the text being edited as a sequence of words and *cursor* is an index into *doc* indicating the current cursor position and *mark* is an optional second cursor indicating a second point in the document. The idea is that the region between *mark* and *cursor* is a selection on which actions (such as invoking the spell checker) operate.

The two events spell and quit_spell are used to mark the beginning and end respectively of the period when spelling is to be checked. During this period, *WP* generates word events where the word in the document at the current cursor position ($doc(cursor)$) is communicated to the spell checker object. The checker will respond with an ok event where a word, w, is passed back to *WP*, whereupon the word in the document at the current position is replaced by w and *cursor* is advanced so as to reference the next word in the document. The VDM notation is used to specify the interactor's state and the effects these operations have on it.

---

state

      doc : *Word**
  cursor : $\mathbb{N}_1$
    mark : $[\mathbb{N}_1]$

internal behaviour

word () *w*: *Word*
ext rd *doc* : *Word**
    rd *cursor* : $\mathbb{N}_1$
pre $cursor \in \text{inds } doc$
post $w = doc(cursor)$

ok (*w*: *Word*)
ext wr *doc* : *Word**
    wr *cursor* : $\mathbb{N}_1$
pre $cursor \in \text{inds } doc$
post $doc = \overleftarrow{doc}[1..\overleftarrow{cursor} - 1] \,\frown\, [w] \,\frown\,$
                $\overleftarrow{doc}[\overleftarrow{cursor} + 1..\text{len } \overleftarrow{doc}] \wedge$
    $cursor = \overleftarrow{cursor} + 1$

insert(*w*: *Word*)
...

forward ()
ext rd *doc* : *Word**
    wr *cursor* : $\mathbb{N}_1$
pre $cursor \leq \text{len } doc - 1$
post $cursor = \overleftarrow{cursor} + 1$

The *word* operation, corresponding to the external word event, simply looks up the word at position *cursor* in *doc* and returns it without changing the values of the state variables. The *ok* operation takes a parameter and substitutes it for the word indicated by *cursor* in *doc*. The value of *cursor* is then incremented.

An obvious problem here is that nothing has been said about what happens when *cursor* gets to the end of the document, but for the purposes of this example, this fact is ignored. The spell and quit_spell induce no change in the state of the system so no corresponding operations need to be defined.

---
rendering

text = *doc*

pos = *cursor*

The rendering contains two components: the text of the document as a single data item and the position in the document of the cursor. This is rather a simplistic model of the system since, in all but the simplest cases in a real system, the whole of the document is not available to the user at the same time. A naïve view of users' reading is also assumed here since the semantics of rendering components implies that an entire rendering component is communicated in a single atomic communication event. The rendering is given as a tuple of named components which are accessible to other interactors via read type events. So, another object may access the document's text at any time by engaging in an event of the form text?x.

15.3.2   The Spelling Checker

The important object in this example is the *Checker*, whose function it is to respond to the word requests from *WP* and respond with an ok at a later time. In order to decide what value to pass back to the *WP*, the user may be required to perform some interaction.

---
interactor *Checker*
events

   spell, quit_spell, word._ , ok._ , ignore, change

external behaviour

(μX • word?w $\longrightarrow$ (is_known $\longrightarrow$ ok!w |
        not_known $\longrightarrow$ (ignore $\longrightarrow$ ok!w $\longrightarrow$ X |
            change $\longrightarrow$ ok!$alt(w)$ $\longrightarrow$ X))) \ {is_known, not_known}

The spelling checker object repeatedly receives a word event and performs either an is_known or a not_known depending on whether or not the word received exists in the dictionary. If the word is in the dictionary, then the checker immediately responds by forwarding the word back to the word processor via an ok. If, on the other hand, the word is not in the dictionary, either that word or a suggested alternative spelling, $alt(w)$, is forwarded via an ok depending on whether the user performs either ignore or change. The is_known and not_known events are hidden from the outside world.

258   Bob Fields, Michael Harrison, Peter Wright

```
state

      dict  :  Word-set
       alt  :  Word ─m→ Word
   current  :  Word

internal behaviour

   word (w: Word)
   ext wr current  :  Word
   post current = w


   is_known ()                          not_known ()
   ext rd dict    :  Word-set           ext rd dict    :  Word-set
       rd current :  Word                   rd current :  Word
   pre current ∈ dict                   pre current ∉ dict
   post true                            post true
```

The state state of the *Checker* object has three components; the dictionary, *dict*, is a set of words, *alt* is a mapping from words to words giving alternative suggestions for words (a restriction here is that *alt(w)* is defined for all words *w* ∉ *dict*) and *current* is the word currently being checked. The *word* operation takes a word as a parameter and stores it in the *current* state component.

The two operations *is_known* and *not-known* perform no calculation: both have postconditions which are true. Their only function is to have preconditions whose value depends on the state, thus restricting the external traces of the system by conditions on the internal state (since an external event may not occur if the precondition of its corresponding operation is not satisfied).

```
rendering
   current_word = current
   altern = alt(current)
```

The rendering of the checker contains two components: the current word (i.e., the one most recently communicated by a **word** event) and the alternative choice for the current word. Actually, this is a simplification of what does in fact happen. In the real Word spell checker, the values of *current* and *alt(current)* (and also any other alternatives which have been found) are rendered visible only when the word is erroneous. For the time being, this simpler specification will be used.

15.4   The User

The previous section contains a specification of the system, and this section begins to consider how the interaction may be treated from the point of view of the user.

The most interesting aspects of the current example arise with a consideration of the actions a user might perform and the information which will be required in order for the user to carry out the action sequences. A typical interaction with the combination of word processor and spelling checker is as follows:

1. spell;

2. choose either ignore or change;

3. choose either quit_spell or go back to step 2.

This is a very coarse analysis of the user's task, and clearly the real work occurs in stage 2 where the decision about whether or not an individual word is correct. This decision step, then, may be further described as follows.

1. Read the current word and alternative.

2. Is it possible to determine the correctness of the word based only on current information?

3. If so, perform ignore or change as appropriate.

4. Is there enough contextual information to decide?

5. If so, perform ignore or change as appropriate.

6. Read the context from the document.

7. Perform ignore or change as appropriate.

The important point to note is that this fragment of the task proceeds by repeatedly checking whether enough information is available; if there is then continuing, otherwise, acquiring some information from the system before proceeding. This aspect of the user's behaviour can be modelled as an interactor. The model captures what the user does only insofar as it is assumed that some other kind of analysis will have generated. The aim is to capture this analysis in a way that will make it possible to consider the system-level implications.


```
interactor UserCheck
events
    spell , quit_spell , ignore , change ,
    current_word.._ , altern.._ , text.._ ,
    can_decide
```


During spell checking, the user can engage in several events: spell, quit_spell, ignore and change form the main interactions with the spell checker and their function is described above. current_word, altern and text are communication events which model the user reading components of the renderings of the *WP* and *Checker* objects. The most peculiar event is can_decide. The intuition behind this is that it performs no real part in the interaction between the user and system, but simply encodes a condition on the internal state of the user and acts as a "guard", constraining the behaviour based on properties of the state. The precondition of the event states that "it is possible to determine the correctness of a word based on the information currently available (in memory)") and its postcondition is true.

```
external behaviour

(μX • current_word?w ⟶ X | altern?w ⟶ X | text?t ⟶ X) ||
spell ⟶ (μY •
              can_decide ⟶ (ignore ⟶ Y ⊓ change ⟶ Y) |
              quit_spell ⟶ Skip)
```

The user may decide to read the current word, alternative suggestion and text of the document at any time (or at least at any time the system makes this possible), represented by the first parallel process in the external behaviour section. Following a spell, the user repeatedly makes a choice between performing change or ignore events, guarded by can_decide. The choice between change and ignore is an internal choice and will be determined by the internal state of the user (see the definition below of the *ignore* and *change* operations).

```
state


current : [Word]
    alt : [Word]
  words : Word-set
   ctxt : Word*
```

The internal state, modelling, perhaps, the user's memory, has five components. *current* and *alt* record the current and alternative words read from the system (which may be absent if the user hasn't yet read the display). *words* is a set of words which the user knows to be correct, even though they may not exist in the system's dictionary (for example, proper names). *ctxt* is the document (or a part of it) read from the word processor.

```
internal behaviour


current_word (w: Word)                  ignore ()
ext wr current : Word                   ext wr current : [Word]
post current = w                            wr alt    : [Word]
                                            rd words  : Word-set
                                            rd ctxt   : Word*
                                        pre current ∈ words ∨ ...
                                        post current = nil ∧ alt = nil

can_decide ()
ext rd current : [Word]
    rd alt     : [Word]
    rd words   : Word-set
    rd ctxt    : Word*
pre ({current, alt} ∩ words ≠ { }) ∨ (ctxt ≠ [])
post true
```

Only three operations have been given as examples of how the internal specification may be constructed. *current_word* simply takes a word as input and stores it in the *current* slot of the state. The operations corresponding to the *altern* and *text* events would be much the same. *can_decide* doesn't really perform any function as such; it doesn't change the state or return any results. It acts as a "flag" or "guard" and can only occur if there is enough information in the state to determine the correctness of the current word (the precondition defined above allows can-decide to occur if either the current or alternative words are known individually, or if the document text is present in memory. The precondition of *ignore* operation states the condition which implies that the current word is correct (thus only allowing ignore to occur for words considered correct), and the postcondition sets both *current* and *alt* to nil in preparation for the next word.

This model of the user's memory is deliberately simplistic, and there are a number of ways in which this could be made more realistic. For example, see [8] and [2] for discussions of models of memory and cognitive processes and the importance of memory in HCI.

So far, then, a model of part of the spelling checker has been developed, along with a model, expressed in the same notation as the system models, of a part of the user's behaviour. The latter describes the sequences of actions a user may perform and also incorporates the information needs of the user in order to carry out the task. The next step is to show how the system and user models may be reasoned about, the ultimate aim being to derive properties which relate to a systems' usability. By way of an introduction, Section 15.4.1 describes and proves a simple functional property of the system, and Section 15.4.2 informally introduces a measure of usability based on requirements on the user's memory. This measure is used to compare two alternative designs for the spelling checker.

15.4.1   Simple Behaviour Properties

To begin with, consider a very simple property which, while not particularly concerned with user-system interaction is one which the system is expected to obey:

> *performing an interaction with the spelling checker starting with a* spell *action, ending with a* quit-spell *and containing only* ignore *actions does not result in the document being changed.*

A mechanism for describing such properties and a calculus for reasoning about them may be defined. The first step is to introduce the concept of an event or sequence of events *inducing* a state change in the system as a result of operations being executed. Induced state changes can be written as "P induces (s, s')", meaning that the execution of process P causes a system initially in state s to be in state s'. An inductive definition of induces is given as a set of proof rules, providing an operational semantics for the external behaviour component of the agent language. The rules come in two flavours: introduction rules allow the behaviour (i.e. the resulting state transitions) of composite processes to be inferred from the behaviour of the components. Elimination rules allow reasoning in the opposite direction, so facts about the behaviour of a composite can be used to infer something about the components. Two examples of introduction rules are

$$\xrightarrow{}\text{-ind-I} \quad \frac{e \text{ induces } (s, s_0), P \text{ induces } (s_0, s')}{e \longrightarrow P \text{ induces } (s, s')}$$

$$\mu\text{-ind-I} \quad \frac{\forall n : \mathbb{N} \cdot (P^n[Stop] \text{ induces } (s, s'))}{(\mu X \bullet P[X]) \text{ induces } (s, s')}$$

And the corresponding elimination rules are

$$\xrightarrow{}\text{-ind-E} \quad \frac{e \longrightarrow P \text{ induces } (s, s')}{\exists s_0 \cdot e \text{ induces } (s, s_0) \wedge P \text{ induces } (s_0, s')}$$

$$\mu\text{-ind-E} \quad \frac{(\mu X \bullet P[X]) \text{ induces } (s, s')}{\exists n : \mathbb{N}_1 \cdot P^n[Stop] \text{ induces } (s, s')}$$

where the notation Q^n means $\underbrace{Q...Q}_{\text{n times}}$.

Note: that this set of rules is deficient in at least one respect: the rules only talk only about the states achieved *after* successful termination of processes. This means that not only is it not possible to reason about non-terminating tasks, it is also impossible to talk about "goals of maintenance", where a procedure is to be followed, possibly resulting in some desired state of affairs, while maintaining some property of the system or environment (an example is driving a car in a straight line) as well as "goals of achievement" where a procedure is carried out in order to achieve a desirable state of affairs.

The theorem about the effect which repeated **ignore** events have on the *doc* state component can now be stated as the inference (15.1). This says that for any pair of states s and s', if the process which performs a **spell** and a **quit_spell** separated by an arbitrary number of **ignore** events achieves the transition from s to s' then it is the case that the *doc* components of the two specifications are identical.

$$\overleftarrow{s}, s: State,$$

$$\frac{(\text{spell} \longrightarrow \mu X \bullet (\text{ignore} \longrightarrow X \mid \text{quit\_spell} \longrightarrow Skip)) \text{ induces } (\overleftarrow{s}, s)}{doc(\overleftarrow{s}) = doc(s)} \qquad (15.1)$$

Proof: The proof follows from the above axioms for **induces** and works by induction on the number of "iterations" around the "$\mu X \bullet ...$" which occur, as outlined below.

h1 $\overleftarrow{s}, s: State,$
h2 $(\text{spell} \longrightarrow \mu X \bullet (\text{ignore} \longrightarrow X \mid \text{quit\_spell} \longrightarrow Skip)) \text{ induces } (\overleftarrow{s}, s)$
1   $(\mu X \bullet (\text{ignore} \longrightarrow X \mid \text{quit\_spell} \longrightarrow Skip)) \text{ induces } (\overleftarrow{s}, s)$ spell and $\longrightarrow$-ind-E
2   $\exists n: \mathbb{N}_1 \cdot P^n[Stop] \text{ induces } (\overleftarrow{s}, s)$ μ-ind-E
3   from $n: \mathbb{N}_1 ; P^n[Stop] \text{ induces } (\overleftarrow{s}, s)$
3.1 $P^1[Stop] \text{ induces } (\overleftarrow{s}, s) \Rightarrow doc(\overleftarrow{s}) = doc(s)$
3.2   from $P^n[Stop] \text{ induces } (\overleftarrow{s}, s) \Rightarrow doc(\overleftarrow{s}) = doc(s)$
         infer $P^{n+1}[Stop] \text{ induces } (\overleftarrow{s}, s) \Rightarrow doc(\overleftarrow{s}) = doc(s)$
      infer $doc(\overleftarrow{s}) = doc(s)$ $\mathbb{N}_1$-induction
c $doc(\overleftarrow{s}) = doc(s)$ $\exists$-elim

Where

$$P = \lambda X \cdot \text{ignore} \longrightarrow X \mid \text{quit\_spell} \longrightarrow Skip$$

■

Such conjectures about the behaviour of a system are, in any case, not very interesting from an HCI point of view: although functional properties of systems can be investigated in this way, not much has been said about properties relating to a system's usability.

15.4.2   Usability and Task-Dependent Properties

An inspection of the *UserCheck* object which encapsulates a part of the task performed by the user when checking the spelling of a document reveals that a number of traces of behaviour are possible. Two traces which are of interest are called Trace 1 and Trace 2 below. They differ only in the position of the text? event where the text of the document is read. By appeal to some notion of short term memory, it seems reasonable to assume that, given a free choice, users are more likely to behave in the way described in Trace 1 since the document's text is read closer to its point of use (the can_decide and ignore or change events. The temporal distance between reading and using an item of information is an indication of how well the user must be able to re-member the information in order to use the system successfully. In this case the distance between reading and using the document's text may be a more significant factor than that between reading and using the current word, because in the former case, much more information is involved.

Trace 1	Trace 2
spell	text?
current_word?	spell
altern?	current_word?
text?	altern?
can_decide	can_decide
ignore or change	ignore or change

The intuition that the temporal distance between events can be a measure of how hard the system is to use suggests a way of assessing rival design solutions. In the next section, several design options, variations on the system model above, are described and the user memory cri-terion applied to them.

15.4.3   Assessing Design Choices

The system model developed in Section 15.2 is incomplete and allows the development to be progressed in a number of alternative ways. The system model, the analysis of the user's task and the machinery developed for reasoning about properties of models can now be used to evaluate these design options.

1. Leave the model as it is. The renderings of both *Checker* and *WP* are made available to the user continuously and the user may interleave interaction with the two tools fairly ar-bitrarily.

2. Introduce two *modes* of the system: "*WP*-mode" and "*Checker*-mode". The editing actions would only be available in the former and ignore and change only in the latter. Some means of switching modes will be provided.

3. Further extend the modedness to control the presentation of renderings as well as the avail-ability of user actions. The rendering and user actions of *WP* are only available in *WP*-mode and similarly for the checker.

The first and last of these options can be seen as representing extremes in the space of design solutions. The latter is closest to the way in which the spell checker component of Microsoft Word is actually implemented, where *WP* and *Checker* are separate overlaid windows. It is ar-gued that the interaction style possible in 1, is more usable than the one characterised by 3. The Macintosh spelling checker pictured in Figure 15.2 is a variant of this latter option, where the modedness extends into the system objects themselves, in that leaving the checker and then re-suming it changes the system's mode so as to check a highlighted region of text rather than the whole document.

The kind of modedness being discussed can be introduced into the system by the addition of an extra parallel object, to enforce constraints on the interactions which can occur. The *Moding-Constraints* interactor, for instance, encodes behaviour of the above type 3.

---

interactor *ModingConstraints*
events

spell , quit_spell , insert.. , forward , set_mark , ignore , change ,
altern.. , current_word..

external behaviour

$(\mu X \bullet \text{pos?}_- \longrightarrow X \,|$
$\qquad \text{text?}_- \longrightarrow X \,| \, ...$
$\qquad \text{spell} \longrightarrow (\mu Y \bullet \text{quit\_spell} \longrightarrow X \,|$
$\qquad\qquad\qquad \text{ignore} \longrightarrow Y \,|$
$\qquad\qquad\qquad \text{change} \longrightarrow Y \,|$
$\qquad\qquad\qquad \text{altern?}_- \longrightarrow Y \,|$
$\qquad\qquad\qquad \text{current\_word?}_- \longrightarrow Y))$

A consideration of the use that is made of the internal state of the user, and in particular looking at when information is stored and used, gives a criterion for choosing one design option over another. Trace 1 above demands less of the user, in terms of memory usage, than Trace 2, and the system which supports both of these (comprising *WP* and *Checker* running in parallel) may be judged more usable less likely to lead to user error than the one which supports only Trace 2 (comprising *WP*, *Checker* and *ModingConstraints*).

15.5   Conclusion

This paper has shown how a formal technique can be used to describe and model aspects of the behaviour of interactive systems and of the users who interact with the systems. The consideration of user attributes and actions at this fine-grained level of detail, coupled with the fact that the same formalism is used for both system and user descriptions, leads to the ability to reason about properties not just of the system in isolation, but of the interaction which takes place between user and system. This approach was used previously in [11] where a technique is described in which an explicit consideration of the user allows additional system constraints or requirements to be derived to improve the system's tolerance of erroneous input by the user. Tolerance of human error is being used as an assessment criterion to allow the relative merits of different design choices to be investigated.

The current work builds on this technique by supporting more sophisticated user and system models and allows more kinds of assessment criteria to be formulated. The use of richer models addresses one of the shortcomings of this earlier work by allowing the effects of user errors on the system to be analysed precisely, rather than being part of an informal identification process. In the example used above, different design solutions can be compared early in the development process using some measure of the mental effort which might be required to operate the different designs. In particular, it can be shown that a design places certain requirements on the user (such as "if the user can remember an item of text for a period x, then it will be possible to use the system effectively"). These requirements may be used as an input to the process of deciding to adopt one solution over another (or alternatively, to perform an assessment of a completed design). Extensions would allow the choice between design alternatives to be made on the basis of other cognitive features, for example, by looking at the mismatch between the information provided by the system and that required to complete the task and making a judgement between designs based on the nature of the relationship between these information categories.

A natural continuation of this work would be to pay more attention to the user model, and a suitable basis for this might be to structure the models around a cognitive architecture such as those described in [10] or [2]. Such a model makes explicit the different types of storage and processing elements which need to be considered in an account of task performance, and defines some of their properties (such as the way in which memory decays). [5] integrates such user models with system specifications in a unified formal framework, in a similar style to the current work. The model may then be used to make further predictions, for instance, about the kinds of user errors which might occur, and with what frequencies (see [3] as an example of predictive models of user error). Predictions about user errors would then feed back into the the next iteration of system design activity.

15.6 References

[1] G. D. Abowd. *Formal Aspects of Human-Computer Interaction*. PhD thesis, University of Oxford Computing Laboratory: Programming Research Group, 1991. Available as Technical Monograph PRG-97.

[2] P.J. Barnard and J. May. Cognitive Modelling for User Requirements. In P.F. Byerley, P.J. Barnard, and J. May, editors, *Computers, Communication and Usability: Design Issues, Research and Methods for Integrated Services*, North Holland Series in Telecommunications, chapter 2.1, pages 101–146. Elsevier Science Publishers, 1993.

[3] M. D. Byrne. Systematic Procedural Error as a Result of Interaction Between Working Memory Demand and Task Structure. Master's thesis, Georgia Institute of Technology, Department of Psychology, 1993.

[4] D. Duke and M. Harrison. Abstract interaction objects. *Computer Graphics Forum*, 12(3):25–36, 1993.

[5] D.J. Duke, D.A. Duce, P.J. Barnard, M.D. Harrison, and J. May. On the Integration of User and System Models. Technical Report ID/WP26, MRC-APU, Cambridge – ESPRIT BRA 7040 Amodeus-2, April 1994.

[6] B. Fields, M. Harrison, and P. Wright. From informal requirements to agent-based specification: an aircraft warnings case study (extended abstract). *ACM SIGCHI Bulletin*, 26(2):65–68, 1994.

[7] C. A. R. Hoare. *Communicating Sequential Processes*. International Series in Computer Science. Prentice-Hall International, 1985.

[8] P. Johnson. *Human-computer interaction: Psychology, task analysis and software engineering*. McGraw Hill, London, 1992.

[9] C.B. Jones. *Systematic Software Development Using VDM*. International Series in Computer Science. Prentice-Hall International, 2nd edition, 1990.

[10] C. Runciman and N. Hammond. User programs: a way to match computer systems and human cognition. In M.D. Harrison and A.F. Monk, editors, *HCI'86 Conference*, People and

Computers: Designing for Usability. BCS HCI Specialist Group, Cambridge University Press, 1986.

[11] P. Wright, B. Fields, and M. Harrison. Deriving human-error tolerance requirements from tasks. In *Proceedings of ICRE'94 The First International Conference on Requirements Engineering, Colorado Springs*, pages 135–142. IEEE, April 1994.

16 The Requirements Engineering of User Freedom

M.D. Harrison
A.E. Blandford
P.J. Barnard

16.1 Introduction

In this paper we explore a group of properties of *interactive systems* (by which we mean the whole system of computers, users and other features of the working environment) that have in common a notion *interaction freedom*. We shall argue that properties within this category are often discussed imprecisely. What we mean by interaction freedom here is the flexibility of an interactive system to switch between activities and the freedom of the user to choose options, and to be aware of his or her own progress. Our aim is to understand these ideas more precisely in terms of an *interaction framework* [6, 3] so that they can be used by cognitive modellers in understanding the consequences of such flexibility on learning or using a computer system, or by system designers in understanding how such properties may be built into an interactive system.

Our aim in this paper is not to make value judgements about when interaction freedom is a good thing, rather we are concerned with an expression of interaction freedom properties that may be used by psychologists and system designers in understanding them and making appropriate judgements. The following examples may help to understand what we are talking about.

- In the context of a walk-up-and-use system, *freedom* might involve the ease with which a user makes choices between system options and decides what action to take next. Interactional freedom is a good thing if it means that a novice user may make mistakes without compromising his or her objectives (such a system might be said to be *human-error tolerant*). It is a bad thing if it means that the user is more likely to follow choices within the walk-up-and-use system that lead away from the required objectives.

- When form filling, interactional freedom will allow the user to enter fields of the form in any order, thereby making it easier to enter information in what is understood to be the most convenient order. It seems clear that it is not always a good idea to provide this freedom, consider in contrast an aircraft recovery procedure that should be followed in every detail in a precise sequence to reduce the possibility of mistake; such a system that supports interactional freedom may not be most appropriate for the task.

A system that permits too much freedom in this manner is likely to cause difficulty for a novice user, but is of benefit to an expert who can exploit the range and power of the interactive system. Our aim is to provide a framework in which these trade-offs may be understood. As a result we would hope that those studying human behaviour may have a conceptual framework in which they can draw valuable conclusions.

As well as providing a neutral conceptual framework of value to behavioural scientists an objective of this paper is to establish interaction freedom requirements and a context in which designers may produce systems that satisfy them. Our intention is that it should be possible to engineer such requirements as part of the design process. We require models or frameworks which can be used to assist the elicitation and formulation of such requirements.

There is a further objective of this paper. Interactional freedom is a property of interactive systems that is of concern from at least two perspectives: the user and the computer system. We therefore continue our development of a formal interaction framework already described elsewhere [6, 3].

We shall begin by identifying a set of notions that could be described as contributing to these requirements of interactional freedom. In describing these notions we shall assume that an interactive system consists of a set of interacting agents. We shall consider this conception of an interactive system in more detail in later sections. Hence in the next section we describe properties of interactional freedom informally. In Section 3 we describe the interaction framework; in Section 4 we describe a formal notion of detour; in Section 5 we describe a number of properties that are associated with interactional potential; in Section 6 we describe history based properties of interaction; and in Section 7 we discuss those properties that are relevant to multiple agents to the interaction.

16.2   Interactional Freedom

Let us consider, informally, what it might mean for an interactive system to have freedom. A number of connected notions are required that concern: the agent that controls the interaction; the amount of choice available to an agent; how robust the agent's interaction is in relation to other activities going on in the system; the extent to which interactions depend on previous events. The notions of freedom that we describe are connected to notions of determinism described in [5]. Non determinism occurs when systems produce unpredictable results: system non determinism occurs because internal system choices, not influenced by users or other environmental factors, determine the result. A process control system therefore will change as a result of processes that are only broadly under the control of the operator and are therefore non deterministic in this sense. Other notions of non determinism, that concern what the user or operator understands is going on, occur when, although it is possible to determine the result, users are unable to do so in practice. Too much user choice may lead to uncertainty about what the result of an interaction will be and where the initiative lies.

16.2.1   Interactional Initiative

The agent that has the *interactional initiative* is the one that *leads* the interaction. In many cases the interactional initiative is clear. For example, in the case of a system like UNIX the initiative is with the user, whereas in many expert systems the system takes the initiative (the user simply has to respond to questions supplied by the expert system). Questions of initiative are important when the user is a novice because a user initiative may leave the novice unable to make progress. It is also important when initiative changes as might happen as a system adapts to the input of the user. Here the adapting process may be initiated by the system leaving the user to recognise these changes and to adapt to them or, alternatively, the user might define them or accept them explicitly. Similar concerns are apparent in dynamic systems where tasks are shared between automated components of the system and the operator. Here initiative is important for recognising how and when the automated system supports or replaces the human operator.

16.2.2   Interactional Potential

Interactional potential is concerned with the scope that exists for exploiting the functionality of the interactive system at any stage in an interaction irrespective of any interactional initiative. For example, some menu based systems designed to support tasks closely may have low interactional potential once a task has been embarked upon, unless the ability to select another task from a menu is always available. A command based interactive system on the other hand is likely to allow a user to invoke the whole functionality of the system at any stage in the interaction and consequently has high interactional potential. Interactional potential is an important idea when considering the training of users. Typically the training process progresses by gradually increasing the repertoire of commands to the user hence gradually increasing the interactional potential of the system, see for example [4]. When we look at this notion more carefully we will see that potential can only be considered in relation to an *objective*. Freedom is a notion that must be seen in the context of the constraining objective that governs the interaction.

A notion that is associated with interactional potential is the idea of an *interactional detour*. Here the concern is with those interactions that are not directly involved in achieving a goal. When we consider interactional detours we may be concerned with interactions that are suboptimal in the sense that they include unnecessary interactions, or they may involve interactions that are actually important. The point is that, at this level, how the agents have caused the detour to occur is not as important as expressing the interactional concepts associated with a detour in general terms. Thus a detour could be: the effect of a user error, and the interaction required to recover from the error; alternatively, it could be an interaction initiated to discover the email address of the person that is to be corresponded with, when the objective is to send a copy of a paper to that person. In the first case the interaction is not necessary, a user need not make mistakes, in the second case it is possible to remember the email address and therefore not to initiate the sequence of events to achieve the subsidiary objective. If it is required that the user remembers the email address then the interaction would be a detour, if it is not then the interaction would not be a detour. It is not our concern to analyse how a decision about what is required is taken, rather we will present a formalism in which distinctions between the cases may be expressed without requiring the particular agent-based analyses.

16.2.3 Interactional Invariance

Whereas the concepts mentioned above may be understood in the context of a system and user pair, other properties require more than two agents to the interaction, or more than one concurrent objective being achieved. *Interactional invariance* is a property that requires that an interaction is not vulnerable to the actions of other agents that are not taking part directly in the interaction. Here we are concerned with the way that interactive system goals are influenced by autonomous or concurrent behaviour which would be the case if we were talking of dynamic systems for example. An interactive system should be capable of supporting certain objectives regardless of the other activities that are going on within the system.

When analysing the extent to which such invariances are true of trajectories we shall be concerned with specific properties of systems that betray potential interferences between attempts to achieve different objectives. Interference can occur between two agents (a system and a user) when trajectories that partially achieve objectives interleave one another, and one achievement affects the outcome of the other. It can also occur between multiple agents when an agent interacts incorrectly in the sense that an appropriate communication is directed to an inappropriate agent.

The property of *misdirected interaction* describes the situations where two agents interact at cross purposes. A typical example of this occurs when a user interacts in a way that is appropriate through one window of a window based system with the wrong window selected [2].

16.2.4 History Based Interaction

Whether or not an interaction will achieve an objective is based on some aspect of the pattern of events that has led to the current situation. We might say that current interaction is tied, in some measure, to the history of the events that have so far been engaged in to achieve the objective. Interactional freedom, at any point in the interaction, can be increased if a reliance on history can be reduced. So for example, an objective that requires the completion of a form will have more interactional freedom if the fields of the form can be completed in any order.

For another example of history based interactions consider the selection of a particular object within a diagram made up of overlapping objects constructed by a drawing package. There are several such systems that depend on the history of how the diagram was constructed [8].

16.3   Interaction Framework

The properties mentioned above are important to our understanding of an interactive system, both the ease with which the system may be used in terms of the demands it makes upon a user and in understanding the constraints that should be applied in the implementation of the computer system. It is clear that the user's freedom in the context of an interactive system depends, in some sense, on some or all of these properties. If we can make these properties more precise then it should ease the implementer's job, and provide understandings of interactive systems that may be useful from the point of view of a human factors specialist. Our aim then is to be more precise and to develop a conceptual and notational basis for expressing these requirements.

We require a framework that can be used analytically as a means of assessing existing systems and provides representations that can be used as a basis for implementing interactive systems. We use the framework that we develop in this section to discuss, and make more precise, detours, potential, initiative, invariance, interference, misdirection, history and so on.

An interactive system consists of a collection of interacting agents $\alpha \in A$. The agents are assumed to have state, some ability to transform states, and a rendering by which other agents may perceive the state of the agent. All agents may be expressed in these terms, for example a human agent will involve cognitive states, and the rendering may include facial expression or tone of voice. Different types of rendering may be appropriate for different types of agent. It shall be assumed that the agents know about part or all of a global state, hence there may be shared context between agents. The main reason for having shared state is to simplify the model and this can be done without compromising the generality of the description.

In understanding how an interactive system achieves its objectives we may consider two courses of action. We may consider the actions that are carried out by the individual agents that contribute to the interaction. Alternatively we may take the viewpoint of an outside observer. Communication or interaction between agents may be perceived from the outside by means of events.

Events

Each agent can potentially participate in a collection of events $alpha(A)$. The state of a system is made up of the state of the agents of the system. An event arises from an inter-action, that is the communication of two agents as they engage in mutually communicative actions. Since communication involves some kind of rendezvous we shall distinguish the agent that initiates the action that causes the communication. An event is therefore associated with an initiating agent. We shall assume that agents engaging in an interaction must have expressive and receptive components. These components may be actions or may be renderings, hence a notice on an automated teller machine explaining how to use it will be a rendering that will be the expressive component of an event that a novice might engage in by reading it.

Another distinction we must make is between event type and event instance. In practice we shall blur the distinction although it is quite clear that we need to be able to distinguish between the possibility of multiple instances of a certain type of event in an interaction trajectory (see below) and the general characteristics of that event. In practice we shall be interested in characteristics of event instances, for example: the source agent; the destination agent.

$$source: Event \longrightarrow Agent$$
$$dest: Event \longrightarrow \mathbb{P}\,Agent$$

When we describe an event instance we can also talk about the state transitions that the event instance triggers. It is important at this juncture to talk further about the possible ways in which an event can be created. The notion of event has a different significance from that which is described in a typical process algebra. In the case of CSP [9] for example both agents must mutually engage in an interaction before an event takes place. In Interaction Framework, it is possible for a system to have some aspect of its rendering in the same state for a substantial period before an event takes place that makes use of it – for example the notice on an automatic bank teller that informs that the display can be adjusted so that it can be read regardless of the height of the user. Many interactions with the teller will not involve any events that make use of this information. When the rendering of the teller machine is used by the customer as an expressive component of an interaction, an event occurs that is part of the interaction trajectory to achieve a particular objective.

In general we shall be interested in the extent to which a system supports a set of objectives. We therefore consider *interaction trajectories*, or partially ordered sets of events, that *achieve* the objectives of a system. In practice there are differences between the sorts of objectives that a "static" office system is designed to support and those which a "dynamic" control system such as an aircraft cockpit is designed to support and we need to consider these differences.

Interaction trajectory

An interaction trajectory is a partially ordered set of events that is observed as the result of the interaction between a number of agents. We say a partially ordered set of events because we may be interested in the possibility of interaction trajectories that involve the blending of parallel events.

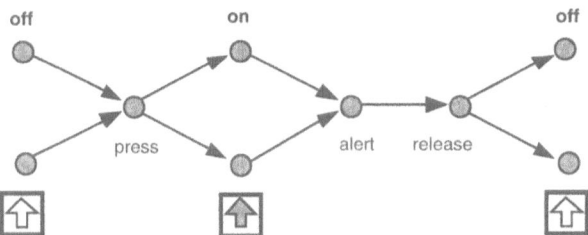

FIGURE 16.1. An example of a fragment of an interaction trajectory

Hence incomparable events are not causally related and may therefore occur in parallel. Typically we are interested in the extent to which an observed interaction trajectory has achieved a desired objective of the system and it shall be assumed that an interactive system is designed to achieve a set of objectives.

Objectives

An objective involves a pre- and post- condition on state which may be linked with the agent who owns the objective in the sense that it is initiated by that agent. It should be noted that it is also possible that the objective is shared and therefore it is no longer appropriate to consider a single agent as owning the objective. The objective to send mail to a particular address therefore might involve a post-condition that a message has been inserted in the letter box that is used by the mail transportation system. If the pre-condition involves a requirement that the address to be sent to is in the state of the sending agent, then retrieving the address again would be a detour in the sense introduced in the previous section. However this does not give a full picture because there are agents which have the property that a precondition, which previously held, fails during the achievement of the postcondition as a result of interfering actions. It is therefore necessary to have an invariant that is always true within the interaction to achieve the objective. The notation: $[\alpha:]\langle p_0, inv, p_n\rangle$ is used to describe an objective (note the square brackets here imply that the owning or initiating agent is optional). We shall be interested in the extent to which an interactional trajectory achieves an objective. An interaction trajectory shall be written $\langle E, \leq\rangle$. We are interested in the state transformations that are triggered by this set of events, hence $\beta: \mathbb{P}(E) \longrightarrow (S \leftrightarrow S)$ is a mapping that takes the interactional trajectory and gives the corresponding state relation that describes the actual effect of the interactive system.

Objective achievement

An event set $\langle E, \leq\rangle$ *achieves* an objective $\alpha: \langle p_0, inv, p_n\rangle$ if for any initial state s_0 that satisfies the predicate p_0 then any s_n for which $\beta(E)s_0 = s_n$ satisfies p_n where $inv(s_i)$ is true for all states s_i that are triggered by the events of the trajectory. We shall write this as $\langle E, \leq\rangle \dashv t$ where $t = \alpha: \langle p_0, inv, p_n\rangle \in T$ and T is the set of objectives of the system.

We are not only interested in event sets that achieve objectives but also event sets that are on track to achieve objectives. We say that $\langle E', \leq\rangle \ll t$ if $E' \leq E$ where $\langle E, \leq\rangle \dashv t$ and $t = \alpha: \langle p_0, p_n\rangle$. The relation between sets E' and E means that each event contained in E that is not in E' is not a predecessor of any of the events in E' and E' is a "beginning" subset of E. We will usually leave the ordering $\leq$ implicit. It should be noted that since we are not concerned with user models we have said nothing in this description about the user's intention to achieve an objective.

16.4   Interactional Detours

One question that we have not answered with the definition of achievement and partial achievement of objectives is whether the interactional trajectory is a good one, or whether the trajectory is "on track" to achieve the objective efficiently. It is clear that if we have a *reachable* system, that is one where you can reach any state from any state then in principle you can always continue to implement any objective wherever you are. We need to capture the idea of an efficient trajectory that is not biased by a system perspective in the sense that it is an efficient use of system resources, and does not have a user bias in the sense that the achievement was made with a clear intention to achieve the objective throughout.

We will define a simple unbiased notion of interactional detour, meaning a suboptimal interaction trajectory as follows:

E is an *interactional detour* with respect to objective t if $F \dashv t$ where $F = E_1 \triangleright E \triangleright E_2$ and there exists an E' such $\sharp(E') \leq \sharp(E)$ for which $E_1 \triangleright E' \triangleright E_2 \dashv t$. Here $\sharp E$ is the length of the longest totally ordered sequence within the partial order E and the symbol $\triangleright$ is defined to *continue* the partial ordering in the sense that every event in the left hand set of $E_1 \triangleright E_2$ precedes the events in the right hand set. In the definition it is assumed that E_1 is non empty because we assume that an interactional detour is not one if immediately on commencing the interaction a detour occurs. Given this definition we can describe optimal interaction trajectories without expressing the criteria for the optimality.

canonical achievement

E is a *canonical achievement* of t if $E \dashv t$ and E contains no interactional detours.

Any F is *detour free* for t if there is a G such that $F \triangleright G$ is canonical for t. It is clear that if $F \triangleright G$ is detour free then F has no interactional detours with respect to t. In other words if the whole is detour free then the parts are detour free.

In practice whether looking up an email address when sending mail to a colleague is an interactional detour or not depends on whether the email address is part of the precondition or part of the invariant. It would be an interactional detour if the precondition required knowledge of the address and no interference could affect the precondition, or if the knowledge requirement is part of the invariant. Our main interest in detours will be in elaborating the idea that an interaction achieves an objective in an efficient way in some sense.

16.5   Interactional Potential

We are interested in a number of questions about interactional potential. At a stage in the achievement of an objective, how many events performed next will continue to achieve the objective? Given an interactional trajectory: how many objectives could be achieved by continuing? How many events performed next would deny the achievement of a particular objective?

The following properties are related to these questions. We shall assume a set of *objectives* $t \in T$, then:

- if $E' \ll t$ then the *event potential* of E' is the set of events e such that $E' \triangleright e$ is detour free for t.

- the *objective potential* of E is the set of objectives $t \in T$ such that E is detour free for t.

- if $E' \ll t$ then there are a number of ways in which the system can lead to a situation where initial objectives, or all objectives are denied, hence we might describe the *denial set* as the set of e such that $E' \triangleright e$ fails to be a partial achievement of any objective. We might also describe the *t denial set* as the set of events that lead to the fact $E' \triangleright e$ is not part of any trajectory that achieves t.

1. A menu based system, in which an initial menu corresponds to a set of fixed objectives that are not achieved until the same menu reappears, will have an objective potential set consisting of t where t is the objective embarked on at the initial menu until the menu reappears. Such a system is cycle based (see [7]). The cycle may be aborted at any stage between displays of the main menu. An appropriate question then is whether the system has an objective potential that contains all the objectives that could be invoked from the menu at any time because an abort followed by a reselection of a menu entry will invoke any one of the objectives. The reason why this is not the case is that these interaction trajectories would not be canonical.

2. We would expect that the interactional phase during which a personal identity number is being input at an automated teller machine should have very small event potential because there should be no scope for trying other options and achieving alternative objectives until security clearance has been achieved.

3. Systems should be designed to minimise the size of denial sets. Any denial set allows the possibility that the interactive system is no longer functional.

16.6   Agent Initiative

We may now consider a number of properties of interactions that relate to the agent's initiative. Most of these properties concern the extent to which a particular agent's actions (that generate events) guide the achievement of an objective, or alternatively might be deterred or inhibited by the activities of other agents.

Taking a view of a trajectory

When considering interactional trajectories we shall be especially interested in events that were initiated by one of the agents. We shall therefore define $\langle E, \leq \rangle \downarrow \alpha$ as restricting the trajectory to the events initiated by the agent α. Hence $\langle E, \leq \rangle \downarrow \alpha = \langle \{e : e \in E \wedge source(e) = \alpha\}, \leq \rangle$. Note the same ordering is assumed of the restricted set. We are further interested in the subset of events that have agent α as either a source or a destination.

$$\langle E, \leq \rangle \updownarrow \alpha = \langle \{e : e \in E \wedge (source(e) = \alpha \vee dest(e) = \alpha)\}, \leq \rangle.$$

Invariance

A system is α-*invariant* with respect to objective $t = \alpha : \langle p_0, inv, p_n \rangle$ if all the events that achieve the objective t are initiated by α – any other events that are initiated by other agents have no *material* effect on the behaviour of the system. This may be made precise as follows: if we take any $\langle E, \leq \rangle$ such that $\langle E, \leq \rangle \dashv t$ then the interaction is α-invariant if given any E' such that $\langle E, \leq \rangle \downarrow \alpha = \langle E', \leq \rangle \downarrow \alpha$ then $\langle E', \leq \rangle \dashv t$.

This property gives us agent invariance because any event initiated by other agents in the system will have no effect on whether the objective is achieved or not. The objective will be achieved at the initiative of the agent alone. Hence for example, an office system which achieves an objective regardless of what is displayed is user invariant. A dynamic system in which other agents, for example the power plant, could update the system so that the original plan for achieving the objective is no longer appropriate, would not be user invariant.

It captures the idea of the agent's initiative because other agents in the system are unable to direct the interaction differently from that envisaged by the agent under which it is invariant.

Misdirected interaction

A number of properties deal with the possibility that agents are at "cross purposes". An action is initiated by one agent to achieve one objective but is interpreted by another agent to mean something else. The problem may occur if a number of objectives are partially achieved from the perspective of one of the agents. There is an additional property that is related to this notion of cross purposes that we shall deal with first.

Multiple objectives may also be achieved through a single stream of interactive behaviour, that is through one pair of agents (α and β). In this case we have an interactional trajectory E which is concerned with the interaction between only two agents ($E \updownarrow \alpha = E \updownarrow \beta$) and partially achieves, without detours, two objectives t_1 and t_2, that is $E \ll t_1$ and $E \ll t_2$. Further we are requiring that E is composed of the events of F and G where $F \ll t_1$ is detour free, and $G \ll t_2$ is detour free. In addition E *interleaves* F and G. When only two agents are involved then inadvertently taking the next step towards the "wrong" objective is only a problem if there is mutual interference between events; that is: performing events in the wrong order will have an effect on the state of the system. This will be made manifest because the original objectives are no longer achieved. An interactional trajectory E is *interference free* with respect to t_1 and t_2 if E is an interleaving of F and G where $F \dashv t_1$ and $G \dashv t_2$ are canonical; it is also case that $E \dashv t_1$ and $E \dashv t_2$ and further, any interleaving of F and G also achieves the objective, that is, any $E' = interleaves(F, G)$ is such that $E' \dashv t_1$ and $E' \dashv t_2$.

Another problem may arise when multiple objectives are being achieved through the use of different agents for each objective (N.B. a computer system itself may be the combination of a number of agents). Interactional dissonance occurs when the wrong or unintended expressive components of one agent are being used by the other. A common example of interactional dissonance is the "unselected window" problem. Here we can imagine the situation in which two objectives are to be achieved by one agent interacting with two other agents. Let us consider an initiating agent α and two further agents β, γ that are to be used to achieve two objectives $t_\beta = \alpha: <p_1, inv_1, p_2>$ and $t_\gamma = \alpha :<p_3, inv_2, p_4>$. Assume further the existence of an interactional trajectory E such that $E \ll t_\beta$ and $E \ll t_\gamma$. We will assume further that the events that make up the trajectory that exclusively relate to the objectives t_β and t_γ are canonical. Hence $E_\beta = E \updownarrow \beta$ is a canonical achievement for t_β and $E_\gamma = E \updownarrow \gamma$ is a canonical achievement for t_γ. The difficulty arises because the event e can be identical with respect to the source but can have more than one target. Hence we think of ϵ as an event type, and e_β targets ϵ at β and e_γ at γ. The problem arises when an event occurs so that the interactional trajectory no longer leads towards one of the objectives, that is it is no longer the case that $E \triangleright e_\beta \ll t_\beta$. However if the other instance had been used it would be the case that $E \triangleright e_\gamma \ll t_\gamma$.

16.7   History

We also argued that constraints on ordering, or the need to remember what has happened already in the interaction, is likely to restrict the freedom of the interaction. How can we express these properties within the interaction framework? Given some objective t we can say that an interactive system is *context independent* for an agent α if given any event whose source is any agent other that α that is the "current event" in the context of a partial detour free achievement for t then the further interaction required to continue to achieve the objective can be determined from that current event. What we are saying is that no memory of the interaction is required in order to achieve the objective.

This property can be expressed formally as follows: if $E_1 \triangleright e \ll t$ and $E_2 \triangleright e \ll t$ where $source(e) \neq \alpha$ then for all partially ordered sets of events F if $E_1 \triangleright e \triangleright F \dashv t$ is canonical then $E_2 \triangleright e \triangleright F \dashv t$ and it is also canonical. A system in which an event is the reading of a rendering of a map (which has no ambiguities or details missing) could be context free if the actions to be carried out depend only on the information that is presented and understood in the map.

A number of properties can be seen as extensions of this context free property. The first is a similar property but legislates that the agent α can determine the interaction predictably although other events not initiated by the agent may not be the same: if $E_1 \triangleright e \ll t$ and $E_2 \triangleright e \ll t$ where $source(e) \neq \alpha$ then there exist partially ordered sets of events F and G such that $E_1 \triangleright e \triangleright F \dashv t$ and $E_2 \triangleright e \triangleright G \dashv t$ where both are canonical trajectories and $F \downarrow \alpha = G \downarrow \alpha$. This property may be required of a plant control system in which the information presented in the rendering of the system should be sufficient for the operator to produce a path to plant closure irrespective of other events that are being generated by the activities of the plant that is being closed.

This set of properties can be extended by saying that some knowledge is required of the interaction, the agent must have some recollection of the history of the interaction. Hence we require that $ht(E_1) = ht(E_2)$ where $ht: \mathbb{P}(Event) \rightarrow \mathbb{P}(Event)$ is some transformation of the past events that must be recalled about the interaction in order to ensure that the interaction is predictable. Hence the idea of history is introduced. Earlier in the paper we discussed the possibility that events could occur in any order, for example where the objective is to complete an electronic form. In this case ht would relate any permutation of a sequence of events. Hence all the possible orders of entries would be mapped, by ht, into a single canonical ordering that could be used as the means of comparison. In the case of the drawing program on the other hand, ht would extract those events that relate to the construction of the diagram and affect the order in which subcomponents of the diagram may be selected, for similar definition in system terms, see [8].

16.8   Conclusion

We have identified definitions of requirements of interactive systems that relate to freedom in interaction. Because we are aware of difficulty in being clear about what the requirements mean, and the fact that we are concerned to enunciate a class of properties that may form the basis of a user centred analysis or a system construction, we have used the interaction framework [6, 3] developed elsewhere to express these properties precisely.

We expect some of the formulations of interaction freedom to be controversial. Perhaps, cognitive modellers will argue that an understanding of initiative or potential cannot be understood without an understanding of user intentions. On the other hand system modellers will argue that interference demands a knowledge of how the state is affected and so on. We are prepared to accept that our formulations may be inappropriate, but would like to see arguments that recognise the interactional flavour of the properties. The questions that must be asked are whether initiative, potential, invariance etc. provide a context in which we can get a better understanding of user, system and other environmental issues.

A user modeller should ask whether for example the concept of interactional detour provides a description of a property that helps to structure an account of the cognitive reasons for detours. We would hope to enter a partnership with such a modeller in which we continue to refine these interactional properties so that they better express, neutrally, some of the concerns that user modellers express.

On the other hand we would hope that system modellers might find that systems that have been constructed with these concepts of agents, events, objectives, expressive and receptive components, interactional trajectories and so on, can be used as generative requirements within the design process. The system modeller's task would be to put flesh on the bones and to understand what the implications of these interactional requirements are on the construction of systems.

Our purpose in this paper is to continue a discussion on interactional freedom, a more specific version of a discussion that we began in 1989 [1]. Here we have chosen a specific set of properties and have used the developing interaction framework to analyse them. We look forward to future contributions.

16.9   References

[1] P. Barnard and M. D. Harrison. Integrating cognitive and system models in human computer interaction. In A. G. Sutcliffe and L. A. Macauley, editors, *People and Computers V.* Cambridge University Press, 1989.

[2] P. J. Barnard and M. D. Harrison. Towards a framework for modelling human computer interaction. In J. Gornostaev, editor, *Proceedings International Conference on HCI, EWHCI'92*, pages 189–196. Moscow:ICSTI, 1992.

[3] A.E. Blandford, M.D. Harrison, and P.J. Barnard. Integrating user requirements and systems specification. In *Computers, Communication and Usability: Design Issues, Research Methods and Integrated Services*, pages 165–196. North Holland Studies in Telecommunication, 1993.

[4] J. M. Carroll and C. Carrithers. Blocking learner errors in a training wheels system. *Human Factors*, 26:377–389, 1984.

[5] A.J. Dix. *Formal Methods for Interactive Systems*. Academic Press, 1991.

[6] M. D. Harrison and P. J. Barnard. On defining requirements for interactions. In *Proceedings of the IEEE International Workshop on Requirements Engineering*, pages 50–54. IEEE, New York, 1993.

[7] M. D. Harrison, C. R. Roast, and P. C. Wright. Complementary methods for the iterative design of interactive systems. In G. Salvendy and M.J. Smith, editors, *Designing and Using Human-Computer Interfaces and Knowledge Based Systems*, pages 651–658. Elsevier Scientific, 1989.

[8] M.D. Harrison, G.D. Abowd, and A.J. Dix. Analysing display oriented interaction by means of system models. In *Computers, Communication and Usability: Design Issues, Research and Methods for Integrated Services*, pages 147–163. Elsevier, 1993.

[9] C. A. R. Hoare. *Communicating Sequential Processes*. Prentice Hall International, 1985.

17 A Framework for Precise, Reusable Task Abstractions

H. Rex Hartson
Kevin A. Mayo

ABSTRACT

Current methods for abstraction of task descriptions within the behavioral view are ad hoc, leading to imprecision, inconsistency, and ambiguity in task- and user-centered interface design representations. However, as interaction designers communicate with software designers and implementers, precise and consistent design representations are crucial.

Our experience with the User Action Notation (UAN) reveals the most difficulty in lower levels of abstraction, those levels just above the articulatory level of task description. This level is crucial in interface design because it is the level at which user actions are used to manipulate interface artifacts, or widgets. Even cases believed to be simple and well understood, such as the `select` task, are seen to be problematic. We argue for inclusion of semantics in task abstraction. We also argue for guiding lower level abstraction within the task-subtask hierarchy by bringing to bear other kinds of abstraction hierarchies, particularly domain-oriented and taxonomical hierarchies.

17.1 Background

17.1.1 Interface as Illusion

Direct manipulation interaction typical of today's graphical user interface (GUI) designs relies on an illusion that attempts to render application entities indistinguishable from the interface artifacts that represent them [12]. In this regard an interface design is successful if the user, facilitating this mimesis through willing suspension of disbelief [6], can manipulate application entities without being conscious of their interface representations. Users have the feeling of engaging real application entities. In the case of such directness, there is no difference to the user between, for instance, a file and a file icon—e.g., dropping a file icon on a folder icon is putting a file in a folder.

To a lesser extent, this kind of directness can also occur in a command-oriented interface, where the name for a file is its representative in the interface. For example, although a filename cannot be manipulated as an object by a user, users seldom think of the distinction between a file and its name.

From most perspectives of analysis and design, supporting this illusion is what interface design is about. We normally speak of interaction as though the illusion were assumed; e.g., no distinction is made between file and file icon. Interaction designers and software engineers work together to create this illusion. However, when interaction designers communicate with software designers and implementers, the reality behind the illusion comes to the surface at the articulatory boundary between interface and non-interface components. Here, designers must communicate precisely about what is behind the illusion in terms of user actions and systems actions. The precision required for this kind of communication requires a structured approach involving semantics in the task abstraction process.

17.1.2 Behavioral and Constructional Views

User interface development can be differentiated into two types: *development of the interaction design* and *development of the user interface software* that implements the interaction. These development types occur in different views, the behavioral and constructional views, respectively [4]. The behavioral view is the working view of people who design and develop interaction components of user interfaces. Here a user interface design is described in terms of tasks and artifacts that comprise interaction in terms of user and interface behavior. In contrast, the constructional view involves development of GUI widgets, algorithms, programming, procedure libraries, control and data flow, state transition diagrams, event handlers, callbacks, and object-oriented representations. This view contains the tools and techniques used to construct the interface software.

A typical interface design and its representation are very large. Abstraction is required in both views to control complexity and to amortize, through reuse, the effort of creating and representing the details. Established methods for abstraction in the constructional view exist in the discipline of software engineering. On the other hand, current methods for abstraction of task descriptions within the behavioral view are ad hoc, leading to imprecision, inconsistency, and ambiguity in task- and user-centered interface design representations. However, as interaction designers communicate with software designers and implementers, precise and consistent design representations are crucial.

In order to achieve precision and consistency in task abstraction we have drawn upon task structuring from the User Action Notation [2, 3] and the Task Mapping Model [8, 9] and the task vocabulary of Lenorovitz et al. [7]. This structure and vocabulary, we argue, can be infused with semantics associated with user actions. In turn, these semantics provide a richer description that supports precision and consistency across behavioral and constructional views.

17.1.3 The User Action Notation, a Behavioral Representation Technique

The User Action Notation (UAN) was created by researchers within the Human–Computer Interaction Project at Virginia Tech as a behavioral interface design representation technique. UAN descriptions are intended to be written by interaction designers and read by all developers, particularly those designing and implementing user interface software. The UAN is a user- and task-centered notation that describes physical (and other) behavior during task performance. The primary abstraction is a *user task*; An interface is represented as a quasi-hierarchical structure of asynchronous tasks, the sequencing within each task being independent from that of others. User actions, corresponding interface feedback, and state change information are represented at the lowest level, i.e., the articulatory level, or level of physical user actions. Higher levels of abstraction hide these details and are used to build the *complete* task structure.

17.2 Abstraction in Task Description

Describing details of user interaction can require much effort and patience. However, the effort a designer puts into detailed task descriptions is an investment that can be reused. In order to control complexity, most methods of task description use abstraction as a means to hide details of tasks at various levels [5]. This is also true in the UAN. The lowest level of abstraction is called the articulation level, the level containing details of keystrokes and mouse buttons. Most of a design, however, is represented at higher levels of abstraction in the UAN, where this low level detail is neither visible nor necessary. Higher levels of a UAN task structure merely make reference to details via "invocations" of lower level tasks. In this way, detailed descriptions are reused in the same way the code of a macro or procedure is reused in software.

More specifically, a task description written in the UAN is a set of user actions and tasks combined with temporal relations such as sequencing, interleaving, and concurrency, to describe time-related user behavior [2]. Each task can then be named and the name later used as a reference to that task. A task name used as a reference is called a macro task because the name is used as a substitute for the whole task description. (Although this is an analogy to programming macros, one should remember that the steps in task macros are performed by users during task performance.) This name reference can be used as a higher level user action in another task description. This is very similar to the way the name of a software procedure is used as a "command" to refer to that procedure within the code of a program; the task name is a surrogate for the task (representing a user invocation of the task), and is an abstraction to hide task details.

In order to explore the concept of task abstraction, we first introduce a simple example in Section 17.2.1, the concept of task parameterization in Section 17.2.2, and a closer look at task semantics in Section 17.3.

17.2.1 Example—The Task of Selecting a File

Consider a UAN description for some task T, containing a sequence of user actions for selecting a file, as shown in Figure 17.1. The ~ is used to denote cursor movement and [and] denote "context of" (file A)—that by which the file icon is manipulated. In this case the context is the whole icon itself. Mv means the mouse button is depressed and M^ means it is released. The expression file A!: is a condition, interpreted as "if file A is not already highlighted, then do the following." And that following feedback action, file A!, represents highlighting file A. Note that separation of the abstract use of the highlighting feedback symbol (!) and the definition of how this highlighting is to be accomplished (a separate declarative definition not shown in this example) allows designers to refer to highlighting before committing to the details of how it will be implemented. This notation is defined and examples given in chapter 6 of Hix and Hartson [4].

TASK: T	
USER ACTIONS	INTERFACE FEEDBACK
~[file A] Mv	file A-!: file A
M^	

FIGURE 17.1. Simple UAN sequence for selecting a file

17.2.2 Parameterization for Reuse of Task Abstractions

Sequences for selection, such as the one in Figure 17.1, are used frequently within interaction designs. Therefore, this sequence is a good candidate for reuse to avoid repeating essentially the same articulatory details every time selection is needed in a design. Selection details can be encapsulated into one task description, that task given a name, and the name used as a reference to the task.

However, the sequence described in Figure 17.1 is specific to the selection of a particular file, file A. If task descriptions are to be reused, they must be written in a more general way, using parameters to distinguish specific instances.

Thus, the sequence of user actions in Figure 17.1 can be generalized to describe user actions for selecting a single object from a set of objects having similar behavior. Hopefully, it can even be used to represent selection of several different types of objects. In order to allow this kind of object substitution in task descriptions, we must use a parameter; that is, file A can be made more general by making it a parameter of the new macro task and calling it object. Figure 17.2 shows a UAN description for this more general selection task:

TASK: select(object)	
USER ACTIONS	INTERFACE FEEDBACK
~[object] Mv	object-!: object!
M^	

FIGURE 17.2. Parameterized description for more general selection macro task

When the description for task T, of Figure 17.1, requires selection of the particular file A, the sequence of user actions in Figure 17.1 is replaced with a reference to ("invocation" of) the parameterized select task macro, select(file A), binding file A as the object during this instantiation of the task.

17.3 Semantics in Task Abstraction—Connecting Illusion and Reality

Figure 17.2 is a good start on a task description for the select task, but it is only a start. So far it describes only clicking on, and highlighting, an object. There is no way to represent the roles of both, for example, a file icon and the file it represents. To associate this icon to a file within an application requires a connection between interface and non-interface components of the system, i.e., a connection to task semantics. This association of meaning must be built into the interface or it does not exist, and designers must include these semantic connections in their design representations.

To make the necessary distinction in the generic case, we adopt the term "entity" to refer to something within the system (e.g., file or system function) and "object" to refer to the interface representation (e.g., icon) of an entity. An entity, therefore, belongs to an application and is not visible to users; an object belongs to an interface and is visible, but illusory.

Expanding the simple UAN description of the select task of Figure 17.2 to include this semantic connection between the actual file (entity) and its iconic representation (object) yields the description in Figure 17.3.

TASK: select(object, entity)		
USER ACTIONS	**INTERFACE FEEDBACK**	**STATE**
~[object] Mv	object-!: object!	selected={entity}
M^		

FIGURE 17.3. Select task description with parameters for semantic connection between interface object and application entity

The difference here, from Figure 17.2, is the inclusion of the third column which indicates a state change, namely the entity becoming selected. (In the third column, selected is the name of a set that contains the names of the entities currently marked as selected.) The object is highlighted—a visible sign that the invisible entity has undergone a state change. It is clear that entity and object referring to it are different but associated.

This distinction between object and corresponding entity introduces additional complexity into the select task description. When we parameterize the select task for reuse, we must include parameters to indicate which interface object is pointed to and which entity is selected.

The reusable task description in Figure 17.3 contains two items that must be bound through parameters to items in the invoking world—object and entity. The former can be an icon, button, scroll bar, or other interface object representing the entity. The latter can be a file, a system function, etc. Generic reference to the task becomes: select(object, entity) and an invocation to select a specific file, say file A, would become: select(file A icon, file A). We have now captured the semantic connection between illusion and reality for this task. In this instantiation for file A, it is now clear that the user clicks on the file icon, the file is selected, and the icon is highlighted.

This interpretation of select crosses the interface/non-interface boundary of a software system because it connects the behavioral act of selecting an object in the interface to the constructional state of an entity being selected in the non-interface system component. As we said at the end of this Section 17.1.1, if user interface designers are to communicate their designs to software designers and implementers with precision, addressing details is obligatory, especially at this cross-boundary connection where reality of the illusion comes to the surface.

Usability issues also arise at this interface/non-interface boundary. Designs that do not give good selection feedback can lead to a task situation where the system "thinks" the user has caused a state change but the user doesn't, or vice versa; state knowledge is not communicated. As examples, consider the lack of feedback in command-line interfaces such as DOS or UNIX.

Our discussion of selection has mostly been oriented toward files and file icons. We might also want to generalize to include selection with other interface objects, e.g., buttons, scroll bars, etc. For example, one might want our select task macro be reusable for selection of a system function (e.g., with a command push button labeled Open). The concept of illusion, as discussed in Section 17.1.1, should apply to buttons as well as file icons, and it does. However, the semantics seem to be a little different. For this discussion we shall also ignore a possible difference in interface feedback (e.g., push button blinking at selection). Clicking on a file icon causes a file to be selected, but clicking on the Open button appears only to activate a system function to open files that are already selected.

Thus, command button selection doesn't *appear* to need the second parameter and would have a different semantics in the State column of the task description. We will return to this discussion of semantic similarity and difference.

Because current task abstraction processes are ad hoc, variation in the way it is carried out lead to ambiguity, imprecision, and inconsistency. Even cases believed to be simple and well understood, such as the `select` task, are seen in this section to be problematic. We have argued here for inclusion of semantics in task abstraction, but we also need a framework and vocabulary for abstractions.

17.4 Framework for Abstraction–Domain-Oriented Hierarchies

In order to provide a framework within which to structure abstraction, we adopted the framework of the Task Mapping Model (TMM). Much like other modeling techniques such as CLG [10], ETAG [11], etc., TMM depicts user task performance in terms of a series of mappings from the user's problem or work domain (the world in which the user wishes to use a computer to solve a problem) to the computer semantic domain (the world of files and application functions) to the computer syntactic domain (the world of commands and grammatical elements) to the articulatory domain (the world of keystrokes, cursor movement, and button presses). In order to use a computer to perform a problem domain task, the user must make a series of mappings to translate the task through this series of domains. Cases where the knowledge necessary to make the mappings is lacking in users and not supported by interface designs, we believe account for a large proportion of usability problems.

As an example, consider the problem domain of document writing, and consider the task, in this domain, of discarding an existing manuscript. In this problem domain, the task might be called `discard manuscript`.

In the computer semantic domain, this same task is expressed using entities (e.g., files) and application functions (e.g., functions to open, close, create, or delete files). The document `manuscript` from the problem domain is represented as a `file` entity in the computer semantic domain, because documents are stored in files. The usual computer semantic term for discarding files is `delete`. Thus, `discard manuscript` in the problem domain maps into the unordered (denoted by the use of set braces) pair {`delete`, `file`} in the computer semantic domain.

The `function-entity` pairs of the computer semantic domain take on a command-like appearance in the computer syntactic domain, referring to specific interface objects, with grammatical ordering. The physical keystrokes and cursor manipulation actions to carry out the syntactic "commands" are expressed in the articulatory domain.

Going to higher levels of abstraction from physical actions in the UAN corresponds to moving from articulatory to computer syntactic to computer semantic to problem domain in the TMM. Thus, the TMM domains provide a domain-oriented hierarchical framework, summarized in Figure 17.4, to guide in establishing structured levels of abstraction for the UAN. In this figure, "grammar" refers to general syntactic aspects of expressions within task descriptions, including ordering of terms and design-, interaction style-, or implementation-dependent terminology. "Action" refers to abstract user actions (e.g., `indicate` and `activate`) from the vocabulary to be discussed in Section 17.5. "Style" refers to a specific interaction style or technique (e.g., a specific kind of "widget"), such as form-filling, menu choices, direct manipulation, or command line interaction.

Levels	Sub-Level	Attributes	Expressions
Semantic Levels		Unordered pairs of functions and entities— *Grammar Abstracted* *Action Abstracted* *Style Abstracted*	{function, entity}
Syntactic Levels	Grammar (G) Syntactic Level	Ordered pairs of functions and entities— *Grammar Specific* *Action Abstracted* *Style Abstracted*	(function, entity) —*or*— (entity, function)
	Grammar-Action (G-A) Syntactic Level	Ordered pairs of functions and entities with actions defined to communicate the pairs— *Grammar Specific* *Action Specific* *Style Abstracted*	Actions to communicate function, entity —*or*— Actions to communicate entity, function
	Grammar-Action-Style (G-A-S) Syntactic Level	Ordered pairs of commands and objects with style specific actions defined to communicate the pairs— *Grammar Specific* *Action Specific* *Style Specific*	Style specific actions to communicate function, entity —*or*— Style specific actions to communicate entity, function
Articulatory Level		Physical user actions necessary to communicate the G-A-S level expressions to the computer	*Written in terms of keystrokes and cursor movement*

FIGURE 17.4. Structured levels of task abstraction

17.4.1 Semantic Levels

We will refer to the highest UAN levels as *semantic levels* of abstraction. A typical interface design expressed in the UAN will have many levels of semantic abstraction, each higher level abstracting more and more detail into its task macros. At every semantic level the general form for a task macro is an unordered pair, {function, entity}, where function denotes an internal application system function and entity denotes an internal application system entity. At the highest level, one might see the entire system abstracted into a pair such as: {manage, database}. The semantic levels are independent of how the functions and entities are represented within an interface design.

Grammar, user actions, and interaction style are all abstracted out of task descriptions at semantic levels. At semantic levels UAN expressions are task names (abstract user actions) connected by temporal relations. In the context of this paper, UAN semantic level user actions are task names expressed as {function, entity} pairs (e.g., {edit, form field}, {open, file}).

17.4.2 Syntactic Levels

Below the semantic levels are the syntactic levels of abstraction. We shall distinguish three kinds of syntactic levels—grammar, grammar-action, and grammar-action-style levels. At the grammar level, the unordered {function, entity} pairs of the semantic levels appear as ordered function-entity (or entity-function) pairs. Grammatical ordering has been added, so that some constraints and implications about specific interface design are already evident, but action and style are still abstract.

The border between the grammar and grammar-action syntactic levels (double line in Figure 17.4) is significant because above this line are only entities and functions and below the line are only user actions used to communicate requests for the entities and functions.

The grammar-action level includes abstract user actions used to request the function, entity pairs of the grammar syntactic level, but the expressions are still independent of specific interaction style (e.g., are not specific to menus, forms, buttons, command lines).

The grammar-action-style level is the lowest syntactic abstraction level, the level just above the articulatory level. Abstractions at this level are of particular importance and interest. This is the level at which user actions are specific to widgets such as menus, forms, and buttons. The grammar-action-style level will be discussed more in Section 17.6.5.

17.4.3 The Articulatory Level

The lowest level of abstraction in the UAN is the articulatory level. The articulatory level is where tasks are described in terms of specific physical user actions required to carry out these functions on a particular implementation platform—e.g., keystrokes of a command line interaction (CLI) or entity selection and menu choices or button presses of a direct manipulation GUI style interaction. The UAN task descriptions in Figures 1, 2, and 3 occur in the articulatory level. However, the UAN is not a notation only for the articulatory level of task description. The UAN covers the higher levels of abstraction, as well, providing notation for representing the entire structure of task abstraction.

17.5 Vocabulary for Abstraction–Taxonomical Hierarchies

By and large, creating task abstractions for reuse is a matter of factoring out similar sequences that recur over task descriptions. The question is: How does one determine what is similar? One can look at articulatory details, but these are very much design dependent. By giving two tasks a similar articulatory design, one can make them look similar, but they may in fact be different semantically. To overcome this difficulty, we sought a precise and consistent vocabulary, so that the appearance at syntactic levels (terms used to describe tasks and their abstractions) will reflect distinctions at semantic levels.

17.5.1 Taxonomy of User Actions by Lenorovitz, et al.

Our need for consistent naming implies the need for a vocabulary, defined in terms of semantics, for identifying elements of abstractions, especially those occurring just above the articulatory level. The user-system interface action taxonomy by Lenorovitz et al. [7], which is built upon the work of Berliner, et al. [1], provides a vocabulary that can be used for precise and consistent naming of certain common user tasks, based on semantic distinctions. We will to use the term "function" for operations that are performed by the computer (usually at the request of the user—e.g., deleting a file) and the term "action" for operations that are performed by the user (e.g., selecting a file).

Figure 17.5 shows an extract from the user-input function/action taxonomy from Lenorovitz et al. [7], adapted here to include their definitions (which contain much of the semantics). A taxonomical structure is a hierarchy with the purpose to classify, with the goal of helping to understand, in this case, user actions being classified and relationships among them. Like the domain-oriented hierarchies of Section 17.4, it does not provide an appropriate model for an entire design representation. That is the job of the task-subtask hierarchy.

For our example task, `select(object, entity)`, we need look at only the parts of this table that include the `indicate` and `activate` action types ; see Figure 17.6. (Note: Monospace font is used for vocabulary terms adopted for use in UAN.)

In Figure 17.6 both `select` and `reference` are ways to `indicate`—`select` by pointing and `reference` by referring to a name.

17.5.2 Clarifying Selection by Pointing

The Lenorovitz et al. definition of `select` is, as shown in Figure 17.6 (with some terminology changes to be consistent with ours): "Opt for or choose an entity by *pointing* to its interface representation." For example, moving the cursor to a `file icon` with a mouse, and clicking the mouse button is an instance of `indicate` by `select`. This definition of `select` needs augmentation for several reasons.

First, as discussed in Section 17.1.1, an entity being selected is only represented in the interface by the object. Pointing (and clicking) to the object causes an internal state change that the system can interpret as selection of the entity.

Second, the basic underlying design of an interface/system will define the semantics for "pointing to." For example, in the case of Macintosh OS, the point of the arrow cursor (sometimes known as the hotpoint of the cursor icon) must enter the object. In other possible platforms, any part of the cursor may enter the object to constitute "pointing to."

Third, although cursor movement in GUI interfaces is usually accomplished via mouse, trackball, touchscreen, or similar input device, our interpretation is broad enough to include discrete cursor movement from object to object by such means as arrow keys or tab/return keys or cursor movement by gesture.

CREATE	ASSOCIATE	NAME	Give title to or attach label to for purposes of identification/reference.
		GROUP	Link together or associate for purposes of identification.
	INTRODUCE	INSERT	Make space for and place an entity at a selected location within the bounds of another such that the latter wholly encompasses the former, and the former becomes an integral component of the latter.
	ASSEMBLE	AGGREGATE	Combine two or more components so as to form a new composite entity.
		OVERLAY	Superimpose one entity on top of another so as to affect a composite appearance while still retaining the separability of each component layer.
	REPLICATE	COPY	Reproduce one or more duplicated of an entity (no links to *master*).
		INSTANCE	Reproduce an original (*master*) entity in such a way as to retain a definitional link to the master—i.e., such that any subsequent changes or modifications made to the master will automatically be reflected in each and every *instance* created therefrom.
INDICATE	SELECT *(POS/OBJ)*		Opt for or choose an entity (e.g., a position or an object) by *pointing* to it.
	REFERENCE		Opt for or choose an entity by invoking its name.
ELIMINATE	REMOVE	CUT	Remove a designated portion of an entity and place it in a special purpose buffer (residual components of the original entity usually close in around *hole* left by *cut-out* portion).
		DELETE	Remove and (irrevocably) destroy a designated portion of an entity.
	STOP	SUSPEND	Stop a process and temporarily hold in abeyance for future restoration.
		TERMINATE	Conclude a process such that it cannot be restarted from the point of interruption, only by complete re-initiation.
	DISASSOCIATE	RENAME	Change an entity's title or label, without changing the entity itself.
		UN-GROUP	Eliminate the common bond or reference linkage of a group of entities.
	DISASSEMBLE	SEGREGATE	Partition and separate an entity into one or more component parts such that the structure and identity of the original is lost.
		FILTER	Selectively eliminate one or more layers of an overlaid composite.
		SUPPRESS	Conceal or keep back certain aspects or products of a process without affecting the process itself (i.e., affects appearance only).
		SET-ASIDE	Remove entire contents of current (active) work area and store in a readily accessible buffer (for future recall).
MANIPULATE	TRANSFORM		Manipulate or change one or more of an entity's attributes (e.g., color, line type, character font, size, orientation) without changing the essential content of the entity itself.
ACTIVATE	EXECUTE __ FN.		Initiate or activate any of a set of predefined utility or special purpose functions (e.g., sort, merge, calculate, update, extract, search, replace).

FIGURE 17.5. Taxonomical hierarchy of user-input actions, extracted from the Lenorovitz et al. [7]

INDICATE	SELECT *(POS/OBJ)*	Opt for or choose an entity by *pointing* to its interface representation.
	REFERENCE	Opt for or choose an entity by invoking its name.
ACTIVATE	EXECUTE __ FN.	Initiate or activate any of a set of predefined utility or special purpose functions (e.g., sort, merge, calculate, update, extract, search, replace).

FIGURE 17.6. Extract from taxonomy for `indicate` and `activate`

Fourth, because our use of the term entity, as introduced in Section 17.4, is narrower than that of the Lenorovitz taxonomy, we need to extend the definition of selection to include both entities and functions.

Finally, since specific designs for select by pointing often require an accompanying action (e.g., depressing or releasing or both of a mouse or trackball button), we extend the definition of select accordingly in Figure 17.7, including the addition of possible feedback.

INDICATE	SELECT (POS/OBJ)	Opt for or choose an entity or function by pointing to the object that represents the entity or function in the interface, with the possible addition of a confirming action. Selection causes an internal and invisible state change signifying selection of that entity or function, along with possible feedback denoting that state change.

FIGURE 17.7. Augmented taxonomy entry for select action

This definition of indicate by select is distinct from indicate by reference. To reference is to "Opt for or choose an entity by invoking its name," as in Figure 17.6.

17.6 Applying the Framework and Vocabulary in Task-Subtask Hierarchies

We have argued for incorporating semantics into our task abstractions for precision and consistency. We have also argued for a more structured approach to task abstraction. To that end, we have introduced a framework and a vocabulary to support task abstraction. We now turn our attention to putting the framework and taxonomy to work in the process of abstraction, in the context of the task-subtask hierarchies of UAN task descriptions.

17.6.1 Task-Subtask Hierarchies

Like most other task-description methods, the UAN produces a task-subtask hierarchy of abstraction among task descriptions. While a task-subtask hierarchy generally works well in the UAN to show the structure of tasks and their decompositions/expansions in terms of lower level tasks, it offers no inherent guidance in how to form levels of abstraction. For UAN users this is not a problem at high and middle levels of abstraction but does become a problem at low levels, particularly at the first level of abstraction above the articulatory level. This is largely because this level is where artifacts/widgets become manifest in the interface design. In this section we bring to bear concepts from the framework of a domain-oriented hierarchy (Section 17.4) and the vocabulary of a taxonomical hierarchy (Section 17.5) to guide abstraction in the task-subtask hierarchy of the UAN. The result is a level of abstraction that contains mainly task macros for the manipulation of interface artifacts.

17.6.2 Semantic Levels of Abstraction

Large parts of most non-trivial interface designs are represented at semantic levels, as {function, entity} pairs, as mentioned in Section 17.4. For example, at the highest level of abstraction for a word processing system, one would find the single most abstract task description: {manage, documents} and so on, down to much more specific tasks, such as {open, file}. Tasks that require files to be opened will invoke the {open, file} task name, with the task details being spelled out at lower levels. In this way, abstraction is used to build a quasi-hierarchical structure (acyclic directed graph) of higher and higher level tasks.

Tasks such as the {open, file} task often will have significant amounts of detail in their decompositions at lower levels, for example to make menu selections and manipulate dialogue boxes with their buttons, scrolled lists, etc. The lower one gets in the task-subtask hierarchy the more variation one sees for these tasks, depending on the interface design.

This transition from high level design-independent task descriptions to low level design-dependent details can be kept clear in the task-subtask hierarchy by bringing some of the structure of domain-oriented hierarchies.

In Figure 17.8 we have illustrated some levels of task-subtask abstraction under the influence of domain-oriented structure. We refer to this figure throughout the rest of the paper. Box A in Figure 17.8 represents the generic form of a task description in the semantic level. Box B contains an instance of a task, for example the {open, file} task, at this level.

17.6.3 Grammar Syntactic Levels of Abstraction

The main difference in going from semantic levels to grammar syntactic levels is that the function-entity (or entity-function) pairs become ordered. The OR in box C of Figure 17.8 denotes that exactly one of a set of tasks connected by this UAN temporal operator will be performed, resulting in the order of either box D or box E.

Using a linguistic analogy, the semantic {function, entity} pairs are canonical, or deep structure, representations of intended operations with no grammatical ordering or other information about how the requests to the system are expressed. In contrast, expressions found in syntactic levels are surface structure or observable representations embodying grammatical order and possibly other interaction style and design dependent information about how user requests are expressed. It is often the case that several different surface structures correspond to the same underlying semantic deep structure.

In a syntactic view of either CLI or GUI designs, it is usual to think of "commands" in the simplest grammatical terms. For example, we often classify the basic interaction paradigm as having either Verb-Noun (V-N) or Noun-Verb (N-V) form. In a GUI selecting a file followed by executing an open function is considered to be in the N-V form. However, in a command line interface the command vi <filename> is considered to be in the V-N form.

Thus, for the {open, file} function-entity pair in a semantic level, a task description in the grammar syntactic level with grammatical ordering that mentions the file entity first would be of the form N-V, as in box D of Figure 17.8. A grammatical ordering that mentions the open function first would be of the form V-N as in box E.

17.6.4 Grammar-Action Syntactic Level of Abstraction

As pointed out in Section 17.4, at and above the grammar syntactic level, one sees functions and entities. In contrast, at the grammar-action level and below, one sees user actions requesting functions applied to entities. To form a grammar-action level representation of the

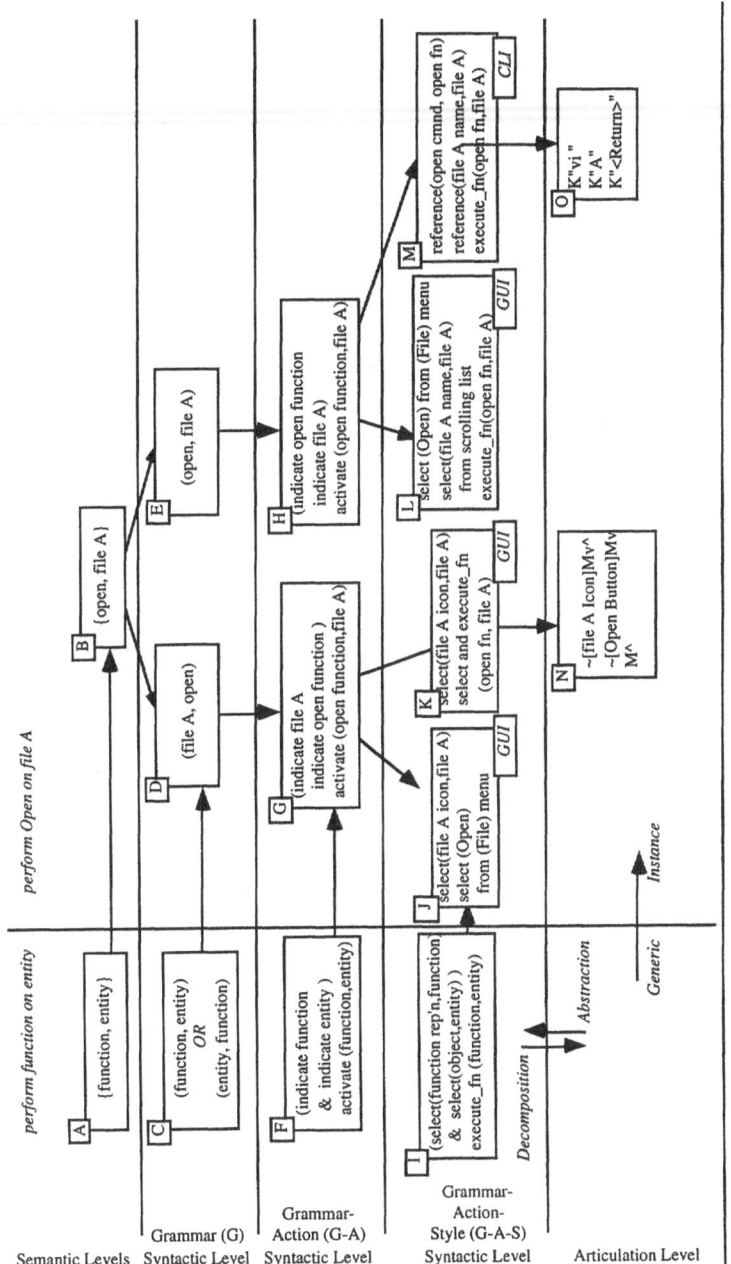

FIGURE 17.8. Domain-oriented hierarchy of abstraction structure

grammar level (entity, function) or (function, entity) tasks, we use the taxonomic vocabulary terms indicate and activate. Box F is the generic form, where the "&" is a UAN temporal operator indicating order independence. The instances of this task, in boxes G and H, do have specific orderings.

Note that in this canonical form of the grammar, both the **N-V** and **V-N** forms of the grammar level appear as indicate-indicate-activate. Both the verb and the noun of the grammar level are represented by an indicate at the grammar-action level, followed an activate, to apply the verb to the noun. The order of the indicate's, however does follow the order of the grammar level.

17.6.5 Grammar-Action-Style Syntactic Level of Abstraction

As stated earlier, in Section 17.4, the grammar-action-style syntactic level of abstraction is important. The articulatory level contains the details of physical user actions without abstraction. Abstraction is a bottom-up process and the grammar-action-style syntactic level, the first level above the articulatory level, is therefore the first level of abstraction. This is the level showing the direct use of basic widgets such as buttons, pull-down menus, scrolled lists, etc. The grammar-action-style syntactic level is especially important because:

- macros at this level are reused the most throughout designs

- much of the interface design activity occurs here

- issues found here (such usability and parameterization) have high impact throughout the rest of the design

- designers spend a significant amount of their time and effort at this level

- this level of abstraction is where the illusion of the interface breaks down and reality behind the illusion must become explicit.

- this is where the look and feel emerge, the artifacts/widgets and the user actions to make them work

Sometimes the articulation level is essentially omitted, leaving the grammar-action-style syntactic level as the lowest level of abstraction expressed in a design representation. Designers or management often make early decisions on interaction style that determine the details behind look and feel of the product. This establishes many of the physical actions (e.g., keystrokes and mouse movements) for the lowest level tasks (e.g., button and menu selection). Once the details of these physical actions are known and agreed upon, designers tend to ignore them by abstracting them away, working only at higher levels. For example, a company designing a security system for banks and airports filled a large wall with a UAN description of their task hierarchy, but articulatory details were never explicitly expressed. The first level of abstraction above the articulatory level (the grammar-action-style syntactic level) was the lowest (most detailed) level they used in their thinking and design discussions. They had already decided on a specific interaction style and the expressions and idioms at that level were well-known to the designers and documented in their custom style guide.

When the interface illusion (discussed in Section 17.1.1) breaks down, it usually occurs at the grammar-action-style level. Although the direct manipulation interaction style makes it seem to the user as though he or she is performing functions directly on application entities, the reality is that the icons, buttons, and menu choices are really commands and parameters in requests to have the system perform the functions. These user requests connect the illusion to reality and the grammar-action-style syntactic level to levels below and above. This realization is crucial in understanding the grammar-action-style syntactic level of interaction. The reality behind the illusion is that mutual task performance is a case of the user communicating to the system what is to be done and the system doing it and giving clear feedback.

Returning to the examples in Figure 17.8, an indicate from box G or H in the grammar-action level typically decomposes into many actions at the grammar-action-style level—e.g., actions for direct use of a scrolled list and several buttons within a dialogue box. For example, box J illustrates a method of performing the task of box G within a GUI design that calls for first selecting a file and then selecting the Open command from the File menu. Box K shows an different GUI design (possibly within the same interface) that also begins with selection of a file, but is completed by selection of, say, an Open button.

Box L contains an example of a grammar-action-style level representation of the open, file task of boxes E and H. Box L also corresponds to a GUI design, using the familiar sequence of selecting Open from the File menu, leading to an "Open dialogue box" in which the users selects a file name from a scrolled list. The Open function is then applied to the selected file by clicking on the Open button in the dialogue box.

A alternative grammar-action-style task method for the open file task of box H is shown in box M. Here the indicate actions of box H are translated into reference actions, implying a command line interaction style where the open command is typed, followed by typing of the file name and some input (e.g., the "return" key) to activate the open command on the file.

17.6.6 Articulatory Level of Abstraction

For completeness, let's continue with our GUI example for opening a file and move to the articulatory level of abstraction. The articulatory details for the hypothetical design of box K are shown in box N, where the user actions are simply selection of the file icon and selection of the Open button. The description in box M leads to quite a different description at the articulatory level, as shown in box O. Box O contains CLI interaction style command syntax one might type to use the Unix "vi" editor to open file A, where K refers to the keyboard string generating device in the UAN, "vi" and "A" are literal strings and "<Return>" is the carriage return key, a single literal keystroke.

Box L would translate, at the articulatory level, first into the physical user actions for making a selection from a pull down menu. Those details will not be given here but (for the Macintosh, for example) would involve moving the cursor to the menu title bar, depressing the mouse button, pulling the cursor down to the choice, and releasing the mouse button. The second and third steps might appear as they are shown in Figure 17.9.

Consider that these steps are performed in the task arena of the Open (file) dialogue box in, say, Microsoft Word. Within this arena consider the specific task of selecting a file by clicking on its name from the scrolled list. We assume the desired file name is visible, a condition of activation that might require other tasks (such as those to manipulate directories) to actualize. Finally the command is activated (via the Open button) to open the selected file. One way (task method) of doing this task, as expressed in the UAN at the articulatory level, is shown in Figure 17.9.

The conclusion of this work is that, at the grammar-action-style level user actions are referred to in the lowest level vocabulary terms such as select, reference, and execute. Additionally, a syntactic form is used to reveal or match a particular interaction style. Thus, a select, when associated with a pull-down menu, has the form: select (x) from (y) menu.

17.6.7 Task Contractions

A literal translation of the form of either box G or box H of Figure 17.8 would require a design having three explicit steps, corresponding to the indicate, indicate, and activate. A GUI design making these three step most explicit might contain icons (or similar GUI interface artifacts) to represent both the function (open) and the entity (file). A third object (e.g., a button) is required to represent explicitly a separate action to execute the function on the entity (i.e., some kind of "Do It" button). After selecting an entity and a function (the order depending on whether the description derives from box G or box H), the user clicks on the Do It button to execute the function on the entity.

TASK: open file (file)		Arena: Open dbx
USER ACTIONS	INTERFACE FEEDBACK	STATE
file name visible in scrolled list:		
~[file name A] Mv	file name A-!: file name A!	selected= {file A}
M^		
~[Open button] Mv	Open button!! *(a second kind highlighting, i.e. blinking)*	
M^		Open function is invoked on the selected file
		Selected file is open

FIGURE 17.9. A possible UAN description for part of the open file task of box L

Boxes L and M are examples where the three user actions of box H are performed explicitly. In some cases, though, when designing for usability, though, we realize that a sequence of three separate actions is extra work for the user. For example, the GUI design of box J, which might represent actions occurring on a Macintosh desk-top, combines the menu selection of the open function and its application to the file. The resulting single action is a *task contraction* used to combine the second select with the execute action. Much like a contraction in a natural language, a task contraction embeds the lexical form of one task within another, usually sharing a terminating action. Thus, in terms of the UAN, the second steps in boxes J and K are task contractions that not only select the Open function but also translate the `activate` of box G into an `execute`, specifying that the Open function is now to be applied to the selected file.

17.6.8 Semantics of Selection Revisited

The discussion in this section on applying the framework and vocabulary in task-subtask hierarchies has revealed the answer to a problem that has continued to escape solution through most of this paper. Our earlier intuition was that a command button is different from a file icon because it leads to an immediate execution of a function. This is only partly right. Consider the syntax in box L, having three separate actions to open a file at the grammar-action-style level (shown here a little more abstractly than in box L, to highlight the connection to vocabulary):

```
select (Open fn)
select (File A)
execute (Open fn, File A)
```

This is an abstract description of one way this task can be accomplished in, say, Microsoft Word™ on the Macintosh™. The `select (Open fn)` corresponds to choosing Open from the File pull-down menu. This menu choice is followed by the Open dialogue box in which the user does the `select (File A)` action by choosing a file name, involving possibly many direct actions on such widgets within the dialogue box as buttons, a pull-down menu (in the guise of a directory name button), and a scrolling list. The operative action (the one that accomplishes selection of the file) is clicking on a file name in the scrolled list.

The user then requests execution of the Open function on the corresponding file, the `execute (Open fn, File A)` action, by clicking on the Open button in the dialogue box or by pressing the return key (defaulted to the Open function). (The function can also be executed by double clicking on the filename during file selection. This variation is a task contraction; the file selection and function execution are contracted into the action of the double click. However, we are presently considering only the case of three separate actions.)

In the case where the three actions are separate, as in box L, how do they compare semantically? Referring to the definition of `select` in Figure 17.7 we see the first two actions, the two `select` actions, are both the same. Both use pointing and clicking to choose an `entity` or a `function` to be used in a subsequent action. The execute action, however, is not the same. Even though it is a point and click task at the articulation level, this is not a select action. This is a case of a task being similar to a `select` task at the articulation level, but not carrying the semantics of a select action per the definition of Figure 17.7. The two parameters for the task are already selected; the `execute` is a pure "`do it`" action, saying when to apply the selected `open function` to the selected `file`.

17.7 Conclusions

This paper is about modeling human-computer interaction for better understanding of interaction, leading to better designs and design representations. We argue for a structured approach to task abstractions that includes semantics, as well as a framework and vocabulary for abstraction. Our approach imposes a notational consistency that aids designer-implementer communication, especially at the "widget" level. Including semantic considerations at this level allows designers to specify interaction so that implementers can properly support the connection between illusion and reality.

Acknowledgments

We wish to thank Jeff Brandenburg, Joe Chase, Deborah Hix, and William Wake for many discussions on this and related topics down in the HCI brainstem-storming room in Femoyer Hall at Virginia Tech.

17.8   References

1.   Berliner, D. C., Angell, D., and Shearer, J. W. Behaviors, Measures, and Instruments for Performance Evaluation in Simulated Environments. In Proceedings of *Symposium and Workshop on the Quantification of Human Performance* , 1964.

2.   Hartson, H. R., and Gray, P. D. Temporal Aspects of Tasks in the User Action Notation. *Human-Computer Interaction. 7* (1992), 1-45.

3.   Hartson, H. R., Siochi, A. C., and Hix, D. The UAN: A User-Oriented Representation for Direct Manipulation Interface Designs. *ACM Trans. on Info. Sys. 8*, 3 (July 1990), 181-203.

4.   Hix, D., and Hartson, H. R. *Developing User Interfaces: Ensuring Usability Through Product and Process*. John Wiley & Sons, Inc., New York, 1993.

5.   Kirwan, B., and Ainsworth, L. K. A Guide to Task Analysis. , 1992.

6.   Laurel, B. K. "Interface as mimesis." Chapter 4 in*User Centered System Design*. Norman and Draper ed. Erlbaum,   Hillsdale, NJ, 1986, 67-85.

7.   Lenorovitz, D. R., Phillips, M. D., Ardrey, R. S., and Kloster, G. V. "A Taxonomic Approach to Characterize Human-Computer Interfaces." *Human-Computer Interaction*. Salvendy ed. Elsevier Science Publishers B. V., Amsterdam, 1984, 111-116.

8.   Mayo, K. A. *Task Mapping Model (TMM) Analysis Manual: A Reference*. TR-93-07, Department of Computer Science, Virginia Tech (VPI&SU), Blacksburg, Virginia, 1993.

9.   Mayo, K. A., and Hartson, H. R. Synthesis-Oriented Situational Analysis in User Interface Design. In Proceedings of *EWHCI'93: Third East-West International Conference on Human-Computer Interaction* (Moscow, August 3-6)., 1993, 134-150.

10. Moran, T. P.   The Command Language Grammar: A Representation for the User Interface of Interactive Computer Systems. *Int. J. Man-Machine Studies. 15* (1981), 3-51.

11. Tauber, M. J. ETAG: Extended Task Action Grammar—A Language for the Description of the User's Task Language. In Proceedings of *IFIP Conference on Human-Computer Interaction—INTERACT'90*   Elsevier Science Publishers B.V. (North-Holland), Cambridge, U.K., August 27-31, 1990, 163-168.

12. Weller, H. G., and Hartson, H. R. Metaphors for the Nature of Human-Computer Interaction in an Empowering Environment: Interaction Style Influences the Manner of Human Accomplishment. *8* (1992), 313-333.

Part IV

Approaches to Formal Specification of
User Interfaces

18   Modelling Interaction Properties for Interactive Case Memories

A. M. Dearden
M. D. Harrison

ABSTRACT

Previous work on formal models for interactive systems has often used text editors and graphics editors as case studies. Consequently the notations developed do not necessarily include all the facilities that may be required in reasoning about other types of interactive system.

In this chapter two possible interaction requirements for an interactive knowledge based system (IKBS), user-initiated recoverability and user-initiated reachability are considered. A two-level model based on the work of Sufrin and He [18] is used to show how these requirements can be expressed formally using the Z notation. This model is unable to support the structuring of specifications from collections of interacting components. Three specification notations, which can support structured specification, are then compared in terms of their powers to express these interaction requirements. We show that none of the specially designed notations is capable of adequately expressing the interaction requirements of user-initiated reachability and user-initiated recoverability in ICMs, although all the notations have been successfully applied to the specification of other types of system.

18.1   Introduction

Previous work on formal expression of properties of interactive systems has often focussed on analysis of document editing, file management and graphical editing systems. Analysis of these systems has supported the development of models which are designed to support the expression of interaction properties, e.g. predictability, honesty, trustworthiness, and conformance [1, 18, 9].

Properties such a such as predictability (the confidence with which a user can predict the outcome of a sequence of operations on the system given the currently perceivable state) are important in systems where the user wishes to determine some result of the interaction completely, e.g. in a word processor or graphics package. However, properties which may be appropriate to document editing systems may not be appropriate to some other types of system. An interactive knowledge based system (IKBS) is a system, based on a model of some domain of knowledge, that interacts with a user in order to deliver advice based on that knowledge model. We should not expect an IKBS to be completely predictable, since if the user were able to predict the output of an IKBS for any given input, they would not need to use the IKBS. Conversely, some properties that are relevant to IKBS may not be so important to the design of document editing systems.

In this chapter we consider one particular type of IKBS, namely an Interactive Case Memory (ICM). ICMs are introduced in section 18.2. The properties we wish to express in a specification are drawn from an analysis of the application of ICMs to support diagnostic problem solving at a help-desk [2, 4]. Some of these properties have been identified by previous research as generally significant for the design of interfaces to IKBS. We compare three different specification notations, all related to the Z notation [17], and all offering the possibility of constructing systems from sets of interacting components, in terms of their powers to express two possible interaction requirements of ICMs. As a baseline we use the two-level model of interactive systems proposed by Sufrin and He [18] with which it is possible to express both requirements, but which does not support the construction of systems from sets of interacting components.

We believe our observations are relevant considerations for any notation designed to support the formal specification of interfaces to IKBS.

18.1.1 Structure of the rest of the chapter

Section 18.2 introduces the concepts of a case memory (CM) and an interactive case memory (ICM), and develops a basic model of the state of an ICM expressed in the Z notation. Section 18.3 develops a set of criteria for choosing a model for describing the interactive behaviour of ICMs. The criteria are based on general desiderata for interaction models, and on two particular interaction requirements that we may wish to specify in developing an ICM, namely user-initiated reachability and user-initiated recovery. Section 18.4 develops a model of an ICM based on the work of Sufrin and He [18], and shows how these interaction properties can be specified using that model. Section 18.5 compares three specification notations, all of which support modular development of interactive systems, in terms of their power to express the requirements identified in section 3, and examines the reasons why these notations are unable to express them. Section summary presents a summary of the results and our conclusions from the investigation.

18.2   Case Memories and ICMs

In this section we introduce the concept of a CM and an ICM as a subclass of IKBS, and describe some of the interaction properties that were identified as relevant in the help-desk case study.

18.2.1 Interactive case memories

Case based reasoning (CBR) is the process of using information from previous incidents to solve new problems. In general CBR involves interpreting the new problem, retrieving a set of stored cases that are judged to be similar (or useful), adapting the solution(s) of the retrieved cases to fit the new situation, and possibly testing and repairing the adapted solution. In recent years Knowledge Based Systems (KBS) based on CBR have gained in popularity and CBR has been successfully applied to a number of commercial and industrial problems [13, 10].

A Case Memory (CM) is a separable software module which conducts the tasks of case storage, problem interpretation, and similarity assessment.

Most CMs developed to date have been based on the assumption that the new problem situation is fully described by a single input to the system [14]. In practical applications this may not be true. For example, if a CM is used in supporting the problem solving operations of a telephone based help-desk, the information about a new problem must be collected incrementally by questioning the customer [2, 4]. An ICM is a system that interacts with a human user in order to collect information about the current problem, interpret the problem and retrieve stored cases. ICMs are a type of IKBS. For an example of an ICM applied to help-desk problem solving see [13].

18.2.2 An initial model for a CM based on Z

Previous work [5] has resulted in the development of a model for CMs which is sufficiently general to model the majority of CMs which have been reported to date. The model enables important properties identified by the CBR research community to be explicated.

The model is based on three sets, Descriptions, Reports and Problem Statements.

† Cases are indexed by elements from the set of Descriptions D.

† The content of a case can be modelled by an item from a set Reports,R. A case is then a Description-Report pair.

† A case base (CB) is a set of cases, or alternatively a relation between D and R. In our help-desk example a description may be lists of symptoms, and a report may be a possible diagnosis, the case base would be the mapping from sets of symptoms to diagnoses.

† A new case is represented by a single statement of the current problem which is modelled as an element from the set of problem statements, *PS*.

† A CM consists of: an enquiry function, Q, which takes as input a CB and a *PS* and returns some ordering over a subset of the CB, together with a particular case base.

We can now give a general description of a CM.

CM _____
| *Cb* : P *Cases*
| *Q* : (D ! R) £ PS ! (*Cases* $ *Cases*)
|_____
| 8 C :D ! R; P :PS †
| Q (C ;P) 2 *Orderings* ^
| dom (Q (C ;P)) [ran (Q (C ;P))   C

In this definition the enquiry function Q takes as input a CB and a PS and returns an ordering over the cases. The definition of orderings used allows for many types of ordering including total ordering, the selection of a single 'best case', or a partial ordering. For details of the model see [3].

The state of an ICM is defined by including a CM, and having a specific value for the current problem statement and a value for the current case ordering.

ICMstate _____
| *CM*
| *currP* :*PS*
| *currCs* :*Cases* $ *Cases*
|_____
| *currCs* = Q (Cb ;currP)

The statement(s) below the middle line of the schema denote invariant constraints that must be satisfied by any ICMstate.

Only three operations will be discussed with regard to the state of an ICM. One operation, change_PS will alter the current value of currP, and consequently update currCs. The operation reset will return the ICM to some initial state. Finally, in some models, a display operation may inform the user of the current state of the case ordering in the ICM. For the purposes of this discussion it is not necessary to specify these operations in detail.

This basic model will be used in sections 18.4 and 18.5 as the basis for developing models of ICMs.

18.3   Requirements for a model of ICMs

In this section we consider what requirements we may have of a software engineering model to support the development of an ICM.

18.3.1   General requirements

It is generally accepted that specifications of interactive systems should model both the state and the behaviour of the system [9, 1, 18]. It is also generally agreed that software engineering notations should support the development of a system in parts or modules. Also it is necessary in an interactive system to reason separately about the state of the system, and that subset of the state that is actually communicated to the user at any time. A suitable notation should support some distinction between these elements.

18.3.2   Interaction requirements for IKBS

During the 1980s a number of critiques of the interfaces to first generation IKBS were developed, for examples see [12] or [16]. An important property which these critiques identified as lacking in first generation IKBS is mixed-initiative dialogue. The dialogue in first generation IKBS tended to follow a question and answer format. The user of the IKBS was expected to act as a data gatherer, while the KBS decided what factors needed investigating and in what order. Throughout the consultation the IKBS kept the initiative. The user was not able to enter observations which they felt were important, or to propose alternative hypotheses for the IKBS to focus on. This limitation not only reduced the acceptability of the system to users [12], but also reduced the problem solving capability of the system and user working together [16].

Analysis of a help-desk application [2] illustrates the importance of flexible dialogue. When a customer first contacts the help-desk any possible previous case may be relevant. As more information is collected the set of cases will be reduced, and cases which at one stage are incomparable may be ordered with respect to one another. This process may be described as *converging* on a case or subset of cases.

It may be that the help-desk operator (HDO) sees a case displayed by the system which they believe is applicable. We may require:

> **reachability** – for any case that is currently displayed in the output case ordering, there is some sequence of operations on the system that will result in that case being brought to the top of the ordering[1].

Notice that this statement requires that the model can discuss the set *possible* future behaviours of the system, without specifying that the user or the system will *necessarily* perform the sequence of actions.

Occasionally the system may converge on a case that is not applicable. This is similar to the problem of finding local maxima in a state-space search. In these situations the HDO may wish to return the system to some prior state in which the HDO remembers having seen a more applicable case. The HDO could then proceed by following a different line of questioning. We may therefore require:

> **recoverability** – for any previous state within the current consultation (i.e. since the last reset operation was performed) there should be some sequence of operations which will return the system to that state.

Finally, both the above properties demand that a sequence of operations should exist but do not discuss the question of how these operations are to be initiated. To fully specify these properties we should also require that the sequence of operations can be initiated by the HDO. Any suitable model for the specification of ICMs must include a distinction between operations initiated by the system and operations initiated by the user. The requirements stated above would then become:

---

[1]In this case *top of the ordering* would be defined to mean that no other case was presented as more relevant than the selected case

user-initiated reachability – for any case which is currently displayed in the output case ordering, there is some sequence of operations that can be initiated by the user which will result in that case being brought to the top of the ordering.

user-initiated recovery – for any previous state within the current consultation there is some sequence of operations that can be initiated by the user which will return the system to that state.

Below we shall assess the ability of various models of interactive systems to express user-initiated recovery and user-initiated reachability.

18.4   A basic model of an ICM process

In this section we use a model based on the work of Sufrin and He [18] to describe an ICM. The model is two-level, in the sense that it uses the state based model of Z (above) as one part of the specification, and then generates a supplementary specification for the behaviour of the ICM, again specified in Z but using the state model as a type. Using this model it is possible to derive formal expressions of the user-initiated recovery and user-initiated reachability. However the behavioural level does not adequately support the structuring of a specification in terms of a set of interacting components.

18.4.1   Sufrin and He's model

Sufrin and He (1990) show how Z can be used to model interactive processes in terms of their sequences of behaviours. To specify a system using Sufrin and He's model we begin with a Z specification of the state and operations that may alter the state.

The behavioural level describes an interactive process in terms of: an alphabet of events in which the process can engage; a behaviour function which relates the set of events to a set of state transitions; an initial state; and a set of traces which specifies what sequences of events are legal traces of the system. Initiative can be described by defining two disjoint subsets of operations on the system, one labelled commands (to indicate user initiated events) and one labelled display (to indicate a display initiated by the system). Further subsets are also described in [18] but are not relevant to our discussion.

To describe the interactive behaviours in which the process might engage constraints can be imposed on the set Trace. Sufrin and He suggest using CSP operators [11] to define the Traces constructively.

For a model of an ICM as a process we use the existing definition of ICMstates given above. We then define an ICMprocess using the following schema:

```
ICMprocess
    command : P E
    display : P E
    fi : P E
    fî : E !7 (ICMstates ! ICMstates)
    ¶ : ICMstates
    Trace : P (seq E)
    fi = dom fî
    display   fi ^ command   fi ^ display \ command = ?
    hi 2 Trace
    8 t₁ ;t₂ : seq E † t₁ ª t₂ 2 Trace )   t₁ 2 Trace
```

We refer to the general structure of this type of schema as a *Process schema*. Sufrin and He define a number of different Process schemata. We have made two minor changes to the model given by [18] by demanding that the behaviour function be deterministic (mapping each event to a function between states rather than a relation), and only one initial state is represented rather than a power set of possible initial states. These changes simplify our later discussion.

The constraints on the ICMprocess schema are that:

† the alphabet, fi, must be the same as the set of events for which state transitions are defined by the behaviour fî;

† the command (those events initiated by the user) and display events are disjoint subsets of the alphabet of possible operations;

† the empty sequence is always a legal trace of the system;

† and any prefix of a legal trace must itself be a legal trace of the system.

To define the behaviour function fî we require that the state transitions associated with all the possible inputs be specified as constraints on the schema ICMprocess. This can be done by describing the state and operations of the system in the normal way as one would for a Z specification, then generating a set of tagged functions defined in terms of schema bindings, which represent the functions in *ICMstates ! ICMstates* corresponding to each possible operation. Finally we map the possible events in fi to the state transition functions. Each possible event-input pair generating an additional constraint on the function fî. Details of the construction are given in [18].

Reachability and recoverability

Using Sufrin and He's model we can express recoverability and reachability and ensure that these state transitions are initiated by the user. To do so we shall need some auxiliary machinery which allows the behaviour function fî to be generalised to a function from sequences of events to state transitions.

Firstly a generic function *map* is defined. *map* takes each element of the list to its image under the function f.

$$[X;Y]$$
$$map : (X \nrightarrow Y) \pounds \operatorname{seq} X ! \operatorname{seq} Y$$

$$8 f : X \nrightarrow Y; s : \operatorname{seq} X; i : \mathbb{N} \mid i \bullet \# s \dagger$$
$$map (f;s) \, i = f (s \, i))$$

The next function fl generalises the behaviour function $\hat{fl}$ to a function that describes the behaviour of the ICM in response to a sequence of events.

$$fl : \operatorname{seq} E \nrightarrow (ICMstates ! ICMstates)$$

$$fl (es) = \underset{9}{\circ} = (map (\hat{fl}; es)))$$

Here $\underset{9}{\circ} =$ represents the distributed composition of functions. Mapping $\hat{fl}$ over a sequence of events *es* produces a sequence of state transition functions. Composing these functions using $\underset{9}{\circ} =$ generates the single function fl that corresponds to the sequential application of the transition functions associated with the events in *es*. Given some original state and a sequence of events fl maps the original state to a new state which is reached by applying the associated sequence of transitions.

Three projection functions that extract different parts of the state of an ICM will be useful in the later discussion. These are:

$$case\_order : ICMstates ! (Cases \, \$ \, Cases)$$
$$top : ICMstates ! \ \mathbb{P} \, Cases$$
$$shown : ICMstates ! \ \mathbb{P} \, Cases$$

$$8 (Cb; Q; currP; currCs) : ICMstate \dagger$$
$$case\_order (Cb; Q; currP; currCs) = currCs$$
$$shown (Cb; Q; currP; currCs) \quad \operatorname{dom} currCs \, [\, \operatorname{ran} currCs$$
$$top (Cb; Q; currP; currCs) = fc_1 : \operatorname{dom} currCs \, [\, \operatorname{ran} currCs \, j$$
$$(8 c_2 : Cases \dagger (c_2; c_1) \, 2 \, currCs) \quad (c_1; c_2) \, 2 \, currCs) g$$

Here *case_order* selects the current case ordering, *shown* represents that subset of cases which are presented to the user, and *top* is the set of cases which are at depth 0 in the case ordering.

Given the definition of fl we can define the reachability of any case in the case ordering by requiring:

$$8 t : Trace; c : Cases \mid c \, 2 \, shown (fl (t) \, f0) \dagger$$
$$(9 t^0 : \operatorname{seq} E \mid t \, \hat{} \, t^0 \, 2 \, Trace \dagger c \, 2 \, top (fl (t \, \hat{} \, t^0) \, f0)))$$

That is, for any *t* in Trace which leads to a state in which the case *c* is shown, there is some sequence of events t^0 such that extending *t* by t^0 gives a legal trace of the system, and that *c* is brought to the top of the ordering by that trace.

To restrict this statement to express user-initiated reachability we can restrict the sequence of events *t* to ensure:

1. that so long as the user initiates the same sequence of commands the result is guaranteed;

2. and that the user can always complete the necessary command sequence.

$8\, t\ :Trace;\ c\ :Cases\ jc\ 2\ shown\ (\text{fl}\,(t)\ \text{\textcircled{0}}\ )\,\dagger$

$(9\ comms\ :seq\ command\ \dagger$

$(8\ t_1\ :seq\ E\ jt_1\ _{\,\text{\tiny n}}\,command = comms\ {}^\wedge t\ {}^a\ t_1\ 2\ Trace\ \dagger$

$\qquad\qquad c\ 2\ top\ (\text{fl}\,(t\ {}^a\ t_1)\ \text{\textcircled{0}}\ )^\wedge$

$(8\ t_2\ :seq\ E\ jt_2\ _{\,\text{\tiny n}}\,command\ \underset{\text{\tiny c}}{}\ comms\ {}^\wedge t\ {}^a\ t_2\ 2\ Trace\ \dagger$

$\qquad (9\ t_3\ :seq\ E\ \dagger$

$\qquad\qquad (t_2\ {}^a\ t_3)\ _{\,\text{\tiny n}}\,command = comms\ {}^\wedge t\ {}^a\ t_2\ {}^a\ t_3\ 2\ Trace)\,)\,)$

Here $a\ \underset{\text{\tiny c}}{}\ b$ denotes that sequence a is a prefix of b. The function $_{\,\text{\tiny n}}$ restricts a sequence to the elements of the sequence that are in a given set. Thus $t\ _{\,\text{\tiny n}}commands$ is the sequence of commands that is embedded within t.

The statement of user-initiated recoverability to any state in the current consultation (i.e. any state since the last reset operation was performed) can be similarly expressed as:

$8\, t\,;t^0\ :seq\, E;\ s_1\,;s_2\ :ICMstate\ jt\ {}^a\ t^0\ 2\ Trace\ {}^\wedge$

$s_1 = \text{fl}\,(t)\ \text{\textcircled{0}}\ {}^\wedge\ s_2 = \text{fl}\,(t^0)\ (s_1)$

$s_1\ 6\ s_2\ {}^\wedge\ reset\ 6\,\text{2\!ran}\ t^0\ \dagger$

$(9\ comms\ :seq\ command\ jreset\ 6\,\text{2\!comms}\ \dagger$

$(8\ t_1\ :seq\, E\ jt_1\ _{\,\text{\tiny n}}\,command = comms\ {}^\wedge t\ {}^a\ t^{0a}\ t_1\ 2\ Trace\ \dagger$

$\qquad\qquad \text{fl}\,(t_1)\ (s_2) = s_1)\,)^\wedge$

$(8\ t_2\ :seq\, E\ jt_2\ _{\,\text{\tiny n}}\,command\ \underset{\text{\tiny c}}{}\ comms\ {}^\wedge t\ {}^a\ t^{0a}\ t_2\ 2\ Trace\ \dagger$

$\qquad (9\ t_3\ :seq\, E\ \dagger$

$\qquad\qquad (t_2\ {}^a\ t_3)\ _{\,\text{\tiny n}}\,command = comms\ {}^\wedge t\ {}^a\ t^{0a}\ t_2\ {}^a\ t_3\ 2\ Trace)\,)\,)$

That is: for any pair of states $s_1\,;s_2$ such that s_2 can be reached from s_1 by some sequence of events t^0 (where $t\ {}^a\ t^0$ is a legal trace of the system) which does not include the reset operation, there is a sequence of commands $comms$ that does not include the reset operation, and that is guaranteed to return the ICM to the original state s_1, whatever events are initiated by the system. The predicate that applies to $comms$ states firstly that any legal trace of the system that embeds $comms$ must have the desired outcome, and secondly that if the user performs any prefix of $comms$ then it is still possible for the user to complete this command sequence.

18.4.2 Limitations of Sufrin and He's model

Sufrin and He's model thus allows the properties of user-initiated recovery and user-initiated reachability to be expressed.

The major drawback of Sufrin and He's model is that no mechanism is provided to allow the structuring a specification as a collection of components. The standard schema calculus of Z is insufficient since there are no rules to describe how the state sets of two Process schemata should be related. Also the schema calculus does not describe how a new behaviour function could be constructed from two behaviour functions which would be of different types (one behaviour function being defined over the state set of each Process).

It is therefore inadequate as a basis for a general notation to support the specification of IKBS.

18.5   Three notations for describing interactive systems

In this section we compare three notations which attempt to describe state and behaviour of a system at a single level and provide mechanisms to support the construction of systems from sets of interacting components. All three notations are related to Z.

The first notation, Object-Z [8] supports the definition of components of a system using *classes*. The definition of a class includes definitions of the allowable operations on an object of the class and a constraint on the permitted behaviour of class objects expressed using a temporal logic.

The second notation, the Agent Language [1], was constructed to demonstrate the possibility of creating notations for describing interactive systems by combining existing notations. An agent includes a definition of the state of the agent and operations on that state, a constraint on the behaviour of the agent expressed using a subset of CSP [11], and a communication component which relates the operations on the state to the messages and channels of the behavioural component.

The final notation, by Duke and Harrison [6], supports the description of a system as a collection of Interactors.

For each notation an outline of a possible definition of an ICM is given and the possibility of describing user-initiated recovery and user-initiated reachability within the notation is considered.

18.5.1   Object orientation and Object-Z

An outline specification of an ICM class in Object-Z is given below.

$$
\begin{array}{|l|}
\hline
\textit{ICMclass} \underline{\hspace{6cm}} \\
\hline
\quad
\begin{array}{|l|}
\hline
Q : \mathbb{P}\,Cases \,!\; PS \,!\; (Cases \,\$\; Cases) \\
currP : PS \\
currCs : Cases \,\$\; Cases \\
Cb : \mathbb{P}\,Cases \\
\hline
8\,C : D \,!\; R; P : PS \dagger Q\,(C;P)\, 2\; Orderings\; \hat{}\\
\qquad\qquad \mathrm{dom}\,(Q\,(C;P)\,) \,[\; \mathrm{ran}\,(Q\,(C;P)\,) \quad C \\
currCs = Q\,(Cb;currP) \\
\hline
\end{array} \\[2mm]
\quad
\begin{array}{|l|}
\hline
\textit{INIT} \underline{\hspace{5cm}} \\
\hline
currP = initP \\
\hline
\end{array} \\[2mm]
\quad
\begin{array}{|l|}
\hline
\textit{change\_PS} \underline{\hspace{4.5cm}} \\
\; -currP ; currCs \\
\; e? : Events \\
\hline
currCs^{0} = Q\,(Cb;currP^{0}) \\
\hline
\end{array} \\[2mm]
\quad
\begin{array}{l}
\vdots \\
\vdots \\
\hline
/\;(currP\;6\;initP\;)\qquad (Cb^{0} = Cb)\,) \\
\end{array} \\
\hline
\end{array}
$$

The specification of the ICM class includes:

† a state invariant, which is equivalent to the schema ICMstate in section 18.2;

† a set of initial states, in this case the single state in which the input problem statement is some initial value;

† a set of operations, only one of which, change_PS is shown in the above class, the prime ^{0} decoration in the operation denotes that the predicate is referring state of the *currCs* and *currP* after the operation has taken place;

† and a history predicate which constrains the possible behaviours of instances of the class, in this case the history invariant states that it is always the case that if the current value of the problem statement is not the initial value then in the next state the CB will unchanged.

Assessing Object-Z

Object-Z provides a model of both state and behaviour. The syntax of the history invariant allows elements of the state to be included in a history expression. However, it is not possible to express the property that any case that the user can see can be reached by some sequence of events, because the temporal logic selected is based on a linear model of time. The statement

$$\diagup \; (c \; 2 \; (\text{dom} \, currCs \, [\; \text{ran} \, currCs) \,) \quad \S \, c \; 2 \; top \, (currCs^0) \,)$$

would be interpreted as requiring that at some future state c would *necessarily* be included at the top of the case ordering. The user would not be able to prevent such an event happening.

The selection of a linear temporal logic is appropriate for the types of re-active objects that the Object-Z language was developed to model. To model possibility would require a branching time temporal logic. Paterno' & Faconti [15] demonstrate the application of a branching time temporal logic to the specification of interactive systems. However the logic used by Paterno' and Faconti, ACTL, is a propositional rather than a predicate logic so it cannot support reasoning about predicates on the state of a system.

A further limitation of Object-Z is that, although the operations can include input or output parameters, it does not represent the initiator of any operation explicitly. It is therefore not possible to discuss any properties related to initiative.

18.5.2   The Agent Language

Abowd [1] builds on the work in Sufrin and He to define the Agent Language specifically for the specification of interactive systems. Each agent is described in three parts:

† of an internal specification which describes components of the state, invariants which apply to the state, and the operations which the agent can engage in;

† an external specification which describes the behaviour using components of CSP;

† and a communication specification which links operations on the state to named channels, which are typed as input, output, or hidden.

An outline for an agent to describe an ICM is shown below.

```
agent ICMagent
internal
    attributes
        T :PS ! Descriptions
        Q :P Cases ! PS ! (Cases $ Cases)
        currP :PS
        currCs :Cases $ Cases
        Cb :P Cases
    invariant
        8 C :Descriptions $ Reports; P :PS †
            Q (C;P) 2 Orderings
        dom (Q (C;P) ) [ ran (Q (C;P) )    C
        currCs = Q (Cb ;currP )
    operations
        changePS (newP :PS)
            change (currP ;currCs)
            pre true
            post currP = newP
:
:
communication
    input keyboard :changePS (newP :PS);reset ( )
    output screen :display (Cs :Cases $ Cases)
external
    „ X † ( (keyboard ;changePS (newP :PS) V (keyboard ;reset ( ) ) ]
            screen display (Cs :Cases $ Cases) ! X )
satisfying
    8 t :Trace †
        # t „ £displayg • # t „ £changePS ;resetg • # t „ £displayg + 1
endagent ICMagent
```

The internal specification of the ICMagent corresponds to the schema ICMstates together with some operations, only one of which, changePS, is shown. The communication component ties each operation to a particular channel. The external specification requires that the traces are made up of recursive invocations (denoted by „ X † f (X)) of a changePS or reset event followed by a display event. Also all possible traces for the ICMagent must satisfy the predicate that the number of changePS and reset events can only ever be equal to or one greater than the number of display events.

Assessing the Agent Language

The agent language specifically includes devices for combining agents to form larger agents.

The communication specification could be used to ensure that changes to the PS could only be performed on an input channel, by using labels such as *keyboard* or *mouse*. The display operation is similarly tied to the channel screen.

The agent language was developed as a prototype to demonstrate the way in which a language for describing interactive systems might be constructed from existing notations. The language chosen to specify the external behaviour of the agent is a subset of CSP. Because CSP is used, the description of the behaviour of an agent can only refer to operations, not to components of the agent's state. Consequently it is not possible to state that the system can reach a state satisfying some predicate, as is required for user-initiated reachability; or that it can recover some previous state.

The agent language supports the distinction between user and system initiative for single operations. Whether this mechanism can be used to specify other initiative based properties in general is more difficult to assess. As we shall see below the labelling of individual operations as initiated by one agent or another is not, in itself, sufficient to describe user-initiated reachability or user-initiated recoverability.

18.5.3   Interactors

A number of models of interactive systems based on the concept of Interactors have been proposed [7]. As a part of the AMODEUS II project Duke & Harrison have developed a Z based notation to describe interactors [6]. Duke & Harrison do not give a name to the basic unit of a specification in their notation, so the term interactor is used ambiguously here to refer both to the notion of an interaction object (an implementation) and to the notational unit used to describe the object.

An ICM could be described using this notation as follows:

$$
\begin{array}{l}
\textit{ICMinteractor} \\
\hline
\quad Q : (D ! R) ! PS ! (Cases \$ Cases) \\
\quad Cb : \mathrm{P}\, Cases \\
\verb|^| \; currP : PS \\
\quad currCs : Cases \$ Cases \\
\verb|^| \; shown : \mathrm{P}\, Cases \\
\hline
\mathrm{O}\; change\_PS \\
\mathrm{M}\; inform \\
\hline
\quad currP = initP \\
\quad 8\, p : PS \,\dagger \\
\quad / (currP = p \;\verb|^|\; (currP^0 \subseteq p)) \\
\qquad\qquad (shown^{00} = top (currCs^{09} \;\verb|^|\; currP^{00} = currP^c))
\end{array}
$$

The specification of the ICMinteractor includes three main sections.

The first section declares components of the state of the interactor. The ^ symbol denotes the fact that the set of cases shown and the current value of the problem statement are visible representations of parts of the state. The invariant that apply to this state are expressed by a separate box labelled *ICMinteractor : inv*. The invariants would be equivalent to the standard invariants in the schema *ICMstates*.

The second section names two operations, change_PS and inform. The change_PS operation is annotated by O to indicate that it is an operation in which the the interactor can participate, but which it does not initiate. The M annotation for the inform operation indicates that it is an operation initiated by the interactor. A full specification would define each of these operations in a similar manner to the definition of operations in Z. For details see [6].

The final section describes an invariant on the behaviour of the interactor. The prime ^{0}notation referring to state elements after one state transition, and ^{00}after two transitions etc. This invariant includes a predicate describing the initial state of the interactor, i.e. that the value of *currP* is some initial value *initP*. It also includes a temporal predicate which states that in the future it is always the case that if the value of *currP* changes between one state and the next, then the next state change will result in *shown* being changed to be the set of cases at the top of the lattice, and the value of currP will be unchanged.

State invariants that hold at all times for an interactor are not included in the main interactor definition, but are recorded in a separate notational unit.

Assessing the interactors model

Duke and Harrison's notation allows explicit representation of state and behaviour, and allows state to be referenced within behavioural predicates. The notation also supports a model of initiative by indicating the initiators of actions. The notation separates perceivable components of the state from hidden components. Also the notation provides a structuring mechanism by allowing operations to be defined separately from the basic state model, and by allowing interactors to be combined to form larger interactors.

The only limitation with respect to the criteria identified in section 18.3, is that the temporal logic used to express constraints on behaviour is based on a linear time model rather than a branching time model. Thus, as with Object-Z it is not possible to state the possibility of reaching particular states.

If a branching time temporal logic were introduced to the Interactors notation the suitability of the notation for our purposes might be improved. Using the symbols G *generally in all futures*, F *in one possible future*, X *in a possible next state*, we could state reachability as:

$$G\ (\ c\ 2\ shown)\ )\quad (F\ c\ 2\ top\ (currCs)\ )\ )$$

Unfortunately this statement still cannot be refined to state user-initiated reachability within Duke and Harrison's model because the logic does not provide a means for discussing the set of operations that might lead to such a state change. Thus although the Interactors model includes a notational device to indicate the initiator of individual actions, it is not possible to consider concepts of initiative over an extended dialogue.

18.6   Summary and conclusions

None of the single-level notations surveyed can be used to express the desired properties of user-initiated reachability and user-initiated recovery.

† Object-Z lacks a representation for discussing initiative, and uses an inappropriate logic for discussing behaviour.

† The Agent Language supports structuring of specifications, separates input and output channels to an agent, but does not allow predicates over the state to be included in the behavioural specification.

† The Interactors model of [6] includes a notational device to indicate the initiator of an action but the logic used to describe behaviour, which is similar to that used in Object-Z, cannot be used to specify initiative over a sequence of actions.

It seems that the goal of devising a single-level formalism which supports specification of both the state and behaviour of interactive systems, allows systems to be constructed from interacting components and supports reasoning about properties such as user-initiative, reachability and recoverability, has not been achieved in any of the models surveyed. An important theoretical question is whether it is possible to construct a (usable) formal specification language that: uses the full power of predicate logic to specify state transitions; supports reasoning over sequences of states; and can be used to structure a specification as a collection of related components. If this is not theoretically possible then we must consider the consequences for the application of formal specification techniques to the design and specification of IKBS and other complex interactive systems.

Acknowledgements:

The authors would like to thank David Duke for many conversations during the development of this work. Andrew Dearden is supported by a CASE studentship from SERC and BTplc.

18.7 References

[1] Gregory D. Abowd. *Formal Aspects of Human-Computer Interaction*. PhD thesis, Unversity of Oxford, 1991.

[2] Derek G. Bridge and Andrew M. Dearden. Knowledge based systems support for help desk operations: A reference model. *Int. J. Systems Research and Information Science*, 5:217 – 234, 1992.

[3] Andrew M. Dearden. The engineering of interactive case memories. DPhil 2nd year report, University of York, Department of Computer Science, September 1993.

[4] Andrew M. Dearden and Derek G. Bridge. Choosing a knowledge based system to support a help desk. *Knowledge Engineering Review*, 8(3):201 – 222, 1993.

[5] Andrew M. Dearden and Michael D. Harrison. A software engineering model for co-operative case memory systems. In M. M. Richter, S. Wess, K.-D. Althoff, and F. Maurer, editors, *Pre-prints from the First European Workshop on Case Based Reasoning*, pages 354 – 359, 1993.

[6] D. J. Duke and M. D. Harrison. Connections from A(V) to Z. Technical Report System Modelling/WP21, AMODEUS II project, ESPRIT Basic Research Action 7040, January 1994.

[7] D.J. Duke, G. Faconti, M.D. Harrison, and F. Paterno'. Unifying views of interactors. In *Proc. International Workshop on Advanced Visual Interfaces*. ACM Press, 1994. To appear.

[8] Roger Duke, Paul King, Gordon Rose, and Graeme Smith. The Object-Z specification language version 1. Technical Report 91-1, Key Centre for Software Technology, Department of Computer Science, University of Queensland, May 1991.

[9] Michael Harrison. Engineering human-error tolerant software. In J. E. Nicholls, editor, *Z User Workshop 91*, pages 191 – 204. Springer Verlag, 1992.

[10] David Hennessy and David Hinkle. Applying case based reasoning to autoclave loading. *IEEE Expert*, October:21 – 26, 1992.

[11] C. A. R. Hoare. *Communicating Sequential Processes*. Prentice-Hall, 1985.

[12] E. T. Keravnou and L. Johnson. *Competent Expert Systems*. Kogan Page, 1986.

[13] Phil Klahr and Gary Vrooman. Commercialising case based reasoning technology. In I. M. Graham and R. W. Milne, editors, *Research and Development in Expert Systems VIII*, pages 18 – 24. Cambridge University Press, 1991.

[14] Christopher Owens. Integrating feature extraction and memory search. *Machine Learning*, 10:311 – 339, 1993.

[15] Fabio Paterno'. Definition of properties of user interfaces using action-based temporal logic. In *Proceedings of the Fifth Internation Conference on Software Engineering and Knowledge Engineering*, 1993.

[16] E. M. Roth, K. B. Bennett, and D. D. Woods. Human interaction with an 'intelligent' machine. In E. Hollnagel, G. Mancini, and D. D. Woods, editors, *Cognitive Engineering in Complex Dynamic Worlds*, pages 23–69. Acedemic Press, 1988.

[17] J. M. Spivey. *The Z Notation: A reference manual*. Prentice Hall, 1989.

[18] B. Sufrin and J. He. Specification, refinement and analysis of interactive processes. In M. D. Harrison and H. W. Thimbleby, editors, *Formal Methods in Human-Computer Interaction*, chapter 6. Cambridge University Press, 1990.

19   LADA — A Logic for the Analysis of Distributed Actions

Alan Dix

Abstract

This paper presents a formalism, LADA, aimed especially at the description of systems and situations which arise during the design and analysis of groupware. We are particularly interested in highly distributed systems and so LADA explicitly models entities (people and things) acting at different unconnected locations. It not only describes the behaviour of the computer software, but also the social protocols required for its successful use. Temporal logic formulae which follow the subjective history of people and other entities are used to simplify the expression of some of the complicated properties required of real systems.

19.1   Introduction

Groupware systems are often distributed either over local area networks or over wider distances. In addition, some systems operate on computers which rarely or never directly communicate over a network, instead relying on email or floppy disk transfers. Traditional distributed systems try to minimise the interference between multiple users and even multiple processes, for example, by locking mechanisms. However, *cooperation* between users suggests that this emphasis on transparency is unacceptable and it is replaced by a desire for mutual awareness [9]. Furthermore, traditional distributed systems rarely deal with systems with infrequent communications (although there have been some recent exceptions notable the Coda File System [8]).

Given these extra complications, it is not surprising that groupware systems are difficult to program and even more difficult to debug. In addition, the consequences of crashes are also more serious as they affect many users simultaneously and may reduce confidence in what are often already socially fragile systems [6, 4, Ch. 13].

One would obviously like some form of argument or proof that the central algorithms of these systems behave as required. Unfortunately, such arguments tend to be very complex also as one has to consider all possible combinations of events, including 'race conditions' and the possibility of deadlock. It is even difficult to state precisely what the requirements are of a system involving several users distributed over several sites.

One would like to use formal arguments to verify correctness, but most popular formalisms for describing and reasoning about software concentrate on single-threaded systems. Even notations for handling concurrent processes, such as CSP [7], do not deal with issues of distribution and operate at a very low-level.

In addition to these requirements on the computer software, the behaviour of the entire groupware system (human and machine) depends on the participants. Designers make explicit and implicit assumptions about their use of the software. For example, it may be assumed that participants never simultaneously work on the same portion of a document. The designer ought to be able to clearly state what assumptions are being made about these *social protocols* and also investigate the consequences when these assumptions fail.

This paper presents a formalism designed especially for describing actions which happen to people and things at different places. It draws on standard temporal logic, but allows one to trace the subjective experience of each person or thing, rather than a single objective history. The augmented temporal logic is itself built upon a semantic model of partially ordered events. The model and logic are presented at a semi-formal level as there is not room for the full formal semantics and it seemed more valuable to explore a worked example.

In the next section we will consider some of the systems which we would like to describe more formally. This is followed by two sections describing the underlying model and the temporal logic based on it. The major bulk of the paper is an extended example: specifying the Liveware database and giving a sketch proof of one form of observational consistency. Finally, we will return to look at some of the wider issues this example raises about LADA itself and specification in this complex domain.

19.2   Background — cooperating at a distance

If two users are cooperating over the same document (spreadsheet, etc.), but are not working at the same site, they can obviously all have copies on their own local machine. However, if several users simultaneously update copies of the same document, problems arise. Systems for asynchronous group working must either prevent such conflicts by the use of locking or include support to handle the multiple versions which arise.

One example is Liveware [11]. This is a database which is shared by the merging of copies as colleagues meet one another. Changes to the database made by one user gradually spread throughout the community of users as different copies of the database meet and merge with one another. A more complex example of a similar principle is multiple source control [1, 3]. This uses version control mechanisms to allow users to update different copies of the same document at different sites. This causes several 'streams' of activity for the same document which can be merged with automated help. In order to avoid sending whole copies of the document, the communication between different sites uses *deltas*, that is differences between versions of the document.

Among commercial systems similar issues arise. Laplink™, the popular PC file transfer tool, allows two file systems to be synchronised based on the date of last update: if the same file exists on both systems, the system overwrites the older version. Of course, if the file has been updated on both file systems, the least recent of the two updates will be lost. Similarly, Lotus Notes™ may have several servers with copies of the same database. If a note is updated on two servers then one update may be lost. This problem is partially ameliorated by the addition of a versioning feature whereby both copies of a note are retained. Although this means that the information is not lost there are potential social conflicts. Imagine that Alison and Brian have each updated the same note on two different servers, but that Alison's update preceded Brian's. After the servers synchronise Alison will find that her updates have been superseded by Brian's. She may wrongfully conclude that Brian actually saw her updates and then rudely ignored them.

This work is being carried out in the context of a project to investigate the use of version support in CSCW systems, and the we believe that the use of appropriate versioning offers the potential to detect such conflicts and offer the participants help in resolving them. However, more complex support system could just mean that problems have simply been put off and will reappear in more complex situations. This emphasises the need for methods to verify that any new systems we propose both work as required and are robust when the social protocols upon which they depend are broken.

Although the principal emphasis in this paper is on asynchronous groupware, the needs in synchronous groupware can be equally pressing. Whenever a system has decentralised control there will be potential for simultaneous conflicting actions. For example, in the Grove synchronous editor, complex algorithms are necessary so that typing can be immediately echoed, but also so that all participants eventually see the same text [5].

19.3   The semantic model

Standard temporal logic and also mathematical time series are based on a linear model of time. A history is modelled as a sequence of states of the world at different times.[1]

$$S_0 \rightarrow S_1 \rightarrow S_2 \rightarrow S_3 \rightarrow S_4$$

Temporal logic operators can then be used to talk about such an history, for example, '$\Diamond P$' says 'eventually P is true' or in other words there is some time t for which P holds in the state at that time (S_t). Given such a model we are forced to specify the order in which all actions have happened. For a synchronous system this is reasonable, but for asynchronous groupware this would hide the very issues we want to discuss, namely simultaneous actions in different locations.

We have therefore adopted a model based on a partially ordered set of events. Each event is the occurrence of an action involving one or more entities, which may be human or machine. Events are only ordered where there is some explicit dependency between them, for example if some entity is involved in both events.

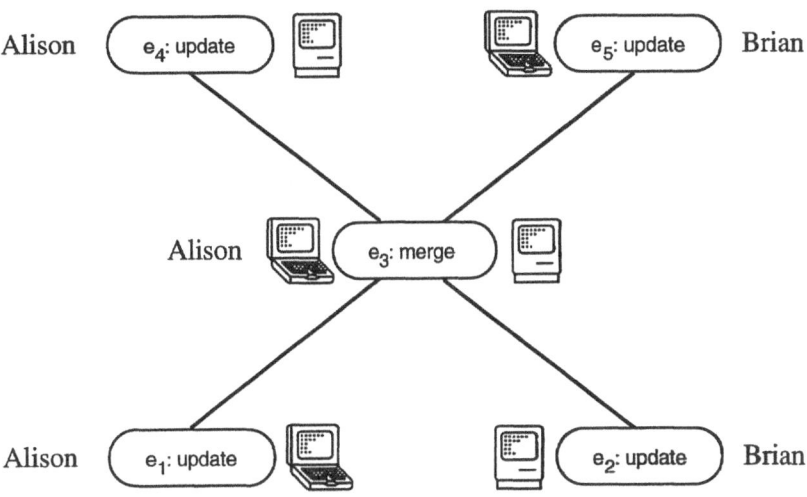

FIGURE 19.1. Event lattice

19.3.1.   The lattice of events

In Figure 19.1, Alison and Brian are working on a document together. Initially Alison is working at home updating the document on the mobile computer, whilst Brian is working on the office computer. Event 'e_1' represents Alison's work and 'e_2' represents Brian's work. Later Alison brings the portable into the office and merges the two versions (event 'e_3'). The next day Alison continues to work in the office, but Brian takes the portable to work on the train. Each update the documents during the day on the two machines (the events 'e_4' and 'e_5' respectively).

The diagram shows the partial order between the events so, for example, e_1 happens before e_3 ($e_1 \text{ p } e_3$) and $e_3 \text{ p } e_5$, but we cannot say anything about the order of e_1 and e_2. This is not just a matter of e_1 and e_2 happening at different places — the important point is that they are unsynchronised. Indeed, one could imagine a similar scenario where the two machines are in the same office, but not connected to one another (although then one would expect some events representing communication between Alison and Brian ... unless they aren't talking). Furthermore, the communication between the two machines could be via a modem.

19.3.2.   Actions and rôles

Let's look more closely at the entities and actions in Figure 19.1. There are four entities: Alison, Brian, the copy of the document on the portable computer and the one on the office desktop computer. There are two types of actions 'update' and 'merge'. The events are instances of these actions and involve a set of participants, who fulfil rôles for the action. The update action requires a person who performs the update and a document which is changed. The merge action requires two documents to merge, and also a person who initiates and controls the merge. There will typically also be some other information about the event, for example, describing the nature of the update. This has been omitted in Figure 19.1, but is also important. Figure 19.2 shows these relationships in a tabular fashion and includes a description of the actual updates.

	Action	Rôle	Entity	Details
e_1	**update**	*person*	Alison	insert "in the town" after line 2
		document	portable	
e_2	**update**	*person*	Brian	delete line 3
		document	desktop	
e_3	**merge**	*initiator*	Alison	
		doc 1	portable	
		doc 2	desktop	
e_4	**update**	*person*	Alison	change line 2 to "had a shop"
		document	desktop	
e_5	**update**	*person*	Brian	change line 3 to "in the country"
		document	portable	

FIGURE 19.2. Events and their participants

19.3.3.   Entity timelines

Finally, we need to add some meaning to the actions. For each action we need to say how it changes the state of its participants. Also for each entity we need to keep track of its state at any time. As the model is distributed we can not ask, for example, about the state of the portable computer at event e_2. However, it is important that the state of the portable is the same at the start of e_3 as it was at the end of e_1. That is, for each entity there is an alternating sequence of states and events which represent its own particular timeline. For example, Figure 19.3 shows the states of the document on the two computers. Depending on our application, we may not want to talk about all of the state of an entity, and for some entities we may not record any state at all. For such entities, the timeline merely records the history of activity of the entity. For example, we can represent the history of Alison and Brian as:

$$Anne_0 \rightarrow e_1 \rightarrow Anne_1 \rightarrow e_3 \rightarrow Anne_2 \rightarrow e_4 \rightarrow Anne_3$$
$$Brian_0 \rightarrow e_2 \rightarrow Brian_1 \rightarrow e_5 \rightarrow Brian_2$$

The symbols *Anne*$_0$, *Brian*$_1$ etc. are there to record the fact that people do have some state (memory etc.) but that we are not going to expand upon it.

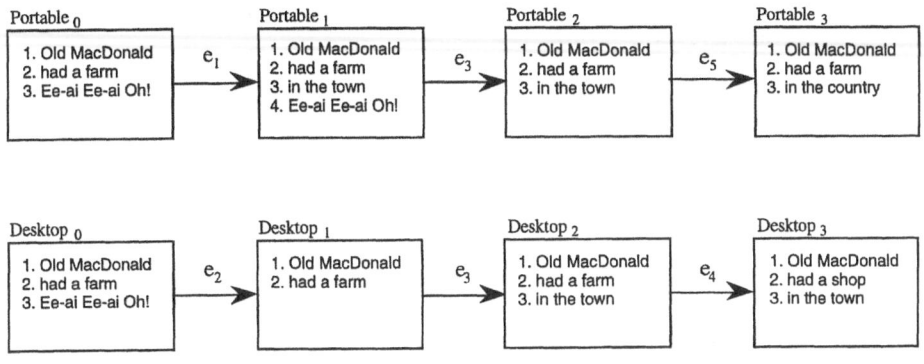

FIGURE 19.3. Document timelines

We are modelling physical entities, such as people, computers and individual copies of a document thus the timeline of any individual entity will be linear — an entity cannot be unsynchronised with itself! This is in contrast to an information entity like the idea of the document "LADA paper". An information entity can have several different versions in different places, and even have several versions on the same device. We of course want to reason about information entities, such as the evolution of a shared document, but to achieve this we need to talk first about the life histories of the individual versions and the way they interact.

As well as this linearity constraint, we could also demand that events are only ordered if some entity has participated in both event, or if there is some intervening sequence of events with this property. To be a little more precise, we can say that an event e_1 is just before another event e_2 if there is no intervening event. We will write this $e_1 \rightarrow e_2$, and define it formally by:

$$e_1 \rightarrow e_2 \quad \Leftrightarrow \quad (e_1 \, \mathsf{p} \, e_2) \wedge \neg \exists e \, st. (e_1 \, \mathsf{p} \, e \wedge e \, \mathsf{p} \, e_2)$$

The *completeness* condition would then be:

$$e_1 \rightarrow e_2 \quad \Rightarrow \quad \exists \text{ an entity } x \, st. \, (x \text{ participates in } e_1 \wedge x \text{ participates in } e_2)$$

Although the linearity condition is a necessary sanity condition for concrete entities, there may be situations where completeness is not required. For example, the ordering of some events may be determined by another observer who is not explicitly included in the model. Thus the completeness condition is left as an optional part of the model which can be imposed if required.

19.3.4.   Alternative histories

The event lattice in Figure 19.1 shows one possible history of the world. There are lot of other things which could have happened, Alison might have taken the portable home after merging the machines, Brian might not have performed any updates and simply waited to see

Alison's version. The full formal model underlying LADA talks about the set of all possible histories. Given a description of the behaviour of the computer systems and the people involved, only some of these worlds can happen. To prove that some requirement holds we need to show that all possible histories which can happen according to these behaviours also satisfy the required property.

More formally: let w be a history of the world — that is, w is an event lattice like the one in Figure 19.1, with associated states of entities etc.. We then denote the expected behaviours of the computer systems and people by $S(w)$ and $P(w)$ respectively and the requirement on the system as a whole by $R(w)$. The requirement holds if:

$$\forall \text{ world histories } w \ (S(w) \wedge P(w) \Rightarrow R(w))$$

The requirements and behaviour can be specified using formulae like that of the completeness condition, but temporal operators act as 'sugar' so that one can avoid talking about the event lattice directly.

19.4   Temporal operators

Standard temporal logic has two principle operators, the diamond operator – 'eventually', that we have already seen and the box operator – 'always'. We could express the old adage that every cloud has a silver lining something like:

$$\square \text{ times are bad} \Rightarrow \Diamond \text{ things get good}$$

Which literally translated says "it is always true that if times are bad then it will eventually be true that things get good".

As eventually can be a long way off, various additional operators are also used. Two of these are 'until' ($\mathcal{U}$) and 'before' ($\mathcal{B}$). The formula 'p $\mathcal{U}$ q' says that p will be true of all states until there is a state where q is true. Similarly 'p $\mathcal{B}$ q' says that before the next state where q is true there will be a state where p is true. The before operator can be defined in terms of until, and visa versa:

$$p \ \mathcal{B} q \ \Leftrightarrow \neg((\neg p) \ \mathcal{U} q)$$

We cannot use these operators directly to distributed actions as there is no simple time ordering. However, each entity has a time ordering, so these operators can be used along a particular entity's timeline. The entity concerned is added as a subscript. For example, we might want to say that whenever a user types the 'send' command the computer will eventually fax a document. This can be written:

$$\square_{user} \text{ types}(user, computer, \text{"send"}) \implies \Diamond_{computer} \text{ faxes}(computer, \text{the file})$$

Notice how this formula starts off by looking at the user's timeline and then in a sense branches off along the computers timeline. In fact, this is quite a complicated behaviour and many properties can be represented with respect to a single timeline. For example, we may want to say that if a user has been updating a document on one computer and then wants to use a different computer, the user ought to ensure that the two computers have performed a merge before starting work with the second. (Notice how difficult it is to express these requirements — this is precisely why a formalism is needed.) We can express this requirement as:

$$\square_u \text{ update}(u, comp_1) \implies \left(\text{merge}(u, comp_1, comp_2) \ \mathcal{B}_u \text{ update}(u, comp_2) \right)$$

This is an example of a social protocol which could be used together with the specification of the system to reason about correctness.

19.5   Example — Liveware

We will now look at the Liveware system in detail and show how one can describe the required properties and go about proving them.

A Liveware database is a collection of individual records which are the units used for update and merging. Each record has a unique identifier generated using the time and user who first created it. So, when two databases are merged the system is able to match records and update the older one to be the same as the newer. The result is that as a group of users meet one another and exchange databases (usually using copies on floppy disk) the data becomes more 'up to date' and information entered by one user gradually permeates throughout the user population. Liveware avoids the concurrent update problem by only allowing a record to be updated by its creator.

19.5.1.   Entity states

To describe the system we need to consider two kinds of entities, copies of the Liveware database and users:

entities: Db, User

At any moment, the database state (Db) has a set of active record identifiers. For each identifier, there is an associated value and also a timestamp of when it was last updated:

state: Db =

records:	$\mathcal{P}$ Id
vals:	records $\rightarrow$ ValD
stamp:	records $\rightarrow$ Time

The identifiers are, as was mentioned, constructed using the creation time and the user who created/owns the record. Also the value set will be assumed to include a special value 'DEL', which will be used to record deleted records:

Id   =   Time × UserName
ValD   =   Val ∪ { DEL }

Given an element id from Id, we will refer to its components as id.t and id.u respectively. Given any database, we can determine the last time it was updated:

$$\text{lasttime} \quad = \quad \max \left(\left\{ \text{id.t} \mid \text{id} \in \text{records} \right\} \cup \textbf{range stamp} \right)$$

We would also expect that records cannot be updated before they are created:

$$\forall \text{id} \in \text{records} \quad \text{id.t} \le \text{stamp(id)}$$

However, although this sounds like a sensible condition, it depends on the way timestamps are generated, in a distributed environment we cannot necessarily assume a global clock. In fact, we will assume a clock that for each action supplies the time as a parameter 'time?'. This will be assumed to satisfy the locally monotonic property:

time 1.

$$\forall e_1, e_2 : \text{Events} \quad e_1 \text{ p } e_2 \Longrightarrow e_1.\text{time?} < e_2.\text{time?}$$

If this is true, then we can assume for any entity 'ent':

time 2.

$$\Box_{ent} \ t = time? \Longrightarrow \Box_{ent} \ t < time?$$

That is any entity will see the parameter 'time?' increase.

The 'state' of users will be considered to consist of their name only:

state: User =
name: Name

Unlike the database state, this will not change. In the following description, we will require the user's name for most actions. In reality this is likely to be obtained once per session when the database is opened, but for simplicity we will ignore this additional system behaviour.

19.5.2.   Action descriptions

We will consider five actions:

create: add a new record
delete: destroy a record
change: change an existing record
look: examine an existing record
merge: merge two copies of the database

The effect of an action is a state transformation of the entities involved in the action. This could be described using any suitable notation, for example, Z schemas with suitable additional semantics. In the descriptions of the actions, some Z conventions will be used. For each entity involved with an action, its state variables before the action will be available in the action's precondition and both these and primed versions available for its post condition. In addition, extra parameters will be included for each action. These will be decorated by either '?' or '!'. The former represent parameters which are inputs to the action and can be used in the actions precondition. The latter are regarded as outputs. In reality, the inputs would often originate with one or other of the participants of an action (in this example mainly the user), but the source of these additional parameters is deliberately left underspecified. Of course, this leaves open the possibility of refining the specification to determine some of the input parameters later during system design.

We now consider the effect of each action in turn, describing the entities involved in the action, the additional parameters and the pre and post conditions of the action. First of all record creation:

action: create   **roles :**   User, Db
                     params: time?: Time, val?: Val, id!: Id

pre: (time?, name) $\notin$ records
post: id!   =   (time?, name)
          records' =   records $\cup$ { id! }
          vals'   =   vals $\oplus$ { id! $\rightarrow$ val? }
          stamp'   =   stamp $\oplus$ { id! $\rightarrow$ time? }

This action is only valid when the new record identifier which will be generated by the action is not already in the database. However, if the database never contains anything that is dated in the future the precondition will always be true. To be precise, the condition on the database is:

$\square_{db}$ lasttime < time?

In fact, we will see that for each action we define:

$\square_{db}$ action(db) $\wedge$ lasttime < time? $\Longrightarrow$ lasttime' $\leq$ time?

This together with the local monotonicity assumption on time will mean that if the database starts in a well timed conditions, it will remain so.

The change action is similar except here the record identifier is required as a parameter:

action: change **roles :**   User, Db
                 params: time?: Time, val?: Val, id?: Id
pre: id $\in$ records $\wedge$ id.u = name $\wedge$ vals(id) $\neq$ DEL
post: records' = records
        vals'   = vals $\oplus \{$ id $\rightarrow$ val ? $\}$
        stamp' = stamp $\oplus \{$ id $\rightarrow$ time ? $\}$

Here the precondition is important, it demands that a valid identifier is given. To be valid, it must both be an identifier that is known to the system but has not been deleted. Liveware records that a record has been deleted by storing 'DEL' in its value. In addition, the record must belong to the user.

The delete operation is identical to change except the value is set to 'DEL':

action: delete **roles :**   User, Db
                 params: time?: Time, id?: Id
pre: id $\in$ records $\wedge$ id.u = name $\wedge$ vals(id) $\neq$ DEL
post: records' = records
        vals'   = vals $\oplus \{$ id $\rightarrow$ DEL $\}$
        stamp' = stamp $\oplus \{$ id $\rightarrow$ time ? $\}$

The look action is even simpler, it performs no state changes at all:

action: look   **roles :**   User, $\equiv$Db
                 params: time?: Time, id?: Id, val!
pre: id $\in$ records $\wedge$ vals(id) $\neq$ DEL
post: val!   = vals(id)

The notation '$\equiv$Db' comes from Z and means 'no change in Db'.

Notice also that the precondition is weaker: users can look at any record, not just their own. Of course, a more sophisticated treatment could consider access control issues, but this will be ignored here.

Finally, we consider the merge operation. This involves two databases, they start possibly different and end up the same. Each record in the final state is the most up to date from the two sources:

action: merge **roles :** $\mathcal{P}$User, Db$_1$, Db $_2$
post: records$_1$' = records$_2$' = records$_1 \cup$ records$_2$
        $\forall$ id $\in$ records $_1$' *st.* stamp$_1$(id) < stamp$_2$(id)
                vals$_1$'(id)   = vals$_2$'(id)   = vals$_2$'(id)
                stamp$_1$'(id) = stamp$_2$'(id) = stamp$_2$'(id)
        $\forall$ id $\in$ records $_1$' *st.* stamp$_1$(id) $\geq$ stamp$_2$(id)
                vals$_1$'(id)   = vals$_2$'(id)   = vals$_1$'(id)
                stamp$_1$'(id) = stamp$_2$'(id) = stamp$_1$'(id)

Notice that there are no preconditions on merge, neither does it actually need any information from the users. A set of users is given as more than one user may be present (and often will be) when databases are merged. However, not all owners of records need be present; the records from all users are synchronised. This does not mean that a user is actually updating another user's records since whichever value is in the final databases will have been set by that user anyhow.

19.5.3.   Generic Actions

In order to simplify the requirements on a system, it is useful to classify the actions into groups of generic actions, giving a class structure to them. Three classes will be used:

$$update(user, db, id) \equiv \quad create \text{ or } change \text{ or } delete$$
$$sees(user, db, id) \quad \equiv \quad update \text{ or } look$$
$$interact(user, db) \quad \equiv \quad sees \text{ or } merge$$

The last class is intended to capture when the user interacts with a database in any way. As a merge involves two databases and possibly several users, it may be part of the generic action in several ways.

19.5.4.   Observational consistency

Now we can capture some of the Liveware properties described in [10]. They note that the collection of Liveware databases at any time are *not* necessarily consistent with one another. However, even though they are not *globally* consistent, they are *observationally* consistent for any particular user. That is although there may be inconsistencies, no one will ever notice!

This statement has several ramifications and one can address it at various levels. However, we will just look at one: if a user sees the same record take on different values, it must always get more up to date.

obs. 1.

$$\square_{user} \ sees(user, db_1, id) \wedge stamp_1'(id) = t \implies$$
$$\square_{user} \left(sees(user, db_2, id) \Rightarrow stamp_2'(id) \geq t \right)$$

With no social protocol this property cannot be guaranteed. Consider for example the following event history for the user, where db_1 and db_2 are separate copies of the database:

$$update(user, db_1, id, val_1) \quad \rightarrow \quad update(user, db_2, id, val_2) \quad \rightarrow \quad look(user, db_1, id)$$

Clearly, the final timestamp of id will be older than the timestamp in the previous event, violating the required condition. We therefore need a social protocol to make the system work. We use similar conditions to the example formula earlier:

social 1.

$$\square_{user} \ merge(user, db_1, db_2) \implies$$
$$\left(\begin{array}{c} sees(user, db_3) \Rightarrow (db_1 = db_3 \vee db_1 = db_3) \\ \mathcal{U}_{user} \quad merge(user, db_1, db_4) \vee merge(user, db_2, db_4) \end{array} \right)$$

social 2.

$$\square_{user}\ sees(user, db_1) \implies$$

$$\left((sees(user, db_3) \implies db_1 = db_3\right)\ \mathcal{U}_{user}\ merge(user, db_1, db_2)\right)$$

The first condition says that between merges the user only interacts with one of the databases which were merged. the second says that when the user has chosen to interact with a database that is the only one which is used until the next merge.

19.5.5.   Sketch proof of observational consistency

The proof is in three main steps. First one proves the equivalent property for a single database following its timeline. That is:

proof. 1.

$$\square_{db}\ id \in records' \wedge stamp'(id) = t \implies \square_{db}\ \left(id \in records' \wedge stamp'(id) \geq t\right)$$

This is proved by induction and case analysis over the actions which a database can be involved in. Indeed, it is trivial to see that no action may reduce a records timestamp.

The second stage is to transfer this result to a user looking at a single database. That is we seek to prove:

proof. 2.

$$\square_{user}\ sees(user, db, id) \wedge stamp'(id) = t \implies$$

$$\square_{user}\ \left(sees(user, db, id) \implies stamp'(id) \geq t\right)$$

Although this involves only the user and one database, it is no longer a linear temporal logic proof. Both the user and the database may have interactions which do not involve one another. In other words, we need to prove temporal properties of entities which take different time paths.[2] For the first time, we really need the additional expressive power of a non-linear logic and can use a general proof rule. Let a and b be any two entities, and e and f two action types which involve them both:

infer 1.

from $\square_a\ P \implies \square_a\ Q$

infer $\square_b\ e(a,b) \wedge P \implies \square_b\ f(a,b) \implies Q$

We simply set P to be $\left(id \in records' \wedge stamp'(id) = t\right)$ and Q to be $\left(id \in records' \wedge stamp'(id) \geq t\right)$. The first part of our proof (*proof 1.*) has therefore fulfilled the condition of the proof rule. Examining each specific action which comprises the generic action 'sees(user,db.id)', we find that all imply that id is in records'. Hence letting both events e and f be 'sees(user,db.id)' we obtain equation *proof 2.*

So far we are still only considering a user's interactions with one database. To prove the full observational consistency property, we need to use the social protocol. This is now a linear temporal logic step and just involves induction and case analysis. The important fact is that the social protocol ensures that the user's interactions are always of the form:

sees(user,db_1) ... sees(user,db   1) merge(user,db 1,db_2) sees(user,db   2)
   ... sees(user,db   2) merge(user,db 2,db_3) sees(user,db   3) ...

The single database version effectively proves the property between merges, but the fact that databases are identical after merges then allows an inductive proof of *obs. 1.*

19.5.6.   Other forms of observational consistency

The proof of simple observational consistency only depended on the system behaviour and the social protocol of the particular user involved. That is, so long as a user obeys the required social protocol any individual record will always get more up to date.

More complex observational properties should look at groups of records. For example, we might like it to be true that two users could agree about their observed history of records. That is, given two records (with ids i and j), and two users (say Alison and Brian), if Alison sees record i updated before record j, we might like Brian to see the same relative ordering. We can define this ordering precisely. We say that Alison sees record i at time t before she sees record j at time 2 (denoted $i@t <_A j@s$) when the following holds:

$$i@t <_A j@s \equiv \Diamond_A \text{ sees}(A,db) \wedge \text{stamp}'(i) \geq t \wedge (j \notin \text{records}' \vee \text{stamp}'(j) < s)$$

This is rather strong as it says that the updates cannot even be first seen at the same time. The weaker equivalent allows this:

$$i@t \leq_A j@s \equiv \neg(j@s <_A i@t)$$

Note that although these are written as partial orders, they will only be guaranteed to be so if Alison obeys her social protocol.

The joint consistency property can then be stated:

obs. 2. – false

$$i@t <_A j@s \quad \Rightarrow \quad i@t \leq_B j@s$$

Unfortunately, this consistency condition (which is what one would expect of a synchronous database) does *not* hold of Liveware. For example, imagine that record i belonged to Alison and j to Brian. They start with identical copies of the database, then in different locations Alison updates record i and Brian updates j. Clearly Alison will see the update to i before j and visa versa for Brian.

Although this stronger form of the consistency property does not hold for any pair of records, it does hold if the records belong to single user. That is:

obs. 3.

$$i.u = j.u \quad \wedge \quad i@t <_A j@s \quad \Rightarrow \quad i@t \leq_B j@s$$

Proving this requires that all three parties (Alison, Brian and the user to whom the records belong) all obey the social protocol. These three need not be distinct leading to two special cases.

• If Alison and Brian both maintain the social protocol, then each will see the other's records in a consistent manner.

• If a single user (say Alison) maintains the protocol, then she will always see her own records as consistent with one another.

Note that in both these cases, we put no stipulations on the other users. This is very important as in a large informal group, we cannot guarantee that everyone else will always fulfil their commitments.

19.6   Lessons about the Logic

Having seen a partially worked through example, we can look again at the underlying formalism and see what can and cannot be done within the logical formulae.

19.6.1.   Additional temporal operators

Several of the steps in the proof of simple observational consistency involved reasoning about a single entity's timeline. The expresion of properties and proofs are then pretty much standard linear temporal logic.

Inductive proofs of 'always' properties is made easier by using the temporal logic 'next state' operator ($\bigcirc$). As with the other operators, this is decorated with the name of the entity which is being traced. For example, the social protocol can be re-expressed as:

social 1a.

$$\Box_{user} \ merge(user, db_1, db_2) \implies$$
$$\bigcirc_{user} \left(\ interact(user, db_1) \lor interact(user, db_2) \ \right)$$

social 2a.

$$\Box_{user} \ sees(user, db_1) \implies \bigcirc_{user} \left(\ interact(user, db_1) \ \right)$$

However, this formulation is only correct so long as the user only engages in interactions with databases. We might have an additional action for users 'drink_cup_of_tea'. If the user, say Brian, were to follow the above formulation of the social protocol it would imply that once an interaction with a Liveware database had taken place, Brian would have to spend the rest of his life with Liveware and *never* drink another cup of tea!

What we really want to say is "in the next state where there is database interaction...". That is, we want to have temporal operators which only look at actions of a particular type. We can denote this by putting the relevant action condition after the entity name in the temporal operator's decoration. For example:

social 2b.

$$\Box_{user} \ sees(user, db_1) \implies \bigcirc_{user:interact} \left(\ interact(user, db_1) \ \right)$$

Similar annotations can be used with the 'always' and 'eventually' operators, but are redundant as the same effect can be achieved in the predicate part:

$$\Box_{ent:action} \ P \quad \equiv \quad \Box_{ent} \ action \Rightarrow P$$

The following two proof rules then allow easy inductive proofs:

infer 2.

> **from** $\Box_{ent:action} P$
>
> **infer** $\Box_{ent} \bigcirc_{ent:action} P$

infer 3.

> **from** initially P **and** $\Box_{ent:action} \left(P \Rightarrow \bigcirc_{ent:action} P \right)$
>
> **infer** $\Box_{ent:action} P$

The first of these is a weakening rule. The second, *infer 3.*, requires information about the initial states of entities, which was mentioned once or twice loosely during the previous proofs, The second part the condition (the inductive part) will usually be discovered by recourse to case analysis on the different types of possible action.

19.6.2.   Resynchronisation

Not every property or proof step can use purely linear temporal reasoning. If they could there would be no need for a new formalism! In the proof of simple observational consistency (*obs. 1.*), we only needed one proof step involving the intertwining of timelines which we could achieve using the inference rule *infer 1*. However, the more complicated observational consistency property (*obs. 3.*) talks about properties of two timelines (in fact three including the record's owner). Furthermore, the Multiple Source Control system [1] uses asynchronous message transfer as well as direct merging and will thus have even more non-linear features.

The logic formulae we have seen so far make it easy to branch onto different entities timelines. Take for example:

$$\square_C \; act_1(C,A,B) \;\Rightarrow\; \big(P(A) \; \mathcal{U}_A \; act_2(A,B)\big) \wedge \big(Q(B) \; \mathcal{U}_B \; act_2(A,B)\big)$$

This says that it is always true along C's timeline that if C engages in the action act_1 then along A's timeline P will hold until A engages in the action act_2 with B and similarly along B's timeline Q would hold until B engages in act_2 with A. We could instantiate this with the following entities an actions:

A	–	Alison
B	–	Brian
C	–	Cupid
$act_1(C,A,B)$	–	Cupid fires his arrows of passion at Alison and Brian
P(A)	–	Alison is unhappy
Q(B)	–	Brian is sorrowful
$act_2(A,B)$	–	Alison and Brian marry

The formula would then read:

"Whenever Cupid fires his arrows of passion upon Alison and Brian, Alison will be forever unhappy until she marries Brian and likewise Brian will be in perpetual sorrow until he marries Alison."

However, the formula does not specify whether the two marriages spoken of are the same event. We could imagine a scenario whereby Alison and Brian are both unhappy and then they marry. Brian is now delighted, but Alison stays unhappy and sadly they divorce (presumably casting Brian once more into the depths of sorrow). Only then does Alison realise the depth of her love for Brian and she remains unhappy until years later they meet again, refresh their romance and remarry.

It makes a good story, but was not what the original formula was meant to express. It allowed one to talk about the diverging timelines of Alison and Brian from one event (the shooting of the arrows), but did not demand that the timelines resynchronise on a single event (marriage). In this example, we could force the required interpretation by adding the requirement to P and Q that no marriage takes place. However, this is both inelegant and will not cope with slightly more complex situations. To allow more general resynchronisation we can label the events:

$$\square_C \; act_1(C,A,B) \;\Rightarrow$$
$$\exists e{:}\mathrm{Event} \; st. \; \big(P(A) \; \mathcal{U}_A \; e{:}act_2(A,B)\big) \wedge \big(Q(B) \; \mathcal{U}_B \; e{:}act_2(A,B)\big)$$

This form of labelling makes the expressive power of the temporal formulae more symmetric (although not completely) at the expense of more complex logic.

Happily, most properties seem to concern relatively little resynchronisation and it is likely that most proofs can be split into mainly linear parts with only occasional non-linear parts. This was certainly the case with the observational consistency proof.

19.6.3.   When logic fails

Although the temporal formulae make it easier to define and reason about properties, they are not complete with respect to the underlying semantic model. Occasionally, properties may need to be stated using the model itself (as was the case with the first time property *time 1.*). Even where the required properties can be stated using the temporal formulae, proofs may have to drop into the semantic domain. This is not a fundamentally difficult process as the formulae can be easily translated into their semantic equivalents to carry out proofs there.

If some constructs seem to recur they may become candidates for later inclusion in the logical level of LADA (as is the case with labelled events), but I am not convinced of the utility of aiming at completeness at the logical level when the semantic level is not unduly complex.

If such a dual level approach seems inelegant to the purist it should be noted that temporal formulae are simply predicates about event lattices. If required they can thus be embedded into properties at the semantic level, giving rise to a 'wide spectrum' notation. For example, we could say:

$$\Box_a \; act_1(a) \;\Rightarrow\; \exists e\text{:}Event \;\; st. \; \left(\Diamond_a \; e\text{:}act_2(a)\right) \wedge \left(\forall f \; f \; e \; P(f)\right)$$

Some care has to be taken over the precise semantics of embedded quantifiers over events.

19.6.4.   Not just atomic events

Whereas most specification notations for interfaces are targeted at continually synchronised systems, LADA is explicitly aimed at the opposite extreme. The entities meet and synchronise at discrete and atomic events. However, there are situations between these two extremes. For example, we may want to describe systems where participants both work separately, but also have protracted periods of synchronised work. During these periods it is reasonable that participants will join and leave the synchronous group. This is not allowed in the current formalism as this would lead to violations of the partial order between events.

Another way in which the atomic nature of events is insufficient to describe interface phenomena is when there are periods of continuous interaction between events. This *interstitial* (that is between actions) *behaviour* become important when studying more detailed interaction. Although it can be ignored then for the highly distributed systems which are the main target of LADA it suggests that appropriate extensions would be valuable for certain target domains. This would bring together the work described in this paper with a longer running study of status/event analysis (e.g., [2] and [4, Ch. 9]).

19.7   Discussion

It is difficult enough to specify and reason about single user interaction – the movement into groupware with the attendant problems of distribution is daunting. We have seen how LADA is designed to address such systems. It has two major features:
- a partially ordered event lattice to express issues of distribution.
- extended temporal logic formulae following individual timelines.

The first of these is not uncommon, although it is important to remember that the use here is to represent events which are totally unsynchronised, rather than simply things which may happen concurrently. The emphasis here is on distribution not concurrency.

The use of temporal formulae is I believe novel and adds considerably to the ease of use and expressiveness of the resulting formalism. This was evident in the worked example where comparatively complex properties of multiple agents and objects were expressed succinctly and proofs of properties nicely factored into linear and non-linear parts.

Acknowledgements

This work was funded by a SERC Advanced Fellowship B/89/ITA/220 and by SERC Grant GR/J08560, "Version Management and Access Control Models for Cooperative Systems".

References

[1]   A. J. Dix and V. C. Miles, *Version Control for Asynchronous Group Work*, YCS 181, University of York, 1992.

[2]   A. J. Dix, Beyond the interface, pp. 171-190 in *Engineering for Human–Computer Interaction: Proceedings of IFIP TC2/G2.7 Working Conference,* Ellivouri, Finland, J. Laron and C. Unger editors, North-Holland, 1992.

[3]   A. J. Dix & R. Beale, *Information Requirements of Distributed Workers*, University of York, 1992.

[4]   A. Dix, A., J. Finlay, G. Abowd and R. Beale, *Human-Computer Interaction*, Prentice Hall, 1993.

[5]   C. A. Ellis and S. J. Gibbs, Concurrency control in groupware systems, *SIGMOD Record,* 18(2), pp.399-407, Proceedings of the ACM SIGMOD International Conference on Management of Data, June 1989.

[6]   J. Grudin, Why CSCW applications fail: problems in the design and evaluation of organisational interfaces, pp. 85-89 in *CSCW'88 Proceedings of the Conference on Computer-Supported Cooperative Work,* ACM SIGCHI & SIGOIS, 1988.

[7]   C. A. R. Hoare, *Communicating Sequential Processes*, Prentice Hall, 1985.

[8]   J. J. Kistler and M. Satyanarayanan, Disconnected operation in the Coda file system, *ACM Transactions on Computer Systems*, 10(1), pp. 3-25, February 1992

[9]   J. Mariani and T. Rodden, The impact of CSCW on database technology, in *Proceedings of the IFIP Workishop on CSCW*, Berlin, April 1991.

[10]   H. W. Thimbleby and David Pullinger, Observations on practically perfect CSCW, in *CSCW Issues for Mobile and Remote Workers*, IEE Colloquium, March 1993.

[11]   I. H. Witten, H. W. Thimbleby, G. F. Coulouris & S. Greenberg, A New Approach to Sharing Data in Social Networks, in *Computer–Supported Cooperative Work and Groupware*, S. Greenberg editor, Academic Press, ISBN 0-12-299220-2, 1991.

---

[1]Branching time interpretations of temporal logic do not use a linear model. However, the branches in the tree represent 'possible' worlds and any particular history is still linear (a path through the tree). The major difference between linear and branching time temporal logics is not in the underlying notion of time, but in the interpretation of the temporal operators. In particular, whether the diamond operator 'eventually' is taken to mean "there is some possible future state where..." or "in any possible future history there will be a state where...".

[2] I'll take the high road and you take the low road, and I'll be in Scotland before you, ...

20 Folding Human Factors Into Rigorous Development

D.J. Duke
M.D. Harrison

ABSTRACT

As part of the ESPRIT Basic Research Action 'AMODEUS-2' we are investigating the role of formal methods in specifying and understanding properties of systems as they relate to usability. This paper summarises a case study in which a formal specification is employed to understand user-significant properties of an interactionally rich audio-visual (AV) environment. We show how user-oriented requirements need to be considered both in the initial abstract task-oriented specification and in the subsequent refinement process.

20.1 Introduction

Despite progress in using formal methods to understand abstract principles and properties of human-computer interaction [1, 3, 10, 9, 15], there is little evidence of this theory being translated into practice. Formal specifications of software systems rarely describe the interaction between users and systems, and [13] is one of the few published examples where formal methods are brought to bear on the problem of describing interaction within a realistic case study. The first contribution of this paper is to show how some of the properties developed in [1, 9] and [15] can be introduced into a specification. For example, state-display conformance [1, 10], honesty [15] and repair [9] are properties that are informed by cognitive models of human-computer interaction, and, by combining their expression with a model of the functional behaviour of a system, it becomes possible to reason about whether the system will adequately support the tasks for which it is intended [1]. Elsewhere [6] we have also suggested that human factors can be folded into a rigorous development *process* by generalising the concept of refinement to encompass these multiple perspectives of the design artefact.

The paper is organised around a specification of the so called ubiquitous computing environment developed at Rank Xerox EuroPARC. This is an audio-visual system intended to support collaboration and general awareness in an office environment [2, 4, 8]. It consists of a number of audio-visual (AV) nodes together with facilities for allowing users to make various AV connections between nodes. Personal nodes are located in offices, and consist of a monitor and speakers that can be connected to other nodes plus a video camera and microphone that allow communication with other workers in the environment. There are also public nodes in various parts of the building, and connection can also be made to external cameras or devices such as video players.

Our goal is to demonstrate how formal specification can be used to understand properties of interaction, and how these properties can in turn influence rigorous software development. An abstract model of the AV system developed in Section 20.2 is used to express properties of the system that will be significant from the viewpoint of its users. Section 20.3 shows how the abstract specification can be reified into a collection of *interactors*. In carrying out this development step we focus on the property of conformance, and discuss why it may not hold in the concrete model. This breakdown leads to design suggestions intended to compensate for this failure and which support the users in achieving their goals. Section 20.4 then concludes the paper with a discussion of the role and limitations of formal methods in folding user requirements into designs.

20.2   An Abstract Model of the AV System

In this section we develop a formal specification of the AV system and describe some of the properties that impact usability. The model is abstract and focuses on the connections and the information *about* a connection that is available to users; in this paper we are unconcerned about how that information is presented or how connections are actually requested. After introducing the basic sets and types used throughout the specification, we define the abstract state of the system using Z schemas [14]. User-oriented properties are then specified in relation to the state.

20.2.1   Preliminaries

The AV specification is centered on two concepts; AV nodes, and the connections that can exist between them. Since Z is a value-based language we need to introduce a means of distinguishing or naming objects whose states might otherwise be identical, and we define two types to represent primitive identifiers or names for individual nodes and connections.

$$[node] \qquad - \text{ identity of AV nodes}$$
$$[conn] \qquad - \text{ identity of connections}$$

Each connection links two nodes in the AV system; the source node *src* is the one that initiates a connection to destination node *dst*.

$$src, dst \quad : conn \rightarrow node$$

Each connection also has a type, for example *glance* or *vphone*, but this information is not needed in the abstract model and is introduced later. Also, only a subset of *conn* is possible at any time, and some connections are never possible, for example making a vphone call to a video player is not (currently) sensible. Although an indication of the reason for failure will be important, it is not necessary to model this reason here; instead, a type is introduced to represent the messages that might be sent to a node, and a relation is used to identify which connections (if any) the message refers to.

$$[mesg] \qquad\qquad - \text{ messages sent to nodes}$$
$$\_ \text{ about } \_ : mesg \leftrightarrow conn \quad - \text{ content of message}$$

20.2.2   Abstract State

Although the abstract of the AV system is small, it is useful to break it into three sections, each defined by a Z schema. The first introduces observations about the system nodes; the set of nodes known to the system is represented by *avnodes*, and for each node the schema records the connections that the node is able to initiate and the messages that the node has received.

$\underline{AVnodes}$ _____

$\quad$ $avnodes : \mathbb{F}\ node$
$\quad$ $initiate : node \twoheadrightarrow \mathbb{F}\ conn$
$\quad$ $messages : node \twoheadrightarrow \mathbb{F}\ mesg$
_____
$\quad$ $\mathrm{dom}\ initiate = avnodes = \mathrm{dom}\ messages$
$\quad$ $\forall n : node \bullet$
$\qquad$ $src(initiate(n)) = \{n\}$
$\qquad$ $\forall con : \mathrm{about}(messages(n)) \bullet src(con) = n \lor dst(con) = n$

The invariant on this schema is governed by the principle that only information relevant to the user of a node should be presented at that node; thus a node can only initiate connections for which it is the source and any connection mentioned in a message to the node must be one involving that node. Not all connections between AV nodes are always possible. We represent the sets of connections that are possible at some time by a set of connection sets, and define a *failures* relation between connections and connection sets such that $(c, cs) \in failures$ when it is not possible to establish c when cs is the current connection set.

$\underline{AVnetwork}$ _____

$\quad$ $possible : \mathbb{F}\ \mathbb{F}\ conn$
$\quad$ $failures : conn \leftrightarrow \mathbb{F}\ conn$
_____
$\quad$ $\forall cs : possible \bullet \mathbb{F}\ cs \subseteq possible$
$\quad$ $failures = \{\ c : conn;\ cs : possible\ |$
$\qquad\qquad\qquad$ $\forall cs' : possible \bullet cs \subseteq cs' \Rightarrow c \notin cs'\ \}$

Both *possible* and *failures* will change over time, for example as users change their access permissions, and as the set of nodes in the system changes. Here we are deliberately abstracting away from the reason for failure; potential causes are considered later. If our task in specifying the system was to analyse and prevent types of failure then the specification would be slightly different. The third aspect to the system concerns the connections, and we identify two sets of interest; connections that have been initiated but not (yet) established, and those that are current.

$\underline{AVconnections}$ _____

$\quad$ $pending : \mathbb{F}\ conn$
$\quad$ $current : \mathbb{F}\ conn$
_____
$\quad$ $pending \cap current = \varnothing$

The abstract state combines the node, network, and connections schemas:

$\underline{AVsystem}$ _____

$\quad$ $AVnodes$
$\quad$ $AVnetwork$
$\quad$ $AVconnections$
_____
$\quad$ $current \in possible$
$\quad$ $\forall cs : possible \bullet src(cs) \cup dst(cs) \subseteq avnodes$

At any time the current connections must be possible, and any connection that is possible must involve the nodes that are available in the system.

20.2.3   General Properties

We have expressed general features of the AV system as an abstract specification; we can now use that specification to understand general principles of the AV system that may be important from the point of view of the user. Four principles are listed below; the first two are expressed formally as desired properties of the system later in this section, the others are formalised in [7].

Privacy: A user should have control over who can make connections to their node, and should be given appropriate notification of connections to their node initiated by other users.

Conformance: The system should allow a user to request just those connections that are possible and which do not involve violation of another user's privacy. Inaccessible connections should not appear to be accessible.

Progress: A connection that has been requested by a user should eventually result in an AV link or, in the event of some failure, result in the user being given appropriate notification.

Feedback: Once a connection has been requested the system should provide the user with suitable feedback about the status of that connection. Hence progress is where a requested connection is eventually delivered, while feedback is about whether the progress will be visible to the user.

20.2.4   Tasks or Objectives

Properties are also important in so far as they enable or hinder the user in achieving specific goals. The purpose of the AV system is to allow users to make connections. This goal can be captured formally as an operation schema where the source and destination of the connection are represented as inputs.

$$
\begin{array}{l}
\textit{Connect} \underline{\hspace{8cm}} \\
\quad \Delta AVsystem \\
\quad \Xi AVnetwork \\
\quad s?, d? : node \\
\hline
\quad \exists\, c : conn \bullet\; src(c) = s? \wedge dst(c) = d? \\
\qquad\qquad\qquad c \in initiates(s?) \\
\qquad\qquad\qquad c \in current' \\
\quad avnodes' = avnodes \\
\quad \forall\, n : avnodes \bullet messages(n) \subseteq messages'(n)
\end{array}
$$

While the invariants on the various parts of the state are sufficient to define the functional behaviour of the AV system they do not necessarily reflect properties of the system that are important to users. Returning to the properties introduced above, a basic concern for a system involving audio and visual monitors is that it should not intrude into personal privacy. To some extent this can be alleviated by allowing users to determine the connections that can be made to their node. However, (perhaps on the advice of a sociologist) we can also insist that even permitted connections must be preceded by a warning message, and strengthen the state invariant accordingly:

$\boxed{\text{privacy-I}}$ $\;\forall\, c : current \bullet \exists\, m : mesg \bullet m \in messages(dst(c)) \bullet m \text{ about } c$

In understanding specifications that capture user-oriented properties it is important to be clear about the interpretation given to predicates. An invariant such as '$m \in messages(n)$' has *practical* as well as the usual proof-theoretic consequences. For example, audio warnings and messages are often transient; while persistence might be obtained by repeating a message over and over it is unlikely to create a comfortable environment for the user. So '$m \in messages(n)$' only requires that the message m is sent to node n; it makes (and can make) no claim about what the user actually has perceived or might perceive at any point in time. This distinction is clarified in Section 20.3 where the concept of an interactor allows us to distinguish between absolute statements about the state of a system and statements about what a user *should* perceive about that state. With these problems and limitations in mind we now consider further properties of the AV system that affect usability, starting with a requirement that a user should always be able to initiate possible connections:

$$\boxed{\text{can-initiate}} \quad \forall\, c : conn \bullet (c, current) \notin failures \Rightarrow c \in initiate(src(c))$$

We might also prevent the user carrying out unnecessary work by legislating that the system should not allow a user to initiate a connection that will fail. That is, the connections offered to a user through the system presentation should reflect the underlying state (connections) of the system; this is one instance of the complementary relationship between state and display studied in [10].

$$\boxed{\text{conformance}} \quad \forall\, c : conn \bullet c \in initiate(src(c)) \Rightarrow (c, current) \notin failures$$

Together, $\boxed{\text{can-initiate}}$ and $\boxed{\text{conformance}}$ suggest that the connections that a user can initiate should be exactly those that will succeed. Since *failures* depends on the *current* state, the connections that a user can *initiate* will in general change after every connection made by any user of the system. Given this, the extent to which these predicates can be realised in practice is limited, and in the next section we suggest how these requirements might be suitably weakened.

20.3 Reification Using Interactors

Reification is a process in which abstract features of a model are replaced by some concrete realisation, and here the abstract features that we are interested in are the means by which information about the AV system is presented to users and the means by which they can modify that system. Although theories exist that support the formal reification of a specification [12] the steps carried out here are informal. Our concern is with how the development steps relate to, or are guided by, the user-oriented properties just discussed.

Figure 20.1 shows the structure of this development. The aim of the hierarchy is to organise the detailed specification into units, called *interactors*, that are significant with respect to user-oriented concerns. An interactor [5, 11] is a specification structure that encapsulates a state, a collection of actions that modify the state, and the *presentation* through which the state can be perceived. Appendix A describes the formal representation of an interactor. The starting point, *AVcore*, captures a single node's perspective of the connections defined and available within the system and will be a basis for investigating conformance properties of the design.

The remainder of this section proceeds as follows. Section 20.3.1 introduces some preliminary definitions, then Section 20.3.2 introduces the first interactor, *AVcore*. Thereafter we focus on the means by which users can request connections and how they can be informed about the state of the system. This involves the interactors enclosed in the box; details of the other interactors and relevant human issues are given in [7].

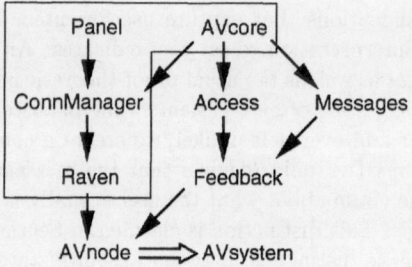

FIGURE 20.1. Interactor Structure for the AV System.

20.3.1 Preliminaries

As before, we begin by introducing basic definitions needed in the remainder of the section, and now we must consider details such as the kinds of connections that can be supported. Because we are not analysing these enumerations in detail, they are introduced as a free type:

$$Ctype ::= \begin{array}{ll} glance & \text{– short one-way visual connection} \\ |\quad vphone & \text{– two-way AV connection, must be accepted} \\ |\quad watch & \text{– AV link to a device} \\ |\quad bgrnd & \text{– visual link to a public space} \end{array}$$

Connections are mapped to their types by a global function $type : conn \rightarrow Ctype$. The reasons why a connection may not be possible should also be defined;

$$problem ::= \begin{array}{ll} notsensible & \text{– cannot ever be made} \\ |\quad notpossible & \text{– for system reasons, e.g. no resources} \\ |\quad notpermitted & \text{– not permitted by the target node} \end{array}$$

we will associate a reason with each *failure*. Finally, in understanding why a connection may not be possible it will be necessary to talk about the types of nodes present in the system. Assuming that this information is invariant, it can be represented by a global function *nodetype*

$$nodetype : node \rightarrow Ntype$$

which maps each node to a value drawn from a free type:

$$Ntype ::= \begin{array}{ll} personal & \text{– node in a private office} \\ |\quad public & \text{– node in a public space} \\ |\quad device & \text{– hardware device such as camera or VCR} \end{array}$$

20.3.2 AVcore

In contrast to the abstract model that centered on a global view of the AV system state, here we are interested in the view that an *individual* AV node has of the system. This is captured in an interactor called *AVcore* which is based on parts of the abstract state extended by three observables which constitute a local equivalent to the *AVnodes* schema. These are the *identity* of the node (*self*), the connections that can sensibly be made (e.g. vphone-ing a device is not sensible) and *reason*, which maps connection failures to an indication of the problem.

$$
\begin{array}{|l}
\hline
AVcore \underline{\hspace{6cm}}\\
\quad self : node\\
\quad AVnetwork\\
\quad AVconnections\\
\quad sensible : \mathbb{F}\ conn\\
\quad reason : (conn \times \mathbb{F}\ conn) \nrightarrow problem\\
\hline
\nabla\ request, permit, deny, link, break : conn\\
\hline
\quad pending = \varnothing\\
\quad \Box identity = identity'\\
\quad \Box sensible = sensible'\\
\hline
\end{array}
$$

By including *AVnetwork* and *AVconnections* the core has information about what connections are possible and why some connections might fail; note that the interactor does not talk about what the user of the node might perceive about the system (it has no presentation). Both points are addressed later in the section; below, we introduce the invariant that holds over all core states:

$$
\begin{array}{|l}
\hline
AVcore :: \mathsf{inv} \underline{\hspace{7cm}}\\
\quad src(\!| pending |\!) = \{self\}\\
\quad \forall c : current \bullet src(c) = self \vee dst(c) = self\\
\quad \mathrm{dom}\ reason \subseteq failures\\
\quad \forall c : conn \bullet c \notin sensible\\
\qquad \Rightarrow\\
\qquad \forall cs : \mathbb{F}\ conn \bullet (c, cs) \in failures \wedge reason(c, cs) = notsensible\\
\hline
\end{array}
$$

The invariant requires that

- each pending connection has *self* as its source,

- *self* is one of the parties to any current connection – the core of a node does not know about connections that may exist between other nodes in the system, and

- a connection that is not sensible will always fail for exactly that reason.

Five actions are introduced at the core level, and at this point our concern is solely with their functional behaviour; later in this section we consider the role of the actions in supporting user tasks and how the user is presented with access to the actions through the interface. The first action, *request*, allows a connection to be added to the pending set provided that it has not already been requested and that it is does not currently exist.

$$
\begin{array}{|l}
\hline
AVcore :: request(c : conn) \underline{\hspace{5cm}}\\
\quad c \notin pending \cup current\\
\hline
\quad pending' = pending \cup \{c\}\\
\hline
\end{array}
$$

The remaining actions are concerned with servicing connection requests, and altering the possible connections by selectively permitting and denying permission. They are not discussed further in this paper, but a full account is contained within [7].

20.3.3 Buttons

AVcore represents the information known to a node but makes no claims about the information that might be perceived by a user of the node. Nor does the specification provide any clues as to how a user can initiate connections. We intend to correct this by developing interactors to model the Raven interface developed at EuroPARC [8]. The first step is to define a 'generic' model of a control panel based on a set of buttons:

[*button*]   – identity of buttons on a display

A *Panel* is an interactor whose state contains a set of buttons; each button is (visually) perceivable and is associated with a label drawn from some set of text objects not considered here. A subset of the buttons may be *pressed*, and this fact may be perceived visually. Not all buttons can be pressed at once, and the set of buttons that are exclusive are represented by a state variable, *exclusive*. See Appendix A for the definition of symbols such as ◁.

$$
\begin{array}{l}
\Phi Panel \\
\hline
\lhd\ label : button \rightarrowtail\!\!\!\!\rightarrow \text{text} \\
\lhd\ pressed : \mathbb{F}\ button \\
\ \ \ buttons : \mathbb{F}\ button \\
\ \ \ exclusive : \mathbb{F}\,\mathbb{F}\ button \\
\hline
\triangledown\ press : button \\
\hline
pressed = \varnothing \\
\ \ \ \Box\ \begin{cases}
\text{dom } label = buttons \\
pressed \subseteq buttons \\
\forall\, a, b : pressed \bullet (\exists x : exclusive \bullet \{a, b\} \subseteq x) \Rightarrow a = b
\end{cases}
\end{array}
$$

The interactor supports a single atomic action, which changes the set of buttons known to be pressed; if a button is pressed then pressing it again releases it. The status of buttons not exclusive to b are unchanged, but any buttons that are exclusive to b must not be pressed afterwards.

$$
\begin{array}{l}
\Phi Panel :: press(b : button) \\
\hline
\ \ \ \text{true} \\
\hline
pressed'(b) = \neg\ pressed(b) \\
pressed'(b) \Rightarrow \forall\, xs : exclusive \bullet \\
\ \ \ \ b \in xs \Rightarrow \forall\, c : xs \bullet c \neq b \Rightarrow c \notin pressed' \\
\ \ \ \ b \notin xs \Rightarrow pressed' \cap xs = pressed \cap xs
\end{array}
$$

20.3.4 Connection Panel

Raven is a system, developed at Rank Xerox EuroPARC, which support panels that can be used to request AV connections. This can be captured by specialising the generic panel mentioned above so that the state is enriched with a function that associates combinations of pressed buttons with (potential) AV connections.

```
┌─ ConnectionPanel ────────────────────────────────────────
│ ▷ AVcore
│ ▷ ΦPanel
│   select : (𝔽 button) ⇸ conn
├──────────────────────────────────────────────────────────
│ Δ request : conn
│   ┌──────────────────────────────────────────────────────
│   □ dom select ⊆ 𝔽 buttons ∧ src⟨| ran select |⟩ = {self}
└──────────────────────────────────────────────────────────
```

Only connections with the node as source can be selected, and only the buttons available on the display can be used to select a connection. There is a simple usability constraint here; any set of buttons that selects a connection should not belong to each exclusive set:

> sensible   ∀ ss : dom select • ¬ (∀ bs : exclusive • ss ⊆ bs)

A connection panel can be used to initiate a request, that is, to add a connection to the *pending* set for the node. This action is described formally by the *request* schema, whose pre- and post- conditions are conjoined to those inherited from the *request* action of the *AVcore* interactor.

```
┌─ ConnectionPanel :: request(c : conn) ──────────────────
│ ∃ bs : 𝔽 buttons •
│     select(bs) = c
│     bs ⊆ pressed
├──────────────────────────────────────────────────────────
│   true
└──────────────────────────────────────────────────────────
```

Although variables in an included interactor cannot be modified by new actions, the effect of the *request* action defined above extends that of *AVcore* :: *request*. Provided that the connection *c* is not pending or current, and that some subset of the pressed buttons selects *c*, the overall effect of *request* is to make *c* into a pending connection. The connection manager allows (a) some buttons to represent both a target and an action, and (b), some targets/actions to be made available through more than one button. Making the specification 'loose' gives us the flexibility to consider design alternatives for the interactor; similarly, we do not require every combination of pressed buttons to correspond to a selected connection.

20.3.5   Raven

Raven contains two groups of buttons, one indicating the possible destinations for AV connections while the other represents the actions that can be carried out; this arrangement can be defined as a specialisation of the ConnectionPanel interactor:

```
┌─ Raven ──────────────────────────────────────────────────
│ ▷ ConnectionPanel
│   actions : button ⇻ Ctype
│   targets : button ⇸ node
├──────────────────────────────────────────────────────────
│ Δ badrequest : conn
│   ┌──────────────────────────────────────────────────────
│   true
└──────────────────────────────────────────────────────────
```

The state of this interactor represents Raven's organisation of buttons in terms of actions and targets. Constraints on the behaviour of a *Raven* interactor are described separately within an invariant schema; again, note that this extends the invariant inherited from *ConnectionPanel*.

Raven :: inv _____

$exclusive = \{\text{dom } actions, \text{dom } targets\}$

$\langle \text{dom } actions, \text{dom } targets \rangle \text{ partitions } buttons$

$select = \{\, ba, bt : button;\ c : conn \mid$

$\qquad\qquad src(c) = self$

$\qquad\qquad bt \in \text{dom } targets \wedge dst(c) = targets(bt)$

$\qquad\qquad ba \in \text{dom } actions \wedge type(c) = actions(ba)$

$\qquad\bullet \{ba, bt\} \mapsto c\}$

Any request initiated using the buttons must be consistent with the assignment of functions to buttons; this is specified by the definition of *select* in the above invariant. We can also be more precise about the state constructed when the user performs the *request* action, in particular the status of buttons afterwards. Since the actual buttons used were hidden by quantification in the *request(c)* action for *ConnectionPanel* we need to reconstruct the specification:

Raven :: *request*(c : conn) _____

$c \notin pending \cup current$

$\exists\, bs : \mathbb{F}\, buttons \bullet select(bs) = clandbs \subseteq pressed$

$pending' = pending \cup \{c\}$

$pressed' = pressed \setminus \{actions^{-1}(type(c))\}$

$actions' = actions \wedge targets' = targets$

The effect of *Request* is extended to the *pressed* variable by requiring that the button for the requested connection type is released after the request has been recorded. Raven's behaviour when a user attempts to invoke *request* outside of its precondition (e.g. to request a connection that already exists) is not described here; see [7].

20.3.6 User Concerns: Feedback and Conformance

The main task that Raven supports is to allow a user to make an AV connection to another node. One property that will assist the user in performing this task is ⟨conformance⟩ between the available actions and the known state of the system. In Section 20.2 we defined this property by requiring that each connection that could be initiated by a node was possible. Here we are concerned with the concrete details of how available connections are presented to users, and so we require some means of reflecting the information about connection availability, captured by the state variables *possible* and *failures*, in the visually perceivable components of the panel.

An obvious way to prevent a user attempting to make certain connections would be to remove the buttons that select those connections from the display. The assumption here is that each button controls a single connection. This is certainly not the case in Raven. Instead, each button is involved in making a number of connections, and removal of a button only makes sense when all connections that may be made using that button are unavailable (doing otherwise would violate ⟨can-initiate⟩). The other problem with the one connection per button model is screen space; it could require an $n \times m$ array of buttons where n is the number of nodes and m is the number of actions. Even for a small AV system of a dozen nodes and 5 possible connection types, the number of buttons/icons might be uncomfortably large, and such a dense array of controls may place a significant cognitive burden on the user. Here is an issue on which the advice of cognitive modellers should be sought. The modelling here makes the issues and trade-offs precise.

Rather than actually remove buttons, selective enabling might be used to force the user to make only requests that can be accepted. If the presentation of a panel interactor is extended with a variable

$\lhd$ enabled : $\mathbb{F}$ button

then an ideal situation would be for the *Raven* interactor to obey

$$select(\! | \, \mathbb{F} \; enabled \, |\!) \subseteq \{ \; c : conn \mid src(c) = self \land \neg \, (c, current) \in failures \; \}$$

This requires that once any target or action has been selected, at most those actions/targets that correspond to possible connections are enabled. Since the set $select(\!|$ $\mathbb{F} enabled \,|\!)$ is exactly those connections that the user can initiate, this requirement is equivalent to the $\boxed{conformance}$ property introduced in Section 20.2. This property will work provided the user of the node is informed of the true state of the AV system. It is not helpful if the only way in which a user can discover the status of the system is by trying to make connections. This relationship between node views and global state is further investigated later in the section. Two further problems with this scheme of selective enabling that have implications on user understanding may be noted:

- It assumes that the action of requesting a connection can be broken into two parts, with feedback on the first provided before the second part is initiated. The scheme will fail if the user can select target and action in parallel, as may occur if a modality such as speech is used. A spoken command such as "glance at Victoria" might be processed as an atomic structure, in which case the presentation would not be updated between the utterance of the action ("glance") and the target ("Victoria").

- More generally, the scheme does not provide conformance between the state of connections and the presentation, but only between the state and the presentation *after* the user has selected either a connection type or a target. Indeed, this may be a strong reason *against* the use of speech to effect requests, since a user may need to plan mentally *what* command they will say before they say it, and until part of the command has been uttered it may not be possible for the system to give adequate feedback about whether the users goal can be achieved. This may be an interesting issue for cognitive psychologists.

It can be seen that the specification of conformance in terms of the interactors is giving information that relates to the way users perceive systems. The notion of conformance defined earlier was concerned with how to inform users about the availability of connections. In extending the specification to encompass the user interface we consider the reasons why a connection might not be possible, and how these reasons affect conformance. It may not be possible to make an AV connection because either:

- the connection is not permitted by the target user, or

- there may be insufficient system resources, or

- it might not be sensible (there are several *types* of connection, some of which only make sense for devices such as video players).

For each reason, it is possible to identify a time frame in which the prohibition is lifted, and from this identify options on how to present information about connection availability:

- Whether a connection is sensible is not a highly volatile property. Unavailability can be presented syntactically by grouping target nodes and connection types according to *node type*.

- Permission, which will also change infrequently, can be presented to the user by enabling just those action or target buttons for which the completed request is permitted.

- Resource availability may be highly dynamic and thus unsuitable for presentation; instead, connection failure due to system limitations can be rendered by messages sent to the node after the user has attempted a connection. Also, it can be argued that users should not be exposed to information about (internal) system resources.

Modification to the interface based on the implications of conformance are described formally in the *ZonedRaven* interactor. Some actions like *glance* are applicable to more than one type of node. This cannot be defined as an enrichment of *Raven* since the latter requires that each action corresponds to a single button. *ZonedRaven* is based on the earlier *ConnectionPanel* specification.

$$
\begin{array}{l}
\textit{ZonedRaven} \rule{4cm}{0.4pt} \\
\hspace{0.5em} \triangleright \ \textit{ConnectionPanel} \\
\hspace{0.5em} \triangleleft \ \textit{enabled} : \mathbb{F}\ \textit{button} \\
\hspace{0.5em} \triangleleft \ \textit{groups} : \textit{Ntype} \to \mathbb{F}\ \textit{button} \\
\hspace{1.3em} \textit{actions} : \textit{button} \nrightarrow \textit{Ctype} \hspace{2.5cm} \text{[No longer a bijection]} \\
\hspace{1.3em} \textit{targets} : \textit{button} \rightarrowtail\kern-1.3ex\rightarrowtail \textit{node} \\
\rule{5cm}{0.4pt} \\
\hspace{0.8em} \text{true}
\end{array}
$$

ZonedRaven, like *Raven*, involves an invariant that can be captured separately:

$$
\begin{array}{l}
\textit{ZonedRaven} :: \mathsf{inv} \rule{4cm}{0.4pt} \\
\hspace{1em} \textit{exclusive} = \{\mathrm{dom}\ \textit{actions}, \mathrm{dom}\ \textit{targets}\} \cup \mathrm{ran}\ \textit{groups} \\
\hspace{1em} \langle \mathrm{dom}\ \textit{actions}, \mathrm{dom}\ \textit{targets} \rangle\ \textit{partitions buttons} \\
\hspace{1em} \textit{select} = \{\, ba, bt : \textit{button};\ c : \textit{conn}\ | \\
\hspace{5em} \textit{src}(c) = \textit{self} \\
\hspace{5em} bt \in \mathrm{dom}\ \textit{targets} \wedge \textit{dst}(c) = \textit{targets}(bt) \\
\hspace{5em} ba \in \mathrm{dom}\ \textit{actions} \wedge \textit{type}(c) = \textit{actions}(ba) \\
\hspace{4em} \bullet\ \{ba, bt\} \mapsto c \}
\end{array}
$$

A consequence of this definition is that any enabled connection fails only if the connection is not possible in the current state (e.g. there is a systems failure).

$$
\begin{array}{l}
\textit{ZonedRaven} \\
\vdash \\
\forall\, c : \textit{select} \langle\!| \ \textit{enabled}\ |\!\rangle\ \bullet \\
\hspace{3em} (c, \textit{current}) \in \textit{failures} \Rightarrow \textit{reason}(c, \textit{current}) = \textit{notpossible}
\end{array}
$$

Since each node has a unique type, we are assuming that nodes are visually grouped with just those actions that apply to that type of node; this is represented by the perceivable 'groups' property.

A further benefit of clustering nodes we suggest might be that the time it takes for a user to locate a target (particularly a personal node) may be reduced. Whether this saving is significant is a question that should be put to a cognitive scientist. Once an action (connection) has been requested by the user of the system by selecting the appropriate buttons it may be useful to disable those buttons until the system has responded to the request:

$$select(\!| \, enabled \, |\!) \cap (pending \cup current) = \varnothing$$

This property is at variance with the current implementation where requesting a current connection causes a message to be sent to the user, informing them that the connection already exists. In summary we can say which buttons we think should be clustered on the basis of the formal *conformance* property. We would like a psychologist to validate this decision and to decide what the most appropriate presentation of the clusters would be.

20.4   Conclusion: Formal Methods, Usability, and Design

The main contribution of the case study undertaken in Sections 20.2 and 20.3 is to show how a user-oriented property such as conformance can be folded into rigorous software development. An important point demonstrated by the AV specification is that abstract principles such as conformance cannot simply be used as invariants over an abstract specification. For example, we described reasons why the presentation of the Raven interface need *not* conform to the internal state. This is not to say that the general principle of state-display conformance [10] is wrong, but simply that it is subjective. It cannot be applied blindly within a development, but instead must be worked into a form that is appropriate for the particular system and the tasks that it supports. With respect to the Raven interface:

- We can for example assume the existence of infinite resources and show that conformance then holds; although this assumption cannot be discharged it does lead to an understanding of where conformance may *fail*. This is valuable in itself, as it may suggest changes to other parts of the design space; for example, clustering buttons.

- We could extend the specification with other interactors that capture the visual and auditory messages sent to a node. A user may be able to make use of the messages to construct a mental representation of the system state. For example, if connections to a certain site are frequently rejected in the morning because of resource limits the user may adjust their behaviour accordingly.

In either case, the way in which a principle like conformance is used or modified within a formal specification must take into account advice that other modelling approaches have to offer. Within rigorous development, a specification has an integrative role in encapsulating inputs from various modelling techniques. This encapsulation is important, for the (obvious) reason that if human factors advice is to impact a design then at some point it must be encoded within the design artefact. The value of a formal specification is that it is both a model that can be used to reason about usability **and** a representation that can be transformed into the final artefact. The difficulty is that it is expressed in a form that is difficult to understand - the specifier therefore has an obligation to make the properties of the specification comprehensible.

We conclude by noting that the use of formal properties in rigorous software development does not *guarantee* that the result will be a usable system (no method, formal or otherwise, can make such a claim). Properties are objective, non-judgemental statements that are either satisfied or refuted by some specification. Other modelling approaches such as task analysis or cognitive models will be called on to assess whether or not the design captured by the formal model is *sufficient* for its intended purpose.

Acknowledgements:

The work reported here was funded by the Commission of the European Union as part of the ESPRIT Basic Research Action 7040 (Amodeus-2). All referenced working papers from the Amodeus-2 project are publically available via anonymous ftp from:

    ftp.mrc-apu.cam.ac.uk::/pub/amodeus

Amodeus is also accessible via the World-Wide Web, URL:

    http://www.mrc-apu.cam.ac.uk/amodeus/amodeus.html

20.5   The Interactor Notation

An interactor consists of a collection of variables representing state and perceivable components, a collection of operation signatures, and a temporal predicate over behaviour. For instance, an *icon* state is a single variable, *state*, and it is perceived using the visual modality ($\triangleleft$) as either highlighted or not highlighted. Other *embellishments* denote observables perceived through the audio (@) and tactile ($\veebar$) senses. Actions initiated by an interactor are introduced using the Δ symbol, other actions in which the interactor participates are tagged ∇.

$$
\begin{array}{|l}
\hline
Icon \underline{\hspace{5cm}} \\
\triangleleft\ highlighted : \mathbb{B} \\
\quad state : State \\
\hline
\Delta\ press, release \\
\hline
state = inactive \\
\Box highlighted \Leftrightarrow (state = active) \\
\hline
\end{array}
$$

$$
\begin{array}{|l}
\hline
Icon :: press \underline{\hspace{3cm}} \\
\quad state = up \\
\hline
\quad state' = dn \\
\hline
\end{array}
$$

Operation names are augmented by the name interactor on which it is defined. Each operation has three sections, a precondition, an *inter* condition (not used in this paper), and a post condition. The pre- and post-conditions follow standard Z practice. Interactors can be built from interactors; a scrollbar for example consists of a perceivable position within a range of values, and a means of changing that position. An 'included' interactor is identified by the symbol $\triangleright$, and is given a name that is used to tag each inherited variable and operation. So variables of *Scrollbar* include *up.state* and *dn.highlighted* and its actions include *up.on* and *dn.off*.

$$
\begin{array}{|l}
\hline
Scrollbar \underline{\hspace{7cm}} \\
\triangleright\ up : Icon \\
\triangleright\ dn : Icon \\
\triangleleft\ pos : \mathbb{N} \\
\quad max, min : \mathbb{N} \\
\hline
\Delta\ slideto : \mathbb{N} \\
\nabla\ up.press, dn.press \\
\hline
pos = min \wedge \Box\ min \le max \wedge pos \in (min .. max) \\
\hline
\end{array}
$$

20.6   References

[1] G. Abowd. Formal aspects of human-computer interaction. D.Phil Thesis, Oxford University Computing Laboratory: Programming Research Group, 1991. Available as Technical Monograph PRG-97.

[2] S. Bly, S. Harrison, and S. Irwin. Media spaces: Bringing people together in a video, audio and computing environment. *Communications of the ACM*, 36(1), January 1993.

[3] A. Dix. *Formal Methods for Interactive Systems.* Academic Press, 1991.

[4] P. Dourish and S. Bly. Portholes: Supporting awareness in distributed work groups. In *Proc. ACM Conference on Human Factors in Computer Systems: CHI '92.* Addison-Wesley, 1992.

[5] D.J. Duke and M.D. Harrison. Abstract interaction objects. *Computer Graphics Forum*, 12(3), 1993. Conference Issue: Proc. Eurographics'93.

[6] D.J. Duke and M.D. Harrison. Mapping user requirements to implementations. Submitted to Software Engineering Journal. Based on Amodeus-2 document sysmod/sm_wp16, 1993.

[7] D.J. Duke and M.D. Harrison. Connections: From A(V) to Z. Technical Report SM/WP29, ESPRIT BRA 7040 Amodeus-2, January 1994. File: sysmod/sm_wp29.ps.

[8] B. Gaver, T. Moran, A. MacLean, L. Lovstrand, P. Dourish, K. Carter, and B. Buxton. Realising a video environment: Europarc's RAVE system. In *Proc. ACM Conference on Human Factors in Computer Systems: CHI '92.* Addison-Wesley, 1992.

[9] M.D. Harrison. A model for the option space of interactive systems. In *Engineering for Human-Computer Interaction: Proc IFIP WG2.7 Conf.* Elsevier, 1992.

[10] M.D. Harrison and A. Dix. A state model of direct manipulation. In M.D. Harrison and H.W. Thimbleby, editors, *Formal Methods in Human Computer Interaction*, pages 129–151. Cambridge University Press, 1990.

[11] H.R. Hartson and P.D. Gray. Temporal aspects of tasks in the user action notation. *Human-Computer Interaction*, 7:1–45, 1992.

[12] C.B. Jones. *Systematic Software Development Using VDM.* Prentice Hall International, second edition, 1990.

[13] L.S. Marshall. Formally describing interactive systems. In C.B. Jones and R. Shaw, editors, *Case Studies in Systematic Software Development*, pages 293–336. Prentice Hall, 1990.

[14] J.M. Spivey. *The Z Notation: A Reference Manual.* Prentice Hall International, second edition, 1992.

[15] B. Sufrin and J. He. Specification, refinement, and analysis of interactive processes. In M.D. Harrison and H.W. Thimbleby, editors, *Formal Methods in Human Computer Interaction*, pages 153–200. Cambridge University Press, 1990.

21 Visual Representation of Formal Specification: An Application to Hierarchical Logical Input Devices

Giorgio P. Faconti
Angelo Fornari
Nicola Zani

ABSTRACT

In this paper we shall describe our experience in the definition of a visual representation for the LOTOS specification of Hierarchical Logical Input Devices. The logical input device model is being used to describe the input functionality of the current generation of graphics standards. An extension of the model has been previously proposed by the authors to take into account the hierarchical structuring of those devices. The model has been formally described and several properties have been investigated by addressing the LOTOS notation, an ISO standard originally developed for the specification of open distributed systems that comes with a graphical syntax. The complexity of such graphical notation makes its use very hard, especially in the early phases of a system specification. Our approach is to develop a simpler notation that, while keeping the basic concepts, focuses on the description of task (process) interrelation by only taking into account the parallel composition operators and is able to express all the required semantics knowledge. The paper, after the introductory remarks, gives a short overview of (G-)LOTOS and of logical input devices. Subsequently, it shows how such devices can be described by means of process-gate network pictures that are elements of a language defined by a graphical grammar. The methodology of operation is described through an example that highlights the advantages of developing a formal specification from drawings.

21.1 Introduction

In the last decade an increasing interest on formal techniques and notations to describe the behaviour of systems and to verify their properties has been noticed. Moving from fundamental works such as [1] and [2], theories have been derived and tools for the development and verification of formal specification have been developed and integrated in Computer Aided Software Engineering (CASE) environments.

The use of well established software development methods and their automation by using CASE tools can improve the production process and the quality of the software, by reducing the number of interventions of programmers and by controlling their activity. In particular, the use of formal methods in the software production cycle, starting from the early phases of specification and, subsequently, in the design and the verification, can prove to be crucial in the production of correct systems.

In the early phases of a system development, very abstract formal descriptions are generally derived from the intended system requirements. The requirements are in most cases informally described in a natural language and are sometimes not very precisely defined. The practical consequence of this fact is that any *suitable* interpretation may be considered to be a *correct* representation of those requirements. Since natural languages are very expressive and very imprecise, one can express any property of a system but it is hard to be sure that someone else will understand exactly the intended meaning of that expression. On the contrary, formal languages are not very expressive, but they are precise. One can't say very much in a formal language, but what it is said is completely unambiguous.

From the above consideration, one may derive the fact that the correctness of the formal expression of system requirements must be proved and that this possibly raises a communication problem among the different constituencies participating in that stage of system development. In fact, formal notations are very hard to read, to not say obscure, for non experts. As an examples the LOTOS notation [3] is somewhat addressed to be the acronym for the Language of Totally Obscure Symbols!

The visual languages approach [4] is a potential mean to add expressiveness to programming language constructs by exploiting the capability of intuition of the intended readers through the use of significative graphical representations in the programming process. In our work we have tried to extend the application of this concept to formal notations, starting form the consideration that in the early phases of a system specification one starts by drawing interconnected boxes to express interaction amongst processes at a very abstract level. A major encouragement to proceed in this direction has been found in the work done within the International Organization for Standardization (ISO) to develop a graphical syntax for the LOTOS notation (G-LOTOS) [7].

21.2 The LOTOS notation

LOTOS [3], standing for Language of Temporal Ordering Specification, was originally developed by ISO/IEC for the specification of open distributed systems and in particular for those related to the Open Systems Interconnection (OSI) architecture. The language is actually an international standard; in fact it is the first and so far, only, specification technique to be standardized.

The language is built from two components:

- *Basic LOTOS* development has been heavy influenced by the Milner's work on A Calculus of Communicating Systems (CCS) [1]. Following the underlying methodology, it provides a notation [5] for defining the temporal relation among the interactions representing the externally observable behaviour of a system. A concurrent system is seen as a process able to interact with other processes by means of *observable actions*, that are atomic entities occurring at interaction points or *gates*, without consuming time. A *finite alphabet* of observable actions is defined for a process, identified only by the name of the gate where they may occur. Processes interact with each other by pure gate synchronization, without exchanging values, so that there is no sense of direction in communications. A *process definition* specifies the behaviour of a process by defining the sequences of observable actions that may occur at the process gates.

- *Full LOTOS* extends Basic LOTOS by giving a finer structure to observable actions and to process interactions; the major advantage being the enhancement of synchronizations with value passing, thus providing for inter-process communication. Actions are identified by a gate name and by a list of zero or more values offered at that gate. The capability to express data value is done by including *type definitions* in the specification. The practical consequence of the inclusion of type definition is that an *infinite number of observable actions* is expressible in Full LOTOS because the values offered at gates may range over infinite sets [6].

For the purposes of this paper, data types and values will not be considered so that reference will only be made to the *Basic* component of the language.

21.2.1   G-LOTOS: a graphical syntax for LOTOS

A graphical syntax (G-LOTOS) [7] has been defined for LOTOS so that each textual behaviour expression has a graphical representation in G-LOTOS. As an example, the definition

process P [g] (n:nat) := g ! n; **stop**

describing the behaviour of process *P* that output a *nat* value on gate *g* and then stops, finds its graphical representation in FIGURE 20.1.

As it can be seen from the figure, the resulting picture is almost complex as the textual notation and its expressiveness is poor, so that it is not intended to be usable for our purposes. However, we have kept in our work the basic concepts and the relevant notation which G-LOTOS has been built from.

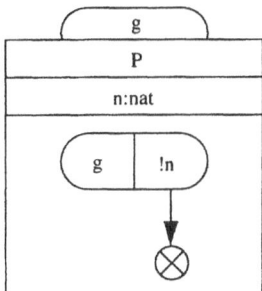

FIGURE 21.1. Graphical representation of process *P*

21.2.2   Basic Concepts and Notation

The language defined by a graphical grammar is the set of pictures that can be derived from such grammar, where a picture is defined as a set of points in a 2-dimensional cartesian space. A graphical grammar is a four-tuple $G = <\Sigma, N, S, P>$ where:

- $\Sigma = \{t_i\}$ is the set of terminal symbols (i.e. the graphics atoms from which a picture is built),
- $N = \{nt_i\}$ is the set of non-terminal symbols,
- S is the starting symbol, and
- $P = \{p_i\}$ is the set of productions so that for each non-terminal symbol $nt_i \in N$ there exist one or more productions $p_i \in P$ of the form:

nt_i **has components** $v_1, v_2, ..., v_n$
       satisfying $c_1, c_2, ..., c_k$
       has attributes $a_1, a_2, ..., a_m$

where $V = \{v_i\} = \Sigma \cup N$, $C = \{c_i\}$ is a set of constraints and $A = \{a_i\}$ is a set of attributes.

$v_1, v_2, ..., v_n$ are the *immediate components* of nt_i; any instance of nt_i is defined to be the set union of exactly one instance of v_1, one instance of v_n, ..., and one instance of v_n, provided that they satisfy constraints $c_1, c_2, ..., c_k, k \geq 0$.

Usual operators $\cap, \cup, \supseteq$, etc. are used to express the constraints that are applied both to terminals and non-terminals as well as to attributes. The special constraint $S : NT$ is used to mean that the picture S can be generated from non-terminal NT. Since nt_i may be used as one of the

352 G.P.Faconti, A.Fornari, N.Zani

components of a more complex picture, attributes a_1, a_2, ..., a_m may need to be defined for it. Moreover, a set of *primitive operators* is assumed to be defined for every picture. When a given non-terminal nt_i occurs many times within the same rule, the j-th occurrence is denoted by $nt_i.j$ both in the definition of its constraints and in that of its attributes. As an example, the following (incomplete set of) productions define the graphical representation for a set of interacting processes as a *process-gate network*:

g_process_net	**has components** *g_process_net_element* *g_process_net* **satisfying** *(g_process_net_element ∩ g_process_net.2) = Φ* ∨ *(g_process_net_element ∩ g_process_net.2) = g_gates_nodes* ∨ *(g_process_net_element ∩ g_process_net.2) = circle*
g_process_net_element	**has components** *rectangle* *process_id* **satisfying** *proces_id ∈ interior(rectangle)*
g_process_net_element	**has components** *g_gates_handle* *g_process_net_element* **satisfying** *common_area(g_gates_handle, g_process_net_element.2) =* *tip(g_gates_handle)*
g_gates_handle	**has components** *planar_line* *g_gate_node* **satisfying** *common_area(planar_line, g_gate_node) =* *point-1(planar_line)* **has attributes** *tip(g_gates_handle) = point-2(planar_line)*

From the above set of productions P, if follows that:

- $S =$ g_process_net
- $N = \{$ g_process_net_element,
    g_gates_nodes,
    g_gates_handle,
    g_gate_node $\}$
- $\Sigma = \{$ rectangle,
    circle,
    planar_line,
    process_id $\}$
- *{common_area, interior, tip,point-1, point-2, ...}* are the primitive operators.

21.2.3   Process-Gate Network

Process-Gate Network (PGN) is a conveient way of expressing graphically the relationship occurring amongst interacting processes: it is a net of process and gates nodes, linked with lines. Process nodes are represented as rectangles containing a process identifier and are standing for process instances; gates nodes are circles containing a gate identifier and are standing for synchronization gates between processes. A network with just one process node (possibly connected with a set of gate nodes) represents a single process instance.

More formally, a PGN is an undirected, bipartite graph (P, G, E) where:

- $P = \{P_1,....,P_n\}$ is an ordered n-tuple of nodes, called *process-node*;
- $G = \{g_1,....,g_m\}$ is a set of m nodes, called *gate-nodes*;
- $E \subseteq P \times G$ is a set of undirected edges, which can only connect process-nodes with gate-nodes.

The graphical composition theorem [8] states that a PGN represents a class of strongly equivalent LOTOS behaviour expressions containing only parallel composition operators, provided that all the process gates are explicitly shown in the net and they are all different. Furthermore, [8] describes an algorithm for deriving from a given PGN one of the behaviour expressions in the class of equivalence it represents.

As an example, FIGURE 20.2 shows a Process-gate net and two derivable LOTOS strongly equivalent behaviour expressions.

$P = \{ P, A, M \}$
$G = \{ p, y, x, d, m, t \}$
$E = \{ (p, P), (y, P), (y, M), (x, A), (x, M), (d, A), (m, M), (t, M) \}$
$(P[p,y] \, ||| \, A[x,d]) \, |[x,y]| \, M[m,t,x,y] \cong (P[p,y] \, |[y]| \, M[m,t,x,y]) \, |[x]| \, A[x,d]$

FIGURE 21.2. Correspondence of PGN and LOTOS behaviour expressions

Consequently, it is possible to define a PGN-based visual language whose semantics is that of the subset of LOTOS behaviour expressions derivable by applying the graphical composition theorem.

21.3   Hierarchical Logical Input Devices

The PGN-LOTOS approach has been used to graphically represent the behaviour of hierarchies of logical input devices (HLID). The concept of HLID has been developed to enhance and to formally describe the input model of the current generation of computer graphics systems [9]. The model has been developed in order to describe a large variety of composed input devices and interaction techniques whilst being as small as possible with respect to the complexity of its specification. The key ideas of this model are:

- the definition of processes internal to the LID is independent from the operating mode setting,
- generic LIDs are uniformly built up from three processes running in parallel with synchronization: they are measure (M), abstraction (A), presentation (P),
- a composed input device, or *cluster*, is represented as acyclic graph with one sink node,
- specific processes, *controlling agents*, are used to constrain the interactions occurring either internally to a LID or between LIDs in a cluster.

21.3.1   Definition of Logical Input Device

A LID is an abstraction used to describe the manipulation of a specific input data type done by a graphics system. Input data type are received and kept in a storage within the *measure* process M. The actual value stored in M determines the state of the LID. Any time the state is updated it is propagated to the *presentation* process P that provides for the feedback to the user. When a trigger action occurs, the measure process propagates the state to the *abstraction* process A which delivers a data item to the system.

The behaviour of a LID, formalized by means of a (pseudo) LOTOS notation, is presented shortly in the following (see [9] for the complete reference):

process M[im_l .. im_j, it_l .. it_m, me, md] : **noexit** :=   (Def. 1)
        im_l ; me ; M[im_l .. im_j, it_l .. it_m, me, md]
        [] ...
        [] im_j ; me ; M[im_i .. im_j, it_l .. it_m, me, md]
        [] it_l ; md ; M[im_i .. im_j, it_l .. it_m, me, md]
        [] ...
        [] it_m ; md ; M[im_i .. im_j, it_l .. it_m, me, md]
endproc

process P[me, eo] : **noexit** :=   (Def. 2)
        me ; eo ; P[me, eo]
endproc

process A[md, od] : **noexit** :=   (Def. 3)
        md ; od ; A[md, od]
endproc

A LID is then specified as parallel composition of the above processes opportunely synchronized. The behaviour of a generic LID is captured by the following process definition:

process LID [im_l .. im_j, it_l .. it_i,eo, od] :=   (Def. 4)
        hide me, md **in**
        (P[me, eo] ||| A[md, od])
        |[me, md]|
        M[im_l .. im_j, it_l .. it_i, me, md]
endproc

21.3.2   Definition of cluster

In order to describe the hierarchical composition of LIDs, let's now introduce the concept of *cluster*. A cluster is recursively defined as:

- let a LID be an atomic cluster;
- let CL_k be an atomic cluster (referred in the following as the *parent* LID),
- let CL_l, ..., CK_{l+k} be a set of clusters (referred in the following as the *childs clusters*) then

    $CL_k \oplus CL_l, ..., CK_{l+k}$:=   (Def. 5)
            hide SG **in** (CL_l ||| ... ||| CK_{l+k}) |[SG]| CL_k

    is a cluster with $\oplus$ being the composition operator if the following conditions hold:

    gates(CL_l) $\cap$ ... $\cap$ gates(CK_{l+k}) = Φ (Eq. 1)

$$SG = gates(CL_k) \cap (gates(CL_l) \cup ... \cup gates(CK_{l+k})) = im\_gates(CL_k) \qquad \text{(Eq. 2)}$$

$$im\_gates(CL_k)_i = od\_gate(CL_j), i = 0, ..., k, j = l + i \qquad \text{(Eq. 3)}$$

with gates(X) being the set of gates of process X, and im_gates(X) and od_gate(X) being respectively the set of input gates to the measure process and the output gate of the abstraction process of LID X. Informally, $\oplus$ creates a hierarchical composition by connecting the abstraction processes of the *child clusters* to the measure process of the *parent* LID.

Different interaction behaviour of the cluster can be obtained depending on the way in which the connections among LIDs are established. Further, once the connections have been defined, the interaction functionality among the components can be described in terms of a controlling agent process. Its task is to impose synchronization constraints over whichever subset of the cluster gates, where for cluster gates we mean every observable gate of the LIDs defining the cluster. Consequently the most general expression of a hierarchy of LIDs is given by:

CLUSTER :=   (Def. 6)
hide SG **in** ((CL$_1$ III ...III CK$_{l+k}$) I[SG]I CL$_k$) I[CG]I CA[CG]

where CA is the controlling agent and CG $\supseteq$ gates(CLUSTER) $\cup$ SG.

21.4 Process-Gate Network representation of HLIDs

The LID's behaviour expression given in (Def. 4) satisfies the requirements for a LOTOS construct to be represented by a PGN so that it can be written as:

- $P = \{ P, M, A \}$
- $G = \{ me, eo, md, od, im_l,....,im_j, it_l, ..., it_i \}$
- $E = \{ (me, P), (me, M), (eo, P), (md, A), (md, M), (od, A), (im_l, M), ..., (im_j, M),$
  $(it_l, M), ..., (it_i, M) \}$

and graphically represented as in the following figure:

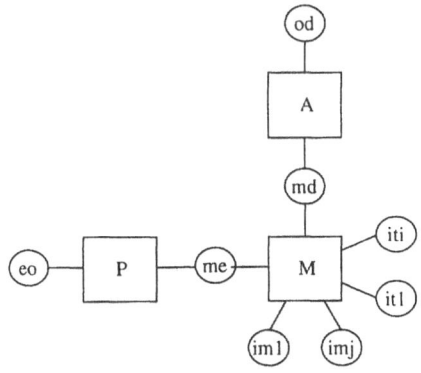

FIGURE 21.3. Graphical representation of a LID's behaviour expression

Encapsulating the behaviour expression within a process definition, as in (Def. 4), results in that an instance of the generic LID is a PGN with just a process node representing that instance; that is:

- $P = \{ LID \}$
- $G = \{ eo, od, im_l,....,im_j, it_l, ..., it_i \}$
- $E = \{ (eo, LID), (od, LID), (im_l, LID), ..., (im_j, LID), (it_l, LID), ..., (it_i, LID) \}$

with the following graphical representation:

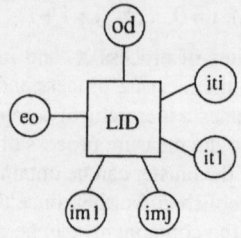

FIGURE 21.4. Graphical representation of a LID's instance

It is easy to verify that the conditions from (Eq. 1) to (Eq. 3) are so that the composition rule given in (Def. 5) and (Def. 6) is conservative in respect to PGN constraints and, consequently, any cluster can be represented through a PGN. In FIGURE 20.5 the hierarchical composition of three LIDs with a controlling agent is shown.

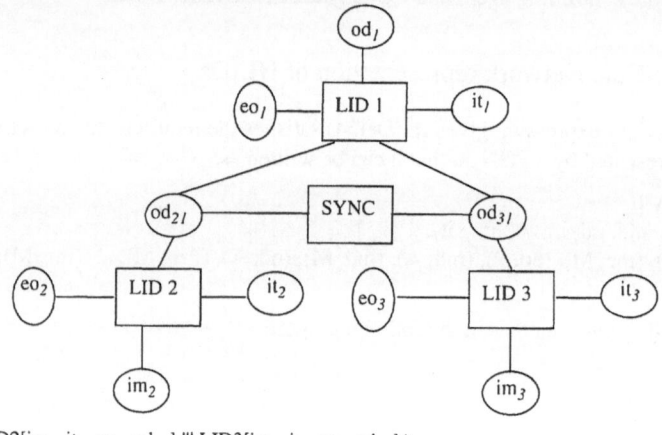

$$((LID2[im_2, it_2, eo_2, od_{2/}] ||| LID3[im_3, it_3, eo_3, od_{3/}])$$
$$|[od_{2/}, od_{3/}]| LID1[od_{2/}, od_{3/}, it_/, eo_/, od_/])$$
$$|[od_{2/}, od_{3/}]| SYNC[od_{2/}, od_{3/}]$$

FIGURE 21.5. Graphical and textual representations of a hierarchy of LIDs

21.5   A visual language for HLIDs

Given the framework described in the previous sections, the main problem to be solved is the derivation of PGN structures from drawings. This can actually be solved by taken a visual language approach: in our case, it has been addressed by adopting the mechanism of the *Picture Layout Grammars (PLG)*[10], which permits to recover the syntactic structure of a visual program by parsing and to add static semantic processing capabilities by extending the attribute mechanism of the underlying graphical grammar [11][12][13].

The approach has several advantages:

- using a grammar to specify the visual language provides a precise definition of the syntax of the language;

- using a parser to recover the language-dependent structure of programs allows the program to be manipulated as a picture;
- since the parser is grammar-driven, a parser for a new visual language is created by merely writing a new grammar.

21.5.1   Picture Layout Grammars

Picture Layout Grammars are only suitable to describe the syntax of a two-dimensional visual language; nevertheless the two dimensions are enough for meaning the most of the composition rules which interested us.

Formally a *PLG* is defined by the six-tuple $G = (\Sigma, N, S, I, D, P)$ where:

- Σ is the set of terminal symbols,
- N is the set of non-terminal symbols,
- S is the starting symbol,
- I is the set of the *parsing attributes*,
- D is the set of domains of the attribute values, and
- P is the set of productions of the form (R, SF, C) where:
  - R is a rewriting rule of the form
    $$N \rightarrow X$$
    $N \rightarrow op(X1, ..., Xn)$ with $X \in N \cup \Sigma$ and *op* is a composition operator,
  - *SF* is the set of semantic functions, and
  - *C* is the set of constraints.

Let *PA* be the set of the parsing attributes, if $p = (R, SF, C) \in P$ with $R = N \rightarrow X/Y$ and Y context of the production, then for any $\alpha \in PA$ the semantic function *SF* contains an assignment of the form $N.\alpha = x.\beta$ with $x \in X \cup Y$, $\beta \in PA$.

The semantic function computes the values of the attributes of the object resulting from the application of the production. In particular, the values of four mandatory attributes, denoted with *L1, L2, R1, R2* and representing either the extent of a shape object or the end-points of a line, are always computed.

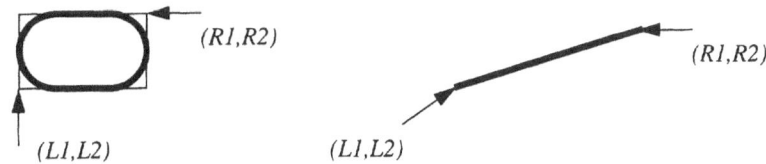

FIGURE 21.6. PLG production mandatory attributes

The constraints of a production describe the relationship occurring amongst the production components; they define spatial constraints or adjacency constraints.

As an example, the production

$$FIGURE \rightarrow over(TOP,BOTTOM)$$

is associated with the constraint

$$TOP.L2 \geq BOTTOM.R2$$

and with the semantic function

$$FIGURE.L1 = min(TOP.L1, BOTTOM.L1)$$
$$FIGURE.R1 = max(TOP.R1, BOTTOM.R1)$$

$$FIGURE.L2 = BOTTOM.L2$$
$$FIGURE.R2 = TOP.R2.$$

Further constraints and semantic functions can be added to production rules to define new composition operators and make the parsing unambiguous.

21.5.2   A Picture Layout Grammar of HLIDs

Following the graphical composition theorem [8], a LOTOS behaviour expression can be derived from a given a PGN structure. Consequently, a Picture Layout Grammar (HLID/PLG) has been developed in order to recognize the syntactical PGN-structure of a drawing which has been subsequently annotated with the necessary semantic information. Given the HLID/PLG and a drawing as input to a spatial parser a LOTOS behaviour expression is automatically generated that can be subsequently analyzed with the tools [14] developed within the Lotosphere ESPRIT Project. The overall architecture of the system is highlighted in the following figure.

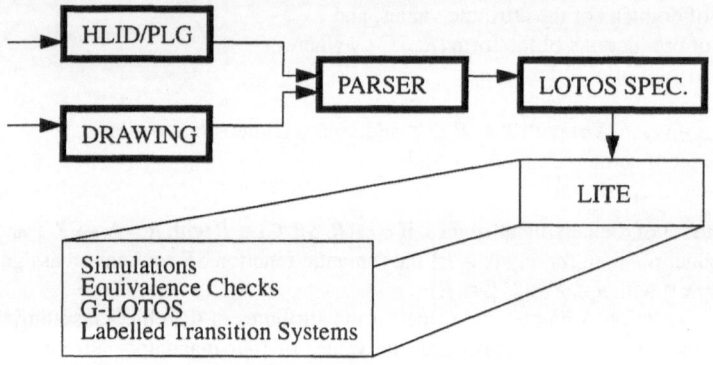

FIGURE 21.7. HLID/PLG-LITE environment

21.5.2.1   A Picture Layout Grammar for generic Process Gate Networks

The definition of a PLG to derive the LOTOS behaviour expression of a generic PGN is straightforward; it contains the sets of terminal and non terminal symbols and the starting symbol

- Σ = {text, line, rectangle, circle}
- N = {*PGN_ELEM, PROC, SYNCHRO, GATE, CONNECT, LINE*}
- $S = PGN$

the sets of attributes and the domains of their values

- I = {*sval, id, posid, class*}
- D = {String, Integer}

and the set of productions P of which only a subset is given here as an example.

The meaning of the attributes and their values are not described in details, as it will require a deep investigation of the grammar that is outside of the purposes of this report.

- A process (*PROC*) is a rectangle containing a text with *class value 1* and *id value 0*

$PROC \rightarrow contains(rectangle,text)$
    $PROC.id = text.sval;$
    $PROC.class = 1;$

- A *PGN_ELEM* has the *class value* of its component

PGN_ELEM → *PROC*
       PGN_ELEM.class = PROC.class;
PGN_ELEM → *SYNCHRO*
       PGN_ELEM.class = SYNCHRO.class;

- A *PGN_ELEM* make out of two adjacent *PGN_ELEMs* is of *class value 1* and must satisfy that both components are also of *class value 1* (i.e. interleaving operator).

PGN_ELEM → *adjacent_to(PGN_ELEM#1,PGN_ELEM#2)[2]*
       PGN_ELEM.class = 1;
       Where: ((PGN_ELEM#1.class == 1) && (PGN_ELEM#2.class == 1));

- Lines attached to rectangles derive their *posid value* from position attributes

CONNECT → *points_to(LINE,~rectangle)*
       *CONNECT.posid = LINE.L1 + 1000*LINE.L2;*

- Synchro-connectors attaching to a connected line have its *posid value*, have *class value 1* and must satisfy the constraint that its previous *posid value* be lower than the *posid value* of the connected line

SYNCHRO → *touches_L(CONNECT, SYNCHRO#1)*
       SYNCHRO.posid = CONNECT.posid;
       SYNCHRO.class = 1;
       Where: SYNCHRO#1.posid < CONNECT.posid;

- Synchro-connectors are build starting from gates

SYNCHRO → *GATE*
       SYNCHRO.posid = 0;
       SYNCHRO.class = 0;
       SYNCHRO.id = GATE.id;

21.5.2.2 An annotated Picture Layout Grammar for HLIDs

The PLG described in the previous section can be specialized in order to derive a complete LOTOS specification of HLIDs.

Since two different type of processes must be distinguished (the LID processes and the Controlling Agent processes), the set of terminal symbols is extended with the punched-card:

- Σ = {text, line, rectangle, circle, punched_card}

a new attribute (*type*) is added to the set of attributes and the *PROC* production is extended so that

PROC → *contains(rectangle, text)*
       PROC.id = text.sval;
       PROC.type = "lid";
       PROC.class = 1;
PROC → *contains(punched_card, text)*
       PROC.id = text.sval;
       PROC.type = "control_agent";
       PROC.class = 1;

The major changes in the grammar are due to the fact the LID gates belong to four different set. In fact, it is necessary to distinguish the actions performed by the component processes of the LID so that this information can be interpreted by the semantic function which will derive the LOTOS specification. This distinction is made by reconsidering the *CONNECT* production and by defining a number of additional constraints. Here the choice has been made to attach the different types of gates to different sides of the rectangle representing a LID process so that

- synchro-connectors attached with a line to the bottom side of the rectangle denote input tokens to the measure process,
- synchro-connectors attached with a line to the right side of the rectangle denote trigger events,
- synchro-connectors attached with a line to the left side of the rectangle denote output tokens from the presentation process, and
- synchro-connectors attached with a line to the top side of the rectangle denote output tokens from the abstraction process.

The *CONNECT* production is consequently split into several productions, of which the one concerning to the input gates to the measure process is shown here:

CONNECT_IM → points_to(LINE,~rectangle)
    *CONNECT_IM.posid = LINE.L1 + 1000*LINE.L2;*
    CONNECT_IM.id = "im_gate";
    Where: ((LINE.R2 == rectangle.L2)
            && (LINE.R1 > rectangle.L1 && LINE.R1 < rectangle.R1))

The spatial parser acts so that at the end of the parsing an annotated PGN structure is produced, from where a specification is generated. The next figure show the processing steps.

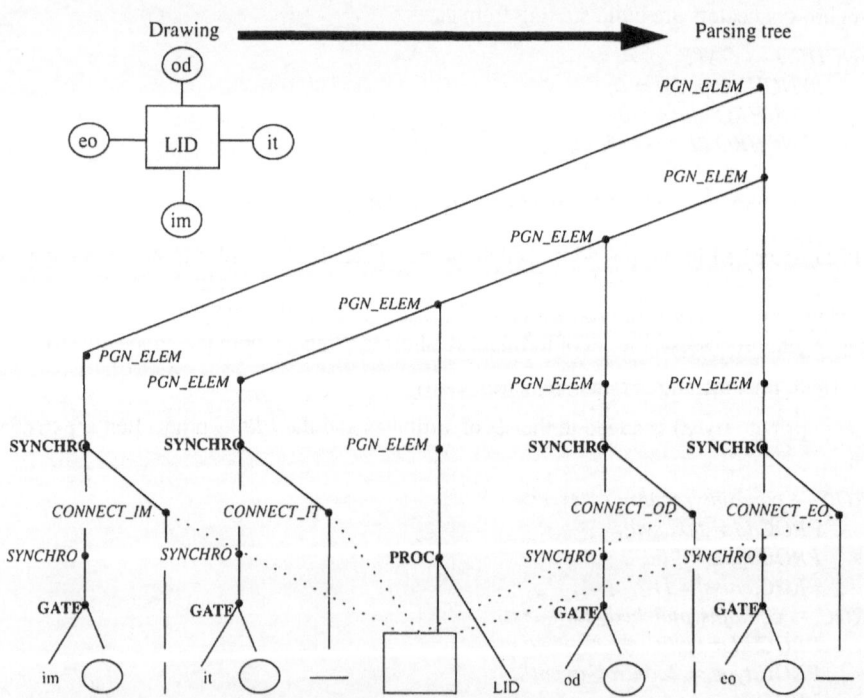

FIGURE 21.8. Spatial parsing tree

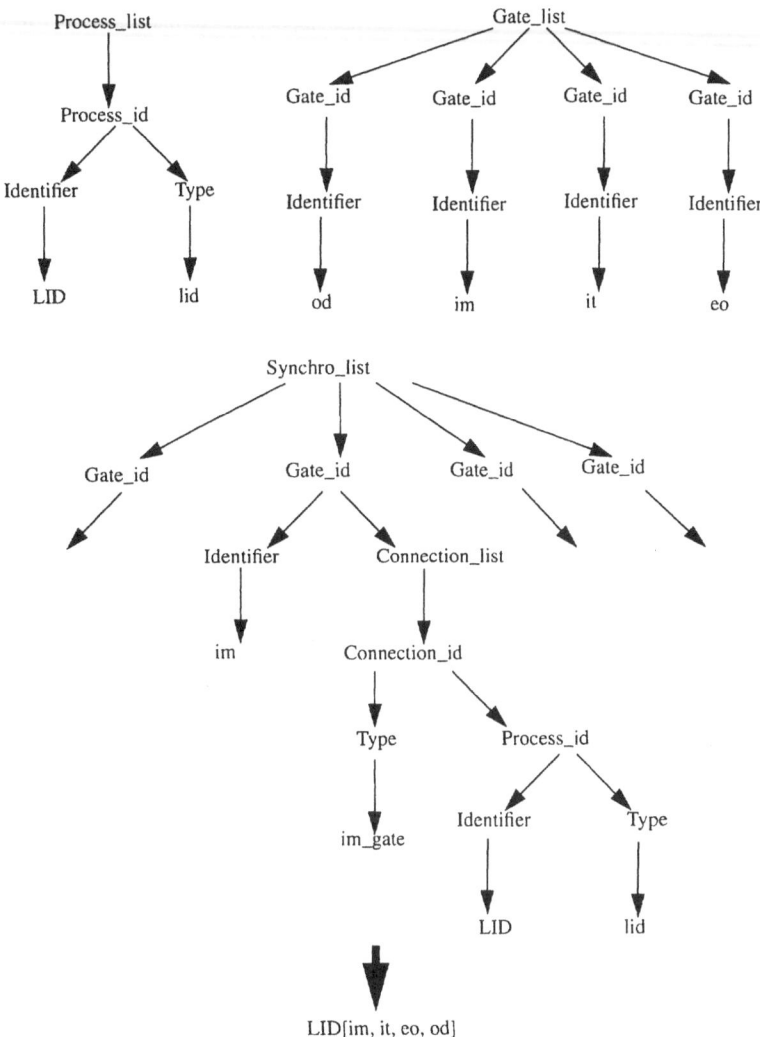

FIGURE 21.9. Annotated PGN structure

21.6 Example

In this section an example is presented which prove how the proposed environment is an efficient tool for supporting the syntactic and the semantic specification of logical input devices. The example is drawn from the color map exemplar found in [15].

The system functional core makes accessible to the interface the concept of color as one of the items describing its internal state: it is represented by a triplet identifying a point in some color space so that:

$$color := \langle x,y,z \rangle , \; x,y,z \in \mathfrak{R}^{+} \tag{Eq. 4}$$

The user is enabled to set the color value by separately entering r, g and b values by means of three instances on the same device; that is, the user performs actions, respectively denoted by r_dev, g_dev and b_dev, defined within a device space that are mapped either to r, g or b values so that:

$$r := f(r\_dev), \; g := f(g\_dev), \; b := f(b\_dev),$$
$$0 \le r, g, b \in \mathfrak{R}^{+} \le 1, \; r\_dev, g\_dev, b\_dev \in \text{Device\_space} \tag{Eq. 5}$$

$$color := g(f(r\_dev), f(g\_dev), f(b\_dev)) \tag{Eq. 6}$$

The interface provide the user with feedbacks for the color value as well as for the r, g and b values.

The behaviour expression of the system specified by using logical input devices is

((RED[r_dev, r_trigger, r_echo, r]   (Def. 7)
    ||| GREEN[g_dev, g_trigger, g_echo, g]
    ||| BLUE[b_dev, b_trigger, b_echo, b])
    |[r,g,b]| COLOR[r, g, b, c_trigger, c_echo, color])
    |[color]| FC[color]

where

- r_dev, g_dev, b_dev are the user actions denoting an input token to the measure process,
- r_trigger, g_trigger, b_trigger are the user actions respectively validating the actual r, g and b values (note that nothing is said on the relationship occurring between triggers and other events),
- r_echo, g_echo, b_echo, c_echo are the events corresponding to the presentation of feedback to the user,
- r, g, b are denoting the actual values for the read, green and blue components of the color in the RGB space,
- color is denoting the actual setting of the color.

It is immediately realized that the graphical representation of the behaviour expression given in (Def. 7) is much more intuitive although being still rigorous, once the composition rules described by the PLG of the previous section are known:

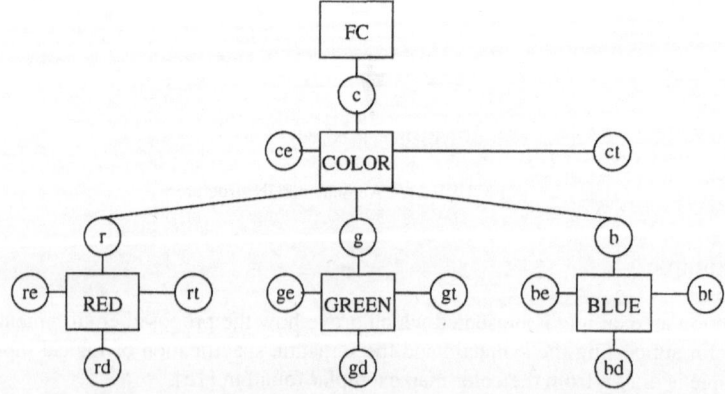

FIGURE 21.10. Graphical representation of the color specification

The behaviour expression described by both (Def. 7) and FIGURE 20.10 only takes into account the synchronization over data paths. Considering the default behaviour of a logical input device, what it can be said is that as soon as a trigger event occurs the corresponding measure value actually set for the triggered device is communicated to a receiving process by gate synchronization. However this doesn't guarantee for the consistency of the interface. As an example the following trace can be derived from the action tree of the behaviour expression

...; r_dev; r_echo; g_trigger; g; c_echo; ...   (Def. 8)

showing that a new value is set and presented for the RED device; the GREEN device is subsequently triggered and its measure value is communicated to the COLOR device that updates accordingly its presentation: at that point the presentations of the COLOR and RED devices mismatch!

The overall methodology to follow in refining the specification, so that any potential inconsistency is removed from the system, is to restrict adopt a constraint based style of specification by defining new processes that impose additional synchronization constraints: in our terminology those processes are referred to as controlling agents.

In this example, a controlling agent must be defined so that input token events are tightly coupled with trigger events for the RED, GREEN and BLUE devices:

process CNTL1[input, trigger] : **noexit** :=   (Def. 9)
        input ; trigger ; CNTL1[input, trigger]
endproc

and the behaviour expression in (Def. 7) must accordingly be changed to:

(((RED[r_dev, r_trigger, r_echo, r]   (Def. 10)
      |[r_dev, r_trigger]| CONTROL1[r_dev, r_trigger])
  ||| (GREEN[g_dev, g_trigger, g_echo, g]
      |[g_dev, g_trigger]| CONTROL1[g_dev, g_trigger])
  ||| (BLUE[b_dev, b_trigger, b_echo, b]
      |[b_dev, b_trigger]| CONTROL1[b_dev, b_trigger]))
  |[r,g,b]| COLOR[r, g, b, c_trigger, c_echo, color])
  |[color]| FC[color]

Again, (Def. 10) can be derived from the following more intuitive graphical representation :

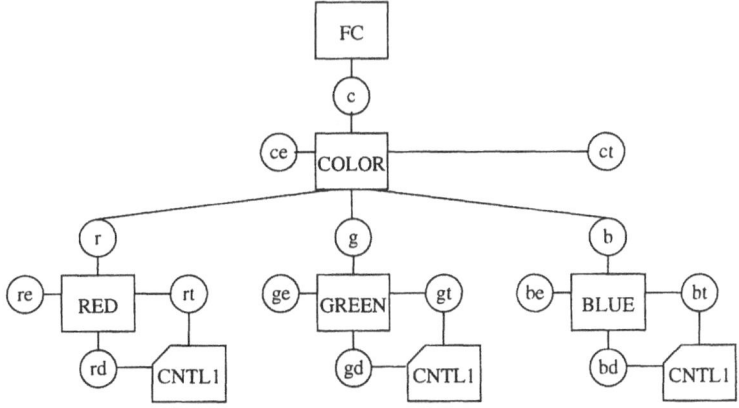

FIGURE 21.11. Adding constraints to the color specification

The above specification is constrained so that whenever actions r_dev, g_dev and b_dev and the corresponding presentations occur, the actual measured values are propagated through synchronization on r, g and b to COLOR which then also updates its presentation.

The specification is may not be yet satisfactory, since the trigger event of the COLOR device is left unrelated. In this case the interface may show presentation values that are consistent by themselves but still do not reflect the color state of the functional core. The introduction of a further constraint is straightforward with the following graphical representation:

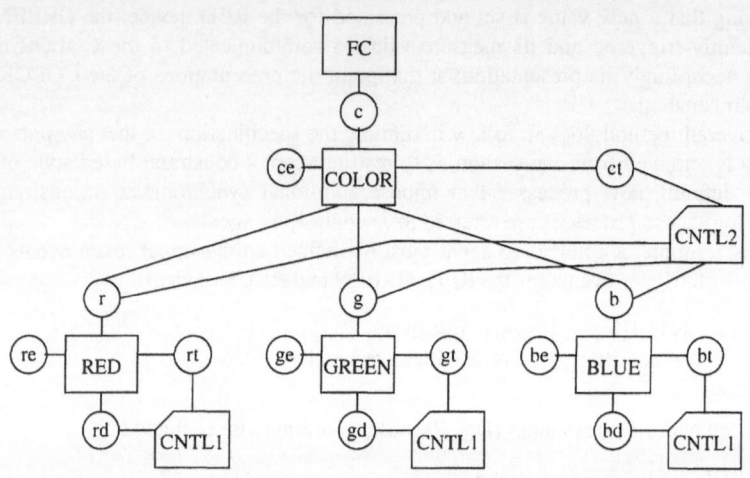

FIGURE 21.12. Adding further constraints to the color specification

where CNTL2 is defined to behave as in the following process definition:

process CNTL2 [r, g, b, c_trigger] : **noexit** :=   (Def. 11)
                r; c_trigger; CNTL2[r, g, b, c_trigger]
                [] g; c_trigger; CNTL2[r, g, b, c_trigger]
                [] b; c_trigger; CNTL2[r, g, b, c_trigger]
endproc

From FIGURE 20.11 the textual LOTOS specification can be derived.

(((RED [r_dev, r_trigger, r_echo, r]   (Def. 12)
            |[r_dev, r_trigger]| CONTROL1 [r_dev, r_trigger])
      ||| (GREEN [g_dev, g_trigger, g_echo, g]
            |[g_dev, g_trigger]| CONTROL1 [g_dev, g_trigger])
      ||| (BLUE [b_dev, b_trigger, b_echo, b]
            |[b_dev, b_trigger]| CONTROL1 [b_dev, b_trigger]))
      |[r,g,b]| (COLOR [r, g, b, c_trigger, c_echo, color]
            |[r,g,b,c_trigger]| CNTL2 [r, g, b, c_trigger]))
      |[color]| FC[color]

Further on the full interface specification can be encapsulated within a process definition that hides a number of gates from being observable:

process COLOR_SET[r_dev, g_dev, b_dev,   (Def. 13)
                         c_trigger,
                         r_echo, g_echo, b_echo, c_echo,
                         color] : **noexit** :=
hide r, g, b, r_trigger, g_trigger, b_trigger **in**
(((RED [r_dev, r_trigger, r_echo, r]
     |[r_dev, r_trigger]| CONTROL1 [r_dev, r_trigger])
  ||| (GREEN [g_dev, g_trigger, g_echo, g]
     |[g_dev, g_trigger]| CONTROL1 [g_dev, g_trigger])
  ||| (BLUE [b_dev, b_trigger, b_echo, b]
     |[b_dev, b_trigger]| CONTROL1 [b_dev, b_trigger]))
  |[r,g,b]| (COLOR [r, g, b, c_trigger, c_echo, color]
     |[r,g,b,c_trigger]| CNTL2 [r, g, b, c_trigger]))
endproc

leading to the following representation of the system

COLOR_SET [r_dev, g_dev, b_dev,   (Def. 14)
                   c_trigger,
                   r_echo, g_echo, b_echo, c_echo,
                   color]
|[color]| FC [color]

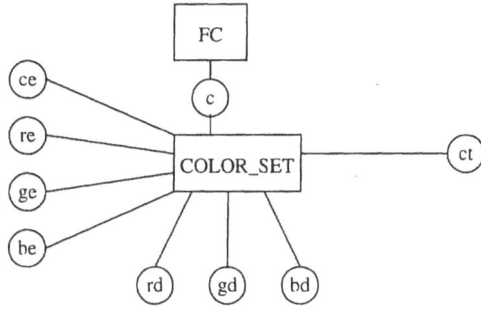

FIGURE 21.13. Encapsulated color specification

It is to be noted that nothing has so far been said about either the actual physical devices or the type of modality used in the interaction; rather the specification has been developed by only taking into account the equations from (Eq. 4) to (Eq. 6).

Assuming, as an example, that the interface is implemented by actually binding the RED, GREEN and BLUE input token events to a mouse device and the c_trigger event to a "button-up" event, we end up the example with the following expressions:

COLOR_SET [r_dev, g_dev, b_dev,   (Def. 15)
                   c_trigger,
                   r_echo, g_echo, b_echo, c_echo,
                   color]
|[color]| FC [color]
|[r_dev, g_dev, b_dev, c_trigger]| MOUSE [r_dev, g_dev, b_dev, c_trigger]

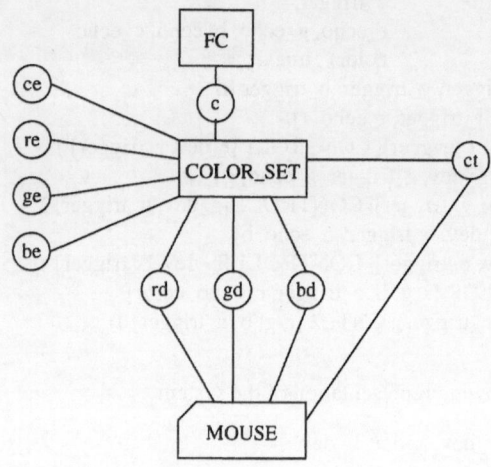

FIGURE 21.14. Encapsulated color specification

where the MOUSE is defined to behave as the following controlling agent:

process MOUSE [red,green,blue,button_up]: **noexit**:=   (Def. 16)
        red; button_up; MOUSE [red,green,blue,button_up]
        [] green; button_up; MOUSE [red,green,blue,button_up]
        [] blue; button_up; MOUSE [red,green,blue,button_up]
endproc

(Def. 15) imposes further constraints with respect to (Def. 13) so that the two are not equivalent specifications. The practical consequence of introducing media and/or modalities within the specification of an interface is that the system behaviour may change while keeping a kind of "week functional equivalence" with respect to user tasks. In many cases, addressing different physical devices may lead to potentially different system behaviour that might not be noticed by the user who is always following his/her mental model of interaction. This intuitive consideration is to be more deeply investigated in future works.

21.7 Conclusions

The relevance of network representations in the context of process algebras, such as LOTOS, has already been recognized since the beginning of the research in this field [16]. Algebraic expressions and graph like box interconnection diagrams play different roles in the field of computer aided software engineering. It is clearly desirable to bridge the gap between the two representations for combining their advantages.

We hope to have shown that Picture Layout Grammars of Process Gate Net are a useful mechanism for the formal interpretation of diagrams that are immediately appealing to intuition.

21.8   References

[1]   A.J.R.G. Milner, *A Calculus of Communicating Systems*, Prentice-Hall, 1990.

[2]   C.A.R. Hoare, *Communicating Sequential Processes*, Prentice Hall International, 1985.

[3]   ISO/IS 8807, Information processing systems - Open Systems Interconnection - *LOTOS - A Formal Description Technique Based on Temporal Ordering of Observational Behaviour*, 1988.

[4]   S.K.Chang, Visual Languages: A Tutorial and Survey, *IEEE Software*, V 4, 1987.

[5]   T. Bolognesi, E. Brinksma, Introduction to the ISO Specification Language LOTOS, *Computer Networks and ISDN Systems*, V 14, 1987.

[6]   H. Ehrig, B. Mahr, *Fundamentals of Algebraic Specification - 1*, Springer Verlag, 1985.

[7]   ISO/IEC JTC 1 SC 21 N 4871, Information retrieval, transfer and management for OSI, *G-LOTOS: DAM1 to IS 8807 on Graphical representation for LOTOS*, 1992.

[8]   T.Bolognesi, A Graphical Composition Theorem for Networks of LOTOS Processes, *Proceedings of the 10th International Conference on Distributed Computing Systems*, IEEE Computer Society, 1990.

[9]   G.P.Faconti, N.Zani, F.Paterno', The Input Model of Standard Graphics Systems Revisited by Formal Specification, *Computer Graphics FORUM*, V 11, N 3, 1992.

[10]   E.J.Golin, *A method for the specification and parsing of visual languages*, PhD Thesis, Brown University, 1990.

[11]   E.J.Golin, S.P.Reiss, The specification of Visual Language Syntax, *Journal of Visual Languages and Computing*, V 2, 1990.

[12]   E.J.Golin, Parsing Visual Languages with Picture Layout Grammars, *Journal of Visual Languages and Computing*, V 1, 1991.

[13]   F.Lakin, Spatial Parsing for Visual Languages, *Visual Languages*, S.K.Chang, T.Ichikawa, P.A.Ligomenides eds., Plenum Press, 1986.

[14]   M.Caneve, E.Salvatori, *LITE Users Manual*, LOTOSPHERE Consortium, EPSRIT II - 2304, Ref. Lo/WP2/N0034/V08, 1992.

[15]   *System Modelling Exemplars*, D.Duke ed., ESPRIT BRA 7040 - AMODEUS, SM/WP 12, 1993.

[16]   G.Milne, R.Miler, Concurrent processes and their syntax, *Journal of ACM*, V 26 N 2, 1979.

22 Grammar-based Formal Specification for the Object-Oriented User Interface Development

Aleš Limpouch

ABSTRACT
Object-oriented programming techniques are considered appropriate for the development of event-driven interactive systems with an object-oriented user interface. Due to the lack of any formalism in object-oriented user interface design and implementation, we utilize our experience in the use of grammar-based notations for the formal specification of user interfaces. This paper proposes a model which combines the Arch and the PAC models with the Bypass mechanism and shows their proper application and interpretation in the decomposition of an interactive system during its development. The adoption of attributed layered translation grammars is proposed for the formal description of the agents in this model. The prototype of the OOGC UIMS system supporting the grammar-based specification of user interfaces is presented in this paper.

22.1 Introduction

The human-computer interface is the fundamental part of each interactive computer system. Its quality determines the applicability of a particular interactive application and the potentional user's attitude toward it. Developing user interfaces, especially in graphical and window environments, has become a time-consuming and complex task. This paper makes an attempt to solve some problems for developers with the control and maintenance of the complexity of user interface development.

For the transparent and flexible user dialogue management, the concept of *User Interface Management Systems* (UIMS) has been introduced. According to [3] "a UIMS is an environment for constructing (prototyping) and managing interactive systems. A UIMS is comprised of a run-time support system and a set of design, specification and evaluation tools." Two general approaches for the user interface development are distinguished: language-based and object-oriented.

22.1.1 Language-based approach

The language-based approach is based on the architecture of the Seeheim model of a UIMS [7]. This architecture splits each application into three components: first, it separates the *application component* (i.e. problem domain) from the *presentation component* (i.e. interaction domain), and finally common control is handled by the *dialogue control component*. These components correspond closely to semantic, lexical and syntactical layers respectively, following standard practice in linguistics and in compiler construction. The Seeheim model of a UIMS is shown, as presented by Green at Seeheim in Figure 22.1.

The separation into problem domain and interaction facilities has been coupled with the hope for general guidelines addressing fast interface development, interface standards, consistent interaction, etc. According to [3] these expectations have not been met, mainly because the Seeheim model is too abstract and does not have sufficient detail for run-time support. Language-based approach is often considered inadequate for the development of modern direct manipulation interfaces. The vertical division into monolithic components in the Seeheim model does not correspond with current modern object-oriented design methods and implementation techniques.

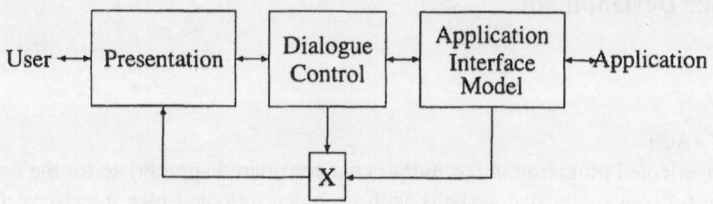

FIGURE 22.1. The Seeheim model

Mullin's model [6] represents an interesting modification of the Seeheim model. The Bypass route (indicated by X in Figure 22.1) is considered the major component of the model and multiple communication links between the components are introduced. The Arch models and Slinky metamodel [1] are the result of another attempt at a revision of the Seeheim model and serves as a good base for the vertical decomposition of an interactive system into layers during its development.

The dialogue control component has always been the most highly developed part of the Seeheim model. Formalisms for the specification of this part can be divided into three major categories: state/transition networks, grammars and event handlers. All have notational peculiarities with different strengths and weakness. According to [5] event handler notations have the greatest descriptive power, but there is a great deal of equivalence in these formalisms with the emphasis on different areas.

22.1.2   Object-oriented approach

Current window-based and direct manipulation graphical user interfaces are often called *object-oriented user interfaces* since their elements are metaphors of real world objects. Interactive systems with an object-oriented user interface should not limit alternatives available to their users. Then they are driven by unpredictable user actions – events. Object-oriented programming techniques are considered appropriate for the development of event-driven interactive systems with an object-oriented user interface.

The first architecture for object-oriented user interfaces was based on the *Model-View-Controller* (MVC) model [4]. Each object is made of three components. The *model* models the state and behaviour of the object in the world (i.e. the model is the object itself). The *view* is the part responsible for the presentation of the object and its state on the screen. The *controller* is the part of the object which handles user's actions and sends events to the model. Taking the example of dice, the model contains the current number on the dice and can generate a new number, the view can present the dice as a cube on the screen, and the controller sends the user's actions, e.g. roll the dice, to the model. The MVC model is a good base for the horizontal decomposition of an interactive system during its development.

An application framework is defined in [12] as a collection of abstract and concrete classes and the interfaces between them, and is the design for a subsystem. It is in fact an application without contents (i.e. "empty application") and is designed to be refined. It can be refined by changing its components or by creating new kinds of components (i.e. new subclasses of existing classes) without affecting the existing classes. This approach has become attractive for the development of interactive systems. The majority of object-oriented application frameworks for the user interface development are based on the MVC model, but usually on a simplified version with the controller integrated to the view object.

Although the abstraction level is raised, developing object-oriented interfaces based on application frameworks is still a hard task. The MVC model does not provide any direction for the vertical decomposition of an interactive system into layers or modules. The handling of more complex dialogues is then often intermixed among several views and their controllers (or event-handling methods). Thus the design and implementation of event-handling methods is a very difficult problem as frameworks give usually no means for dialogue control (proper handling of user action sequences), the clear management of contextual data changes within dialogue states, and support for history of dialogue.

Another model called PAC (Presentation, Abstraction, Control) is described in [2]. The PAC model gives the possibility of decomposing a user interface into a set of *agents* that can communicate together in several ways. The Presentation defines the input and output behaviour of the application as perceived by the user. The Abstraction part implements the functions that the application is able to perform. The Control part maintains the mapping and the consistency between the Abstraction and Presentation. It is intended to hold the context of the overall interaction between the user and the application. The structure of the PAC model is shown in Figure 22.2. PAC is a logical model that helps identify the structure of interactive applications and does not provide any formalism for the specification of agents.

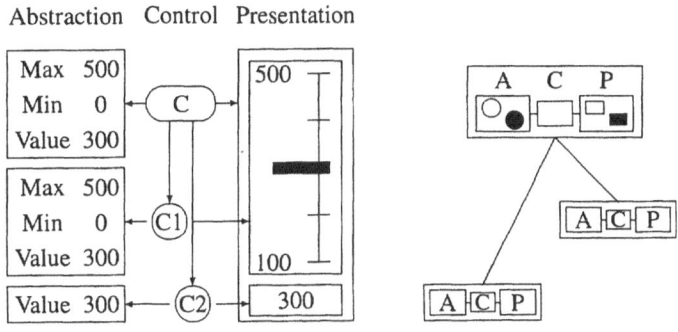

FIGURE 22.2. The PAC model

22.1.3   Our approach

In [8, 9] we presented a theoretical framework for the user interface development, which was based on the language-based approach. We proposed an extension to attributed translation grammars, which covers some important needs for the dialogue design and makes it possible to create a formal description of the user interface. Our extension of the translation algorithm enabled us to design the GRAMCOMP UIMS (generator and run-time system) which was based on the Seeheim model.

A number of experiments with the GRAMCOMP system have been made. During the experiments, the system proved to be useful for rapid prototyping of specific user interfaces. Complete redesign of the user interface for a special CAD system was accomplished with the help of the given formalism. The major advantages appear to be proper handling of user action sequences during the dialogue, support for context help, history and undo facilities, and clear management of contextual data changes within states of dialogue.

Due to the lack of any formalism in the object-oriented user interface development, we would like to utilize our experience and to use grammar-based notations for the formal specification of object-oriented user interfaces. This paper shows how combination of the Arch and the PAC model with the Bypass mechanism and their proper application and interpretation can help in the decomposition of an interactive system during its development. The adoption of attributed layered translation grammars is proposed for the formal description of the agents in our model. The prototype of our OOGC UIMS system which supports the grammar-based specification of user interfaces is presented.

22.2   Design model for interactive systems

In the world of object-oriented programming, the development of interactive systems does not really start from scratch. Developers usually have pre-built components at their disposal, at least a database management system (DBMS) or an interaction toolkit (e.g. X Window System). An interactive system is then decomposed during the design phase into layers, modules and objects, which simplifies the implementation of the system.

The Arch model (shown in Figure 22.3) constitutes a good base for the vertical decomposition of interactive systems. It consists of five components [1]:

- The *Domain-Specific Component* controls domain-related data and performs domain-related functions.

- The *Interaction Toolkit Component* implements the physical interaction with the user.

- The *Dialogue Component* has responsibility for task-level sequencing and maintaining consistency between domain-specific and user-interface-specific abstractions.

- The *Presentation Component* mediates the Dialogue and the Interaction Toolkit Components and provides a set of toolkit-independent objects (often called "interactors") for the Dialogue Component.

- The *Domain-Adaptor Component* mediates the Dialogue and the Domain-Specific Components, and also reorganizes domain-related data and provides domain-oriented functions required for user dialogue tasks.

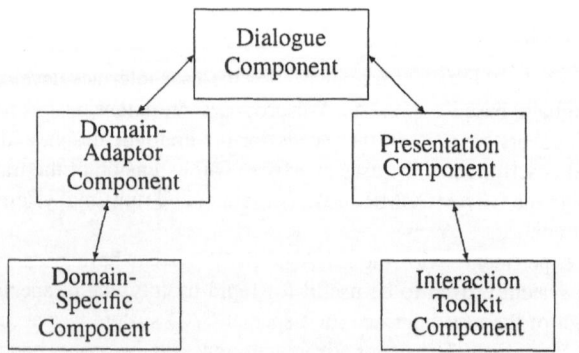

FIGURE 22.3. The Arch model

The coupling of functionalities into the components of the Arch model is left dependent upon the goals of the developers, their weighting of development criteria, and the type of system to be implemented. The concept of the Slinky metamodel [1] enables the shift of functionalities from component to component within the architecture of the Arch model.

The PAC model serves as a good base for the horizontal decomposition of an interactive system during its development. Then we would like to propose an idea to combine the Arch and PAC models and apply the PAC model to all components of the Arch model. Thus objects in each component can be divided into three groups: Presentations, Abstractions and Controllers.

The group of Abstractions contains objects which represent models and their structure, for example: a CAD database in the Domain-Specific Component; user-defined diagrams in the Domain-Adaptor Component; tables of grammar rules in the grammar-based Dialogue Component; model of interactors in the Presentation Component; and tables of event mappings and frame buffers in the Interaction Toolkit Component.

The group of Presentations contains objects, which are involved in presentation of Abstractions, for example: a display list of CAD systems in the Domain-Specific Component; layouts of user-defined diagrams in the Domain-Adaptor Component; a tree hierarchy of toolkit-independent objects in the Dialogue Component; window objects in the Presentation Component and key events or drawing tools in the Interaction Toolkit Component.

The group of Controllers contains agents which link the Abstractions and Presentations, transform them, and also maintain relationships with other agents. Agents can perform, for example, the following tasks: updating the display list according to changes in the CAD database in the Domain-Specific Component; controlling user-defined diagrams derived from the CAD database in the Domain-Adaptor Component; processing sequences of task-level events in the Dialogue Component; connecting interactors and window objects in the Presentation Component; and translating events according to mapping tables.

It seems clear, that five components of the Arch model are only general modules. These components will be decomposed into a few layers or modules during the development of an interactive system for maintenance and other reasons. It turns out that each module can be decomposed into PAC objects. PAC triplets are connected within the components, layers or modules through agents (Controllers) in a similar way as in the original model. We leave as a matter of design decision, whether they are connected between components directly or through some component manager agent. Multiple connections of the components and modules enable adoption of multi-threaded processing. We can also mention that the vertical decomposition in the Arch model is prepared for the development of client-server systems.

Another problem which should be observed is providing rapid graphics output and complex semantic feedback for graphically intensive applications, such as CAD or GIS systems. The original Arch Model connects the components only in the way shown in Figure 22.3. It seems necessary for Presentations of the Domain-Specific Component, e.g. display lists, to be connected directly with the Interaction Toolkit Component, which provides graphics output functions. For similar reasons they should be connected to the Presentation Component for continuous changing of some domain-dependent values, e.g. position indicator, during the dragging of a domain object.

The given problem can be solved by agents (Controllers), which serve as a bypass between the domain-specific and user-interface-specific parts, but are still included in the Dialogue Component. The Bypass agents directly connect domain-specific Presentations (or Controllers) and user-interface specific Abstractions (or Controllers). For example, a special agent connects the display list of CAD systems with a graphics output controller for direct graphics output. This agent also provides proper windows and graphics contexts. Figure 22.4 illustrates the proposed combination of the Arch and PAC models with additional Bypass agents.

As a short example we will describe the usual command of graphical applications, which enables one to input a sequence of points. For example, in CAD systems such sequences can be interpreted as polylines or curves, while in GIS systems it might be interpreted as linear

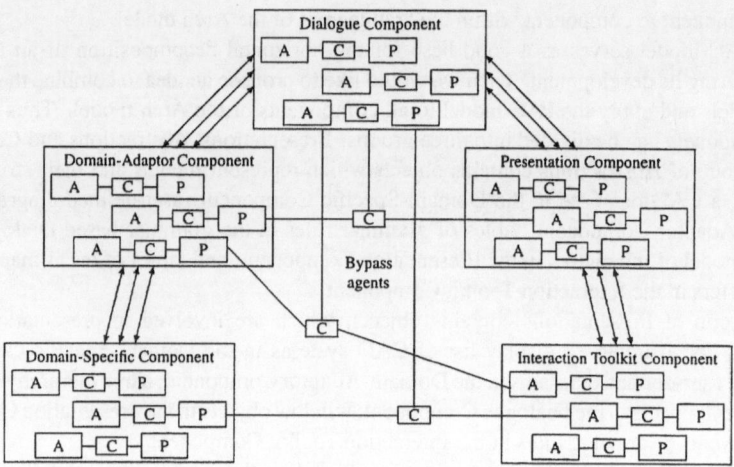

FIGURE 22.4. The proposed model

topographic objects. Such a command should enable the user to input new points, to remove the last specified point, and to change line attributes within this command. Then the designed system should provide some button on the screen for selecting this "polyline" command and then, the user can select a particular sequence of points in the active window. For example the new point in the sequence is selected by a click on the left mouse button and the other options "remove last point" or "line attribute command" might be selected from the menu, which is popped up by a click on the right mouse button. The system should enable the user to leave the active window and continue in another window with the same drawing area. An experienced user might also like to input a new point in user coordinates from some command line within the system. The position of the mouse cursor in the user coordinate system should be presented in a coordinate indicator. This command is deactivated by selecting any button for graphics manipulations within the drawing area, e.g. graphics object selection.

Allocations of objects, functions and agents within the polyline example in our model might be made as follows:

Domain-Specific Component: a database of graphical objects; an agent which stores the polyline in the database after completion of the polyline command.

Domain-Adaptor Component: a list of points kept during the input of the point sequence; an agent which provides proper handling of the graphics echo during the input of the point sequence; an agent which updates the coordinate indicator on the basis of mouse move events.

Dialogue Component: an agent for handling the input of the point sequence; an agent for the specification of line attributes; three bypass agents for transmitting mouse move events, for direct output of the graphics echo, and for updating the coordinate indicator.

Presentation Component: the coordinate indicator; drawing area objects; the command line; point, menu a text interactors; an agent which transforms tokens received from basic interactors into task-level events for the Dialogue Component.

Interaction Toolkit Component: an agent which provides graphics output functions; an agent which translates events into keyboard symbols and mouse events.

22.3   Controller specification based on grammars

As mentioned above, the proper handling of sequences of user's actions is one of the principal problems in the development of object-oriented user interfaces. The event handling in event-driven systems is based on some combination of event-handling loop and event handlers, but the principle is the same. Events are retrieved from an event queue within an event-handling loop and then dispatched to the corresponding event handler (controller, event-handling method of view). The handling of more complex dialogues and clear management of contextual data changes within dialogue states are still very difficult. Controllers (agents) in the Dialogue Component are supposed to be responsible for the handling of such sequences and for the contextual data management. Thus our aim was to find some formalism for the description of these agents.

From our experience with the GRAMCOMP UIMS [8, 9], attributed translation context-free grammars are very suitable formalism for the handling of sequences of user's actions. Our experiments have shown that grammars provide an accurate specification notation for the user interface development. Translation grammars define, in fact, a transformation of one language into another. In terms of user interfaces, this means that sequences of events (input symbols) are translated into sequences of computer actions (output symbols). Attributes are added for the management of contextual data changes. In our experiments, attributed translation grammars proved to be able to describe complex tasks and contextual data changes in a clear and manageable way.

But we have met some traditional drawbacks of the grammar approach. Conventional context-free grammars fail in the support of several layers of abstraction which are required for the decomposition of dialogue into elementary sequences and for their concurrent processing. This is, in fact, the main reason for the claims that grammars are not suited for the development of direct manipulation user interfaces. The use of layered grammars can increase modularity, facilitate the decomposition of complex interactive systems without losing of context management, and allow concurrent processing of user actions.

For this purpose we can use a layered translation grammar LG defined as pair $LG = (G, R)$, where

G is a set of translation grammars, where grammar G_i, $1 \leq i \leq m$ is defined as a tetrad $G_i = (N^{G_i}, T^{G_i}, P^{G_i}, S^{G_i})$, where

N^{G_i} is a set of non-terminal symbols;

$T^{G_i} = (I^{G_i} \cup O^{G_i})$ is a set of terminal symbols, where

I^{G_i} is a set of input symbols,
O^{G_i} is a set of output symbols;

P^{G_i} is a set of rules in the form

$$(r^{G_i})\, X_0^{G_i} \to X_1^{G_i} X_2^{G_i} \dots X_{n_r G_i}^{G_i},$$

where $n_r G_i \geq 0$, $X_0^{G_i} \in N^{G_i}$, $X_k^{G_i} \in (N^{G_i} \cup T^{G_i})$ for $1 \leq k \leq n_r G_i$;

S^{G_i} is the start symbol;

$R = (t, S^{G_r})$ is relation, where $t \in T^{G_s}$, $1 \leq r,s \leq m$.

Thus the layered grammar is a set of grammars which allows us to consider certain terminal symbols as start symbols of another grammar. The bottom layer comprises productions of all terminal symbols from top-level layer which are start symbols of further grammars. By using non-terminals, we can describe states and their sequences within an layer.

Another drawback of grammars seems to be the weak description of possible relations of symbols between grammars in the traditional approach. To overcome this problem, the declarative capability of terminal symbols can be enhanced with an indication of corresponding events and agents. We proposed an enhancement of attribute mechanism in traditional grammars in [8, 9]. A set of inherited attributes can be assigned to each input symbol and a set of synthesized attributes can be assigned to each output symbol for this purpose. Then each input symbol can be supplemented with corresponding event and a set of corresponding agents (or grammars) which restricts the agent to processing events generated only by these corresponding agents. In a similar way, each output symbol can be supplemented by a set of corresponding Abstractions or Presentations as well as a set of agents (or grammars) for which events and messages are generated. These supplementary indications (attributes) can be used for easier maintenance and more effective processing in the whole system.

Thus, we propose to use the attributed layered translation grammar for the specification of agents in the Dialogue Component of our model. One grammar corresponds to each agent. Input symbols can be considered as task-level events received by the agent. All input symbols which are start symbols of further grammars define agents in the bottom layer of the Dialogue Component. Output symbols can be considered as Abstractions or Presentations corresponding to the agent as well as events generated by the agent.

The semantic processing of input symbols then means computation of synthesized attributes and/or start (processing) of the corresponding agent in the bottom layer. The semantic processing of output symbols means sending messages to Abstractions or Presentations as well as generating events or sending messages to another agents, e.g. agents in the other components of the model. Generated messages can also create and manipulate bypass agents. In this way the attributed layered translation grammar enables developers to decompose the top-level dialogue into tasks which can be performed concurrently by different agents and also to manage updates of Abstractions and Presentations according to contextual data changes during the dialogue.

22.3.1 Polyline example

In our polyline example the input of the point sequence is handled by an agent in the Dialogue Component. This component can be described by an attributed layered translation grammar and the polyline command will be specified by one attributed translation grammar in this layered grammar. We will show the grammar for the polyline agent in detail in this subsection.

The polyline agent is defined by the attributed translation grammar $POLYG = (N, I \cup O, R, S)$. We use following sets of symbols (these symbols are typeset in different capitalization and type styles for their easier distinction):

set of non-terminal symbols:
$N = \{POLYLINE, PSTART, PEND, PLIST, PDELETE\}$;

set of input symbols:
$I = \{point, remove, line\_attrib, exit\}$;

set of output symbols:
$O = \{$**EXITCMD, SAINTER, EAINTER, SAECHO, EAECHO, SAECHOBYPASS, EAECHOBYPASS, SALIST, EALIST, ADDPOINT, DELPOINT**$\}$.

The start symbol S of this grammar is the non-terminal symbol $POLYLINE$.

The input of the point sequence is then specified by the following set of rules *R*:

(1) POLYLINE → PSTART PLIST exit PEND

```
PSTART    {DrawAreaAgentID := POLYLINE.DrawAreaAgentID}
PLIST     {InListID        := PSTART.SyListID;
           InInterIDList   := POLYLINE.InInterIDList
                                           + PSTART.SyInterID;
           InLineAttr      := POLYLINE.InLineAttr}
exit      {event:   exit;
           grammar: POINTG, ARCG}
PEND      {InListID        := PSTART.SyListID;
           InInterID       := PSTART.SyInterID;
           InBypassID      := PSTART.SyBypassID;
           InEchoID        := PSTART.SyEchoID}
POLYLINE  {SyLineAttr      := PLIST.SyLineAttr}
```

This rule divides the agent operation into three parts: initialization, input of point sequence, and closing parts. This agent is deactivated by the *exit* symbol. The associated semantic rule denotes that it accepts only an event `exit` issued by agents corresponding to grammars POINTG and ARCG which are other grammars of the layered grammar. Other semantic rules mostly copies agent identifiers (interactor, drawing area, echo, echo bypass, and point list agents) or line attributes.

(2) PSTART → **EXITCMD EALIST SAINTER SAECHO**
           SAECHOBYPASS

```
EXITCMD       {event:   exit;
               grammar: POINTG, ARCG}
EALIST        {message: createListAgent;  return : agentID}
SAINTER       {message: createInputAgent; return : agentID}
SAECHO        {message: createEchoAgent;  return : agentID}
SAECHOBYPASS  {SrcID           := SAECHO.agentID;
               TgtID           := PSTART.DrawAreaAgentID;
               message: createBypassAgent(SrcID,TgtID);
               return : agentID}
PSTART        {SyListID        := EALIST.agentID;
               SyInterID       := SAINTER.agentID;
               SyBypassID      := SAECHOBYPASS.agentID;
               SyEchoID        := SAECHO.agentID}
```

This rule describes the initialization part of the agent. The agent issues the `exit` event and deactivates the agents corresponding to the POINTG and ARCG grammars. Then the agent creates point list, interactor, echo, and echo bypass agents by means of messages associated by the given semantic rules. Agent identifiers are saved into attributes at the end of rule for later processing.

(3) PEND → **EAECHOBYPASS EAECHO EAINTER EALIST**

```
EAECHOBYPASS  {message:destroyAgent; target:PEND.InBypassID}
EAECHO        {message:destroyAgent; target:PEND.InEchoID}
EAINTER       {message:destroyAgent; target:PEND.InInterID}
EALIST        {message:destroyAgent; target:PEND.InListID}
```

This rule describes the closing part of the agent in which the agent destroys the point list, interactor, echo, and echo bypass agents.

(4) $PLIST^0$ → point **ADDPOINT** $PLIST^1$ PDELETE $PLIST^2$

```
point      {event: point; source: PLIST0.InInterIDList}
ADDPOINT   {InX              := point.X;
            InY              := point.Y;
            InLineAttr       := PLIST0.InLineAttr;
            message: addPoint(InX,InY,InLIneAttr);
            target : PLIST.InListID}
PLIST1     {InListID         := PLIST0.InListID;
            InInterIDList := PLIST0.InInterIDList;
            InLineAttr       := PLIST0.InLineAttr}
PDELETE    {InListID         := PLIST0.InListID;
            InInterIDList := PLIST0.InInterIDList}
PLIST2     {InListID         := PLIST0.InListID;
            InInterIDList := PLIST0.InInterIDList;
            InLineAttr       := PLIST1.SyLineAttr}
PLIST0     {SyLineAttr       := PLIST2.SyLineAttr}
```

This rule describes the input of the point sequence. The agent accepts the new point in the form of the `point` event issued by agents given in the `InInterIDList` attribute. Then it sends the `addPoint` message to the point list agent. Other semantic rules mostly copies agent identifiers (interactor, drawing area, echo, echo bypass, and point list agents) or line attributes. Correct handling of the "remove" option in the polyline command is ensured by the generating of *PDELETE* non-terminal symbol for each point. The rule guarantees in this way that this agent is not able to process more *remove* than the *point* symbols.

(5) $PLIST^0$ → line_attrib $PLIST^1$

```
line_attrib {event: line_attrib;
             if (line_attrib.LineAttr = nil) {
                LINEATTRG.InLineAttr := PLIST0.InLineAttr;
                use (modal) grammar: LINEATTRG
                line_attrib.LineAttr:=LINEATTRG.SyLineAttr;
             }}
PLIST1      {InListID         := PLIST0.InListID;
             InInterIDList := PLIST0.InInterIDList;
             InLineAttr       := line_attrib.LineAttr}
PLIST0      {SyLineAttr       := PLIST1.SyLineAttr}
```

This rule describes changing of line attributes during the polyline command. The agent accepts the line_attrib event issued by any agent. An agent associated to grammar LINEATTRG is started only in the case when line attributes are not set. The indication modal denotes that the polyline agent waits for an completion of the line attributes input.

(6) PLIST → e

```
PLIST          {SyLineAttr := PLIST.InLineAttr}
```

This rule is auxiliary empty rule for correct processing.

(7) PDELETE → remove **DELPOINT**

```
remove     {event: remove; source: PLIST.InInterIDList}
DELPOINT {message: deletePoint; target: PDELETE.InListID}
```

This rule describes processing of the "remove" option of the polyline command. The agent accepts the *remove* symbol in the form of the remove event issued by agents given in the InInterIDList attribute. Then it sends the deletePoint message to the point list agent.

(8) PDELETE → e

This rule is auxiliary empty rule for correct processing.

The given attributed translation grammar is an ambiguous grammar. These conflicts can be resolved by preferential use of one rule according to the context of the polyline command.

The polyline command can be used in the context of the attributed layered translation grammar in the following rule:

(k) TASK^0 → polyline TASK^1

```
polyline {event: polyline;
          POLYG.DrawAreaAgentID := TASK0.InDrawAreaAgentID;
          POLYG.InLineAttr       := TASK0.InLineAttr;
          use (non-modal) grammar: POLYG;
          polyline.LIneAttr      := POLYG.SyLineAttr}
TASK1     {InLineAttr            := polyline.LineAttr}
TASK0     {SyLineAttr            := TASK1.SyLineAttr}
```

This rule describes processing of the button for the selection of the polyline command. The top-level agent accepts the polyline event and starts the agent corresponding to the given grammar POLYG. The indication non-modal denotes that the top-level agent does not wait for an completion of the polyline command.

The given specification looks rather complicated, but the polyline command is probably one of the most complicated commands for processing. The generation tool described in the next section is able to complete some semantic rules, e.g. the semantic rules which simply copy inherited attributes into inherited or synthesized attributes. Then it is not necessary to specify the majority of the semantic rules given above. However, the given mechanism enables developers to specify the handling of contextual information accurately. The full specification of the layered attributed translation grammar is then prepared for various tests of dialogue correctness and missing items.

22.4   User interface generation tool

In the previous sections, we presented the model for a UIMS and the grammar-based formalism for the specification of agents in the Dialogue component of our model. For our experiments with presented mechanisms, we have proposed the OOGC UIMS which supports the implementation of object-oriented user interfaces based on the given model. The presented formalism for the specification of agents gives us the possibility to design a prototype of a user interface generation tool which makes rapid prototyping of object-oriented user interfaces possible.

Grammar-based notation enables us to use the Constructor–Executor model for the design of the structure of the OOGC UIMS. The whole system consists of three parts:

- Constructor – OOGCGT generation tool

- Executor – OOCA run-time system

- Interaction Toolkit – OOGF framework

The attributed layered translation grammar defines a set of agents in the Dialogue Component of a developed interactive system. This grammar constitutes the input into the Constructor tool which generates a set of agents. These generated objects are then used by the object-oriented Executor which controls the overall management of dialogue processing and event handling within the system. The interaction toolkit provides a set of user interface objects and interactors for the system.

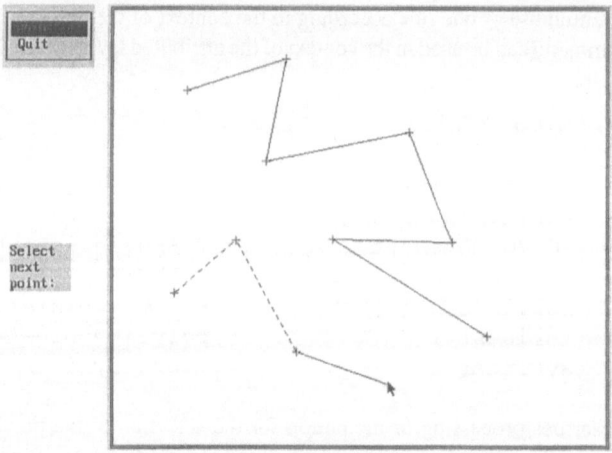

FIGURE 22.5. The sample screen of the polyline example

The prototype of a simple version of the OOGCGT generation tool was implemented. It provides a text-based editing environment for the creation of attributed layered grammars as well as a compiler for the generation of agent class definitions and tables, which are necessary for the Executor part. The generation tool contains several simple options for checking of grammar correctness and missing items. The prototype of the OOCA run-time system consists of a set of abstract classes for the event dispatching and grammar symbol processing. The OOGF framework represents simple toolkit which implements a small set of user interface objects and interactors. The current UIMS system has been implemented for IBM PC computers in Borland Pascal and C++ languages. Some experiments with the system were done for small testing applications. One of them (the polyline example) is shown in Figure 22.5.

More sophisticated version of the system is currently under development. This version will support the specification of agents in a visual form, a certain method for the specification of agents in the other components of the proposed model, some object-oriented way for the specification of Abstractions, and a visual editor for Presentations. These tools should then be connected to each other by means of a certain expert tool, which will support the maintenance of links among developed objects, layers, modules and components. It is expected that the next generation of the environment will support the use of user-defined tools instead of provided tools.

22.5   Conclusion

The model for the development of interactive systems has been proposed. It combines the Arch and PAC models with additional Bypass agents which handle direct communication between components. The given model enables developers to take advantage of both vertical and horizontal decomposition for designed interactive systems and to develop clear structures in them. Some experiments with the proposed model were done for small testing applications. One of them (the polyline example) was presented in this paper. The proposed model and its decomposition scheme are currently used for the design of a large-scale geographic information system (GIS) based on the redesign of an existing middle-scale land Information system (LIS) [10]. The development environment based on the proposed model is currently being prepared within the OOGC UIMS system.

The formalism based on the attributed layered translation grammar amended with agent indications was introduced for the specification of agents in the Dialogue Component of the proposed model. The specification of the polyline example was presented. Investigations are currently being done with the aim of finding all features and capabilities of the proposed formalism. We hope that it might be used for the specification of agents within all components of our model.

The OOGC user interface management system supporting the development of object-oriented user interfaces based on the proposed model was designed. The prototype of the OOGC UIMS was implemented. The system is based on the Constructor–Executor model. The prototype of the user interface generation tool supporting the specification of agents based on the attributed layered translation grammar was developed. Many tools, which enable developers to construct object-oriented user interfaces, and to maintain their whole complexity, are expected in the next version of the system.

Formalisms for the description of presentation and abstraction objects is another future topic of investigations. Hopefully, some grammar based notation might be used for this purpose. This aim would give us the possibility to introduce a complete uniform formal method suitable for the specification of object-oriented user interfaces.

Acknowledgements:

The author would like to express his thanks especially to Prof. Bořivoj Melichar for valuable suggestions in problems of attributed translations and Prof. Pavel Slavík with his valuable suggestions and ideas during the development of the GRAMCOMP UIMS.

22.6   References

[1] A Metamodel for the Runtime Architecture of an Interactive System. The UIMS Tool Developers Workshop. *SIGCHI Bulletin*, 24(1):32–37, 1992.

[2] J. Coutaz. PAC, an implementation model for dialog design. In *Proceedings of the INTERACT'87*, pages 431–436. Elsevier, 1987.

[3] D.A. Duce, M.R. Gomes, F.R.A. Hopgood, and J.R. Lee, editors. *User Interface Management and Design*. Proceedings of the Workshop on UIMS and Environments, Lisbon, June 4-6, 1990. Springer, Berlin, 1991.

[4] A. Goldberg. *Smalltalk-80 Interactive Programming Environment*. Addison-Wesley, Reading, MA, 1983.

[5] M. Green. A Survey of Three Dialogue Models. *ACM Transactions on Graphics*, 5(3):244–275, 1986.

[6] J. Mullin. *Dialogue Specification, Analysis and Implementation in a User Interface Management System*. PhD thesis, University of Strathclyde, 1991.

[7] G.E. Pfaff, editor. *User Interface Management Systems*. Proceedings of the Workshop on UIMS, Seeheim, Nov. 1-3, 1983. Springer, Berlin, 1985.

[8] P. Slavík and A. Limpouch. User Interface Design Based on the Theory of Formal Languages. Research Report DC-91-02, Czech Technical University, Prague, 1991.

[9] P. Slavík and A. Limpouch. User Interface Design Based on the Theory of Formal Languages. Research Report DC-93-03 (revised version of the report DC-91-02), Czech Technical University, Prague, 1993.

[10] TopoL 3.0. Reference guide, Help Service – Mapping, Prague, 1994.

[11] A. Weinand, E. Gamma, and R. Marty. ET++ – An Object-Oriented Application Framework in C++. Proceedings of the ACM Conference on Object-Oriented Programming, Systems, Languages and Applications. *SIGPLAN Notices*, 23(11):46–57, 1988.

[12] R.J. Wirfs-Brock and R.E. Johnson. Surveying Current Research in Object-Oriented Design. *Communications of the ACM*, 33(9), 1990.

23 Petri Net Based Design of User-Driven Interfaces Using the Interactive Cooperative Objects Formalism

Philippe A. Palanque
Rémi Bastide

ABSTRACT

The research work presented here belongs in the domain of formal specification of human-software interaction. More precisely, we are concerned by the applying a formal specification technique in the various stages of the construction of an user-driven application, the kind supported by most of the current UIMS. We use the Interactive Cooperative Objects (ICO) formalism, in which structural (or static) aspects are described in an object-oriented framework and dynamic (or behavioral) aspects are described with high-level Petri-nets. The formalism, a case study and some of its expected benefits are presented here.

23.1. Introduction

The specific problems related to the engineering of user-driven interfaces are now widely recognized and well identified. Theoretical and practical work in this area are numerous, and, although starting from the same empirical evidences, present very various solutions [1, 16, 9].

In spite of this diversity, some constants are standing out in the proposed solutions and this witnesses the fact that the main features of the domain are now being well mastered. In the recent formal approaches (such as those presented in the 1993 York workshop on formal methods), the following characteristics are always present :

- *A description encompassing both the state and the event aspects of interactive applications*: both aspects are equally important for the mastering of the behavior of an interactive system. This point also stems from the reactive nature of modern interactive systems which evolve in a discrete manner according to their inner state and to the events they receive from their environment. Earlier systems were mostly transformational by nature, and thus a state-based approach was well suited to model them. Modern graphical systems are most often programmed in an event-driven approach [7], but a purely event-driven design often leads to unmanageable code, due to the scattering of the system's state.
- *The handling of both data structure and control structure*: as the object-oriented approach has shown, a complex system can only be mastered if both its structural (or static) and behavioral (or dynamic) aspects are captured in an unified notation. Formal methods in HCI integrate these two components often by trying to merge as seamlessly as possible two formalisms dedicated to one or the other of these two aspects.
- *The need for structuring mechanisms*: as any other software component, the user interface must be understandable, reusable and open to evolution. Any formal approach must therefore offer structuring constructs, in order to produce components of tractable size so that their validation keeps simple. These structuring constructs must also ensure that previously designed components may be extended or reused in different contexts.
- *The need for an easy description of parallelism*: this may appear surprising at first glance. Firstly, interfaces are often programmed using conventional sequential programming

languages. Secondly, the user who drives the interaction with the software has only very limited potential for concurrent activities. Nevertheless, the need for a description of concurrency is of prime importance, even if the user only interacts with the software through a purely sequential device such as a keyboard, because user-driven systems have the goal to allow the user to follow conceptually concurrent tasks, by freely interacting with several parts of the software without any predefined path or schedule. Those tasks are usually concurrent, in the meaning that they evolve independently most of the time, but must synchronize and cooperate when they have to access shared data. It is therefore necessary, starting from the specification phase, to use a formalism allowing to represent this conceptual concurrence.

- *The need for formality*: the approaches mainly based on tools have shown their limitations. Most of recent proposals are based on formal notations, most often using formalisms borrowed from other parts of computer science instead of providing yet another "ad-hoc" notation. Thus the design of the interface takes advantage of the advances performed in other domains of computer science. This need for formality stems from the difficulty to ensure the proper functioning of interfaces design in an event-driven environment. Such environments resemble real-time or reactive systems which are known to be difficult to design, to verify and to test. Several formalisms that are now used in the field of interface design have first proved their modeling power in the field of real-time systems (e.g. LOTOS, Petri Nets, Temporal Logic, CCS, CSP).

- *The accounting for temporal aspects*: The explicit handling of time-related properties is becoming more and more important, especially in multi-modal systems or in animated interfaces, where there is time-based system evolution. It should be possible to deal properly with concerns such as alarms, and calendar-driven events.

In this chapter, we present a formalism called Interactive Cooperative Objects (ICO), specially built for the design, the specification and verification of interactive software.
Section 23. 2 presents the ICO formalism in an informal way. Section 23.3 details in which way this formalism matches the five criteria given above. In section 23.4 we describe a complete example of a simple application featuring a user-driven interface. The last section (section 23.5) shows how a formal verification may be performed.

23.2. Definition of Interactive Cooperative Objects

The formal definition of the ICO formalism is rather lengthy, since it needs to cope with concepts borrowed both from the object oriented approach (classification, inheritance, polymorphism, dynamic instanciation and use relationship) and from the Petri nets theory. Therefore, only an informal definition is given here, but the interested reader may refer to [13] for more details.
The ICO formalism is an object-oriented language specially designed for the modeling and implementation of event-driven interfaces [3, 15]. In this language, all objects are instances of a class which describes four components: services, behavior, state-space and presentation. ICOs may be thought of as a strongly typed object language in the spirit of Eiffel [12] with the peculiarity that the behavior of the objects is not described by algorithmic constructs, but instead is given in terms of Petri nets, which allow for an easy description of concurrency, both inside and object and between objects.

The services of an ICO class define its visible part, and are methods that may be called by clients of an instance of that class. Those services may either be functional, and return information on the data structure of the instance, or be procedural, and represent a request for the execution of a processing.

The **ObCS** (Object Control Structure) of a class fully defines the behavior of its instances: it describes how the availability of the services evolve over time, how the service requests are processed by the instance according to its inner state, the operations the instances may perform on their own behalf, and the services they may require from other objects. The formalism used to describe both the behavior and the state space of the objects is a dialect of high-level Petri nets called Petri nets with objects (PNO), which is further described in section 3.2.

Each service is associated with one or several ObCS' transitions. A service request may be accepted only when one of its associated transitions is enabled, and it is performed by the occurrence of such a transition. Services of a class ICO which are at the user's disposal are called **user services**. An ObCS may include transitions which are not associated to any service: they correspond to the object's spontaneous activity.

The presentation of a class states the external look of its instances. This presentation is a structured set of **widgets**.

The user / system interaction will only take place through those components. Each user action on a widget may trigger one of the ICO's user service. The relation between user services and widgets is fully stated by the **activation function** which associates to each couple (widget, user action) the service to be triggered.

In an interactive application modeled by ICOs, each window will be modeled by an ICO class. When modeling a window by an ICO, the sequencing and synchronization constraints for the user actions are expressed in the ObCS. Transitions relate to the services, stating their availability, and user services relate to widgets through the activation function. Thus the active or inactive state of the widgets may be known by looking at the ObCS' marking: the fact that no transition associated to a service is enabled by the current marking means that this service is not currently available to the user.

In our approach, Petri nets are encapsulated in objects, thus defining their behavior and state space. The tokens flowing in the ObCS are references to other objects, featuring an ObCS of their own.

23.3. Rationale for the use of the Interactive Cooperative Object formalism

From this informal definition of the ICO formalism, we may now explain how ICOs match the five requirements stated in the introduction.

23.3.1. State and events in modeling

In order to compare several state-based and event-based modeling we introduce a very general representation for a reactive system. This representation is not aimed to serve as a design formalism, but merely to serve as a comparison device. In this representation, a reactive system is characterized by three components:

• the set of its possible states, denoted by S, from which the current state is denoted by s_c and the initial state by s_0,

• the set of events to which it reacts, denoted by E, from which the incoming event is denoted by e_i,

• the set of actions it can perform, denoted by A.

The system's response to an event is to perform one of its actions, which may result in a change of state. The action performed depends on both the incoming event and the current state ($a = f(s_c, e_i)$), and the state reached (s_r) after the occurrence of the action depends on both the previous state and the incoming event ($s_r = g(s_c, e_i)$). We call f the *reaction* function and g the *side-effect* (state-changing) function.

All the formalisms for the description of reactive systems aim at defining S, E, A, f and g in a more or less explicit way, often providing a graphical notation designed to enhance the readability of models and generally putting the emphasis on one of the definition's components.

In the rest of this section, we use a toy example to illustrate the difference between event-based and state-based modeling, and show how Petri nets allow for a mixed approach.

The system considered as example is defined as follows:

• $S = \{S1, S2, S3, S4\}$, $s_0 = S1$

• $E = \{Ev1, Ev2\}$,

• $A = \{A1, A2, A3, A4\}$,

• f : S X E → A, such that
  $f(S1,Ev1) = A1$,
  $f(S2,Ev1) = f(S3,Ev1) = A2$,
  $f(S4,Ev2) = f(S3,Ev2) = A3$,
  $f(S2,Ev2) = A4$,

• g : S X E → S, such that
  $g(S1,Ev1) = g(S3,Ev2) = S2$,
  $g(S2,Ev1) = g(S4,Ev2) = S3$,
  $g(S3,Ev1) = S4$,
  $g(S2,Ev2) = S1$.

23.3.1.1. State-based modeling

In state-based modeling, the emphasis is put on the system's states, which are explicitly enumerated. The best suited formalisms for this approach are state diagrams and their extensions (statecharts [8], Augmented Transition Networks (ATN) [22], ...).

In state-based modeling, the system is represented by a quadruplet <S, O, T, s_0> where:

• S and s_0 are as stated above,

• O is the set of state changing operators,

• T is the transition function such that T : S x O → S.

In finite state automata (FSA), O = E and T is equivalent to the side-effect function, which means that the reaction function is not modeled. Models derived from FSA, such as ATN, take into account the reaction function by defining O such that O ⊆ E x A.

The system considered as example may be modeled by an ATN as shown in Figure 23.1.

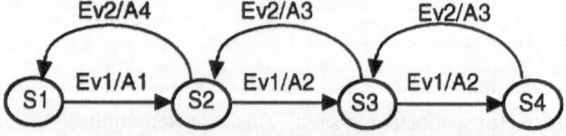

FIGURE 23.1. State-based modeling of the toy example

The emphasis put on the system's states is highlighted by the graphical notation, since each state has a dedicated graphical representation. On the opposite, the elements of the sets A and E are duplicated in the model (e.g. the association Ev1/A2 is duplicated between states S2-S3 and S3-S4; association Ev2/A3 is also duplicated), and those sets may only be built by sorting out the inscriptions on the arcs. Moreover, if one wants to know from which state a given operation may occur, every state of the model must be studied. Likewise, the set of actions possibly triggered by a given event is not made explicit, and must be built in the same way.

When there is much concurrency in the system, this leads to an automaton with a very large number of states, and the replication of events and actions hinders the readability and the conciseness of the model.

23.3.1.2. Event-based modeling

Most current UIMSes rely on an event-based approach where the focus is on the set of possible events to which the system has to respond. In practice, events and event-handlers are embedded in general purpose programming languages [7].

In event-based modeling, the system is represented by a quintuplet $<V, E, A, O, v_0>$ where:

- E and A are the Event and Action sets as stated above,
- V is a set of state variables,
- v_0 is the initial value of the state variables,
- O is a set of operators such that $O \subseteq E \times C \times A \times SI$ where C is a set of conditions (Boolean expressions on the state variables) and SI is a set of instructions consisting solely of affectations to state variables.

The system considered as example may be modeled with an event formalism, as shown in Figure 23.2.

```
V = {v}, v0 = 1 and v : integer.
O = {      <Ev1, v=1, A1, v:=2>,
           <Ev1, v=2, A2, v:=3>,
           <Ev1, v=3, A2, v:=4>,
           <Ev2, v=4, A3, v:=3>,
           <Ev2, v=3, A3, v:=2>,
           <Ev2, v=2, A4, v:=1>}.
```

FIGURE 23.2. The toy example modeled by an event formalism

The event-handlers to be produced in a programming language may be deduced trivially from this description. There is one event-handler for each event Ev_i in E, built by selecting from O all the quadruplets in which Ev_i appears. The event-handler for Ev1 is shown in Figure 23.3.

```
Handler Ev1 is begin
          Case v of
          1 : A1; v:=2;
          2 : A2; v:=3;
          3 : A2; v:=4;
          Endcase
EndHandler;
```

FIGURE 23.3. An example of an event handler

With such a formalism, the events appear very clearly. However, it is difficult to know which events may trigger a given action. This can only be achieved by searching for that action in all the event-handlers. Moreover, it is almost impossible to ensure that the action may actually be triggered, because the triggering depends on a state whose reachability is unknown. The set of all the possible states of the system is not explicit; we can only know that this set of states is a subset of the Cartesian product of the state variables' domains. Of course, this problem does not appear in this toy example since there is only one state variable. Finally, as in the state-based approach, actions are duplicated in the models.

23.3.1.3. Petri nets-based modeling

Petri nets [17] is a widely known formalism for modeling the behavior of concurrent systems. Presented for the first time by C.A.Petri in 1962 it has since been the focus of a lot of research work. The main uses of PN are for discrete event simulation and modeling complex systems such as communication protocols or distributed databases [6]. The major advantages of PN in such areas are their expressiveness with regards to concurrency related concerns (synchronization, parallelism), their graphical representation, their mathematical foundation (which allows for analyzing the models in order to statically prove important properties), and their executability.

Petri nets are often ranked amongst the state-based formalisms, which may be due to a hasty assimilation with finite state automata.

A Petri net is defined by a quintuplet <P, T, Pre, Post, M> where:
- P is the set of places,
- T is the set of transitions,
- Pre is the forward incidence function representing the input arcs of the transitions,
    Pre : PxT → N
- Post is the backward incidence function representing the output arcs of the transitions,
    Post : PxT → N
- M is the distribution function (such that M : P → N) of tokens in the places, stating the number of tokens in each place of the net.

A Petri net models a system by a set **places** (pictured as ellipses) and a set of operations (called **transitions** and pictured as boxes). The state of a system is modeled at any moment by a distribution of **tokens** in the net's places. Places and transitions are connected by directed arcs, which define when each transition is allowed to **occur**, and what the effect of its occurrence will be. A transition is allowed to occur when each of its input places holds at least one token; The occurrence of the transition consumes a token in each input place and sets a token in each output places. Moreover, an integer **weight** n is associated with each arc by the forward and backward incidence function, thus allowing to take or set n tokens in places at a time. Generally, a transition occurrence may consume or produce tokens.

When modeling a reactive system with Petri nets, there is a need to represent the interface between the system being modeled and its environment. To this end, two approaches may be followed:
- consider a subset of T as interface transitions, which are triggered by the environment,
- consider a subset of P as interface places, in which the environment may deposit tokens.

The former is not suited to the modeling of reactive systems because it considers that the environment directly triggers actions in the system, whereas the latter allows to represent the fact that an incoming event may trigger different actions in the system. Moreover, in this second approach each event is directly modeled in the system by the deposit of a token in an interface place.

The system taken as example may be modeled by a Petri net as shown in Figure 23.4.

Events are made explicit in the model by places without incoming arcs called event-places. Contrarily to the state-based approach, events are not duplicated in the model. Actions are represented by transitions; they also appear explicitly and are not duplicated, contrarily to both state-based and event-based modeling.

The set of states is not directly shown, preventing the model from combinatory explosion. Instead, the structure of the set of states is modeled by the state-places (the ones which are not event-places). In the toy example there are three state-places - P1, P2 and P3 - but actually four different states: (1, 0, 0), (0, 2, 0), (0, 1, 1) and (0, 0, 2). However, Petri net theory allows for the easy calculation of the set of states, which is provided by the net's reachability graph.

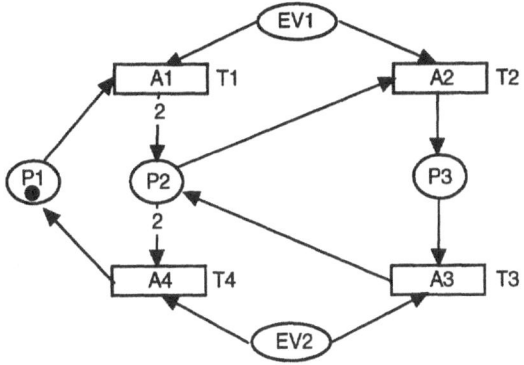

FIGURE 23.4. Modeling by a Petri net of the toy example

The reaction function (associating events to actions) is clearly stated by the arcs from event-places to transitions. This function is explicit neither in the state-based nor in the event-based approach. Finally, the side-effect function is described by the arcs between the transitions and the state-places. Let's remark that Petri nets allow to model a reaction function which is not deterministic (and also provide mathematical tools to check if it is or not), but as expected, any side-effect function will be deterministic.

23.3.2. Petri nets and data handling

Over time, several extensions of the basic PN model have been developed to increase their modeling power. In the Interactive Cooperative Objects formalism, we use a kind of High-Level Petri Nets (HLPN) called Petri Nets with Objects (PNO) [20]. We will now present informally the PNO model over a simple example, by showing how it relates to the basic PN model.

The example chosen to illustrate the use of PN is an excerpt from the modeling of a Flexible Manufacturing System (Figure 23.5).

The *Drill* operation may occur if there is an available drill, an a part to be drilled in the inventory. After the drilling, the part is set on a conveyor belt while the drill is waiting to be cleaned (in place *Waiting for attendant*). When an attendant shows up, the clean transition may occur and the drill returns to the *Available drills* state. Drilling and cleaning may occur at the same time if there are several drills, and the *Clean* transition depicts a synchronization (it may occur only if there is both an attendant and a drill waiting).

As it appears in this example, several important features are not taken into account by conventional PN: Firstly, the tokens flowing in the net are undifferentiated entities, and thus PN deal merely with control structure and forget data structure. Secondly, basic PN do not allow to structure a system's model in several hierarchical level, and the nets rapidly reach too big a size to remain easily manageable. Lastly, the expressiveness of the basic model is insufficient (for example, simple operations such as counting are difficult to express).

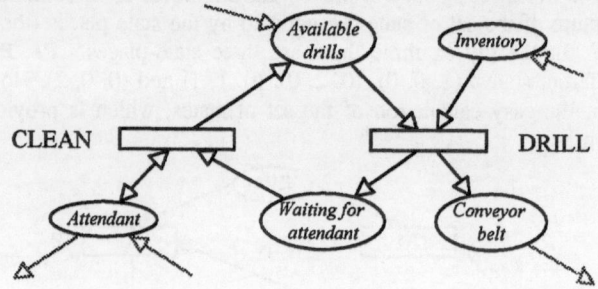

FIGURE 23.5. Modeling a flexible manufacturing system by means of PN.

Several High-Level Petri Net models have been developed in order to tackle some or all of those problems. To overcome the problem of data structure, we have presented the Petri Nets with Objects formalism where the net's places may hold objects (in the sense of Object-Oriented languages such as Eiffel [12]) instead of simple tokens. To handle those objects, the transitions have an action part, which may request creation or deletion of objects as well as invocation of their methods.

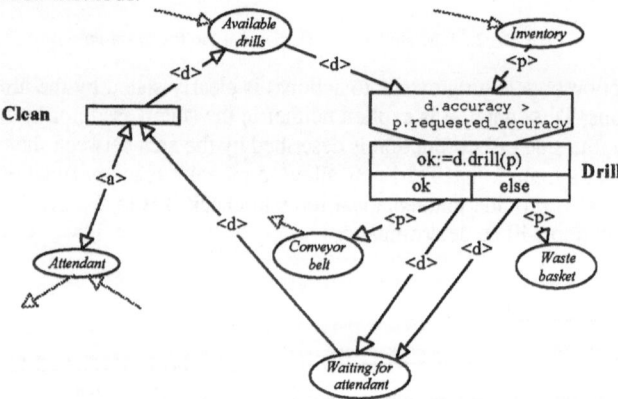

FIGURE 23.6. Modeling a flexible manufacturing system by means of HLPN.

We now extend the previous example to highlight the features of PNO: Arcs are now labeled with variables that act as transitions formal parameters, and allow to specify the flow of objects in the net. During a transition occurrence, objects in the input places are bound to the variables through a semi-unification mechanism. Transition *Drill* features a **precondition** *(d.accuracy> p.requested_accuracy)* which is a Boolean expression allowing it to select incoming tokens according to their values (in our case, the precondition selects a drill which precision is greater than the precision required for the part). This transition also features an **action** part *(Ok := d.drill(p))* stating the method to be called during its occurrence. Finally, the transition features a set of **emission rules** (displayed at its output side), allowing to express the fact that a transition occurrence may produce different outcomes according to the value of the objects it handles. At the end of a transition occurrence, the emission rules are evaluated; One is chosen among the true ones, and only arcs associated to this emission rule are activated. In our example, the part is put on the conveyor belt only if drilling completed properly (Boolean variable Ok is true), and otherwise discarded in the waste basket. The drill is set into place *Waiting for attendant* whether the drilling operation has been successful or not.

23.3.3. Structuring techniques for Petri nets

The main difficulty encountered when modeling a system by means of High-Level Petri Nets is to cope with large nets. Their complexity exceeds the understanding abilities of designers, and they are difficult to analyze, to modify and to reuse. Facing this problem, designers may follow two approaches.
The first one is **hierarchical refinement**. It consists in substituting a part of a net by a net which is somehow equivalent. The equivalence may be essentially graphical without dealing with net behavior as in [19]. When the behavior is taken into account, the substituted part may be a single transition [21] or place; it may also be a net [2] and then different kinds of behavior equivalencies may be considered [18]. The reduction techniques of [4], aimed at simplifying a net, are also related to this approach.
Hierarchical refinement, however, presents some limitations: The system is still modeled with a single net and, at the most detailed level, it may be very large. This net is a rigid whole, the same sub-net may be found in several places, and the designer cannot focus on a part of the system independently of the others.
The second approach does not recursively include nets, but instead considers nets communicating with each other ; Each net models a part of the system and their **composition** results in a model of the whole system. Our formalism is based on this approach, which is favored by object-oriented design.

23.3.4. Description of concurrency using Petri nets

Petri nets are especially at ease for modeling concurrent systems. They allow to describe how parallelism is produced, how several branches of the processing may proceed sequentially and independently, and how parallelism may be reduced by synchronization, when parallel branches need to cooperate or to exchange data. Moreover, all the algorithmic control structures are easily modeled by Petri nets.

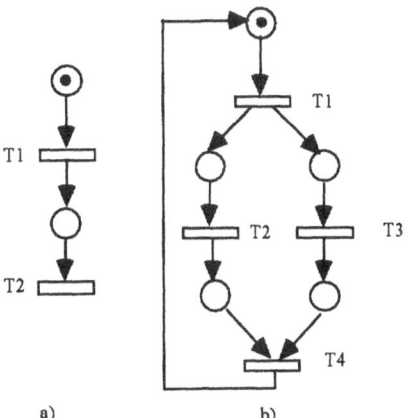

FIGURE 23.7. Petri nets constructions for modeling concurrency

Picture 7.a. highlights how a sequence of operations is described in the Petri nets formalism. In this case, the operation modeled by transition T2 may only occur after T1. The Figure 23.7.b. shows how one may describe the production of parallelism within a system. After transition T1 occurs, two threads of control (modeled by the transitions T2 and T3) may proceed independently and concurrently. Transition T4 models a reduction of parallelism within the system, which is a synchronization between the threads initiated by transition T1.

23.3.5. Verification of models using Petri nets

The use of ICOs allows the designer to use mathematical properties of Petri nets for validation of the models. A lot of results are available in that area ([11] among others) and we give some examples of results which may be used for event-driven interfaces.
There are two ways to analyze a Petri net:
- to prove marking-independent properties by the calculation of **place and transition invariants**. This analysis results solely from the intrinsic structure of the net.
- to prove properties of a marked net by the construction of the **reachability graph**. This kind of analysis is only valid for a given initial marking.

Since the initial marking of the ObCS of an object is defined by the class it belongs to, these two kinds of validations can be used for our means.

The mechanisms for the objects' cooperation are defined in such a way that the validation of a model may be processed in two separate steps:
- *unitary validation* studies the behavior of a single object, making a "good cooperation" assumption upon its relationships with other objects; that is, the servers of the object are able to process all its requests, and its clients send as many requests for its services as it may process;
- *cooperation validation* studies the behavior of a set of objects according to the way they are cooperating through the client-server relationship; it enables to know whether the objects cooperate in such a way that each server fulfills the needs of its clients, that is whether the cooperation preserves the objects' behavior properties set out by the unitary validation.

When modeling an interface, unitary validation enables to prove that the dialogue of each window is designed in such a way that it meets the requirements. Cooperation validation concerns both ICO / non-ICO and ICO / ICO cooperation: the former enables to ensure that the user's requests may be satisfied by the application's functional kernel and that the ICO's presentation reflects the state of the functional kernel, and the latter is needed as soon as an application may open several windows.

The dialogue's properties we want to check are those specified in the application's interface requirements. These properties may be stated either in terms of command sequences which may be issued by the user and processed by the application - e.g. each *update* command may be followed either by a *save* command or by a *cancel* command -, or in terms of the states which may or may not be reached by the application - e.g. a list box may be able to contain any number of items or not be able to contain less than a given number of items.
In fact, the properties which may be required of an interface are not so numerous and for the most part may be listed :
- the **absence of deadlock** is the possibility for the user to issue another command whatever was the sequence of previous ones;

- the **predictability of a command** is the fact that the user must be able to foresee the effect of a command. That is, a command must always be processed in the same way in a given context;
- the **reinitiability** is the possibility for the user to reach the initial state of the window, or a given predefined state;
- the **availability of a command** may take three different forms:
  - the command must be available at any moment, whatever state the application is in (e.g. a *help* command),
  - the command must be available for at least a specified number of times, eventually through any sequence of commands,
  - the command must always become available, that is the user may always issue a command sequence after which the command is available again;
- the **succession of commands** indicates in which order some commands may be issued; for instance a given command must or must not be followed by another one, immediately after or with some other commands in between;
- the **exclusion of commands** which must never be available at the same time (or on the contrary must always be available simultaneously);
- the **bound of a state variable** of the application corresponds to the fact that the number of elements of some resource handled by the application is restricted (or is not);
- **integrity constraints** between the values of some application's state variables.

23.3.6. Summary of ICO's key features

We may now summarize to which extend the ICO formalism matches the six criteria presented in the introduction in this chapter.

As demonstrated in section 23.3.1. ICOs allow for an integrated description of both the state and the event aspects of interactive applications. This is achieved by distinguishing in the models several places meant to represent the incoming of events while the other places represent the state space of objects that implement the application.

The control structure aspect of an application is described in the ObCS of an ICO by a high-level Petri net, formalism which is widely used (in the real time community) and particularly well suited to describe complex behaviors. We have shown in section 23.3.2. how Petri net modeling integrates with the objects oriented approach to allow for the modeling of data.

The structuring mechanisms available for high level Petri nets have been detailed in section 23.3.3., our formalism allows both for hierarchical refinement necessary in a top down design and for composition better suited for a bottom up design which the reuse of previously designed components.

Petri nets are one of the few formalisms dealing with concurrency in a formal way yet providing a graphical notation which favors readability and communication between designers.

Section 23.3.5 has shown how the formal definition of ICOs may be used to provide mathematical verification of models and to prove properties related to the external behavior of the application. Moreover, various extensions to Petri nets have been proposed in order to deal with time in the models, allowing to express and verify time-related properties.

23.4. Modeling an application

In this section we will show how to model a database browsing application by following a stepwise design process. A window is modeled by an ICO class, as for example the one shown in Figure 23.8; its presentation defines the window's layout, and its ObCS the window's dialogue.
First, we present the informal user interface specification of the application. Next, we detail the non-interactive objects that are interface independent. Then, we define the ICO of the window displayed to the users.

23.4.1. Informal specification

The example chosen to illustrate the use of the formalism is a fairly common one: an editor for tuples in a relational database table. This editor allows adding new tuples into the database, deleting tuples, selecting tuples from those already stored and changing their values. Of course, our goal is to provide a fully user-driven dialogue, as opposed to a menu-driven one.
The overall look of the interface is shown in Figure 23.8. Three different areas can be distinguished in that window:
- The editing area, in which the attributes of a selected tuple may be edited through the use of standard interface components (radio buttons, check box, simple-line entry field).
- A scrollable list (list box) shows the tuples of the table, presenting them by their distinctive attribute (a primary key). Items in this list may be selected by clicking on them with the mouse.
- A command zone in which database operations (creation, deletion, ...) may be launched by clicking on command pushbuttons.

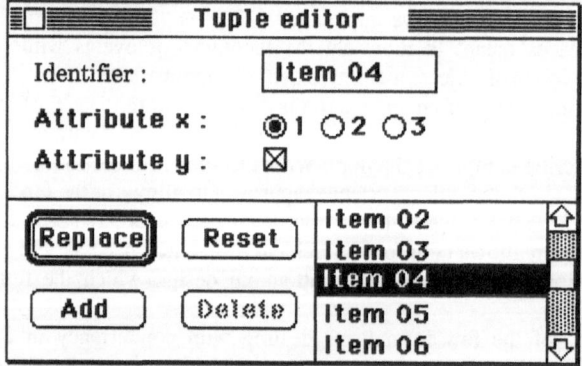

FIGURE 23.8. Overall look of the window

The actions available to the user change through time and depend on the state of the dialogue. Those dialogue rules are expressed here informally. One of the goals of the ICO modeling is to make formal and non ambiguous such natural language informal requirements:
- It is forbidden to Select a tuple from the table when another one is being edited.
- It is forbidden to Quit the application while the user is editing a tuple. In any other case it must be possible to quit.
- It is forbidden to Delete a tuple whose value has been modified by the user.

- After a modification of the current tuple, only the actions Add, Replace and Reset are available.
- The user must be able to act on the items of the editing area at any time.
- Only tuples that satisfy the integrity constraints may be added to the database.

23.4.2. Non interactive objects: Tuples

Our case study yields two object classes: class Tuple, which corresponds to the non-interactive application kernel, and class Editor, which is modeled by an ICO.
The class Tuple is detailed in Figure 23.9. The instances of this class are passive entities, used only as a data structure, and thus they do not feature an ObCS (to be more precise, the ObCS is trivial: each service is available at any moment).

```
Class Tuple
Services
  Display;              -- Display the tuple values in the editing area
  Add;                  -- Add the tuple to the database table.
  Copy :<o : Tuple>;    -- Creates a new object identical to the current one
                        -- Does the tuple satisfy the integrity constraints?
  Correct :<r : BOOLEAN>;
  Delete;               -- Delete the tuple
```

FIGURE 23.9. The Tuple class

23.4.3. Modeling the tuple editor

The class Editor is a full fledged ICO, featuring services, an ObCS and a presentation part. The description of the class, may be seen in Figure 23.10. The ObCS is shown in Figure 23.11, while the presentation, which consists of the widget list and the activation function, is detailed in Figure 23.12.

```
Class Editor
Services
  Reset; Replace; Edit; Delete; Quit; Add;
ObCS (see Figure 23.11)
Presentation (see Figure 23.8 and Figure 23.12)
end
```

FIGURE 23.10. The Editor class

The Editor's ObCS (Figure 23.11) must be read in the following way:
• *Initialization:*
The initial marking of the ObCS' net depends on the actual contents of the database at the time the window is opened (when the ICO is created). Figure 23.11 shows an initial marking: the places *list, selected* and *edited* are empty, and the place *default* contains the template for the first item to be edited. If the table was not empty, one tuple would be automatically selected while all the others would be in the place *list.*
• *Processing:*
From this initial state, only the two services **edit** and **add** (or transitions T1 and T2) may occur.

The occurrence of the **edit** service removes the template token from the place *default*, modifies its value and puts it back in the same place.

The occurrence of the **add** service depends on the precondition o.correct, which checks integrity constraints on the object, eventually producing a modal error dialogue. If the precondition holds, the token is moved from the place *default* to the place *selected*.

From now on, the table has one tuple. As the place *selected* is the only one holding a token, only the **edit** and **delete** services may occur. The occurrence of the **delete** service puts the PNO back in its initial state. The inhibitor arc between the place *List* and the **delete** service of the transition T3 means that this transition may only occur if the place is empty. The occurrence of the **edit** service results in creating a local copy of the tuple and depositing the original (o) and the copy (dup) in the place *edited*.

While the place *edited* holds a token, several services may occur:

- Modify the value of the copy by the occurrence of the service **edit**.
- Replace the original by the copy through the service **replace**.
- Cancel all changes by the occurrence of the service **reset** (the copy is then deleted).
- **Add** the edited tuple to the table; the added tuple becomes selected, while the original one becomes unselected.

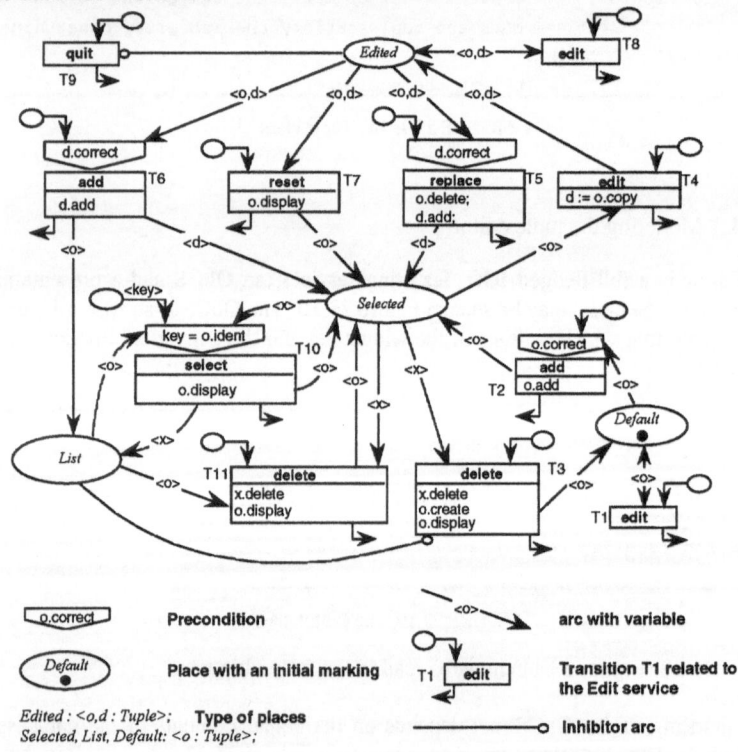

FIGURE 23.11. The ObCS of the class Editor

If this **edit / add** cycle is performed a number of times, we will reach the state where the place *selected* is empty, the place *edited* holds one token - a tuple whose identifier value is "Item 04" -, and the place *list* contains at least tokens corresponding to tuples items 02, 03, 05 and 06. This picture shows three activated pushbuttons, which correspond to the currently allowed user operations on the database. The active or inactive state of the pushbuttons is fully determined by the possible occurrence of the transitions they relate to in the ObCS. For example, the delete button is not activated, since place *selected* holds no token.

Figure 23.12 shows both the list of widgets associated to an Editor and how the user can request a user service. All the widgets of the editing area trigger the *Edit* service since their purpose is only to inform the dialogue that an editing action has been performed.

23.5. Verification of the example

In this section we will fill the gap between the mathematical tools available for studying properties of the nets and the validation of a concrete system by showing how results of the Petri nets theory may be used to prove properties of the behavior of an application modeled by Interactive Cooperative Objects.

In the following sub-sections we detail the unitary validation of the Tuple Editor application according to the two techniques described above (i.e. calculation of invariants and calculation of the reachability graph). Due to space reasons we do not treat the cooperation validation here.

Widget	User's action	Activated service
PushButton Add	Click	Add
PushButton Delete	Click	Delete
PushButton Replace	Click	Replace
PushButton Reset	Click	Reset
PushButton Close_Box	Click	Quit
RadioButton 1	Click	Edit
RadioButton 2	Click	Edit
RadioButton 3	Click	Edit
EntryText	Any (Click, Keyboard, ...)	Edit
CheckBox	Click	Edit
ListBox	Click	Select

FIGURE 23.12. The activation function

23.5.1. Calculation of invariants

As an example, we will analyze the ObCS' net of an Editor. This analysis of invariants is based on the calculation of both conservative and repetitive components in the ObCS of the Editor.

23.5.1.1. Calculation of conservative components

P= {Default, Edited, List, Selected}
T = {T1, T2, T3, T4, T5, T6, T7, T8, T9, T10, T11}
Analyzing the PNO corresponding to the ObCS of the Editor consist in looking for the positive solution of the equation $f^T.C=0$; these solutions are found doing additions and subtractions between lines and columns of matrix C which is the result of the operation Post-Pre where Post represents, for each transition, the variables labeling outputs arcs, and Pre represents, for each transition, the variables labeling the input arcs of the transition. .

The initial marking of the ObCS of the ICO is only one token in the place Default . The conservative component is thus Default+Edited+Selected = 1.

Remark: only the place *List* does not belong to a conservative component.

23.5.1.2. Calculation of repetitive components

For this calculation, we are looking for sequences of transitions s such that C.s = 0
The set of repetitive components is:
T4+T5; T2+T3; T4+T6+T11; T1; T4+T7; T8; T9; T10.
which corresponds to the services:
Edit-Replace, Add-Delete, Edit-Add-Delete, Edit-Reset, Edit, Quit, Select.
Remark : all transitions belongs to at least one repetitive component.

It results from the calculation of place invariants that the set of places {*Default, Selected, Edited*} is a **conservative component**, that is, the number of tokens in this set of places never changes whatever transition is fired, and remains as it was in the initial marking of the net [11]. In our case, there is always one and only one token (one tuple or a couple of tuples) in one of these three places, whatever state the dialogue is in. Moreover, the place *List* is unbounded (i.e. it may receive any number of tokens).

It results from the calculation of transition invariants that the following transition sequences are **repetitive** and **stationary** :
T4+T5; T2+T3; T4+T6+T11; T1; T4+T7; T8; T9; T10.
More precisely, the occurrence of any of these transition sequences does not change the distribution of tokens in the places, except for the sequences T2.T3 and T4.T5 which replace one tuple of the *Default* and *Selected* place respectively by another newly created one. Of course, the value of tokens which are moved by the transition occurrences may be changed.

Let's examine what can be proven:
- there is absence of deadlock because each transition belongs to a repetitive sequence which may occur from the initial marking.
- the commands *edit* and *add* are predictable because all transitions associated to each of them have as input a different place of the conservative component (for the edit command, T1 has *Default*, T4 has *Selected* and T8 has *Edited*, and only one of them may be enabled since there is only one token for these three places). The *delete* command is predictable because T11 has an input arc from place *Selected* and T3 has an inhibitor arc from the same place.
- the reinitiability results from the fact that each transition belongs to a transition sequence which is stationary and may occur from the initial marking (more precisely: it is always possible to reach a marking where there is only one token in the *Default* place, but this tuple does not have the same name as the initial one, due to the occurrence of transition T3)
- availability of commands:
  - *edit* is always available: there is always one token in one of the places *Default, Selected* or *Edited*, and thus one of the transitions T1, T4 or T8 may occur;
  - *quit* is not available only if the *Edited* place contains a token, but it becomes available again after the occurrence of T5, T6, or T7;

- all the other commands may become available again because all transitions may occur once and the net is reinitializable, and thus the net (without the *quit* transitions) is live;
- the bounds of state variables and integrity constraints are expressed by the net invariants. In the current case, we only have that {*Default, Selected, Edited*} is a conservative component and *List* is an unbounded place. But PNOs enable to consider invariants concerning not only the location of tokens in places, but also their value [20].

23.6. Conclusion

This chapter has presented the Interactive Cooperative Objects formalism, which is based on high-level Petri nets and on the object-oriented approach. This formalism is dedicated to the specification, design and verification of software featuring a user-driven interface, such as those covered by the CUA norm. We have presented how this formalism meets five important criteria, mandatory for a seamless integration of the life cycle of an interactive application. A simple case study has been presented to highlight the main features of the formalism.

Due to its Petri net roots, the ICO formalism is well suited when the dialogue between the user and the system proceeds in a discrete way. We are now studying how to apply this formalism to describe the continuous interactions encountered in direct manipulation software and animated user interfaces.

As this formalism is aimed at software design, the techniques needed to automatically generate the code for the user interface and the contextual help system have been published in [13] and [14] respectively.

23.7. References

[1]   Abowd G.D. Agents: Communicating interactive processes, *proceedings of Interact'90* Elsevier p.143-148 Cambridge August 1990.

[2]   André C. Use of the Behavior equivalence in Place-Transition Net Analysis, *Application and Theory of Petri Nets*, IFB 52, Springer, 1982.

[3]   Bastide R., Palanque P. Petri nets with objects for the design, validation and prototyping of user-driven interfaces, *proceedings of Interact'90* Elsevier p. 625-631. Cambridge August 1990.

[4]   Berthelot G. Transformations and decompositions of Nets. In [5].

[5]   Brauer W. *Petri nets: Applications and relationships to other models of concurrency.* W. Brauer, W. Reisig, G. Rosenberg editor, LNCS 254 &255, Springer Verlag.

[6]   Bruno G., Alessandro B. Petri-net based Object-Oriented modelling of distributed systems. *OOPSLA'86*, 1986.

[7]   M. Green: A survey of three dialogue models. *ACM Transactions on Graphics* 5, 3 (July 1986), 244-275.

[8]   D. Harel: Statecharts: A visual formalism for complex systems. *Science of Computer Programming* 8, 231-274, 1987.

[9]   Harrison M., Duke D. Abstract models for interaction objects, *Internal report, dependable computing systems center*. University of York.

[10] K. Jensen: Coloured Petri nets and the invariant method. In: A. Pagnoni and G. Rozenberg (eds.): *Applications and Theory of Petri Nets*, Informatik-Fachberichte 66. Springer-Verlag, Berlin, 1983.

[11] K. Lautenbauch: Linear algebraic techniques for place/transition nets. In [5].

[12] Meyer B. *Object oriented software construction*. Prentice Hall, 1988.

[13] Palanque P. *Modelling user-driven interfaces by means of Interactive Cooperative Objects*. Ph.D. Dissertation of University Toulouse (France). 1992.

[14] Palanque P., Bastide R., Dourte L. Contextual help for free with formal dialogue specification, *proceedings of. HCI International* 1993.

[15] Palanque P., Bastide R., Sibertin C., Dourte L. Design of User-Driven Interfaces using Petri nets and Objects, In *proceedings of 5th Conference on Advanced Information Systems Engineering* (CAISE'93). LNCS N° 685, Springer-Verlag, 1993.

[16] Paterno F. Definition of Properties of User Interfaces Using Action-Based Temporal Logic, *Proceedings of the 5th International Conference on Software Engineering and Knowledge Engineering* SEKE'93, June, 16-18 1993

[17] Peterson J.L. *Petri net theory and modeling of systems*. Prentice-hall. 1981. ISBN 0-13-661983-5.

[18] Pomello L. Some equivalence notions for concurrent systems, an overview. G. Rozenberg edit., *Advances in Petri Nets' 85*, LNCS 222, 1985.

[19] Reizig W. Petri Nets in Software Engineering; in [Brauer...86].

[20] C. Sibertin-Blanc. High level Petri nets with data structure. In: *6th European Workshop on Petri Nets and Applications* (June 1985, Espoo, Finland).

[21] Valette R. Analysis of Petri Nets by Stepwise Refinements; *Journal of computer and system science* 18, 3; 1979.

[22] Wood W.A. Transition network grammars for natural language analysis. *Communications of the ACM* 13, 10, pp. 591-60, October 1970.

24 User Centred System Modelling Using the Template Model

Christopher Roast
Michael Harrison

ABSTRACT

Abstract models of interaction may be used to support the development of interactive systems by providing frameworks in which properties of a proposed interface can be specified and reasoned about without necessarily requiring an implemented artifact. In this paper we illustrate such a model. We introduce extensions that identify and clarify system components that have user significance. These extensions enable system properties of the model to be linked to user requirements that may, for example, have their basis in experiment. These extensions form the basis for the *template model*.

The *template model* is used to express usability requirements for a system that may support a user's recognition of its state. Two requirements are described, namely *output correctness* and *structural consistency*. *Output correctness* requires that displayed information reflects state accurately and comprehensibly. *Structural consistency* requires that all task relevant changes are *consistently* reflected in system output.

24.1 Introduction

One of the main concerns of Human Computer Interaction research is that system design is *user centred*. The observation is often made that system designers do not design for the effective use of others. The problem is that users often have different goals and predispositions from designers. For this reason, ideally, the system *and* its operating environment should be modelled during development. Since most HCI is concerned with a single user and a single system, it is reasonable to think of the user as the primary environment in which the system interacts. To ensure usability requirements are met we should consider modelling system users (possibly multiple users co-operating) in conjunction with the system. In practice, this is difficult to achieve, systems are deterministic and finite, however users are impossible to model or generalise with the accuracy that would be required to support system design. Typically, user models are only used for evaluation, and are not in a form that would relate to a design representation, see for example [17]. Because system models do give a direct representation of a design and can be provided formally they give a degree of precision and accuracy that: (i) supports reliable development and refinement, and (ii) emphasises constraints necessitated by the eventual product.

This paper presents a means of introducing user oriented issues into interactive system development using a system model that includes abstractions relevant to the role and resources of intended users. In this way we are able to consider the user, possibly several users with different viewpoints upon the system, and express usability requirements by making simple though explicit assumptions about users' psychological and cognitive activities. We would hope that such assumptions would be presented in a form that would make it possible to validate these assumptions.

We use the abstract model of interaction in order to describe two general system properties that support ease of use: *observational predictability* and *reactivity*. We argue that although these system properties can support ease of use they are unrepresentative of users' capabilities and are too restrictive upon system behaviour. These limitations serve as a motivation for the concept of *template abstractions*. Template abstractions are system abstractions required to be of psychological or task relevance to users, hence they serve as a means of focusing upon the users' perspectives of a system. Template abstractions are used to extend the abstract model, giving the *template model* [15]. Using the template model, we are able to re-define notions similar to *observational predictability* and *reactivity* that are more realistic and representative of users' requirements.

24.1.1   Modelling in HCI

Human Computer Interaction modelling research comes in three categories: user, system and design process modelling. User and system perspectives are aimed at enabling the comprehension of interactive systems and their use [4] to assist the design problem. By contrast design process modelling captures how information relevant to interface design is used, see [14]. This paper concerns the first two of these categories.

User modelling analyses users' mental and physical resources with the aim of understanding the activity of interaction. As a result, qualitative and quantitative measures of ease of use can be established based on cognitive parameters ([2, 5, 16]). These measures are based on: (i) a detailed description of the system; and (ii) the use of psychological concepts not necessarily related to system components. The disparity between these sources of information prohibits the constructive use of user models in software development [3]. This can be contrasted with the role of system models in HCI. System models enable requirements to be expressed in terms of abstractions that can be related directly to the system being developed while avoiding unnecessary detail. In this way system models support development. The main problem for system models is that usability requirements are not easily expressed using system concepts. Requirements such as ease of use and appropriateness for task are seen as primarily psychological and environmental properties, not as system properties. In general, system models are normally inadequate as a means of expressing usability requirements of systems.

24.1.2   Abstract System Models

Dix, Harrison, Runciman and Thimbleby have proposed that abstract models of interactive behaviour of systems may be used as a means of overcoming this problem, by providing a minimal formal framework with components germane to interaction and purpose of use, see [8, 9]. Abstractions in these models are designed to express properties of direct relevance to use, and thus avoid system details that may distract from a user centred perspective.

In this paper we shall use a simple state-based model similar to that of [11]. The model consists of: a set of system states S, one of which is identified as the initial state $s_0 \in S$; a set of system outputs D; the output for any state is given by a 'view' function $v : S \rightarrow D$; and an input alphabet K. Each input is assumed to identify a function over states, i.e. $k \in S \rightarrow S$ for each $k \in K$. Thus, an abstract model of interaction is given by the tuple: $\langle S, s_0, D, v, K \rangle$. The state based model gives a deterministic and synchronous account of interaction that is adequate for modelling stand alone interactive systems. In general, we shall write $s(\langle k_1...k_n \rangle)$ to denote the state $k_n(...(k_1(s_0))...)$.

Two system properties that form the basis for our notions of *output correctness* and *structural consistency* may be expressed using this state based model. The template model, which extends this model, employs abstractions that make reference to intended use.

Observational Predictability

Interfaces are often difficult to use because inadequate information is output for users to maintain an understanding of system state. The first property assumes that users base their future actions on an understanding of state. *Observational predictability* (see [10] for elaborations of this property) may support the user's comprehension of state by ensuring that state information can be determined from the system output. A property that captures aspects of this idea is as follows:

Definition 1 *A state based system* $\langle S, s_0, D, v, K \rangle$ *is* **observationally predictable** *iff:*

$$\forall s, s' \in S : v(s) = v(s') \Rightarrow s = s'$$

In short, this property requires that the view function v has an inverse (v^{-1}). Although observational predictability may prevent interaction in which users are mistaken about the state of the system, it has limited applicability:

- Observational predictability cannot be seen as a general constraint upon interactive systems because many applications require a system state that is more complex than can be output completely at any one time. Few systems, apart from the simplest, can adhere to this property.

- This property, stated baldly, gives no clue about whether a user might be able to exploit it. We cannot rely upon the user being able to reliably recognise displays which are identical and displays which are not and to make the necessary interpretations.

Reacting

The second property captures a basic requirement of interactive systems, namely, that they react immediately to user inputs. This can be contrasted with 'batch-like' systems in which a mass of inputs are made prior to any response being given by the system.

A system is interactive if it is responsive to inputs. A reactive system is interactive in a stricter sense, it responds whenever an input causes a state change: in the state $s \in S$, the input $k \in K$ has an effect if and only if $s \neq k(s)$. Thus, a state based model will be termed *reactive* if it responds to effects upon its state:

Definition 2 *A system* $\langle S, s_0, D, v, K \rangle$ *is* **reactive** *iff:*

$$\forall s \in S, k \in K : s \neq k(s) \Rightarrow v(s) \neq v(k(s))$$

Here we have the same problem as we had with observational predictability. We must consider whether or not the formal notion corresponds to user perceived reactivity. *Reactivity* demands that a system responds immediately to state changes, users may benefit from this response if they reliably recognise it. Thus in order to perceive a *reactive* system as such, the user must be attentive to the changes that can be recognised through the outputs. As with observational predictability we must somehow accommodate what user capabilities are in this context.

The two properties, defined above, both represent system properties that may be capable of supporting ease of use. Both properties fail to take the capabilities of users into account. In addition, observational predictability imposes unrealistic constraints upon interactive systems. The following section addresses these problems by introducing a more user-oriented perspective through the use of template abstractions.

24.2   User Perspectives

24.2.1   Template Abstractions

Expressing system constraints, that involve information relevant to user interactions, requires the use of abstractions of the state-based model's components. As we have said already, these relate to particular tasks and particular user perceptions. Hence *observational predictability* is extended to focus on what the user sees or knows about in relation to particular tasks. Hence we define a system property that expresses what is actually used to perform the task, which shall be called *output correctness*. Similarly, *reactivity* can be modified to apply to system components as opposed to the entire system state, and to accommodate users' perceptions of input and output. The modified property is called *structural consistency*. We shall describe these user or task related structures in terms of three *template abstractions*: results, display templates and input templates.

Results

It is clear that the information that is required by users to determine the successful completion of their tasks should be made accessible to them — for example, 'the document' represented within a word processor. Dix describes this information, whether or not it is accessible, as *the result* of the system state [8]. The benefit of identifying a general state abstraction such as the result is that system properties can be focused towards supporting the system's proposed use. The tasks which a system is intended to support may depend upon differing abstractions of a system's state. For instance, while word processing, the task of ensuring a document's content is correct may be independent of features of its printed form, such as page layout, font size, etc. Alternatively, the task of satisfying document presentation requirements may depend on page format and font size while ignoring content. By contrast, more low level tasks such as correcting text will depend upon the current cursor location, and possibly the content of a cut and paste buffer. Other more administrative tasks may only concern the document's location on a storage device. Thus for different tasks (and sub-tasks) differing state abstractions with a status similar to *the result* may be identified.

Since a number of system components may be of interest while performing tasks, we shall model this by considering a collection of results (R) each of which extracts information relevant to a task. Each *result* $r \in R$ is modelled as a function from states to a range of values $(\mathcal{U}_r)$.

Definition 3 *A result $r \in R$ is a function upon states which extracts information necessary for users to determine if a task (or sub-task) is complete.*

$$r : S \to \mathcal{U}_r$$

Identifying results for a particular application, can be seen as a product of task analysis. A definition of appropriate tasks will ideally include a description of the objects that will be the focus of users activities; such objects represent ideal candidates for results within the template model, see [7].

Display Templates

More is required than the notion of result, observational predictability is unrepresentative of user capabilities. For example displays that are identical may not be reliably recognised as such by users, and vice versa. Display templates are used to tackle this problem by abstracting away from those display details that users do not consider when evaluating system output.

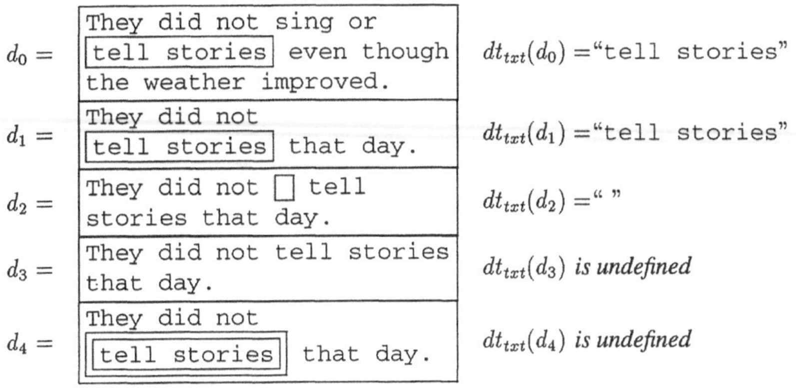

$d_0 =$
> They did not sing or
> tell stories even though
> the weather improved.

$dt_{txt}(d_0) =$ "tell stories"

$d_1 =$
> They did not
> tell stories that day.

$dt_{txt}(d_1) =$ "tell stories"

$d_2 =$
> They did not □ tell
> stories that day.

$dt_{txt}(d_2) =$ " "

$d_3 =$
> They did not tell stories
> that day.

$dt_{txt}(d_3)$ is undefined

$d_4 =$
> They did not
> tell stories that day.

$dt_{txt}(d_4)$ is undefined

FIGURE 24:1. The values extracted by a display template dt_{txt} for five displays.

A system display usually contains detail that is irrelevant to users' perceptions of what it represents. For example, although the choice of colour scheme used by an interface can impact upon user performance, the particular choice is irrelevant to content. We wish to 'hide' display details, or any other form of output for that matter, which are not concerned with content, and do this by defining *display templates*. *Display templates* are a means of referring to perceived display features such as menus, icons, cursors, etc. independently of details not affecting their perceived role. For example, whether a cursor is rendered as an underscore, vertical line or inverse video is immaterial to its role. Thus, *display templates* focus upon output details recognised as potential sources of information relevant to task ([12]). As with *results*, it may be the case that the designer is *hypothesising* about the information that the users will require in achieving some goal.

To model the connection between user perceptions of results we identify a set of *display templates*, that have a corresponding meaning to results, called Dt. Each display template will be treated as a partial function from displays to a range of values $(\mathcal{U}_{dt})$. It should be noted that there is no reason why we should not generalise this notion of output template to any mode of output not just displays. Hence D could be any output medium.

Definition 4 *A* **display template** $dt \in Dt$ *is a partial function upon displays which extracts details that can be perceived by users as potential sources of information.*

$$dt : D \twoheadrightarrow \mathcal{U}_{dt}$$

By modelling display templates as partial functions we take into account the fact that whatever feature a display template extracts, it may not always be present in the output. For example, although a cursor may determine a position on the display, it can be absent, in which case no location can be determined by it. Another illustration of a display template is given in figure 24.1. Here the display template dt_{txt} is assumed to extract the text framed in the display, the figure shows what values dt_{txt} may extract for various displays. Applied to d_3 and d_4, dt_{txt} is taken to be *undefined* since there is no framed text in d_3, and d_4 has text within a different form of frame.

Particular details of any display template depend upon understanding of users' perceptions and expectations. The specification of individual display templates can draw upon existing knowledge of how people perceive certain types of information as well as contextualised empirical studies of users' perceptions of output techniques.

Input Templates

State and display abstractions reflect the tasks and perceptions of intended users. The same idea can be applied to system inputs. Thus a notion of *input template* should identify input sequences perceived as units of input by users. In this way we are able to take into account the fact that users may not perceive individual inputs (elements of K) as completed actions. For instance, the property of *reactivity* requires that the system reacts to inputs that are effective in the sense that they change the state of the system. If users' perceptions of input differ from the actual inputs then the property is of little benefit and may confuse users. Input templates may be used to identify classes of inputs at a broader granularity than K. For example, we can suggest a variety of activities that may be treated as unitary actions by users when interacting with a word processor: saving a file; changing the font being used; spell checking a document; inserting words, symbols and letters. Each of these activities could be perceived by experts as unitary actions while using the system, despite being composed of numerous physical inputs. However, for novices it may be the case that they are not perceived. Thus, differing input templates can be associated with differing classes of activity.

Abstractions similar to input templates can be found in psychological modelling, task analysis and dialogue design. For instance, Schiele and Green identify *simple tasks* "for which distinct action sequences have to be learned, and which roughly correspond, at least for the novice, to the application of individual functions or commands in a given system." ([16]). Alternatively, Card et al. introduce the notion of *method* as "a sequence of inputs for executing a unit task that forms a well integrated segment of users behaviour" ([5]). Similarly the identification of input sequences suggestive of input templates is evident in dialogue design (see [1, 6]).

To model the various perceptions of input to a system we shall identify sets of *input templates*, It. Each *input template* ($it \in It$) is a function over input sequences that extracts perceived actions (represented by a set A_{it}). We can envisage an input template as being similar to a function that parses the input and returns an abstraction based upon non-terminals within a grammar.

Definition 5 *An* **input template** $it \in It$ *is a function on input sequences:*

$$it : K^* \to A_{it}^*$$

An input template extracts the sequence of actions that an input sequence is perceived as producing, this may not be what it actually produces.

Individual input templates may be identified by empirical and observational techniques in the same way as display templates.

We now have all we need to relate system models of interactive behaviour to what is actually perceived by groups of users in carrying out tasks.

24.2.2   The Template Model

Definition 6 *A* **template interaction model** *consists of a tuple:*

$$\langle S, s_0, D, v, K, R, Dt, It \rangle$$

The first five elements of this correspond to those of the state based system model. The last three elements are sets of template abstractions determined by an analysis of intended task and user perceptions: a set of results (R), a set of display templates (Dt) and a set of input templates (It), respectively.

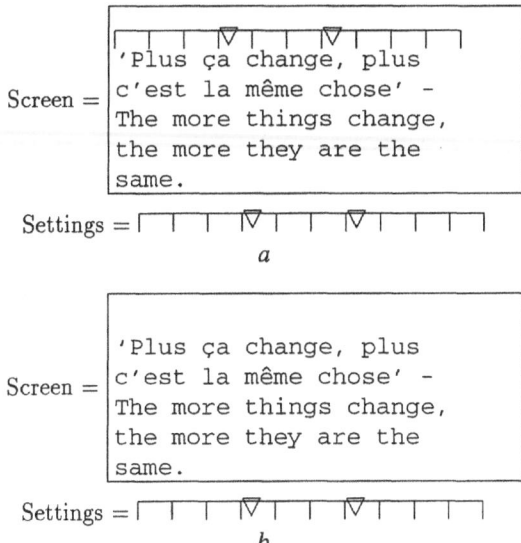

State *a* shows tabulation settings accurately. State *b* has the same settings as *a* but they are not displayed.

FIGURE 24.2. Different depictions of the same tabulation information.

Since the template model includes templates abstractions, it is naturally oriented towards accommodating users perceptions of the system and the tasks it supports. The template model may now be used to define usability properties that incorporate notions of what is seen, or known or understood.

24.3   Template Model Properties

24.3.1   Supporting the User

To support the user's evaluation of system state it is necessary that particular information be communicated to the user. Within the template model, state information relevant to users' tasks is represented by the set of *results* (R). Those aspects of the system that can be reliably communicated to the user to support the task that is being carried out are modelled by display templates from Dt. Results and display template are *coupled* in the sense described above. We consider additional requirements of such a coupling.

Result values can only be communicated to users if the system outputs correct information in a recognisable form. One clear requirement is that the display template values generated are determinable from, and associated with, some result. This ensures that the output information is computed from information relevant to the users' tasks.

The relationship between *display template* and *result* may not be static. It is possible that mode for example, which may be regarded as an additional component of the state, will determine whether or not the information is actually output in some state and therefore modifies the nature of the relationship. For example, the presentation of tabulation information within a word processor can often be toggled on and off (see figure 24.2). The presence of information output by a display template has to be contrasted with the display template being undefined. Thus, we require that only defined display template values are functionally related to result values:

$$\forall s_1, s_2 \in S : \left(\begin{array}{c} r(s_1) = r(s_2) \ \wedge \\ v(s_1) \in \text{ran } dt \ \wedge \\ v(s_2) \in \text{ran } dt \end{array} \right) \Rightarrow dt(v(s_1)) = dt(v(s_2))$$

This property requires that each possible result value determines a uniquely defined display template value. The display template either takes the value determined from the result value or it is undefined. This property is not sufficient to ensure that result values are always available to the user so long as they are perceivable. For example, displayed tabulation information may show tab positions yet abstract over tab justification (e.g. 'left-tab', 'right-tab', etc.), in spite of the fact that this information is extracted by the result.

In order to ensure that display template values reliably indicate underlying result values, we require that result values be determined from display template values:

$$\forall s_1, s_2 \in S : \left(\begin{array}{c} dt(v(s_1)) = dt(v(s_2)) \ \wedge \\ v(s_1) \in \text{ran } dt \ \wedge \\ v(s_2) \in \text{ran } dt \end{array} \right) \Rightarrow r(s_1) = r(s_2)$$

If two displays have the same defined display template value, then the underlying result associated with the template has the same value. This means that the user can always determine result values from the display template values. Combining these two constraints we obtain:

$$\forall s_1, s_2 \in S : \left(\begin{array}{c} v(s_1) \in \text{ran } dt \ \wedge \\ v(s_2) \in \text{ran } dt \end{array} \right) \Rightarrow (r(s_1) = r(s_2) \Leftrightarrow dt(v(s_1)) = dt(v(s_2)))$$

Thus, we obtain a one-to-one correspondence between display template values and result values whenever the display template is defined.

To express this constraint as a template model property, we require that it holds between each result and a display template. We shall term this property *output correctness*.

Definition 7 *The template model $\langle S, s_0, D, v, K, R, Dt, It \rangle$ is* **output correct** *iff, there is some injective mapping f from R to Dt such that:*

$$\forall r \in R, s_1, s_2 \in S :$$
$$\left(\begin{array}{c} v(s_1) \in \text{ran } dt_r \ \wedge \\ v(s_2) \in \text{ran } dt_r \end{array} \right) \Rightarrow (r(s_1) = r(s_2) \Leftrightarrow dt_r(v(s_1)) = dt_r(v(s_2)))$$

Where dt_r is $f(r)$.

For each result a unique display template is identified, and when the display template is defined it consistently reflects the value of the result.

24.3.2   Structuring Interaction

As we have argued, template model enables the formulation of interactive properties based on additional task related template abstractions. We now show how we can improve the definition of *reactivity* using these ideas. We are concerned here with the nature of changes brought about by user interactions.

Successful interaction usually requires that users maintain some understanding of the system's state. Ideally, whenever the state changes, users will need to amend their understanding appropriately. *Reactivity* addressed this point in general terms by only demanding that any state change was reflected in some display change. Normally the new state can be only partly conveyed to users. What is conveyed often focuses upon the differences between the new and preceding state. We have defined *results* to be of primary relevance to the performance of tasks and therefore changes in the results are of most significance to users. Thus, the differences between a new and preceding state communicated to users should reflect *result* values that have changed.

Result changes provide another level of significance. The very nature of their changes indicates an implicit structure of the application domain that may be employed by the user as tasks are performed. The changing results may identify interdependencies between system components. For example, within a drawing package circles and squares may be constructed with various line widths. Two results may be of relevance to use: the line width used for drawing circles, and that used for squares. If line width is a global parameter shared by both operations, then the two results will be interrelated since a change in one will alter the other. Alternatively, if line width were local to each operation, then the two results could change independently. These two possibilities represent alternative interactive structures. Our use of the template model does not 'prefer' either of these possibilities, but requires that whichever is implemented it is consistently reflected by system behaviour.

We concentrate on how structured interaction supports the users' determination of changes to results, as opposed to the determination of particular values. Since, this type of property is concerned primarily with change, for any display template (dt), result (r) and input template (it), we shall identify the following sets of input sequences:

$$\Delta_{dt}, \Delta_r, \Delta_{it} : \mathcal{P}(K^*)$$

where, Δ_{dt} is the set of input sequences that determine a display in which the display template dt has changed and is defined:

$$\Delta_{dt} \doteq \{p^\frown\langle k\rangle \in K^* : dt(v(s(p^\frown\langle k\rangle))) \neq dt(v(s(p))) \wedge v(s(p^\frown\langle k\rangle)) \in \text{ran } dt \}$$

Δ_r is the set of input sequences that determine states in which the result r has changed.

$$\Delta_r \doteq \{p^\frown\langle k\rangle \in K^* : r(s(p^\frown\langle k\rangle)) \neq r(s(p))\}$$

Δ_{it} is the set of input sequences that represent a completed input for that input template:

$$\Delta_{it} \doteq \{p^\frown\langle k\rangle \in K^* : it(p) \neq it(p^\frown\langle k\rangle)\}$$

In other words, it indicates when a significant action (represented by A_{it}) has been executed by the user.

Given any display template, result and input template, we can consider possible relations concerning their dynamic behaviour. A variety of simple relations are represented by differing constraints upon the Venn diagram in the figure 24.3. The notion of *reactive* can be re-expressed in terms of the template model in a variety of ways. Below we consider a number of suitable constraints:

- If a system is to react immediately and consistently to result changes then we should require that display template and result changes coincide: $\Delta_r = \Delta_{dt}$.

  This property does not allow a display template to appear without a corresponding result change. A more realistic, less demanding constraint is for a display template change to indicate a possible result change: $\Delta_r \subseteq \Delta_{dt}$.

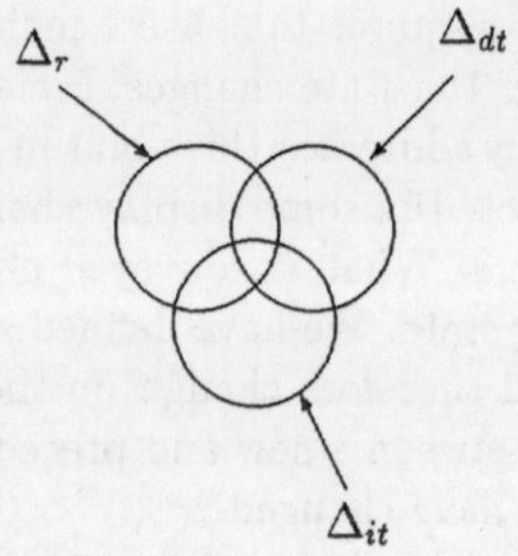

FIGURE 24.3. Venn diagram of Template Model Abstractions

- As input templates represent actions, as percieved by intended users, we can require that such actions produce result changes. In this way input templates can be classified by the results they create. Hence, the completion of an input template it can be constrained to co-incide with changes to a result r: $\Delta_r = \Delta_{dt}$. As above, this may be too restrictive in which case we can consider the weaker constraint: a result should not change, other than when an associated input template is completed: $\Delta_r \subseteq \Delta_{it}$.

We shall propose the last of these properties is representative of *structurally consistent* interactive behaviour.

Definition 8 *The template model* $\langle S, s_0, D, v, K, R, Dt, It \rangle$ *is* **structurally consistent** *iff, there is some injective mapping f from R to $Dt \times It$, such that:*

$$\forall r \in R : (\Delta_r \subseteq \Delta_{dt_r}) \wedge (\Delta_r \subseteq \Delta_{it_r})$$

Where $f(r)$ is (it_r, dt_r).

For each result a display and input template are uniquely identified and the result will only change when the input template is completed. When this occurs the display template appears.

24.4   Conclusions

An abstract system model has been described in which interface properties can be formulated and evaluated without the need to develop a prototype system. Our approach differs from other system level descriptions of interactive systems because we include structures that are relevant to the user's perspective upon interaction. This makes it possible for us to include hypotheses about the way the system is likely to be used in a typical environment. The *template model* introduces abstractions which are formally characterised *and* required to correspond to psychologically relevant, or task relevant, information. This enables mathematical properties to be linked closely with user requirements.

The template model has been used to express *structural consistency* which relates input structures to changes in the state information relevant to a user's tasks. In addition to identifying structural constraints upon interaction, we have also addressed the accurate output of relevant state information. The template model property of *output correctness* has been developed as a means of ensuring that when information is output it accurately represents state information. Unlike *observational predictability*, *output correctness* does not require that such information is always output. This formalises a more realistic system constraint.

24.5   References

[1] H. Alexander. Structuring Dialogues using CSP. In Harrison and Thimbleby [13], pages 273–295.

[2] P. Barnard. Interacting Cognitive Subsystems: A Psycholinguistic Approach to Short-term Memory. In A. Ellis, editor, *Progress in the psychology of language*, volume 2, chapter 6. Lawrence Erlbaum, 1985.

[3] P. Barnard and M. D. Harrison. Integrating cognitive and system models in human computer interaction. In A. G. Sutcliffe and L. A. Macauley, editors, *People and Computers V*, pages 87–104. Cambridge University Press, 1989.

[4] P. J. Barnard and M. D. Harrison. Towards a Framework for Modelling Human Computer Interactions. In J. Gornostaev, editor, *Proceedings International Conference on HCI, EWHCI'92*, pages 189–196. Moscow:ICSTI, 1992.

[5] S. K. Card, T. P. Moran, and A. Newell. *The Psychology of Human Computer Interaction*. Lawrence Erlbaum, 1983.

[6] G. Cockton. Three Transition Network Dialogue Management Systems. In P. Johnson and S. Cook, editors, *People and Computers: Designing the Interface*, pages 135–144. Cambridge University Press, 1985.

[7] D. Diaper. *Task Analysis for Human-Computer Interaction*. Ellis-Horwood, 1989.

[8] A. J. Dix. *Formal Methods for Interactive Systems*. Academic Press, 1991.

[9] A. J. Dix, M. D. Harrison, C. Runciman, and H. W. Thimbleby. Interaction models and the principled design of interactive systems. In H. Nichols and D. S. Simpson, editors, *European Software Engineering Conference*, pages 127–135. Springer Lecture Notes, 1987.

[10] M. D. Harrison, G. D. Abowd, and A. J. Dix. Analysing Display Oriented Interaction by means of System Models. In P.F. Byerley, P. J. Barnard, and J. May, editors, *Computers, Communication and Usability: Design issues, research and methods for integrated services*, pages 147–163. Elsevier, 1993.

[11] M. D. Harrison and A. J. Dix. A state model of direct manipulation. In Harrison and Thimbleby [13], pages 129–151.

[12] M. D. Harrison, C. R. Roast, and P. C. Wright. Complementary methods for the iterative design of interactive systems. In G. Salvendy and M.J. Smith, editors, *Designing and Using Human-Computer Interfaces and Knowledge Based Systems*, pages 651–658. Elsevier Scientific, 1989.

[13] M. D. Harrison and H. W. Thimbleby, editors. *Formal Methods in Human Computer Interaction*. Cambridge University Press, 1990.

[14] A. MacLean, R. M. Young, and T. P. Moran. Design Rationale: the argument behind the artifact. In *Proceedings ACM Conference CHI'89*, pages 247–252, 1989.

[15] C. R. Roast. *Executing Models in Human Computer Interaction*. PhD thesis, Department of Computer Science, University of York, 1993.

[16] F. Schiele and T. R. G. Green. HCI formalisms and cognitive psychology: the case of task action grammar. In Harrison and Thimbleby [13], pages 9–62.

[17] R.M. Young and J. Whittington. Using a knowledge analysis to predict conceptual errors in text-editor usage. In J.C. Chew and J. Whiteside, editors, *CHI'90 Conference Proceedings*, pages 91–97. Addison Wesley, 1990.

25 Understanding Direct Manipulation Interaction Algebraically

Roger Took

ABSTRACT

Attempts to explain human computer interaction in an abstract and generic way have up to now resorted to a functional notation, in which input is identified with the arguments to a function, and output with its result. The semantics of the interaction is expressed in the evaluation of the function itself. This has some drawbacks, in particular the difficulty of expressing the semantic or temporal dependence between input and output events, which is a major characteristic of direct manipulation interaction. This paper presents an alternative algebraic formulation, which captures centrally these IO synchronisations and dependencies.

25.1 Introduction

There have been a number of attempts to represent human-computer interaction - essentially the relationship between input and output - in ways that are both abstract and tractable. Firstly, there is Dix et al's [6, 5, 4] *PIE* model, in which an interpretation function I maps sequences of input actions P (for *Program*) to system (output) effects E:

$$P \xrightarrow{I} E$$

Or more conventionally:

$I : \text{seq } Input \rightarrow Output$

Secondly, there is by now a rich collection of mechanisms used to provide an interactive capability in functional languages [1, 7, 8, 11, 12, 13]. The earliest and most intuitive of these is called *streams* [10], and is closely related to the *PIE* model. Using streams, an interactive program is a stream processing function S from sequences of input to sequences of output:

$S : \text{seq } Input \rightarrow \text{seq } Output$

The *PIE* model and streams are equivalent functional representations, since we can derive one from the other. We can construct I from S:

$I = last \circ S$

That is, the *PIE* interpretation function I can be derived by taking the last element in the sequence of output generated by S. Similarly, the stream function S can be constructed by recursively concatenating the results of applying I (here $+$ appends an element to the end of a sequence, *front* takes the whole list except its last element, and $\langle \rangle$ is the empty sequence):

$$
\begin{aligned}
S(inputs) &= S(front(inputs)) + I(inputs) \\
S\langle \rangle &= \langle \rangle
\end{aligned}
$$

On the other hand, the *PIE* model and streams differ in important respects. The *PIE* model is an attempt to elucidate interaction in such a way that properties such as reachability (of one program state from another), predictability (of the effect of an input), and observability (of state via display) can be generically expressed (see [4]). In contrast, streams are designed to be *executable* interactively. Only one execution of S suffices to *implement* an interactive sequence, whereas I has to be repeatedly executed. For example, S might directly generate the interactive equivalence:

$$S\langle i_1, i_2, i_3 \rangle = \langle o_1, o_2, o_3 \rangle$$

whereas using I, following the conversion above, requires multiple invocations of I:

$$
\begin{aligned}
S\langle i_1, i_2, i_3 \rangle &= & S(front\langle i_1, i_2, i_3 \rangle) + I\langle i_1, i_2, i_3 \rangle \\
&= & S\langle i_1, i_2 \rangle + I\langle i_1, i_2, i_3 \rangle \\
&= & S(front\langle i_1, i_2 \rangle) + I\langle i_1, i_2 \rangle + I\langle i_1, i_2, i_3 \rangle \\
&= & S\langle i_1 \rangle + I\langle i_1, i_2 \rangle + I\langle i_1, i_2, i_3 \rangle \\
&= & S(front\langle i_1 \rangle) + I\langle i_1 \rangle + I\langle i_1, i_2 \rangle + I\langle i_1, i_2, i_3 \rangle \\
&= & S\langle \rangle + I\langle i_1 \rangle + I\langle i_1, i_2 \rangle + I\langle i_1, i_2, i_3 \rangle \\
&= & \langle \rangle + I\langle i_1 \rangle + I\langle i_1, i_2 \rangle + I\langle i_1, i_2, i_3 \rangle \\
&= & \langle \rangle + o_1 + o_2 + o_3 \\
&= & \langle o_1, o_2, o_3 \rangle
\end{aligned}
$$

However, both these functional representations more strictly describe *batch* programs, where all the input may be submitted before any output is produced. The next section illustrates how such functional formulations must be specially evaluated in order to be acceptably *inter*active. The inference is that functional representations are incapable of describing the following critical distinguishing characteristics of direct manipulation interaction:

- the synchronisation, especially alternation, of input and output.

- the dependence of input upon previous output.

This paper presents an alternative algebraic representation [2, 9] at a similar level of abstraction and genericity which builds in these direct manipulation characteristics centrally. We first of all illustrate in more detail the deficiencies of functional representations.

25.2   Functional Representations of Interaction

Functional programs are simply *expressions*, and their execution is just by *evaluation*. There are two main justifications for functional languages. Firstly, programs in them are *referentially transparent*. That is, if we declare $i = E$, then expression E can be *substituted* for i throughout, without changing the meaning of the program. This would certainly not be the case in an imperative program which contained the statement $i := E$, where the *state* of i is allowed to be *updated*. Secondly, the evaluation of a functional program can procede in any order. This is known as the *Church-Rosser* property [10]. These two properties make functional programs *tractable*: they can be manipulated mathematically without changing meaning. Thus they are an ideal medium both for constructing and reasoning about application programs.

How can we exploit these benefits of functional expression in *interactive* programs? A number of difficulties are immediately evident. There something intuitively state-oriented about interactive programs. Whether writing a document or updating a database, the user typically has a notion of the *current* state of the object being modified. Secondly, in interactive programs we are typically not interested in a single *end* result, but in a *sequence* of *intermediate* results by which the user keeps track of the task in hand.

The first problem can be resolved by exploiting the equivalence between *history* and *state*. That is, the history of operations on a state is an equivalent representation for the state itself, so long as the initial state is known and the operations are deterministic. The second problem can be partially resolved by expressing output also as a *sequence* of effects, as in streams.

For example, consider a radically simple bank teller machine dedicated just to your account, and to which you may repeatedly input a number in order to make a withdrawal, and which responds (as well as by delivering your money which we ignore here) by displaying the current balance (for simplicity we assume that you can go into the red). A functional implementation can exploit the historical representation as sequences of numbers input and output (Here : prepends an element to the beginning of a sequence):

$$withdraw(\langle\rangle, balance) = \langle\rangle$$
$$withdraw(amount : rest\_of\_input, balance) =$$
$$(balance - amount) : withdraw(rest\_of\_input, balance - amount)$$

This handles the iterative nature of interaction by a *recursive* call to *withdraw*, and handles state by passing it as an explicit parameter between calls of *withdraw*. The first line terminates the recursion when the input is the empty sequence. The type of the *withdraw* function is thus:

$$withdraw : seq\ Int \times Int \to seq\ Int$$

The state itself can be hidden from the environment of the program by defining an enclosing function which conveniently also sets the account state to its initial value:

$$bank(inputs) = withdraw(inputs, 10)$$

For example, here is the evaluation of the interaction with *bank* driven by the input sequence $\langle 1, 3, 2 \rangle$:

$$
\begin{aligned}
bank&\langle 1,3,2\rangle \\
&= withdraw(\langle 1,3,2\rangle, 10) \\
&= (10-1) : withdraw(\langle 3,2\rangle, 10-1) \\
&= (10-1) : (10-1-3) : withdraw(\langle 2\rangle, 10-1-3) \\
&= (10-1) : (10-1-3) : (10-1-3-2) : withdraw(\langle\rangle, 10-1-3-2) \\
&= (10-1) : (10-1-3) : (10-1-3-2) : \langle\rangle \\
&= \langle 10-1, 10-1-3, 10-1-3-2\rangle \\
&= \langle 10-1, 10-1-3, 4\rangle \\
&= \langle 10-1, 6, 4\rangle \\
&= \langle 9, 6, 4\rangle
\end{aligned}
$$

The type of *bank* is thus:

$$bank : seq\ Int \to seq\ Int$$

Clearly input and output need not be sequences of the *same* type of thing, and we can easily make more realistic refinements to this representation by assuming sequences of ever more complex types for input and output. Thus by relying on this recursive implementation, we can express a general functional representation for interaction which reveals the closeness of the historical and state-based representations:

$$
\begin{array}{|l}
\overline{\underline{[Input, Output]}} \\
\quad Interact : seq\ Input \to seq\ Output \\
\hline
\quad Interact(inputs) = Interact'(inputs, initial\_state)
\end{array}
$$

$$
\boxed{
\begin{array}{l}
=[Input, Output, State] \rule[-2pt]{0pt}{12pt}\\
\quad Interact' : \text{seq } Input \times State \to \text{seq } Output \\
\hline
Interact'(\langle\rangle, state) = \langle\rangle \\
Interact'(input\_event : rest\_of\_input, state) = \\
\qquad\qquad view(new\_state) : Interact'(rest\_of\_input, new\_state) \\
WHERE \\
\qquad new\_state = op(input\_event, state)
\end{array}
}
$$

Here, *Input*, *Output* and *State* are generic types; that is, they are open to instantiation. The internal function

$$
\boxed{
\begin{array}{l}
=[Input, State] \rule[-2pt]{0pt}{12pt}\\
\quad op : Input \times State \to State
\end{array}
}
$$

expresses the essential semantic update operations of any interactive application (in a large implementation, the *Input* may of course discriminate between a range of possible operations on the *State*, but we can still package this functionality into *op*). Note that this function operates on the variable *state*, but its result defines *new_state*, thus preserving referential transparency. In the *bank* example, *op* is in effect the function:

$$
op : Int \times Int \to Int
$$
$$
op(amount, balance) = balance - amount
$$

The other internal function:

$$
\boxed{
\begin{array}{l}
=[Output, State] \rule[-2pt]{0pt}{12pt}\\
\quad view : State \to Output
\end{array}
}
$$

expresses the essential interactive generation of *Output* from the current *State*. So for example we might use *view* to refine *bank* so that it includes some more graphic representation of the state of the account, such as changing the colour of the displayed balance depending on whether the account is in the red or the black.

There remain two outstanding problems. Firstly, interaction is *open-ended*. That is, we do not expect to have to complete our input sequence of actions before getting to see any of the output. In fact this property is what essentially distinguishes interactive programs from *batch* programs, where the whole input must be delivered in advance of receiving any of the corresponding output. Functionally, however, we cannot express this requirement. Interactive programs with the type seq *Input* → seq *Output* are simply functions between sequences, and their semantics is preserved independently of the relative order of delivery of the sequences.

In practice, functional implementations of such interactive programs rely on a particular evaluation strategy built into the run time system of the language. The strategy used is called *normal order* evaluation, which proceeds by evaluating the outermost (leftmost) function applications first. The upshot is that parameters to a function do not have to be fully evaluated before the function can deliver a result. In particular, the seq *Input* parameter to an interactive program of form *Interact* may be delivered incomplete, in the sense that the tail of the sequence is unspecified (this also requires special provision in the language implementation). For example, we might have the sequence of *Input* $\langle 1, 3, 2, \ldots \rangle$, where we represent the possibility of further *Input* from the user by the ellipsis. Using normal order evaluation, the function *bank* applied to this input can be evaluated:

$$bank\langle 1,3,2,...\rangle$$
$$= withdraw(\langle 1,3,2,...\rangle, 10)$$
$$= (10-1): withdraw(\langle 3,2,...\rangle, 10-1)$$
$$= 9: withdraw(\langle 3,2,...\rangle, 9)$$
$$= 9:(9-3): withdraw(\langle 2,...\rangle, 9-3)$$
$$= 9:6: withdraw(\langle 2,...\rangle, 6)$$
$$= 9:6:(6-2): withdraw(\langle ...\rangle, 6-2)$$
$$= 9:6:4: withdraw(\langle ...\rangle, 4)$$

At this point the evaluation simply hangs waiting for new input, but in the meantime we may assume that any results that have been fully evaluated (i.e. the numbers 9, 6, 4) are output as soon as they are evaluated. Thus we expect the program to exhibit standard interactive behaviour. By contrast, the first evaluation of $bank\langle 1,3,2\rangle$ above used *applicative* order evaluation. Here no output would have been delivered until the input sequence terminated. Worse than this, strictly applying applicative order evaluation results in a right-left order of evaluation of the input sequence. Thus the output would in fact have been delivered in reverse order from the input!

Normal order evaluation, however, does not solve all our interactive problems. Normal order evaluation is essentially output driven. That is, the program will output all it can until it is halted by lack of input. Thus under this strategy there is no way of specifying that some output should *not* be delivered until some input is received. Unfortunately, interactive output, as well as containing the results of some dynamic evaluation of the current (hidden) state, is often packaged in *static* data that is defined in advance in the program. For example, we might wish to refine our *bank* program so that instead of simply outputting the raw number, some helpful message was prepended, so that interaction should proceed ($>$ is the system prompt):

```
> 1
Balance: 9
> _
```

In order to implement this we would need to update *withdraw* so that the *view* function included this message (the output of *withdraw* is now a sequence of strings):

$$withdraw(amount: rest\_of\_input, balance) =$$
$$\langle \text{"}Balance:\text{"}, print(balance - amount)\rangle: withdraw(rest\_of\_input, balance - amount)$$

Unfortunately, under normal order evaluation the statically defined part of the output message, since it is immediately evaluable, will appear *before* the relevant input has been given:

```
Balance:
> 1
9
```

Implementations of functional interaction must resort to more complex primitives in order to resolve this I/O synchronisation problem [7, 11]. In order to understand that such a program works as required, the reader, it can be argued, must know as much about its non-declarative implementation details, in particular its evaluation strategy, as the reader of an imperative program. For this reason we lose the original tractability that was the major justification for the functional approach.

Thus there are fundamental difficulties in representing interaction functionally. Firstly, the problem of output packaging is simply an instance of a general problem of I/O synchronisation that is inherent in the functional representation of interaction. Essentially, *any* interleaving of input and output is semantically acceptable, simply because their relative ordering is not represented at all and is thus open to implementation. From the user's point of view, of course, a strict alternation of input and output is just about the only acceptable ordering. This is especially the case in direct manipulation systems, where input is relatively dense. While it is formally the case that the history of input determines the current display (at least in a single-user deterministic system), we certainly cannot expect the user to do without a screen representation of this. Indeed the point of direct manipulation systems is that the whole current state is displayed to the user who consequently does not have to remember any input history. The exceptions prove the rule: mouseahead, in which the user preconstructs the effects of his actions before they are actually displayed, is tolerable only over short input sequences.

Secondly, as Buxton [3] argues, the *pragmatics* of low-level direct manipulation input may be critical to usability, so that it is dangerous to abstract away from this. Such input only makes semantic sense in the context of the previous output.

25.3   An Algebraic Representation

The distinguishing feature of the functional representations of interaction above is that *input* is identified with the arguments to a function, and *output* with its result. This is a rather operational view, in that input and output are primarily linked *semantically* (i.e. by the evaluation of the function). The alternative algebraic representation presented here links input and output also *syntactically*, in that *expressions* of interaction contain both input and output operations.

An algebraic specification consists firstly of a *syntax*, conventionally called the *signature*, which generates a set of *terms* in the same way that a grammar generates a set of sentences in a natural language. This term language must secondly be given a semantics. Just as in a natural language two syntactically distinct sentences:

The dog bit the man
The man was bitten by the dog

may mean the same thing, so under the semantics of an algebraic specification two distinct terms may denote the same value. As in natural language we often define meaning by giving synonyms or paraphrases, so in an algebraic specification we define semantics by specifying *equivalences* over sets of terms. This is expressed as a set of *equations* between terms. Just using the equations we can tell whether any two (finite) terms from the language of the signature are equivalent in meaning or not. Thirdly, since not all syntactically possible terms may be meaningful, an algebraic specification may contain a set of *exceptions*, which are terms whose meaning is intended to be unevaluable. Exceptions are one way of representing *partial* algebras.

There are a number of ways in which we use the equations as rules to decide on semantic equivalence. Firstly, terms are allowed to contain *variables* which stand for any syntactically correct (sub-)term. So if our equations contained:

The x bit the y = The y was bitten by the x

then so long as we replace (instantiate) x and y consistently with nouns, we can use this equation to generate a whole set of pairs of equivalent sentences, including the pair above. Terms with no variables are called *ground* terms, in that they are fully instantiated.

Secondly, we can *substitute* equivalent terms for each other. So if we had the equation (or had derived the equivalence):

man = masculine human

then we could generate the equivalence:

The dog bit the man = The dog bit the masculine human

Finally, we can exercise *transitivity* (if $a = b$ and $b = c$ then $a = c$). So from the equivalences above we can also derive:

The dog bit the masculine human = The man was bitten by the dog

Thus the equations allow us to generate sets of semantically equivalent terms. This is thought of as an equivalence *relation* (i.e. one that is reflexive, symmetric and transitive) over the whole set of terms generated by the syntax of the signature. Each set of terms equivalent under this relation is considered to be an abstract unit of meaning (i.e. a value), for example the value '*Dog biting man in the past*'-ness. The set of these abstract values forms what is called the *quotient term algebra*. The exceptions *exclude* terms from this algebra. For example, if we had the exception:

The book bit the x.

then we semantically exclude all sentences generated by instantiating the variable x. Such sentences are meaningless.

A more conventionally mathematical algebraic specification uses a more restricted, but therefore more precise, syntax than the natural language used in the illustration above. Each *terminal* symbol of the specification (*word* by analogy with natural language) is considered to be an *operator*, which returns (or just has) a value of some sort by virtue of being applied to other values (*operands*) that have been similarly returned by operators. In order that the terms generated not be infinite, some operators do not require operands, and so are *constant* in value. An algebraic signature expresses the required sort of operands, and the sort of returned value, for each operator. Here algebras are presented in a Z-like box, in which the upper section is the signature, containing operators and their operand and return sorts, the middle section contains equations, and the lower section contains exceptions.

For example, the algebra of natural numbers, including a predecessor operator, can be expressed:

$$
\begin{array}{|l}
\hline
\quad Nat \underline{\hspace{6cm}} \\
\quad zero :\rightarrow NAT \\
\quad succ, pred : NAT \rightarrow NAT \\
\hline
\quad pred\,(succ\ n) = n \\
\hline
\quad pred\ zero \\
\hline
\end{array}
$$

Thus *zero* is a constant (operator) of sort NAT, and *succ* and *pred* are operators that require a natural number operand and whose returned value is also of sort NAT. The equation gives the semantic relation between *pred* and *succ*. All our algebraic notation will be in *prefix* form (i.e. operator first followed by a list of operands), and so the brackets here are strictly unnecessary but are included for clarity. In this equation n is a variable (it is not declared in the signature), and from the syntax it is clear that it stands for any value of sort NAT. Thus abstract values of this algebra are represented by ground terms like:

zero
succ zero
succ (pred (succ (succ zero)))

among which there may be equivalences such as:

$$zero = pred\,(succ\,zero)$$
$$succ\,(succ\,zero) = succ\,(succ\,(pred\,(succ\,zero)))$$

but from which are excluded any terms equivalent to the exception *pred zero* (for example, the term *pred* (*succ* (*pred zero*))). (We might also specify that the algebra be *strict*, in which case all terms which *use* an exceptional term are also exceptions, such as *succ* (*pred zero*)).

An algebraic specification may contain *many* as opposed to, as here, a single sort of value. The sorts represent sets of distinct values all of some particular kind, and are the essential repository of meaning in the specification. However, this meaning can only be revealed by enumerating all the sets of equivalent ground terms of each sort by the techniques outlined above. That is, meaning lies in the signature, equations and exceptions only, and we can presume nothing else.

25.3.1   Representing Direct Manipulation Interaction

We use a many-sorted algebra with sorts *DEEP_STATE*, *DISPLAY* and *EVENT*. We understand *DEEP_STATE* to be the set of states of the underlying application, *DISPLAY* to be the set of screen states, and *EVENT* to be the set of possible input values. The *constructors* of *DEEP_STATEs* are the operators *input* and *start* (*start* is a constant, intended to be the initial state). *EVENT* has no constructor in this algebra, and so the algebra is generic over *EVENT*:

DMI [*EVENT*]

$input : EVENT, DISPLAY \rightarrow DEEP\_STATE$
$output : DEEP\_STATE \rightarrow DISPLAY$
$start :\rightarrow DEEP\_STATE$

We give no equations for this algebra, and so each of its possible ground terms is a distinct abstract value. These values are of two sorts, *DEEP_STATE* or *DISPLAY*. For example, here is a list of smaller terms of each of these sorts (we assume that *e*1 and *e*2 are constant *EVENT*s):

DEEP_STATEs	*DISPLAYs*
start	*output start*
*input e*1(*output start*)	*output*(*input e*1(*output start*))
*input e*2(*output*(*input e*1(*output start*)))	*output*(*input e*2(*output*(*input e*1 (*output start*))))

This is a very abstract representation of interaction, since it is little more than a syntax. Yet this is precisely its strength, in that we hereby specify the synchronisation of input and output and the dependence of input upon previous output, prior to any application, or indeed user interface, semantics.

Refining this high level specification into a particular direct manipulation interactive system clearly requires additional detail in the sorts, and equations to specify semantic relationships between the operations of *input* and *output*. We do this in two stages. The first stage preserves the generality of the representation over applications and user interfaces, but introduces some semantics. The second stage we illustrate here by specifying a direct manipulation banking system along the lines of the functional example above.

Abstract Semantics

We need to make clearer what we might mean by *DEEP_STATE*, *DISPLAY*, and *EVENT*. Conventionally, application state is a mapping between references and values. The references are necessary to distinguish between similar values in the same state, and also to identify *different* values which represent an update *across* states. The display screen in a direct manipulation system can also be thought of as a mapping between some possibly geometric references like screen locations and graphical objects such as icons. Thus we *select* an icon under direct manipulation by clicking at its location. We can construct an algebra of *State* which captures generically this mapping between references *REF* and values *VALUE*:

$$\underline{State\,[REF,\,VALUE]}$$
$$\Delta : REF, VALUE, STATE \rightarrow STATE$$
$$\nabla : REF, STATE \rightarrow STATE$$
$$\Box :\rightarrow STATE$$
$$select : REF, STATE \rightarrow VALUE$$

$select\ r\ (\Delta\ r\ v\ s) = v$	[1]
$select\ r\ (\Delta\ r'\ v\ s) = select\ r\ s$	[2]
$select\ r\ (\nabla\ r'\ s) = select\ r\ s$	[3]
$select\ r\ \Box$	[4]
$select\ r\ (\nabla\ r\ s)$	[5]

Here Δ is an update operation on a $STATE$ which adds to the $STATE$ a new mapping between a REF and a $VALUE$. For example, a mapping between a REF r and a $VALUE$ v can be added to a $STATE$ s by:

$$\Delta\ r\ v\ s$$

This is a term representing a new $STATE$. Similarly, ∇ is a $STATE$ operation which *deletes* a reference from a $STATE$. Thus:

$$\nabla\ r\ s$$

is a $STATE$ from which REF r (and its mapping) has been removed. The *meaning* of these operations is given by the definition of *select*, which specifies how $VALUE$s are looked up in a $STATE$. For example, $\Box$ is the constant $STATE$ in which nothing can be *selected*, since $select\ r\ \Box$ is unevaluable by exception [4]. Consider also the $STATE$:

$$\Delta\ r_1\ v_1\ \Delta\ r_2\ v_2\ \Delta\ r_1\ v_3\ \Box$$

This represents a state in which reference r_1 maps to value v_1, and reference r_2 maps to value v_2. Note that $STATE$s in fact record the whole history of updates. Here, for example, r_1 has been updated from a previous value of v_3. It is clear that r_1 has value v_1 in this state if we *select* r_1 in it, and evaluate the result according to the equations (it is a minor but important feature of the evaluation that *distinct* variables must be instantiated by *distinct* values):

$$select\ r_1\ (\Delta\ r_1\ v_1\ \Delta\ r_2\ v_2\ \Delta\ r_1\ v_3\ \Box) = v_1 \qquad \text{[by equation 1]}$$

Thus in Δ-update it is unimportant whether the REF already exists in the $STATE$, since only the new mapping will be looked up by *select*. We can *select* r_2 by a similar evaluation:

$$select\ r_2\ (\Delta\ r_1\ v_1\ \Delta\ r_2\ v_2\ \Delta\ r_1\ v_3\ \Box)$$
$$= select\ r_2\ (\Delta\ r_2\ v_2\ \Delta\ r_1\ v_3\ \Box) \qquad \text{[by equation 2]}$$
$$= v_2 \qquad\qquad\qquad\qquad\qquad\qquad\qquad \text{[by equation 1]}$$

However, if we attempt to *select* a *REF* that has either been deleted or never existed in a *STATE*, then the exceptions ([4] and [5]) tell us that this cannot be evaluated. For example, *select*ing a non-existent *REF*:

$$select\ r\ (\Delta\ r_1\ v_1\ \Delta\ r_2\ v_2\ \square)$$
$$=\ select\ r\ (\Delta\ r_2\ v_2\ \square) \hspace{3cm} \text{[by equation 2]}$$
$$=\ select\ r\ \square \hspace{4cm} \text{[by equation 2]}$$
$$-unevaluable \hspace{3.5cm} \text{[by exception 4]}$$

Similarly, *select*ing a ∇-deleted *REF*:

$$select\ r_2\ (\Delta\ r_1\ v_1\ \nabla\ r_2\ \Delta\ r_2\ v_2\ \square)$$
$$=\ select\ r_2\ (\nabla\ r_2\ \Delta\ r_2\ v_2\ \square) \hspace{2.5cm} \text{[by equation 2]}$$
$$-unevaluable \hspace{3.5cm} \text{[by exception 5]}$$

At this level we are concerned simply to say that such terms are unevaluable. In a practical implementation, and in particular in an interactive system, we would of course handle these exceptions in some more graceful way.

State, as intended, is generic over *REF* and *VALUE*, in that we do not *construct* values of these sorts in the algebra (*select* is a *selector*, not a constructor). For our purposes in direct manipulation systems, we wish to *reuse State* to specify both the application's *DEEP_STATE*, and the *DISPLAY* states of the screen. We accomplish this reuse by instantiating the generic sorts *REF* and *VALUE*, and by a simple syntactic renaming of the constructed sort *STATE* (/ means 'replaces'):

$$Surface == State[LOC, ICON]\{DISPLAY\,/\,STATE\}$$

Thus what we here call the *Surface* is a *State* whose basic values are *DISPLAY*s, which are mappings between screen locations *LOC* and *ICON*s. The *Surface* remains generic over *LOC* and *ICON* whose meanings we leave open to interpretation.

A fundamental constraint which direct manipulation places on applications is some knowledge of the *Surface*. That is, the application must be able to *dereference* the *DISPLAY* against some denotation within its semantics, so that the application can interpret what user *EVENT*s mean. There are two ways in which this can be achieved. The application's *DEEP_STATE* may retain a complete knowledge of the *State* of the *DISPLAY*, in particular the *LOC*ations of *ICON*s, and so be able to map directly from screen locations to application denotations. This has two disadvantages. Firstly, the application is dependent upon device geometry (*LOC* may be pixel coordinates, for example). Secondly, user manipulation of the *ICON*s on the *DISPLAY* (for example, updating their *LOC* by moving them to another place on the screen) necessitates updating the mappings from *LOC* to denotations in the *DEEP_STATE*.

It is far better that the application retain only a symbolic representation for the *ICON*s, independent of their *DISPLAY LOC*ations. The *DEEP_STATE*, that is, should ideally retain a mapping between *ICON*s (rather than *LOC*s) and application denotations. In addition, the application is likely to need mappings between its own internal references and values in order to maintain its semantics. The references in *DEEP_STATE*, therefore, consist both of *ICON*s and what we can call here *LABEL*s. We can now define the application state (*Deep*) as another *State* mapping between *ICON*s or *LABEL*s and *VALUE*s, in which each state is a *DEEP_STATE* (*VALUE* is unchanged):

$$Deep == State[ICON\ |\ LABEL, VALUE]\{DEEP\_STATE\,/\,STATE\}$$

The semantically augmented, but still general, specification of direct manipulation interaction can be given by combining the *DMI* syntax (in which *EVENT*s are here *LOC*s) with the algebras for the *Surface* and *Deep* States:

$\underline{\quad DMI+ \quad}$_____
| $DMI[LOC]$ |
| $Surface$ |
| $Deep$ |
| $cpply: VALUE, DEEP\_STATE \rightarrow DEEP\_STATE$ |

| $input\ loc\ (output\ s) = apply\ (select\ (select\ loc\ (output\ s))\ s)\ s$ | [6] |

Note that this means that the $State$ operations ($\triangle$, ∇, $\square$, and $select$) are here overloaded (they work on $Deep$ as well as $Surface$ $States$), but this causes no ambiguity. In addition here we need a general application function $apply$, which takes a $VALUE$ (from the $DEEP\_STATE$) and effects a $DEEP\_STATE$ change. $apply$ is necessary since some $VALUE$s in the $DEEP\_STATE$ will be $operations$, which would otherwise have to be implemented as higher-order functions. To do this would break our simple equational semantics.

The single equation [6] in $DMI+$ is our main generic expression of direct manipulation interaction in this formalism. It is to be understood as follows. For any $DEEP\_STATE$ s, its $DISPLAY$ is $output\ s$. If the user clicks with the mouse at a particular screen location loc of sort LOC, then the effect is to change s into the $DEEP\_STATE$ $input\ loc\ (output\ s)$. This is the left-hand side of equation [6]. The equation goes as far as is possible in the abstract to defining the semantics of this in terms of $apply$ing some application defined $VALUE$ (which may be a constant or an operation) to s. The particular application $VALUE$ which is to be applied is extracted by a process of double dereferencing of the two sorts of $State$. Firstly, the $ICON$ under the location loc is extracted from the $DISPLAY$ $output\ s$:

$select\ loc\ (output\ s)$

Then this $ICON$ is used to extract the application $VALUE$ which is its semantic denotation:

$select\ (select\ loc\ (output\ s))\ s$

Finally, this $VALUE$ is applied to the $DEEP\_STATE$ s:

$apply\ (select\ (select\ loc\ (output\ s))\ s)\ s$

The exact semantics of $apply$ must be left to particular specialisations of $DMI+$.

$DMI+$ is intentionally a very abstract representation of what is going on under direct manipulation interaction of the semantic feedback from some application. A major feature of its generality is the way in which it abstracts from the precise effect of each user input. This is important, since user input in direct manipulation interaction (for example a click at a screen location) may have two types of denotation within the application semantics: it may specify an $operator$ or an $operand$. At the level of $DMI+$ we wish to preserve independence of more specific user interface design decisions such as whether the operator must be specified before the operand or vice versa.

Concrete Semantics

In order to show how $DMI+$ is both a general characterisation of this sort of interaction, and can also be specialised to produce more specific designs for particular applications, we address the simple $bank$ example above. Consider an interface which looks like:

This can be specified by the following algebra, which is an extension of $DMI+$:

```
┌─ Bank ──────────────────────────────────────────────────────────
│ DMI+
│ withdraw :→ VALUE
│ balance, current :→ REF
├──────────────────────────────────────────────────────────────────
│ start =
│     △ balance 1000
│     △ current 0
│     △ [WITHDRAW] withdraw
│     △ [£10] 10
│     △ [£20] 20
│     △ [£50] 50 □                                              [7]
│ output s =
│     △ 1 [WITHDRAW]
│     △ 2 [£10]
│     △ 3 [£20]
│     △ 4 [£50]
│     △ 5 | select balance s | □                                [8]
│ apply withdraw s = △ balance (−(select balance s) (select current s)) s   [9]
│ apply v s = △ current v s                                     [10]
└──────────────────────────────────────────────────────────────────
```

Bank first of all [7] defines the *start DEEP_STATE* by giving initial values for the internal references *balance* and *current*, followed by the denotation of the *ICON*s as either the operation *withdraw* or the constants 10, 20 and 50 (we assume that arithmetic is also imported here). Equation [8] says that the *output DISPLAY* of a *DEEP_STATE s* consists of fixed mappings between *LOC*ations 1, 2, 3, and 4 and the *ICON*s on the screen, and a mapping between *LOC* 5 and an iconic *projection* of the value of *balance*. For brevity we do not define this projection, but its meaning is obvious. Thus the *layout* of the *DISPLAY* does not change in this application. The last two equations ([9] and [10]) define the semantics of *apply* within the *Bank* application. For simplicity of presentation we make the assumption of prioritised pattern matching in this evaluation. Thus equation [9] matches *withdraw*, while equation [10] matches any *VALUE v* *except withdraw*.

So the effect of *apply*ing *withdraw* to some *DEEP_STATE s* is to update the internal reference *balance* to the value of *balance* less the value of *current*. The effect of *apply*ing *withdraw* to any other *VALUE v* is to set *current* to that *VALUE*. Since we initialise *current* to 0, the *DEEP_STATE apply withdraw s* is always defined.

Take as an example an interactive session in which the user first selects the $\boxed{£20}$ $ICON$, then changes her mind and selects the $\boxed{£50}$ $ICON$, and finally selects the $\boxed{\text{WITHDRAW}}$ $ICON$ and so withdraws £50 from the $balance$ in the bank. The new $balance$ is displayed in the lower $ICON$. We assume that the LOCs $1\ldots5$ are logical screen locations for which pixel coordinates are a concrete realisation. This interactive session can be represented in a single expression:

$$input\,1\,(output\,(input\,4\,(output\,(input\,3\,(output\,start)))))$$

We can show the evaluation of this in stages. Let us call the first $DEEP\_STATE$ generated after $start$, D. The first input event ($LOC\,3$) selects the $\boxed{£20}$ $ICON$, and this sets $current$ to the value 20:

$$
\begin{aligned}
D &= input\,3\,(output\,start) \\
&= apply\,(select\,(select\,3\,(output\,start))\,start)\,start && \text{[by equation 6]} \\
&= apply\,(select\,\boxed{£20}\,start)\,start && \text{[by equations 1 and 2]} \\
&= apply\,20\,start && \text{[by equations 1 and 2]} \\
&= \Delta\,current\,20\,start && \text{[by equation 10]}
\end{aligned}
$$

The second input event ($LOC\,4$) is delivered in the context of the $output$ of $DEEP\_STATE$ D, and changes $current$ to 50 (the evaluation is abbreviated) in a new $DEEP\_STATE$ D':

$$
\begin{aligned}
D' &= input\,4\,(output\,D) \\
&= apply\,(select\,(select\,4\,(output\,D))\,D)\,D && \text{[by equation 6]} \\
&= apply\,(select\,\boxed{£50}\,D)\,D && \text{[by equations 1 and 2]} \\
&= \Delta\,current\,50\,D && \text{[by equation 10]} \\
&= \Delta\,current\,50\,\Delta\,current\,20\,start
\end{aligned}
$$

The third input event ($LOC\,1$) $select$s the $\boxed{\text{WITHDRAW}}$ $ICON$, and D' is finally updated with a new value for $balance$:

$$
\begin{aligned}
input\,1\,(output\,D') & \\
&= apply\,(select\,(select\,1\,(output\,D'))\,D')\,D' && \text{[by equation 6]} \\
&= apply\,(select\,\boxed{\text{WITHDRAW}}\,D')\,D' && \text{[by equations 1 and 2]} \\
&= apply\,withdraw\,D' && \text{[by equations 1 and 2]} \\
&= \Delta\,balance\,(-\,(select\,balance\,D')\,(select\,current\,D'))\,D' \\
& && \text{[by equation 9]} \\
&= \Delta\,balance\,(-\,1000\,50)\,D' && \text{[by equations 1 and 2]} \\
&= \Delta\,balance\,950\,D' && \text{[by standard arithmetic]} \\
&= \Delta\,balance\,950\,\Delta\,current\,50\,\Delta\,current\,20\,start
\end{aligned}
$$

Thus equational evaluation, rather than moving from input to output as in the functional representations, here provides equivalences between interaction oriented terms like the one we started with in this example, and ever deeper semantics in terms of $DEEP\_STATE$s.

25.4 Dialogue Issues

Clearly here the icon $\boxed{\text{WITHDRAW}}$ is an $operator$, while the others (i.e. $\boxed{£10}$, $\boxed{£20}$ and $\boxed{£50}$) are its $operands$. Given this interface, there is a design decision as to whether the user should be required to select an operand first, followed by the operator, or vice versa. The interaction specified above allows any order of invocation, since there is always (even initially) a notion of a current amount to be withdrawn. Thus if the user inadvertently clicks twice on WITHDRAW, she will withdraw the current amount twice.

If we wish to tighten the interactive *dialogue*, for example to exclude the above error, then this can be achieved by a simple update to the equations. It requires a new equation to replace [9]:

$$apply\ withdraw\ s = \nabla\ current\ \Delta\ balance\ (-\ (select\ balance\ s)\ (select\ current\ s))\ s$$

[9a]

This equation now *deletes* current from any $DEEP\_STATE$ from which a withdrawal has just been made. Thus an attempt to make a second withdrawal becomes unevaluable by exception [5]. Clearly we should give some error message in this case, but this is more an implementation detail.

Equation [9a] also has the effect of imposing a strict *operand-operator* dialogue on the interaction. That is, we cannot select WITHDRAW until we have selected an amount to be withdrawn. However, we may still change our mind about the amount to be withdrawn. Thus dialogue can be modified by relatively simple adjustments to the semantics of the interaction.

25.5   Interpretation

As noted above, an algebraic specification is ultimately considered to be its quotient term algebra, i.e. the set of sets of equivalent values under the equations (and excluding the exceptions). It is a *specification* to the extent that we can provide more concrete algebras (sets of values and operations on these) that preserve the abstract relationships. Concrete algebras that do this are called *models*. In order to decide whether a particular concrete algebra is in fact a model for an algebraic specification, we first of all must declare the mapping between the abstract and concrete values and operations. Conventionally this is done using an interpretation function $[\![\_]\!]$. For example, we can declare an interpretation for NAT (the concrete values $(+1)$ and (-1) are the increment and decrement functions respectively):

$$[\![zero]\!] = 0$$
$$[\![succ]\!] = (+1)$$
$$[\![pred]\!] = (-1)$$

In order for a concrete algebra to be a model, there must exist a *homomorphism* between the concrete algebra and the abstract algebra. That is, for any abstract operator op_A and abstract value a the following equation must hold:

$$[\![op_A(a)]\!] = [\![op_A]\!]([\![a]\!])$$

For example, using NAT:

$$[\![succ\ zero]\!] = [\![succ]\!]([\![zero]\!])$$
$$1 = (+1)(0)$$
$$1 = 1$$
$$true$$

25.5.1   Varieties of Interpretation

An algebraic specification represents a *class* of concrete algebras since there may be a number of concrete algebras which can act as homomorphic models for the abstract specification. Consider numbers represented in the Roman numeral system. A feature of our interpretation of NAT is that we have made a *one-to-one* interpretation from the abstract numbers (sets of numerically equivalent terms) into some concrete algebra like Roman or Arabic numerals. This is known as an *initial* interpretation. However, our interpretation need not be one-to-one in order to preserve homomorphism. In particular, we may end up with models which contain *more* or *fewer* concrete values, and both of these may be useful interpretations of the specification.

Final Interpretations

Under a final interpretation we need generate only the *minimum* set of concrete values which is necessary to preserve the abstract semantics of the operators. For example, the abstract $Bank$ above has possible $DEEP\_STATE$ values:

$$\triangle \, current \, 50 \, start$$
$$\triangle \, current \, 50 \, \triangle \, current \, 20 \, start$$

These are abstractly distinct since there are no equations to relate them. Under an initial interpretation we would have to provide some history-preserving concrete representation with a different value corresponding to each of these. However, if the only observation that we can make of these values is to *select* the most recent *current* mapping (which is the case in $Bank$) then there would appear to be no need to record previous mappings. Thus under a final interpretation we could represent $DEEP\_STATE$s simply using a set of variables (*current*, *balance* etc) whose previous values might be overwritten. In this concrete representation the above two abstract values would be indistinguishable (i.e. they would both be modelled by $start$ with $current$ set to 50).

Loose Interpretations

Just as we might *conflate* abstract values in an interpretation so long as we do not lose the homomorphic property, so we might also *decompose* abstract values into more concrete values than are abstractly necessary. Such interpretations are called *loose*. For example, in $Bank$ we suppose just the five LOCs $1 \ldots 5$. These are clearly not sufficient to provide an *implementation* of direct manipulation, in which the user expects to be able to click at *any* pixel coordinate within the area of an $ICON$:

So an implementation of $Bank$ would for example need to make a loose interpretation of LOC 1 as the *set* of possible pixel coordinates via which (WITHDRAW) might be *select*ed.

25.6   Conclusions

This paper presents an algebraic representation of interaction which is at a similar level of abstraction and genericity to the various functional representations, but which captures more explicitly the essential characteristics of direct manipulation interaction: IO synchronisation and dependence. What we have not addressed here is the expression of *properties* over interaction. It is evident even in our simple $Bank$ example that the interface is not *predictable*. That is, we can select (WITHDRAW) in ignorance of the amount to be withdrawn, unless we happen to remember the amount $ICON$ that was last selected. Clearly in implementation we might highlight this $ICON$. This property here seems expressible by comparing initial and final interpretations of the specification, but the precise formulation of this requires further research.

25.7   References

[1] P. Achten, J. van Groningen, and R. Plasmeijer. High Level Specification of I/O in Functional Lanuages. In J. Launchbury and P. Sansom, editors, *Functional Programming, Glasgow 1992*, pages 1–17. Springer-Verlag, Workshops in Computing Series, 1993.

[2] M. Bidoit. Algebraic System Specification and Development - A survey and annotated bibliography. In M. Bidoit, H.-J. Kreowski, P. Lescanne, F. Orejas, and D. Sannella, editors, *LNCS 501*. Springer Verlag, 1991.

[3] W. Buxton. Lexical and Pragmatic Considerations of Input Structures. *ACM Computer Graphics*, 17:31–37, January 1983.

[4] A. Dix. Abstract, Generic Models of Interactive Systems. In D. M. Jones and R. Winder, editors, *People and Computers IV: Proc. HCI '88*, pages 63–77. Cambridge University Press, September 1988.

[5] A. J. Dix, M. D. Harrison, C. Runciman, and H. Thimbleby. Interaction Models and the Principled Design of Interactive Systems. In H. Nichols and D. S. Simpson, editors, *Proc European Software Engineering Conference*, pages 127–135. Springer Verlag, 1987.

[6] A. J. Dix and C. Runciman. Abstract Models of Interactive Systems. In P. Johnson and S. Cook, editors, *British Computer Society Conference Proc., "People and Computers: Designing the User Interface"*, pages 13–22. Cambridge University Press, 1985.

[7] A. Dwelly. Synchronizing the I/O Behaviour of Functional Programs with Feedback. *Information Processing Letters*, 28:45–51, 1988.

[8] A. D. Gordon. An Operational Semantics for I/O in a Lazy Functional Language. In *Proc. Conf. on Functional Programming Languages and Computer Architecture*, pages 136–145. ACM, June 1993.

[9] I. Van Horebeek and J. Lewi. *Algebraic Specifications in Software Engineering*. Springer-Verlag, 1989.

[10] P. Hudak. Conception, Evolution, and Application of Functional Programming Languages. *ACM Computing Surveys*, 21:359–411, September 1989.

[11] P. Hudak and R. S. Sundaresh. On the Expressiveness of Purely Functional I/O Systems. Technical Report YALEU/DCS/RR-665, Yale University, December 1988.

[12] P. W. M. Koopman. Interactive Programs in a Functional Language: A Functional Implementation of an Editor. *Software - Practice and Experience*, 17:609–622, September 1987.

[13] S. Thompson. Interactive Functional Programs: a Method and a Formal Semantics. Technical Report No. 48, UKC Computing Laboratory, November 1987.

26 Using an Abstract Model for the Formal Specification of Interactive Graphic Systems.

Juan Carlos Torres
Buenaventura Clares

ABSTRACT

Algebraic specification has been widely used for the formal specification of graphic systems. Normally, specification languages use only very simple geometrical concepts as graphical theoretical support, which results in complex specifications.

The specification of interactive graphic systems has found a good formal model in the concept of 'interactor'. An interactor is an abstraction of an entity in interactive graphics capable of both input and output. Interactors have been formally specified using CSP-like languages, but without any graphic abstract conceptual support.

In this paper we discuss the integration of a formal abstract model (the graphic object concept), an algebraic specification language and synchronization mechanisms. Binding these concepts allows us to carry out a property oriented description of interactive systems, with a high level of abstraction.

26.1 Introduction

Algebraic specification languages have been used to specify graphic systems, mainly graphic standards [1,2,9]. These works have used general purpose specification languages, which are not well suited for the specification of graphic systems, because the specification of a graphic system should allow us to determine not only the system state but also the resulting image. The origin of this problem is that the image is not part of the system state, but is, in fact, an interface. So, it is necessary to specify what should happen on the two sides of this interface: graphic system and human observer. This can be accomplished in three different ways:

· Fixing the interface structure, that is the image generation system structure. This will allow us to deduce the resulting image from the values passed to it.

· Using a specification language that allows us to express the representation of the drawing elements using graphic primitives. The specification of the visualization of any element will be then carried out describing how it is built using the primitive elements. The image corresponding to these simpler elements will be specified and tested on the two sides of the interface.

· Embedding a formal description of graphic elements within the specification language.

We have decided to use the third approach, employing our graphic object formalism to describe graphic elements [12,13]. This formalism is an extension of the Fiume raster graphics theory [6], including a precise mathematical definition of some object composition operations.

The formal specification of interactive graphic systems can be supported by the concept of interactor [5]. An interactor is an abstraction of an entity in interactive graphics capable of both input and output. Interactors have been formally specified using LOTOS, a CSP like language, but without any graphic abstract conceptual support [11]. An interactor is an architectural abstraction with four active components (see Figure 26.1):

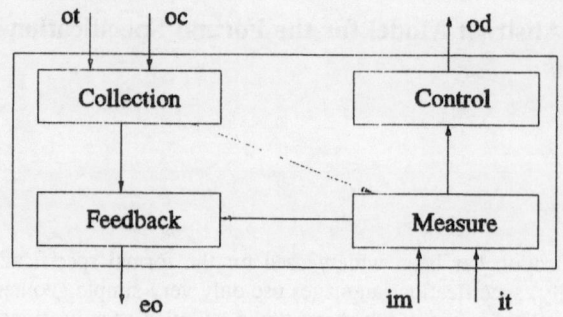

FIGURE 26.1. Internal structure of an interactor.

○ *The collection*, which gives a high level description of the external appearance.

○ *The feedback*, which produces the external appearance.

○ *The measure*, which builds a high level input data.

○ *The control*, which delivers the produced input data.

We consider that the specification of interactive graphic systems can be made easier by using an abstract model to represent graphic information, and propose to bind the abstract model with a concurrent algebraic specification language. The final section of this paper shows a specification of an interactor based on this approach.

26.2 The abstract model

This section contains a brief summary of the graphic object concept [12,13], which is an extension of the graphic object concept of Eugene Fiume [6]. Our formalism is based on four main concepts: geometrical transformation [14], volume, aspect and presence.

A *geometrical transformation*, $\tau: \mathbb{R}^n \rightarrow \mathbb{R}^n$, is a bijection, which holds the following property

$$\forall X, Y \in \mathbb{R}^n \ \forall \beta \in [0,1] \subset \mathbb{R} => \tau(\beta \cdot X + (1-\beta) \cdot Y) = \beta \cdot \tau(X) + (1-\beta) \cdot \tau(Y)$$

Informally, a graphic object is an abstraction of a system with a strong geometrical and visual content. The geometrical and visual information must specify the space occupied by the object and its visual appearance. We shall call these two concepts presence and aspect of the graphic objects. The *aspect* of a graphic object describes its visual appearance (colour, transparency, reflection coefficient, etc.), and other non-geometrical attributes (density, type of material, etc.).

The *presence* of a graphic object describes its space occupance, that is the multiplicity with which an object occupies space. Presence is a countable property.

A *ζ-structure* on a field **K** is a set, Z, on which the following operations are defined:
·   An internal binary operation, +, called addition for which Z is a commutative group.
·   An external operation over the field **K**, *, called product by scalar, for which $(Z, +, *)$ is a vectorial space.

· Two internal binary operations, $\cup$ and $\cap$, called   union and intersection, and one internal unary operation, $\sim$, called complement, for which Z is a boolean algebra. The empty element is the neutral element of the vectorial space.
· An internal binary operation, $\times$, called product, satisfying the following properties: associativity, commutativity, and existence of identity element, and the neutral element of the vectorial space acts as an absorbent element.

It could be interesting to show that such an algebraic structure could exist. Let us choose the subset of integer values between 0 and 2^p-1. It is easy to see that the addition, internal product and product by scalar can be defined as the normal operation modulus 2^p, and that boolean operations can be defined as bit by bit operations. More complex sets may be derived considering records of simple integer subsets.

To manage the presence and aspect of a graphic object we define the algebraic structures presence and aspect domains. An *aspect domain or aspect space*, δ, is a set of aspect values which is a ζ-structure. In the same way, a *presence domain or presence space*, π, is a set of presence values which is a ζ-structure.

Formally, a *volume*, V, is a subset of $\mathbb{R}^n$. The *volume* of a graphic object is the portion of space where the object is, that is where we have some information about the object.

Definition 26.1. A universe of graphic objects, u, is a triple $u=(\pi,\delta,n)$ where π and δ are a presence domain and an aspect domain respectively, over the same field, and n is the euclidean space dimension.   □

Definition 26.2. A *graphic object*, in the universe $u=(\pi,\delta,n)$, is a pair (μ,α), where μ is a function, called *presence function*, defined as $\mu: \mathbb{R}^n \rightarrow \pi$, and α is a function, called *aspect function*, defined as $\alpha: \mathbb{R}^n \rightarrow \delta$ □

The set of graphic objects in a universe, u, will be denoted as $\Omega(u)$.

A graphic object may be described giving the aspect and presence value for every volume point. A rectangle can be defined as:

$$\text{Rectangle}(P_1,P_2) = (\mu, \alpha)$$

where:

$$\mu(P)= \begin{cases} 1 & \text{if } P \leq P_2 \wedge P \geq P_1 \\ 0 & \text{otherwise} \end{cases}$$

$$\alpha(P) = k \cdot \mu(P)$$

and k is the aspect value for the rectangle.

Every graphic object has an associated volume, which may be defined as the zone of the space in which the object information is enclosed. The *volume* V associated to a graphic object $O=(\mu,\alpha)$ is the set of points holding that

$$\text{Vol}(O) = \{P \in \mathbb{R}^n \mid \alpha(P) \neq 0 \vee \mu(P) \neq 0\}$$

It is possible to formally define modelling operations which give a powerful algebraic structure to the graphic object set. Over the set of graphic objects the following operations are defined: geometrical transformation, addition, product by scalar, union, intersection, complement, object product, object circular product and geometrical transformation. For any two given objects, $O_1=(\mu_1,\alpha_1)$ and $O_2=(\mu_2,\alpha_2)$, and any given value $k \in K$, these operations are computed by the following expressions [13]:

Geometrical transformation $\qquad T(O) = (\mu \cdot T^{-1}, \alpha \cdot T^{-1})$

Addition: $\qquad\qquad\qquad O_1 + O_2 = (\mu_1 + \mu_2, \alpha_1 + \alpha_2)$

Scalar product: $\qquad\qquad k*O_1 = (k*\mu_1, k*\alpha_1)$

Union: $\qquad\qquad\qquad O_1 \cup O_2 = (\mu_1 \cup \mu_2, \alpha_1 \cup \alpha_2)$

Intersection: $\qquad\qquad\quad O_1 \cap O_2 = (\mu_1 \cap \mu_2, \alpha_1 \cap \alpha_2)$

Complement: $\qquad\qquad\quad \sim O_1 = (\bar{\mu}_1, \bar{\alpha}_1)$

Product: $O_1 \times O_2 = (\Sigma_{\delta(O1,O2,P)} \mu_1(P_1) \times \mu_2(P_2), \Sigma_{\delta(O1,O2,P)} \alpha_1(P_1) \times \alpha_2(P_2))$

$\qquad$ where $\qquad \delta(O_1,O_2,P) = \{ (P_1,P_2) \mid P_1 \in Vol(O_1), P_2 \in Vol(O_2) \text{ and } P=T_t^{[P]1}(P_2) \}$

Circular Product: $O_1 \otimes O_2 = (\Sigma_{\delta c(O1,O2,P)} \mu_1(P_1) \times \mu_2(P_2), \Sigma_{\delta c(O1,O2,P)} \alpha_1(P_1) \times \alpha_2(P_2))$

$\qquad$ where $\qquad \delta_c(O_1,O_2,P) = \{ (P_1,P_2) \mid P_1 \in Vol(O_1), P_2 \in Vol(O_2) \text{ and } P=T_c^{[P]1}(P_2) \}$

The set of graphic objects for any universe is a ζ-*structure*. Graphic object operations allow us to model complex graphic objects from simpler ones.

It is also possible to define graphic object functions, which map graphic objects onto graphic objects [15]. A *graphic object function*, $F[\beta]$, with parameter ß, from universe u_1, $u_1=(\pi_1,\delta_1,m)$, to universe u_2, $u_2=(\pi_2,\delta_2,n)$, is a function whose action over any object, $O \in \Omega(u_1)$, is the object of $\Omega(u_2)$ given by:

$$F[\beta](O) = (f_p[\beta](\mu), f_a[\beta](\alpha))$$

where

$$f_p[\beta](\mu) = \mu': \mathbb{R}^n -> \pi_2$$

$$f_a[\beta](\alpha) = \alpha': \mathbb{R}^n -> \delta_2$$

are two functionals called presence component and aspect component of the object function.

As an example, let us contemplate a changing colour function, assigning colour k to any object point with non zero aspect. This function may be defined as $F[k](O) = (f_p[k](\mu), f_a[k](\alpha))$ where

$$f_p[k](\mu) = \mu$$

$$f_a[k](\alpha) = \alpha'$$

and

$$\alpha'(P) = \begin{cases} 0 & \text{if } \alpha(P)=0 \\ k \in \delta_2 & \text{if } \alpha(P) \neq 0 \end{cases}$$

One immediate application of this concept is to represent graphical operations within a graphic system, in an abstract way, whose information is symbolized by graphic objects. They can be used to represent operations such as hiding a component on an interface, changing its colour, or extracting some part from it.

To model the visualization process we can use the Fiume raster graphic theory, deriving a Fiume object as a visual representation of every graphic object. We can now derive a Fiume graphic object, $O_f = (Z_o, I_o)$, equivalent to a graphic object, $O = (\mu, \alpha)$. To do this, it is necessary to map the Fiume colour space onto an aspect domain. Given an injective function, $G: C \longrightarrow A$ where $C \subseteq \mathbb{R}^c$ is a Fiume colour space and A is an aspect domain, for any graphic object $O = (\mu, \alpha)$ we define its visual representation as the Fiume graphic object given by:

$$O_f = (Z_o, I_o)$$

where

$$Z_0 = \{ P \subseteq \mathbb{R}^n \mid \mu(P) > 0 \} \subseteq \mathbb{R}^n$$

$$I_0 = G^{-1}(\alpha(P)): Z_0 \longrightarrow C$$

We consider the visual representation of any graphic object (in $\mathbb{R}^n$ with $n \leq 4$) as that of the Fiume object which corresponds to its equivalence class. It should be noticed that the visual equivalence relationship could be defined in different ways, affecting the visual representation of some graphic objects as Fiume objects. Of course this implies that the visual representation of several graphic objects can be the same. Two graphic objects, $O_1 = (\mu_1, \alpha_1)$ and $O_2 = (\mu_2, \alpha_2)$, defined in $\mathbb{R}^n$, are *visually equivalent*, $O_1 \approx O_2$, if their aspect and presence functions satisfy the following condition

$$\forall P \in \mathbb{R}^n => \mu_1(P) > 0 \text{ iff } \mu_2(P) > 0$$

and

$$\text{if } \mu_1(P) > 0 \text{ then } \alpha_1(P) = \alpha_2(P)$$

The visual equivalency relationship between graphic objects is an equivalence relationship.

This correspondence between Fiume objects and graphic objects allows us to use graphic objects as a modelling concept which supports the Fiume visualization formalism.

26.3 The specification method

GRALPLA is an algebraic specification language developed at Granada University. For a GRALPLA specification it is possible to build a prototype automatically in a high level language. This prototype can be used as a first version of the system for the implementation, or as a reference implementation.

The specification of a system using GRALPLA consists of a collection of modules which are written and translated independently. The specification of each module has six parts: header, dependencies, constructors, functions, axioms and synchronization. A correct module is formed with a sequence of these components in the order described (see Figure 26.2). The remainder of this paragraph describes the syntax and semantics of these sections [7,8].

· Header. This section contains the name of the module (object_id), which is also the name of the carrier set, and an optional list of formal parameters, used to build generic modules. The parameter list is a list of identifiers, which are used as types for generic modules. The actual type for each identifer is fixed when using the module. The signature of these parameters is obtained from their specifications.

· Dependencies. This section gives a list of the modules which are used by the actual module. Object_id is a module identifier which is used in the specification of the actual module. That is, the actual module may use its carrier set and all its functions. The list of

<Specification_Module> ::= Header [Dependencies] Constructor
                            Functions Axioms [Syncronization]

<Header> ::= **[parametric] [graphic] object** object_id
                [[parameter_id {,parameter_id}]]

<Dependencies> ::= **import** { object_id [[type_id {,type_id}]]}

<Constructors> ::= **Constructor** {function_id : [type_id { , type_id}] -> object_id
                    where function_id [var_id {,var_id}] = Expression}

<Functions> ::= **Functions** { function_id [< selector_id, {selector_id} >] :
                    type_id { , type_id} -> type_id { , type_id} }

<Axioms> ::= **Axioms** [**var** { var_id {, var_id} : type_id ;}]
                    {function_id (Term {,Term}) [.selector_id] = Expression}

<Expression> ::= Term | **if** (Condition) Expression **else** Expression **Endif**

<Condition> ::= function_id [(Term {, Term }) [.selector_id]]
                    (= | > | < | < >) Term | Boolean-Expression

<Term> ::= function_id [(Term {,Term}) [.selector_id]] | var_id | Constant |
                    Boolean-Expression | Integer-Expression | ERROR [String]

<Syncronization> ::= **Syncronization** { **do** function_id (var_id { , var_id}) =
                    Condition }

FIGURE 26.2. Summary of the GRALPLA Syntax

types must appear when the used module has parameters, they act as actual parameters for
this instance of the generic module.

· Constructors. This section contains the constructor signature. Constructors are a special
kind of function, every constructor returns only one result of the carrier set type. They are
used to create objects of this type, so any module must have at least one constructor.
Function_id is the constructor name. The type list is employed optionally to allow the use
of parameters when creating an object (i.e. the dimension of an array).

· Functions. This section contains the signature of the module functions. Any function
may return more than one result, in this case selectors must been included to identify every
result. Any function definition has four components: the function identifier, an optional list
of selector identifiers, a list of argument types, and a list of result types. Any function must
have at least one argument and one result.

Axioms. This section contains the axioms that hold for this module. Every axiom is an equation, whose left hand side is a function. To write the equation it is possible to use auxiliary variables, whose only purpose is to establish relations within the axiom. The variable declaration uses a pascal-like structure. Every axiom refers to one module function, whose arguments may be functions. Expressions may be conditional ones. Integer and boolean expressions are built up with integer or boolean terms and operators.

Axioms are interpreted as directional equations: what appears on the left hand side can be carried out as explained on the right hand side.

The error conditions are described, indicating that the corresponding function returns ERROR, as result.

Integrating the graphic object theory with the algebraic specification language implies the inclusion of graphic objects as a basic type in the specification language, thus allowing the definition of elements which are graphic objects, for which volume, presence and aspect can be determined. In some way this implies using a certain degree of model based specification, as we are fixing, directly or indirectly, the representation of the module as a graphic object.

Defining an element as a graphic object implies the inclusion of the consultor functions aspect and presence in the specification module. This can be carried out in two different ways. Firstly, it is possible to define these functions explicitly. The module shown in figure 26.3 is a specification of a rectangle, defined as a graphic object.

Graphic Object Rectangle

Constructors
  rectangle: Point, Point, Colour -> Rectangle;

Functions
  aspect: Point, Rectangle -> Colour;
  presence: Point, Rectangle -> Int;
  is_in: Point, Rectangle -> Bool;
  surface: Rectangle -> Real;

Axioms
  var P,P_1,P_2: Point, C: Colour, R: Rectangle;

  is_in(P,rectangle(P_1,P_2,C)) = if (($P > P_1$) and ($P < P_2$)) true else false;
  aspect(P,rectangle(P_1,P_2,C)) = if (($P > P_1$) and ($P < P_2$)) C else 0;
  presence(P,R) = if (is_in(P,R)) 1 else 0;
  surface(rectangle(P_1,P_2)) = if(rectangle(P_1,P_2)=0) 0 else (P_1.X-P_2.X)*(P_1.Y-P_2.Y);

FIGURE 26.3. Specification of a rectangle

The second possibility is to fix a representation for the graphic object defined in the module using graphic object modelling operations. The aspect and presence functions are automatically included, and it is not necessary to write any axioms to specify them. This can be done including a where clause for every constructor. The rectangle can be specificated as a product of two lines (see Figure 26.4).

Graphic Object Rectangle;

Constructors
rectangle: Line, Line -> Rectangle;
where rectangle(L_1,L_2) = L_1 , L_2;

Functions
surface: Rectangle -> Real;

Axioms
var L_1,L_2: Line;

surface(rectangle(L_1,L_2)) = if(rectangle(L_1,L_2)=0) 0 else length(L_1)*length(L_2);

FIGURE 26.4. Specification of a rectangle fixing its internal representation

To specify the visualization of the different elements, it is necessary to express the relationship between the graphic objects and the image. This is done using the Fiume theory, as described above.

At present a non concurrent implementation of GRALPLA is available, which generates a C++ code [15].

26.4 Specifying interactive systems

W. Mallgren proposed an algebraic formalism to specify interaction [10]. This facilitates the integration of the specification of interactive and non-interactive components, but Malgren's proposal has two drawbacks: specifications are very complex with many axioms, and there is no method to ensure that the specification is deadlock free.

To overcome these disadvantages, we propose the inclusion of an explicit synchronization mechanism in the specification language.

Let us take the specification of a buffer of one element [10] (see Figure 26.5). This specification needs to guarantee that the function **get** is not performed when there is no data, and that the function **put** is not performed when the buffer is full. To study these conditions we need a model of concurrent operation. Let us assume that all the functions are implemented using the following scheme, based on a conditional critical region:

Code for Operation Op
    when Op_is_allowed do
        Implementation_of_Op

The condition Op_allowed must be expressed using the specification module information, which can be:

· The module state [10]
· Module variables
· Module functions

Object Buffer

Constructors
   buffer: -> Buffer

Functions
   Get <v,R>: Buffer -> Int, Buffer
   Put: Buffer, Int -> Buffer

Axioms
   var T:Buffer; x: Int;

   Get(Put(T,x)).v = x
   Get(Put(T,x)).R = Buffer

FIGURE 26.5. Specification of a buffer

The first option implies adding functions to manage the module state, and is the main cause of the complexity of Malgren's specifications. The complete specification of the buffer using this solution is shown in figure 26.6.

Using module variables to express synchronization restrictions will, of course, need the addition of new functions to manage these variables, and new axioms. Further, it imply a design step as it fixes the representation for some module state information.

Operations

   $init   -> state

   Put:wait   state -> boolean
   Get:wait   state -> boolean

   Put$return   state × integer -> state
   Get$return   state -> state

Axioms
   ∀ S∈state x,y∈integer

   Put:wait($init,x) = false
   Put:wait(Put$return(S,x),y) = true
   Put:wait(Get$return(S),x) = false

   Get:wait($init) = true
   Get:wait(Put$return(S,x)) = false
   Get:wait(Get$return(S)) = true

FIGURE 26.6. Malgren's specification of a buffer.

Object Buffer

Constructors
> buffer: -> Buffer

Functions
> Get <v,R>: Buffer -> Int, Buffer
> Put: Buffer, Int -> Buffer
> Full: Buffer -> Bool

Axioms
> var T:Buffer; x: Int;
>
> Get(Put(T,x)).v = x
> Get(Put(T,x)).R = Buffer
> Full(Put(T,x)) = true
> Full(Get(T).R) = false
> Full(Buffer) = false

Synchronization
> do Get(T) when Full(T)
> do Put(T,x) when not Full(T)

FIGURE 26.7. Specification of a buffer adding module functions to express synchronization

The third solution is more natural, as it only implies the addition of the consult functions required to express the synchronization mechanism (see Figure 26.7). The synchronization block includes the specification of all the synchronization constraints, thus increasing readability. For any function in the synchronization block, its guard must be true to allow the operation to process.

This structure facilitates the definition of correctness, which can be established for the sequential and concurrent component of the specification independently. The correctness of the concurrent component must ensure, at least, that there is no state for which one, or more, functions are not allowed forever.

Definition 26.3: A **free operation** is a function which may modify the module state and which either does not appear in the synchronization section, or which appears but whose guard is true.   □

A function may always be a free operation, but normally a function will be a free operation only when the module is at determined states. For example, in the buffer example, 'Get' is a free operation only when 'Full' is true.

Definition 26.4: A **deadlock** is a module state at which there is one, or more, functions blocked and whose guard cannot be changed by any free operation.   □

Definition 26.5: A specification is **formally correct** if its operational component is complete and consistent and its synchronization block ensures that the module cannot reach any deadlock state.   □

We will now give a characterization of deadlock free specifications, based on two additional concepts.

Definition 26.6: A set of **synchronized functions**, f_s, is a non empty set of functions which are affected by the synchronization block.   □

In the preceding example the following synchronized function sets exits: {Get,Put}, {Get}, {Put}.

Definition 26.7: The set of **control functions**, f_c, related to a synchronized function set, f_s, for a given module state, is the set of module functions that can make the guard of some function in f_s become true.   □

In the previous example the f_c sets related to each f_s are, at any module state:

$$f_s = \{Get,Put\} \quad => \quad f_c = \{Get,Put\}$$
$$f_s = \{Get\} \quad => \quad f_c = \{Put\}$$
$$f_s = \{Put\} \quad => \quad f_c = \{Get\}$$

Lemma 26.1: A specification reaches a deadlock state if and only if for some module state there is a synchronized function set f_s, whose control function set f_c is included in it, $f_c \subset f_s$, when all the guards for the functions in f_s are false.

Proof. We will begin by showing that when a deadlock is produced, the lemma condition must been satisfied. Let us suppose that a deadlock has been produced, in this case there must be a set of synchronized blocked functions, f_g, whose guard must be false. The existence of deadlock implies that there is no free function which can make any of these guards become true, and thus the control functions associated with f_g must be contained in f_g. Obviously the reciprocal is also correct.   □

Theorem 26.1: A specification cannot reach any deadlock state if and only if it is not possible, for any module state, that a synchronized function set exists whose guards are all false and whose control function set is included in it.

Proof: Evident.   □

It is easy to see that the buffer specification is deadlock free. This result allows us to validate the specification of an interactive system.

26.5 Examples

We will now apply these concepts to carry out the specification of an interactor[7,8]. The external appearance of the system can be represented as a graphic object, and thus, the graphic output representation can be the visual representation of this graphic object. The interactor must have five external functions (see Figure 26.1):

· Input measure: lower level input data.
· Input trigger: indicates the moment when the measure must apply its function.
· Output data: higher level output result, which may be returned to a higher level interactor or system.
· Output control: higher level description of the output part.
· Output trigger: indicates when the output control must be applied.

The specification can be developed noticing that:

- All the data can be considered as graphic objects.
- The interactor has only two external synchronization signals.
- oc and im can be modelled as consulting functions over external modules.

The specification scheme for an interactor is shown in figure 26.8. The representation of an interactor is a graphic object built up using the output data and the measure. Whenever one of these components changes, the interactor representation (and its visualization) change. The first axioms assert that the result of an input trigger is to change the interactor measure. The second axiom expresses the action of an output trigger. The output data is obtained as a graphic object expression of the actual measure.

The remainder of this section presents some examples of specification. Figure 26.9 shows the structure of a scrollbar, using a graphic representation for an interactor, which is a modification of the representations introduced by Duke [3] and Paterno [4]. This representation tries to emphasize two important facts:

- The existence of two orthogonal information flows: that of control and that of measure.
- That the echo information is derived from the internal graphic object representation.

Graphic object Interactor

import LowerLevelSystem, HigherLevelDescription;
    //   These modules provide two functions:
    //   GetInputMeasure: LowerLevelSystem -> Graphic_Object;
    //   GetOutputControl: HigherLevelDescription -> Graphic_Object;
Constructor
    Interactor: Graphic_Object,Graphic_Object -> Interactor;

Graphic representation
    Interactor(O1,O2) = Func(O1,O2);

Functions
    InputTrigger: Interactor -> Interactor;
    GetOutputData: Interactor -> Graphic_Object;
    OutputTrigger: Interactor -> Interactor;
    GetMeasure: Interactor -> Graphic_Object;   // Internal auxiliary functions

Axioms
    var I: Interactor, O1,O2: Graphic_Object, LLS: LowerLevelSystem,
          HLD: HigherLevelDescription;

    InputTrigger(Interactor(O1,O2)) = Interactor(O1,GetInputMeasure(LLS));
    OutputTrigger(Interactor(O1,O2)) = Interactor(GetOutputControl(HLD) ,O2);
    GetMeasure(Interactor(O1,O2)) = O2;
    GetOutputData(I) = func(GetMeasure(I));

FIGURE 26.8. Specification scheme for an interactor.

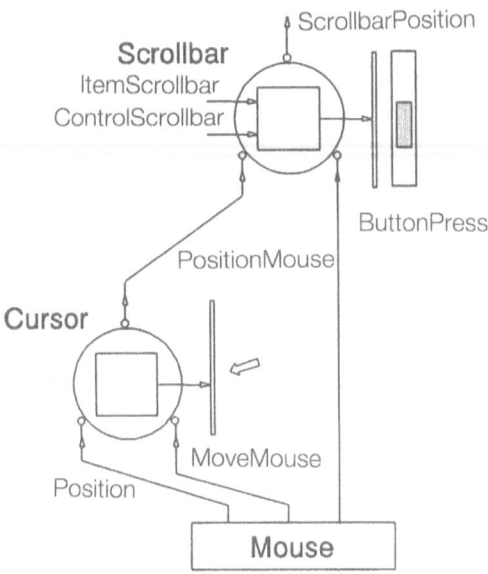

FIGURE 26.9. Structure of a scrollbar

The specification module **cursor** is shown in figure 26.10. We assume that there exits a proccess 'Mouse', which controls the mouse device, and which can activate the interactor trigger. It, also, also has an external function which returns the mouse position:

$$Get\_Position: Mouse -> Point;$$

Graphic Object Cursor;

Constructor
    Cursor: Point -> Cursor;

Graphic representation
    Cursor(P) = Line(P-dx,P+dx)+Line(P-dy,P+dy); // dx and dy are constant

Functions
    PositionMouse: Cursor -> Point;   // Deliver the cursor position
    MoveMouse: Cursor -> Cursor;   // Input Trigger. Activated by mouse.

Axioms
    var C: Cursor, P,Px,Py: Point;

    PositionMouse(Cursor(P)) = P;
    MoveMouse(Cursor(P)) = Cursor(Get_Position(Mouse));

FIGURE 26.10. Specification of a cursor.

We will now specify the module Scrollbar. This module uses the cursor, and is triggered by the mouse. We will assume that a function exists which builds up a rectangle from its two opposite edges, the border colour and the interior colour. We need an external module which gives the output control data, and manages the output trigger (see Figure 26.11).

Graphic Object Scrollbar;
import Mouse, ExternalModule;

Constructor
Scrollbar: Point, Point, Point, Point -> Scrollbar;
// inferior corner, diagonal, interior rectangle diagonal, measure

Graphic representation
Scrollbar(P1,P2,P3,P4) =
rectangle(P1,P1+P2,white,black)+rectangle(P1+P4,P1+P3+P4,grey,black);

Functions
ScrollbarPosition: Scrollbar -> Position;   // get Scrollbar position
ControlScrollbar: Scrollbar -> Scrollbar;   // outputtrigger
ButtonPress: Scrollbar -> Scrollbar;   // Mouse Trigger

SetPosition: Scrollbar, Point -> Scrollbar;   // Internal Functions
SetControl: Scrollbar, Point, Point, Point -> Scrollbar;

Axioms
var S: Scrollbar; P1,P2,P3,P4,Pa,Pb,Pc: Point;

ScrollbarPosition(Scrollbar(P1,P2,P3,P4)) = P4;
SetPosition(Scrollbar(P1,P2,P3,P4),Pa) = Scrollbar(P1,P2,P3,Pa);
SetControl(Scrollbar(P1,P2,P3,P4),Pa,Pb,Pc) = Scrollbar(Pa,Pb,Pc,P4);

ScrollbarPosition(ButtonPress(S)) = SetPosition(S,PositionMouse(Cursor));
ControlScrollbar(S) = SetControl(S,GetExternalData);

FIGURE 26.11. Specification of a scrollbar

26.6. Conclusions

This paper has studied the use of the graphic object formalism for the formal specification of interactive graphic systems. We have focused on the possibility of extending algebraic specification languages to specify interactive graphic systems, using the graphic object theory as a support. The proposal is based on the union of three components:

· Graphic objects, which are an abstract model of graphic entities.

· An algebraic specification language.

· A synchronization mechanism embedded in the specification language.

Binding these components implies some degree of representation of the system state, but our approach has several advantages. Firstly, it allows the generation of a running prototype of the system during the earlier states of development, and secondly it contains a precise semantic of the graphic information processed.

The synchronization mechanisms have been confined to the interior of the specification modules, this allows us to test each module independently.

The strength of this approach has been shown carrying out the specification of an interactor based description of a scrollbar, using the proposed specification language.

At present we are working on the developments of an extended version of the GRALPLA language for concurrent systems specification, adding the do/when clauses. We are also interested in investigating the possible combination of some kind of partial state representation, which may be used to simplify the specification of some systems, and which may assist the design and implementation process.

26.7 References

[1]   Duce D.A., "Formal Specification of Graphics Software". Ed. Earnshaw R.A., *Theoretical Foundation of Computer Graphics and CAD*. Springer-Verlag 1988. pp.543/574.

[2]   Duce D.A., "GKS, Structures and Formal Specification", *Proceeding of Eurographics'89*. North-Holland, 1989.

[3]   Duke D.J., Harrison M.D., *Abstract Interaction Objects*, Computer Graphics Forum, Vol.12, N.3 (EUROGRAPHICS'93), pp.25-36. (1993)

[4]   Faconti G., Paterno' F., *A visual environment to define composition of interacting graphical objects*. The Visual Computer, Vol.9, pp. 73-83, (1992).

[5]   Faconti G., Paterno' F., An Approach to the Formal Specification of the Components of an Interaction. In C. Vandoni, D.A. Duce(ed.), *EUROGRAPHICS'90*, pp. 481-494, North Holland (1990).

[6]   E.L. Fiume, *The Mathematical Structure of Raster Graphics*, Academic Press, Boston (1989).

[7]   M.Gea, J.C. Torres, F.L. Gutierrez, B. Clares, V. del Sol, Prototipado a partir de especificación algebraica: Especificación de sistemas gráficos. *CEIG'93: Congreso Español de Informatica Gráfica*, Granada, Spain (1993).

[8]   M. Gea, J.C. Torres, Object Oriented Prototyping of Graphic Applications from Algebraic Specification, *Fourth Eurographics Workshop on Object Oriented Graphics*, Sintra, May 1994.

[9]   Gnatz R., *An Algebraic Approach to the Standarization and the Certification of Graphics Software*, Computer Graphics Forum, Vol.2, N.2, 1983. pp.153-166.

[10]   W.R. Mallgren, *Formal specification of interactive graphic programming languages*, MIT Press, Cambridge (1982).

[11]   Paterno' F., Faconti G., On the use of LOTOS to describe Graphical Interaction. In A. Monk, D. Diaper, M. Harrison, (ed.), *People and Computer VII: Proc. of the HCI'92 Conference*, pp. 155-173, British Computer Society (1992).

[12]   J.C. Torres, *Abstract representation of graphic systems. Graphic object theory*, PhD Dissertation, Department of Lenguajes y Sistemas Informáticos, University of Granada, Granada, Spain (1992).

[13]   J.C. Torres; B. Clares, *Graphic Objects: A Mathematical Abstract Model for Computer Graphics*, Computer Graphics Forum, **12**(5), pp. (1993).

[14]   J.C. Torres, V. del Sol, B. Clares and D. Martín, Definición algebraica de transformación geométrica. *CEIG'91: Congreso Español de Informatica Gráfica*, Madrid, Spain (1991).

[15]   J.C. Torres, B. Clares, A Formal Approach to the Specification of Graphic Object Functions, *EUROGRAPHICS'94*, Oslo, September 1994.

List of Participants

P.J.Barnard
MRC Applied Psychology Unit
15 Chaucer Road, Cambridge CB2 2EF, U.K.

R.Bastide
L.I.S., Universite' Toulouse I,
Place Anatole France, 31042 Tolouse Cedex, France

D.Bell
Philips Research Labs,
Cross Oak Lane, Redhill, Surrey, RH1 5HA, U.K.

N. O. Bersen
Center for Cognitive Science, Roskilde University,
P.O. Box 260, DK-4000 Roskilde, Denmark

H. de Bruin
Erasmus University Rotterdam, Computer Science Department
P.O. Box 1738, 3000 DR Rotterdam, The Netherlands

F.Bodart
Facultes Universitaires Notre-Dame de la Paix, Institut d'Informatique,
rue Grandgagnage, 21, B-5000 NAMUR, Belgium

A.Dearden
University of York, Department of Computer Science,
York, Y01 5DD, U.K.

A.Dix
University of York, Department of Computer Science,
York, Y01 5DD, U.K.

D.A. Duce
Rutherford Appleton Laboratory, Informatics Department,
Chilton DIDCOT, Oxon OX11 0QX, U. K.

D.Duke
University of York, Department of Computer Science,
York, Y01 5DD, U.K.

G.Faconti
CNUCE - C.N.R.
Via S.Maria 36, 56126 Pisa, Italy

B.Fields
B.Fields, University of York, Department of Computer Science,
York, Y01 5DD, U.K.

J.D.Foley
GVU Center & College of Computing, Georgia Tech,
801 Atlantic Drive, Room 241, Atlanta, GA 30332-0280, USA

T.Elwert
Computer Science Department, University of Rostock
Albert Einstein-Str.21, 18051 Rostock, Germany

M. van Harmelen
36, Brightwell Walk, Manchester M4 1LZ, U.K.

R.Hartson
Virginia Tech, Departement of Computer Science,
562 McBryde Hall, Blacksburg, VA 24061-0106, USA

M.Harrison
University of York, Department of Computer Science,
York, Y01 5DD, U.K.

V.Hassinen
Unda Oy
Kutojantie 7, FIN-02630, Espoo, Finland

W.D.Hurley
Computer Science Department, University of Pittsburgh,
330 Alumni Hall, Pittsburgh, PA 15260, USA

A.Limpouch
Department of Computers, Faculty of Electrical Engineering, Czech Technical
University,
Karlovo nam.13, 121 35 Prague 2 Czech Republic

P.Markopoulos
Computer Science Department, QMW University of London,
Mile End Road, London E1 4NS, U.K.

M.Mezzanotte
CNUCE - C.N.R.
Via S.Maria 36, 56126 Pisa, Italy

P.A.Palanque
L.I.S., Universite' Toulouse I,
Place Anatole France, 31042 Tolouse Cedex, France

S.Pangoli
CNUCE - C.N.R.
Via S.Maria 36, 56126 Pisa, Italy

F.Paterno'
CNUCE - C.N.R.
Via S.Maria 36, 56126 Pisa, Italy

C.R.Roast
Computing and Management Sciences, Sheffield Hallam University,
100 Napier Street, Sheffield S11 8HD, U. K.

S.Schreiber
Institute of Computer Science, Munich University of Technology,
Arcisstr. 21, 80290 Munich, Germany.

S.Sciacchitano
CNUCE - C.N.R.
Via S.Maria 36, 56126 Pisa, Italy

P. "Noi" Sukaviriya
GVU Center & College of Computing, Georgia Tech,
801 Atlantic Drive, Room 241, Atlanta, GA 30332-0280, USA

R.Took
University of York, Department of Computer Science,
York, Y01 5DD, U.K.

J.C.Torres,
Dpt. Lenguajes y Sistemas Informaticos, E.T.S.I. Informatica,
Avd. Andalucia 38, Universidad de Granada, E-18014, Granada, Spain.

J.Vanderdonck
Facultes Universitaires Notre-Dame de la Paix, Institut d'Informatique,
rue Grandgagnage, 21, B-5000 NAMUR, Belgium

Focus on Computer Graphics

(Formerly EurographicSeminars)

User Interface Management and Design. Edited by D. A. Duce, M. R. Gomes,
F. R. A. Hopgood, J. R. Lee. VIII, 324 pages, 117 figs., 1991

Advances in Computer Graphics Hardware III. Edited by A. A. M. Kuijk.
VIII, 214 pages, 88 figs., 1991

Advances in Object-Oriented Graphics I. Edited by E. H. Blake, P. Wisskirchen.
X, 218 pages, 74 figs., 1991

Advances in Computer Graphics Hardware IV. Edited by R. L. Grimsdale,
W. Straßer. VIII, 276 pages, 124 figs., 1991

Advances in Computer Graphics VI. Images: Synthesis, Analysis, and
Interaction. Edited by G. Garcia, I. Herman. IX, 449 pages, 186 figs., 1991

Intelligent CAD Systems III. Practical Experience and Evaluation. Edited by
P. J. W. ten Hagen, P. J. Veerkamp. X, 270 pages, 116 figs., 1991

Graphics and Communications. Edited by D. B. Arnold,
R. A. Day, D. A. Duce, C. Fuhrhop, J. R. Gallop, R. Maybury, D. C. Sutcliffe.
VIII, 274 pages, 84 figs., 1991

Photorealism in Computer Graphics. Edited by K. Bouatouch, C. Bouville.
XVI, 230 pages, 118 figs., 1992

Advances in Computer Graphics Hardware V. Rendering, Ray Tracing and
Visualization Systems. Edited by R. L. Grimsdale, A. Kaufman.
VIII, 174 pages, 97 figs., 1992

Multimedia. Systems, Interaction and Applications. Edited by L. Kjelldahl.
VIII, 355 pages, 129 figs., 1992. Out of print

Advances in Scientific Visualization. Edited by F. H. Post, A. J. S. Hin.
X, 212 pages, 141 figs., 47 in color, 1992

Computer Graphics and Mathematics. Edited by B. Falcidieno, I. Herman,
C. Pienovi. VII, 318 pages, 159 figs., 8 in color, 1992

Rendering, Visualization and Rasterization Hardware. Edited by A. Kaufman.
VIII, 196 pages, 100 figs., 1993

Visualization in Scientific Computing. Edited by M. Grave, Y. Le Lous,
W. T. Hewitt. XI, 218 pages, 120 figs., 1994

Photorealistic Rendering in Computer Graphics. Edited by P. Brunet,
F. W. Jansen. X, 286 pages, 175 figs., 1994

From Object Modelling to Advanced Visual Communication. Edited by
S. Coquillart, W. Straßer, P. Stucki. VII, 305 pages, 128 figs., 38 in color, 1994

Photorealistic Rendering Techniques. Edited by G. Sakas, P. Shirley, S. Müller.
X, 448 pages, 155 figs., 16 color plates, 1995

Interactive Systems: Design, Specification, and Verification.
Edited by F. Paternó. X, 447 pages, 176 figs., 1995

Springer-Verlag
and the Environment

We at Springer-Verlag firmly believe that an international science publisher has a special obligation to the environment, and our corporate policies consistently reflect this conviction.

We also expect our business partners – paper mills, printers, packaging manufacturers, etc. – to commit themselves to using environmentally friendly materials and production processes.

The paper in this book is made from low- or no-chlorine pulp and is acid free, in conformance with international standards for paper permanency.